Local Aviation Collections of Britain

For
John Berkeley and Mike Ingham
Pioneers both

Front cover: Mosquito prototype W4050 at the de Havilland Aircraft Museum, London Colney, Hertfordshire, following its exacting restoration, 2016. *Garry Lakin-DHAM*

Rear cover:

English Electric Lightning F.53 ZF579 at the Gatwick Aviation Museum, Charlwood, Surrey. *Richard Hall*

Ken Wallis at the controls of Bensen B.7 G-APUD at Shoreham, 1959. It is now part of The Aeroplane Collection and displayed at the Museum of Science and Industry, Manchester. *KEC*

Star performer at special events at Bruntingthorpe, Leicestershire, Handley Page Victor K.2 XM715 *Teasin' Tina*. *Darren Harbar*

Handley Page Herald 100 G-APWA in 1959. Today, *Whisky-Alpha* is preserved at the Museum of Berkshire Aviation, Woodley. *Handley Page*

Hawker Hunter GA.11 WV256 at the Cornwall Aviation Heritage Centre, Newquay Cornwall Airport. *Ken Ellis*

Local Aviation Collections of Britain

In search of the treasures the UK's nationals envy

Ken Ellis

Crécy Publishing Limited

Local Aviation Collections of Britain

First published in 2017 by Crécy Publishing Limited

A CIP record for this book is available from the British Library

ISBN 9781910809112

Printed in Malta by Gutenberg Press Limited

Crécy Publishing Limited
1a Ringway Trading Estate, Shadowmoss Road, Manchester M22 5LH
www.crecy.co.uk

Geoffrey de Havilland Jnr piloting the prototype Mosquito W4050 on its maiden flight at Hatfield, 25th November 1940. Today this machine is displayed at its place of birth Salisbury Hall, London Colney; the home of the de Havilland Aircraft Museum. It is the only surviving British World War Two aircraft prototype. *British Aerospace*

Contents

Foreword
Ian Thirsk

Head of Collections Royal Air Force Museum

When Ken Ellis asked me to write the foreword to *Local Aviation Collections of Britain* I was hugely flattered, if not to say a little nervous! Ken is someone I have always looked up to for he is undoubtedly *the* authority on the UK aircraft preservation movement and a genuine enthusiast. His many seminal works such as *Great Aviation Collections of Britain* adorn my office bookshelves and not a day goes by without my consulting his masterpiece series *Wrecks & Relics*.

I first met Ken when he became the editor of *FlyPast* magazine back in the 1980s. Like many enthusiasts of my generation, *FlyPast* was the 'voice' (and in many ways the 'social glue') of our movement and Ken's writings informed, inspired and encouraged us to achieve great things. In those days I was working as a volunteer at the Mosquito Aircraft Museum (now the de Havilland Aircraft Museum) at Salisbury Hall, overseeing the restoration of Mosquito TT.35 TA634 – an aircraft which is also significant to Ken as you will see later on. I have more than a passing interest in the Mosquito, instilled by my father who worked for de Havilland at Hatfield plus regular sightings of T.3 RR299 passing overhead during the summer months. Salisbury Hall was my local museum and I still recall the privilege, honour and excitement of being allowed to work on a 'real' Mosquito while, at the same time, helping to safeguard a unique collection of great local relevance. My volunteer involvement developed my interest in the Mosquito even further and in 1986 Ken published my first article in *FlyPast*, a great turning point for me.

I have been fortunate enough to develop that volunteer passion and involvement into a career and today, as Head of Collections at the Royal Air Force Museum, am privileged to oversee one of the great national collections. As such, I know from first hand experience the tremendous part played by local collections in securing the aviation heritage of this country.

This is an excellent and comprehensive book in the traditional Ellis style, detailed, engaging and highly informative. The depth of information is truly phenomenal and I never fail to be impressed by the degree and scale of Ken's research. I particularly enjoyed Ken's introductory chapter *Local Heroes*, especially the reference to exhibits in local museums having national or even global significance. Ken is quite right to point out that not all 'crown jewels' are in the nationals. For example take the de Havilland Museum's premier exhibit, the Mosquito prototype W4050 – surely that is an airframe of international significance. However, what shines through is it that this book is really about people, the achievements of those unsung volunteer enthusiasts.

Ken is a modest unassuming individual with a huge passion for his subject. He remains a source of inspiration and encouragement to others and I thoroughly recommend this, his latest book.

Introduction
Local Heroes

In search of the treasures the UK's nationals envy

When I was down on my knees, trying to persuade my lovely publishers that this was a viable book, one of the straplines I came up with was: 'In search of the aeronautical treasures Britain's national museums envy'. Back in 2013 I penned *Great Aviation Collections of Britain*, devoted to the 'nationals'; the RAF Museum, Science Museum etc. I was worried that *some* readers would regard all the other collections as inferior and intended to write the 'sequel' extolling the virtues of the 'regionals'. The word 'envy' was deliberately chosen; just because an exhibit is with a local museum doesn't mean that it lacks national, or even global, significance.

Let's steal a portion of the introduction from *Great Aviation Collections* as it sums up why this book needed doing: "But *we're* great!" I hear the team at Newark exclaim. And at Martlesham Heath, Weston-super-Mare, Speke Airport, Sunderland, Dumfries and Galloway, and all points in between. You get the picture... All over the UK there are museums with exhibits that the directors of 'nationals' would love to drool over in their own galleries. There are also venues out there with collections that far surpass some of the nationals in terms of the *number* of aircraft held."

So, this book is here to prove that not all the 'crown jewels' are in the nationals. Indeed, there are a handful of museums dealt with here that are close to, or closing in on, the stature of a 'national' and should really been seen in that light. The Brooklands Museum, de Havilland Aircraft Museum, The Helicopter Museum, Newark Air Museum and Solent Sky are certainly in this league. Some of the institutions herein are run by full-time staff; others function on a totally volunteer basis. We need to banish the notion that 'part-time' or 'amateur' means second-rate and that 'local' or 'regional' implies out of touch or inadequate. On the contrary, it has always been my opinion that unlike the 'big boys' these museums are more welcoming, their exhibits more accessible and, depending where you live, nearer!

What is and isn't covered

Local Collections of Britain concentrates on the *pure* aviation museums of the British Isles. By that I mean those *devoted* to an aeronautical theme, not those that exhibit an aeroplane or two as part of a wider collecting policy. The entries are listed county-by-county for England, with Scotland, Wales and Northern Ireland following – in much the same manner as the biennial tome *Wrecks & Relics*.

The narrative on each museum is less about what it is like today – you should really *go and find that out for yourself* – but aims to tell the story of how the present set-up came about, its background and aims. The emphasis is on *aeronautica*; if the reader is looking for a catalogue of the names of chairmen, curators, managers and the like, this is not for you. Equally, there are thousands who have slaved to establish these organisations, sweated over restoration projects, steadfastly mown the grass and so on. Some of these 'local heroes' get a mention within the narrative; but this is purely a personal choice as it would be impossible to cover them all.

As well as being exclusively an aviation museum, the venue must regularly open to the public with no need to pre-book. 'Regularly' is generally regarded as *at least* open at weekends – that's Saturday *and* Sunday – from spring to autumn, with a few exceptions. For completeness, each section is concluded with *brief* details of the venues that fall outside of this coverage along with reminders of the national collections. For the latter, you'll need *Great Aviation Collections of Britain*. Websites are given so that readers can plan visits: as ever in this day and age these are given for information only; no recommendation of content is to be implied. Of course, greater details can be had from the latest edition of *Wrecks & Relics*.

Tables and profiles

Tables provide an at-a-glance view of the extent of each collection. These are arranged by type and details including the year built and approximate (or occasionally precise!) arrival dates are given. Regular *W&R* readers will have no problems with these and, if you seek more, then it is time to refer to your library of past editions! 'Ownership' or 'custodianship' of airframes in this book is not to be inferred as definitive. As might be expected, in the 'private sector' many exhibits are on loan, be that short, medium or even permanent: no attempt has been made to delineate such status, or to name names. As museums regularly change their displays, exhibits listed or profiled may not be on public show. As with any aspect of a visit to a museum, readers are urged to check with the venue beforehand to avoid any disappointment.

As well as a narrative on each venue and an inventory of airframes (if applicable), the most important or interesting exhibits come under the spotlight through exhibit profiles – or 'biographies'. These are a personal selection to show the flavour and *some* of the highlights of each venue. Some are clearly 'hot shots', others the reader may not have given a second glance to until now; my aim is to show that even humble types have a place in our heritage. To avoid repetition, a degree of rationing has had to be enforced. If, for example, the reader is keen on Museum B and can't understand why its Gloster Meteor is not profiled, that would probably be because Museum K has one that *is* featured.

When choosing an aircraft to profile, the emphasis has been unapologetically on British designed and built aircraft and I'm aware that trainers, communications types, helicopters, gliders, microlights etc are thinner on the ground than they deserve. In general – and rules are made to be broken – cockpits, incomplete airframes, unmanned aerial vehicles (aka drones) and the like are not profiled. The engine(s) noted with each profile are those that the airframe would have most likely been powered by and are not necessarily fitted on the exhibit. The biographies do not attempt to list every oil change, service and re-spray in an exhibit's history. The assumption is that most readers will know the historical importance of the majority of types, but rarer ones are given a deeper description. Additionally, I attempt to outline the merit of an exhibit in terms of its significance locally and nationally.

Seemed like a good idea at the time

The collecting policies of the featured museums vary considerably; and there are still a few that hang on to the 'it's an aircraft, it's available – let's have it' approach. Unlike the 'nationals', the collections herein can readily adopt a 'local' or 'regional' theme for their exhibits and that link increases the importance of an airframe. Others specialise by topic: Weston-super-Mare's incredible The Helicopter Museum being the most obvious example while one of the Newark Air Museum's keynotes is trainers. It is quite possible that a particular airframe may be very important to one museum but if moved to another venue might be of little merit. Just because an airframe, or any object, is rare does not mean it *has* to be preserved; the commonplace can often have greater importance.

So far in this trilogy, *Lost*, *Great* and *Local*, I've refrained from comment on life, the universe and everything. Now's the time! I was chewing the cud with a curator of lengthy experience, who I'm not going to name, about the future of aviation museums. While discussing collecting policy, we got talking about the spread of types that would satisfy the average 'punter'. He explained that too often collections can become obsessed with the esoteric, appealing to only a small proportion of the people that come through the door. He also felt that row upon row of airframes failed to impress visitors; their eyes were drawn to certain aircraft, or the way they were presented. He went on to explain his "dream ticket" aviation museum and I quote: "It does not need many aircraft: 'Joe Public' spends less time per visit [than in years gone by]. A gift shop full of 'tat' and a good café will take up a goodly amount of the time. You'll need a biplane, a Spitfire, a Harrier, a Concorde and *perhaps* a colourful helicopter – job done!" He also went on to add: "These don't even *need* to be the real thing, as long as they are good replicas, they [the general visitor] won't mind."

'My' curator shares a view I've had for a long time. Great strides have been made in getting airframes under cover, but the sheer number 'preserved' in Britain means that aim will remain mission impossible. Besides, there's nothing nicer than walking around an open air aircraft park. In coming years, it's not roofs that will matter; it will be an ever dwindling number of willing hands – the 'local heroes' that make a museum function. "We desperately need 'new blood', or I can see us cutting the number of days we're open, or stopping special days." That's a conversation I had in early July with a northern England curator. The need for 'new blood' is a refrain I've heard for decades.

Britain's aviation heritage is told by an amazing number of museums and collections and I hope that the variety of exhibits outlined in this book shows just how lucky we are. While I'm not advocating the harsh 'minimalist' observation put forward above, I've long been on record that there are *too many* airframes held in British museums, be they 'local' or 'national'. A glance through the exhibit lists in the chapters that follow show astonishing duplication; across collections and within them. One museum has three fast jets of the same variant. A recent visit to central England found two volunteers gallantly rubbing down an aircraft that I knew was on its third lick of paint in four decades. Yet examination of the main wheel bays and the rear fuselage showed that this far from relevant type should really have been put out of its misery. The 'lads' working on it, both in their 70s, could have been transforming the prospects of the much more significant exhibit thirty feet away. On asking why this was not the case, the answer was: "It's not its turn."

What's needed is to coolly assess if an airframe really should be an exhibit *at all*. Is it really A Good Thing? For too long, museums have been 'scrap-averse'. There is nothing wrong in admitting that time and circumstances have overtaken a particular exhibit. We cannot be far off one of the nation's too many Vulcans becoming so 'senile' that 'euthanasia' would be the most efficient solution.

A 'cull' would enable that most precious, and diminishing, resource – our 'local heroes' – to maximise their time and efforts on *really deserving* types. Some 'surplus' aircraft *might* be passed on to other museums; but that doesn't address the 'glut': it just moves the problem around. We have to be brave and start axing some airframes for the sake of others, admitting that what must have seemed like a good idea at the time is no longer fit for purpose. The aviation heritage 'movement' needs to grasp the nettle and thin out its stock: Joe and Josephine Public won't mind and it's the heroic thing to do.

Ken Ellis
People's Republic of Rutland
July 2017

Myddle Cottage, 13 Mill Lane, Barrowden, Oakham, LE15 8EH
ken@sillenek.com

Acknowledgements

As with *Lost Collections of Britain* and *Great Aviation Collections of Britain*, there are people in every edition of *Wrecks & Relics,* and each copy of *FlyPast*, who have contributed to my knowledge of the UK's aviation heritage. The wealth of aeronautical legacy that Britain basks in is a tribute to a vast army of amateurs and professionals, all united by their enthusiasm for the subject.

My thanks to: **Elfan Ap Rees**, The Helicopter Museum; **Dave Arkle**, The Aeroplane Collection; **Alan Beattie**, Yorkshire Aircraft Preservation Group; **Steve Beebee** at *FlyPast*; **Philip Birtles**, de Havilland Aircraft Museum; **Ben Brown**, Sywell Aviation Museum; **David Burke**; **John Camp**, Boxted Airfield Museum; **Dave Charles**, North East Land, Sea and Air Museum; **Mike Davey**, 'Aggie-Paggie' and others; **Lewis E Deal MBE**, Spitfire and Hurricane Memorial Museum and Medway Aircraft Preservation Society; **Alan Doe**, Montrose Air Station Heritage Centre; **Bill Fern**, South Yorkshire Aircraft Museum; **Murray Flint**; **Ken Fostekew**, Museum of Berkshire Aviation; **Ron Fulton**, BDAC – Old Sarum Airfield Museum; **Guy Gainey**, Speke Aerodrome Heritage Group; **Chris Gilson** at *FlyPast*; **Richard Hall**, Lightning XS420 at Farnborough; **Graham Haynes**, Bentwaters Cold War Museum; **Howard Heeley**, Newark Air Museum; **Keith Hill**; **Mike Hodgson**, Thorpe Camp Visitor Centre; **Harry Holmes**, Avro Heritage Museum; **Jonathan Horswell**; **Jonathan Howard**, Prince G-AMLZ; **Daniel Hunt**, Wings World War Two Remembrance Museum; **Dianne James**, Midland Air Museum; **John Kenyon**, a Northern Aircraft Preservation Society founder and helping to establish the Wight Aviation Museum; **Dougie Kerr**, Solway Aviation Museum; **Tim Kershaw**, Jet Age Museum; **Howard King**, Martlesham Heath Control Tower Museum; **Garry Lakin**, de Havilland Aircraft Museum; **Richard 'Digger' Mason**, Fenland and West Norfolk Aviation Museum; **Trevor J Matthews**, Lashenden Air Warfare Museum; **Peter Michallat**, The Helicopter Museum; **Peter Mills**, Gatwick Aviation Collection; **Naylan Moore**, South Yorkshire Aircraft Museum; **John Nixon**, Millom Discovery Centre; **Geoff Nutkins**, Shoreham Aircraft Museum; **Andrew Panton**, Lincolnshire Aviation Heritage Centre; **Ivor Ramsden**, Manx Aviation and Military Museum; **Davie Reid**, Dumfries and Galloway Aviation Museum; **Ian Richardson**, Yorkshire Air Museum; **Graham Rood**, Farnborough Air Sciences Trust; **Colin Savill**, Newark Air Museum; **Jim Simpson**, Morayvia; **James Stables**, South Yorkshire Aircraft Museum; **Ralph Steiner**, de Havilland Aircraft Museum; **Rob Taylor**, Speke Aerodrome Heritage Group; **Julian Temple**, Brooklands Museum; **David E Thompson**; **Richard Turner**, Boxted Airfield Museum; **Graham Vale**, East Midlands Airport Volunteers Association; **Bob Wealthy**; **Bill Welbourne**, Fenland and West Norfolk Aviation Museum; **Neil Werninck**, Montrose Air Station Heritage Centre; **Jeff Williams**; **Keith Williams**, E L Wisty. And those who contributed photos, they are credited with their work.

Alan Curry, **Mike Ingham** and **Dean Wright** reviewed the draft in what became a hectic roller-coaster as this mammoth evolved. Despite their efforts, the responsibility for mistooks is awl mein!

John Berkerley, formerly of the Midland Aircraft Preservation Society and the Midland Air Museum, and **Mike Ingham**, a founder-member of the Northern Aircraft Preservation Society, patiently answered my questions on the origins of these groups, and on many different aspects of the evolution of Britain's incredible aviation heritage movement.

Many thanks go to **Ian Thirsk** for his kind foreword. The development of what is now the de Havilland Aircraft Museum has always been a source of inspiration and pleasure to me. I've known Ian a long time and his progression from helping out on Mosquito TA634 to his present post as Head of Collections at the Royal Air Force Museum is a shining example of how the 'grass roots' are vital to the 'nationals' – the over-riding message of this book.

Patience personified, the team at Crécy Publishing – **Gill Richardson**, **Jeremy Pratt** and designer **Rob Taylor**, backed my ever-expanding vision for this work with only the occasional roll of the eyes from ceiling to floor and back again! Most of all my thanks to Pam and feline Rex for their own respective brands of support over the many, many months of this project: I could not have achieved this without their encouragement.

The author with the fuselage of the Pennington 'Flying Flea' at Torver Mill, Cumbria, during its removal on 12th March 1994. Fully restored in 1995, it is now on display at the Solway Aviation Museum. *Alan Curry*

CHAPTER 1

Moments in Time
A Chronology of Britain's Aviation Museums

While grappling with this monster, an essential tool to keep things vaguely on track was a scribbled timeline linking the birth, and sometimes the deaths, of Britain's aviation museums and collections. Then it dawned that if it was useful to me, readers would likely appreciate it. This brings together all three books on the subject. *Lost Aviation Collections of Britain,* published in 2011, which charted the most prominent institutions that have gone by the wayside. In 2013 *Great Aviation Collections of Britain* appeared, charting the 'nationals', in order of their aeronautical 'baptism': Science Museum, Imperial War Museum, Shuttleworth Collection, Fleet Air Arm Museum, Royal Air Force Museum Hendon and Cosford, Museum of Army Flying, Imperial War Museum Duxford, the Ulster collections, National Museum of Flight Scotland. Museums and collections given here follow the guidelines in the introduction, so aviation venues with limited opening times, or prior access required, are not included. Likewise, since the 1960s there have been many preservation groups that have been set up with no intent to open to the public; some still going strong, others demised. These are also not listed.

Above: Alcock and Brown departing Lester's Field, Newfoundland, at the start of their epic transatlantic flight on 14th June 1919. Their Vimy was handed over to the Science Museum at the opening of its new buildings on 15th December 1919. This marked the start of a permanent aviation exhibition and the origins of the National Aeronautical Collection. *Rolls-Royce*

1897	In London, the South Kensington Museum, which became the Science Museum in 1909, staged a temporary display, the 'International Exhibition of Motors and Their Aeroplanes'. Included was the Lilienthal glider imported from Germany by T J Bennett in March 1895. This was presented to the Science Museum in 1920 and is today in store.
Aug 1909	Percy Pilcher's Hawk glider of 1896 was presented *on loan* to the Royal Scottish Museum (RSM – National Museum of Scotland from 1995), Edinburgh. This was the first complete fixed wing aircraft to be placed with a museum. (It was displayed at South Kensington in early 1913 – see below.) The Pilcher was taken on a permanent basis on 24th March 1920 and is still with the museum in Scotland, regretfully stored.
26th Nov 1913	The Science Museum took delivery of the Cody Military Aeroplane from Farnborough. This was the first whole, powered aircraft to join a British museum on a permanent basis; it is also the oldest surviving British military aeroplane. It was the 1930s before it went on regular display.
5th Mar 1917	The War Cabinet authorised the collection of potential exhibits for the proposed National War Museum; quickly renamed the Imperial War Museum.
15th Dec 1919	The Alcock and Brown transatlantic Vickers Vimy was handed over to the Science Museum at the opening of its new buildings. This marked the start of a permanent aviation exhibition and the origins of the National Aeronautical Collection.
1920 to 1923	The Imperial War Museum staged a major exhibition within the Crystal Palace, Sydenham, London. Included was an extensive collection of aircraft: the Bristol F.2b Fighter, Royal Aircraft Factory BE.2 and RE.8, and the Sopwith Camel that are still with the museum were part of this original display.
7th Jul 1936	The Imperial War Museum at South Lambeth was officially opened.
1944	Air Historical Branch (AHB) began the allocation of airframes and artefacts for 'museum' purposes. This essentially kicked off the process that led to the RAF Museum in 1972. As an example, Avro Lancaster I R5868 was listed as an 'AHB aircraft' on 14th July 1945.
15th May 1959	Mosquito W4050 was officially unveiled at London Colney and the museum dedicated to it was opened – it had arrived by road in September 1958. This was called the Mosquito Aircraft Museum by 1974 and in the 1990s it adopted the title de Havilland Aircraft Museum – Chapter 12.
Oct 1959	The Air Ministry conducted an audit of the historical artefacts held by RAF stations.
24th Jun 1961	Short Sunderland ML824 arrived at Pembroke Dock, Wales, for the Short Sunderland Trust. It was opened to the public on a regular basis – see Chapter 33.
21st Oct 1962	A meeting in Manchester on 21st October 1962 transformed an ad hoc group of enthusiasts into the Northern Aircraft Preservation Society (NAPS). Officially constituted in January 1963, Britain's first 'organised', enthusiast-based preservation group was born. On 3rd November 1962 NAPS took delivery of Avro Avian G-EBZM. NAPS changed its name to The Aeroplane Collection in 1974 and the organisation still has the Avian, displayed at the Museum of Science and Industry, Manchester. Brief mention in Chapter 5; full details Chapter 18.
10th Nov 1962	The Solway Group of Aviation Enthusiasts took on Hawker Hart K4972; donating it to the RAF Museum in October 1963. This group founded the Solway Aviation Museum, see 1983 and Chapter 7.
1963	The Shuttleworth Collection, of vehicles and aeroplanes, opened to the public on a full-time basis. The first occasional open day was staged in 1957. The collection's founder, Richard Shuttleworth, had begun collecting historic aircraft in 1932.
31st Aug 1963	Peter Thomas opened his Skyfame Aircraft Museum to the public at Staverton. This was Britain's first commercial, dedicated aircraft museum.
May 1964	The Fleet Air Arm Museum at Yeovilton opened to the public.
Sep 1964	The station collections at RAF Colerne and RAF St Athan opened on an occasional basis.
1966	The British Historic Aircraft Museum was established at Rochford, Southend Airport. It was billed as "Britain's first national aircraft collection".
Sep 1966	The station collection at RAF Finningley opened on an occasional basis.
Mar 1969	The Airborne Forces Museum opened at Aldershot.
1970	The station collection at RAF Cosford, open on an occasional basis since 1968, took the name Aerospace Museum Cosford.
Apr 1970	The British Historic Aircraft Museum was declared moribund at Southend, having never opened to the public.
Apr 1970	The Lashenden Air Warfare Museum opened to visitors.

26th Jun 1970 Avro Lancaster VII NX611 (G-ASXX) flew into Squires Gate to become the centrepiece of the Reflectaire Museum. The Lancaster was the main acquisition of the Historic Aircraft Preservation Society; it had arrived at Biggin Hill from Australia on 13th May 1965. The assets of HAPS were transferred to Reflectaire Ltd in 1968. NX611 is now at the Lincolnshire Aviation Heritage Centre, East Kirkby – Chapter 16.

19th Jul 1970 The Lincolnshire Aviation Museum opened at Tattershall – Chapter 16.

1971 The Kent Battle of Britain Museum opened at Hawkinge – Chapter 14.

21st Mar 1971 The Sunderland Trust was dissolved: Sunderland ML824 moved to the RAF Museum at Hendon.

5th Jun 1971 Keith Fordyce's Torbay Aircraft Museum opened at Higher Blagdon, Devon.

1972 Collecting historic aircraft since 1970, Sir William Roberts established the Strathallan Aircraft Collection at Strathallan with occasional open days; by 1975 it was open on a regular basis.

1972 The Brenzett Aeronautical Museum Trust opened its doors. It was renamed the Romney Marsh Wartime Collection by 2014 – Chapter 14.

27th May 1972 The Historic Aircraft Museum opened at Southend, with the majority of the airframes gathered by the former British Historic Aircraft Museum included in its exhibits.

15th Nov 1972 The Royal Air Force Museum was officially opened at Hendon.

1973 Aircraft Preservation Society of Scotland (*Aviation* Preservation Society of Scotland from 2000) was formed. Independent of but working closely with the nascent Museum of Flight – see 7th July 1975 – the society's aircraft collection is largely based at East Fortune.

14th Apr 1973 After a couple of occasional open days from 1971, the Newark Air Museum was officially opened at Winthorpe – Chapter 23.

Jetstream T.1 XX492 framing Newark Air Museum's Hangar No.2, with No.1 to the left. *Ken Ellis*

1974	The Cornwall Aero Park opened at Helston. It changed its name to the Flambards Triple Theme Park by 1986, later becoming the Flambards Village Theme Park and today is the Flambards Experience – Chapter 6. From 1988 the substantial aviation content was trimmed down and by 2008 was minimal.
Nov 1974	Museum of Army Flying opened to the public at Middle Wallop. Under the name Army Air Corps Museum it had been available on an occasional basis from March 1968.
1975	The North East Vintage and Veteran Aircraft Association opened a display at Lambton Castle, Chester-le-Street. In 1977 the move was made to Usworth, Sunderland, and in 1979 it was renamed the North East Aircraft Museum – see 1979.
7th Jul 1975	Museum of Flight opened to the public on an increasingly regular basis at East Fortune. The former airfield had been used as a large object store for the Royal Scottish Museum from early 1971.
1976	The Mitchell Memorial Hall opened at Southampton. Its name later changed to the R J Mitchell Spitfire Museum. See May 1984 for its next iteration and Chapter 11.
1976	The Ulster Folk and Transport Museum opened at Cultra Manor, Belfast. This was the first permanent exhibition of aircraft in Northern Ireland.
8th May 1976	The Norfolk and Suffolk Aviation Society opened its museum at Flixton. It moved to its present site on 24th April 1977.
11th Jul 1976	The Nostell Aviation Museum, run by the South Yorkshire Aviation Society, opened at Nostell Priory. As the South Yorkshire Aircraft Museum it relocated to Firbeck in 1982, open on Sundays. See 29th May 2001 and Chapter 31.
Sep 1976	The Wales Aircraft Museum opened at Rhoose, Cardiff Airport. It was run by the South Wales Historic Aircraft Preservation Society, which was formed on 1st March 1967.
17th Jul 1977	The Dumfries and Galloway Aviation Museum opened at Tinwald Downs – Chapter 32.
1978	The Imperial War Museum opened up Duxford airfield to the public. The museum had acquired the entire site in February 1976 and for some time before that had used it as a large object store.

The Norfolk and Suffolk Aviation Museum embraces aviation in all its forms as this section of the main display hangar shows: left to right, Sea Harrier FA.2 ZA175, Provost T.1 WV605 and the basket of Thunder Ax7 hot-air balloon G-BJZC. 'Flying' above are Rogallo-winged hang-gliders, Wasp Falcon 4 and Antonov C.14. *Ken Ellis*

2nd Jan 1978	Skyfame Aircraft Museum at Staverton closed its doors; most of the collection was absorbed by the Imperial War Museum, Duxford.
2nd Apr 1978	The Midland Air Museum opened at Coventry Airport – Chapter 29.
25th Oct 1978	Douglas DC-3 EI-AYO flew into Wroughton to inaugurate the Science Museum's transport aircraft collection.
1979	The Second World War Aircraft Preservation Society, founded on 14th August 1977, established its collection at Lasham and opened regularly to the public.
1979	Stan and David Brett opened the Rebel Air Museum at Andrewsfield (Great Saling). The museum closed in 1986, re-emerging at Earls Colne, as the Earls Colne Aviation Museum, in 1991.
1979	The North East Aircraft Museum opened on a limited basis at Usworth. In 1987 the museum was available on a full-time basis. In 2012 it was rebranded as the North East Land, Sea and Air Museum – Chapter 22.
1st May 1979	The Aerospace Museum Cosford opened on a full-time basis. It was renamed the RAF Museum Cosford on 22nd June 1998.
27th May 1979	The Loughborough Leicestershire Aircraft Preservation Museum and Preservation Society opened to the public at Castle Donington, East Midlands Airport.
1981	The Bomber County Aviation Museum opened at Cleethorpes. It was run by the Humberside Aircraft Preservation Society, which was founded in 1975 at Goxhill. The Cleethorpes operation closed in 1987 but the museum re-located to Hemswell, re-opening to the public in 1989.
May 1981	The control tower at the 100th Bomb Group Memorial Museum was dedicated to the men of the 'Bloody Hundredth' at Thorpe Abbotts – Chapter 20.
13th Jun 1981	The Spitfire Memorial Building opened at Manston. On 7th October 1988 the Hurricane Memorial Building was inaugurated and the Spitfire and Hurricane Memorial Museum was created – Chapter 14.
Jun 1982	The Tangmere Military Aviation Museum opened – Chapter 28.
1983	The Solway Aviation Society opened its visitor centre at Carlisle Airport, Crosby-on-Eden. On 18th May 1996 the full-blown Solway Aviation Museum was opened – Chapter 7.
30th Mar 1983	The Manchester Air and Space Museum opened. It became the Air and Space Gallery of the Museum of Science and Industry in 1985 when it merged with its next door neighbour – Chapter 18.
10th May 1983	The contents of the former Historic Aircraft Museum were auctioned at Southend.
1984	The East Midlands Aeropark opened at East Midlands Airport – Chapter 15.
May 1984	The Hall of Aviation opened at Southampton. On 12th May 2004 it was rebranded as Solent Sky – Chapter 11.

Travelling tail-first, Sandringham VH-BRC passing what was the Vosper Thorneycroft yard at Woolston, before crossing the River Itchen to be off-loaded ready for installation in the Hall of Aviation at Southampton on 1st March 1983. *Science Museum*

Nov 1984	The Loughborough Leicestershire Aircraft Preservation Museum and Preservation Society moved out of East Midlands Airport and settled at Bruntingthorpe. It changed its name to the Bruntingthorpe Aviation Collection, but was moribund by mid-1985. See also Chapter 15.
5th May 1985	The City of Norwich Aviation Museum opened at Norwich Airport – Chapter 20.
Dec 1985	The Lincolnshire Aviation Museum at Tattershall Thorpe closed its doors. The majority of the collection moved to East Kirkby but was soon wound down.
1986	The East Essex Aviation Museum opened at Clacton on Sea – Chapter 9.
1986	The Wellesbourne Wartime Museum opened at Wellesbourne Mountford – Chapter 29.
Apr 1986	Battle of Britain Memorial Flight Visitor Centre opened at Coningsby – Chapter 16.
31st May 1986	After a first, occasional, open day on 11th August 1985, the Yorkshire Air Museum was officially opened on a full-time basis – Chapter 31.
20th Jun 1987	Fenland Aircraft Preservation Society opened its museum at West Walton Highway – Chapter 20. The group took on the name Fenland and West Norfolk Aviation Museum in 1995.
19th Jul 1987	Lincolnshire Aviation Heritage Centre opened at East Kirkby – Chapter 16.
1988	The North Weald Aviation Museum opened – Chapter 9.
1988	Founded in 1978, the Shoreham Aircraft Museum opened on a permanent basis – Chapter 14.
17th May 1988	The Jet Heritage Aviation Museum opened. It was re-established in August 1999 as the Bournemouth Aviation Museum – Chapter 8.
30th Sep 1988	The Strathallan Aircraft Collection closed.
10th Oct 1988	Contents of the Torbay Aircraft Museum auctioned.
11th May 1989	The Caernarfon Air Museum – later Caernarfon Airport Airworld Museum – opened at Caernarfon aerodrome – Chapter 33.
Nov 1989	After two 'seasonal' trial openings at Weston-super-Mare in 1978 and 1979 (under the name British Rotorcraft Museum) the International Helicopter Museum opened on full-time basis. The museum was renamed The Helicopter Museum in 1998.
1991	The Brooklands Museum, Weybridge, opened – Chapter 27.

Restored Concorde G-BBDG awaiting 'passengers' at Brooklands. *Terry Dann*

1992	The Gloucestershire Aviation Collection opened on an occasional basis at Hucclecote. This came to an end on 29th October 1995, but the organisation relocated to Gloucestershire Airport, Staverton, and became Jet Age Museum. Doors closed on 1st October 2000, but returned in fine style – see August 2013 and Chapter 10.
1993	The Museum of Berkshire Aviation opened at Woodley – Chapter 3.
23rd Mar 1993	Vulcan B.2 XH558 touched down at Bruntingthorpe having been acquired by C Walton Ltd. The collection grew under the British Aviation Heritage banner; this was effectively the start of the Cold War Jets Collection – Chapter 15.
9th Jul 1993	The National Battle of Britain Memorial and visitor centre was unveiled at Capel le Ferne. With the opening of 'The Wing' on 28th March 2015 it took on full-blown museum status – Chapter 14.
1994	The Air Defence Battle Command and Control Museum was officially opened at RAF Neatishead – Chapter 20. It was renamed the RAF Air Defence Radar Museum on 1st January 1999.
1994	The Metheringham Airfield Visitor Centre opened – Chapter 16.
26th Mar 1994	The Carpetbagger Aviation Museum (later the Carpetbagger Secret Warfare Museum) opened at Harrington – Chapter 21.
17th Jul 1994	The Thorpe Camp Visitor Centre opened at Tattershall Thorpe – Chapter 16.
1996	The Island Aeroplane Company opened up to the public at Sandown, Isle of Wight. It was rebranded and expanded as the Front Line Aviation Museum in 1998.
Jan 1996	Wales Aircraft Museum closed at Cardiff Airport.
1997	The Earls Colne Aviation Museum at Earls Colne, closed.
1997	The RAF Manston History Museum opened – Chapter 14.
1998	The RAF Wickenby Memorial Museum (later renamed Collection, not Museum) opened at Wickenby – Chapter 16.
14th Nov 1999	The Front Line Aviation Museum closed at Sandown.
2000	Bristol Aero Collection began regular open days at Kemble but had to close its doors on 28th May 2012. See June 2017 and Chapter 10.
Sep 2000	The Martlesham Heath Aviation Society opened its control tower museum – Chapter 26.
Nov 2000	The Manx Aviation and Military Museum opened – Chapter 13.
2nd Jun 2002	The Twinwood Airfield 1940s Museums opened at Twinwood Farm – Chapter 2.
29th May 2001	Having relocated from Firbeck, the South Yorkshire Aircraft Museum's Aeroventure was officially opened at Doncaster. It had been opened on a 'preview' limited basis since 24th August 2000 – Chapter 31.
21st Jul 2001	The Sywell Aviation Museum opened at Northampton Airport – Chapter 21.
27th July 2002	The 306th Bomb Group Museum opened at Thurleigh – Chapter 2.
2003	The Davidstow Moor RAF Memorial Museum was inaugurated – Chapter 6.
2003	The Wings World War Two Remembrance Museum opened at Redhill. It closed in November 2009. See 20th March 2010 – Chapter 28.
14th May 2003	The Aviation Visitor Park (later the Runway Visitor Park) opened at Manchester Airport – Chapter 18.
28th Jun 2003	Farnborough Air Sciences Trust opened up at Farnborough – Chapter 11.
Apr 2004	The Gatwick Aviation Museum began 'regular' opening, on alternate Sundays, despite planning restrictions – Chapter 27.
18th Aug 2004	The Concorde Visitor Centre opened to public visits at Filton; the facility closed in late 2010 – Chapter 10.
2005	The Bomber County Aviation Museum closed as Hemswell.
May 2005	The Highland Aviation Museum opened at Inverness – Chapter 32.
2006	The Ulster Aviation Collection was established at Long Kesh, Northern Ireland. The largest collection of historic aircraft in all of Ireland, it is available on an occasional basis. Run by the Ulster Aviation Society, founded in 1968, its first aircraft, a Grumman Wildcat, was acquired in April 1984.
Apr 2007	Previously open only on Sundays, the Montrose Air Station Heritage centre opened on a full-time basis – Chapter 32.
20th May 2007	The Bentwaters Cold War Museum opened – Chapter 26.
11th Aug 2007	The Davidstow Airfield and Cornwall at War Museum opened – Chapter 6.
late 2007	The Airborne Forces Museum at Aldershot closed. Most of the exhibits were subsumed into 'Airborne Assault' which opened at the Imperial War Museum, Duxford, on 8th December 2008.
Oct 2009	The Second World War Aircraft Preservation Society closed down at Lasham.

20th Mar 2010	The Wings World War Two Remembrance Museum re-opened at Balcombe – Chapter 28.
29th May 2011	The Boxted Airfield Museum was opened – Chapter 9.
Jul 2011	The RAF Burtonwood Heritage Centre opened – Chapter 5.
1st Jul 2012	Established at MoD Boscombe Down and available on a limited access basis there from 1st July 2000, the Boscombe Down Aviation Collection opened the Old Sarum Airfield Museum on a full-time basis – Chapter 30.
29th Mar 2013	Classic Air Force opened at Newquay Cornwall Airport, St Mawgan, and closed in 2015 – Chapter 6.
Aug 2013	Jet Age Museum re-opened (see 1992) in its brand new building at Gloucestershire Airport, Staverton – Chapter 10.
28th Sep 2014	RAF Defford Museum opened in Croome Park – Chapter 29.
Sep 2015	The Cornwall Aviation Heritage Centre opened at Newquay Cornwall Airport, St Mawgan – Chapter 6.
8th Oct 2015	The Avro Heritage Museum at Woodford was officially unveiled ready for the public debut on 13th November – Chapter 18.
10th Oct 2015	Morayvia opened at Kinloss – Chapter 32.
11th Nov 2015	The 453rd Bomb Group Museum was officially opened at Old Buckenham, ready for its first season, starting in the spring of 2016 – Chapter 20.
25th Mar 2016	The Gatwick Aviation Museum opened officially at Charlwood – Chapter 27.
6th May 2016	The Stowe Maries Great War Aerodrome was officially opened – Chapter 9.
summer 2017	Aerospace Bristol due to open – Chapter 10.

CHAPTER 2
BEDFORDSHIRE

Reich Wreckers
306th Bomb Group Museum

Thurleigh
www.306bg.co.uk

While an unpretentious brick building might seem an unlikely home for a subject as big as a unit of the USAAF's famous 'Mighty Eighth', the 306th Bombardment Group Museum is more than up to the task. As with many venues in this book, what the 306th museum lacks in scale, it makes up for abundantly in setting the mood and character of a momentous era. Known as the 'Reich Wreckers', the 306th BG's B-17 Flying Fortresses arrived at Thurleigh, to the north of Bedford, in September 1942.

Prior to the arrival of the Americans, from January 1942 Thurleigh hosted fleeting RAF detachments, including the Wellingtons of 18 Operational Training Unit. It was also home to the ground elements of the newly re-formed 160 Squadron

Above: A B-17G Fortress of the 'Triangle-A', the 306th Bomb Group, returning to the fold at Thurleigh as depicted by artist Keith Hill in his full colour painting 'Thurleigh's Guiding Light'. *Courtesy and copyright Keith Hill Studios – www.aviation-artist.com*

as it prepared to move to India to join up with its Liberator IIs in February. As such Thurleigh had the slightest of RAF heritage before it became USAAF Station 111 and the 306th arrived from Wendover in Utah. At 293ft above mean sea level, the base offered a commanding view of the surrounding countryside. To the west the land falls away into the vale of the River Ouse and its tributaries – this allowed for some dramatic 'pop-up' arrivals at the airfield!

The oldest operational bomb group in the Eighth Air Force, on 9th October 1942 the 306th carried out its debut raid and was in the first wave to strike German targets. After 342 gruelling missions, the 306th stood down in April 1945 having remained loyal to its base at Thurleigh until it departed for the Continent in December. That gave it the longest 'tenancy' of any British-based bomb group.

In the late 1940s Thurleigh was selected for complete regeneration as the National Aeronautical Establishment, a vast 'super-Farnborough' with a 5-mile long runway intended to keep the UK at the forefront of aviation technology. Construction did not get underway until the early 1950s and by then the plans had been scaled back. The classic three-runway pattern of wartime Thurleigh was swallowed as a 10,500ft by 300ft runway was laid east-west. Known as the Royal Aircraft Establishment (RAE) Bedford, limited operations began in 1954 and it was formally opened in June 1957. All went quiet in March 1994 when the airfield was shut down and the process of selling off the site began.

The north-western enclave was acquired by motor racing driver Jonathan Palmer and turned into a unique facility, the Bedford Autodrome. Jonathan, himself a pilot, was keen to commemorate the airfield's wartime exploits and he turned to Ralph Franklin, who had worked at the RAE for 38 years and was an acknowledged expert in the airfield's USAAF days. Collecting artefacts and planning displays began and a growing number of volunteers rallied to the cause. There were few surviving 1940s buildings in which to set up the museum but on the northwest perimeter, close to what had been the bomb dump, was one listed as 'SAA' on original site maps. This turned out to stand for Small Arms and Ammunition, and this former weapons store turned out to be ideal. The building was occupied in January 2002 and the 306th BG Museum was officially opened by Jonathan Palmer on 27th July that year.

The Thurleigh team have achieved a remarkable museum. Its main focus is of course the 306th and among the wealth of material is a tribute to ball turret gunner Sgt Maynard H 'Snuffy' Smith of the 423rd Bomb Squadron. Aged 32, he was a 'grandfather' among his fellow personnel, who were a decade or so younger. On Smith's first mission, to the U-boat pens at St Nazaire, France, on 1st May 1943 his Fortress was riddled with flak as it pulled away from the target. A fire in the mid-section was so intense that three of the crew baled out – never to be seen again. Smith helped the badly injured tail gunner, used the waist guns to fend off Luftwaffe fighters and fought the blaze as the crippled bomber returned to England. Riddled with holes, the B-17 made an emergency landing and was declared a write off. At a ceremony at Thurleigh, Smith was presented with a Medal of Honor by US Secretary of State for War, Henry L Stimson.

The social impact of a US bomb group 'dropping in' on Bedford is also a theme at the museum; the famously 'Over-paid, Over-sexed and Over-here' visitors. There's a fascinating 'Home Front' exhibition and a charming 'GI Brides' tableau. The latter includes a parachute silk wedding dress; from the immediate Thurleigh area 148 girls married 'Yanks'.

One of many displays within the 306th Bomb Group Museum at Thurleigh, including a ubiquitous Willys Jeep. *Ken Ellis*

Big Band Shrine
Twinwood Airfield 1940s Museums

Twinwood Farm
www.twinwoodevents.com/museums

Control towers seem to have an atmosphere all of their own. All have stories to tell, but perhaps the example at Twinwood Farm, has more than most. The unit most associated with the airfield was 51 Operational Training Unit, headquartered at another Bedfordshire station, Cranfield. The Blenheims, Beauforts and Beaufighters of the OTU used Twinwood as a relief landing ground from the summer of 1941 to mid-1945. Fighter units were also temporarily resident, with Mustangs being the most common type. Military flying stopped at Twinwood by 1948, although it saw occasional use by light aviation through to the 1970s.

Down the road in Bedford, a potent element of the American war effort established its operating headquarters – USAAF Major Glenn Miller and his orchestra. The famous orchestra leader, composer and trombonist, whose arrangements of 'American Patrol', 'In the Mood', 'Moonlight Serenade' and 'Tuxedo Junction' are as emotive today as they ever were, was at the height of his popularity. From Bedford, Miller and his entourage could radiate out to give morale-boosting performances far and wide. Using a couple of flat-bed trailers as the stage, the band, its bevy of singers and the great man himself enthralled a huge crowd in the lee of Twinwood's tower on 27th August 1944. As it turned out, this was to be Miller's only open-air concert presented in Britain. A Noorduyn UC-64 Norseman dropped into Twinwood on 15th December 1944; it was picking up Glenn Miller to take him to Paris. The aircraft and the 40-year-old band leader were never seen again, sparking endless theories about what had happened and turning Twinwood into a place of pilgrimage.

From 2002 David Wooding created the Twinwood Arena from the former airfield. A purpose-built outside events facility, this has become home to a wide range of gatherings, exhibitions and sporting occasions. No expense was spared on restoring the control tower and it has been turned into a visitor centre devoted to the history of the airfield and a shrine to Glenn Miller.

Above: Glenn Miller and his orchestra performing at Wattisham during the summer of 1944. *KEC*

Also within is an extensive exhibition of the superb work of local aviation, military and transport artist, Keith Hill. The tower was officially opened on 2nd June 2002 by Beryl Davis, a British-born vocalist with Miller's original orchestra. Naturally, the occasion was used for a Miller-style concert of 'swing' classics and this was the start of the annual Twinwood Festival. Based in the tower, the Glenn Miller Museum is a part of the heritage 'package' on offer at Twinwood. Other elements included the Twinwood Aviation Museum which holds a large collection of RAF and USAAF artefacts, material from local wartime crash sites and much on the night-fighter role of 51 OTU. Two former RAF accommodation blocks contain exhibitions: Hut 37 housing 'Under Fire' on the wartime fire service while Hut 44 has been returned to its wartime status by the Summer of '44 living history group.

Also in Bedfordshire
Shuttleworth Collection
The famous collection is at Old Warden Aerodrome, near Biggleswade, and is rightly considered to be a national treasure. It is covered in depth in the sister volume *Great Aviation Collections of Britain*. **www.shuttleworth.org**

RAF Signals Museum
Located within RAF Henlow, the collection is a fascinating insight into military radio communications. **www.rafsignalsmuseum.org.uk**

When in Bedfordshire...
Dominating the skyline to the south of Bedford at Cardington are the two awesome 700ft-long airship sheds. The northern-most example, No.1, was built on site and completed in 1916. The second was dismantled at Pulham, Norfolk, in 1928 and re-erected alongside its cousin. A year later, the R-101 commercial airship, a cruise liner of the skies, first took the air from Cardington. On 4th October 1930 it departed east-bound with on its maiden voyage, only to crash in France; just six of the 54 on board survived. With this disaster, Britain's airship programme was terminated. Since then the giant structures have been used for all sorts of experimentation and from 1981 occasionally modern-day airships have been built and flown, but with little success so far. Upkeep of the buildings costs a fortune, but any thoughts of demolishing one, or both, of these breath-taking cathedrals would be to rob the nation of a reminder of an incredible era.

Famous landmark to the south of Bedford, Cardington's airship sheds. *Ken Ellis*

CHAPTER 3
BERKSHIRE

Royal County Custodians
Museum of Berkshire Aviation

Woodley
www.museumofberkshireaviation.co.uk

Lincolnshire, East Anglia and Yorkshire are all areas of Britain that spring easily to mind as centres of considerable aeronautical activity and heritage. By contrast, nestled to the west of London, the Royal county of Berkshire has an incredible story to tell and, since 1993, has had the Museum of Berkshire Aviation (MBA) to take on the task. County boundaries have changed, but during World War Two 21 airfields came under the Berkshire 'flag'. From 1944 there was an over-riding theme at Berkshire airfields – D-Day. For this, USAAF Ninth Air Force Douglas C-47 Skytrain and C-53 Skytrooper transports and Waco CG-4 Hadrian and Airspeed Horsa assault gliders descended on Aldermaston, Greenham Common, Membury and Welford. From 1950 Aldermaston was transformed into the Atomic Weapons Research Establishment and Greenham Common also rose to fame as the site of 'nukes'. During the 1950s Greenham was a rotational base for the Boeing B-47 Stratojets of the USAF's Strategic Air Command. Deterrence was again the mission from 1983 when the base hosted the ground-launched Boeing BGM-109 Tomahawk cruise missiles of the 501st Tactical Missile Wing and tolerated the much-publicized 'peace camps' along the boundary fence. With the Berlin Wall down and the Soviet Union no more, the missile trucks left in 1991 and Greenham Common became an industrial estate. Welford maintains a US military presence in the shape of a vast materiel storage complex.

Above: Herald 100 G-APWA getting airborne from what is believed to be Radlett in 1959. Today, *Whisky-Alpha* again wears BEA colours. *Handley Page*

Only White Waltham is a home to aviation today, with a thriving light aircraft population. The airfield gained fame during World War Two as the headquarters of the Air Transport Auxiliary organisation. Civilian pilots, male and female, ferried aircraft from the factories to their British operational bases, or back for modification, or to and from maintenance units. White Waltham also featured prominently in another aspect of aviation in Berkshire – manufacturing. After the war, the airfield was used as the flight test centre for Fairey, its Fireflies and Gannets contrasting with the company's advanced rotorcraft it was endeavouring to develop. In 1960 Fairey was acquired by Westland and the factory at Hayes turned to building Scout and Wasp helicopters, which also 'beat the circuit' at White Waltham.

White Waltham was also used as a test site for the Slough-based R Malcolm company from 1936; this had become ML Aviation by 1946. Among the varied design and engineering projects undertaken was the inflatable wing ML Utility type developed from 1954 and tested at White Waltham. (An example is displayed at the Museum of Army Flying at Middle Wallop, Hampshire.) Later the company developed a series of rotary winged remotely piloted drones and a diminutive Sprite of the 1970s is on show at the MBA. The 19th century Elliotts of Newbury furniture manufacturer took up glider and aircraft production post-war. As well as primary gliders for the Air Cadets, it built a series of high-performance sailplanes, the Olympias; two Elliott gliders are on show at the MBA.

Woodley's heritage

But it is Woodley that is best known for its contribution to aircraft design and manufacture. Frederick G Miles and his brother George developed a family of light aircraft and trainers, initially through the Phillips and Powis company, taking the name Miles Aircraft in 1943. The company collapsed in 1946 and Handley Page took over the factory. Since the MBA's opening in 1993, a close association has been maintained with the Miles Aircraft Collection and there is a very strong Miles theme across the museum.

Origins of the MBA belong with the Berkshire Aviation Group, a group enthusiasts determined to chart the heritage of the county and particularly the Miles connection. Items collected included the outer wings of Master advanced trainers and a small upper fuselage section from a Marathon airliner and a vast number of smaller artefacts. A place on the former Woodley aerodrome was the ideal location and a temporary exhibition was staged there in May 1991 with Graham Johnson's Magister recreation, 'L6906' as the centre piece and this became the museum's founder airframe. During 1992, Handley Page Herald G-APWA, in the care of The Herald Society, arrived by road from Southend. Using a Robin hangar that had previously been part of the Miles technical school, the museum was officially opened on 27th March 1993. During 1996, negotiations that had started three years previously bore fruit with the arrival of the Martinet from Iceland. Restoration of this airframe has been a long and challenging undertaking, highlighting the capabilities of MBA's volunteers. The opening of the museum concentrated minds and locals and individuals from far and wide contributed items to swell the exhibits. With the new century, fund-raising began to increase the size of the museum. Thanks to a bequest from former Miles employees, the late Bob Brown, the floor area of the MBA was doubled when the Robert Brown Hall was opened on 24th May 2008.

Magister recreation 'L6906' was used to raise awareness and help generate funds for the Museum of Berkshire Aviation in the early 1990s. *KEC*

A one-sixth scale wind tunnel model of the Miles M.52 supersonic experimental project, which was cancelled in early 1946. *Ken Ellis*

Fairey Jet Gyrodyne XJ389
1955 | Compound helicopter | One 520hp Alvis Leonides radial

As part of its post-war strategy, Fairey established a rotary wing division to exploit compound helicopters, which combined a main rotor with fixed wings and conventional propellers. The first step was the Gyrodyne, which first flew on 5th December 1947 from White Waltham. The nine-cylinder Leonides piston engine buried within the fuselage drove the rotor blades and a tractor propeller mounted on the end of the starboard stub wing to counter rotor torque in addition to providing forward thrust. This machine was involved in a fatal crash on 17th April 1949. At that point testing of the second Gyrodyne was halted.

By the time of the accident, after considerable experimental work on ground rigs, designer Dr J A J Bennett had perfected the next step, the Jet Gyrodyne. This time, the Leonides was required to work even harder for its living. It drove two pusher propellers mounted on stub wings and, via a clutch, a pair of modified centrifugal compressors from Rolls-Royce Merlins that pumped kerosene into pressure jets at the tips of the 60ft diameter rotor blades. These jets allowed the rotorcraft to take-off and land vertically, but the main rotor could also 'coast' unpowered, allowing for auto-rotation for a controlled, rolling landing if needs be.

Jet Gyrodyne XJ389 on a sortie out of White Waltham in 1955. *Fairey Aviation*

The second Gyrodyne, civil registered as G-AJJP, was transformed into the new 'jet' guise. Although it first took to the air at White Waltham in January 1954, it was not until 1st March of the following year that a full transition from one flight phase to another, and back, was achieved by John Dennis. At first this machine was given the military serial XD759, but this was later amended to XJ389. The Jet Gyrodyne paved the way for the tip-jet powered Ultra-Light Helicopters of 1955 and the giant 90ft diameter rotor, 33,000lb all-up weight Rotodyne transport of 1957. (For more on both of these see Chapters 29 and 25.) With these two projects up and running XJ389 was no longer required and it was struck off charge on 1st December 1960 going into the hands of Sqn Ldr Alan Jones and 424 Squadron Air Training Corps at Southampton. (Sqn Ldr Jones was instrumental in setting up the museum now known as Solent Sky, see Chapter 11.) By the summer of 1979 the Jet Gyrodyne was taken on by the RAF Museum at Cosford and it was placed on loan to the MBA in June 1994.

Handley Page Herald 100 G-APWA
1959 | Medium range airliner | Two 1,910shp Rolls-Royce Dart 527 turboprops

After 18 years on display outside, the Yorkshire Air Museum scrapped Herald 213 G-AVPN, keeping its cockpit section. This brought the UK population of whole examples of the twin turboprop to three: Woodley's G-APWA, Norwich's G-ASKK and Duxford's G-APWJ. Held within the wider Imperial War Museum collection, *Whisky-Juliet* is arguably the 'national' airframe, however the author would nominate the Woodley example as of equal stature and better provenance. Either way, with a total production run of 50, with three intact museum airframes, the Herald can boast a healthy proportion of survivors.

Swift action in 1948 allowed Handley Page (HP) to take on assets of the collapsed Miles Aircraft at Woodley and Handley Page (Reading) Ltd was established that July. Before the liquidators were brought in, Miles had started testing the Marathon four-engined airliner, but it was in a league that the ailing company should never have strayed into. It took a company of HP's stature to put the Marathon into production but the line was closed in 1951 with a total of 43 built, the bulk being handed to a reluctant RAF as navigator trainers.

Miles had schemed a scaled-up version of the Marathon, the M.73, and these plans were dusted down, given considerable improvement and the HPR.3 Herald, powered by a quartet of Alvis Leonides Major radials, was born. Built at Woodley, the prototype first flew on 25th August 1955 at HP's airfield at Radlett. Twenty-one months previously, Fokker had flown the first F.27 Friendship, propelled by two well-proven Rolls-Royce Darts. The Dutch company had a head-start and had opted for the powerplant of the future, the turbine. The first Herald went back into the workshop and emerged as the slightly stretched Dart-powered HPR.7, flying for the first time on 11th March 1958. Two years later HP's arch-rival Avro put its twin-Dart 748, aimed at the same market, into the air. Eight Heralds were built at the Berkshire site, the last in December 1961. Production transferred to Radlett, concluding in August 1968 with the 50th example. HP had really missed the boat.

Built within sight of where it now stands, *Whisky-Alpha* was the first production Dart-powered Herald and it had its maiden flight at Woodley on 30th October 1959. It wore the colours of launch customer British European Airways (BEA), the scheme that it again wears today. As the development and demonstration airframe, G-APWA was destined for a varied life; a sample of which will have to suffice here. Thirty-four days after its first flight and with its certificate of airworthiness nine days old, *Whisky-Alpha* set off for demonstrations at Nice, France, on 3rd December 1959. Upon return, it was briefly used by BEA for trials of its Scottish 'Highlands and Islands' services. From March 1960 the Herald was demonstrated in West Africa and Brazil and Argentina and in July it was at Upavon for evaluation by the RAF and the Royal Australian Air Force. Jersey Airlines kicked off orders for the slightly longer Series 200 and leased *Whisky-Alpha* for route proving trials in 1961. With a 21-seat VIP interior, G-APWA set off in January 1962 on a Royal tour of Latin America, with HRH Prince Philip completing 99 of the 126 flying hours as captain. The tour, which included sister ship G-APWC, went down the eastern side of the continent, crossed the Andes mountain range and returned up the Pacific coast. For the outbound and homeward Atlantic crossings, podded underwing fuel tanks were fitted. The regal theme continued in 1962 when another regal pilot, King Hussein of Jordan, charted *Whisky-Alpha* for his honeymoon with Princess Muna in Morocco in July.

In February 1964 G-APWA was sold to Brazilian airline Sadia de Transportes Aereos taking on the registration PP-ASV, but by March of the following year, it was back in the UK and wearing the identity G-APWA again. A lease to British Midland Airways in 1966 was followed late that year with a return to Brazil, this time as PP-SDM. It came back to the UK in July 1976 joining British Air Ferries, based at Southend, again becoming *Whisky-Alpha*. It was kept busy with a series of leases and charters; among others it worked in France, Egypt, Libya and Zimbabwe. By 1982 it was stored at Southend, very likely facing the scrapman's axe. Thanks to considerable efforts by the late Roger Hargreaves, saviour of several airliners (including the Britannia at the former Liverpool Airport, see under Merseyside) G-APWA was passed to what became The Herald Society in 1992 and it was moved to its birthplace, Woodley. The re-assembly task was daunting; the restoration required even more so. The volunteers who worked on *Whisky-Alpha* have created a stunning exhibit and an imposing 'gateway' to the museum.

Miles Martinet TT.I TF-SHC
1943 | Target-tug | One 870hp Bristol Mercury XXX radial

Volunteers at Woodley have been working on the substantial restoration of this machine for over two decades. The team started with a wreck that had endured the ravages of Icelandic weather for 28 years and unsurprisingly much of its structure is new, or considerably reworked. As such some readers may call this a replica, or perhaps a re-creation. That does not diminish the worth of this exhibit as it stands for a family of advanced trainers that started with the ground-breaking Miles

Martinet TF-SHC during the opening
of the MBA's Robert Brown Hall on
24th May 2008. *Ken Ellis*

Kestrel of 1937. Getting on for 5,000 of the production version, the Master, the Martinet target-tug and the Queen Martinet target drone were produced, making TF-SHC the most tangible reminder of a very important RAF type.

    Built at Woodley in 1943 as MS902, the Martinet was issued to 27 Maintenance Unit (MU) at Shawbury on 21st October 1943 and in the following November it was ferried to 76 MU at Wroughton where it was packed for shipping, along with sister ship MS903. The SS *Isobell* docked at Reykjavik in Iceland in January 1944 but it was not until 19th July 1945 that MS902 appears to have become active. On that date it was taken on charge by Reykjavik-based 251 Squadron and coded 'AD-X'. The squadron was tasked with air-sea rescue and weather reconnaissance using Lockheed Hudsons, Boeing Fortresses and Vickers Warwicks until it was disbanded on 30th October 1945. The day after 251 closed its doors, MS902 was transferred to the Reykjavik Station Flight. On 18th July 1949 it was struck off RAF charge, although it very likely was out of use by 1946 at the latest. The Martinet was acquired by the Akureyri Flying Club and civilian registered as TF-SHC. It was based at the airstrip alongside the town of that name on Iceland's northern coast. A sortie on 18th July 1951 ended badly with a forced landing on a farm at Kópasker just inside the Arctic Circle on the north eastern tip of the island. This was almost certainly the last ever flight by a Martinet, or other members of the family. The hulk languished at Kópasker until July 1979 when it was salvaged by the Iceland Aviation Historical Society and it was put into store at Reykjavik Airport, its one-time base. Negotiations began in 1993 to bring the Martinet back to Woodley and the wreckage arrived in the UK in March 1996.

Miles Student 2 G-MIOO
1957 | Military trainer/liaison | One Turboméca Marboré IIF3 turbojet

Being a prototype, or a one-off, or extremely rare is not necessarily sufficient to make an aircraft worthy of becoming a museum piece, but occasionally a number of pointers coincide to secure preservation. At first glimpse, the inclusion of the Student gives the impression that MBA's collecting policy has gone 'off piste' as it is not a child of the county. However, the collection's remit is to act as a repository for all things Miles. This attractive, but abortive, jet was the last throw of the dice for the dynasty, being marketed well into the 1970s.

    After the demise of Miles Aircraft in 1947, Frederick G Miles moved to Redhill and established a design consultancy. Brother George took over the design office of de Havilland-owned Airspeed at Portsmouth. There he conceived the DH.115 Vampire jet trainer, the prototype first flying in November 1950. George joined 'FG' at Redhill and in December 1951 and among several projects refined what became the M.100 Student jet trainer. In January 1954 Hunting carried out the maiden flight of the Jet Provost and the following year the RAF began evaluating the type with a view to 'all-through' training on jets. George Miles set about building the Student, which he believed offered much more potential than the 'JP'. It could accommodate a pupil and instructor in the then fashionable side-by-side layout with another two people, somewhat cramped, behind in the liaison role. Access was via a pair of car-like doors. The engine was buried in the upper centre section, offering scope for a variety of powerplants, or even twin turbojets alongside one another. Construction was kept as simple as possible, facilitating licence production. By the time George piloted the prototype on its maiden flight, from Shoreham wearing the 'B Condition' (or trade-plate) marking G-35-4, on 15th May 1957, the Jet Provost had been snapped up by the RAF.

    F G Miles Ltd continued to market the Student, which was civil registered as G-APLK in March 1958. Interest from the South African Air Force brought about the armed Mk.2 version and G-APLK first flew in this guise on 22nd April 1964. With the military serial XS941, it carried out weapons clearance flights at the Aeroplane and Armament Experimental Establishment, Boscombe Down, during the summer of 1964. After this the Student 2 was retired at Shoreham, going to Ford for storage in late 1967 until 1971. In November 1973 G-APLK was re-registered to Miles-Dufon Ltd and returned to airworthiness at Shoreham, carrying out a noise monitoring contract for Hawker Siddeley on an HS.125 executive jet at Hatfield between March and October 1974.

George Miles, designer and test pilot of the Student, G-35-4, outside the airport building at Shoreham, 1957. *Miles Aircraft*

In October 1984 the Student was acquired by Peter Hoar, a pilot for aviation film and TV specialists Aces High and a Miles devotee, and ferried to Duxford. It was re-registered as G-MIOO – the closest the alphabet could get to M.100. Engine problems on 24th August 1986 resulted in a forced landing in which Peter was badly hurt; it was the type's last flight, having clocked up around 280 hours total time. The wreck was passed on to the Vintage Aircraft Team at Cranfield, moving to Bruntingthorpe by the beginning of 1995. Aces High's proprietor, Mike Woodley – another Miles fan and benefactor of the rare and the unusual – took on the Student in November 1996, keeping it at North Weald and then Dunsfold. The following year the appropriately named Mr Woodley presented G-MIOO on loan to the MBA. Since then, volunteers at Woodley have worked hard on this fascinating piece of Miles heritage.

Museum of Berkshire Aviation aircraft

Type	Identity	Built	Origin	Acquired	Notes
Broburn Wanderlust	–	1946	Britain	28 Nov 1992	glider
EoN Primary	–	1948	Britain	2004	glider
EoN 460-1	–	1965	Britain	27 May 2009	glider
Fairey Jet Gyrodyne*	XJ389	1949	Britain	Jun 1994	see profile
Fairey Gannet T.5	XG883	1957	Britain	24 Mar 1996	–
Handley Page Herald 100*	G-APWA	1959	Britain	28 Aug 1992	see profile
McBroom hang-glider	–	1974	Britain	1993	–
Miles Magister I	'L6906'	1940	Britain	26 Apr 1991	substantial recreation
Miles Martinet TT.1	TF-SHC	1943	Britain	Mar 1996	see profile
Miles Student 2	G-MIOO	1957	Britain	1997	see profile
Westland Scout AH.1	XP895	1963	Britain	13 Oct 2010	composite

Notes: * – illustrated in the colour section

Also in Berkshire
Maidenhead Heritage Centre

Exhibits include a tribute to the incredible contribution and gallantry of the men and women of the Air Transport Auxiliary which was headquartered at nearby White Waltham. **www.atamuseum.org**

When in Berkshire...

In Windsor, alongside the Thames in Alexandra Gardens, Barry Avenue, is the Sydney Camm Memorial, including a full-scale model of Hurricane 'R4229' in the colours of 249 Squadron, honouring the place of birth and youth of Hawker designer Sir Sydney Camm. The replica was commissioned and financed by the Sir Sydney Camm Commemorative Society. **www.sirsydneycamm.org**

CHAPTER 4

BUCKINGHAMSHIRE

Trenchard Museum and James McCudden Air Power Heritage Centre

Within RAF Halton, southeast of Aylesbury, these two exhibitions concentrate on the history of the base, home of the famed RAF apprentices. As well as a huge array of exhibits, a couple of gliders and cockpits, there is Folland Gnat T.1 XR574 on show. Open Tuesdays, or by prior arrangement. **www.raf.mod.uk/rafhalton**

The Heritage Park – Pitstone Green Museum

Located north of Tring and run by Pitstone and Ivinghoe Museum Society volunteers, the centre includes a World War Two room, within which is an Avro Lancaster cockpit recreation that uses many original fittings. Open bank holidays and Sundays. **www.pitstonemuseum.co.uk**

Above: A famous image of a 91st Bomb Group B-17F Fortress 'buzzing' the tower at Bassingbourn. Sadly, the brilliant Tower Museum has had to close its doors – here's hoping it's only an intermission. *Tower Museum Bassingbourn*

CAMBRIDGESHIRE

Imperial War Museum, Duxford

'Duxford', as it is mostly simply known, is of course a national institution boasting its own active airfield with regular major events and airshows. It is covered in depth in the sister volume *Great Aviation Collections of Britain*. **www.iwm.org.uk**

Tower Museum Bassingbourn

Due to circumstances beyond the control of the volunteers from late 2015 the exceptional museum within tower of the former USAAF Station 121, famed as the base of the B-17 Fortress *Memphis Belle*, was closed for an indefinite period. Hoping that the issues can be overcome, keep an eye on the website. **www.towermuseumbassingbourn.co.uk**

Bottisham Airfield Museum

As this book closed for press, members of the Bottisham Airfield Museum Group were readying an application to the Heritage Lottery Fund towards their plans to open an exhibition dedicated to the airfield's resident units, in particular the USAAF's P-51 Mustang-equipped 361st Fighter Group. Keep an eye on the website for developments. **www.bottishamairfieldmuseum.org.uk**

Transatlantic Gateway
RAF Burtonwood Heritage Centre

Burtonwood
www.rafburtonwood.com

Up to November 2008, people travelling along the M62 motorway near Warrington could see five hangars adjacent to the eastbound carriage as they hurtled past. These looked so out of place that most passers-by must have wondered if the area had ever really been an airfield. Since these massive edifices were demolished, from the motorway only those with long memories could appreciate the heritage of the site. Along that stretch the M62 has as its foundation the 9,000ft post-war runway that handled everything from Douglas C-47 Skytrains to Convair B-36 Peacemakers. Prior to April 1988 there were other clues, this time to the south of the six-lane highway that links Liverpool with Hull. There was a massive parking apron, an airport-like terminal and an imposing control tower. These were constructed in 1953 and personnel getting off USAF Military Air Transport Service (MATS) airlifters were greeted by a sign declaring 'Gateway to Europe'. The tower came crashing down on 17th April 1988 as the base at Burtonwood continued to contract and succumbed to bulldozers. On what the Americans called Site 8, was Header House, a warehouse a mile long and in the late 1950s it was the largest of its kind in Europe. By 2012 this area had been developed, including an inevitable hypermarket.

Construction of Burtonwood airfield started in 1938, with a standard three-runway layout, extensive dispersal sites and a huge 'factory' area to the south. Known as the Burtonwood Repair Depot, it was operational by May 1940. With its proximity to Liverpool – with its docks and Speke airport both handling vast numbers of airframes, engines and spares coming across the Atlantic – Burtonwood was ideally located for the USAAF to use as a maintenance, repair and storage centre. It was handed over becoming Station 590, Base Air Depot (BAD) 1, in June 1942 and extensive construction work was initiated. From July 1943 to May 1945 BAD 1 accepted, assembled, modified or repaired a grand total of 11,575 aircraft of over 25 types, including 4,381 Republic P-47 Thunderbolts and 4,243 Boeing B-17 Flying Fortresses. Additionally 30,386 engines were overhauled, 38,526 machine guns were serviced and 71,422 parachutes repaired and packed. At its wartime peak, BAD 1 was home to 18,500 personnel. (See the Boxted Airfield Museum – Chapter 9 – for a rare survivor of Burtonwood at this time.)

Above: The ramp on Burtonwood's 'A' Site on the northern side of the airfield, looking towards the Technical Site, with B-17s, B-24s, P-47s and RAF Mosquitos, circa late 1945. *RAF Burtonwood Heritage centre*

This empire was returned to the RAF on 5th May 1946, but with the beginning of the Berlin Airlift in 1948, the Americans were back, using Burtonwood as an air transport and storage hub. The Cold War had arrived and by the mid-1950s it was the largest American base outside the continental USA. Flying ceased in 1959 and – for the second time – Burtonwood reverted to the RAF, on 18th June 1965. Once again, the 'Stars and Stripes' were destined to return. When France withdrew its forces from NATO, huge supply dumps had to be relocated and Burtonwood was perfect for the task. On 2nd January 1967 the base was transferred to the US Army and remained so until July 1993 when the last 'Yanks' departed.

In 1987 the Burtonwood Association was formed to keep former personnel in touch and to make sure that the base's place in history was assured. In the late 1980s a small visitor centre run by volunteers was opened in a building alongside the former main gate; this later moved to rooms within the massive Header House. By the end of the decade redevelopment of the former US Army facility meant that another venue had to be found. Entrepreneur Ray Phillips acquired Sites 4 and 5 to the east of the former airfield and began to develop the area as Gulliver's World Warrington, the second of his Gulliver's entertainment complexes; the first of which was at Matlock in Derbyshire. In February 2011 Ray offered a building and the RAF Burtonwood Heritage Centre became a reality, opening to the public five months later. Since then the exhibits have expanded and in December 2015 the forward fuselage of Douglas DC-4 N31356 arrived from North Weald. It represents the C-54 Skymasters and other transports that made the Burtonwood apron busier than any airport in the UK of the 1950s.

Also in Cheshire
Hooton Park Trust

The trust is managing the heritage of the precious Grade II* listed World War One hangars on the former airfield site alongside the River Mersey. Also based at Hooton is The Aeroplane Collection (TAC), which started life as the pioneering Northern Aircraft Preservation Society. Although Hooton Park falls outside the remit of this book it would be criminal not to chart TAC's seminal contribution to aircraft preservation in the UK. This is dealt with in Chapter 18. **www.hootonparktrust.co.uk** **www.theaeroplanecollection.org**

Hooton Park Trust / The Aeroplane Collection* aircraft

Type	Identity	Built	Origin	Acquired	Notes
Auster J/1N Alpha*	G-AJEB	1946	Britain	28 Jun 1975	–
de Havilland Vampire T.11*	XD624	1955	Britain	20 Mar 2011	–
de Havilland Canada Chipmunk T.10*	G-AOUO	1950	Canada	Mar 2017	–
de Havilland Canada Chipmunk T.10*	WK640	1952	Canada	Mar 2017	–
Fairey Gannet T.2	–	1956	Britain	20 Jul 2012	cockpit
Luton Minor*	G-AFIU	1938	Britain	1971	–
Mignet 'Flying Flea'	–	1936	France	2011	fuselage
Miles Messenger*	'G-AHUI'	1946	Britain	22 Aug 20002	composite project
Miles Gemini*	'GAKHZ'	1947	Britain	22 Aug 20002	composite project
Slingsby Tutor	BGA.466	1946	Britain	31 Aug 2014	glider
Slingsby Tutor*	BGA.473	1947	Britain	10 Jun 2012	glider
Supermarine Spitfire I	–	1940	Britain	2015	cockpit
UFM Easy-Riser	–	1981	USA	9 Apr 2004	–

Hack Green Secret Nuclear Bunker
A former Cold War regional government bunker near Nantwich. Among other attractions is Hunting Jet Provost T.4 XS179. **www.hackgreen.co.uk**

Part of The Aeroplane Collection's display at Hooton Park, 1946-built Auster J/1N Alpha G-AJEB.
Dave Arkle – The Aeroplane Collection

CHAPTER 6
CORNWALL and DEVON

Museum First, Beach Later
Cornwall Aviation Heritage Centre

Newquay Cornwall Airport
www.cornwallaviationhc.co.uk

'Visit us in the morning and the beach in the afternoon' is a jingle on the Cornwall Aviation Heritage Centre's welcoming website. Opened to the public in September 2015, this is one of the UK's newest aviation museums, but it is not the first to have been set up at Newquay Cornwall Airport, the former RAF St Mawgan, as we shall see. The airfield opened in a limited manner during 1942, but it was late 1943 before facilities were such that units could be accepted on anything other than a temporary detachment basis. To the west was the disastrous airfield at Trebelzue which had proven to be inoperable, hence the development of the land to the immediate east as St Mawgan. A variety of types could be found at St Mawgan during the 1940s, mostly Douglas Dakotas; the airfield was reduced to care and maintenance in 1947.

Above: Guided tours of the VC-10 tanker are a highlight of a visit to the CAHC. *Ken Ellis*

St Mawgan re-opened in the first days of 1951 in the role that it is most associated: maritime patrol. Equipped with Avro Lancaster GR.3s, the School of Maritime Reconnaissance was followed by the Anti-Submarine Warfare Development Unit, with Avro Shackletons. Frontline and operational training Shackleton units were the main residents through to the late 1960s. From 1956 air-sea rescue helicopters became part and parcel of the airspace around St Mawgan; in turn Westland Whirlwind, Wessex and Sea Kings – the latter bowing out in 2008. In preparation for the Hawker Siddeley Nimrods that replaced the Shackletons from late 1969 the massive Hangar 404 was built. The importance of St Mawgan was further emphasized with its role as a master diversion airfield and the building of hardened aircraft shelters (HASs) for major exercises and temporary detachments. With the disbanding of 38 Squadron in October 1992 the wind down of the RAF presence began and today it is a small enclave within the civil airport.

Classic interval

Amid great pomp, the Coventry-based Classic Air Force (CAF) established itself at Newquay during 2012, using Hangar 404. It was opened to the public on 29th March 2013, only for CAF to throw in the towel two years later and retreat back to Coventry where it rapidly curtailed flying operations and museum status. Some background to CAF is required, before it takes its place in any second edition of *Lost Aviation Collections of Britain*. Starting off as an air taxi and charter set-up based on Jersey in the late 1960s, in 1977 it took the name Air Atlantique and expanded into freight charters with a fleet of Dakotas. Air Atlantique moved to Coventry Airport, Baginton, in the mid-1980s and its activities multiplied; the airline fleet extended to Douglas DC-6s and Lockheed Electras via several associate companies. Typical of the breed, the Dakotas worked hard, some were modified as maritime pollution sprayers but they rose to fame offering enthusiast flights and joy-rides to and at airshows. This side of things became known as the Air Atlantique Classic Flight and de Havilland Dragon Rapides were acquired along with an eclectic mix of 'warbirds' and vintage light aircraft. Regulation changes eventually meant that public category operation of Dakotas was no longer viable and the final members of the fleet were retired or sold on.

In 2011 a new visitor attraction, entitled AIRBASE – Festival of Flight, was launched at Coventry and in February the following year the Classic Aircraft Trust was established, taking on a dozen or so aircraft donated by Air Atlantique co-founder, Mike Collett. Visitor figures were not encouraging and on 30th September 2012 AIRBASE closed and the intention of migrating to Newquay, under the CAF banner, was announced. As the move to Cornwall advanced, during 2013 a split-site operation was chosen with the maintenance base remaining at Coventry. Weekend opening to the public at Coventry resumed in April 2014. At Cornwall the decision was taken to acquire some sizeable 'hardware' to add to the airworthy and static CAF airframes. The Vickers Varsity from the Imperial War Museum at Duxford was brought by road at great cost with the BAC One-Eleven and Vickers VC-10 flying in during 2013.

The re-location to Newquay was always high-risk. 'Bucket and spade' visitors take a lot of persuading to pull away from the beaches and attractions of the seaside. For those who did turn up, the potential money-spinner of a flight 'around the bay' proved to be well beyond the pockets of most 'punters'. Basing aircraft in the West Country while the engineering facility remained bolted to the Midlands made for many 'dead runs' ferrying to and fro. This also applied to airshow appearances, with aircraft facing long and expensive positioning flights, probably pushing up appearance fees. By March 2015, the airworthy elements of CAF had returned to the Midlands and the remainder of the exhibits faced uncertainty.

Hawker Hunter GA.11 WV256 has been returned to the days of mid-1955 when it served 26 Squadron at Oldenburg in West Germany as an F.4. *Ken Ellis*

Largest in Cornwall

Thankfully volunteers who had pitched in with CAF came to the rescue and the Cornwall Aviation Heritage Centre (CAHC) was formed. The expensive Hangar 404 was forsaken and a dispersal and a HAS on the western perimeter, close to the present-day RAF St Mawgan enclave, were secured. The static display airframes, along with the awesome responsibility for the two jetliners, were handed over by CAF. With little time, frantic work got the new collection up and running and ready for opening up in September 2015 for what one of the team described as "a near vertical learning curve!" In far more practical accommodation, with a warm welcome for visitors and a policy of allowing as much access to the exhibits as possible, CAHC has seen its visitor figures increasing. The 'beach later' approach mentioned at the beginning is working well with the marketing of a venue that is admittedly a distance from the attractions of Newquay itself. CAHC is the largest aviation heritage attraction in Cornwall and Devon and its well-motivated team deserves success.

British Aircraft Corporation One-Eleven Srs 539GL ZH763
1980 | Medium range airliner | Two 12,000lb st Rolls-Royce Spey 512-14DWE turbofans

Of the four BAC One-Eleven 'bus-stop jets' preserved in Britain, two are held by 'nationals' (the Duxford Aviation Society and the National Museum of Flight Scotland) and both served with British Airways. The other two contrast with that pair dramatically: the development and trials Series 475 G-ASYD at the Brooklands Museum, Surrey (Chapter 27), and the CAHC's example, which last flew in military trials. In the days before four-figure Airbus production runs, with 249 built between 1965 and 1991 (nine of which were completed in Romania) the One-Eleven was an UK success story.

This example was built at Hurn, Bournemouth, for British Airways as G-BGKE, carrying out its maiden flight on 26th January 1980. Destined to work out of Birmingham Airport, *Kilo-Echo* was delivered to the airline on 3rd March, taking the fleet name *County of Gwynedd* initially, before adopting *County of West Midlands*. This machine carried out the last British Airways One-Eleven service on 30th March 1991, staging Munich-Manchester. Nineteen days later it was ferried to its birthplace at Hurn and placed in open store. It started a new life as a trials test-bed when it was acquired by GEC Ferranti Defence Systems in June 1991 for lease to the Defence Research Agency (DRA). It was delivered to the DRA site at Thurleigh on 29th July and again put into store. With the impending closure of Thurleigh, *Kilo-Echo* was transferred to Farnborough before going to Boscombe Down and in January 1994 it was given the military serial ZH763.

At Boscombe the One-Eleven was adapted for trials of the Enhanced Surveillance Radar, flying in this guise until 2002. By this time DRA had become defence specialist contractor QinetiQ from January 2003 ZH763 was converted into the Large Flying Laboratory with a large, removable, belly radome and a port fuselage side-mounted radome. During March 2007 the One-Eleven took part in Phases 1 to 5 of QinetiQ's Surrogate Unmanned Air Vehicle trials where ZH763 flew under the command and control of a pilot in the Tornado Integrated Avionics Research Aircraft (TIARA), Panavia Tornado F.2A ZD902. These flights were to pave the way for fighter aircraft to control 'swarms' of drones. The jetliner made its last flight with QinetiQ on 21st December 2012 and entered its third storage phase. QinetiQ donated ZH763 to the Classic Air Force and with Flt Lt Mark 'Hasty' Hasted as captain it was ferried from Boscombe Down to Newquay on 26th April 2013 – making the last flight by a One-Eleven in the UK.

One-Eleven ZH763 last served as QinetiQ's Large Flying Laboratory. The attachment points for the side-mounted radome can be seen behind the roundel. *Ken Ellis*

Cornwall Aviation Heritage Centre aircraft

Type	Identity	Built	Origin	Acquired#	Notes
BAC One-Eleven Srs 539GL	ZH763	1980	Britain	26 Apr 2013	see profile
Clutton FRED Srs 3	G-BKVF	1991	Britain	Sep 2015	–
Colomban Cri-Cri	G-MCXV	1986	France	Sep 2015	–
de Havilland Sea Devon C.20	XK895	1956	Britain	13 Feb 2013	–
de Havilland Venom FB.50	J-1649	1956	Britain	Apr 2013	cockpit
English Electric Canberra T.4*	WJ874	1954	Britain	30 Jul 2013	–
English Electric Lightning F.53	ZF580	1967	Britain	Sep 2014	–
Evans VP-2	G-BTSC	1980	USA	Sep 2015	–
Everett Gyroplane Srs 1	G-ULPS	1987	Britain	Sep 2015	–
Fieseler Fi 103 V-1	–	–	Germany	Sep 2015	replica flying-bomb
Hawker Sea Hawk FGA.6	WV798	1954	Britain	Jul 2012	–
Hawker Hunter T.8C	WT722	1955	Britain	9 Jul 2012	–
Hawker Hunter GA.11	WV256	1954	Britain	13 Jul 2012	–
Hawker Siddeley Harrier GR.3	XV753	1969	Britain	19 Jun 2013	–
Monnett Sonerai I	G-BJBM	1983	USA	Sep 2015	–
Scheibe SF.28A Tandem Falke	G-CCIS	1978	Germany	Sep 2015	–
Stern ST-80 Balade	G-BWVI	1978	France	Sep 2015	–
Vickers Varsity T.1*	WJ945	1953	Britain	9 Jan 2013	–
Vickers VC-10 K.3	ZA148	1967	Britain	28 Aug 2013	–

Notes: * – illustrated in the colour section. # Dates prior to September 2015 relate to arrivals for the former Classic Air Force. RAF St Mawgan's long-term 'gate guardian', Avro Shackleton AEW.2 WL795 was disposed of in December 2015 and is located close to the CAHC site. At the time of writing, it was hoped to open this up to the public in due course, but it is managed independently from CAHC.

Moorland Double
Davidstow Airfield and Cornwall at War Museum

www.cornwallatwarmuseum.co.uk

Davidstow Moor RAF Memorial Museum

www.davidstowmemorialmuseum.co.uk
Davidstow Moor

Somewhat bizarrely there are two aviation museums, side-by-side, on the former technical site located in the north western corner of RAF Davidstow Moor. This isn't overkill; both offer different coverage. With respect to the two venues, it is the airfield that dominates memories of a visit. Built on common land with the strict proviso that it be returned as much as practical to its former status, Davidstow Moor opened for business in October 1942. At 970ft above mean sea level it is the highest airfield ever built in Britain. As common land and with minor roads making use of the runways and perimeter tracks, it is a delight to walk on. The tower and several other period buildings survive on the northern side; to the southwest the site is covered with forest, but the runways and 'peris' are extant. Davidstow Moor was the domain of Coastal Command, at first maritime patrollers in the form of Lockheed Hudsons, Armstrong Whitworth Whitleys, Vickers Wellingtons and Warwicks. From May 1944 operations changed to long-range strike in the form of potent Bristol Beaufighter TF.Xs with 144 Squadron and 404 Squadron RCAF taking up residence. The moorland airfield was reduced to care and maintenance status in September 1944 and reverted to agriculture by the end of the following year. Today, when the weather is clement, you can watch microlights or radio controlled aircraft using the wide expanses of the northwest-southeast runway. But the best time to experience this dramatic location and its commanding views is when the only noise is the sheep grazing allowing the atmosphere of this aeronautical treasure to envelope you.

The tower and the sheep at Davidstow Moor – one of the most atmospheric of Britain's former airfields. *Ken Ellis*

Usually referred to as 'Cornwall at War', the full title of the larger museum is the Davidstow and Cornwall at War Museum. During the summer of 2016 the skyline changed considerably with the erection of a display hall allowing the aircraft to come indoors. Displays are spread over a dozen or so buildings, four of which were built in 1942. The heritage if the airfield is of course covered, but the remit of Cornwall at War is wider, embracing the Army, the Royal Navy and the 'home front', from the Great War to the Falklands conflict.

The spark that started the adjacent Davidstow Moor RAF Memorial Museum, or the 'Memorial Museum' as the locals call it, was the need to create a monument in memory of those who served at the airfield. The simple local stone memorial that stands at the entrance to both museum sites was dedicated in 2003. The 'Memorial Museum' occupies what was the sergeants' shower block and within it is room after room of carefully presented artefacts telling the story of the personnel, units and locals that came together on the moor to do long-ranging battle. The words on the memorial sum up the mood that airfield and its museums generate: 'They flew by day and night and gave their lives to keep forever bright that precious light of freedom'.

The sergeants' shower block is now the Davidstow Moor RAF Memorial Museum. In the foreground is the simple, but moving, commemoration to the valour of Coastal Command personnel. *Ken Ellis*

Davidstow Airfield and Cornwall at War Museum aircraft

Type	Identity	Built	Origin	Acquired	Notes
de Havilland Vampire T.11	XK627	1956	Britain	2012	fuselage
Fairey Gannet ECM.6	XG831	1957	Britain	16 Feb 2008	–
Fieseler Fi 103 V-1	–	–	Germany	2012	replica flying-bomb
Hawker Hunter F.6	XG164	1956	Britain	15 Jul 2014	composite
Northrop Chukar D.1	XW999	1971	USA	26 Sep 2009	target drone
Northrop Chukar D.2	ZG347	2000	USA	26 Sep 2009	target drone
Northrop Shelduck D.1	XZ791	c1984	USA	26 Sep 2009	target drone

Also in Cornwall
The Flambards Experience

This multi-faceted visitor attraction at Helston includes 'Britain in the Blitz' and the 'Aviation Experience: A Century of Pioneering Flight', the latter including a Concorde cockpit. If you are in this area, a trip to RNAS Culdrose, HMS *Seahawk*, is also worthwhile; there is a public viewing area on the eastern perimeter. **www.flambards.co.uk**

When in Cornwall...

You've got to go to Land's End... Among the many attractions is Bölkow Bö 105D 'G-CDBS' helicopter in the colours of the Cornwall Air Ambulance. **www.landsend-landmark.co.uk**

And in Devon
Cobbaton Combat Collection

Described as the largest private collection of military vehicles and wartime memorabilia in the southwest, exhibits includes a Horsa glider replica that was used in the movie *A Bridge Too Far*. **www.cobbatoncombat.co.uk**

A Bölkow Bö 105D in the colours of the Cornwall Air Ambulance is among the attractions at Land's End. *Ken Ellis*

CHAPTER 7
CUMBRIA

Pioneers of the Borders
Solway Aviation Museum

Carlisle Lake District Airport
www.solway-aviation-museum.co.uk

As noted in the Introduction, the 'locals' are more than capable of making the curators of the 'nationals' drool over exhibits and the predecessors of the all-volunteer Solway Aviation Museum (SAM) is a shining example of this, having made a contribution to the RAF Museum and helped to start Britain's jet 'warbird' movement. Following the adage never to leave a stone unturned, members of the Solway Group of Aviation Enthusiasts had heard that the Nelson Tomlinson School at Wigton, Cumberland, still had a 'biplane' used by the Air Training Corps (ATC) during World War Two. On 17th March 1962 off they went and there it was – in the roof space of an out-building. No engine or undercarriage, but most of Hawker Hart Trainer K4972 nevertheless. A deal was struck and the airframe was gingerly lifted down on 10th November 1962 and taken to Crosby-on-Eden, the present-day Carlisle Lake District Airport. Britain's 'stock' of Hawker military biplanes had doubled.

Above: Vulcan B.2 XJ823 has been drawing visitors to Carlisle Airport since it touched down in January 1983. *Ken Ellis*

(Since 1962, discoveries in Afghanistan and from-the-ground-up restorations to flying condition elsewhere have swollen the number of Hawker biplanes in the UK still further. The recovery of K4972 was an example of a *very early* acquisition of an important airframe by a 'local' organisation of enthusiasts, but it was not the first; if only by a matter of days. Turn to Chapter 18 for more.)

The Hart was the Solway group's founder airframe, but wise decisions were made relating to K4972. It was offered to the RAF Museum on 16th October 1963 and gratefully accepted; it travelled to Henlow within days. By early 1968 it was at St Athan, being restored by staff of 4 School of Technical Training. The very badly damaged port lower wing was replaced with one found at an ATC unit in Maidenhead. Rolls-Royce pitched in with a 510hp Kestrel X found in Sheffield; a propeller was held in RAF Museum stock. In 1972 the Hart went on display at Hendon and, apart from a break during 1992 to 2002, it's still proudly displayed there.

On 9th May 1969 former Central Air Traffic Control School de Havilland Vampire T.11 WZ507 touched down at Carlisle, having been acquired by the renamed Solway Aviation Group (later Society). Permission had been granted to park it at the airport and in January 1977 it was joined by Gloster Meteor NF.14 WS832 which arrived by road from Pershore. At this point WZ507 disappeared into one of the hangars and it did not emerge again until 1980. The Vampire had been kept in such good condition that it had caught the eye of Alexander 'Sandy' Topen, the leading light of the Vintage Aircraft Team, and he had arranged an exchange with the enlightened Solway team. Led by Sandy, a working party involving several volunteers from Solway worked away on the Vampire. On 9th January 1980 it was placed on the civil register as G-VTII – taking the 'Is' as '1s', this stands for Vampire T.11. On 17th February *Double-India* had its post-restoration maiden flight and became the first private civilian operated former military jet in the UK. The Vampire was ferried to Duxford in the early summer of 1981 and, as this book closed for press, *India-India* was being operated by the Vampire Preservation Group at North Weald.

RAF Crosby-on-Eden opened for business in February 1941 and throughout its short existence, readying aircrew for combat was the main theme. The Hawker Hurricanes and Typhoons of 59 Operational Training Unit (OTU) gave way to the Bristol Beauforts and Beaufighters of 9 OTU from September 1942 until the Douglas Dakotas of 109 OTU arrived in August 1944. The RAF pulled out in late 1946. Thankfully, in 1960 Carlisle Corporation recognised the importance of the airfield to both the city and the region, setting it up as Carlisle Airport; since 2009 it has been operated by Stobart Aviation.

Landmark collection

The fourth aircraft in the collection was Avro Vulcan B.2 XJ823 which flew in during January 1983, instantly becoming a landmark at the airport. The Vulcan was to have a more subtle influence on the group; when the time came to set up a telephone line for the group, arrangements were made to have the number end in '823'. Clubbing together to acquire the V-bomber were David Hutchinson and Tom Stoddart. Former RAF engineer Tom has been a stalwart supporter of the collection and today is the museum's technical director, lending his long experience of aircraft maintenance to the day-to-day activities of the museum. The Vulcan generated much visitor interest and the Solway team started to open up on Sunday afternoons with a display of artefacts in a small building while fund-raising for larger exhibition space began.

During 1990 the contents of the former Blue Streak museum at RAF Spadeadam was handed over. With additions from other sources, this has evolved into a major exhibition and place of pilgrimage in its own right at SAM. Hidden within sprawling moorland to the northeast of Carlisle, Spadeadam today is a major weapons range and the venue for many RAF and NATO exercises. With de Havilland Propellers (Hawker Siddeley Dynamics from 1963) as the lead contractor, Blue Streak was a medium range ballistic nuclear missile which was developed from the mid-1950s. Spadeadam was chosen as the site for some of the trials and potentially as the first operational base and a silo and launch pads were built. Tests, including the Rolls-Royce/Rocketdyne RZ.2 motor, were carried out at Spadeadam until the entire project was axed in 1960. Blue Streak went on to become the first stage booster of the European Launcher Development Organisation rocket and was used from 1964 to the mid-1970s. Visitors with no interest in rocketry get very quickly engrossed in SAM's Blue Streak Room and its 'space race' folklore.

The RAF Museum's Hawker Hart Trainer shortly after restoration, in 1971. Its place at Hendon was made possible by the museum's forebears. *KEC*

The Solway Aviation Museum was formally opened up to on 18th May 1996, thanks to a long campaign of fund raising and considerable support and encouragement from the airport management. The present-day building has permitted great expansion of exhibition space and the workshop has doubled in size over the years. Outside, the aircraft park has taken on more airframes, although so far trundling the Vulcan up what is a considerable slope has not been possible. The quality and extent of displays within SAM is amazing, the Crosby Room details the fascinating history of Carlisle Airport including a life size working copy of the tower control desk. The airfields of Cumbria and across the border into southern Scotland are also covered and special events and education days are often staged. The fiftieth anniversary of the founding of the Solway Group of Aviation Enthusiasts was celebrated in 2011 and the occasion was taken to initiate feasibility studies to put the aircraft collection under cover. The team at Solway has steadfastly developed and matured the Solway Aviation Museum; today it is a valued regional asset that is still pioneering.

Above: Third aircraft for Solway and proudly displayed to this day, Meteor NF.14 WS832 on the ramp at the Royal Aircraft Establishment, Llanbedr, in 1962. *via Arthur Pearcy*

SAM's Blue Streak Room provides a fascinating insight into Britain's part in the 'space race'. *Ken Ellis*

McDonnell Phantom FGR.2 XV406
1968 | Multi-role fighter | Two 12,250lb st Rolls-Royce Spey 201 turbofans

Just over a dozen whole 'Phabulous' Phantoms are with museums in Britain, including an F-4D and an F-4S from the USAF and the US Navy respectively and an F-4J(UK) at the Imperial War Museum, Duxford. The remainder are Spey-powered FG.1s and FGR.2s, with the latter in the majority. Solway has a particularly fine example and its place at Carlisle is far more relevant than might at first appear. Built at St Louis, Missouri, XV406 touched down at Aldergrove, Northern Ireland, the home of 23 Maintenance Unit (MU) on 29th October 1968. It transited to Holme-on-Spalding Moor in late November, having been designated to test an EMI-developed reconnaissance pod. XV406 was prepared to accept the new device and was ready for flight test by mid-1969. It was issued to 'A' Squadron of the Aeroplane and Armament Experimental Establishment at Boscombe Down on 16th January 1970 for service evaluation of the pod, before returning to Holme in June 1971.

On 18th September 1972 XV406 was flown to Coningsby to for 228 Operational Conversional Unit (OCU) before joining its first frontline unit, 54 Squadron – also at Coningsby – on 1st August 1973. From the days of the Hunter onwards, RAF fighter units frequently 'borrowed' other machines from fellow squadrons, for a couple of days, or a matter of weeks. XV406 had its share of these short-term shuffles, for example during August 1973 it was briefly with 41 Squadron, which shared the ramp at Coningsby. The following month it started to serve another Coningsby unit, 54 Squadron. It moved to Wattisham and 111 Squadron on 24th April 1974, migrating with the unit to Leuchars on 23rd October 1975. XV406 was back at Wattisham on 13th January 1978, with 23 Squadron, transferring to 56 Squadron across the ramp in September 1982. It departed Wattisham on 18th July 1983 for another stint with 228 OCU at Coningsby and XV406 decamped with the unit to Leuchars in April the following year. The stay at Leuchars was relatively long, during 1988 it transferred to the base's frontline units, 43 Squadron from June and 'Treble-One' from November before resuming work with 228 OCU in December.

On 15th May 1990 XV406 was ferried to St Athan for decommissioning. It was issued for display purposes to 14 MU at Longtown, Carlisle, a huge non-airfield storage and distribution site that had handled all US-supplied spares for British Phantoms since 1968. XV406 arrived at 14 MU on 14th November 1991 and was officially unveiled a week later. A press release gave its total flying time as 4,674 hours, but did not stop there: of its 4,367 landings, 3,310 were to a full-stop, while 1,030 were 'rollers' or 'go-arounds' and on 27 times it engaged airfield arrester wires. The sprawling 14 MU disbanded in September 1996 and as the site wound down, it was decided to hand on XV406 to SAM; it arrived at Carlisle Airport on 22nd April 1998.

Wearing the colours of its last unit, 228 OCU, Phantom FGR.2 XV406 is an imposing exhibit at Carlisle. *Ken Ellis*

Mignet 'Flying Flea' 'G-ADRX'
1936 | Single-seat ultra-light | One Citroën H2 (2CV) piston

There is an infestation of diminutive 'Flying Fleas' in collections throughout Britain. These vary from those built in the type's hey-day from 1935 up to the beginning of World War Two. Some flew, some 'hopped', most thrashed about at nought feet! These were built by studying Henri Mignet's French language book *Le Sport de l'Air*, or more likely the Air League's translation *The Flying Flea – How to Build it*, or the serialisation in the magazine *Practical Mechanics*. Others were constructed in the 1960s and beyond; most following the 'plans' (such as Mignet supplied) to the letter; others being less perfectionist. All of the post-war ones were for static purposes, although rumours have persisted about illicit flights! The 'Flea' is often seen as a comic creation; this is unfair as it sired the British permit to fly system and was the launch pad for homebuilding worldwide.

The choice of which Flea to profile was easy; as co-writer of *Henri Mignet and his Flying Fleas in 1990* and founder of the Flying Flea Archive, the author had a role in the acquisition and restoration of the example now at SAM, and it is a child of Cumberland to boot. This machine was built in Ulverston in what is believed to be 1936 by Ronnie Jolly. Fitted with a two-cylinder Anzani, flight was attempted but ended, typically for the type, in a nose-over with damage to the propeller and main wing after a hectic week of trying to get aloft. Put into store, immediately post-war it was acquired by Bill Pennington who wanted the engine for several projects, including powering a boat. The airframe was stored in a former mill at Torver in Cumberland. Bill eventually sold the Anzani to the owner of a three-wheeler sports car – perhaps a Morgan – for spares.

Investigations by the author and John Nixon of the South Copeland Aviation Group coincided in 1992 and negotiations began with Mrs Doreen Pennington. John, an officer at HM Prison Haverigg on the site of the former RAF Millom, and his team were working hard to establish a museum in a wartime building outside the 'wire'. (See below for the irrepressible John's latest project.) The RAF Millom Museum opened during Easter 1993 to much acclaim. At the same time, John had developed a workshop within the prison where inmates could work as part of their rehabilitation. The locally-built Flea would be both an ideal exhibit and a restoration project and Mrs Pennington readily agreed that the time had come for the little aircraft to leave its home of nearly five decades. The airframe was removed from the mill on 12th March 1994 and a year-long project began to restore the HM.14 to display standard. Searches for an affordable Anzani or a Douglas proved fruitless but a Citroen 2CV flat-twin fitted the bill perfectly. Painted in an attractive pale blue and silver dope and wearing the period, but unallocated at the time, registration 'G-ADRX' the Flea went on show in the museum in 1995. Alongside was a sign that never ceased to raise eyebrows: "This aircraft was restored by the inmates and staff of HMP Haverigg. As a project it is totally unique and proves that positive things can be achieved in a prison environment. We hope you like the results of our efforts."

John had to give up his curatorship of the RAF Millom Museum in 2007 and the organisation became a limited company, leasing the building from the prison service. The museum expanded at rapid rate, taking on a large warehouse in Haverigg and lots of airframes were acquired. What many believed to be the inevitable occurred in August 2010 when both sites were closed and the contents sold off to meet debts. The Flea was rescued from this debacle and on 7th September 2010 it moved to its present home at SAM. This required quick reactions from the Carlisle team but, as SAM's David Kirkpatrick said at the time: "it's a piece of Cumberland's heritage and perfect for us, besides we're used to thinking on our feet!"

With John Nixon leading the way and Davie Reid of the Dumfries and Galloway Aviation Museum at the centre section, the main wing of the Flying Flea emerges at Torver, 12th May 1994.
Alan Curry

Sikorsky Whirlwind HAR.21 WV198
1952 | Utility helicopter | One Pratt & Whitney R1340-AN-1-57 Wasp piston engine

In the early 1950s Yeovil-based Westland took the brave step of breaking away from fixed wing aircraft manufacture and entering the burgeoning helicopter market. The company was exceptionally shrewd in deciding not to re-invent the wheel, instead coming to a licence agreement with the American Sikorsky company. Westland did not stick with cloning US types, but redesigned, re-engined and refined so much that their products could be considered as 'stand alone' types. Chances are that the Whirlwind sitting in SAM's aircraft park might be overlooked, but it is a US-built example and served with the Fleet Air Arm's first-ever operational helicopter squadron.

First flown at Sikorsky's Hartford, Connecticut, plant on 16th October 1952 it was destined for the Fleet Air Arm as HAR.21 WV198. It was the equivalent of the US Navy's HRS-2 and given the Bureau of Aeronautics serial number 130191 for administrative purposes. It was shipped to Britain and taken on charge at Gosport on 19th November and, along with nine others (WV189 to WV197), was turned around quickly and embarked in the aircraft carrier HMS *Perseus* which departed Portsmouth bound for the Far East on 12th December. The HAR.21s were to be deployed by 848 Squadron, for the type's debut frontline use, in the jungles of Malaya against communist insurgents in a conflict labelled with classic British understatement as 'The Emergency'. There were high hopes for the Whirlwinds, but it was an evaluation and it was accepted that there would be accidents and incidents. Based at Sembawang, Singapore, WV198 was coded 'K' – markings it again wears today. It rolled over on its side when one of the front undercarriage units collapsed during an autorotative forced landing on 25th November 1954; there were no injuries to the two crew. By declutching the rotor drive most helicopters can autorotate; glide under a degree of control via the free-wheeling main rotor. On 3rd September 1956 the engine failed on take off and WV198 suffered a heavy landing from about 15ft and it was returned to Sembawang for repair. On 12th November the pilot of WV196 was killed when autorotation failed and helicopter plunged to the ground and erupted in a fireball. The following day, all the HAR.21s were grounded.

Shipped back to Britain, WV198 was prepared for display at the Royal Tournament, held at London's Earl's Court in June 1958. It was being used as a travelling recruitment airframe by 1959, based mostly at Lee-on-Solent and Fleetlands. By 1976 it had been handed over to the Sea Scouts at Gosport, but was disposed of by 1979 to a scrap dealer in Portsmouth. Recognising it for what it was, pioneering 'vintage' helicopter collector and operator Jim Wilkie acquired WV198 and brought it to Carnforth in Lancashire in May 1981. On 25th January 1982 Jim civil registered the HAR.21 as G-BJWY. Jim founded the Helicopter Museum of Great Britain at Heysham and by October 1982 WV198 was on show, painted in US Marine Corps colours. With the closure of Jim's set up WV198 was passed on to the National Fire School at Chorley by the summer of 1989. It was placed on its side in a simulated crash scene – a situation it had experienced for real 35 years previously in the Malayan jungle. WV198 moved for a short spell to Warmingham, Cheshire, in 1990 before travelling to Firbeck and the South Yorkshire Aircraft Preservation Society the following year. This important waypoint in the history of Royal Navy helicopter evolution joined SAM on 13th November 1992.

Whirlwind HAR.21 WV198 with former Royal Saudi Air Force Lightning F.53 ZF583 to the left. *Ken Ellis*

Solway Aviation Museum aircraft

Type	Identity	Built	Origin	Acquired	Notes
Auster J/5L Aiglet Trainer	G-APLG	1958	Britain	Apr 1995	–
Avro Vulcan B.2	XJ823	1961	Britain	24 Jan 1983	–
Bede BD-5 Micro	G-BDTT	c1976	USA	2012	–
Bensen B-8M	G-BRHL	1989	USA	2012	–
Cessna 152 II	G-BNNR	1981	USA	2011	–
de Havilland Vampire T.11	WZ515	1953	Britain	May 1990	–
DH Canada Chipmunk T.10	WB584	1950	Canada	Dec 2012	composite
DH Canada Chipmunk T.10	WB670	1950	Canada	13 Dec 2012	–
English Electric Canberra T.4	WE188	1953	Britain	Apr 1988	–
English Electric Lightning F.53	ZF583	1968	Britain	8 Jan 1989	–
Gloster Meteor NF.14	WS832	1954	Britain	15 Jan 1977	–
Hawker Hunter F.51*	E-425	1956	Britain	26 Nov 2008	–
Hawker Siddeley Trident 1C	G-ARPP	1965	Britain	19 Aug 2009	cockpit
Hunting Jet Provost T.4	XS209	1964	Britain	24 Jun 2006	–
McDonnell Phantom FGR.2	XV406	1968	USA	22 Apr 1998	see profile
Mignet 'Flying Flea'*	'G-ADRX'	1936	France	7 Sep 2010	see profile
Percival Sea Prince T.1*	WP314	1953	Britain	Aug 1998	–
Sikorsky Whirlwind HAR.21	WV198	1952	USA	13 Nov 1992	see profile
Slingsby Grasshopper TX.1	'WZ784'	1952	Britain	2001	glider

Notes: * – illustrated in the colour section.

Also in Cumbria
Lakeland Motor Museum

At Blackbarrow, near Ulveston. As well as a barrage of wonderful cars, there's 'Flying Flea' 'G-ADYV', Solar Wings Typhoon G-MBCG microlight and Cameron N-77 G-BNDV hot-air balloon for those who prefer looking upwards! www.lakelandmotormuseum.co.uk

Solar Wings Typhoon microlight G-MBCG 'flies' from the ceiling of one of the display halls at the Lakeland Motor Museum. *Ian Humphreys*

Millom Discovery Centre

There is much of interest within but from the point of view of this book John Nixon's section on the aviation of the area, in particular the former RAF Millom, is well worth visiting. (For more on John see the profile on the Flying Flea in the Solway Aviation Museum section, above.) A 'star' item is an outer wing from a Blackburn Botha, signed by Millom veterans. Phase One of John's exhibition was unveiled in the summer of 2014; he's hard at work on Phase Two. www.millomdiscoverycentre.co.uk

Windermere Jetty

The former Windermere Steamboats Museum is due to re-open during 2017. A previous exhibit was the unique Slingsby T.1 Falcon BGA.266 water-glider that was tested on Lake Windermere in February 1943 – here's hoping that it will make a re-appearance. Keep an eye on www.windermerejetty.org

Aeronautical Wonderland
Bournemouth Aviation Museum

Bournemouth Airport
www.aviation-museum.co.uk

Variety has been a hallmark of Bournemouth Airport ever since the days it was established as RAF Hurn in the summer of 1941. Today, the Airbuses and Boeings plying schedules, charters or in and out for maintenance contrast with the specially modified Dassault Falcon 20s operated by Cobham Aviation on contract to the UK armed forces. Training, general and executive aviation companies, fixed and rotary winged, complete the busy vista. Dorset's proximity to France and Normandy in particularly added to the galaxy of aircraft that were stationed during the war years, especially in the run-up to D-Day. Types including Armstrong Whitworth Whitleys and Albemarles; de Havilland Mosquitos, Hawker Typhoons and North American Mustangs for the RAF and Martin B-26 Marauders and Northrop P-61 Black Widows for the USAAF made Hurn their home. From 1944 British Overseas Airways Corporation staged limited services and other airlines joined in until Heathrow was ready for business during 1946-1947.

Above: A general view of the Bournemouth Aviation Museum looking west, with the airport to the right. From the foreground to the back: Vampire T.11, Harvard T.2b, Provost T.1, Jaguar GR.1, Hunter F.6A, Vulcan B.2MRR cockpit and, to the left: Viscount 806 and Canberra PR.7s cockpits. *Terry Dann*

From the early 1951s Vickers established a flight test base at Hurn, before creating a final assembly facility which, in turn, produced Varsities, Viscounts and BAC One-Elevens. Flight Refuelling began operations from Hurn in the 1970s and has had a presence ever since, the company taking on the name of its founder, Sir Alan Cobham, in 1994. Adding further to the diversity was the civilian-operated Fleet Requirements Unit, providing target facilities for Royal Navy ships, using de Havilland Sea Hornets and Hawker Sea Furies from the 1950s, through to English Electric Canberras and Hawker Hunters up to the unit departing for Yeovilton in 1971. Development as an airport commenced in the late 1960s. This all adds up to an impressive heritage and the Bournemouth Aviation Museum (BAM) serves to tell that story.

Jet origins

The origins of Bournemouth Aviation Museum go back to businessman Mike Carlton wanting to acquire something more potent than North American Harvard IIA G-TEAC, painted in RAF colours as 'MC280' that he had operated from early 1979. Mike was the managing director of the Brencham Group, owning a diverse range of companies. One of these was Glos-Air at Bournemouth Airport (Hurn) and in September 1981 Spencer Flack's spectacular all-red Hawker Hunter F.51 G-HUNT was ferried from Stansted to its new Dorset home. A year later, Mike also acquired two-seater T.7 G-BOOM. Even though he had two jets, the call-sign *Hunter One* had always appealed to Mike and it was taken as the name for the stable. As a shrewd businessman, he decided that a separate concern should be created for his new-found 'hobby' and so the Brencham Historic Aircraft Company came about in June 1983. The huge expansion of the flying side of Hunter One needs only the briefest treatment here; for full details take a look at sister volume *Lost Aviation Collections of Britain*. While on holiday in Zimbabwe, Mike and his wife Kathy took a flight as passengers in a Republic Seabee amphibian from the waters near the Kariba Dam on 31st August 1986. The aircraft crashed on take-off, killing all on board. In due course Brencham ceased trading and auction house Christie's was brought in to oversee the sale of the collection at Bournemouth on 1st October 1987.

Out of this came a new company, Jet Heritage Ltd (JHL) was inaugurated on July 1988 with Hunter Wing Ltd as its holding organisation. Hunter G-BOOM, Gloster Meteor TT.20 G-LOSM and a pair of Jet Provosts formed the caucus of the fleet. As well as running these for airshow, film and promotional work, JHL specialised in the maintenance of classic jets and running similar aircraft for third parties. There was also an intention to establish a museum, so that the *working* collection could be enjoyed by not just airshow audiences. This was inspired by the Battle of Britain Memorial Flight Visitor Centre at Coningsby. To this end, the Jet Heritage Aviation Museum was opened to the public on 17th May 1998. Sadly, JHL ceased trading on 19th August 1999 and the pioneering venture came to a halt.

Out of adversity – adaptation

Thanks to setting up of the Jet Heritage Charitable Foundation in 1994, the museum element survived the collapse of JHL. On 27th August 1999 the Bournemouth Aviation Charitable Foundation Ltd arose, ultimately taking the form of the all-volunteer run BAM. With a wealth of aircraft types operating at Bournemouth and much goodwill towards BAM, the collection prospered ranging from light aircraft 'lodging' to airliners. Hurn remained a centre for 'vintage' jets and the aircraft of de Havilland Aviation, Source Classic Jet Flight and other operators helped to swell the museum ramp. Channel Express Handley Page Herald 401 G-BEYF flew its last service on 9th April 1999 and on 26th May was presented on loan to BAM. On 17th November 2004 another airliner joined the fold: former European Aviation BAC One-Eleven Series 530 G-AZMF. This local product, which first flew at Hurn on 4th March 1972, extended BAM's policy of allowing visitor access whenever possible and was used as the venue for some memorable parties and other occasions. It seemed as though the rollercoaster days of the past were over.

Then, to quote a BAM press release in late 2007: "Bournemouth Airport dropped a bombshell". Expansion plans meant that the management was not prepared to renew the lease on the museum hangar; the land was destined to be a car park. (There are obvious advantages to basing a museum at an airport: increased 'footfall', take-offs and landings for visitors to watch, resident aircraft as ready 'exhibits' and ease of delivery of airworthy exhibits. But over the decades there have been numerous instances when airport-based museums have discovered that they do not feature in future plans: quite rightly aviation heritage is the first thing to jettison when expansion beckons.) When the doors shut at BAM on 19th December 2007, it seemed very unlikely that any form of recovery could be made.

During the early months of 2008 all manner of possibilities were explored and salvation was found close to home. On the southern boundary of the airport, overlooking the taxiway and runway, is top Dorset visitor attraction Adventure Wonderland Bournemouth. An aviation museum to further tempt visitors was an obvious advantage to the park's management and BAM was invited to relocate – an offer that was readily accepted. The collection needed rationalising and the Herald and One-Eleven could not be accommodated. The former was scrapped during July 2008 with the cockpit being acquired by a dealer; the latter departed the airport in November to become a teaching aid in Newcastle. Thankfully in July 2015 the BAM team were able to secure the cockpit of 'their' Herald and it returned to the fold. During 2013 and 2014 the forward fuselages of a Boeing 737 and another One-Eleven have been secured, once again allowing visitors to 'get on board'. The Mayor of Christchurch, Cllr David Flagg, presided over the officially opening of the 'new' BAM on 24th October 2008. Since then BAM's volunteers continue to work hard to tell the story of Dorset's aviation heritage in a vibrant and imaginative manner.

Chichester-Miles Leopard G-BKRL
1988 | Light jet transport | Two 300lb st Noel Penny NPT301-3A turbojets

This diminutive twin-jet was the prototype of what was hoped would become a family of personal transports to replace long-established twin piston-powered types. There have been several attempts to break into this market, mostly by US-based outfits, but the Leopard was a unique departure for a British concern. Ian Chichester-Miles established Chichester-Miles Consultants (CMC) in the early 1980s to develop his concept of a four-seater, constructed largely of glass fibre reinforced plastic with localised carbon fibre strengthening and powered by a revolutionary British small turbojet. Four people could be accommodated under a forward-hinging canopy. The design was intended to be scaled-up to produce six, or perhaps even eight-seat versions.

Detailed design and construction of *Romeo-Lima* was carried out under contract from CMC by Wiltshire-based Designability Ltd. Test pilot Angus McVitie carried out the first flight, at Thurleigh, Bedford, on 12th December 1988 and much of the 50 or so hours that the prototype clocked. Established in 1972 by Noel Penny, Coventry-based Noel Penny Turbines specialised in the development of small turbofans for industrial, marine and aviation applications. The company ceased trading in 1991, leaving CMC with a prototype built around an engine that was no longer available. A second example, with a significantly beefed up airframe and undercarriage was built and this was fitted with a pair of US-built Williams FJX-1 turbofans which, at 700lb st, gave over twice the thrust of the NPTs of G-BKRL. This machine, registered G-BRNM, had its maiden flight on 9th April 1997 and carried out a limited test programme. A six-seat version, the Leopard Six, was announced in March 2001 but soon the entire programme was curtailed. The second example, *November-Mike*, was put on show at BAM in 2004 and was joined the following year by G-BKRL. On 26th March 2008 G-BRNM left BAM, moving to the Midland Air Museum, see Chapter 29.

CMC Leopard G-BKRL at North Weald, June 1991. *KEC*

Hawker Hunter F.6A XG160
1956 | Day fighter | One 10,000lb st Rolls-Royce Avon 203 turbojet

Mention the September 1958 Farnborough airshow and the chances are that the debut of the revolutionary, giant Fairey Rotodyne compound helicopter or the incredibly advanced Blackburn NA.39 (the Buccaneer to be) will not get a look in. Everyone at the show was left spellbound by 22 Hawker Hunter F.6s in formation and performing two loops; nothing like it has ever been seen again. Leading this incredible achievement was Sqn Ldr Roger Topp, later Air Cdre R L Topp AFC. The aircraft comprised the Wattisham-based 111 Squadron's famed aerobatic demonstration team, the 'Black Arrows', with several aircraft and pilots 'borrowed from other frontline units to make up the numbers. What seems to have escaped the coverage at the time was that in the last days of August the Hunters gathered at Odiham, nine miles to the west, to practise. During those sessions Topp led 24 Hunters in a perfectly executed loop.

Of the two Hunters that made up the 'Odiham 24', but did not perform at Farnborough, one survives: XF515 is based in the Netherlands with the Dutch Hawker Hunter Foundation, British-registered as G-KAXF. At the time of writing, *Xray-Fox* was airworthy, but grounded at the behest of the British Civil Aviation Authority, following the Shoreham airshow disaster of 22nd August 2015. As regards the 'Farnborough 22', five survive intact, plus another that is a cockpit section. One is on display at a museum in Germany, one with a collection in Australia; another is decidedly airworthy at Cape Town, South Africa, as ZS-AUJ. The cockpit of XE584 is displayed in the Wirral, Merseyside – see Chapter 19. That leaves two whole examples; XG194, Sqn Ldr Topp's aircraft, is kept at its former base of Wattisham (Chapter 26), but only one is on regular public display: XG160 at BAM.

Flown for the first time on 5th September 1956, Hunter F.6 XG160 was built by Armstrong Whitworth at Bitteswell and was issued to 5 Maintenance Unit at Kemble on 12th October. It was first operational with the 'Fighting Cocks', 43 Squadron, at Leuchars before moving for a short stint with 92 Squadron at Middleton St George in 1957. Coded 'U', XG160 joined 111 Squadron in early 1958, the unit settling in to Wattisham on 18th June 1958 from North Luffenham and North Weald before that. At Odiham and at Farnborough, the gloss black Hunter was flown by Flt Lt Mike Thurley. During early 1961 'Treble-One' made the leap from the Hunter to the English Electric Lightning F.1A. Hunter XG160 had gravitated to 229 Operational Conversion Unit (OCU) at Chivenor by early 1965. The OCU was renamed at the Tactical Weapons Unit (TWU) on 2nd September 1974 and moved to Brawdy. During XG160's time with the TWU it was converted to F.6A status, being fitted with a brake parachute in a fairing over the jet exhaust and given the ability to carry 230 gallon drop tanks on the inboard weapons pylons as a standard fit. On the last day of July 1978 TWU became 1 TWU, but work remained as before for its large Hunter fleet, with detachments often being made back to XG160's previous base at Chivenor. Its flying life over, XG160 was ferried to Scampton where it joined the Trade Management Training Squadron as instructional airframe 8831M.

In late 1994 the Hunter was donated to the Royal Jordanian Air Force for use by its Historic Flight and in January 1995 XG160 arrived at Bournemouth for restoration by Jet Heritage. The following month it was allocated the British civil registration G-BWAF to RV Aviation. With its 'Black Arrows' provenance rediscovered, it was decided that it was best that XG160 stayed in Britain and not be flown; It joined BAM in early 2000.

The jaw-dropping 22 Hunter formation – including BAM's XG160 – performing at Farnborough, September 1958. *KEC*

Bournemouth Aviation Museum aircraft

Type	Identity	Built	Origin	Acquired#	Notes
American AA-5B Tiger	G-BFZR	1979	USA	Sep 2013	–
Avro Vulcan B.2MRR	XH537	1959	Britain	29 Oct 1991	cockpit
BAC One-Eleven Srs 479	ZE432	1973	Britain	30 Apr 2014	forward fuselage
Boeing 737-229	G-CEAH	1975	USA	8 Dec 2013	forward fuselage
CMC Leopard*	G-BKRL	1988	Britain	18 Feb 2005	see profile
de Havilland Vampire T.11	XE856	1954	Britain	6 Sep 2005	–
English Electric Canberra PR.7	WT532	1955	Britain	5 Jul 1999	cockpit
English Electric Lightning F.53	ZF582	1968	Britain	21 Sep 2004	cockpit
Gloster Meteor NF.14	WS776	1954	Britain	5 Feb 2005	–
Handley Page Victor K.2	XL164	1961	Britain	24 May 2013	cockpit
Handley Page Herald 401	G-BEYF	1963	Britain	9 Jul 2015	cockpit
Hawker Hunter F.6A*	XG160	1956	Britain	Jan 2000	see profile
Hawker Siddeley HS.125 CC.3	ZD620	1982	Britain	29 Oct 2015	fuselage
North American Harvard T.2b*	KF388	1945	USA	Jul 2000	composite
Northrop Shelduck D.1	XR346	1960	USA	–	target drone
Percival Provost T.1	WW450	1953	Britain	10 Oct 2005	–
Piper Cadet 161	G-TLET	1989	USA	5 Jun 2013	–
SEPECAT Jaguar GR.1	XX763	1975	GB/France	26 Sep 2009	–
Vickers Viscount 806	G-OPAS	1958	Britain	5 Dec 2006	cockpit
Westland Wessex HAS.3	XT257	1967	USA/GB	20 Jan 2005	–
Westland Wasp HAS.1	XT431	1965	Britain	21 Dec 2013	composite

Notes: * – illustrated in the colour section. # Dates prior to August 1998 relate to arrivals for the former Jet Heritage Museum.

Also in Dorset
Tank Museum

Bovington is home to the world's finest international collection of armoured fighting vehicles (AFVs). Within the massed arrays of tanks is the forward section of General Aircraft Hamilcar assault glider TK718, complete with a Tetrarch light tank within its cavernous fuselage. Hamilcars were designed to fly large pieces of equipment and weaponry, including the Tetrarch, into battle zones. The newly built Vehicle Conservation Centre includes another 100-plus AFVs and Saunders-Roe Skeeter AOP.12 XM564 observation helicopter. The VCC is occasionally opened to the public, keep an eye on the website. **www.tankmuseum.org**

CHAPTER 9
ESSEX

Holding the Line
Stow Maries Great War Aerodrome

Stow Maries
www.stowmaries.org.uk

Some of Britain's dwindling operational aerodromes have their origins as primitive flying fields during World War One. For the majority, traces of those days a hundred years ago have been obliterated with the march of time and development. That is not the case with Stow Maries, which has claim to be Europe's most complete surviving Great War aerodrome. Member of Parliament for Maldon and Secretary of State for Culture, Media and Sport, the Right Hon John Whittingale officially opened the active aerodrome and heritage centre on 6th May 2016, at the beginning of the centenary celebrations of Royal Flying Corps (RFC) station Stow Maries.

In the early evening of 19th January 1915 the nature of warfare changed for the people of Great Britain. A pair of Zeppelin airships dropped bombs on Great Yarmouth and King's Lynn, in each case killing two people, injuring many more and destroying buildings. Compared with the slaughter that must have gone on in the trenches of the Western and Russian Fronts that day these losses were but pinpricks. But the souls lost were *civilian*; the harsh realities of unlimited warfare had come to wreak havoc on a defenceless population. The government acted swiftly and a network of landing grounds was established, from which frail biplanes with minimal target information were intended to climb relentlessly to height and engage the new 'terror weapon'.

Above: The end of a perfect day, manoeuvring BE.2e replica 'A2767' into a hangar at Stow Maries. *Terry Dann*

So it was that a motley collection of aircraft belonging to 37 (Home Defence) Squadron arrived at the recently completed Stow Maries aerodrome in September 1916, to bolster the anti-Zeppelin defences of London and the Home Counties. These machines belonged to the unit's 'B' Flight, one of the detachments administered from the headquarters at Woodham Mortimer, near Maldon. The others were at Goldhanger, on the coast near Orsey Island, and Rochford, today's Southend Airport. There seems to have been very little activity by 'B' Flight during 1916, but its pilots got more and more attuned to the task in hand during 1917 when the squadron staged 149 'ops' in a total of 236 hours of flying time. The longest sortie was flown by Captain C A Ridley on 25th May 1917 in Daimler-built Royal Aircraft Factory BE.12a A6318, who departed Stow at 17:12 hours for a 4 hour, 4 minute patrol. On 22nd June 1918 *all* of 37 Squadron – by then an RAF unit – moved into Stow Maries, staying until its machines flew off to Biggin Hill on 17th March 1919 to disband there four months later. During its tenure at Stow Maries 37 Squadron operated diverse types: Royal Aircraft Factory BE.2s, BE.12s, RE.7s and SE.5As; Sopwith Pups, 1½ Strutters and Camels. With the departure of the biplanes, Stow Maries reverted to the farmland it had been in 1915 and there was every prospect that 100 years later nobody would ever be able to tell that there had been an aerodrome there.

Swinging the propeller of the real Be.2e A2767 at Stow Maries in 1917. *Courtesy Stow Maries Great War Aerodrome*

Turning back time

Much of the land that had been occupied by the aerodrome had been known as Flambirds Farm and this name was rekindled. The locale and the farm are believed to have been the inspiration for Kathleen Peyton's *Flambards* – with an 'a' – novels from the 1960s which resurfaced in the late 1970s as a television series. The storyline mixed country life romps with early aviation. (See Chapter 6 for a Flambards theme park!) All the wooden structures that had formed the camp at Stow Maries were 'recycled' and over the decades the brick buildings were reduced to storage and then dereliction. With the coming of the 1970s and increasing awareness of the heritage of bygone military sites, there was a call for something to be done to prevent total decay at Stow. Time continued to slip by but the results of a survey by the Royal Commission for Historic Monuments published in 1997 underlined the site's importance.

In 2008 motor racing engineer and wildlife photographer Russell Savory was looking for a new location for his company; the legendary RS Performance, famed for transforming production-line vehicles and potent classics such as the Caterham. (Take a while to look at the 'Wildlife' section of the Stow Maries website for examples of Russell's astonishing imagery.) Savory was entranced by Stow Maries, not only did it offer great workshop facilities, it was a superb environment for rare birds and he was well aware of the allure of the RFC. Russell and a business partner acquired the 79-acre site including two dozen Great War era buildings in need of a lot of tender, loving care. The Engine and Doping Workshops were the first to be reborn and it was these that the high-tech RS Performance occupied. By then Russell was convinced that the whole site needed to be brought back into use and the most appropriate was as an aerodrome. Miracle of miracles in modern Britain, a 'new' airfield was created.

The Squadron Offices building was set aside for use as a museum-cum-visitor centre, the former Airmen's Mess Hall appropriately became the tea room and an impressive memorial was erected in December 2010. In that year the site was declared a Conservation Area and in the summer of 2012 the Great War period buildings were given Grade II* listing. The land was put on the market again in late 2012 and Russell Savory led a campaign to secure Stow Maries as a national asset. With the support of Essex County Council, Maldon District Council, the National Heritage Memorial Fund and English Heritage from December 2013 Stow Maries Great War Aerodrome Ltd was established, successfully acquired the site and achieved charitable status.

With genuine World War One aircraft being as rare as hen's teeth and, even if available, costing a king's ransom, the search for winged examples focussed on replicas. Besides, the ethic at Stow Maries is not to envelope aircraft in the equivalent of glass cases, but to display them – ideally in the air. Two major partners have brought airworthy aircraft to the historic aerodrome. The World War One Aviation Heritage Trust's machines are built to the highest period specifications in Wellington, New Zealand, by The Vintage Aviator Ltd. Well-known British specialist operator Bianchi Aviation Film Service based its Great War aircraft from 2015. Others, including airworthy plans- or kit-built scale replicas, are resident at Stow Maries. Wonderful though these are, they are beyond the scope of profiling in this book; that said the Bianchi Fokker E.III has 'an age', celebrating its fiftieth anniversary in 2017.

What has been achieved at Stow Maries is a unique combination of aerodrome, heritage centre and wildlife environment; proof that aviation and nature can go hand in hand.

Stow Maries Great War Aerodrome aircraft

Type	Identity	Built	Origin	Acquired	Notes
Airco DH.2	–	2016	Britain	15 May 2016	static, scale, replica
Blériot XI*	'10'	1999	France	24 July 2015	airworthy replica
Fokker E.III	'107/15'	1967	Germany	28 Jul 2016	airworthy replica
Gotha G.V	–	2016	Germany	May 2016	cockpit, replica
Manning-Flanders MF.1	G-BAAF	1975	Britain	Apr 2017	static replica
Morane-Saulnier 'N'	'MS824'	1970	France	24 Jul 2015	airworthy replica
Nieuport 17	'N1977'	1997	France	11 Nov 2016	airworthy replica
Royal Aircraft Factory BE.2e*	'A2767'	2013	Britain	10 Mar 2015	airworthy replica
Sopwith Pup	'A673'	1977	Britain	9 Oct 2011	static replica
Sopwith 1½ Strutter	'A8274'	2016	Britain	May 2016	cockpit, replica
Sopwith Camel*	'N6377'	1973	Britain	20 Apr 2016	airworthy replica
Sopwith Camel	–	–	Britain	30 Apr 2015	replica, to be airworthy
Sopwith Snipe	'F2367'	2011	Britain	7 Aug 2015	airworthy replica

Notes: * – illustrated in the colour section. The DH.2, Gotha, 1½ Strutter and Pup are static replicas; other than the Pup, all were constructed on site by volunteers. The airworthy replicas are owned by partners, eg: the Blériot, Fokker, Morane-Saulnier and both Camels by Bianchi Aviation Film Service; the BE.2 and Snipe by the World War One Aviation Heritage Trust.

Wolfpack Lair
Boxted Airfield Museum
Boxted
www.boxted-airfield.com

Two Nissen huts huddled together on the western edge of the former USAAF Station 150, Boxted, serve to remind visitors of the wartime days of what is now peaceful Essex farmland. Close to the Boxted Airfield Museum is a dilapidated building that has its foundations on what was a T2 hangar. The field in between is where the 'boss' of the 56th Fighter Group (FG), Major Hubert 'Hub' Zemke parked his Republic P-47 Thunderbolt nearly 75 years ago. On the southern boundary is Langham Lodge, which 'The Wolfpack' made its headquarters; Zemke referring to it as 'The Wheelhouse'. This is a just a part of Boxted's fascinating heritage.

Work started on the construction of Station 150 in the spring of 1942 and on 10th June 1943 the 386th Bombardment Group – 'The Crusaders' – arrived with Martin B-26 Marauders. The 386th BG's 'Widowmakers' vacated in September heading further west to Great Dunmow. Two months later, the peace was shattered with the arrival of the North American P-51B Mustangs of the 354th FG. On 11th January 1944 the unit's Major James Howard was awarded the Medal of Honor for single-handedly defending a bomber stream until his ammunition was expended. 'The Wolfpack' descended on Boxted on 18th April 1944, having previously been based at Halesworth. Immediately post-war, Boxted became an RAF station, including the DH Mosquitos of 25 Squadron in residence from 1946, but the following year operations ceased.

'Hub' Zemke's P-47D *Oregon's Britannia* parked at Boxted – a stone's throw from the present-day museum. *Boxted Airfield Museum*

Marauder tribute

Former 386th BG radio operator Henry Farwell officially opened the Boxted Airfield Museum on 29th May 2011. With the help of a Heritage Lottery Fund grant, the volunteers of the Boxted Airfield Historical Group (BAHG) have achieved a superb testament to Station 150. The first Nissen hut on site was built to order and serves as the shop, café and BAHG's special events venue. Next door is the exhibition building which utilizes an original Nissen hut from the airfield, acquired in 2007. To maintain originality as much as possible of the outer and inner corrugated skin has been saved and re-used.

As well as the exhibitions, there is a small chapel area and with it a roll of honour. Among the names commemorated is that of 2nd Lt Elwood D Raymond of the 'Wolfpack's' 61st Fighter Squadron. On 18th September 1944 he was returning from an anti-flak mission in support of the Arnhem landings when his P-47D 42-36057 'UN-F' crashed in mud flats at Southminster on the Essex coast. Parts from his aircraft provide a stark reminder of the young men who never returned to Boxted.

Providing considerable interest at Boxted open days is the rear fuselage of B-26C Marauder 41-35253 that served with the 323rd BG's 454th Bomb Squadron, not far away at Earls Colne. Like most of its breed, '5253 was named; at first *Black*

The rear fuselage of B-26C 41-35253 at Boxted. *John Camp*

Magic IV then *Mr Shorty*. The later was in honour of James Richard Gray III, the son of the B-26's captain, 1st Lt Dick Gray. The intention was to have nose-art in the form of a little mountain boy holding a rifle, but a suitable artist was not to hand. This B-26 took part in 96 missions including the 323rd's last one of the war, to Erding in Germany on 25th April 1945.

Mr Shorty was scrapped at Burtonwood – see *Transatlantic Gateway* in Chapter 5 – in June 1945, the hulk going to a scrapyard in Warrington. Twenty-nine years later the rear fuselage was salvaged and put into store at Duxford, before it was acquired by the Rebel Air Museum at Andrewsfield and later at Earls Colne. When Rebel closed in 1997, it was placed into store, going into BAHG's care in 2011. This impressive survivor is owned by the trustees of nearby Marks Hall and is on loan to BAHG. The hall was headquarters for the USAAF's Ninth Air Force and the operations offices for the 323rd BG. Trailer mounted, this relic is wheeled out on special occasions as a tribute to all Marauder men; the team hope that one day they will be able to display it inside the museum, but for now it is only available for viewing on open days. There may be little tangible where Marauders, Mustangs and Thunderbolts once growled but the museum is a shining example of what can be achieved with determination and passion.

One of Riddle's Raiders
East Essex Aviation Museum

Clacton on Sea
www.eastessexaviationsociety.org

Before the lifeboat pulled away, its crew paid their respects. A small crowd had gathered on the beach to the east of Clacton on Sea, towards Jaywick, where the body of a 26-year-old American lay. Pennsylvania-born Flt Off Raymond Earl King had run out of luck on 13th January 1945. Ditching his ailing North American P-51D Mustang in the waters off Clacton seemed his only chance. King survived the impact, but he succumbed to exposure in the bitterly cold sea. He was one of 'Riddle's Raiders', named after Lt Col Kyle L Riddle, the boss of the Wattisham-based 479th Fighter Group. King was assigned to the 436th Fighter Squadron and that day he was flying Inglewood, California-built P-51D 44-14574 '9B-J' *Little Zippie*.

Forty years later the East Essex Aviation Society was formed principally around the idea of salvaging *Little Zippie*. In the summer of 1986 its volunteers opened up the East Essex Aviation Museum in Martello Tower 'A', one of two built in 1805 on the west bank of the River Colne at Point Clear, near St Osyth. Tower 'B' was demolished in the mid-1970s – no easy feat. Martellos cropped up all over Britain's eastern coasts during the Napoleonic War to deter invasion. The Mustang was recovered on 16th August 1987 and its fuselage became the main exhibit, along with a moving memorial to its pilot. Inside the tower are two floors crammed with memorabilia. The roof gives commanding views, allowing visitors to ponder on what its garrison might have seen in the early years of the 19th century had the French come to 'visit' and to stare at the waters, which can turn from benign to deadly in the blink of an eye.

Lt Hans J Grasshoff of the 436th FS alongside P-51D
Little Zippie at Wattisham. Grasshoff flew this
Mustang on occasions. KEC

A well-known, and posed, 'scramble' of 56 Squadron pilots at North Weald in 1941. Left to right: Plt Off A G H Rouse, Flt Lt A V Gifkins, Plt Off R H Deugo RCAF and Sgt K M Stewart-Turner. Only Rouse survived the war, leaving the RAF as a Wing Commander. *KEC*

Hurricane Force
North Weald Airfield Museum

North Weald
www.nwamuseum.co.uk

When it came to choosing what type of aircraft should the 'gate guardian' at North Weald, there was no debate. Hawker Hurricanes first appeared at the Essex fighter station in May 1938 and the last ones arrived in early 1945 with 285 Squadron. No wonder the locals referred to North Weald as 'The Hurricane Airfield'. Unveiled on its plinth near the main entrance on 19th April 2009 the replica Hurricane wears the markings of 56 Squadron. Like the choice of aircraft, the squadron markings were also easy to pick – 56 Squadron spent no less than 13 years at 'Weald, starting with Armstrong Whitworth Siskins in 1927. The unit followed the RAF's fighter evolution through Bristol Bulldogs, Gloster Gauntlets and Gladiators and it was the squadron that introduced the Hurricane to the airfield in May 1938. The Hurricanes of 56 were present at North Weald for two stints during the Battle of Britain; they were last based there from December 1940 to the summer of 1941. The parish signs in North Weald Bassett feature the Hurricane as the main subject and the magazine of the North Weald Airfield Museum is called, you've guessed it, *The Hurricane*.

During the summer of 2016 North Weald celebrated its centenary, the Royal Aircraft Factory BE.2s of 39 Squadron's 'A' Flight moving in during the first week of June 1916. The airfield had closed by early 1920, but not for long. It was 56 Squadron that brought back operational fighters in 1927 and the RAF was to remain until February 1958 when the Hawker Hunter F.6s of 111 Squadron – the 'Black Arrows' – left for North Luffenham. During that time, a bewildering procession of squadrons (over 50) and other units helped to make North Weald one of the most famous of RAF stations. North Weald has become a thriving civil aerodrome, with a healthy number of historic and classic aircraft in residence.

Cosmopolitan bonds

Since the late 1980s it has been the task of the North Weald Airfield Museum to chart this rich and varied heritage. At first the building it occupies looks incongruous, located a distance from the main airfield site, but this was RAF North Weald's Station Office, 'Ad Astra House', an exhibit in its own right. In front is an obelisk that was a gift from Norway to the people of North Weald in June 1952. Ties between the airfield and the Royal Norwegian Air Force are strong and are regularly commemorated. Enveloping the Norwegian memorial is an imposing arc of Portland stone that commemorates all who served on the airfield; this was dedicated on 3rd September 2000. It includes a Debt of Honour that charts 267 men, women and children that lost their lives. To quote the museum website: "no distinction has been drawn between death in the face of the enemy or in an accident on or around the airfield. All served and all paid the supreme sacrifice."

After the memorials, inside the museum are four themed rooms and the depth of the displays is breath taking – but there's a huge subject to tackle. The Wulstan Tempest Room charts the exploits of a Zeppelin killer. On 1st October 1916 while piloting a Royal Aircraft Factory BE.2 2nd Lt W J Tempest of 39 Squadron Royal Flying Corps intercepted and shot down the Zeppelin L31 over Potters Bar, for which action he was awarded the DSO. The death of Kapitänleutnant Heinrich Mathy, the exceptional airship commander of the Great War, dealt a crippling blow to Imperial Germany. The Victor Beamish Room zooms in on the Battle of Britain. As station commander during 1940 Wg Cdr Beamish was not expected to fly operationally but as the 37-year-old could find no regulation that actually *forbade* him from doing so, he had his own Hurricane kept ready for action. Credited with seven 'kills' and nine 'probables', he was awarded the DSO and DFC during this period.

During World War Two North Weald was a cosmopolitan community and the Scott-Madden Room is dedicated to those serving from Canada, Czechoslovakia, New Zealand, Norway, Poland and the two US 'Eagle' Squadrons as well as British personnel. This is named after Wg Cdr David Scott-Madden, who led the North Weald Wing during 1942 and was instrumental in making the Norwegian 331 and 332 Squadrons into a renowned fighting force. The Roger Topp Room takes the North Weald story into the jet age and it was opened by the man himself, Air Cdre R L Topp AFC, on 19th April 2009. (More about Roger's time with the 'Black Arrows' can be found in Chapter 8, the Bournemouth Aviation Museum.) Among other displays, there is one outlining the 'Blitz' – North Weald and the surrounding area were on the receiving end of Luftwaffe attacks during 1940-1942.

'Ad Astra House', home of the North Weald Airfield Museum was RAF North Weald's Station Office. *Ken Ellis*

North Weald's 'gate guardian', a Hurricane replica in the colours of 56 Squadron. *Ken Ellis*

Also in Essex
Bradwell Bay Military and Science Museum

Opened in 2015, the museum is based on curator James Harvard's collection, accrued over twenty years. Located on the edge of the former World War Two airfield, a Jaguar and Lynx have been added to the external display. **https://bradwellmilitarymuseum.co.uk**

Bradwell Bay Military and Science Museum aircraft

Type	Identity	Built	Origin	Acquired	Notes
SEPECAT Jaguar T.2A	XX146	1974	GB/France	Apr 2017	–
Westland Lynx HMA.8	ZD266	1983	Britain	2016	–

Purfleet Heritage and Military Centre

This incorporates the **Hornchurch Wing** exhibition with an incredible wealth of aviation artefacts. There are extensive other displays, all housed in the incredible Royal Gunpowder Magazine 18th century arsenal.

Ridgewell Airfield Commemorative Museum

Established in USAAF Station 167's former hospital. Displays – including the Tony Ince Collection – are dedicated to the 381st Bomb Group and RAF units. **www.381st.com**

Thameside Aviation Museum

Located within East Tilbury's Coalhouse Fort, a 1860s Victorian Casemate Fortress, TAM has had an exhibition within the walls since 1984 and displays include much on the Battle of Britain over Essex. **www.aviationmuseum.co.uk** | **www.coalhousefort.co.uk**

Vulcan Restoration Trust

The trust maintains Vulcan B.2 XL426 in live condition at London Southend Airport and stages regular open days and events. As this book went to press, the Vulcan Restoration Trust revealed the brilliant news that Hangar 6 had been secured to house XL426, initially for a five-year period. Keep an eye on **www.avrovulcan.com** for developments.

Boxkite to Airbus
Aerospace Bristol

Filton
www.aerospacebristol.org

By the time readers get to this page, if all has gone well, Britain's latest aviation museum will have opened in grand style at Bristol's former Filton airfield. This is Aerospace Bristol and doubtless a lot of the press reporting will have used words like 'latest' and 'brand new'. Amid the Champagne and the canapes there will have been a small caucus of stalwarts who will toast one another because this venture didn't start overnight, it can trace itself back to 1992, if not further. This massive project will have cost just shy of £20 million with financial backing from Airbus UK, BAE Systems, Rolls-Royce, the Heritage Lottery Fund, other funding agencies and the Bristol Aero Collection Trust. Members of this last-named organisation have stuck tooth and nail to the vision of commemorating the industrial aviation achievements of Bristol and the surrounding area and have shown exceptional tenacity through many ups and downs that were finally vindicated with the unveiling of Aerospace Bristol.

The 'Bristol' part of Aerospace Bristol is geographic; applying to the city and the region's many achievements in aeronautical development. It is also specific, relating to the Bristol Aeroplane Company which was founded by Sir George White at Filton in February 1910 as the British and Colonial Aeroplane Company. From 1920 it was known as the Bristol Aeroplane Company and it became one of the most iconic of the UK's aviation industrial giants. Types that contributed to this hallowed status included the Boxkite, Bristol Scout and F.2b Fighter, Bulldog, Blenheim, Beaufighter, Brabazon and Britannia.

Above: Rolling Concorde G-BOAF into nearly completed exhibition hall at Filton, 7th February 2017. *Aerospace Bristol*

In February 1960 Bristol became a part of the British Aircraft Corporation (BAC) and Filton's last product was probably its most famous of all, the Anglo-French Concorde supersonic airliner. BAC and Hawker Siddeley joined forces in 1977 to create British Aerospace, restructuring as BAE Systems in 1999. Two years later BAE Systems divested itself of its Airbus elements and at Filton, Airbus UK carried on the present work of building wings and other structures for the European multi-national. Bristol as a company did not just build aeroplanes; from 1920 it created aero engines thanks to the genius of Roy Fedden. The engine division morphed into Bristol Siddeley in 1959 which seven years later was acquired by Rolls-Royce. At Patchway, Rolls-Royce continues to manufacture and develop aero engines, marine powerplants and other products. Hence Aerospace Bristol aims to show the contribution of Bristol and its successors, Rolls-Royce and Airbus plus other enterprises and the City of Bristol and the region to aviation history.

Dogged determination

Bristol Aero Collection (BAC) came into being during 1992 and began the process of collecting artefacts, large and small, with the intention of establishing a museum, ideally at Filton. Thanks to Meggitt Aerospace, space was found at the factory at Banwell, to the east of Weston-super-Mare. This was very appropriate as in the later part of the war Banwell was the production site for the Bristol-run shadow factories that used Weston-super-Mare for assembly and flight test. Beauforts, Beaufighters and Hawker Tempest IIs were built at Banwell. Also taking advantage of this kind offer was Roger Hargreaves, the leading light of the Britannia Aircraft Preservation Trust, who located Britannia 308 G-ANCF and the cockpit of Series 101 G-ALRX, which was presented to BAC in December 2013. (See Chapter 19 for a tribute to Roger.) Changing needs at the site meant that BAC had to relocate in 1996; but the base supplied in the formative years by Meggitt was a vital launch pad.

August and September 1996 was a frenetic time as the growing collection was moved to a leased hangar at the former RAF airfield at Kemble, later to be renamed Cotswold Airport. The nature of Kemble was such that the public could gain access, vital for fund-raising and increasing awareness. Occasional open days were staged and from early 2000 these became regular and popular. The collection expanded while formulating plans and putting into gear. During 2006 BAC faced another move, this time within the perimeter of Kemble, to Hangar E2 – a far better facility. While the distance was tiny compared with ten years previously when the collection decamped from Somerset to Gloucestershire, the logistics and sheer toil involved was still daunting. In April 2012 BAC announced that the lease on its hangar was not going to be renewed and that it would be moving yet again – to Filton. The last public day at Kemble was held on 28th May and the well-tried skills of packing up and shifting came back into play. The vast 'Brabazon Hangar' at Filton (see below) swallowed the airframes as momentum was gained on the museum project. In the same way that Banwell had helped to springboard BAC, so Kemble provided vital time to consolidate and mature the blueprint for the future.

The Concorde 'effect'

With the end of Concorde operations, bringing an example back to its birthplace at Filton made a lot of sense. With the blessing of British Airways, Airbus UK and BAE Systems, *Alpha-Fox* made the type's last ever flight on 26th November 2003. BAC was part of this from long before the touchdown, having established BAC Trading Ltd to run a visitor centre in conjunction with Airbus UK. An apron and reception area were built and the Concorde Visitor Centre opened to the public, on a pre-booked basis, on 18th August 2004. Developments on the airfield brought about the closure of the facility in late 2010 and Airbus UK put *Alpha-Fox* into a careful 'care and maintenance' programme. That year saw extensive exhibitions and gatherings under the 'BAC 100' banner, celebrating the centenary of the Bristol company and Filton. In the spring of 2011, BAE Systems – the operator of the airfield – announced its closure and on the last day of the year all went silent at Filton.

Plans for a permanent exhibition were announced by the Concorde Trust in October 2006; this was to take the form of a large, almost totally glass-walled building, on the northern perimeter. Outline planning permission was granted in July 2008 but concern was expressed that the plans were too 'Concorde-centric' with the remainder of Filton's incredible heritage almost side-lined. The collection of material amassed by BAC was a ready-made museum in the waiting. In the same year that the airfield closed, 2011, the Concorde Trust announced the Bristol Concorde Aviation Museum but by May it had to declare that its bid to the Heritage Lottery Fund (HLF) had been unsuccessful. Guidance from BAC increased on the project and in May 2012 BAC and the Concorde Trust merged to become the Bristol Aero Collection Trust and the pace began to increase. The new venture was called the Bristol Aerospace Centre, soon changed to Aerospace Bristol. In December BAE Systems pledged the land and buildings that the present-day museum is centred upon, including the two Grade II listed 'Belfast Truss' hangars from World War One. The next HLF application was announced as a winner in May 2013. A campaign to bring a Bristol 170 Freighter back from New Zealand was launched in late 2016: this is a major 'hole' in important UK types that *should* have a home in Britain. Construction of the Concorde hall began during 2016 and G-BOAF was rolled into it on 7th February 2017 to await the grand opening at the end of the summer.

Filton links

At the time this book closed for press, the exact number of airframes due to go on show in the first phase of Aerospace Bristol was unconfirmed, but some of the airframes mentioned in the listing deserve greater explanation. As will be seen under Farnborough, Hampshire, the Beagle 206 began life as the Type 220 as the Bristol design office attempted to broaden the market base of Filton products. The Sea Harrier is fitted with a Rolls-Royce Pegasus 104 vectored thrust turbofan, which was conceived by Bristol Siddeley. The Government Aircraft Factory Jindivik target drone was the first application of the exceptionally adaptable Armstrong Siddeley Viper turbojet in the early 1950s which from 1959 became a Bristol Siddeley product. Initially Fairey was the UK design authority overseeing the British Jindivik programme but with the company's absorption into Westland in 1960, Filton took more and more responsibility for the drone, including possible extension of its roles. (For more on the Beagle 206 and Jindivik, see the Farnborough Air Sciences Trust in Chapter 11.) Until the programme was terminated in November 2001, major elements of the Hawker Siddeley HS.146 and BAE Systems Avro RJX airliner family had been built at Filton. Well-known microlight designer Mike Whittaker worked as an engineer with British Aerospace at Filton and his MW-4 microlight had the distinction of being the last aircraft to be designed, built and flown at Filton.

Scheduled to go on show inside Aerospace Bristol are the last traces of an aircraft that is famous, but perhaps for the wrong reasons. This was the Type 167 Brabazon, which boasted a capacity for 100 passengers in spacious, luxurious surroundings, a dozen crew and eight coupled engines driving four contra-rotating propellers providing a cruise of 250mph. With an all-up weight of 290,000lb at the time it was the largest and most complex commercial aircraft – anywhere. To accommodate it, the runway at Filton needed extension westwards, necessitating the almost total demolition of the village of Charlton and elaborate rerouting of local roads. A massive new assembly hall, with a 'footprint' of 8 acres, was created. This inevitably became known as the 'Brabazon Hangar' and it still survives, although significantly it has avoided listing and may not have a role in the redevelopment of the former airfield site.

When test pilot 'Bill' Pegg captained the Brabazon on its maiden voyage on 4th September 1949 the undertaking was estimated to have cost between £12 and £15 million – an eye-watering financial commitment in a country still enduring food and fuel rationing. Inevitably the axe fell on the Brabazon and only the prototype – undeniably an incredible technical achievement – clocked up around 400 hours. It and the unfinished second example were scrapped in 1953. A wheel, nearly 5ft high and a piece of fuselage skin carrying its airliner's name, latterly on show in the former Bristol Industrial Museum, are all that remains.

For the founders of the Bristol Aero Collection taking those first steps in 1992, it has been a long journey to Aerospace Bristol. The time in between has involved more than its fair share of packing cases and low-loaders, but perseverance has triumphed.

A wheel, nearly 5ft high and a piece of fuselage skin from the Bristol Brabazon airliner on show at the former Bristol Industrial Museum in 1995. These items are destined for display at Aerospace Bristol. *Ken Ellis*

British Aircraft Corporation/Sud Concorde 102 G-BOAF
1979 | Supersonic airliner | Four 38,050lb st Rolls-Royce/SNECMA Olympus 593
Mk.610-14-28 turbojets

Of the total production run of 20 Concordes, seven are preserved in the UK: the prototype G-BSST at Yeovilton; the pre-production G-AXDN at Duxford and G-BBDG at Brooklands (Chapter 27); and four British Airways workhorses at East Fortune, Heathrow, Manchester and Filton's G-BOAF. Arguably the most important example is the French-assembled 001 which was the first to take to the skies, on 2nd March 1969 at Toulouse, France, in the hands of André Turcat and team. From a purely national point of view, it is G-BSST that dominates. Brian Trubshaw piloting it from Filton's runway 38 days after the its French counterpart. There are a lot of Concorde zealots that would argue that all of the seven deserve 'star' treatment, but in determining which to profile in this book, two score higher than the others. Large chunks of *Delta-Golf* at Brooklands were built at the British Aircraft Corporation factory there which makes its presence there very appropriate. Likewise *Alpha-Fox* at Filton: it was the ultimate one built, both at Filton and of the type; the last of a long line of 'Bristol' products (the British element of Concorde started off as the Bristol Type 223); and the final one of the twenty to fly. That ticks a lot of boxes!

Registered as G-BFKX, Concorde 100-016 lifted off from Filton's on 20th April 1979. It was prepared for the bizarre joint venture between British Airways (BA) and Air France and Dallas-based Braniff International that had been inaugurated on 12th January 1979. Braniff offered a service from Dallas to Washington DC at subsonic speeds and then a supersonic run to either London or Paris and return. It all sounded simple enough until US trade laws and Federal Aviation Administration (FAA) procedures were taken on board. For the US sector, Braniff flight and cabin crew had to be engaged and for the Atlantic crossing, BA or Air France personnel took over. The Concordes involved could not be owned by a non-US airline; hence G-BFKX was registered not to BA but to British Aerospace. Equally the Concordes had to be American

A moment of history, Concorde G-BOAF making its last-ever touch down, back at its Filton birthplace: 26th November 2003.
Tony McCarthy

registered, so from 14th December 1979 *Kilo-Xray* became G-N94AF, a hybrid British-American identity. Technically, the 'G' needed taping over once a Braniff crew were in charge and this needed uncovering before tackling the Atlantic. The author understands that a duplicate set of flight documentation was kept on board, so that FAA-related paperwork was in the cockpit on the legs to and from Dallas and that this was substituted with British bureaucracy for the transatlantic phase. Sanity was restored in May 1980 when Braniff ditched the agreement.

On 12th June 1980 Concorde 100-016 took up the registration that had been intended for it from birth, as hinted at in its Anglo-American identity, G-BOAF. While flying between Christchurch and Sydney on 12th April 1989 *Alpha-Fox* suffered the first of several upper rudder separations that for a while bedevilled the Concorde fleet. It landed safely. Tragically, that was not the case for Air France's F-BTSC flying AF4590 from Paris Charles de Gaulle to New York John F Kennedy on 25th July 2000. The images of it climbing away trailing a massive plume of flame are unforgettable. It crashed shortly afterwards, killing all 109 on board and four people on the ground. The Concorde fleet was grounded immediately. Filton and Toulouse worked furiously with BA and Air France on the Return to Flight programme and G-BOAF was the first with the modifications, test flying on 17th July 2001; going back into service on 7th November.

With the decision taken to retire the Concordes from service, *Alpha-Fox* flew as BA9010 on a sortie out of Heathrow for a blast over the Atlantic, carrying out a stream landing back at its base with G-BOAE and G-BOAG. On 26th November 2003 Captains Les Brodie and Mike Bannister piloted *Alpha-Fox* on its, and the type's last ever flight, touching down watched by huge crowds at Filton. That was its 6,045th landing, its total flying time coming to 18,257 hours during which it had achieved 5,639 supersonic flights. As with all seven of the BA Concordes, G-BOAF remains the property of the airline.

Bristol Bolingbroke IV 9048
1942 | Patrol bomber | Two 920hp Bristol Mercury XV radials

In Finland, Blenheim IV BL-200, built under licence in 1944 and flown by the Finnish Air Force until June 1957 is the sole intact surviving Blenheim. Across the planet other 'Blenheims' are preserved, but all are Canadian-built Bolingbroke IVs. The Royal Canadian Air Force (RCAF) wanted large numbers of Blenheims and Fairchild Aircraft of Longueuil, Quebec, was contracted to build Bolingbroke IVs from 1939. A crew trainer, the Mk.IVT, followed the patrol bomber version and the last was struck off charge in 1947; it is from these stocks that so many survived to the present day. The Blenheim transformed the prospects for the Bristol company, with over 6,000 of all variants being built, by the parent company, shadow factories and under licence. The design allowed for a family of types to be developed: the Beaufort and the Beaufighter.

Filton's 'Boly' is the only whole example in Britain outside of the 'nationals' or Duxford's wonderful airworthy example. Mk.IV 9048 was built at Longueuil and was brought on charge by the RCAF on 8th October 1941. It was issued initially to 8 (Bomber Reconnaissance) Squadron and given the code 'YO-F'. As part of Western Air Command it was based at Sea Island, Vancouver, and detached to Alaska for coastal patrol duties in each case. It was used for a famous series of stills released by the Director of Public Information in Ottawa, showing it flying through snow-covered Alaskan mountains. By the spring of 1942 the Bolingbroke had transferred to crew training duties, serving with British Commonwealth Air Training Plan with 3 Bombing and Gunnery School (BGS) at MacDonald, Manitoba and finally 7 BGS, Paulson, also in Manitoba.

Aviation heritage owes a huge debt to Canadian farmers, rural contractors and homesteaders, not least Wes Agnew of Hartney, Manitoba. From 1946 into the early 1950s the RCAF offered equipment at very reasonable rates to locals in an attempt to overcome chronic shortages of aluminium, rubber and other useful commodities. All over Canada, individuals bought up war surplus airframes and towed them on their undercarriage to where they could be robbed of parts to help repair a tractor, a roof, or provide a cart with new wheels. Farmers the world over are genetically programmed never to throw anything away and this meant that in the 1960s and beyond, there were rich pickings to be found in the undergrowth at farmsteads close to former air bases.

Bolingbroke IV 9048 of 8 (Bomber Reconnaissance) Squadron RCAF during a detachment to Alaska in 1941. *Director of Public Information Canada*

Bolingbroke 9048 was struck off charge with the RCAF at Paulson on 21st August 1946. Paying no more than a couple of hundred dollars for each airframe, Wes Agnew bought at least 17 Bolingbrokes, including 9048, and this 'fleet' decorated his property for decades. The majority of these went on to museums or become restoration projects, including Duxford's 'flyer'. Snapped up by famous warbird operator David Tallichet, 9048 was moved to Chino, California, in 1972 before going through a series of US-based owners. By 2003 it was back at Chino and available for disposal, being shipped to Filton in June 2006.

Bristol Britannia 101 G-ALRX
1953 | Long range airliner | Four 3,900shp Bristol Proteus 705 turboprops

Ordinarily, the profiles do not extend to cockpits; however the story of this Filton-built prototype and its life of just 51 flying hours over 43 days deserves telling. Bristol chief test pilot A J 'Bill' Pegg took the prototype Britannia, G-ALBO, for its maiden flight at Filton on 16th August 1952. This machine was joined by G-ALRX on 23rd December 1953 and Bill was again in command for its first excursion. On 4th February 1954 he was piloting G-ALRX with eleven others on board, including flight test engineers Ken Fitzgerald and Gareth Jones. Alongside Bill was Captain D Malouin from Dutch national airline KLM with other worthies from its management in the cabin. Keeping them company was Dr Archibald Russell, Bristol chief designer, Dr Stanley Hooker, chief engineer of the Bristol engine division, and Mr Farnes, senior sales manager – no pressure on the pilot, then!

The reduction gear on the starboard inner Proteus failed and the turboprop disintegrated, starting a severe fire. Sanctuary at Filton was impossible; surrounded by houses and factories it was no place to take a blazing airliner. The tide was low in the Severn Estuary and Bill shut down the starboard outer, yelled to everyone to brace for impact and committed to a forced landing. He pulled off a flawless belly landing in the mud, the Britannia slid along for about 400 yards and ground to a halt. Not only had the sludge cushioned the landing, it had extinguished the fire. All on board scrambled out with only minor injuries and waded to firmer ground to await the rescue crews. James Hamilton-Paterson, in his superb *Empire of the Clouds – When Britain's Aircraft Ruled the World* summed the exploit up: "It was a tribute not only to first-rate piloting but to an immensely strong airframe." In all, 85 Britannias were built; oddly KLM never took delivery of one!

There was no time to recover the precious airframe before the Severn rolled back in and its salt water put paid to G-ALRX ever flying again. After accident investigations the fuselage was used for cabin fitment trials and other tasks at Filton. Chopped down to just a forward fuselage it was passed on to the Aeromedical and Safety School at Boscombe Down. After a fair bit of lobbying, Roger Hargreaves of the Britannia Aircraft Preservation Trust (Chapter 19), succeeded in acquiring this important artefact and on 10th December 1995 it was moved to Banwell, along with the nascent Bristol Aero Collection (BAC) airframes. It migrated to Kemble and on 23rd December 2013 it was gifted to BAC to take up a prominent place in the Aerospace Bristol exhibition.

Both of the prototype Britannias (G-ALRX left, G-ALBO left) in British Overseas Airways colours on a sortie out of Filton, January 1954. *Bristol Aeroplane Company*

Bristol Type 173 Series 1 XF785
1952 | Transport helicopter | Two 545hp Alvis Leonides 73 pistons

In an attempt to diversify after World War Two Bristol set up a helicopter division with Raoul Hafner as chief designer. The company developed Britain's first production helicopter, the Sycamore, and the Type 173, the country's first twin-rotor design. (For more on Hafner, the Sycamore and the operational version of the 173, the Belvedere, see The Helicopter Museum, Chapter 25.) Although it may be that in the first phase of Aerospace Bristol, the Type 173 does not get included, it is nevertheless an important artefact. It represents the start of Bristol's most complex rotorcraft and shows just how long such a project can take to come to fruition. In 1947 the Ministry of Supply expressed great interest in a transport helicopter for use as an 'airliner', flying crane and possible military purposes. Hafner put forward the contra-rotating twin rotor, twin-engined Type 173 utilizing as many parts and sub-structures as possible from the Type 171, the Sycamore to be.

It was 1951 before the prototype, civil registered G-ALBN, was ready to test. Chief test pilot for Bristol rotorcraft, Charles 'Sox' Hosegood, carried out the first ground run on 5th May 1951. It was November before confidence had grown enough for tethered hovering. Sox carried out the first 'free' hover on 3rd January 1952 but it was full of control and resonance problems. C H Barnes described in *Bristol Aircraft since 1910* that Sox: "found difficulty in moving in any direction but backwards". The following day Sox took G-ALBN up again only to bring it back down for a heavy landing; the undercarriage, rear fuselage and rotors were badly damaged. Developing Britain's first and, as it transpired, only twin-rotor helicopter family was going to be a long and involved process. It was not until 24th August 1952 that Sox was able to fly around the airfield, enabling him to transit to Farnborough for the SBAC airshow the following month.

The prototype was given the military serial XF785 in October 1953 and Sox carried out deck landing trials on the aircraft carrier HMS *Eagle* in November. After that it reverted to its civil registration and continued development flying until the late 1950s when it was retired. Having been financed by the state, it was transferred to Henlow with the instructional airframe number 7648M on 10th July 1960 and placed into store to await the creation of the RAF Museum. In the late 1980s it was transferred to Cosford, for further storage. Realising its importance, the Bristol Aero Collection took over custodianship of it at Kemble on 3rd January 2002. There it was available for public inspection, almost certainly the first time it had been viewed by appreciable numbers of people since Farnborough 50 years before. In January 2013 the Type 173 made the journey to Filton, returning to its birthplace.

The Bristol 173 in military guise. Behind it is the long gone control tower and, behind the trees the World War One hangars that form part of the Aerospace Bristol site. *Bristol Aeroplane Company*

Aerospace Bristol aircraft

Type	Identity	Built	Origin	Acquired	Notes
BAC/Sud Concorde 102*	G-BOAF	1979	GB/France	26 Nov 2003	see profile
BAC/Sud Concorde 100	–	–	GB/France	1997	cockpit, engineering mock-up
Beagle 206 Srs 1	G-ATDD	1965	Britain	May 1996	cockpit
Bristol F.2b Fighter#	'A7288'	2010	Britain	10 Jul 2010	static replica
Bristol Scout#	'A1742'	1962	Britain	2017	static replica
Bristol Babe III#	'G-EASQ'	1972	Britain	Nov 1994	static replica
Bristol Bolingbroke IV#	9048	1941	Britain	25 Jul 2006	see profile
Bristol Beaufighter	–	c1942	Britain	2017	cockpit
Bristol Britannia 101#	G-ALRX	1953	Britain	23 Dec 2013	cockpit, see profile
Bristol 173 Srs 1	XF785	1952	Britain	3 Jan 2002	see profile
Bristol Sycamore HR.14	XJ917	1957	Britain	30 Apr 1993	–
Bristol Sycamore HR.14	XL824	1957	Britain	2015	–
GAF Jindivik 103B	A92-708	1975	Australia	27 Aug 1997	target drone
Hawker Siddeley Sea Harrier FA.2	ZD610	1985	Britain	30 Sep 2015	–
Hawker Siddeley 146 RJX100	–	2008	Britain	6 Dec 2013	unfinished airframe
Whittaker MW-4	G-MBTH	1982	Britain	2013	–

Notes: * – illustrated in the colour section. At the time of going to press, it was not know just how many of the airframes held would go on show. Other than Concorde *Alpha-Fox* and *one* of the Sycamores, those marked with a # are *believed* to be involved.

The Jet Age exhibition hall with the Gloster E28/39 replica in the centre. Clockwise, from the left: Meteor TT.20 WM234, Javelin FAW.9 XH903 and Meteor F.8 WH364. *Courtesy Jet Age Museum*

The cockpit of Vulcan B.2 XM569 is an imposing exhibit at Jet Age. *Les Woodward*

Gloster's Guardians
Jet Age Museum

Gloucestershire Airport
www.jetagemuseum.org

Like its near neighbour, Aerospace Bristol, the all-volunteer Jet Age Museum has led a nomadic life. While the end result took quite some time to achieve, it was certainly worth the effort and fortitude involved. Jet Age Museum commemorates another great name of the British aircraft industry – Gloster. By 1992 the Gloucestershire Aviation Collection (GAC) was collecting artefacts and airframes at Hucclecote, east of Gloucester. Also known as Brockworth, this was the factory and airfield of the Gloster Aircraft Company from 1929 until all traces of aviation manufacture had gone in 1964. Dedicated to charting the history of Gloster through a museum, GAC's volunteers also had their eyes on the story of the jet engine, hence the adoption of Jet Age Museum title. Gloster and jets had been synonymous since the company designed and built Britain's first jet – and the world's first practical jet – the E28/39 which had its maiden flight on 15th May 1941. GAC's founder airframe at Hucclecote was Meteor T.7 WL360 in 1992, quickly followed by bulky Javelin FAW.9 XH903. The Javelin is still with the collection; WL360 was disposed of in 1997.

As might be expected of a 'brown field' site close to a large town and adjacent to a motorway, demands for the redevelopment of Hucclecote were pressing. In late 1995 GAC had to vacate its building and its last public open day was held on 29th October. There were hopes that Hucclecote could again provide a base as negotiations with the developers continued on and off through to 2001. During 2005 a scheme in conjunction with Brockworth Enterprise School to create a visitor centre devoted to the heritage of the site was mooted, but was shelved in mid-2008.

Almost seamlessly, in 1995 GAC found a new home at Staverton, Gloucestershire Airport, close to Cheltenham. Having completed the complexities of the relocation no time was lost in opening up to the public on an occasional basis. While Staverton does not have the heritage of Hucclecote, it has a fascinating pedigree, as well as a wide variety of RAF units; other names linked with it include Folland, Rotol, Dowty and Flight Refuelling. Dowty's propellers division is now under the GE Aviation banner; the company's undercarriage business is now part of Safran. Both GE and Safran maintain factories at Staverton. Another part of GE Aviation, since 2007, is what started as the famous Smiths instrumentation business and by the 1950s was known as Smiths Industries. Among the company's many market leading products was the Autoland system – enabling aircraft to land 'blind' – and head-up displays. The Hawker Siddeley Trident forward fuselage on display at Jet Age is a tribute to this achievement.

Early in 2000 it was apparent that GAC would have to vacate its hangar and another 'final' open day was held, on 1st October. In an incredibly hectic 72 hours from 28th December 2000 to New Year's Day 2001 the aircraft, engines and myriad other items were moved. Most of the airframes were moved to other locations at Staverton, others were dispersed nearby. All the time the GAC team did not give up on the idea of a permanent home. Undaunted, other plans were laid: Heritage Lottery Funding pursued, local authorities lobbied.

On 11th February 2011 the breakthrough was achieved. Tewkesbury Borough Council, already a benefactor and alert to diversifying the tourist appeal of the region, realised the merit and potential of an aviation museum: planning permission was granted at Gloucestershire Airport for Jet Age. After that the pace quickened and the first ground was cut on the new building in August 2012. The first full season was envisioned as 2014, but the opportunity was taken to exploit local interest and from late August 2013 Jet Age staged what was called 'Opening Lite'. This helped to whip up publicity and allowed the volunteer team to 'shake down' its procedures before the big event. There was only one person on the 'hit list' to officiate at the full and proper opening ceremony: Captain Eric 'Winkle' Brown CBE DSC AFC RN. Eric had been at Cranwell when the Gloster E28/39 was being readied for flight and later got to fly it and a host of other jets. With the great man unveiling a plaque, the all-new Jet Age Museum opened its doors in fine style just over 14 years since it had had to close them in what was then considered a temporary 'blip'.

Filling the gaps

While getting the hardware to tell the tale of British jet development was relatively easy, with a wide choice of surviving Gloster and other products available, the task of showing the company's earlier days was much more difficult. The acquisition of a Gladiator from a wind-blown mountain in arctic Norway is detailed in the profiles that follow. From the earliest days of GAC, it was realised that replicas would play an important role. The choice of the Gamecock, the RAF's last fighter with a wooden airframe – until of course wood was 'rediscovered' for the exceptional de Havilland Mosquito – which first flew at Hucclecote in 1925 proved to be a wise one. The completed item belies the fact that it was a complex and challenging project. Before construction could start, drawings had to be recreated as very few originals survived.

The Gamecock team was led by Roff T Jones, a former Gloster senior designer and hundreds of plans to the highest standard were created. Barry Denton led the build team with work getting underway in earnest during the summer of 1998. The Bristol Jupiter VII radial is an original on loan from the RAF Museum and reconditioned by the Rolls-Royce Heritage Trust; the propeller is also an original.

While the first Gloster E28/39 jet had its official maiden flight at Cranwell in May 1941, it had already had air under its wheels at its birthplace, Hucclecote. During initial taxying trials on 8th April, 'Gerry' Sayers' test report read as follows: "The aeroplane left the ground on each of these three runs. The actual flights being about 6ft off the ground and varying in distance from 100 to 200 yards along the ground." With this incredible heritage, pictures and artwork of the E28/39 would just not do at Jet Age Museum something far more tangible was needed. The Staverton example is the last of a 'production run' of three full-size fibreglass models produced by the Sir Frank Whittle Commemorative Group and paid for by 'The Reactionaries' – former colleagues of Whittle. The first two are externally displayed at Lutterworth – where Whittle first test ran his engine – and at Farnborough (Chapters 15 and 11 respectively), where much of the test flying was carried out. Thanks to The Reactionaries, funds from GAC members and Tewkesbury Borough Council, the moulds were also used to create the example with Jet Age. Unlike the previous two, which essentially are imposing works of art, the Staverton E28/39 sits on replica undercarriage and is far more detailed, including a fitted out cockpit. With the original taking pride of place in the Science Museum in London and displayed in 'flying' guise, Jet Age's E28/39 provides the only opportunity to get close to the world-beating prototype conceived by Gloster and Whittle.

Gloster Gladiator II N5914
1937 | Day fighter | One 840hp Bristol Mercury VIIIA radial

With respect to the exceptional Gamecock reproduction and the array of Gloster jets, the exhibit with the most notable provenance is the Gladiator. Visitors to Jet Age Museum can follow the restoration of this project; a rare example of the RAF's last biplane fighter. The British Gladiator population stands at seven, including the Staverton example. Two are airworthy, at Duxford and Old Warden, one is under restoration to fly for the 'warbird' world; two are on show at the RAF Museum, Hendon and another is held by the Fleet Air Arm Museum at Yeovilton. That a 'local' museum has achieved such a high-profile airframe is a testament to Jet Age's 'reach'.

Germany started to invade Norway on 8th April 1940 and Britain rushed forces in an attempt to prevent the enemy consolidating its hold. The Norwegian coastline posed frightening strategic implications for any future blockade of Britain by the Kriegsmarine. At Filton, Bristol, 263 Squadron was put on alert and 18 Gladiators flew via Sealand, near Chester, to Prestwick, arriving on 20th April. The following day, Fleet Air Arm pilots ferried the biplanes to deck of the aircraft carrier HMS *Glorious*. On the 24th, *Glorious* was cruising along the Norwegian coast and 263's Gladiators flew off to settle on the frozen Lake Lesjaskog, southwest of Trondheim. The inevitable happened: within 24 hours, the Luftwaffe bombed the ice, collapsing the 'airfield' from under the RAF and Fleet Air Arm aircraft parked there. About 13 Gladiators were taken out of action, including N5628 which is poignantly displayed at Hendon. *Glorious* shuttled more Gladiators across the North Sea including, it is believed, N5914 and Hawker Hurricanes from 46 Squadron. (Fresh from the factory at Hucclecote, N5914 was rushed to Prestwick in late April 1940 where it was placed on charge with the local Ferry Flight prior to embarking for Norway.)

By the end of May, RAF operations were being conducted from the airfield Bardufoss, northeast of Narvik, and an airstrip at Skaanland, near Bødø; both beyond the Arctic Circle. The plan by then was to hold the port of Narvik in the hope of creating a bridgehead there. On 2nd June 1940 New Zealand-born Plt Off James L Wilkie in N5914 and Fg Off Louis R Jacobsen in N5681 took off from Bardufoss at 14:30 hours to patrol the Narvik area. Both Gladiators were engaged by a pair of Messerschmitt Bf 110s of I Gruppe, Zerstörergeschwader (I./ZG 76). North of Narvik, Leutnant Helmut Lent shot down N5914 and the 20-year-old Wilkie was killed. The 'Kiwi' was buried with full military honours in the New Cemetery at Narvik. Jacobsen was able to return to Bardufoss, but was one of ten of 263's pilots who perished when *Glorious* was sunk on 8th June. Eight Gladiators and ten Hurricanes had managed to land back on the carrier as British forces pulled out.

The fuselage frame of Gladiator N5914.
Courtesy Jet Age Museum

Gladiator N5914 remained where it fell, on high ground at Lille Haugfjell near Narvik. In December 1998 the wreckage was salvaged in a 'combined operation' involving the Fleet Air Arm Museum (FAAM), the Royal Norwegian Air Force Museum and Jet Age personnel. The latter had amassed a large amount of Gladiator airframe components to help with two domestic projects, including the example now on display at Bødø. From this, Yeovilton and Jet Age gained sufficient to form restoration projects; FAAM's based on a Lake Lesjaskog example, Jet Age was allocated the remains of N5914, plus wings and parts from other examples. To thank FAAM for its help, Jet Age volunteers worked on that project alongside their own and on 17th July 2002 'N5574' was handed over to Yeovilton. The restoration of N5914 is a challenging and long term project, but will produce a very significant exhibit in due course.

Gloster Meteor F.8 WH364
1959 | Day fighter | Two 3,600lb st Rolls-Royce Derwent 8 turbojets

With a selection of Meteors to go for in Jet Age's 'fleet', the F.8 represents the most numeric RAF frontline version, boasts a varied service life, has connections with two test pilots and was a well-known Gloucestershire landmark for three decades. Built by Armstrong Whitworth at Baginton, Coventry, F.8 WH364 was issued to 29 Maintenance Unit (MU) at High Ercall on 4th February 1952. At North Weald, 601 (County of London) Squadron Royal Auxiliary Air Force began converting from de Havilland Vampire F.3s in August 1952 and was basking in the luxury of receiving brand new Meteor F.8s. The first two aircraft were taken on charge on the 11th: WH364 adopting the code 'B' and WH349 'C'.

During summer camp at Takali, Malta, Fg Off N D Norman reacted perfectly on 24th June 1954 when WH364's canopy disintegrated around him; the 25-year-old bringing the Meteor back for a faultless emergency landing. This was Desmond Norman who on 13th June 1965 carried out the first flight of a British success story, the prototype BN-2 Islander, which he had designed with John Britten. (See under Solent Sky, Chapter 11, for the BN-1.) In its damaged state, WH364 could not go home to North Weald with the rest of 601 and it was issued to 137 MU at Safi on Malta for repair and storage. For a matter of weeks in June and July 1956 WH364 was active again, on charge with the Station Flight at Takali. In October 1957 WH364 flew south to Libya, for a spell with the Station Flight at Idris until it returned to Safi in March the following year. The Meteor's last spell of flying from Malta was again at Takali, this time as part of the station's Communications and Target Towing Squadron, from October 1960 until a minor flying accident put it back into storage at Safi on 8th August 1961.

The Meteor was ferried to the UK and issued to 5 MU at Kemble on 17th August 1962. The RAF still had need of the twin-jet in the 1960s and WH364 was dusted down and delivered to Binbrook, where it was placed on charge with 85 Squadron on 4th December 1964. Coded 'U' WH364 carried out target facilities work from the fighter station until it was finally retired, back to 5 MU, on 18th November 1969. During 1971 WH364 was given the instructional airframe number 8169M and in the following year was placed on a plinth near the main gate. It was painted in 601 Squadron colours, in the markings of the commanding officer's mount of 1952, with dramatic red and black stripes on the fin and rudder. (The actual machine was WK722 'A' which appeared in those colours in the static display at the Royal Review of the RAF, held at Odiham in July 1953.) The Meteor was taken down off the 'gate' in April 1992 having previously been acquired by the Avon Air Museum for possible restoration by Meteor Flight. This did not come about and WH364 was acquired by Jet Age patron Peter Cadbury and donated to the museum. Peter had been a production test pilot with Hawker at Langley up to 1943, flying Hurricanes. He transferred to Gloster at Hucclecote, testing Typhoons off the production line, moving to Moreton Valence by 1946 to work on early Meteors. WH364 was delivered to Staverton on 10th September 2003.

Meteor F.8 WH364 on the 'gate' at RAF Kemble, March 1972. *Roy Bonser*

Gloster Javelin FAW.9 XH903
1959 | All-weather fighter | Two 11,000lb st Bristol Siddeley Sapphire 210 turbojets

There are ten Javelins extant in the UK, two consisting of forward fuselages only. That makes the two in the custody of Jet Age an impressive percentage of the population! The second airframe to join the Gloucestershire Aviation Collection (GAC), XH903 in on loan from the RAF Museum. It was built at Hucclecote in early 1959, making its first flight from the small runway at its birthplace; the sortie terminating a short distance to the southwest at the test airfield at Moreton Valence. Hucclecote was *not* the place for circuits in something the size and weight of a Javelin!

On 27th February 1959 XH903 was issued to 19 Maintenance Unit (MU) at St Athan for service preparation and on 1st May it joined 23 Squadron at Coltishall, taking the code 'K'. In June 1960 it was back at Moreton Valence, as an early candidate for upgrade to FAW.9 status, when Mk.7s were fitted with Sapphire turbojets equipped with limited reheat, for use above 20,000ft. This work was completed in January 1961; XH903 again going to 19 MU. On 14th February 1961 XH903 took the code 'G' – it was to keep this for the rest of its service life – with 33 Squadron at Middleton St George (now Durham Tees Valley Airport). In February and March it was briefly with 29 Squadron at Leuchars. Back at Middleton, XH903 served with 33 until the squadron disbanded there on 17th November 1962. Four days later the Javelin was on the ramp at Laarbruch, West Germany, having joined 5 Squadron. The unit moved to Geilenkirchen in December and it retired its last 'Flat Irons' (as Javelins were nicknamed) in October 1965, to take on English Electric Lightnings. On 15th October XH903 was accepted at 27 MU Shawbury which at the time was a 'graveyard' for the type. FAW.9 XH903 was spared and issued to RAF Innsworth, a non-airfield site between Gloucester and Cheltenham, for display purposes on 23rd August 1967. For a while it carried the erroneous serial number 'XM903'. Taken on by GAC on 19th May 1993 it was moved to Hucclecote, relocating to Staverton three years later.

Jet Age Museum aircraft

Type	Identity	Built	Origin	Acquired	Notes
Airspeed Horsa replica	–	2010	Britain	2010	–
Avro Vulcan B.2	XM569	1963	Britain	6 Feb 1997	cockpit
de Havilland Vampire T.11	XD506	1954	Britain	28 Feb 1998	–
English Electric Canberra TT.18	WK126	1954	Britain	Oct 1995	–
Gloster Gamecock	'J7904'	1997	Britain	9 Aug 1998	reproduction
Gloster Gladiator II	N5914	1940	Britain	Dec 1998	see profile
Gloster E28/39	'W4041/G'	2005	Britain	Jun 2004	replica
Gloster Meteor F.III	EE425	1945	Britain	Jan 2000	cockpit
Gloster Meteor T.7	VW453	1949	Britain	22 Apr 2013	–
Gloster Meteor T.7	WF784	1951	Britain	Mar 1997	–
Gloster Meteor F.8	WH364	1952	Britain	10 Sep 2003	see profile
Gloster Meteor NF(T).14	WS807	1954	Britain	Jul 1997	–
Gloster Meteor TT.20	WM234	1952	Britain	16 Apr 2014	composite
Gloster Javelin FAW.4	XA634	1956	Britain	23 May 2015	–
Gloster Javelin FAW.9*	XH903	1958	Britain	19 May 1993	see profile
Hawker Hunter F.4	XE664	1955	Britain	21 Feb 1999	cockpit
Hawker Hurricane	'V6799'	1968	Britain	2 Jul 1997	replica
Hawker Typhoon I	–	1942	Britain	2004	forward fuselage
Hawker Siddeley Harrier T.2	XW264	1969	Britain	28 Jun 1994	cockpit
Hawker Siddeley Trident 3B-101	G-AWZU	1971	Britain	28-11-13	forward fuselage

Notes: * – illustrated in the colour section.

Also in Gloucestershire
Bristol's City Museum and Art Gallery

Inside are treasures from all walks of life in a lively and well-presented manner. Dominating the atrium is a replica Bristol Boxkite, built in 1964 for the film *Those Magnificent Men in Their Flying Machines*. **www.bristolmuseums.org.uk**

M-Shed

Situated in Bristol's breath-taking 'Floating Harbour' area, not far from the SS *Great Britain*, this visitor attraction vividly tells the story of the city and the area. Handing from the ceiling of one of the halls is 1936 Mignet 'Flying Flea' G-AEHM on loan from the Science Museum. A huge store, called **L-Shed**, contains many treasures from the former Bristol Industrial Museum: behind-the-scenes tours can be arranged by prior application. **www.bristolmuseums.org.uk**

'Flying' in the atrium of Bristol's City Museum an Art Gallery, a *Magnificent Men* replica Boxkite. *British Aircraft Corporation*

Bristol Britannia XM496 Restoration Society

The society cherishes *Regulus*, which made the last-ever flight by a Britannia when it flew into Kemble airfield – now Cotswold Airport – on 14th October 1997. Open on Sundays and for special events. **www.XM496.com**

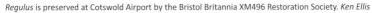

Regulus is preserved at Cotswold Airport by the Bristol Britannia XM496 Restoration Society. *Ken Ellis*

First in the Air
Farnborough Air Sciences Trust

Farnborough
www.airsciences.org.uk

Trenchard House, the main Farnborough Air Sciences Trust – FAST – building, was just a year old when a frail biplane took to the air just a stone's throw away on 16th October 1908. Constructed by the Royal Engineers the previous year, it those days the building served as the headquarters of the Balloon School. Exactly a century later a faithful replica of the pioneering British Army Aeroplane was unveiled as the centrepiece of FAST's tribute to Samuel Franklin Cody.

Like many organisations charted in this book, FAST is not just about aeroplanes and artefacts, the building it occupies is one of the oldest aviation-related structures in Britain – an exhibit in its own right. In August 1914 the Balloon School was taken over by the Officer Commanding the Military Wing of the Royal Flying Corps (RFC) as his headquarters before departing to France the following year. This man's glittering career was to lead to the label 'Father of the Royal Air Force' and the full title of Marshal of the RAF Hugh Montague Trenchard, 1st Viscount Trenchard, GCB OM GCVO DSO. The Old Balloon School, or Royal Aircraft Establishment (RAE) Building G1, was named Trenchard House by FAST in the great man's honour.

The name 'Farnborough' is irretrievably linked with the pioneers of flight and aeronautical research. The progression from the Balloon Factory to the Royal Aircraft Factory and the re-alignment into the RAE in 1918 is well known. The creation of

Above: Samuel Franklin Cody making history of Farnborough Common in British Army Aircraft No.1A, 16th October 1908.
Courtesy FAST

RAE propelled the Hampshire airfield to the pinnacle of aerospace technological achievement. Farnborough also witnessed the initial steps of the RFC in May 1912 when the first units, 1 and 2 Squadrons, were formed at the airfield with a motley collection of aeroplanes. From 1948 Farnborough also earned fame as the venue for the British aviation industry to showcase its wares in annual airshows; going biennial – and increasingly international in content – from 1964. Farnborough remains a major research and development site, with QinetiQ – as the inheritors of the RAE's mantle – in the Cody Technology Park campus and BAE Systems at the Farnborough Aerospace Centre, among others. From 1994 trials flying from the airfield stopped and today it is a major centre for corporate jet operations.

National landmarks

All of this is a vast heritage and an almost impossible story to tell, but from November 1993 that challenge was taken up by FAST. With the contraction of the Defence Research Agency – as RAE had become in April 1991 – at Farnborough there was great concern that the historic Main Factory Site (MFS), a direct link to the days of the Balloon Factory, would be at risk. The misgivings were two-fold: none of the buildings had listed protection, and, for the future untold quantities of artefacts and archives charting eight decades of achievement. For the latter there was already a firm basis, RAE had run a museum since at least the 1950s and, ironically, it was last located within Building G1 – which became FAST's Trenchard House.

Work to collate potential exhibits, from photographs to wind tunnel models, was made all the easier from 30th April 1996 when FAST moved into building R52, within the wind tunnel complex. With great respect to this huge effort and the work to chronicle, restore and display this enormous cache is still carrying on, it was relatively straightforward. The major effort, led by FAST but with considerable input from local government and other agencies, lay with campaigning to secure the future of nationally important buildings within the MFS. In December 1996 endless meetings, surveys, feasibility studies yielded fruit when six structures were given Grade II listing and in 2002 the 24ft Wind Tunnel and the Transonic Wind Tunnel were enhanced to Grade I. Without all of this work it is quite possible that the landscape at Farnborough would have been robbed of these incredible significant waypoints in aeronautical engineering. Adding pace to all of this activity, the Ministry of Defence invited tenders for the MFS land and in 2000 the area was acquired by a developer.

The developer was determined to mark the heritage of the site and FAST was offered the Old Balloon School, vacating R52 and moving in during the autumn of 2002. The external fabric of each of the listed buildings on the MFS was restored by the developer at a cost running into many millions of pounds. Another FAST initiative was also taken up, in dramatic and pleasing style; the 1910 airship hangar was conserved, relocated and re-erected in skeletal form as a monument to the early days of flying at Farnborough. Within the Farnborough Business Park, these buildings form what is known as the Royal Aircraft Establishment Heritage Quarter and have found other uses – see later. Across at Trenchard House, FAST opened its doors to the public on 28th June 2003. As is described below, the team threw themselves into another project to honour Farnborough's most famous pioneer on the centenary of him taking to the air.

The displays inside FAST are intriguing; in the early days of developing a supersonic transport, RAE scientists evaluated the 'M-wing' layout before opting for the Concorde's ogival delta. *Ken Ellis*

Unveiling the replica British Army Aircraft No.1 at the Farnborough Air Sciences Trust, 16th October 2008. *Ken Ellis*

Cody's legacy

American-born Samuel Franklin Cody came to Britain while touring with his 'Wild West' show; though he is not to be confused with William Frederick 'Buffalo Bill' Cody of greater fame in that form of entertainment. Samuel developed skills in building and flying large kites, initially as another 'spectacular' for his pageants. Eventually, the kites could lift a man aloft and the British Army became interested as a cheaper and more practical means of observation than gas balloons. Cody was appointed Chief Kiting Instructor in April 1906 at the Balloon Factory, the precursor of the Royal Aircraft Factory. He was quickly involved in the creation of the airship *Nulli Secundus* (Second to None) of 1907. (A replica of this flying machine is on show at the RAF Museum Hendon.)

Lessons garnered from the airship gave him a command of engines and propellers and in 1907 Cody decided to 'power up' one of his man-lifting kites with a 15hp French-made Buchet engine. The next step was a much larger machine but essentially adopting the layout of the powered kite. Cody named his creation British Army Aircraft 1A. On 16th October 1908 all was ready and he made several 'hops' in straight runs. Then, from a starting point near the Swan Inn on the eastern edge of Farnborough Common he made the first powered, controlled and sustained flight in the UK. The statistics were: distance 1,390ft, height of around 30ft, flight time 27 seconds, average speed around 27mph.

Cody had parted company with the Balloon Factory by April 1909 but stayed on at Farnborough, developing his flying machines in a ramshackle hangar on Laffan's Plain. That October he became a British citizen. On 27th August 1912 his Military Trials Biplane was declared the winner of a competition for an aircraft for the newly-formed RFC. This machine, with the serial number 301 was issued to 4 Squadron, which had formed at Farnborough on 16th September. It was followed by a second, 304; and this is preserved at the Science Museum in London. Cody and a passenger were killed while testing a new machine on 7th August 1913; he was mourned as a national hero.

In January 2007 the team at FAST embarked on a major project, the construction of a replica of British Army Aircraft 1A to be unveiled on the centenary of its maiden flight. This was daunting enough, in terms of time scale and the challenges of recreating a flying machine long since extinct. Unlike most of the aircraft exhibits at FAST, the finished product could not be displayed externally, and with a span of 53ft the Cody was going to need a substantial building. As the replica came together, so did plans for the Cody Pavilion which would act as a shrine to the great pioneer and give FAST a much-needed area in which to carry out special events. All of this came together spot on time on 16th October 2008. Captain Eric 'Winkle' Brown CBE DSC AFC RN, the doyen of RAE test pilots, officiated at another ceremony at FAST on 7th August 2013 by unveiling a statue of Cody on the centenary of his death.

Time marches on and nothing remains the same. Farnborough is used to change, the arrival of balloons, kites and then aircraft must have been a huge upheaval to the areas denizens in 1907. With the closure of the RAE's old site it looked as though an entire era was going to erased. The incredible aviation heritage that is Farnborough has been secured in fine and appropriate style.

Beagle 206X G-ARRM
1961 | Light transport | Two 260hp Continental IO-470D pistons

The Beagle 206 was the reason for the Beagle company being created and, along with a large dose of British bumbling, was a main reason for the collapse of the UK's last stab at large scale light aircraft manufacture. Thanks to the intervention of no less than three museums – including FAST – the prototype 206 has survived. *Romeo-Mike* has only a tenuous link with Farnborough, appearing at the 1961 and 1962 Society of British Aircraft Constructors (SBAC) airshows, and is a good example of the 'Where do you put it?' conundrum. As will be seen, until 2011 this 'orphan' has had a long list of 'foster homes'.

Derived from the Type 220 design study by Bristol – see under Aerospace Bristol, Chapter 10 – the prototype Beagle 206X was first flown at Shoreham by John Nicholson on 15th August 1961. It was always envisaged as interim; the second example (the 206Y G-ARXM) which appeared a year later was substantially redesigned. During *Romeo-Mike's* time at the September 1961 SBAC display, HRH Prince Phillip was invited to take the controls during one of many 'flag waving' demonstration flights. G-ARRM was back at Farnborough in September 1962 but its development role was rapidly coming to an end as it was far from the intended production standard. It was retired at Shoreham by the end of 1964 and stored.

With the demise of Beagle in early 1970 a 'rescue' was staged and on 11th August 1970 the Beagle 206X was moved to Duxford where the Imperial War Museum (IWM) was in the earliest phases of occupying the site, initially as a large artefact store. Taking on *Romeo-Mike* was a brave move, as it lacked anything to do with 'Imperial' or 'War'! Ambitious plans to re-use the former Pullman railway carriage works in Brighton as a transport museum brought G-ARRM to the town's Preston Park area on 29th April 1978. That scheme came to nought and the Beagle moved the short distance west to its birthplace at Shoreham, where it was hoped that some form of exhibition could be created. By 1990 staff at the IWM had run out of plausible-sounding reasons why *Romeo-Mike* fitted the collecting policy.

Beagle made a big statement at Farnborough in September 1962 with the 206Z G-ARRM, E.3 (or 'Auster AOP.11') G-ASCC and the 218 G-ASCK. *KEC*

Thankfully the Surrey-based Brooklands Museum, with 'manufacturing' firmly part of its remit, took over custodianship of the Beagle, and this remains so today. G-ARRM took its fourth road journey, arriving at Brooklands on 17th November. With the establishment of the Bristol Aero Collection (BAC) – predecessors of Aerospace Bristol – an appropriate and welcoming 'home' was found. *Romeo-Mike* was on the road again, travelling to Banwell, Somerset, in January 1994 and then to Kemble in the summer of 1996. In May 1996 BAC was presented with the cockpit of Beagle 206 Series 1 G-ATDD by the Science Museum. This was a more compact exhibit for what was a peripheral element of the Bristol story. Meanwhile there were schemes for G-ARRM again at Shoreham and the twin made its second road-borne arrival on 23rd May 2005. The plan was to restore the prototype ready for celebrations of the fiftieth anniversary of its first flight in August 2011. After this came road trip No.8, to Farnborough on 10th December 2011.

STOP PRESS: Road journey No.9 took place on 3rd August 2017 when *Romeo-Mike* returned to Brooklands – Chapter 27 – for the new 'Aircraft Factory' exhibition.

English Electric Lightning T.5 XS420
1965 | Advanced trainer | Two 13,200lb st Rolls-Royce Avon 301 turbojets

Several aircraft within the FAST collection are on loan and Richard Hall's Lightning is one of those. While it was not directly associated with Farnborough, XS420 is a particularly fine two-seat T.5 and is a great example of many aircraft in British museums that owe their existence to the commitment of individuals. Don Knight took XS420 for its first flight, from Samlesbury, on 23rd January 1965 and it was issued to 226 Operational Conversion Unit (OCU) at Coltishall on 29th April. Thanks to XS420's owner Richard Hall, there follows an account of how, on 31st January 1973 at Coltishall XS420 nearly joined the 76 Lightnings, from the RAF fleet of 280, that were written off.

That day the T.5 was crewed by Captain Gary Catren of the USAF and Flt Lt George Smith. There was nothing out of the ordinary with the take-off run until 140 knots was reached. There was an indication that No.1 reheat had failed. Notwithstanding this, Catren elected to continue by selecting 100 per cent cold power on No.1 while at the same time pulling back on the stick to raise the nose wheel. Upon reaching 155 knots the nose still refused to lift and the pilot had the impression that the aircraft was not accelerating in the normal way. With just 1,500 yards of runway left Catren decided to abort. What happened next is open to debate but Smith thought he heard Catren say the word 'Chute', or it could have been an expletive! The brake chute was pulled slightly before the reheat was cancelled which set the chute on fire, considerably adding to XS420's predicament. Despite braking, the aircraft hit the runway barrier at around 100 knots and did not come to a stop for a considerable distance afterwards. It ended up with the nose wheel buried in the ground although both crew walked away unhurt. Repairs complete, XS420 was back on charge with 226 OCU on 22nd August 1973.

The Lightning was transferred to Binbrook in September 1974 and its natural metal colour scheme was replaced by camouflage. On 18th September 1976 XS420 was issued to the Lightning Training Flight (LTF) at Coningsby. During its time with LTF it took up the codes 'V', 'Y' and finally 'DV'. Normally based at Binbrook, runway work necessitated LTF to detach to Coningsby until the spring of 1978. Last recorded flight for XS420 was 26th May 1983 by which time it had a total of 2,296 hours, 55 minutes on the clock. It was stored until 12th October 1987 when it was towed out and placed on Binbrook's decoy line. Offered for sale by tender on 17th February 1988 XS420 was sold to a company called Tadorna Holdings and taken by road to Narborough, Norfolk, on 25th July. Murray Flint, a leading light in the Fenland and West Norfolk Aircraft Preservation Society (see Chapter 20) acquired XS420 and it was moved to West Walton Highway, Norfolk, on 8th May 1994. Murray moved the T.5 to his home at Walpole St Andrew, Norfolk, on 11th July 1998 for restoration. Repainted in 226 OCU colours it was displayed in the static park at the International Air Tattoo, Fairford, in July 2003. After the show it was delivered to FAST, arriving on 3rd September. Ownership was transferred to Neil Airey and Heather Graham of Lakes Lightnings in August 2006. It was purchased by Richard Hall and Mike Potten in June 2012; Mike selling out his share in June 2013. As Richard declares: "the story continues..."

Government Aircraft Factory Jindivik 104AL ZJ496
1983 | Unmanned target drone | One 2,500lb st Armstrong Siddeley Viper 201 turbojet

Rules are meant to be broken, in the introduction it was boldly announced that "unmanned devices" would not be profiled... well, here's the exception. Powered by a 2,500lb static thrust turbojet, with a length of 26ft 8in, a span of 20ft 9in, a maximum take-off weight of 3,650lb and a top speed of 564mph the Australian designed and built Jindivik target drone is an appreciable aircraft. A total of 267 units – over half the complete production run – was acquired for operation by the Royal Aircraft Establishment (RAE) all based at Llanbedr in Wales. The first shipment arrived in Britain in 1957 and the Jindivik entered service in 1960. In a world that is increasingly dominated by unmanned aerial vehicles, the Jindivik provided a wealth of experience for British remotely controlled aircraft.

Enough justification... The Jindivik – Aboriginal for 'hunted one' – was developed by the Government Aircraft Factory (GAF) at Fisherman's Bend, Melbourne, Australia, in the late 1940s. To prove the aerodynamics the prototypes, called Pikas, were piloted; the first one getting airborne on 31st October 1950. Powered by an Armstrong Siddeley Adder, the prototype Jindivik had its maiden flight on 28th August 1952. After a dozen Adder-powered examples, all production examples had Viper turbojets. Jindiviks took off from a wheeled trolley and landed using a centrally mounted skid.

The FAST Jindivik was part of the last batch built by Aerospace Technologies of Australia, as GAF was renamed in July 1987. Allocated the Royal Australian Air Force serial A92-901 – which it still carries on its fin – it was given the Ministry of Defence serial ZJ496 when it arrived at Llanbedr in the spring of 1998. This machine had 18 flights, the last of which is believed to have taken place in September 2001. A fascinating and important part of Britain's aviation heritage, ZJ496 joined FAST on 10th May 2005.

Hawker Hunter T.7 WV383
1955 | Advanced trainer | One 7,700lb st Rolls-Royce Avon 122 turbojet

FAST boasts two Hunter T.7s, but it is the famous one named *Hecate – Lady of the Night* that takes 'star' billing. It had a life as a frontline single-seat fighter and over a quarter of a century of cutting edge research flying – the bulk of that 'across the way' at Farnborough airfield. Hugh Merewether took Hunter F.4 WV383 for its maiden flight, from Dunsfold, on 12th July 1955. It was accepted for service on 23rd August and joined the RAF Flying College at Manby on 19th December. A belly landing on 27th January 1956 put paid to its first RAF career. It was returned to Dunsfold in 1958 and converted to T.7 status by fitting a new two-seat cockpit and spine fairing; this work was completed on 3rd July 1959. Gütersloh in West Germany was WV383's next assignment, from 8th January 1960 when it joined the Station Flight, acting as a reserve for the based units. This work continued at nearby Jever from 24th April 1961. WV383's last RAF posting was to Kai Tak, Hong Kong, with 28 Squadron from 1964 until the unit retired its Hunters in December 1966. Ferried back to the UK, WV383 settled in to 5 Maintenance Unit (MU) at Kemble for storage.

Dusted down, WV383 began many years of service with the Royal Aircraft Establishment (RAE) at Farnborough from 21st July 1971. Destined for the Flight Systems Department, WV383 was flown to Cranfield where the Institute of Technology installed two head-up displays (HUDs) and equipment to allow the lead pilot to monitor television imagery of what lay ahead. At this stage WV383 was providing a 'head *down*' view to the left-hand seater; his colleague acting as safety pilot with 'eyes out'. Refit completed, WV383 was back at Farnborough on 13th September 1973 but it was over a year before the first sorties were flown 'in anger'. Low-light television (LLTV) allowed for sorties in poor visibility and, in time, at night. Jaguar B.08 XW566 – see below – was also used for this task. By January 1976 the Hunter was flying as low as 250ft at night and the trials pilot was viewing imagery via the HUD. A return to 5 MU was made on 31st August 1976 and WV383 returned to the Flight Systems Department in the RAE's 'raspberry ripple' colour scheme two months later. By 1980 night vision goggles (NVG) were in use and the LLTV had been exchanged for a forward-looking infra-red (FLIR) system. It was at this stage that WV383 gained the legend *Hecate – Lady of the Night* on the nose, after the torch-carrying Greek goddess.

By 1987 WV383 was readied for a new experimental role, evaluating the Ferranti pod-based Penetrate system. *Flight* magazine for July 1988 described the pod's role: "Designed to enhance an aircraft's ability to perform covert high-speed low-level penetration at night and in adverse weather, Penetrate uses a radio altimeter for accurate terrain-referenced navigation. The output is displayed in the form of a digital map and is also coupled to the pilot's HUD. The pilot can select progressive HUD enhancements, depending on the visibility. These range from obstruction cues, through ridgeline overlays, to full perspective displays of the terrain. For flight trials, Penetrate has been built into a pod housing a video camera and recorder to play back the flight and check the accuracy of [the] terrain-referenced navigation. The system uses a 400-megabyte optical disc to store the central digital database, which contains a map." On 1st April 1991 RAE was renamed the Defence Research Agency and test flying at Farnborough was being wound down and moved to Boscombe Down. *Hecate* flew to its new base on 24th March 1994 but by 1998 had been retired and placed in store. This incredibly adaptable aircraft was moved to FAST by road on 13th April 2000.

A Harrier GR.5 of 1 Squadron in close company with a GAF Jindivik over Cardigan Bay in 1989. *British Aerospace*

SEPECAT Jaguar B.08 XW566
1971 | Advanced trainer | Two 7,305lb st Rolls-Royce/Turboméca Adour 102 turbofans

Entering service with the RAF in September 1973 the Anglo-French Jaguar strike fighter and advanced trainer served for 34 years, including combat during the Gulf War of 1991. It was also a major export success and was licence produced in India. The Jaguar was a collaborative programme between Breguet in France and the British Aircraft Corporation (BAC); the first prototype flying in France on 8th September 1968. The organisation established to oversee the venture basked in the name Société Européenne de Production de l'Avion d'Ecole de Combat et d'Appui Tactique; unsurprisingly, most people adopted the abbreviation SEPECAT when referring to it! Jaguars are widely preserved in the UK: FAST's example was the first British-built two-seater and served at Farnborough, working with the collection's Hawker Hunter T.7 WV383 on low-light operations. Jaguar B.08 XW566 was the last of eight prototypes and the first British two-seater. The flight programme was three years old by the time it was rolled out at Warton on 1st June 1971 and the airframe used 80 per cent production-standard assemblies. Its maiden flight, of 46 minutes including some supersonic time, was in the hands of Paul Millett on 30th August. After initial trials it was briefly dispatched to the Aeroplane and Armament Experimental Establishment at Boscombe Down where it was put through rough field operation with a weapon load of four 1,000-pounders – two in tandem on the centre-line station, one on each inner pylon – and drop tanks on the outers. XW566 returned to Warton for a decade of development flying, including low-light television (LLTV) optics and helmet-mounted data display.

After 718 flights with BAC – British Aerospace from 1977 – XW566 was transferred to the Royal Aircraft Establishment (RAE) at Farnborough on 3rd February 1982 to continue work on LLTV with a centre-line mounted pod. It was ferried to 5 Maintenance Unit at Kemble in April, returning in June resplendent in the RAE's 'raspberry ripple' colour scheme. With RAE XW566 worked hard, as well as LLTV trials, it was used to evaluate Smiths Industries head-up displays and worked on a Southampton University-led experiment for the Institute of Sound and Vibration Research. Its last sortie was on 17th June 1985 but RAE still was not through with XW566. The Avionics and Sensors Department used it for electro-magnetic compatibility research, including simulated lightning strikes. The Jaguar was transferred to FAST on 9th June 2004.

Farnborough Air Sciences Trust aircraft

Type	Identity	Built	Origin	Acquired	Notes
Airbus Defence and Space Zephyr 6	–	2008	Britain	Mar 2017	see notes
Beagle 206 Srs 1X	G-ARRM	1961	Britain	10 Dec 2011	see profile
Cody British Army 1A	–	2007	Britain	16 Oct 2008	replica
English Electric Canberra B(I).6	WT309	1955	Britain	Feb 1998	cockpit
English Electric Lightning T.5*	XS420	1965	Britain	3 Sep 2003	see profile
Folland Gnat T.1*	XP516	1963	Britain	8 Jun 2004	–
GAF Jindivik 104A	ZJ496	1983	Australia	10 May 2005	target drone, see profile
Hawker Hunter T.7*	WV383	1955	Britain	13 Apr 2000	see profile
Hawker Hunter T.7	XL563	1957	Britain	Apr 2014	–
Hawker Siddeley Trident 3B-101	G-AWZI	1971	Britain	15 Dec 2004	cockpit, on loan
Hawker Siddeley Harrier T.4	XW934	1973	Britain	28 Aug 2007	–
Northrop Chukar D.2	ZG631	1996	USA	Oct 2008	target drone
Royal Aircraft Establishment X-RAE.1	–	1981	Britain	2001	drone
SEPECAT Jaguar B.08	XW566	1971	GB/France	8 Jun 2004	see profile
Short MATS-B	–	1982	Britain	2005	target drone
Sud SA.330E Puma	XW241	1968	France	29 Aug 2007	–
Sud Gazelle HT.2	XW863	1973	France	11 Jun 2013	–
Westland Scout AH.1	XP848	1962	Britain	3 Sep 2015	–
Westland Scout AH.1	XT633	1966	Britain	3 Sep 2015	–
Westland Wasp HAS.1	XV631	1969	Britain	11 Feb 2010	cockpit
Westland Lynx HAS.2	XZ166	1975	Britain	Oct 2009	cockpit

Notes: * – illustrated in the colour section. The Zephyr is a prototype solar-powered high-altitude 'pseudo-satellite' – an unmanned air vehicle capable of staying aloft for days. It was designed and built at Farnborough.

SEPECAT Jaguar T.2 XW566 on show at FAST. In the background is the wind tunnel complex. *Ken Ellis*

When in Farnborough

As explained under the section of the Farnborough Air Sciences Trust, above, development of the former Main Factory Site led to the establishment of the **Royal Aircraft Establishment Heritage Quarter** within the Farnborough Business Park. Here can be found the relocated and skeletal 1910 balloon hangar and the famous wind tunnel structures. The former Weapons Testing Building, Q134, is now called The Hub and includes a display entitled 'The Secret Factory' and the Aviators Café. Also within The Hub is the National Aerospace Library, which is open to the general public. **www.historicfarnborough.co.uk** Dramatically displayed on the roundabout to the north of the airfield, close to the Southwood Golf Course, is the **Whittle Memorial**, a full-scale model of the Gloster E28/39 jet as a tribute to Sir Frank Whittle. For more details take a look at Jet Age Museum, Gloucestershire.

Maritime Romance
Solent Sky

Southampton
www.solentskymuseum.org

Draw a circle based on the Solent Sky building in Southampton with a radius of, say, 25 miles. Within can be found such famous locations as: Beaulieu, Calshot, Chattis Hill, Eastleigh, Gosport, Hamble, Lee-on-Solent, Portsmouth and Woolston. Across the waters of the Solent and well within our imaginary circle, is the Isle of Wight with an aviation heritage all of its own. The Solent and Southampton Water supply even more character with Hythe and Southampton serving as flying-boat terminals and the coastline between the great maritime city and the Isle of Wight provided the course for the famous Schneider Trophy in its final years.

The curators of some museums find the collecting policy of their institution restricting, or difficult to achieve; not so the team at Solent Sky, their remit is full of potential and they tell the story of an incredible region – past and present – remarkably well. Not surprisingly, maritime aviation and the allure of the Spitfire feature highly in the extensive exhibitions. Dominating the main display hall is the Short Sandringham commercial flying-boat which graphically illustrates an era that ran from Supermarine pioneering flying-boat services from Woolston in 1919 to the demise of Aquila Airways and its Short Sunderlands and Solents in 1958. During early 2017, Solent Sky announced that it had been granted £64,800 from the Heritage Lottery Fund to create an exhibition to further capitalise on the lavish era entitled 'Romance of the Flying-Boat'. With the Sandringham as the centrepiece, visitors will also be able to sample the opulence of first-class cruising with Imperial Airways through a recreation of the interior of a typical 1930s flying-boat. As part of a vivid Supermarine tribute, Solent Sky reminds visitors that there was more to the company than the Spitfire, the Schneider Trophy S.6A contrasts with a Scimitar naval strike fighter – the last to carry the hallowed name.

Sandringham 4 VH-BRC dominates the ground floor at Solent Sky. Surrounding it, clockwise from bottom left: Sea Vixen FAW.2 XJ571, 'Flying Flea' 'G-ADZW', BN-1 G-ALZE, Tiger Moth BB807 and the Airwave hang-glider prototype. *Terry Dann*

The museum wasn't always called Solent Sky, nor was it in its current location. The origins go back to the work of 424 Squadron Air Training Corps – which today has its headquarters adjacent to the museum – and most importantly Sqn Ldr Alan Jones – the present director of Solent Sky. (The squadron was custodian of the Fairey Jet Gyrodyne that is on show at the Museum of Berkshire Aviation, Chapter 3.) Alan was determined that Southampton should honour Reginald Joseph Mitchell, the designer of the Spitfire, and the work of Supermarine. His determination was vindicated in 1976 – the 40th anniversary of the first flight of the prototype Spitfire – with the opening of the Mitchell Memorial Hall in a former dance hall near the Civic Centre. The two founder airframes, the S.6A and Spitfire F.24 were on loan from the RAF Museum and remain on show. By 1979 the name had changed to the R J Mitchell Spitfire Museum and visitor figures proved that a larger exhibition space was called for.

Plans for what is the present Solent Sky building were formulated in the early 1980s. Collaboration with the Science Museum provided the national museum with the answer of where to put a *very* large object in its care, and the new museum with an impressive and relevant centrepiece. The Sandringham required careful planning as it was essential to position it within the structure long before final fitting out: the other exhibits and installations were placed *around* it. With its coverage dramatically expanded to tell the story of aviation in all its forms across the region, the museum's name needed changing. The new identity was revealed in May 1984 when the Southampton Hall of Aviation was opened to the public. On 12th May 2004 former Fairey chief test pilot Lt Cdr Peter Twiss and motor racing legend Sir Jack Brabham presided over the rebranding to Solent Sky.

At first glance some of the exhibits do not have a Solent connection. The statue of Roy Chadwick, the famed Avro designer, and the replica Avro 504J are reminders that his early days in charge of the Avro design office, were at Hamble, not in Manchester. de Havilland does not spring to mind as having a link with the region. The company bought out Portsmouth-based Airspeed in 1940 and in the following year production of Oxfords began at the Christchurch factory, 25 miles to the west along the Dorset coast. Post-war Sea Venoms, Vampire trainers and Sea Vixens, among others, were built there. The hang-glider on show was the prototype of a long line of such conveyances, produced by Airwave Gliders of Shalfleet on the Isle of Wight. The name 'Wight' on the incredible quadruplane replica – a flying 'Venetian blind' – provides a clue to its relevance. Originating in 1916, the single-seat fighter prototype was produced by the aviation division of well-known Cowes-based shipwrights, J Samuel Wight and Company, trading as Wight Aircraft. To finish on another Southampton association, in the 1930s a much revered model manufacturer had its origins in the town. The International Model Aircraft Company produced complete, elastic band-powered, flying models and used the jingle – 'Flies Right Off the Ground' – FROG. Not long after this Frog was adopted as a trading name and 1:72 scale plastic kits followed, one of the early ones appropriately being a Short 'Empire' flying-boat. Such is the magic of an incredible region!

de Havilland Sea Vixen FAW.2 XJ571 negotiating a roundabout (backwards!) near Guildford on its way to exhibition at the Brooklands Museum, 6th December 1994. It travelled in similar style to Southampton on 5th February 2003. *British Aerospace*

The Wight Quadruplane in its original form at Somerton on the Isle of Wight, September 1916. *KEC*

Britten-Norman BN-1 G-ALZE in its original form at Bembridge in 1951. *Peter Green Collection*

Britten-Norman BN-1F G-ALZE
1951 | Light aircraft | One 55hp Lycoming O-145-A piston

In 1949 two former inmates of the de Havilland Technical School at Hatfield began construction of a single-seat parasol monoplane of their own design, at Bembridge on the Isle of Wight. They were John Britten and Desmond Norman, giving their initials to the craft's designation, BN-1. The two entrepreneurs were determined to get into aircraft manufacture and to this end they had purchased Bembridge aerodrome and, on its southern boundary, the flying club and its hangar, and the famous Propeller Inn. Desmond made its first 'hops' on 4th August 1950 but it was badly damaged when its 40hp JAP J-99 failed on take-off during a later flight. It was substantially redesigned and rebuilt as the BN-1F, with a Lycoming 'flat-four'. At this point, references to the name 'Finibee' crop up apparently based on how the designation read backwards; there is no evidence that this was an official label. *Zulu-Echo* was tested in the new guise at Bembridge on 26th May 1951. This *may* have been with Desmond at the controls, or with Fairey production test pilot Geoffrey Alington flying it. Either way, Geoffrey piloted it two days later on what is described as its 'official' test flight. The BN-1F was withdrawn from use in April 1953 and stored in a boathouse in Bembridge Harbour.

After the BN-1 John Britten and Desmond Norman's early ventures included the revolutionary Micronair atomiser for aerial crop-spraying and they also dabbled in hovercraft development. The Lycoming from the BN-1F was used to power a rudimentary wind tunnel set up by John Britten in the garden of his Bembridge home. Beyond that their talents combined to produce the world-beating BN-2 Islander, from 1965. (Take a look at the section on Jet Age Museum in Chapter 10 and Meteor F.8 WH364 for Desmond's 'weekend warrior' experience with 601 Squadron Royal Auxiliary Air Force.) The pioneering Britten-Norman design was salvaged from the Bembridge boathouse in the late 1970s and G-ALZE moved to the RAF Museum Cosford by 1979 where it was restored and placed on display. It left Cosford in early 1985 for Southampton and has been on display ever since. Needless to say, an Islander has long very high on Solent Sky's 'wants' list – in April 2017 the museum got more than it bargained for...

Britten-Norman BN-2 Mk.III-2 Trislander G-RLON
1975 | Short range airliner | Three 260hp Lycoming O-540-E4C5 pistons

For a short while, Solent Sky was custodian of the only museum Trislander in Britain. Not content with generously passing on one of its long-serving fleet for posterity, Aurigny Air Services also donated its last-ever example, G-BEVT, to the Duxford Aviation Society on 21st June 2017. Surrounded by warplanes at Duxford, the society runs the active one of Britain's *two* 'national' airliner collections – the other being the Science Museum's reclusive gathering at Wroughton. Fourteen years after John Britten and Desmond Norman flew the diminutive BN-1 – see above – they were at the controls of what became a world-beater, the prototype BN-2 Islander, G-ATCT, on 13th June 1965. The company has had several changes of name and ownership during its life: today its factory site is at Bembridge, Isle of Wight, with flying conducted from Lee-on-Solent. Still in limited production, the twin-engined BN-2 has achieved in excess of 1,250 units manufactured. The rugged type is still in great demand and residual values remain high in the secondary market which explains why only one example of the twin is in a British museum; at the National Museum of Flight Scotland.

Radical thinking resulted in transformation of the Islander into one of the most distinctive airliners ever: the eighteen-seat, three-engined Trislander. The fuselage was stretched and the extra engine was mounted up on the fin. The designers, John Britten and Desmond Norman, piloted the prototype, G-ATWU, on 11th September 1970. This was a conversion of the second prototype twin-engined BN-2 and it was followed by 72 production examples from 1971 to 1984. A small number remain in service. The Solent Sky example was built at Gosselies, north of Charleroi, Belgium, by Fairey Britten-Norman and first flew, as G-BCXW, on 2nd June 1975. It arrived at Bembridge two days later for fitting out, ready for its customer, Air Pacific of Suva, Fiji. It was delivered on 27th June 1975, registered as DQ-FCF. It next served from George Town, Cayman Islands, with Cayman Airways as VR-CAA *Cayman Unity*, from 21st January 1980. The Trislander returned to Britain on 14th July 1987 taking up the appropriate registration G-OCTA with Octavia Air at Staverton.

Guernsey-based Aurigny Air Services started operating the tri-motors in June 1971. Solent Sky's example began its association with the airline on 7th June 1991, initially with the name *Snowy*. G-OCTA was re-registered as G-ITEX on 21st June 2000 before becoming G-RLON – denoting its colour scheme promoting Royal London Insurance – on 26th April 2002. With the Trislanders being replaced by Dornier 228 twin turboprops, *Oscar-November* was retired in February 2017. G-RLON was flown to Lee-on-Solent on 5th April 2017 to await space being prepared for it at Southampton. That final touchdown was its 105,130th landing and the Trislander completed 32,604 flying hours. On accepting *Oscar-November* Solent Sky's Sqn Ldr Alan Jones summed up its importance to the museum: "The Britten-Norman story is very much a local one. The aircraft... served as part of a fleet of Trislanders that for forty years plied their route from Southampton to Alderney, a familiar sight and with its distinctive engine sound became they almost a part of life in the city. For over thirty years the story of Britten-Norman has been told by Solent Sky."

Folland Gnat F.1 XK740
1957 | Lightweight fighter | One 4,700lb st Bristol Siddeley Orpheus 701 turbojet

William Edward Willoughby Petter had designed the Lysander and Whirlwind, among others, for Westland and the exceptional Canberra for English Electric. His last creation was the Gnat lightweight fighter, a compact single-seater intended to reverse the increasing complication of fighters and that could be licence built by nascent aircraft industries. The RAF had no requirement for such a machine, but the Ministry of Supply (MoS) backed the project, ordering six Gnat F.1s for development purposes. The 'suits' hoped that the little fighter would attract export orders and they were right; Finland, India and Yugoslavia ordered examples from the production line at Hamble – just down Southampton Water from Solent Sky. India went on to built 193 as the Ajeet, proving Petter's point when it was nicknamed the 'Sabre Slayer' during the Indo-Pakistan wars of 1965 and 1971. The Gnat was developed in the late 1950s into a two-seat advanced trainer, the T.1, serving the RAF from 1959 to 1979.

Sqn Ldr 'Teddy' Tennant carried out XK740's first flight from Chilbolton – 20 miles northwest of Solent Sky – on 6th March 1957. It was the third of the half-dozen F.1s ordered by MoS. Tennant took it up the following day for 36 minutes and handed it over to Indian Air Force pilots to try it out. It was accepted by the MoS on the 26th and in the following September

Folland Gnat F.1 XK740 was used for most of its flying life for Bristol Siddeley Orpheus trials. *Bristol Siddeley*

was displayed at the Farnborough airshow. It was transferred to Bristol Siddeley at Filton for development work with the Orpheus turbojet from 13th December 1958. By March 1960 it was fitted with an Orpheus 100 to help with development of the trainer version. Released from the MoS trials fleet on 13th February 1961 XK740 joined the travelling recruiting airframes of 71 Maintenance Unit at Bicester and was allocated the instructional airframe number 8396M. By the summer of 1967 it was kept at Church Fenton and used on the 'northern' circuit of shows and special events and had gained the colours of the 'Red Arrows' aerobatic demonstration team. Struck off charge on 17th January 1974, it was transferred to the RAF Museum at Cosford. Earmarked for the Hall of Aviation, XK740 was returned to its birthplace, Hamble, in early 1987 where it was refurbished at what was then a British Aerospace plant. On 6th March 1987, the thirtieth anniversary of its first flight, XK740 was handed over to the Southampton Hall of Aviation, on loan from the RAF Museum.

Saunders-Roe SR.A/1 TG263
1956 | Flying-boat fighter| Two 3,850lb st Metropolitan-Vickers Beryl F2/4 turbojets

The war against Japan in the Far East and the Pacific had thrown up a need for fighters that could operate without the need for scarce runways. In early 1944 the Saunders-Roe (Saro) design team, working at the company-run flying-boat modification and maintenance base at Beaumaris on Anglesey, came up with a revolutionary answer: a single-seat twin-jet flying-boat fighter. Specification E6/44 was written around this idea and three SR.A/1 prototypes were ordered. All were built at Saro's East Cowes factory on the Isle of Wight – 12 miles to the south of Solent Sky. Chief test pilot Geoffrey Tyson took the first one, TG263, off from the mouth of the Medina River off Cowes on 16th July 1947. During development flying he evolved a quick reaction take-off technique, by retracting the wing floats as soon as the hull was up on the step, the drag was lowered considerably and the SR.A/1 could conduct the flying-boat equivalent of a scramble. Flown by Tyson, TG263 caused a stir at the Farnborough airshow that September. By this time any practical use for the SR.A/1 had vaporised but trials continued; it was transferred to the Marine Aircraft Experimental Establishment at Felixstowe on 11th June 1948. The other two SR.A/1s were written off, one fatally, in 1949 and on the last day of the year the programme was terminated.

Ferried back to Saro, TG263 alighted on the Medina on 22nd May 1950. It was given the 'B Condition' ('trade plate') identification for company trials, but it is thought not to have ventured out much. It gained a lot of publicity during the summer of 1951 when it landed on the Thames and was moored close to the Houses of Parliament as part of the attractions for the Festival of Britain. This was its last excursion; it was grounded and roaded to the College of Aeronautics at Cranfield where it became part of the famous 'Library of Flight' of significant and esoteric airframes. One of the co-axial Beryl turbojets from TG263 was passed on to Donald Campbell for use in his jet-powered hydroplane, the Bluebird K7, which was launched in 1955. Campbell went on to achieve seven records between 1955 and 1964 in this sleek vessel. Campbell was killed in the K7, fitted with a Bristol Siddeley Orpheus, on Coniston Water on 4th January 1967. The jet flying-boat was acquired for Peter Thomas's Skyfame Museum and it was moved there on 16th October 1966. When Skyfame closed in 1978, TG263 was part of the mass rescue arranged by the Imperial War Museum (IWM) and it was taken to Duxford where it was put through a restoration programme. In 1993, TG263 moved to Southampton where it remains, on loan from the IWM, as a bizarre local product.

Saunders-Roe SR.A/1 TG263 moored on the River Medina in front of the Columbine Hangar at East Cowes, July 1947. *KEC*

Short Sandringham 4 VH-BRC
1943 | Flying-boat airliner | Four 1,200hp Pratt & Whitney R-1830 Twin Wasp radials

Six Short four-engined flying-boats survive, three in the UK, one each in France, New Zealand and the USA. The first Sandringham conversion of a Sunderland appeared in November 1945 with much cleaner aerodynamics and a maximum capacity of 45 passengers on two decks. The Solent Sky example was built by Shorts at Rochester on the River Medway in Kent as Mk.III JM715 for the RAF. It was taken on charge at the flying-boat base at Wig Bay, north of Stranraer, on 3rd July 1943. It was not issued for operational service and was put into store, care of the resident 57 Maintenance Unit (MU). In 1945 JM715 was upgraded to GR.V status by substituting its Bristol Pegasus radials for Pratt & Whitney Twin Wasps. This was probably done by Scottish Aviation at Greenock on the Clyde between April and July 1945. On 30th July 1945 it was back in the care of 57 MU.

Shorts at Sydenham, Belfast, acquired JM715 on 30th April 1947. It was converted to a Sandringham 4 for Tasman Empire Airways Ltd (TEAL) of Auckland, New Zealand, as ZK-AMH *Auckland*. It set off on delivery from Poole Harbour on 15th October 1947 and served TEAL as a stop-gap until the arrival of its more suitable Short Solents in 1949. It was sold to Barrier Reef Airlines of Brisbane, Australia, becoming VH-BRC, named *Beachcomber* in May 1950. Ansett Airways bought out Barrier Reef in 1952 and *Beachcomber* was used for the service from Rose Bay, Sydney, to Lord Howe Island, off Australia's eastern coast. *Romeo-Charlie* was outfitted to carry 42 passengers in four cabins, with a flight crew of five. Construction of a runway bisecting the southern portion of Lord Howe Island brought to an end Ansett's flying-boat era in 1974.

Beachcomber and Sunderland V VH-BRF *Islander* (now with Fantasy of Flight in Florida and last flown in 1996) were sold to flying-boat legend Captain Charles Blair for his Antilles Air Boats organisation, based in the British Virgin Islands. US-registered as N158C and named *Southern Cross*, the Sandringham set off eastwards for its new home on 28th November 1974. In the Virgin Islands *Southern Cross* became VP-LVE. In 1976 and 1977 Blair captained *Southern Cross* to Ireland, operating variously out of Foynes on the Shannon, and Bantry Bay. Blair, having married film star Maureen O'Hara in 1968, was using the flying-boat to visit the in-laws! On 19th August 1976 Blair brought *Southern Cross* to Belfast Lough, thereby completing a leisurely circumnavigation of the globe; as JM715 this flying-boat had last been in Belfast 29 years before. On both transatlantic trips, *Southern Cross* also visited Calshot Spit on the Solent. Charles Blair's incredible 45,000-hours and 50-year flying career ended in the crash of a Grumman Goose on 2nd September 1978 en route St Croix to St Thomas.

Southern Cross touched down on Lough Derg in western Ireland on 24th October 1980 and on 2nd February 1981 transited to Calshot from where a UK consortium hoped to operate it on charters. It was beached on the former seaplane slipways at Lee-on-Solent, but the enterprise came to nought. Here was a golden opportunity for the Science Museum to acquire an iconic flying-boat, adding to the growing transport collection. With the help of the National Heritage Memorial Fund, *Southern Cross* was bought in November 1981. It could have been moved to the storage site at Wroughton in Wiltshire, but negotiations were staged with another, much more appropriate venue. Due to open in early 1984 was the ambitious Hall of Aviation in Southampton, close to the banks of the River Itchen and opposite what had been the Supermarine factory at Woolston. *Southern Cross* would become the centre-piece of the new museum, a home adjacent to where passenger-carrying flying-boats had last operated in the 1950s.

On 1st March 1983 the Sandringham was eased back down the slipway at Lee-on-Solent and on to a specialist Mexefloat barge by members of the Army Marine Unit, based at nearby Marchwood, and was towed up Southampton Water to Ocean Village. There *Southern Cross* was off-loaded at the new marina on the 2nd and repainted as *Beachcomber* of Ansett in the coming weeks. With building work at a stage where the largest exhibit could be moved in, VH-BRC was carefully manoeuvred over a main road and winched into its new home.

Southampton University Man-Powered Aircraft
1961 | Single-seat experimental | One human!

American industrialist Henry Kremer launched a competition in the late 1950s to stimulate new approaches to aviation, particularly in airframe structures. A series of prizes was offered, the first being for £5,000 – about £125,000 in present-day values – and a lot of interest was generated, particularly in academic institutions where different departments could co-operate on a practical project. The Department of Aeronautics at Southampton University rose to the challenge and design of SUMPAC – Southampton University Man-Powered AirCraft – was initiated in July 1960. Construction began the following January with a complex pedal system driving a pusher propeller; the airframe was made largely of spruce and balsa and covered in see-through cellophane. The wing had an area of 300 square feet yet the empty weight was only 128lb. Sustained flight was calculated to last only seconds and at first racing cyclists were considered as potential pilot-cum-powerplant. It was soon realised that what would really fit the bill was an athletic pilot who would instinctively recognise the necessary control inputs: the incredibly experienced Derek Piggott was the natural choice.

In his superb autobiography, *Delta Papa – A Life of Flying* (Pelham, London, 1977) Derek described the first faltering trials as "a series of minor disasters. With a design like this, where every ounce of excess weight must be saved, there are bound to be a few items which prove too weak because of unexpected loads." The first real flight, at four o'clock in the afternoon at Lasham on 9th November 1961 is vividly recalled: "I eased back on the stick, the pedals suddenly began to slip a little and all became easier. Tremendous excitement! I pedalled harder trying to make it stay up for as long as possible.

The delicate, see-through SUMPAC at Solent Sky. *Ken Ellis*

One wing began to drop and we turned slowly off the line of the runway. My reactions were slow as I thought out the required aileron and rudder movements to stop the turn. Gradually she responded and the wings came level again. The elevator control was very sensitive and the aircraft pitched up and down as I over-controlled. This caused extra drag and suddenly there was the rumble of the wheel on the grass."

Take-off had occurred at a giddy 19.8mph, Derek achieved an 'altitude' of 5ft 8in and the flight lasted eight seconds. As the light faded, the team wheeled SUMPAC away into the hangar and carefully de-rigged it. Validating the flight took time: "Months afterwards we realised that history had been made that day..." This was the first true man-powered flight in the UK. SUMPAC went on to achieve several other flights and the head of the design team, David Williams, flew it a couple of times. Turns were achieved, but never anything like the controlled figure-of-eight the Kremer prize was after.

The Southampton University team had disbanded by 1964 and the project was handed on to a team from Imperial College, London. This was led by Alan Lassière, the chairman of the London Man-Powered Aircraft Group. The propulsion system – the pedals and gears – and the 'pylon' mounting for the pusher propeller were among the modifications. Trials began in late 1965 from West Malling but on 12th November 1965, with John Pratt at the pedals, SUMPAC was badly damaged and the decision was taken to abandon future trials. The airframe was repaired and it was presented to the Shuttleworth Collection at Old Warden in 1966. With a span of 80ft, the SUMPAC was a snug fit suspended from the rafters of one of Old Warden's hangars and an approach from the Hall of Aviation to take it on was gratefully received. The fragile craft was moved to Southampton in 1984 and gently lifted into its perch 'flying' from the exhibition hall's beams.

Supermarine S.6A N248
1929 | High-performance floatplane | One 2,300hp Rolls-Royce 'R' piston

One of many jewels on display inside London's Science Museum is the Supermarine S.6B floatplane S1595 and the beautiful Schneider Trophy. Flt Lt John Boothman flew it to secure the hotly competed international trophy in perpetuity for Great Britain on 13th September 1931 at 340.05mph. What is often overlooked is that another of the RAF High Speed Flight's high-performance Supermarines survives: S.6A N248. This machine competed in the 1929 contest and was held in reserve for the 1931 event; both of which were staged from Calshot Spit, seven miles down Southampton Water from Solent Sky. But N248 has an even closer association: it was built at Woolston, just across the River Itchen from the museum. N248 and Spitfire F.24 PK683 were the founder members of the museum, being installed in the Mitchell Memorial Hall in 1976; both are on loan from the RAF Museum.

Fg Off Richard 'Batchy' Atcherley was the pilot for S.6 N248, competition number '8', during the competition staged on 7th September 1929. He cut the turning point at Hayling Island and was disqualified. Despite that, he managed to clinch closed circuit records in both the 50km and 100km categories, at 332.49mph and 331.0mph, respectively. During 1931 N248

Framed by the cowling of Spitfire F.24 PK683, Supermarine S.6A N248 inside the Mitchell Memorial Hall. Portrait of R J Mitchell on the left. *KEC*

was brought up to near S.6B status, under the designation S.6A. In June Flt Lt Linton Hope took N248 for a practice flight from Calshot. Part of the cowling detached, necessitating an emergency landing. As he brought the floatplane down, it was caught by the wake of a passing vessel and N248 overturned. Hope clung to a float and was quickly rescued. The S.6A was salvaged, repaired and was test flown on 6th September 1931 – cutting it fine for the 'race' which was to be staged seven days later. The use of inverted commas on the word 'race' is because only Great Britain was competing; as long as Boothman kept to the rules, the Schneider was the nation's. With the competition number '4' N248 would have been raced by Fg Off L S Snaith, but his services were not required.

The purpose of the S.6s had gone and by 1939 N248 was noted dismantled in a hangar at Eastleigh. It emerged to take a role in the 1942 film *The First of the Few*, directed by and starring Leslie Howard. The film was the story of the man that Howard was portraying, Reginald Joseph Mitchell, designer of the S.6, some exceptional flying-boats and the peerless Spitfire. The S.6A was back at Eastleigh on 22nd June 1946 mounted on a flat-bed lorry being shown off to the public at the Victory Air Pageant. During that year N248 was presented to Southampton Corporation. At around this time it was painted as the second S.6B, S1596, competition number '7'. The S.6A was frequently displayed at Southampton's Royal Pier – the former commercial flying-boat terminal – near the cruise liner and ferry port and less than a mile from the present-day Solent Sky; it was kept at Eastleigh when not 'on duty'. The floatplane was much in demand, for example it was present at the Festival of Britain in London during the summer of 1951 – the Saunders-Roe SR.A/1 was also at the event. In 1966 the S.6A left Southampton and the following year was at the former Supermarine factory at South Marston. There a team from the British Aircraft Corporation restored it – *still* as 'S1596' – to take part in the centenary celebrations of the Vickers company. (Vickers acquired Supermarine in 1928.) In 1968 the S.6A was at Abingdon for the fiftieth anniversary of the RAF celebrations. Installed in the Mitchell Memorial Hall in 1976, the opportunity to return 'S1596' to its rightful identity of N248 was taken by the time the S.6A crossed to the new building in 1984.

Solent Sky aircraft

Type	Identity	Built	Origin	Acquired	Notes
Airwave hang-glider	–	1980	Britain	1987	–
Avro 504J replica	'C4451'	1991	Britain	14 Nov 1991	–
Britten-Norman BN-1F	G-ALZE	1951	Britain	Mar 1985	see profile
Britten-Norman Trislander	G-RLON	1975	Britain	5 Apr 2017	see profile
de Havilland Tiger Moth	BB807	1935	Britain	Sep 1988	–
de Havilland Vampire T.11	XE998	1955	Britain	2005	–
de Havilland Sea Venom FAW.22	WM571	1954	Britain	24 Dec 1988	–
de Havilland Sea Vixen FAW.2	XJ571	1960	Britain	5 Feb 2003	–
DHC Chipmunk T.10	WK570	1952	Canada	2002	cockpit
Folland Gnat F.1	XK740	1957	Britain	6 Mar 1987	see profile
Hawker Siddeley Harrier GR.3	XV760	1969	Britain	2010	cockpit
Mignet 'Flying Flea'	'G-ADZW'	1994	France	May 2000	–
Saunders-Roe SR.A/1	TG263	1946	Britain	1993	see profile
Saunders-Roe Skeeter Mk.8	G-APOI	1957	Britain	3 Aug 2008	–
Saunders-Roe Skeeter AOP.12	XL770	1958	Britain	1987	–
Short Sandringham 4*	VH-BRC	1943	Britain	2 Mar 1983	see profile
Slingsby Grasshopper TX.1	WZ753	1952	Britain	1989	–
Slingsby Cadet TX.3	XN246	1959	Britain	1988	–
Southampton University SUMPAC	–	1961	Britain	Jul 1984	see profile
Supermarine S.6A	N248	1929	Britain	7 Feb 1976	see profile
Supermarine Spitfire F.24*	PK683	1946	Britain	7 Feb 1976	–
Supermarine Swift FR.5	–	1955	Britain	1996	cockpit
Supermarine Swift F.7	XF114	1957	Britain	2005	–
Supermarine Scimitar F.1	XD332	1966	Britain	10 Mar 1999	–
Wight Quadruplane	'N546'	1987	Britain	1988	replica

Notes: * – illustrated in the colour section.

Also in Hampshire...
Museum of Army Flying
At Middle Wallop, the headquarters of the Army Air Corps is this very impressive museum also offers great views of the activity on the busy airfield. This is a national collection and it is covered in depth in the sister volume *Great Aviation Collections of Britain*. www.armyflying.com

Gliding Heritage Centre
Lasham is the home of the Lasham Gliding Society, one of the world's largest gliding clubs. Established in August 2013 the Gliding Heritage Centre is a 'working' collection with many of the 'exhibits' regularly being flown. A second hangar is planned and longer opening hours, but for now visitors will get a warm welcome on Sunday afternoons. www.glidingheritage.org.uk

New Forest Airfields Museum and Education Centre
Opened on 29th May 2016 the centre is based on the former back-up generator building of post-war RAF Sopley, Southern Radar, near Bransgore. A short distance to the southwest was the USAAF advanced landing ground of Winkton. Limited open days, more details at: https://fonfasite.wordpress.com/the-education-centre

Sammy Miller Motorcycle Museum
Set up in 1964 at New Milton, the number of exhibits is breath-taking, nearly 400 'bikes' in four galleries. Also on show is Morane-Saulnier Rallye G-EISO, a sort of motorbike of the air. www.sammymiller.co.uk

When in Hampshire
Calshot Castle and Heritage Area
The former RFC and RAF marine aircraft base hosted the last Schneider Trophy races, in 1929 and 1931. The final Sunderlands flew away in October 1953 and Calshot closed as an RAF station in May 1961. Much of the site is accessible to the public,

The flying-boat station at Calshot Spit in the late 1920s. Today much of this amazing time capsule survives. *KEC*

allowing a glimpse of a unique time capsule. There are plenty of displays on Calshot's aviation days within the castle and great views of the Solent. **www.english-heritage.org.uk/visit/places.calshot-castle**

When on the Isle of Wight

There has not been a dedicated aviation museum on the island since 1999, but there's certainly scope for one! In and around Cowes there is some aviation interest to be found.

At The Prospect in the delightful High Street in Cowes is a real gem, the **Sir Max Aitken Museum**. Set inside an 18th century sail-maker's loft, this was the home of Sir Max Aitken Bt DSO DFC from 1947 until his death in 1985. Most of the exhibits are marine in nature, but there is an exhibition of his night-fighting days with 601 (County of London) Squadron. **www.sirmaxaitkenmuseum.org**

Across the River Medina at East Cowes, inside the iconic Columbine Hangar – where Saunders-Roe built many flying-boats, ending up with the enormous Princess – is the **Classic Boat Museum Gallery**. (See the image of the SR.A/1 jet flying-boat for this incredible building in its heyday.) The museum is devoted to boating memorabilia and the aviation 'flavour' is limited, but it is well worth the visit. **www.classicboatmuseum.org**

Prototype Legacy
de Havilland Aircraft Museum

London Colney
www.dehavillandmuseum.co.uk

Writing on a toilet wall is not to be condoned, but there can be mitigating circumstances. Sketches of aerofoils in one of the loos at Salisbury Hall, London Colney, helped to spark Britain's first dedicated aviation museum. The scribbles were not vandalism; it was a way to capture a moment of inspiration. At the time Salisbury Hall was not a stately home, it was the drawing office and prototype assembly workshop for de Havilland. The design team was relocated to the hall in October 1939, close enough for ease of communication with Hatfield but far enough away should the Luftwaffe decide to attack the airfield and factory. A concrete base went down, a hangar was erected and the requisitioned hall turned into drawing offices with a common room, a canteen and washrooms. Chief designer Ronald Eric Bishop and his team were working to create a fast, unarmed twin-engined aircraft that could lend itself to being a fighter, a bomber and a photo-recce platform. To save precious strategic commodities, the new machine was to have an airframe that used as much wood as possible. This was the birthplace of the Mosquito – the 'Wooden Wonder'.

Major Walter Goldsmith moved into the moated manor house in 1958. A substantial dwelling on the site can be traced back to the Ninth Century, if not before. The present house was built in the 1670s and boasts some illustrious residents, including King Charles II and Eleanor 'Nell' Gwynne, who occupied a cottage in the grounds. In more recent times, Lady

Above: Members of the restoration team arranged in front of the Mosquito prototype. Project manager Bob Glasby is seventh from the left, and Ian Thirsk eighth from the left. *Garry Lakin-DHAM*

Mosquito TT.35 TA634 with Salisbury Hall in the background. *Stuart Howe*

Randolph Churchill, along with her son, Winston, during 1905 and in the 1930s Sir Nigel Gresley, designer of locomotives such as *Flying Scotsman* and *Mallard* stayed a while. Getting to know his new home, Walter was bemused by the drawings of wing sections on the wall of a toilet. He also pondered the large patch of concrete adjacent to the hall; what was that all about? He asked around and soon discovered that less than two decades earlier, the concrete had been the base of a hangar, the house had been a design office for de Havilland and the very first Mosquito had been built there. Not just the Mosquito: the Airspeed Horsa assault glider, the Vampire single-seat jet fighter and the Hornet twin-piston fighter all came off the drawing boards at the hall. Salisbury Hall was vacated by DH in 1947, but it was not done with aviation: Walter Goldsmith was captured by the most recent era of Salisbury Hall's long heritage.

One of the people Walter got to know as he unfolded the past was Bill Baird, who worked in the DH public relations department. Bill had spent a lot of time 'hiding' W4050 since it had left the haven of Salisbury Hall. The 'Top Brass' saw no value in it; merely that it was occupying space that could be earning money. Walter was restoring the hall with the help of a Ministry of Works and Buildings grant and was keenly aware that one of the terms of the funding was that the finished product be opened regularly to the public. The needs of Bill and Walter coincided and it was agreed that DH would lend W4050 to the Goldsmith project, but no cash would be forthcoming. As the prototype could not be left to stand outside the organisations that had formed the considerable 'supply chain' that produced 7,781 Mosquitos, in Britain, Australia and Canada were contacted. This resulted in £1,800; an early example of corporate 'sponsorship'. If that seems a derisory amount, in 1958 that was enough to dismantle a Robin hangar, transport it to London Colney, lay down a concrete base and re-erect and re-clad the structure. In September 1958 W4050 returned to its birthplace and was publically unveiled on 15th May the following year. From this humble beginning came the exceptional present-day museum.

First of its kind

Salisbury Hall became the prototype *dedicated* aviation museum – the first of its kind in Britain. While the Imperial War Museum and the Science Museum have had airframes on charge since 1920 and 1913 respectively, both have a much wider remit than aviation. The Shuttleworth Collection – aircraft *and* vehicles – traces its origins to 1932; but it was the 1960s before it opened, at first only occasionally, to the public. By saving the only surviving World War Two combat prototype, the small band of people who had brought W4050 home had sown the seeds of an explosion of preservation activity, particularly in the 1960s and 1970s: as charted in Chapter 1, *Moments in Time*, and throughout this book.

Displays inside the Robin hangar multiplied and the story of Hatfield and de Havilland became a part of the coverage. The second of many airframes arrived in January 1968 in the form of Venom NF.3 WX853 from the 'gate' at Debden. As custodians of the first Mosquito, an example of a late production machine could not be passed up and TT.35 TA634 arrived from Liverpool in September 1970. The volunteers appreciated that this could not live outside for long and more covered space was a priority. The donation of a Swiss Air Force Vampire FB.6, which flew into Hatfield in the summer of 1974 added to the need to formalise the collection. Negotiations during that year resulted in the acquisition of the freehold to the site

Discovered in a kibbutz in Israel, the wing of Mosquito TR.33 TW233 in a freight bay at Heathrow in July 1980. It is now part and parcel of the magnificent restoration of FB.VI TA122. *Stuart Howe*

occupied by the hangar and its surroundings. The name Mosquito Aircraft Museum (MAM) – which for a long time had been the unofficial name – was formally adopted, also in 1974. In 1977 the de Havilland Aircraft Museum Trust Ltd was established, taking up charitable status. The necessary elements were in place for raising cash towards and exhibition hangar. By 1982 the impressive sum of £65,000 – no lottery hand outs or crowd-funding in those days – had been raised and construction started. The Mk.35 was rolled into the warm and dry, along with several other airframes. By the early 1990s MAM adopted a title that had been presaged back in 1977 when it became the de Havilland Aircraft Museum. This was a far more appropriate name for what had become a major collection and a powerful tribute to the de Havilland dynasty.

Members of the museum, I know, forgive the author singling out someone who made a dramatic impact on MAM – Stuart Howe. An acknowledged expert on all things Mosquito; his books on the subject were on and off the shelves like fiddler's elbows during the writing of this section. He was a determined 'ferret', be it for a small component or an entire airframe. An astounding example of this was the museum's *third* Mosquito: FB.VI TA122, that saw operational service in the closing months of World War Two, which Stuart negotiated for from the Royal Netherlands Air Force Museum. This had no wing, but undaunted, Stuart set about a search for a replacement and a lead from warbird operator Robs Lamplough set him off in the direction of an Israeli kibbutz at Beit Alfa. This ended up with the arrival of an El Al Boeing 747 freighter at London's Heathrow Airport in July 1980. Among more mundane items in its cavernous hold was the relatively light, but very bulky entire wing from former Israel Air Force Mosquito TR.33 TW233. After a long restoration, TA122 is whole, thanks to inspired 'footwork'. Stuart also knew how to galvanise people to donate and how to merchandise. His skills in the latter direction were reflected in the expansion of the RAF Museum Hendon shop – Stuart's full time job for many years. While he had the drive of a zealot, he was kind, considerate and set about his goals with a grin on face. Stuart Howe died on 14th April 2004; the fabric of today's DHAM reflects his endeavours at every turn.

The composite forward fuselage of DHAM's Airspeed Horsa, with a model of the assault glider to the left. *Ken Ellis*

Missing links

In April 1965 the hallowed name of de Havilland was swallowed within Hawker Siddeley; the company had been acquired in January 1960, but traded as a division for five years. This explains the appearance of Hawker Siddeley types in the table and the relevance of the Cierva C.24 is dealt with in the profile section. On 12th September 1941 test pilot George Errington was in command of the prototype Airspeed Horsa DG597 as it was towed aloft from the Great West Aerodrome, Harmondsworth; these days swallowed within the enormity of London Airport, Heathrow. The Horsa assault glider had been designed on the drawing boards at Salisbury Hall; Airspeed having been bought up by de Havilland in 1940 and the drawing office was amalgamated.

Another aircraft was conceived at Salisbury Hall and, like the Mosquito, it was a shapely twin-engined warplane. This was the Hornet, which had its maiden flight at Hatfield in the hands of Geoffrey de Havilland Jnr on 28th July 1944. Sadly, no intact example of this magnificent-looking fighter survives. The largest element of one, the rear fuselage of 1950-built Sea Hornet NF.21 VX250, is to be found at Salisbury Hall. This machine was reduced to produce at St Davids in Wales in December 1956 and the carcass dumped at the fire training compound. The remains were salvaged by Mosquito maestro Tony Agar – see the Chapters 16 and 31 – in 1972 and the rear fuselage presented to MAM. Also on show, and always attracting curious glances, is a concrete mould used to form the Hornet's fuselage; the Mosquito was made in the same manner. Fuselages were made in two halves; not unlike the way a plastic kit is assembled. After the plywood had been moulded, fittings would be applied to the inner surfaces and then the two halves would be joined along the vertical centre line using a 'Vee' shaped butt joint reinforced by plywood strips in rebates, inside and out.

Although always marketed as a Hawker Siddeley product, the Trident three-jet airliner was a de Havilland-originated design, the Type 121. The substantial former British Airways Trident 2 forward fuselage, like several other exhibits at DHAM, is open to public inspection. Another jetliner fuselage represents the last aircraft to be built at Hatfield, the HS.146. This prototype of this four-jet first flew at Hatfield on 3rd September 1981 with the last example leaving in 1993, by which time production was consolidated at Woodford. Rebranded and re-engineered as the RJ (Regional Jet) series, the programme was terminated in 2003. DHAM's example is a Series 100, built at Hatfield in November 1983, going on to serve in Brazil, the USA and Canada before returning to the UK in May 1989. It flew with Air UK as G-UKPC before transferred to Jersey European Airways as G-JEAO in 1994. Retired in 2009 to Filton it was parted out for components and the fuselage was secured by the museum.

14:45 hours on the dot

Geoffrey de Havilland Jnr was at the helm of the prototype Mosquito for its first flight from Hatfield on 25th November 1940. To help celebrate W4050's 75th birthday, the Heritage Lottery Fund (HLF) said 'yes' to a grant of £41,000 towards the epic four-year restoration of this incredibly significant survivor. At 14:45 on 25th November 2015 W4050 was rolled out at exactly the time that it started its maiden flight at Hatfield.

As noted above and in the profile below, the survival of W4050 is down to it avoiding several corporate attempts to have it scrapped or burnt; each time it was quietly moved to another site to keep the Hatfield-based 'suits' off the scent! When Major Walter Goldsmith offered to display the 'orphan' W4050 at Salisbury Hall, its clandestine custodians seized the opportunity. Eventually, Hatfield agreed to recognise the status quo by presenting W4050 on permanent loan. With the advent of the restoration grant, HLF could not pour money into an artefact that was on loan and BAE Systems agreed to officially hand over ownership. At the 75th anniversary ceremony a representative of the multi-national presented a scroll that settled a 'problem' of many decades and a national treasure that had relied on skulduggery for its initial survival assumed perpetuity at its birthplace. No only did HLF agree to help with the rebirth of W4050, another £62,200 was handed over in 2015 towards the museum's new project, a £1.5m display hall. Treasures such as the Comet 1 fuselage will be able to go indoors when the project is finished.

Cierva C.24 G-ABLM
1931 | Autogiro | One 120hp de Havilland Gipsy III piston

A first glance this exhibit looks out of place: de Havilland didn't 'do' rotorcraft and Cierva – that was Spanish wasn't it? Father of the Autogiro – a name he registered as a trademark – Don Juan de la Cierva Codorníu settled in Britain and established the Cierva Autogiro Company in March 1926. Design and engineering expertise was to be found aplenty so licences were granted to several manufacturers. de Havilland was basking in the spectacular success of the Moth two-seat biplane and wanted to extend the marketplace; more seats and a cabin was the answer. The Puss Moth, Leopard Moth and Hornet Moth 'family' were aimed at this demand. Cierva believed that the comfort of the Puss Moth could be achieved in an Autogiro. de Havilland seconded C T Wilkins to the task and the C.24 came together at Stag Lane, Edgware. Cierva's Hanworth workshop created the three-blade rotor, all other construction was entrusted to DH. The 'compact' three-seat layout of the Puss Moth was adopted; behind the pilot sat two passengers in staggered seats that allowed togetherness while avoiding being shoulder-to-shoulder and minimising fuselage width. The tricycle undercarriage was radical, as was a water ballast system for trimming. The Gipsy engine could spin up the otherwise 'free-wheeling' rotor to reduce the take-off run.

Cierva carried out the test the first flight, at Stag Lane in September 1931. Straight away G-ABLM proved to be disappointing, both in control and performance. The C.24 is reported to have cost £10,000 to develop – £550,000 in present-day prices and a fortune for the task in hand in the early 1930s. A dorsal fin and end-plates to the tailplane were fitted in October 1931 and this improved directional stability, but it was clear that the three-seater was only ever going to carry a pilot and one passenger. From 27th May to 9th June 1932 Cierva took G-ABLM for a 1,430-mile tour of Europe, carrying out

Cierva C.24 G-ABLM at the Fifty Years of Flying event at Hendon in July 1951. *Roy Bonser*

The 'flight line' at the impressive former Liverpool Airport, Speke, Merseyside: Britannia 308 G-ANCF and Jetstream 41 G-JMAC. *Ken Ellis*

Museum of Berkshire Aviation, Woodley, Berkshire: Miles Magister 'L6906', Miles Student 2 G-MIOO, Miles Martinet TT.1 TF-SHC, Fairey Jet Gyrodyne XJ389. *Ken Ellis*

Museum of Berkshire Aviation, Woodley, Berkshire: Handley Page Herald 100 G-APWA. *Ken Ellis*

Cornwall Aviation Heritage Centre, Newquay Cornwall Airport, Cornwall: Vickers Varsity T.1 WJ945. *Ken Ellis*

Cornwall Aviation Heritage Centre, Newquay Cornwall Airport, Cornwall: English Electric Canberra T.4 'VN799'. *Ken Ellis*

Solway Aviation Museum, Carlisle Lake District Airport, Cumbria: Mignet Pou du Ciel 'G-ADRX'. *Ken Ellis*

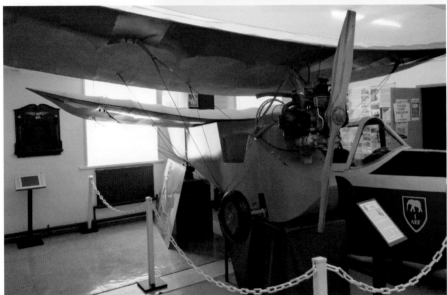

Solway Aviation Museum, Carlisle Lake District Airport, Cumbria: Hawker Hunter F.51 'XG190'. *Ken Ellis*

Solway Aviation Museum, Carlisle Lake District Airport, Cumbria: Percival Sea Prince T.1 WP314. *Ken Ellis*

Bournemouth Aviation Museum, Bournemouth Airport, Dorset: CMC Leopard G-BKRL. *Terry Dann*

Bournemouth Aviation Museum, Bournemouth Airport, Dorset: North American Harvard T.2b KF388. *Terry Dann*

Bournemouth Aviation Museum,
Bournemouth Airport, Dorset:
Hawker Hunter F.6A XG160.
Terry Dann

Stow Maries Great War Aerodrome,
Stow Maries, Essex: Blériot XI
replica G-BPVE. *Terry Dann*

Stow Maries Great War Aerodrome, Stow Maries, Essex: Sopwith Camel replica 'N6377'. *Terry Dann*

Aerospace Bristol, Filton, Gloucestershire: BAC/Sud Concorde 102 G-BOAF. *Aerospace Bristol*

Jet Age Museum, Gloucestershire Airport, Gloucestershire: Gloster Javelin FAW.9 XH903. *Les Woodward*

Farnborough Air Sciences Trust, Farnborough, Hampshire: Hawker Hunter T.7 WV383. *Ken Ellis*

Farnborough Air Sciences Trust, Farnborough, Hampshire: English Electric Lightning T.5 XS420. *Richard Hall*

Farnborough Air Sciences Trust, Farnborough, Hampshire: Folland Gnat T.1 XP516. *Ken Ellis*

Solent Sky, Southampton, Hampshire: Short Sandringham 4 VH-BRC. *Terry Dann*

Solent Sky, Southampton, Hampshire: Supermarine Spitfire F.24 PK683. *Terry Dann*

de Havilland Aircraft Museum.
London Colney, Hertfordshire:
de Havilland Mosquito TT.35
TA634. *Ken Ellis*

de Havilland Aircraft Museum.
London Colney, Hertfordshire:
de Havilland Comet 1B F-BGNX.
Ken Ellis

de Havilland Aircraft Museum.
London Colney, Hertfordshire:
Hawker Siddeley HS.125 Srs 1
G-ARYC. *Ken Ellis*

RAF Manston History Museum, Manston, Kent: Gloster Meteor TT.20 ;WD615'. *Ken Ellis*

RAF Manston History Museum, Manston, Kent: Westland Wessex HU.5 XS482. *Ken Ellis*

East Midlands Airport Aeropark, East Midlands Airport, Leicestershire: Armstrong Whitworth Argosy 101 G-BEOZ. *Jon Wickenden*

East Midlands Airport Aeropark, East Midlands Airport, Leicestershire: Avro Vulcan B.2 XM575.
Jon Wickenden

Thorpe Camp Visitor Centre, Tattershall Thorpe, Lincolnshire: English Electric Lightning F.1A XM192. *Ken Ellis*

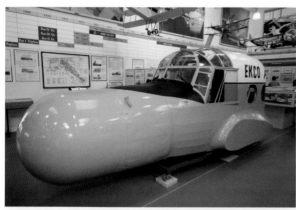

Avro Heritage Museum,
Woodford, Greater Manchester:
Avro XIX Srs 2 G-AGPG:
Ian Humphreys

Avro Heritage Museum,
Woodford, Greater Manchester:
Avro Vulcan B.2 XM603:
Ian Humphreys

Runway Visitor Park, Manchester Airport, Greater Manchester: Hawker Siddeley Nimrod MR.2 XV231.
Terry Dann

Museum of Science and Industry, Manchester, Greater Manchester: Avro Triplane replica. *Terry Dann*

Museum of Science and Industry, Manchester, Greater Manchester: Avro Type F replica. *Terry Dann*

Museum of Science and Industry, Manchester, Greater Manchester: Avro Avian IIIA G-EBZM. *Terry Dann*

City of Norwich Aviation Museum, Norwich Airport, Norfolk: Fokker Friendship 200 G-BHMY. *Terry Dann*

City of Norwich Aviation Museum, Norwich Airport, Norfolk: Westland Whirlwind HAR.10 XP355. *Terry Dann*

Sywell Aviation Museum, Northampton Airport, Northamptonshire: Hawker Hunter F.2 WN904. *Terry Dann*

North East Land, Sea and Air
Museums, Sunderland, North East:
Westland Widgeon G-APTW.
Ken Ellis

North East Land, Sea and Air
Museums, Sunderland, North East:
FMA Pucará A-522. *Ken Ellis*

North East Land, Sea and Air Museums, Sunderland, North East: North American F-86D Sabre 16171.
Jon Wickenden

Newark Air Museum, Newark, Nottinghamshire: Supermarine Swift FR.5 WK277. *Ken Ellis*

Newark Air Museum, Newark, Nottinghamshire: Scottish Aviation Bulldog T.1 XX634 and Bulldog classroom instruction module. *Ken Ellis*

Newark Air Museum, Newark, Nottinghamshire: Hawker Siddeley Sea Harrier FA.2 ZA176. *Ken Ellis*

demonstrations and liaising with European licencees. Also that year, Cierva test pilot 'Reggie' Brie flew G-ABLM in the Brooklands to Newcastle air race of 6th August, averaging 103.5mph. Brie was at the controls at Castle Bromwich on 18th October 1932 when G-ABLM was damaged in an accident. This may well have put paid to the C.24's flying and in 1935 it was presented to the Science Museum. It was in the static at the Fifty Years of Flying event at Hendon in July 1951, but otherwise remained in the museum's large object store at Hayes. G-ABLM was at Hatfield by 1973 for a restoration at the hands of Hawker Siddeley apprentices. It moved down the road to London Colney in the summer of 1980, on loan from the Science Museum.

de Havilland Hornet Moth G-ADOT
1937 | Biplane tourer | One 130hp de Havilland Gipsy Major 1 piston

Market forces being as they are, other than the Tiger Moth, examples of de Havilland's famous light aeroplane family of the 1920s and 1930s are rare commodities in museums. DHAM has the only example of a Hornet Moth in a British museum; it saw active service during World War Two *and* has a Hertfordshire connection. Ordered by Sir Ralph Leigh Hare, G-ADOT was built at Hatfield in 1937 and based by the baronet-pilot at Norwich's Mousehold aerodrome. Along with a large number of sundry light aircraft it was impressed for military service and, camouflaged and with the serial number X9326, it was issued to 2 Coastal Patrol Flight (CPF) on 29th February 1940. The flight was one of six set up around the British coast to look for enemy activity as a way of alleviating the work of the hard-pressed Coastal Command, from the autumn of 1939. Using a mixture of light aircraft, the worth of the CPF's is difficult to assess, but the presence of *any* aircraft would act as a deterrent to a U-Boat. Based at Abbotsinch – now Glasgow Airport – 2 CPF's beat was the imposing Clyde Estuary. Their work done, the CPFs were disbanded in May 1940. For the rest of the war Hornet Moth X9326 took the role of a 'hack', a general duties runabout. It served with: 1 School of Technical Training at Halton (from May 1940); 6 Air Observer and Navigator School at Staverton (November 1940); 24 Group Communications Flight, also at Staverton (1941), 23 Operational Training Unit at Pershore (1941) and finally 5 Group Communications Flight at Swinderby (May 1944).

Retirement from military life came comparatively late, going to 5 Maintenance Unit at Kemble on 2nd January 1946. Offered for disposal it was bought up, along with other types, by Air Commodore Whitney Willard Straight's Straight Corporation and transferred to its subsidiary, Western Airways at Weston-super-Mare, to get it ready for a return to life as a civilian and it became G-ADOT once again on 20th May 1946. It was acquired by the Herts and Essex Aero Club at Broxbourne on 4th June. It served faithfully for 13 years; its certificate of airworthiness lapsing in October 1959. It was kept at Stapleford Tawney, where the Herts and Essex had moved from Hertfordshire in the 1950s. By the early 1960s the engineless Hornet Moth was in a garden at Stoke Ferry, Norfolk, as a child's plaything. This may seem to be a flippant use of a classic, but this probably saved it for posterity. It gravitated to the Shuttleworth Collection at Old Warden and by the early 1970s was at Hatfield. *Oscar-Tango* joined DHAM in 1977 and was an early candidate for the museum's workshop, rolling out from there and going on display in 1987.

Hornet Moth G-ADOT showing its economic needs for display space. *Ken Ellis*

de Havilland Mosquito W4050
1940 | Fighter/bomber | Two 1,460hp Rolls-Royce Merlin 21 pistons

By their very nature, prototypes lead a perilous existence. Those that survive the rigours of test and development might be dusted down and sold on to a customer, but most likely they will be scrapped as there is no profit in sentiment. Only with the dramatic expansion of the 'heritage movement' from the late 1950s have prototypes been sought out for saving and manufacturers been so moved as to hand on these treasures for posterity.

Without question, the most important airframe at the DHAM is W4050, the only surviving British World War Two combat aircraft prototype. The very first Avro Lancaster, Handley Page Halifax, Hawker Hurricane, Supermarine Spitfire, Vickers Wellington – to name a few British giants – are long since gone. Likewise the initial Boeing Flying Fortress, Consolidated Liberator, Curtiss Warhawk, North American Mitchell and Republic Thunderbolt as examples of US legends. The EAA Air Venture Museum at Oshkosh, Wisconsin, has a XP-51 Mustang, but *not* the seminal NA.73X prototype. Then of course there are the inaugural German, Italian and Japanese combat types to consider. All of these are extinct.

This is not the case for the Mosquito, but this is just part of the story. The prototype is on show to the public in the *very* place in which it was designed and conceived. The survival of W4050 is an incredible tale that involves a string of visionary and determined DH employees, a man who bought a ramshackle hall in Hertfordshire and discovered its 'unseen' heritage and a team of people who founded, expanded and run Britain's oldest established pure aviation collection. In October 1939, the month after World War Two broke out DH chief designer Ronald Eric Bishop and his team re-located to Salisbury Hall from Hatfield, less than four miles to the north. The aircraft factory was too tempting a target for the Luftwaffe and the hall represented a quiet, out-of-the-way, yet neighbouring retreat. A hangar was erected and inside a mock-up of a private venture twin-engined fighter-cum-bomber was hastily erected and the initial design was given the go-ahead.

From 1939 the little building resounded to the clamour of construction while rooms in the hall witnessed the creation of thousands of drawings. The prototype Mosquito was taking shape. The revolutionary machine was dismantled and taken by road to Hatfield for flight testing. As well as the prototype, three development prototypes were also built at Salisbury Hall. With a one-piece wing and fragile fuselage, taking Mosquitos on lorries to Hatfield was time-consuming and costly. In May 1941 Geoffrey de Havilland Jnr paced out a field alongside Salisbury Hall and decided to fly the second example (the first Mk.II night-fighter W4052) for the 'hop' to Hatfield on the 15th. Two more early 'Mossies' took the airborne option on September 14 (W4053) and December 5 (W4073), touching down minutes later at Hatfield.

Wearing the B Condition (or 'trade plate') identity E-0234 and overall yellow colours, Geoffrey took the prototype 'Wooden Wonder' on its first flight on 25th November 1940. It flew to Boscombe Down for evaluation by the Aeroplane and Armament Experimental Establishment on 19th February 1941, by which time it was wearing the RAF serial W4050. After its 12th flight at Boscombe on the 24th, Gordon Slade was taxying the prototype over rough ground when the tail wheel jammed and the fuselage fractured. W4050 was hastily fitted with the fuselage intended for the first photo-recce prototype, W4051; this had also been built at Salisbury Hall. The prototype re-flew on 14th March. Evaluation at Boscombe was completed on 23rd May 1941. Back at Hatfield W4050 was used for stall investigations before it was grounded in October while Merlin 61s were fitted and it flew with these in June 1942, reaching 40,000ft on its second sortie. It next had Merlin 77s installed, going back into the air on 8th October 1942. At the end of the month John de Havilland flew W4050 to 29,000ft at an incredible 439mph – 20mph *faster* that a production Spitfire HF.VIII at the same altitude. The prototype was tested by Rolls-Royce at Hucknall from 1st March to 10th June 1943 but its life as a development airframe was running out.

In December 1943 W4050 was flown for the last time but it was put to good use as an instructional airframe. In 1946 it was transferred to the DH Aeronautical Technical School which was then at W4050's birthplace, Salisbury Hall. (Also at 'The Tech' at that time was the DH.88 Comet G-ACSS, famed for winning Sir MacPherson Robertson's air race from England to Australia in October 1934. Today, the almost totally reconstructed G-ACSS is held in airworthy condition at the Shuttleworth Collection, Old Warden.) W4050 appeared in the static park at the 1946 and 1947 Society of British Aircraft Constructors displays at Radlett, a mere two miles to the east of the hall. When DH moved out of Salisbury Hall in 1947 the prototype 'Mossie' started a somewhat migratory life, with periods in store at the DH-run aerodrome at Panshanger, the company factory at Hawarden, near Chester, before settling again on Hatfield. Several times the significant, but industrially redundant, airframe faced destruction but common sense, and the occasional subterfuge, prevailed. When Walter Goldsmith acquired Salisbury Hall, the pressure of space at Hatfield and the major's wish to foster his home's aviation legacy coincided. In September 1958 W4050 was again moved to Salisbury Hall, on long-term loan, and it was put into a hangar similar to the one it had been built in 18 years previously.

To help celebrate W4050's 75th birthday, the Heritage Lottery Fund (HLF) said 'yes' to a grant of £41,000 towards the epic four-year restoration of this incredibly significant survivor. This precious prototype has been conserved to the configuration in which it last flew, from the first half of 1943, with two-speed, two-stage supercharged Merlin 77s. With the advent of the restoration grant, HLF could not pour money into an artefact that was on loan and BAE Systems agreed to make the prototype's existence official. At the 75th anniversary ceremony a representative of the multi-national giant presented a scroll that transferred ownership to DHAM; W4050 had secured perpetuity at its birthplace and was officially a national treasure.

Mosquito W4050 in the Robin hangar at Salisbury Hall, 1974. In the foreground is a Molins 6-pounder 57mm cannon which was fitted to the Mk.XVIII. *Stuart Howe*

de Havilland Mosquito TT.35 TA634
1945 | Target-tug | Two 1,690hp Rolls-Royce Merlin 113/114 pistons

The choice of Mosquito W4050 for a profile was an obvious one, but with *three* whole airframes to choose from at London Colney, why stop there? The FB.VI would appear to 'out-weigh' the TT.35, but the author's preference goes beyond this rationale, TA634 was the first 'warbird' he ever clapped close eyes on; sitting in the huge No.1 Hangar at Liverpool Airport, Speke, in the late 1960s. The spotty, long-haired youngster was awe-struck by the Merlins dripping oil into huge trays and it was worth all the angst of sneaking in from Bank's Road, avoiding the patrol van and bunking back out again. Besides, TA634 had been brought to Liverpool through agitation by the Merseyside Society of Aviation Enthusiasts (MSAE), an organisation that the author joined thanks to the inspiration of that Mosquito. More on the activities of MSAE in Chapter 18.

Built at Hatfield as a B.35, TA634 was destined to see no operational service as a bomber, being ferried to 27 Maintenance Unit (MU) at Shawbury on 14th April 1945, where it was destined to spend the best part of seven years in storage. It was issued to Brooklands Aviation at Sywell on 22nd February 1952. Brooklands had a contract to convert Mk.35s to target-tugs and went on produce 205 TT.35s, the last one, RV349, being completed in May 1954. Work on TA634 was completed five months after arrival at Sywell. It was fitted with a ML Aviation-built airflow-driven winch mounted at the forward end of the bomb bay, a reel for 2,000 yards of cable to which a banner (flat and flag-like) or a sleeve (windsock-like) target were attached. Behind the bomb bay guide rails were fitted and around the tail guard wires installed to prevent snagging. The undersides were painted in distinctive yellow and black diagonal stripes, while the remainder of the airframe was silver dope.

After the conversion, TA634 was taken on charge by 22 MU at Silloth on 23rd July 1952. It was 17 months before the Mosquito started to earn its keep with the RAF; it was issued to 4 Civilian Anti-Aircraft Co-operation Unit (CAACU) at Llandow on the last day of 1953. Alas, this was all too brief, 4 CAACU amalgamated with 3 CAACU at Exeter in May 1954. TA634 did not make the migration; instead it moved into the care of another Llandow unit, 38 MU. The Mosquito returned to duty on 20th March 1956 when it was accepted at Sylt in West Germany, where units rotated for Armament Practice Camps; TA634 also flew in this guise from Ahlhorn and Schleswigland. From 26th June 1957 the TT.35 was back in the dark at 27 MU. On 10th September 1959 TA634 got to catch up with 3 CAACU at Exeter, where it took the code '53'. It worked hard, mostly tugging targets across the range at Manorbier in southwest Wales. With Gloster Meteor TT.20s taking over the role, a ceremonial final Mosquito flypast was staged at Exeter on 9th May 1963, with TA634 taking part. Eighteen days later the TT.35 was taken on charge by 23 MU at Aldergrove and the target towing gear was removed. TA634 was declared a non-operational airframe on 14th June and was available for disposal.

In Liverpool the aforementioned MSAE was campaigning to have a Mosquito displayed at Speke Airport. Member Don Stephens, author of the first two editions of *Wrecks & Relics*, lobbied local and national politicians. They caved in during 1965 and parted with £720 (£14,400 in present day values; average salary that year was around £800) went to the Ministry of Defence and TA634 was flown to Speke on 6th November. And there it stayed with no apparent will, or plan, for its future. All this changed in the early months of 1968 when a follow up to the successful film *633 Squadron*, released in 1964, was gearing up. Use of TA634, at the production company's cost and for a reported fee of £1,000, was agreed and on 31st May TA634 became G-AWJV, registered to the Lord Mayor, Aldermen and Citizens of the City of Liverpool at the Municipal Buildings in Dale Street. Returned to flying condition, the TT.35 was test flown by Neil Williams on 17th June and ferried to Bovingdon where the filming took place. Directed by Boris Sagal and starring David McCullum as the improbably named Quint Munroe, *Mosquito Squadron* employed three other 'Mossies': T.III RR299 and Mk.35s RS709 and RS712. Lots of footage was used from *633 Squadron* which explains why TA634 was painted as 'HJ896' and carried the codes 'HT-G', to blend in with the 'takes' from the previous film. Like many 'follow ons', *Mosquito Squadron* was not a patch on its predecessor. On 16th July 1968 returned to Speke, clocking up a total time of 742 hours, 50 minutes and, as it turned out, its last flight.

By then certainly the Lord Mayor and Aldermen and perhaps the Citizens of the City of Liverpool were beginning to wonder why they had a World War Two 'bomber' taking up valuable space in a hangar at the airport. The Mosquito Aircraft Museum was an obvious and deserving place for it and TA634 made the road journey to London Colney on 29th September 1970. The Mosquito was repainted in the colours of the aircraft flown by Gp Capt P C Pickard DSO** DFC of 487 Squadron RNZAF during Operation JERICHO against the Amiens prison on 18th February 1944. Pickard and his navigator, Flt Lt J A Broadly DSO DFC DFM failed to return in Mk.VI *F-for-Freddie*. After the opening of the display hangar in 1984 TA634 was subject to a comprehensive restoration and was completed in the colours of a Pathfinder Force Oakington-based Mk.XVI '8K-K' of early 1945.

Mosquito TT.35 TA634 in flight with two others, probably during its time in West Germany 1956-1957. *via Stuart Howe*

de Havilland Vampire FB.6 J-1008
1949 | Fighter-bomber | One 3,350lb st de Havilland Goblin 3 turbojet

Although Mosquito variants kept the DH design team at Salisbury Hall busy throughout the war, the next major project started in May 1942 – the DH.100 Spider Crab single-engined jet fighter. Thankfully, during the gestation of this superbly adaptable machine the name was changed to Vampire. Geoffrey de Havilland Jnr took the prototype for its maiden flight on 29th September 1943. Like the Mosquito, the Vampire became a massive success for DH, in single-seat fighter form and, later as a two-seat night-fighter and finally the T.11 trainer. Single-seaters are rare in British museums; DHAM boasts a fine example of a British-built export FB.6.

In 1948 the Swiss Air Force ordered its first jets, 75 Vampire FB.6s, which were delivered from Hatfield between 1949 and 1950. The country went on to licence build another 100, before moving on to a similar agreement for DH Venoms. The DHAM example was an early delivery and part of a large batch refurbished between 1960 and 1960; work included pressurising the cockpit and adding a Martin-Baker Mk.2 ejection seat. From the 1970s the Vampire fleet was wound down, and J-1008 was donated to the Mosquito Aircraft Museum, flying from Dubendorf to Hatfield on 20th August 1974. It was transferred to London Colney on 11th May 1975 and put through a restoration programme in 1994.

Swiss Air Force Vampire FB.6 J-1008 shortly after arrival at Hatfield, August 1974. *Stuart Howe*

de Havilland Sea Venom FAW.22 XG730
1957 | Naval all-weather fighter | One 5,300lb st de Havilland Ghost 105 turbojet

Originating in 1949 the Venom was a 'growth' development of the Vampire, using the much more powerful Ghost turbojet and a new, thinner wing with swept leading edge. It mirrored the career of the Vampire, the single-seat version being adopted widely by the RAF and export customers. A radar-equipped two-seater night/all-weather fighter was developed for the RAF and the Fleet Air Arm (FAA). The Sea Venom was the FAA's first all-weather jet fighter and by the late 1950s was helping to pioneer guided missiles into service. DHAM's Sea Venom was built at Hawarden, Chester, and was first flown from there on 1st August 1957. It was issued to 891 Squadron at Merryfield on 10th December but moved to nearby Yeovilton in October 1958. These were its shore-bases, but 891 carried out several cruises in HMS *Bulwark*. Yeovilton was to remain XG730's operating base through to its retirement. From 4th November 1959 it was with 894 Squadron, attached to HMS *Albion*, taking the codes '499' plus 'eyes' and a 'shark's mouth' – the markings it again wears today. On 25th January 1960 XG730 transferred to 893 Squadron, which embarked in HMS *Victorious*, as its last operational unit. The squadron stood down in February 1960, in readiness for converting to the DH Sea Vixen FAW.1. XG730 was dispatched to the Royal Navy Aircraft Yard at Sydenham for a modification programme. Final use came with the Yeovilton-based, Airwork-operated Air Direction Training Unit from November 1965.

The Sea Venom made its last flight, from Yeovilton to Lee-on-Solent, on 7th July 1970, bringing its total time to 1,163 hours, 40 minutes. There it was prepared to join a carrier for one last time by the resident Marine Aircraft Repair, Transport and Salvage Unit. XG730 was moved by road to Portsmouth and craned on board HMS *Hermes* for its decommissioning ceremony. (*Hermes* was converted to a helicopter carrier and then in 1981 it was given a ski-jump so that it could take BAe Sea Harriers. As it turned out, this was just in the nick of time; the following year the carrier had a pressing engagement in the South Atlantic!) Taken back off *Hermes*, XG730 was delivered to HMS *Dryad* at Southwick, for display. From there it was acquired by the Mosquito Aircraft Museum, arriving at London Colney on 28th October 1978.

Sea Venom FAW.22 XG730 at Salisbury Hall in the colours of 894 Squadron, complete with 'shark's mouth', that it wore 1959-1960. *Stuart Howe*

de Havilland Dove 8 G-AREA
1961 | Light transport | Two 400hp de Havilland Gipsy Queen 70 Mk.3 pistons

'One careful owner'... phrasing to beware of, it can't be true. So what about: 'One careful owner, the same one that designed and built it'. This is the story of *Echo-Alpha*, DHAM's Dove 8, one of the first aircraft a visitor to London Colney will see. With all-metal construction, tricycle undercarriage and a generous cabin size, DH got the Dove right from the beginning. The prototype first flew, from Hatfield, on 25th September 1945 and the last of 542 units came off the line in 1968. From 1951 all Doves were built at Hawarden, Chester. The type was recruited by the RAF and the Fleet Air Arm as the Devon and Sea Devon, respectively. A fair number of Doves are preserved in the UK, but *Echo-Alpha* has an impressive – if relatively compact – pedigree. Built at Hawarden in 1961, G-AREA was used initially as a demonstrator for the Mk.8, but soon settled down to work as an inter-factory shuttle and general communications runabout. For 35 years it plied all manner of personnel about the UK and into Europe, all the time based at Hatfield. *Echo-Alpha* was registered to de Havilland until July 1963 when that was changed to Hawker Siddeley and from 1977 it was a British Aerospace asset. Its Certificate of Airworthiness lapsed on 8th September 1987 and the Dove was stored at Hatfield, awaiting a suitable moment for it to go to London Colney. It was not until 2000 the *Echo-Alpha* moved to its new home.

de Havilland Comet 1A F-BGNX
1953 | Long range airliner | Four 5,500lb st de Havilland Ghost 50 Mk.4 turbojets

The fuselage of Comet 1XB F-BGNX has been restored to gleaming natural metal and the colours of Air France. The airframe is the largest surviving element of the first phase of the revolutionary jetliner's career. Starting with the mysterious loss of BOAC's G-ALYP near the isle of Elba, off the western Italian coast on 10th January 1954, the Comet was the centre of a massive and painstaking crash investigation process. At the end of this the design re-emerged as the Series 4 in 1958, but by then the long-range jetliner 'race' was opening up and its technological lead was a thing of the past. (See Chapter 15 the for the Comet 4.)

    F-BGNX was the first of three Comet 1As for national flag-carrier Air France and, by definition, it was the airline's first jet transport. First flown, at Hatfield, on 6th May 1953, *November-Xray* was delivered to Le Bourget, Paris, on 12th June. The Comets flew to Rome, Italy, Dakar in French West Africa (present-day Senegal) and Beirut, Lebanon. Time was taken off the schedules to attend the September 1953 Farnborough airshow as a static exhibit. Two days after BOAC's *Yoke-Peter* plummeted into the Ligurian Sea with the loss of all on board, Air France grounded its trio of Comets.

    As the investigation gained pace and the Royal Aircraft Establishment (RAE) at Farnborough became the centre for one of the most intense crash investigations in aviation history; Comets were being gathered to take part in all manner of tests. The Ministry of Supply approached Air France and acquired F-BGNX in April 1954, but it was not until 27th June 1956 that it was ferried to the RAE, with the British registration G-AOJT temporarily applied; DH chief test pilot John Cunningham was at the controls. In August the Comet was dismantled and the wings and fin were used for structural testing. By 1957 the fuselage had been cocooned, joining a number of Comet carcasses littering Farnborough. In the early 1970s F-BGNX was moved to the fire training compound and its future looked bleak. The cocooning process had been skilfully done and this not only helped to preserve an increasingly important artefact, but seemed to deter the fire crews from committing serious damage. Entreaties from the Mosquito Aircraft Museum were listened to and on 20th March 1985 the Comet fuselage arrived at London Colney, carefully negotiating the tight turns and narrow access roads to its new home. A restoration programme is busy returning F-BGNX to a polished and impressive state, to remind visitors of the cutting edge technology of the early 1950s. (See Chapter 15 for the story of a Comet that got away.)

Comet 1A F-BGNX was displayed statically at the September 1953 Farnborough airshow. *Peter Green Collection*

Hawker Siddeley HS.125 Series 1/521 G-ARYC
1963 | Corporate transport | Two 3,100lb st Bristol Siddeley Viper 521 turbojets

de Havilland was morphed into Hawker Siddeley in 1963 and the last aircraft to carry the famous name was a gamble that turned out to be Britain's most successful commercial jet with close on 1,600 built in a production life of half a century. This was the HS.125 executive jet which from 1993 became a Raytheon product assembled in the USA from British-built airframes; the last examples being completed in 2012. By then the design had grown in size and evolved from turbojet to turbofan power. In the early days, the new twin-jet was to be called the 'Jet Dragon', harking back to the DH Dragon and Dragon Rapide biplanes of the 1930s; thankfully its designation 'One-Two-Five' was far catchier for the 1960s.

The first examples were widely known as DH.125s and *Yankee-Charlie* was the first completed to the Series 1 production standard. The maiden flight took place at Hawarden on 12th February 1963. It was handed over to Bristol Siddeley Engines (BSE) at Filton on 24th July where it was used for trials and certification of the Viper 520, 521, 522 turbojet series. From the mid-1960s G-ARYC was engaged in shuttling personnel from Filton to Toulouse for the Concorde programme and its BSE/SNECMA Olympus 593s. By 1966, G-ARYC had adopted Rolls-Royce titles and logos. *Yankee-Charlie*'s last flight took place on 7th September 1973 at Filton, clocking up a total time of 4,565 hours, 35 minutes. In March 1976 the HS.125 was taken by road to Hatfield and stored, in readiness for presentation to the Mosquito Aircraft Museum, where it was delivered in 1979. The jet carries BSE titles on the port side and Rolls-Royce to starboard.

de Havilland Aircraft Museum aircraft

Type	Identity	Built	Origin	Acquired	Notes
Airspeed Horsa	–	c1944	Britain	1996	fuselage
Cierva C.24	G-ABLM	1931	Britain	Jul 1980	see profile
de Havilland Humming Bird	J7326	1924	Britain	25 Mar 2003	–
de Havilland Tiger Moth	G-ANRX	1939	Britain	1976	–
de Havilland Queen Bee	LF789	1943	Britain	13 Apr 1986	–
de Havilland Hornet Moth	G-ADOT	1935	Britain	1977	see profile
de Havilland Comet replica	–	1990	Britain	2001	–
de Havilland Dragon Rapide	G-AKDW	1945	Britain	1994	–
de Havilland Mosquito prototype	W4050	1940	Britain	Sep 1958	see profile
de Havilland Mosquito FB.VI	TA122	1945	Britain	26 Feb 1978	–
de Havilland Mosquito TT.35*	TA634	1945	Britain	Oct 1970	see profile
de Havilland Mosquito TT.35	TJ118	1945	Britain	1973	cockpit
de Havilland Vampire FB.5	VV217	1948	Britain	12 Aug 2009	–
de Havilland Vampire FB.6	J-1008	1949	Britain	11 May 1975	see profile
de Havilland Vampire NF.10	WM729	1952	Britain	22 Jun 1994	cockpit
de Havilland Vampire T.11	XJ772	1955	Britain	29 Mar 1994	see profile
de Havilland Venom FB.4	WR539	1956	Britain	Nov 1992	–
de Havilland Venom NF.3	WX853	1955	Britain	Jan 1968	–
de Havilland Sea Venom FAW.22	XG730	1957	Britain	28 Oct 1978	see profile
de Havilland Dove 8	G-AREA	1961	Britain	2000	see profile
de Havilland Comet 1A	G-ANAV	1952	Britain	2016	cockpit
de Havilland Comet 1A*	F-BGNX	1953	Britain	20 Mar 1985	see profile
de Havilland Comet 2	–	1953	Britain	14 Jun 1996	cockpit
de Havilland Comet C.2(R)	XK695	1956	Britain	17 Dec 1995	cockpit
de Havilland Sea Vixen FAW.2	XJ565	1960	Britain	31 Oct 1976	–
de Havilland Heron 2D	G-AOTI	1956	Britain	19 Aug 1995	–
de Havilland Canada Chipmunk T.10	WP790	1952	Britain	1976	–
Hawker Siddeley Trident 2	G-AVFH	1971	Britain	Jul 1982	forward fuselage
Hawker Siddeley HS.125 Srs 1*	G-ARYC	1963	Britain	Mar 1976	see profile
Hawker Siddeley HS.146-100	G-JEAO	1983	Britain	27 Jul 2009	fuselage

Notes: * – illustrated in the colour section.

CHAPTER 13
ISLE OF MAN

Island Salute
Manx Aviation and Military Museum

Isle of Man Airport
www.maps.org.im

Aircraft have a 'pull' all of their own, but one of the aims of this book is to highlight that there is far more to aviation than just wings or rotors. Across Britain's aeronautical museums can be found all sorts of items that extend our knowledge into other, fascinating aspects. A classic example of this can be found among the thousands of items at the Manx Aviation and Military Museum; these range from the Brazilian-built twin-turboprop airliner 'guarding' the buildings to a pair of brass Bofors anti-aircraft shell casings. At about 13:20 hours on Sunday 3rd September 1939 one of the guns of 41 Battery, Manx Regiment opened fire and someone had the presence of mind to collect the spent cases – why? At 11:15 that morning Prime Minister Neville Chamberlain had announced that a state of war existed with Germany: that Manx Regiment Bofors was the first gun of Britain's forces to have fired in World War Two.

The museum is run by the volunteers of the Manx Aviation Preservation Society (MAPS), which was formed in 1994. From day one, the society wanted to embrace not just civil and military aviation but the entire military history of the Island since the beginning of the 20th century. Opening to the public in November 2000, the Manx Aviation and Military Museum is located on the southwestern perimeter of Isle of Man Airport, close to the threshold of Runway 08; some of the buildings it occupies were used by the Fleet Air Arm as HMS *Urley* from the summer of 1944. The museum is dedicated "to the Manx men and women who served their Island in the cause of freedom; to those people of other nations who were brought to our shores by wartime service and to all those who, in war and peace, lost their lives in the Isle of Man in aviation accidents."

Above: Former Fleet Air Arm buildings are part of the museum site. *Courtesy Manx Aviation and Military Museum*

In 2005 the trustees of the Manx Regiment Old Comrades Association decided to loan their collection to MAPS and the Museum of the Manx Regiment relocated from Tromode, near Douglas. The Manx Regiment exhibition gives a detailed history of its wartime service of this Light Anti-Aircraft unit, with uniforms, weapons, equipment and photographs. Among the treasures is a very rare self-propelled Bofors gun and the whole collection makes up Britain's most comprehensive museum of a Light Anti-Aircraft Regiment – which is where we came in.

Swords into ploughshares

Activity at the busy Isle of Man Airport can be viewed from the museum and, inside, the exhibitions show that airliners were at the very beginning of what was then called Ronaldsway. Services to England and Ireland started in 1933. It was July 1940 when 1 Ground Defence Gunnery School settled in, having previously been at North Coates on the Lincolnshire coast. Trainee anti-aircraft gunners used a variety of machine guns and cine guns with moving targets provided by Hawker Harts, Westland Wallaces and Lysanders. The unit was renamed as 3 RAF Regiment School in June 1942; disbanding in February 1943.

Later that year construction teams had arrived to transform and expand the airfield and lay down 'hard' runways. It reopened as HMS *Urley*, a Fleet Air Arm station specialising in training in the art of torpedo attack. Mostly in use was the potent, but challenging, Fairey Barracuda, plus some of the ubiquitous Fairey Swordfish. The Navy pulled out in January 1946 and Ronaldsway settled back into the world of commercial aviation. On display outside is a 1979-built Embraer Bandeirante 20-seat twin turboprop in the colours of Manx Airlines. Headquartered at the airport, Manx Airlines flew a variety of types from 1982 to 2002. The Island's other military airfields, Andreas (1941 to 1946) and Jurby (1939 to 1963) and Ronaldsway's 1930s rival for commercial services, Hall Caine, near Ramsey, are also charted at the museum. The Island's aviation and military history is in good hands at Ronaldsway.

Manx Aviation and Military Museum aircraft

Type	Identity	Built	Origin	Acquired	Notes
Embraer Bandeirante P1	G-BGYT	1979	Brazil	2007	–
Bristol Bolingbroke IVT	9041	1941	Britain	21 Jun 2004	cockpit

When at Isle of Man Airport

Chances are that visitors will have arrived through the airport, if not take the time to visit the terminal to discover a typically Manx aeroplane – tail-less like the Island's famous cats! 'Flying' within the building since 2001 has been the one-off Manx Eider Duck; a single-seat pusher light aircraft. It was developed in the 1960s with the assistance of Jurby-based Peel Cars but never flew.

Commercial and military aviation subjects are covered at Ronaldsway. *Courtesy Manx Aviation and Military Museum*

'Flying' inside the terminal at Isle of Man Airport is the one-off Eider Duck. *Terry Dann*

CHAPTER 14
KENT

Place of Pilgrimage
National Battle of Britain Memorial

Capel le Ferne
www.battleofbritainmemorial.org

Sitting atop of the cliff, whimsically contemplating the English Channel and what lies beyond, the pilot figure at the memorial to 'The Few' at Capel le Ferne is deeply moving. It is made all the more so by walking away from him and taking a wider look at the site. He is perched in the middle of a gigantic three-bladed propeller cut into the grass in much the same way as the ancient chalk figures to be found on the South Downs and elsewhere. A walk along the Foxley-Norris Wall, with all the names of 'The Few' etched into it, evokes quiet thoughts about the summer of 1940 and the conflict that raged in the skies above and across Britain. The recently opened Wing visitor centre is superbly done, all the more so because it vividly explains the events nearly eight decades ago to younger generations who benefitted subliminally from the outcome of the airborne clash. There are two replicas of a Hurricane and Spitfire to remind visitors of the shape and size of the principal defenders but they are almost superfluous as the message is so powerfully brought across by the stonework.

Above: Harry Gray's exceptionally evocative pilot figure, looking out across the Channel at the Capel le Ferne. The base carries badges of the units that took part in the Battle of Britain. *Ken Ellis*

The memorial was unveiled on 9th July 1993. The Foxley-Norris Wall, named in honour of former Battle of Britain Hurricane pilot and the first president of the Battle of Britain Memorial Trust, ACM Sir Christopher Foxley-Norris GCB DSO OBE, was inaugurated in July 2005. The Wing, shaped like the Spitfire's elliptical planform, includes a special presentation called the 'Scramble Experience' and was inaugurated on 28th March 2015. Fully appreciating the significance of the statue and the wall, pedestrian access to those is free and need not involve a visit to the remainder of the site.

The website explains how that incredible statue carved by Harry Gray came about. The sculptor "found it difficult to come up with a design he was happy with. Then one day, during a break, Harry's trainee sat down and adopted a contemplative pose that provided [Harry] with the inspiration that had previously eluded him." The figure is clad in an Irvin jacket not just to protect him from the coastal aspect; it hides his uniform so that his rank and his nationality remain unknown. This is an important aim at Capel; the Foxley-Norris Wall *names* 'The Few' but does not reveal, nationality, rank or awards. The website also carries a story that I hope I'm forgiven for repeating, it sets the meaning of this place so well. In 1993 HM Queen Elizabeth the Queen Mother flew by helicopter to unveil the memorial. The pilot suggested that they turn back as conditions were poor. The Queen Mother is reported to have declined the offer, because: "My boys never turned back". No wonder Capel is dubbed a modern day place of pilgrimage.

Frontline Scramble
Kent Battle of Britain Museum

Hawkinge
www.kbobm.org

Driving to the west of Hawkinge village, it is difficult to imagine that an all-grass airfield with an illustrious past once existed among the endless houses. The A260 is called Spitfire Way, which provides a clue and as you turn west, you enter Aerodrome Road. This follows the northern perimeter of the airfield and to the south are roads that pay homage to the heritage of the area, including Woodcock Gardens – 17 Squadron based the single-seat Gloster biplane at Hawkinge in 1926 – and Defiant Close – 141 Squadron briefly detached some it is turret-fighters in June 1940. Further along Aerodrome Road is the Kent Battle of Britain Museum, which opened its doors in 1971 and uses the Operations Block and the Armoury; survivors of what was RAF Hawkinge.

From the summer of 1917 Hawkinge was a departure point for aircraft heading for France and the trenches and for machines coming back to 'Blighty'. By the following year it was acting as an Aircraft Acceptance Park. From 1920 it was a fighter station – a role it kept all the way through to the end of 1945. A sequence of types such as Sopwith Snipes, Hawker Furies, Gloster Gladiators gave way to Hawker Hurricanes in late 1939. From the evacuation of Dunkirk, late May 1940, Hawkinge was in the frontline and it was to host an unending array of detachments as it was used as a forward operating base; Hurricanes were the main type for the rest of 1940, Spitfires almost exclusively using the airfield up to 1945. From 12th August to 7th September 1940 the Luftwaffe bombed Hawkinge six times – twice on 15th August. Early raids caused much damage and peppered the flying field, but it remained in use with fighters threading their way through the craters. The last RAF Spitfires – Mk.IXs of 122 Squadron and the Mk.21s of 1 Squadron – departed in October 1945. The RAF maintained a presence at Hawkinge, including gliders, until January 1962 and the disposal process began in 1966. In the summer of 1968 the sound of Merlin engines returned, the airfield was ideal as a set for the filming of the 1969 released *Battle of Britain*.

Hurricane Is of 501 Squadron scramble from Hawkinge, August 15, 1940. *501 Squadron Association via Andy Thomas*

With the Hawkinge wartime operations block in the right background, a trio of Hurricane replicas in the colours of 32 Squadron. In the background, the inevitable march of housing. *Courtesy Kent Battle of Britain Museum*

The Hawkinge Aeronautical Trust was established and from 1971 a small parcel of land on the northwest perimeter, including two wartime buildings was developed as the Kent Battle of Britain Museum. The museum has expanded to six buildings. This is an array of airframes, mostly full-size replicas of Hurricanes and Spitfires, several of which were veterans of the *Battle of Britain* film. With respect to these, the real gems at Hawkinge are hundreds of items culled from 'digs' of wartime crash sites in the 1960s and 1970s. The Armoury appropriately holds a collection of land-based and airborne weaponry together with what is claimed to be the most complete collection of 1940 uniforms, flying equipment and insignia; both RAF and Luftwaffe. There is also a 'Wall of Honour' upon which are over 600 autographs of Battle of Britain pilots and aircrew, famous and far less so.

Kent Battle of Britain Museum aircraft

Type	Identity	Built	Origin	Acquired	Notes
Boulton Paul Defiant I	'L7005'	2002	Britain	28 May 2015	replica
de Havilland Moth	'G-AAAH'	1981	Britain	2003	replica
de Havilland Tiger Moth	'N9181'	1940	Britain	2005	–
DFS Grunau Baby	'D-3-340'	1938	Germany	1989	glider
Fieseler Fi 103 V-1	–	1964	Germany	1987	replica flying-bomb
Fokker Dr.I	'425/17'	1978	Germany	1994	replica, plus another
Gotha G.IV	–	2004	Germany	2012	replica forward fuselage
Hawker Hurricane I	'N2532'	1999	Britain	1971	replica, plus several others
Messerschmitt 'Bf 109'	'14'	1968	Germany	1971	replica, plus two others
North American Harvard T.2B	FX442	1944	USA	1999	–
Supermarine Spitfire prototype	'K5054'	1984	Britain	2010	replica, plus another
Supermarine Spitfire I	'N3289'	1968	Britain	1971	replica, plus several others

LAWM's superb Riechenberg on the apron at Headcorn in August 2013 after its restoration in Germany. Behind is Nord Pingouin G-ETME (a Messerschmitt Bf 108 Taifun development) in Luftwaffe colours as Yellow 14. *Richard Foord – LAWM*

They Raced the Eagles
Lashenden Air Warfare Museum

Headcorn
www.lashendenairwarfaremuseum.co.uk

"They raced the eagles, mounting high above the unforgiven lands. They wrote their names across the sky with fiery hearts and burning hands," so reads the memorial plaque at the Lashenden Air Warfare Museum. The stirring words serve as tribute to the combat units that flew briefly from what was a rudimentary Advanced Landing Ground (ALG) known as Lashenden: Canadian 403 and 421 Squadrons and the American 354th Fighter Group. As an ALG its life was expected to be a frenzy of fighter operations for a short while followed by sweet silence and a return to agriculture as the aircraft hopped into liberated France to finish the job. While all that might have been temporary, the aerodrome that grew up on the site from the 1950s is a lovely venue. Headcorn thrives with flying schools – both fixed wing and rotary, a parachute centre, special events and concerts are staged; it's even possible to take a ride in a Supermarine Spitfire. The atmosphere is very welcoming, none more so than the long-founded Lashenden Air Warfare Museum (LAWM).

At this point it's as well to point out that there was an ALG called Headcorn, five miles *northeast* of the township of the same name that reverted to farmland in 1945. The Lashenden ALG, two miles *southeast* of Headcorn town, has for decades wisely adopted the name Headcorn. Light aircraft were using the area that became the Lashenden ALG by 1927. The Spitfires of 421 Squadron Royal Canadian Air Force touched down on 6th August 1943 and the following day they were joined by 403 Squadron. Operations from Lashenden lasted only until the 20th when both units took the short 'hop' eastwards to Headcorn. The ALG was then prepared for the arrival of the North American P-51B Mustangs of the Ninth Air Force's 354th Fighter Group, comprising the 353rd, 355th and 356th Squadrons. The Americans roamed far and wide, on occasion as far as the Polish border, conducting bomber escort and ground attack missions. On 18th June 1944, the 354th departed Lashenden for France and the immediate area fell quiet. In the 1950s Lashenden was revived, as Headcorn aerodrome, and has never looked back since.

Experience tells

Heading for its fifth decade, LAWM has its origins in material collected by members of the Maidstone branch of the Royal Air Forces Association in the late 1960s. Thanks to the generosity of the aerodrome owner, the volunteers were offered a building in early 1970 and that Easter LAWM was opened. The first airframe acquired was the piloted V-1 flying bomb, the Fieseler Fi 103R-IV – profiled below. Much of the museum content is based on crash site recoveries – 'digs' – and the scope and level of presentation is exceptional. Two examples will have to suffice. On 6th September 1940 Sgt S Karubin of the Polish 303 Squadron operating from Northolt was piloting Hurricane I V7290 and he engaged a Heinkel He 111. Return fire from the Luftwaffe bomber downed *C-for-Charlie* and it crashed at Pembury, Kent. Karubin took to the silk and was slightly injured. Three months later, on 15th November, Feldwebel Otto Jaroš of the 3rd Staffel of Jadgeschwader 26, based at Audembert, France, was flying Messerschmitt Bf 109E-1 6353 *Yellow 9*. Just after lunch, he encountered Sgt E Wright in a Hawker Hurricane of 605 Squadron and the RAF pilot got the better of him. Jaroš baled out and started five years in captivity; *Yellow 9* impacted at Hordon on the Hill in Essex. In each case, LAWM uses the components help to tell the story along with a narrative about the parts, their place in the aircraft and their purpose.

A German U-boat towing a Fa 330 rotary winged observation platform aloft. LAWM has an example brought to Farnborough in 1945. *KEC*

In March 1994 the museum acquired Focke Achgelis Fa 330A-1 100549 from the Merseyside Aviation Society – see Chapter 18. With this under its belt, LAWM became the only non-national museum to display two genuine World War Two German aircraft. Introduced into service in 1942 the Fa 330 Bachstelze (Water Wagtail) was a means of dramatically extending the 'reach' of U-boats. A single-seat gyrokite, it was towed behind a submarine allowing its pilot to see for many miles around. All Fa 330s, believed to be about 200, were built by Weser Flugzeubau at Hoykenkamp, Bremen. Designed to be packed into a small, water-tight container and therefore compact and easily moved around it is no wonder that 25 Fa 330s survive; LAWM's example being one of the five in Britain. The museum has expanded its displays ever since its inception and, due to have opened by the time these words appear, is a brand new display hall which will dramatically increase the amount of material that can be exhibited, with the Reichenberg as the centrepiece. LAWM is part and parcel of what makes Headcorn such a lovely and vibrant aerodrome.

Fieseler Fi 103R-IV 'Reichenberg'
1944 | Piloted flying-bomb | One 6600lb st Argus As 014 pulse-jet

An ever more desperate Germany was considering ways to hit high-value targets with precision in an attempt to stave off the invasion of Europe and slow down the inevitable. The V-1 flying-bomb and later the V-2 ballistic missile were formidable weapons, but could only be aimed at 'generalised' targets – towns or industrial areas. Minds turned to the notion that what was needed was a pilot who would *stay* with his aircraft, thereby making sure of a direct hit. Under project Reichenberg V-1 'doodlebugs' were to be turned into pilot-guided weapons. Design work was carried out by Deutsche Forschungsanstalt für Segelflug (DFS) and the modification of standard V-1s for testing purposes was carried out by Henschel. There were four versions: Fi 103R-I single-seat-glider for aerodynamic testing; 'R-II two-seat glider trainer; 'R-III single-seater with Argus pulse-jet: all of these had skid landing gear and flaps. The Fi 103R-IV was the operational version and had no flaps, no skid and a nose containing a 1,874lb warhead with a plywood nose cone.

The first trial launches were undertaken from Heinkel He 111H 'motherships' in the summer of 1944, flying out of Lärz. The first two examples crashed, killing the pilots. Test flying was thereafter carried out by Flugkapitän Hanna Reitsch and Hauptmann Heinz Kensche (who was killed during the testing, on 5th March 1945). Two factories manufactured Reichenbergs, at Dannenberg and Pulverhof, both using slave labour. The Japanese, of course, went on to deploy this form of warfare, the Kamikazes. For the Germans, the name given to any such airmen was Selbstopfermänner (selfless ones) but thankfully this hideous weapon was never used in anger. Approximately 175 were produced before the project was abandoned in the spring of 1945. *Diver! Diver! Diver!* by Brian Cull and Bruce Lander (Grub Street 2008) records that zealot Hanna Reitsch was furious at the ditching of the project. She blamed the failure of: "higher authority to appreciate that the

Suicide Group was no stunt, but a collection of brave, clear-headed and intelligent Germans who seriously believed after careful thought and calculation that by sacrificing their own lives they might save many times that number of their fellow countrymen and ensure some kind of future for their children."

The museum's Fi 103R-IV was captured at Dannenburg in the American zone and was brought to Britain in 1945. It was displayed at the German Aircraft Exhibition at the Royal Aircraft Establishment at Farnborough from 29th October to 9th November 1945. It passed through a number of Army bomb disposal units, including Horsham until discovered near Rochester by the museum in 1970 stored outside in a very poor condition. The bottom of the cockpit had corroded through, the rear fuselage was broken and it was due to be scrapped. Far too good for such a fate, it was acquired and moved to Headcorn. Temporary repairs and a cosmetic paint job were carried out to buy time until the funds and expertise were available for a proper restoration. In November 2007 the 'R-IV was taken to Geisenhausen, near Munich, where Axel Kuncze and his team at Auktionshaus fur Historic Technik carried out a five-year restoration. Work included replacing the non-original nose cone and wing spar, skinning the rear fuselage, recovering the wings with the correct grade ply and fitting out the cockpit. All of this work returned the Reichenberg to how it was when displayed at Farnborough in 1945. This impressive exhibit came back to Lashenden on 4th March 2013. Since then it awaited the moment when it could become the central exhibit in the new display building; this was achieved on 2nd July 2017.

Lashenden Air Warfare Museum aircraft

Type	Identity	Built	Origin	Acquired	Notes
English Electric Lightning F.53	ZF587	1968	Britain	17 May 2001	cockpit
Focke Achgelis Fa 330A-1	1000549	1944	Germany	22 Mar 1994	–
Fieseler Fi 103R-IV Reichenberg	6/2080	1944	Germany	1970	see profile

Kent's Flagship
RAF Manston History Museum

Manston
www.rafmanston.co.uk

Once a major aviation centre with huge potential, Kent Airport, widely known as Manston, ground to a halt on 15th May 2014. It was two years away from celebrating its centenary. Attempts to kick start operations since appear to have petered out, so now it seems as though only its exceptional heritage remains. Two museums are to be found on the former airport, both within sight of one another. But it is not a case of hissing and booing from across the road; they complement each other perfectly. Both the Spitfire and Hurricane Memorial Museum (below) and the RAF Manston History Museum, do what it says on the tin!

One of the exhibition halls at the RAF Manston History Museum. Huntair Pathfinder microlight in the foreground, Canberra B.15 and Victor K.2 cockpits at the rear. *Ken Ellis*

Opened in 1997, the RAF Manston History Museum is run by the volunteers of the RAF Manston History Society and is centred upon a former Motor Transport building. The bulk of the displays are centred on the airfield's amazing military history but from the late 1950s commercial activity expanded at Manston, including scheduled services and the airport was at the forefront of what was then called 'Inclusive Tours' charters to European sunspots. To the praise of the Manston team, the displays go beyond the specific and appeal to visitors with wider tastes; extensive support displays are very absorbing and the wartime street re-creation is exceptional.

The Royal Naval Air Service used the field from 1916 as a landing ground for anti-Zeppelin patrollers. Westgate Bay was used for floatplane operations. The Great War airfield was in the area where the former passenger terminal is located. The airfield was extended and improved and training became the main occupation. From the very day the RAF was created, 1st April 1918, Manston dropped its naval links and became a Training Depot Station with Avro 504s and Airco DH.4s among others. In April 1944 the look of the airfield had been transformed after massive engineering work. Manston's proximity to the Continent put it in the frontline, but also was in an ideal position to accept damaged aircraft limping back from 'ops'. The east-west runway was widened and extended – to become the longest in southern England at the time – grass over-runs provided, the FIDO fog-dispersing system installed and parking space radically increased. Manston had become a master diversion airfield, a role it kept up until the RAF pulled out in 1999. The Americans moved in during the summer of 1950, mainly with fighter-bombers, leaving eight years later. A bewildering array of units and types has been based throughout the airfield's long history and an appreciable chunk of this book would be needed to do it real justice. The many airfields of Kent all have their story to tell but Manston is the county's flagship and the team at the RAF Manston History Museum have created a vibrant and comprehensive tribute.

Gloster Meteor TT.20 WD646
1951 | Target tug | Two 3,700lb st Rolls-Royce Derwent 8 turbojets

The only Allied jet to see operational service in World War Two, the Gloster Meteor evolved from single-seat interceptor into a two-seat advanced trainer and night-fighter. Design and manufacture of the night-fighter series was handed over to Armstrong Whitworth (AW), a fellow member of the Hawker Siddeley Group since 1935. Based upon the T.7 trainer, but with long span wings and an elongated nose for the radar the first version was the NF.11, the prototype flying in November 1950 and the type entered RAF service in the summer of 1950. A tropicalised version, the NF.13, flew in December 1952. The NF.12 featured US-built radar and first appeared in April 1953; the final variant, the clear-canopied NF.14 following six months later. AW devised a target-towing version of the NF.11 in the late 1950s, to replace DH Mosquito TT.35s – see Chapter 12. The principal modification was a pylon on the upper starboard centre section which carried a podded ML wind-driven winch. Only one 'straight' NF.11 survives intact (at Weybourne, Norfolk – Chapter 20) plus a trio of cockpits; the Manston example has ben returned to NF.11 guise, serving with a Kent-based squadron.

Meteor NF.11 WD646 first flew at Bitteswell on 12th October 1951 and was delivered to the Central Signals Establishment at Watton on 15th November. Here it was used for radar trials until it was retired to 5 Maintenance Unit (MU) at Kemble on 22nd December 1958. It was allocated to the TT.20 conversion line and was transformed by AW at Bitteswell between April and November 1961 when it was taken on charge by 33 MU at Lyneham. It was issued to 3 Civilian Anti-Aircraft Co-operation Unit (CAACU) at Exeter on 24th January 1962 and coded 'R'. Final service started on 6th October 1970 when WD646 joined 5 CAACU at Woodvale. It was retired, for the second time, on 10th December 1971, going to 1 School of Technical Training at Cosford with the instructional airframe number 8189M. It was not used as a teaching aid and by 1973 had moved to the care of 2030 Squadron Air Training Corps at Sheldon, Birmingham, and it was to stay nearly two decades. By 1993 the TT.20 had been acquired by 39 Restoration Group at North Weald but the group was wound up in late 1997. It was acquired by the Manston example and trucked to its new home on 15th November 1997. It has been painted to represent NF.11 WD615 which served 85 Squadron as 'A' from nearby West Malling from September 1951 to April 1954.

Lockheed T-33AN Silver Star Mk.3 21231
1954 | Advanced trainer | One 5,100lb st Rolls-Royce Nene 10 turbojet

Derived from the Lockheed P-80 Shooting Star, America's first truly operational jet fighter, the trainer version 'T-Bird' gained as great a fame as its forebear and a vastly longer service life. There are ten T-33s in British museums, all but the Manston example Lockheed-built, powered by Allison J33s, and served with the French Air Force up to the mid-1970s. One deserves a profile, and the choice of this Canadian, Rolls-Royce-propelled example was not just a case of singularity. French T-33As certainly visited the UK during their service, but lack any real tie-in other than being a shapely, early jet. The Royal Canadian Air Force (RCAF) based Silver Stars with its fighter units in France (1952 to 1967) and West Germany (1955 to 1993) and the type frequently visited the UK. Canada started operating Silver Stars from January 1953, retiring the last example, by which time they were designated CT-133s, in March 2002. With Rolls-Royce Nenes the Silver Stars had a strong British 'flavour', the Manston example is kept indoors and has been painted to represent a USAF 'T-Bird' that was based at the airfield. This all serves to knock the French examples into a cocked hat!

The Manston example was built by Canadair at Cartierville, Montreal, Quebec, and was taken on charge by the RCAF as 21231 on 26th March 1954. Lockheed designated the Nene-engined version the T-33AN; licencee Canadair called them Type CL-30 and built 237 examples for the RCAF. T-33AN 21231 was struck off charge on 23rd February 1967. There is nearly

Manston's Silver Star wears the colours of a T-33A of the 512th Fighter Bomber Squadron, based at the airfield 1952 to 1954. A Rolls-Royce Derwent is displayed alongside it. *Ken Ellis*

a 20-year gap before the 'T-Bird' surfaces again, this time on the US civil register as N10018 in California in 1986. The jet went through several keepers and registrations: N134AT in California from early 1987; N333DV in 1992 and N36TH with owners in Texas, Michigan and back to California up to 1999. As N36TH the T-33AN touched down at North Weald on 29th July 1999 wearing the colour scheme of the USAF aerobatic demonstration team, the 'Thunderbirds'. Registered in the UK as G-BYOY on 8th June 2000, the Silver Star appears not to have been flown since its transatlantic ferry flight. This was the museum's second acquisition sourced from North Weald; the Silver Star crossed the Thames at Dartford by road and headed for its new home on 3rd February 2010. It has been painted in the colours of a 'T-Bird' general duties runabout for the 512th Fighter Bomber Squadron of the 406th Fighter Bomber Wing. The 512th flew Republic F-84 Thunderjets and then North American F-86 Sabres from Manston from July 1952 to November 1954 when it moved to Soesterberg in the Netherlands.

RAF Manston History Museum aircraft

Type	Identity	Built	Origin	Acquired	Notes
de Havilland Canada Chipmunk T.10	WP772	1952	Canada	1999	–
English Electric Canberra B.15	WT205	1955	Britain	14 Oct 2000	cockpit
English Electric Lightning F.6	XR770	1965	Britain	3 Mar 2015	–
Fieseler Fi 103 V-1	–	2004	Germany	2004	replica flying-bomb
Gloster Meteor TT.20*	WD646	1951	Britain	15 Nov 1997	see profile
Handley Page Victor K.2	XL190	1961	Britain	6 Feb 1999	cockpit
Hawker Hunter F.6A	XG226	1956	Britain	2003	cockpit
Hawker Siddeley Buccaneer S.2B	XV352	1967	Britain	1999	cockpit
Huntair Pathfinder	–	c1982	Britain	2003	–
Lockheed T-33A/N Silver Star Mk.3	21231	1954	USA	3 Feb 2010	see profile
Nieuport 17	–	2004	France	2005	replica, plus another
Panavia Tornado GR.1	ZA325	1980	GB/Ger/Italy	2010	cockpit
PZL Iskra TS-11	G-BXVZ	1977	Poland	Aug 2013	–
SEPECAT Jaguar GR.3A	XZ106	1976	GB/France	21 Nov 2008	–
Short 330-100	G-SSWP	1979	Britain	Aug 2004	cockpit
Slingsby Cadet TX.3	XA312	1953	Britain	1999	glider
Slingsby Grasshopper TX.1	XA231	1953	Britain	1999	glider
Sopwith 1½ Strutter	–	2004	Britain	2005	replica
Westland Whirlwind HAS.7	XN380	1960	USA/GB	13 Oct 2001	–
Westland Wessex HU.5*	XS482	1963	USA/GB	2000	–

Notes: * – illustrated in the colour section.

MAPS project leader Lewis E Deal (at podium) during the unveiling of Hurricane II 'BN230' at Rochester, 22nd April 1988. *KEC*

Icons
Spitfire and Hurricane Memorial Museum

Manston
www.spitfiremuseum.org.uk

Between 1939 and 1945 a dozen Hawker Hurricane squadrons were based at Manston, mostly for relatively brief detachments. As for Supermarine Spitfires, they eclipsed the Hurricanes with a total of 28 individual units; several of these taking up residency more than once. This data is more than enough, perhaps, to have started this unique museum devoted to both of these iconic fighters. But the main driving force that created the Spitfire and Hurricane Memorial Museum was that in 1955 the newly appointed Officer Commanding RAF Manston, Gp Capt W G Oldbury DFC, wanted a Spitfire as a 'gate guardian'. The nature of Manston is such that public roads run close to, and even through, the sprawling base and Spitfire XVI TB752 became a well-known and much-loved landmark. So much so, that when it was threatened with removal and reduction to spares in 1970 the people of Ramsgate and of Thanet district kicked up such a fuss that is was allowed to stay on duty. The clamour even got as far as mention in the House of Commons. This highlighted the need to protect the long term of this historic aircraft that was permanently kept outside. In 1978 the newly established Medway Aircraft Preservation Society (MAPS) found itself without its debut project and TB752 required a repaint and probably much more. This co-incidence of need led directly to the inauguration of the Spitfire Memorial Building.

The legacy of this amazing museum is inextricably linked with MAPS and this chapter happily goes 'off message' to include what is essentially a workshop. Both Hurricane LF751 and Spitfire TB752 are profiled below and their stories inter-weave with the background to the museum. The restoration of a Ministry of Defence (MoD) aircraft by a volunteer organisation was ground-breaking in its day. The Medway Branch of the Royal Aeronautical Society established MAPS in the autumn of 1977 as a self-contained group of volunteers who were prepared to tackle the restoration of a Short Sandringham flying-boat. (Take a look at Chapter 11 for a possible candidate.) This ambitious project did not come about and, as explained above, the restoration of Spitfire TB752 was substituted. This was fortuitous as the workshop that MAPS was able to secure – and still occupies – was in the former Motor Transport Repair Bay at Rochester aerodrome. This measures 48ft by 16ft – not four-engined flying-boat friendly!

Meetings to discuss the restoration of TB752 began in April 1978 and the then Officer Commanding RAF Manston, Wg Cdr Colin Campbell, his team and representatives of the MoD smoothed the way. The restoration was so thorough that it was clear that the Spitfire needed to go into the protective confines of a building, but that would negate its 'gate guardian' role.

The scheme to put TB752 inside an 'all glass' structure' was born and this led to the Spitfire Memorial Building on 13th June 1981. Safe inside and supported by all manner of supporting displays, the Spitfire was flanked by two external 'guardians', English Electric Canberra PR.3 WE168 and Gloster Javelin FAW.9 XH764. (To illustrate the frailty of display airframes, both the Canberra and the Javelin were offered up for tender in November 1989 and were carted away by an Essex-based scrap dealer. The interior fittings of the cockpit of the Canberra are part of the Norfolk and Suffolk Aviation Museum – see Chapter 26.)

The experience gained by the MAPS team from TB752 led to a 'commission' to restore former gate guardian Hurricane II LF738 for the RAF Museum. This brought about the arrival of LF751 and a two-pronged project that would also provide a Hurricane to keep the Spitfire company. The exceptional restoration of LF751 was unveiled at Rochester on 22nd April 1988. It was installed in the expanded building the following September and on 7th October the Spitfire and Hurricane Memorial Museum was inaugurated. Restoring TB752 for the MoD was a unique event; the opening of a privately-funded building to contain a 'gate guardian' was without precedent and now a volunteer run museum was on site. (The museum is administered by the RAF Manston Spitfire and Hurricane Memorial Trust.) In 1993 the third 'arm' of the museum was opened up; the Merlin Café. From the very beginning this emporium developed a loyalty with visitors, volunteers and airfield staff; it makes visiting the Manston museums a day-long experience and contributes to the upkeep of the Spitfire, Hurricane and the displays.

Medway's incredible workshop

As mentioned in several places within this book, the 1960s and 1970s saw the birth of organisations with names ending in 'Aircraft Preservation Society'. Today, only five are active. (Others, like the Northern Aircraft Preservation Society took on a new name; in that case The Aeroplane Collection – see Chapter 18.) The Britten-Norman Aircraft Preservation Society is restoring the oldest surviving BN-2 Islander, G-AVCN, at its birthplace at Bembridge, Isle of Wight. The Lincolnshire Aircraft Preservation Society has existed in two iterations; in the 1960s as a predecessor to the Lincolnshire Aviation Museum and presently acting in support of the Lincolnshire Aviation Heritage Centre at East Kirkby amending its name by substituting the word *Aviation*. (See Chapter 16 under *Pathfinders* and *Lancaster Base* respectively.) The Fenland and West Norfolk Aircraft Preservation Society runs the museum at West Walton Highway, Norfolk, and is covered in Chapter 20. Founded in 1973 and unique in adopting 'APS' as a *prefix* not a suffix, the Aircraft Preservation Society of Scotland bases itself at East Fortune with the National Museum of Flight Scotland and in 2000 slightly rebranded itself as the *Aviation* Preservation Society of Scotland.

It was amid the 'APS era' that the Medway Aircraft Preservation Society was born in 1977, becoming an all-volunteer not-for-profit company limited by guarantee in 1988. As will be seen in the 'Also in Kent' section at the end of this chapter, the Rochester workshop is open to visitors, but in truth it falls out of the terms of reference given at the beginning of this book. That said, to not cover the work of this skilled and innovative organisation would be a crime. The work speaks for itself, but if more persuasion were needed in October 2010 MAPS received the Queen's Award for Voluntary Service. As part of this, that year, HRH the Duchess of Cornwall visited the workshop to view progress on the Boulton Paul Defiant. As a result, she became an honorary member of 'The MAPS chaps' and in December 2011 agreed to be their patron.

Two of the projects have been to airworthy status; the most demanding being Spitfire PR.XI PL965 (G-MKXI) for Chris Horsley which consumed an estimated 45,000 man hours. Mark Hanna, of the Old Flying Machine Company, carried out the first test flight on 23rd December 1992. Today, the Mk.XI is part of Peter Teichman's Hangar 11 Collection at North Weald. Of all of the Spitfires restored at Rochester the oldest surviving Mk.I, K9942, displayed at the RAF Museum Cosford has by far the greatest provenance. This machine entered service with 72 Squadron on 24th April 1939, serving until 5th June 1940; it has been restored to its status during that time. Among the pilots that flew K9942 was Fg Off James Brindley Nicolson, who carried out 14 operational sorties in it between 15th November 1939 and 23rd March 1940. While serving with 249 Squadron, Nicolson became Fighter Command's only Victoria Cross holder after he was involved in an engagement with a Junkers Ju 88 and Messerschmitt Bf 110s on 16th November 1940. The workshop has undertaken static restoration of engines, including several Rolls-Royce Merlins, Bristol Hercules XII, Daimler Benz DB 603 and a Junkers Jumo 003 turbojet and well as a long list of sub-assemblies.

The current MAPS project, Scion II G-AEZF at Heston in April 1947 while in service with Gatwick-based Air Couriers. It will be completed in its original floatplane guise. *KEC*

The current project is hopefully destined for local display as it is a Rochester-built aircraft. The Short Scion was a six-seat general purpose aircraft, which could be operated on conventional wheeled undercarriage or on twin floats. The prototype first flew at Gravesend on 18th August 1933 and Short manufactured a total of 16 at Rochester before handing over production rights to Pobjoy Air Motors and Aircraft, also at Rochester. The MAPS example, G-AEZF, was the last of six Pobjoy examples, powered by a pair of that company's revolutionary Niagara radials. Completed as a floatplane, its maiden flight was from the waters of the River Medway on 9th December 1937. Converted to a landplane in 1941, it was out of use by mid-1954. Its survival since has been truly remarkable but when it arrived at Rochester in 2013 it is best described as an engineless 'basket case'. The wizards at MAPS have made incredible progress with the Scion and it is being restored to floatplane status and will be a tangible link with Rochester's long association with the Short dynasty and marine aircraft especially. This ambitious project has been made possible by a substantial grant from the Rochester Bridge Trust recognising the importance of aircraft restoration and the aviation heritage of Medway and its river.

Medway Aircraft Preservation Society restoration projects

Aircraft	Built	Received	Dispatched	Location / status
Supermarine Spitfire XVI TB752	1945	7 Jul 1978	13 Jun 1981	Manston – see profile
Gloster Meteor F.8 WK914	1952	1980	Oct 1983	Malta Air Museum, Takali, Malta
Republic F-84F Thunderstreak FU-6	1952	Oct 1983	28 Mar 1990	RAF Museum Cosford, stored
Hawker Hurricane II LF738	1944	8 Feb 1984	28 Jun 1995	RAF Museum Cosford
Hurricane II LF751	1944	20 Mar 1985	22 Apr 1988	Manston – see profile
Supermarine Spitfire XI PL965	1944	1987	23 Dec 1992	Airworthy as G-MKXI, North Weald
Piper Tri-Pacer 150 G-APXU	1952	Jul 1991	8 Oct 1996	Airworthy with Stamford owner
Northrop Shelduck D.1 'XT005'	c1965	1992	2016	MAPS, stored
Short Sherpa G-14-1	1953	10 Mar 1993	3 May 2006	Ulster Aviation Collection, Long Kesh, Northern Ireland. Fuselage. Profiled in *Great Aviation Collections of Britain*
Supermarine Spitfire V BL614	1942	Mar 1995	20 Oct 1997	RAF Museum Hendon
Fairchild Argus II 'FS628'	1943	21 Oct 1997	5 Jun 1999	RAF Museum Cosford
Supermarine Spitfire I K9942	1939	19 May 1998	31 Oct 2000	RAF Museum Cosford
Bristol Sycamore HR.12 WV783	1950	2002	Sep 2003	RAF Museum Hendon
North American Harvard II FE788	1941	2003	30 Aug 2005	Airworthy as G-CTKL, Biggin Hill
Douglas Dakota 3 KG437	1944	Apr 2003	19 Jan 2006	RAF Museum Hendon, cockpit
Fairey Battle I L5343	1939	Jan 2006	19 Oct 2008	RAF Museum Hendon
Boulton Paul Defiant I N1671	1938	24 Apr 2009	6 Dec 2012	RAF Museum Cosford
GEC-Marconi Phoenix ZJ303	c1995	Jul 2012	2014	BAE Systems, Rochester, display
Short Scion II G-AEZF	1937	13 Jun 2013	–	Current project

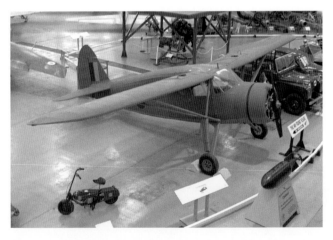

Fairchild Argus II 'FS628', another MAPS success, on show at the RAF Museum Cosford.
Ken Ellis

Hawker Hurricane II 'BN230' (LF751)
1944 | Day fighter | One 1,280hp Rolls-Royce Merlin XX piston

Both of the Hurricane and Spitfire that give their name to the museum are on loan from the RAF Museum and are examples of the exceptional work of the Medway Aircraft Preservation Society (MAPS). Assembled and flight tested at Langley, LF751 was issued to 22 Maintenance Unit at Silloth on 19th March 1944 for pre-service preparation. Twenty days later it was taken on charge at Long Marston with 1681 Bomber Defence Training Flight (BDTF), as part of the replacement of the flight's four Curtiss Tomahawks. The BDTF was a 'touring' unit, working with neighbouring bomber operational training units (OTU) by 'bouncing' their 'victim', allowing the gunners to respond and bring their guns to bear on the 'enemy'. This was far more choreographed than might at first seem, but it was not without risk. The BDTF disbanded on 21st August 1944 and three days later LF751 was re-employed in the same sort of work with 24 OTU at Honeybourne. Coded 'UF-V', the Hurricane was part of the OTU's 'C' Flight which provided adversary training for gunners in Wellington IIIs. Three days before 24 OTU disbanded, on 21st July 1945, LF751 was downgraded to instructional airframe status, with the airframe number 5466M. LF751's whereabouts in the late 1940s cannot be confirmed, but by 1952 it was at Waterbeach. There it was slowly being denuded of parts, along with former 43 Squadron and Royal Aircraft Establishment test-bed Mk.II Z3687 and Mk.II PG539, which had previously served with 30 OTU. (Having been used for laminar flow aerofoil trials on behalf of Armstrong Whitworth's flying-wing programme, from 1944 to at least 1946, Z3687 was wingless.) The Hurricanes were donors for Mk.II LF363 which was on charge with the Waterbeach Station Flight and flown on special occasions. Much in need of a major overhaul, LF363 was ferried to Langley on 30th September 1955 where Hawker had agreed to undertake a rebuild. Going in the same direction was the 'bundle' of Hurricane airframes. At Langley, not only did a newly invigorated LF363 return to the skies, but a composite static Mk.II, with the identity LF751, was created for 'gate guardian' duties back at Waterbeach. (LF363 went on to become a founder member of the Historic Aircraft Flight at Biggin Hill in 1957; which the following year was renamed the Battle of Britain Flight.)

Waterbeach was reduced to satellite airfield status in August 1963 and the Hurricane's duty there was complete. It was moved to the 18th century Bentley Priory, near Stanmore, again as a display airframe. Famed as the World War During 1968 the Hurricane was used for in a non-flying capacity for the film *Battle of Britain* at both Henlow and the studios at Pinewood. Returned to 'The Priory', by the mid-1970s LF751 was camouflaged and painted with the codes 'FB-B', as used by 'A' Flight of 24 OTU. MAPS took delivery of former 'guardian' of the Biggin Hill Chapel of Remembrance, Hurricane II LF738 on 8th February 1984 at the Rochester workshop. It was destined for a painstaking restoration and display at the RAF Museum Cosford. From the moment strip down commenced, it became obvious that LF738 was in need of major work with many parts in need of replacement or rebuild. Eyes turned to LF751 at Bentley Priory: could it repeat its role as a donor airframe? It arrived at Rochester on 20th March 1985. As its strip down commenced, it became obvious that LF751 was *also* in need of the same sort of treatment. Hopes had always been high that Spitfire XVI TB752 – see below – inside Manston's Spitfire Memorial Building since the summer of 1981 would be joined by a Hurricane. In a similar arrangement that had been reached with Hawker at Langley in 1955 concerning LF363 and LF751, it was agreed that MAPS would restore LF738 for the RAF Museum and LF751 for the projected display at Manston. Both projects would benefit from the same 'learning curve' and the sourcing and recreation of parts. Among the items utilised in LF751, the control column came from a Hurricane that crashed at West Malling in September 1940 and the 'spade grip' came from an example that force-landed at Manston in May 1940.

As the restoration continued, considerable thought was put into the markings that LF751 would be finished in. In the early hours of 19th August 1942 Operation 'Jubilee', the amphibious raid on the French port of Dieppe commenced. The first aircraft over the scene, leading the Tangmere Wing, was Hurricane II BN230 *A-for-Ack*, flown by 43 Squadron's charismatic commanding officer, Sqn Ldr Daniel Albert Raymond Georges Le Roy du Vivier DFC* CdG – simply 'Danny' to his colleagues. On the beaches the mostly Canadian forces suffered considerably on what was always intended and an 'in-and-out' operation. In the skies, Fighter Command losses reached 111 aircraft; 61 pilots were killed or taken prisoner. With the 'Fighting Cocks', 43 Squadron, three aircraft were lost and Canadian F/Sgt H Wik was killed. It was decided that as Spitfire TB752 had a combat history while LF751 did not, Danny's BN230 would be an excellent complementary scheme. MAPS estimated that 22,000 man hours and £18,000 were expended on the restoration. When LF751 was unveiled at Rochester as 'BN230' 'FT-A' on 22nd April 1988, the extent of the work was abundantly evident. On 7th October the Spitfire and Hurricane Memorial Museum was inaugurated, and the iconic pair have been on show ever since.

The exuberant Sqn Ldr 'Danny' Le Roy du Vivier in the cockpit of the original Hurricane II BN230, 1942. Below the cockpit was the RAF Ensign, the Belgian flag and the black and white chequerboard marking of the 'Fighting Cocks', 43 Squadron. *KEC*

Supermarine Spitfire XVI TB752
1945 | Day fighter | One 1,580hp Rolls-Royce Packard Merlin 266 piston

Painted on the port side under TB752's windscreen, alongside the name *Val*, are four Luftwaffe crosses. In the space of 13 days in the spring of 1945 four different pilots flying TB752, 403 Squadron's 'scratch' Spitfire, downed four enemy aircraft. After all it had been through, in 1970 TB752 faced potential oblivion, but 'people power' rallied to save it for Manston, and for Kent. In the autumn of 1977 the Medway Branch of the Royal Aeronautical Society established the Medway Aircraft Preservation Society (MAPS) to restore a Short Sandringham flying-boat. This did not come about, instead TB752 became the first of an exceptional series of restorations from a tiny workshop at Rochester; very nearly 40 years later that exceptional work continues.

Built at the giant Castle Bromwich factory near Birmingham as a high-back Mk.XVI TB752 was issued to 33 Maintenance Unit (MU) at Lyneham on 21st February 1945. Three days later it was transferred to 84 Group Support Unit (GSU) at Lasham. This was a 'readiness pool', bringing Spitfires up to the latest combat specification and keeping them at ready-to-go status for issue to units in Europe. On 17th March 1945 the Spitfires of 66 Squadron touched down at Schijndel in the Netherlands, having set off from armament practice camp at Fairwood Common and broken the journey overnight at Manston on the 16th. Among the unit's compliment was TB752, coded 'LZ-F' and two days later it began its frontline career, escorting Douglas Bostons and North American Mitchells. On the 25th Plt Off D Hugo, flying TB752, was in trouble. The port main leg had failed and he was 'waved off' at Schijndel and advised to fly to Eindhoven, with far more extensive facilities, to force land. Hugo must have breathed a sigh of relief when he carried out a safe landing: he and TB752 would live to fight again. Not for long in the young pilot officer's case. Flying TB521 on 11th April German flak caught the Spitfire and he was killed. Repaired, TB752 re-entered the fray on 19th April 1945, joining 403 Squadron Royal Canadian Air Force (RCAF) at Diepholtz in Germany and given the codes 'KH-Z'. On fighter units, the aircraft *Z-for-Zebra* often was the unit 'scratch' aircraft; nobody's 'chosen' mount, but available for any pilot. And so began the 13 days in which those 'kill' tallies painted near the windscreen came about:

Spitfire TB752's victories

Date	Pilot	Victim
21st Apr 1945	Sqn Ldr 'Hank' Zary DFC	Messerschmitt Bf 109
25th Apr 1945	Fg Off David Leslie	Focke-Wulf Fw 189
1st May 1945	Fg Off Robert Young	Focke-Wulf Fw 190
3rd May 1945	Fg Off 'Fred' Town	Heinkel He 111

Notes: There is strong justification confirming Town's He 111 as the final Luftwaffe aircraft shot down by Allied forces during World War Two.

'Hank' Zary was newly established as the commanding officer of 403 Squadron and 21st April was his first 'outing' with the unit, piloting TB752. With four Bf 109s already under his belt, he came back an 'ace', having achieved the required five victories with another Messerschmitt dispatched. On the 25th David Leslie also came back with something – a 'kill' and flak damage. For the second time TB752 required the attentions of a Repair and Salvage Unit (RSU): following its landing accident it had been sorted out by 409 RSU at Diest. RSUs were remarkable, and unsung, outfits. They followed the combat units as they advanced across Europe, staying on some airfields for a matter of only days before decamping and relocating; using truck-based workshops with minimal other facilities. TB752 was patched up by a working party from 410 RSU at Goch and within 24 hours was back with 403 Squadron. 'Bob' Young's kill was certainly an Fw 190; it is believed to be a long-nosed Fw 190D 'Dora'. Five days after Fred Town downed the Heinkel He 111, VE-Day was celebrated. No.403 Squadron disbanded at Reinsehlen on the last day of June and TB752 was issued to 83 GSU at Dunsfold on 2nd August. By then the role of the GSUs had reversed; no longer issuing aircraft *out* to combat units, but *receiving* them for re-allocation. Indeed, the day before they were officially re-designated as Group Disbandment Centres, but it was some time before the hard-worked GSU teams caught up with that paperwork! TB752 was at Dunsfold perhaps only for hours, being transferred straight away to 29 MU at High Ercall.

The Spitfire was to spend 68 months in the huge storage hangars at High Ercall. It had one moment of respite, attending the Battle of Britain display at Scampton in mid-September 1949. The RAF had not done with its war veteran, on 19th April 1951 it was taken on charge by 102 Flying Refresher School (FRS) at North Luffenham. Pilots finding themselves 'driving a desk' for a period, or away from the flight lines for other reasons, attended an FRS to get up to speed with new procedures. Time at 102 FRS was fleeting, the following month TB752 moved to 103 FRS at Full Sutton. A spell at 49 MU Colerne from October 1951 and a return to 29 MU in August 1953 could have been a prelude to the smelter, but the Spitfire had more to offer. Coded 'F', on 23rd November 1953 TB752 was taken on charge at 5 Civilian Anti-Aircraft Co-operation Unit, Llanbedr. CAACUs were staffed and run by contractors, hence the 'Civilian' bit and provided facilities for army gunnery units – something to shoot at! A year later TB752 was retired to 33 MU at Lyneham and *may* have taken part in the filming at Kenley of *Reach for the Sky*, released in 1956.

Officially declared a non-effective airframe at Lyneham on 13th December 1954, TB752 was allocated to Manston for 'gate guardian' duties on 28th September 1955 although it was the following year before it took up its post. This Spitfire can lay claim to no less than three 'maintenance numbers', serial numbers allocated to non-flying airframes: 7256M and 7279M

Spitfire XVI TB752 'on guard' at Manston, February 1975. Behind is Javelin FAW.9 XH764. *Roy Bonser*

during its gate guardian days and 8086M when it entered the custodianship of the RAF Museum. At some stage, TB752 gave up its all-over natural metal scheme for camouflage. Lewis E Deal, the project leader on the restoration of TB752 and the guiding light on all MAPS projects since, wrote *The Manston Spitfire TB752* (North Kent Books, 1981) and a section describes a change in TB752's fortunes: "The year 1970 almost saw the end of TB752's life, not only at Manston but for all time. Spares and parts for the Spitfires flying with the Battle of Britain Flight were urgently required to enable the Spitfires to keep flying... TB752 was selected for removal and dismantling for the parts that could be utilised. The RAF and the Ministry of Defence had not, however, reckoned on the reaction from the Civic Heads [of Ramsgate] and the people of Thanet to the possible loss of 'their' Spitfire. The day came for TB752 to be removed from Manston, but with only an hour to go, and the transporter waiting, the pleas for the aircraft to remain in Kent were finally successful and the order was countermanded. The people of the Isle of Thanet breathed again – but it was indeed a very, very close call."

It was from this moment that it was realised that the real long term survival of the Manston Spitfire lay with bringing it indoors, before further decades in the Kent coastal air took their inevitable toll due to corrosion. Meetings in early 1978 gave rise to the unique arrangement that is detailed at the beginning of this chapter. On 7th July 1978 TB752 was entrusted to the MAPS team and moved to Rochester. The proviso was that the Manston Spitfire be all trim and back on duty for the Battle of Britain Day celebrations to the following year – no pressure there then! TB752 was officially handed over on 15th September 1979. Returned to the colours it wore with 403 Squadron it initially carried *three* kill tallies; it was to be some years before Fg Off Town's downing of the He 111 was confirmed.) Fund raising for the Spitfire Memorial Building gained momentum and TB752 was unveiled in its home on 13th June 1981.

Advanced Outpost
Romney Marsh Wartime Collection

Brenzett
http://theromneymarsh.net/wartimecollection

During 2014 the museum run by the Brenzett Aeronautical Museum Trust was 'rebranded' as the Romney Marsh Wartime Collection to reflect the full extent of its intent. Established in 1972, with extensive items recovered from crash sites across the county and beyond, the museum is housed in what was a wartime hostel for the Women's Land Army. Not surprisingly, this aspect of World War Two has always featured prominently in the displays. Established in June 1939 the Land Army resulted from the experience during World War One as the nation came to grips with the removal from agriculture and industry of vast numbers of men. It was not until October 1949 that the Women's Land Army was stood down. This may seem a long time after the war but the task of returning personnel from Europe, the Middle and Far East was a lengthy operation.

The Brenzett museum occupies a building used by the Women's Land Army as a hostel during World War Two. *Ken Ellis*

The museum is located in the southwest corner of a triangle of land that was transformed from agriculture into an Advanced Landing Ground (ALG) which was officially named Brenzett but was known to the locals as Ivychurch. Construction began in the last weeks of 1942 with two Sommerfeld steel mat runways laid down and rudimentary wooden buildings erected. First use was for just a couple of days in the middle of September 1943 when the Supermarine Spitfire IXs of 122 Squadron arrived from the nearby ALG at Kingsnorth. All went quiet again until a trio of North American Mustang III units, 129 and the Polish 306 and 315 Squadrons, arrived in July 1944. Intensive operations into Europe came to an end in October and the ALG was returned to the landowner in 1945. As might be expected, there is much within the museum on life at ALGs and outside there is a memorial dedicated to all those who lost their lives while serving from Kent's dozen such airstrips; it was unveiled on 7th August 1994.

Among the extensive aviation displays is the recovered forward fuselage of Hawker Hurricane I V7350. Sgt Frank Walker-Smith of Croydon-based 85 Squadron was flying this machine in the afternoon of 29th August 1940 when he was shot down in an engagement with Messerschmitt Bf 109s. Walker-Smith took to his parachute and was wounded. The Hurricane impacted at Etchington in Kent but was destined to become four decades later a stark testament to the Battle of Britain.

Romney Marsh Wartime Collection aircraft

Type	Identity	Built	Origin	Acquired	Notes
de Havilland Vampire T.11	XK625	1956	Britain	Nov 1989	–
Douglas Dakota 4	G-AMSM	1943	USA	1979	cockpit
English Electric Canberra B.2	WH657	1952	Britain	1987	cockpit
English Electric Canberra PR.9	XH136	1959	Britain	2014	cockpit
Hawker Hurricane I	V7350	1940	Britain	1989	cockpit

Rural Idyll
Shoreham Aircraft Museum

Shoreham
www.shoreham-aircraft-museum.co.uk

A walk through in the delightful village of Shoreham, to the north of Otford, is all that you would expect: church, shops, wonderful pubs and the River Darent running through a very picturesque valley. In High Street, at the staunchly non-superstitious No.13, is perhaps the most unimaginable venue for an aviation museum. This is the Shoreham Aircraft Museum; one of the most delightful destinations in this book and must be put on your 'To Do' list *now*! The collection's origins go back to 1978 when local enthusiasts, with a passion for the Battle of Britain, combined and a permanent display was opened to the public in 1988. This team of dedicated, hard working and totally welcoming stalwarts have made sure that since then the museum has never looked back. The exhibitions have been extended, regular special events are staged and, to top it all, its tea room is a legend in its own right!

Many of the exhibits come from local aviation 'archaeology' 'digs'. There are several museums – no names, no pack drill – where such items litter displays, trailing rust and decay with at best, unintelligible labels, and nothing to inspire the imagination at all. Not at Shoreham, the displays are changed frequently, the whole place is vivid, inviting, informative. Backing up the aviation theme is a tasteful treatment of the 'Home Front'. No.13 is the home of Geoff and Lesley Nutkins, the museum occupies a series of spacious outbuildings with an idyllic cottage garden where visitors can reflect on what they have seen, probably with a cup of tea and a fabulous cake created by Lesley and her team. Geoff is the modest founder of the collection and a gifted aviation artist – samples of his exceptional work are displayed on the walls of the tea room. His portraiture of Battle of Britain pilots and others sets him apart: you do not need to read the signature to know when you are looking at a 'Nutkins'.

A view from the main exhibition building at Shoreham of the tea room: sippin' among the hops! *Ken Ellis*

Two of many

The two most substantial exhibits provide just a taste of what awaits the visitor to Shoreham. In the middle of 2008 the team took delivery from Norway of a partially restored forward cockpit section of a Junkers Ju 88A-1 'Schnellbomber' (high-speed bomber) and this became the centrepiece of a new wing at the museum which opened in 2010. Built in 1940 this exhibit served with a Luftwaffe bomber unit during the Battle of Britain before it was sent to the Eastern Front. It wears the colours of Kampfgeschwader 54, famed for its 'Totenkopf' (skull) badge and having fought on all of the European fronts. This is the basis of a long term project which will create a complete Ju 88 cockpit, including the rearward-facing radio-operator/gunner's position.

Prominent in the main display building is the forward fuselage and engine from an unidentified Tangmere-based 607 Squadron Hawker Hurricane I. The Shoreham team describes it as one of their best ever 'digs'. The narrative alongside the exhibit takes up the story of Sgt John Landsell and his lasting testament. "He was involved in combat with the Messerschmitt Bf 109 of Hauptmann Nuemann of Jadgeschwader 27 on 17th September 1940 at 3.40pm... John's Hurricane was set on fire and he was forced to take to his parachute. Sadly, it would seem that this did not fully [deploy] and he fell to his death. His Hurricane dived at full throttle into a hop garden in Beltring in Kent. This was witnessed by a young lad by the name of John Grimes. Forty-six years later John was to be key in finding this aircraft. We had tried for some time to locate the aeroplane but had been hampered in our search by an old underground sprinkler system which affected [our] metal detectors... Just as all seemed lost, John arrived on the scene. In 1940 the crash site had been one of three hop gardens, but now it was one large wheat field with no obvious sign of the havoc of that summer day. It seems impossible but John eyed the lie of the land and paced 100 steps into the corn field, pin-pointing the crash site exactly!" The 'dig' yielded what has become an impressive, and poignant exhibit; on the control column the gun button was still set to fire and the Rolls-Royce Merlin ranks as being one of the best ever recovered, complete with supercharger.

Remembering 'The Few'

In 2006, the Shoreham team embarked on an ambitious and demanding scheme to erect permanent memorials to all of the Battle of Britain pilots who lost their lives within a ten-mile radius of the village. In each case the aim is to erect a memorial stone at, or as close as possible to, the spot were each of these brave young men made the ultimate sacrifice. The sixth memorial was dedicated to Fg Off Robin McGregor 'Bubble' Waterston of 603 Squadron on 29th September 2009, adjacent to the entrance of the Royal Artillery Barracks at Woolwich in London. Waterston tragically lost his life during the early evening of 31st August 1940 when he was shot down in Supermarine Spitfire I X4273, which crashed in Repository Road, outside the barrack gates. This humbling project continues and funds from activities at the museum and donations from visitors have made it possible: the heroes of High Street.

Also in Kent
Dover Museum

A wide ranging and lively collection, including a replica V-1 'doodlebug' flying-bomb. **www.dovermuseum.co.uk**

Historic Dockyard Chatham

A huge number of naval attractions, large and small, set to rival Portsmouth. Among them is 1953 Westland Dragonfly HR.5 WG751. **www.thedockyard.co.uk**

The Shoreham Aircraft Museum's Ju 88A-1 cockpit. *Courtesy Shoreham Aircraft Museum*

Medway Aircraft Preservation Society

At Rochester aerodrome, read all about the workshop in *Icons*, above. **www.mapsl.co.uk**

Royal Engineers Museum and Library

To the north of Chatham, the museum has the catch-line: 'Local Heritage – Global Impact' and proves that military engineers have always been a crucial element of the British Army. Aeronautical exhibits include the medals of Major James McCudden VC DSO* MC* MM, born in nearby Gillingham, a pre-1914 military balloon basket and 1980 Hawker Siddeley Harrier GR.3 XZ964. **www.re-museum.co.uk**

When in Kent

Take the A249 north out of Sittingbourne and cross the impressive Kingsferry Bridge on to the Isle of Sheppey and head for Eastchurch and Leysdown, avoiding the copious hoards of jellied eels and liquor vendors. Within the middle of Eastchurch is an impressive memorial to the aviation pioneers of the island and marking the first Royal Navy aviators who took tuition from Eastchurch aerodrome, in 1911. The following year this was formalised as the Naval Flying School and Eastchurch became the ancestral home of the Royal Naval Air Service. Further east, beyond Leysdown on Sea, is Muswell Manor – 'The Birthplace and Cradle of British Aviation'. The manor became the clubhouse of the Royal Aero Club and the flying field in front of it was the world's first organised flying ground. On 2nd May 1909 J T C Moore-Brabazon became the first *British* pilot to fly in Britain, taking a Voisin biplane aloft from Muswell Manor. (S F Cody – see *First in the Air* Chapter 11 – was an American citizen when he flew at Farnborough on 16th October 1908.) Two days after Brabazon's exploit, Orville and Wilbur Wright visited to meet up with the Short brothers to discuss production of Wright Flyers. The Shorts had established the world's first aircraft factory at Leysdown, building versions of the American's Flyer biplane. Here are several memorials and plaques at Muswell and there is something quite elemental about the site; the launch pad of British aviation. **www.muswellmanor.co.uk**

A microlight on the turf in front of Muswell Manor during the celebrations of the centenary of Brabazon's flight of 2nd May 1909 from that very spot. *Ken Ellis*

CHAPTER 15
LEICESTERSHIRE

Big Thunder
Cold War Jets Collection

Bruntingthorpe
www.bruntingthorpeaviation.com

Motor vehicle test and development, storage and rectification; aircraft parking and reclamation centre; light industry; film location venue; corporate hospitality, agriculture – these and more are roles carried out at present-day Bruntingthorpe. All of these utilise a former airfield to the full and employ many people, directly and indirectly. Another activity goes on, also in diverse forms. Bruntingthorpe is a throbbing, vibrant centre for aviation heritage, almost all of it run by volunteers. This mixture of business and pleasure is the result of the passion of one family and without that catalyst none of the 'fun' side of this astounding institution would exit. The Walton family's love of aviation has created a national institution and a place of pilgrimage.

Truth be told, the Cold War Jets Collection and all of the other aviation heritage activities that go on at Bruntingthorpe do not fall into the definition of coverage outlined at the beginning of this book. If you have read this far, you will also appreciate that rules are made to be broken and that these pages are full of exceptions. Open only on Sundays or on special occasions it may be, but to omit the phenomenon that is Bruntingthorpe would be a crime. Besides, as it is only 20 miles or so to the west of the desk where these words are being churned out, the author is likely to get raided and lynched!

Above: Star performer at Bruntingthorpe special events, Victor K.2 XM715 *Teasin' Tina. Darren Harbar*

A Douglas RB-66B Destroyer tucking up the gear at Bruntingthorpe, May 1960. *KEC*

Irresistible impulse

In November 1942 the Vickers Wellington-equipped 29 Operational Training Unit began aircrew instruction at Bruntingthorpe. The unit flew its final sorties in May 1945 but by that time the airfield had other, more secretive, residents. From September 1944 Frank Whittle's Power Jets established a flight test centre; out of the way of prying eyes, but close enough to the Leicester and Lutterworth development sites. It was from Bruntingthorpe that the pioneer had his first flight in a jet aircraft. A gifted pilot since the mid-1920s, Whittle decided to taxi Gloster Meteor I EE221, fitted with a pair of Power Jets W.2/700s, on 19th October 1945. After a couple of runs, in his own words, he: "yielded to an irresistible impulse to take off"; after a low speed circuit, he carried out a perfect landing. He returned three days later for another, more lively, 45-minute sortie. A unique occasion: self-taught to fly a jet, propelled by engines of his design. Four months before Whittle's excursions in EE221, Armstrong Siddeley Motors also based its flight test operations at Bruntingthorpe. Both organisations moved on early in 1946 and in October the airfield went into care and maintenance.

In the mid-1950s construction teams transformed the look of the airfield, the northeast-southwest runway was dramatically lengthened, new taxiways and extensive hardstandings were laid, a large Butler hangar was erected on the northeast perimeter along with a lot of buildings. The Americans were coming: Strategic Air Command was to use the base for jet bomber deployments, a frontline outpost of the Cold War. Administered by the 3912th Air Base Squadron (ABS), Bruntingthorpe was ready for business in February 1957. Thirty Boeing B-47E Stratojets descended in early 1958 for the first of what were to become known as 'Reflex Alert' exercises. This was not to last long, in September 1959 control of the airfield was transferred to USAF Europe and the 7542nd ABS. With the motto 'Big Thunder' and a badge of a bomb-totin' eagle against a lightning flash, the arrival of the 7542nd heralded resident aircraft, not just temporary inmates. The Douglas RB-66 Destroyers of the 19th Tactical Reconnaissance Squadron, part of the 10th Tactical Reconnaissance Wing, arrived in August 1959. The 19th moved out in August 1962 and Bruntingthorpe was returned to RAF control, becoming an unmanned satellite of Wittering. That enormous runway was a great temptation to Wittering's resident Victor units, 100 and 139 Squadrons, and during 1963 and 1964 at least it was used for 'rollers'. It would be a lovely coincidence if Victor XM715 visited during its days with 100 Squadron, long before it took up permanent residence in 1993. Non-airfield parts of the site began to be sold off from November 1965 and the remainder was disposed of in March 1973.

First steps to a heritage site

In 1972 the Rootes Group acquired 600 acres of the airfield and set up a motor vehicle proving ground; this was later run under the aegis of Chrysler UK and then Peugeot-Talbot. Bruntingthorpe's association with the Leicestershire-based Walton family began in 1983 when C Walton Ltd bought the entire site. The test track was retained; some of the area returned to agriculture and other elements were to be developed. In the same year that the aviation enthusiastic Walton family acquired Bruntingthorpe, in the northwest of the county the Loughborough Leicestershire Air Museum (LLAM) at East Midlands Airport was in trouble. (More on this organisation can be found in the sister volume *Lost Aviation Collections of Britain* and see the section *Across the Runway* below.) The airport management announced the launch of the East Midlands Aero Park and these plans did not involve LLAM, its site had to be vacated by November 1983. Without hesitation, the Waltons offered a temporary home at Bruntingthorpe and over a frenetic weekend, 19-20th November, the collection moved in lock, stock and barrel. Well almost... Avro Vulcan B.2 XM575 had to be left behind; there were hopes that it would follow, but it never did. LLAM changed its name to the Bruntingthorpe Aviation Collection but by mid-1985 all of this had ground to a halt and it petered out. The Dassault Mystère IVA was inherited by what became the Cold War Jets Collection.

Also during 1983 warbird restorer and pilot Nick Grace approached the Walton family requesting that his British Aviation Heritage (BAH) stage airshows at Bruntingthorpe in the hope that they could become regular occurrences and that the airfield might become a centre for airworthy historic aircraft. Two displays were staged in 1984 and 1985. Nick was restoring former Irish Air Corps Supermarine Spitfire Tr.IX ML407 (G-LFIX) and it first flew on 16th April 1985 from St Merryn. What became known as the 'Grace Spitfire' appeared frequently at Bruntingthorpe up to 1988. Tragically, Nick was killed in a car accident on 14th October that year and the BAH 'project' came to nought. From July 1992 Sandy Topen's Vintage Aircraft Team received permission to move in from Cranfield but its operations were wound down in 1996.

'Big Thunder', The Vulcan and Cold War warriors

The Walton family turned its passion for aviation into hardware on 23rd March 1993. There was not a dry eye on the airfield when Avro Vulcan B.2 XH558 touched down; everyone was convinced they were witnessing the last-ever flight by the legendary delta. C Walton Ltd had acquired the former Vulcan Display Flight aircraft and, in the words of David Walton: "we couldn't see it scrapped, or [go] overseas and this airfield is a perfect home". That year was the turning point, the start of an exceptional family collection. An airshow was organised and it took its name from the motto of the USAF's 7542nd ABS, 'Big Thunder'. In a salute to Nick Grace it was run under the revived BAH banner. The year was rounded off with a V-bomber 'double' when Handley Page Victor K.2 XH715 arrived on 19th November. Two more 'Big Thunder' displays followed before morphing into a cavalcade of taxying jets under the 'Rolling Thunder' title. In one form or another, these signature events continue to the present day.

By the turn of the new century, the Walton family collection had taken on its current Cold War Jets label with regular openings on Sundays. On 12th June 2002 a former Olympic Airways Boeing 747-212 touched down and, after removal of the engines and some fittings, it joined the line-up. This was not the first of its type at the airfield; another example flew in September 1994. That was purposefully destroyed in a trial conducted in May 1997 on behalf of the Civil Aviation Authority and the US Federal Aviation Administration investigating ways of containing explosions in the cargo holds. Airliners have become a familiar scene at Bruntingthorpe as it is now a leading parting out centre recycling such giants.

Following negotiations with the Walton family, in 2000 the Vulcan to the Sky Trust started the at times tortuous process to put Vulcan XH558 back in the sky, as a civilian. The story of *The* Vulcan is well known and need not be gone into in depth here – see also Chapter 31 for details of its current home. XH558 had its first flight after restoration on 18th October 2007. It departed to Lyneham on 12th June 2009, returning to salute its former base on its farewell tour in 2015.

Among the individuals and organisations that co-exist alongside the Cold War Jets Collection, two require greater mention. On 24th June 1988 English Electric Lightning F.6 XR728, flown by Flt Lt Chris Berners-Price, flew in from Binbrook for the Lightning Preservation Group (LPG). With the determination to keep an example 'live', LPG volunteers have surpassed themselves with the progress made. Not content with XR728, LPG secured F.6 XS904 which had been in use for target facilities work with British Aerospace at Warton. Piloted by test pilot Sqn Ldr Peter Orme, this machine flew to Bruntingthorpe

The Lightning Preservation Group's F.6 XR728 taxying at Bruntingthorpe after its last flight, 24th June 1988. *Roy Bonser*

Line up of three of Bruntingthorpe's Buccaneer S.2Bs. Front to rear: Cold War Jets XX900 and T-Bag's XX894 and XW544. Behind is Comet *Canopus* and Boeing 747-212B 'G-ASDA'. *Ken Ellis*

on 21st January 1993 completing the last flight of the type in the UK. Since then LPG have taken on a pair of cockpits, F.3 XP703 and T.5 XV328, and all of F.3 XR713 which used to 'guard' the main entrance at Leuchars. Aware that keeping the two F.6s taxying into the long-term would involve housing them, LPG came up with the novel scheme of acquiring a Quick Reaction Alert 'shed' from Binbrook and re-assembling it at Bruntingthorpe. In one fell swoop, LPG managed to conserve two of their airframes and preserve an otherwise neglected piece of Cold War heritage.

Lovingly known as 'T-Bag' – standing for The Buccaneer Aviation Group – the operation was originally called the Buccaneer Preservation Society. A talented and tenacious set of enthusiasts care for a *quartet* of Hawker Siddeley Buccaneer S.2s, intending to keep all of them running. Founder member was the Cold War Jets Collection S.2B XX900 which arrived in October 1994. In sequence three other S.2Bs arrived: XX894 in September 2003, XW544 in October 2004 and XX889 in May 2011. To quote one of the crew: "One is not enough – four is more like critical mass!"

Aero Spacelines / Boeing Super Guppy 201 F-BTGV
1970 | Large capacity freighter | Four 4,912shp Allison 501-D22C turboprops

By far and away the aircraft that draws the most curious looks at Bruntingthorpe is not military, looks vaguely like an airliner but was best summed up by a fascinated visitor in August 2016 as "an airship with wings". To add to its novelty it is French-registered; so what merit does it have in an English collection? Well, the clue is the eight-foot tall word 'Airbus' on the fuselage side... From 1971 into the mid-1990s four of these bulbous giants plied the airways of Europe carrying large sub-assemblies, including wings, for the BAC/Sud Concorde and for the growing family of Airbus airliners. *Golf-Victor* and its three colleagues were regular visitors to Manchester, picking up wings built at Hawarden, Chester, taking them for final assembly at Toulouse, France. One of these giants is preserved at Toulouse (F-BPPA – the second Guppy), another at Hamburg's Finkenwerder plant (F-GDSG, No.3): the major Airbus nations. Without the vision of the Walton family, there is every reason to believe that Britain – a major participant in Airbus – would have missed out on this unsung but important contribution to the UK aerospace industry. The fourth Super Guppy is still airworthy; acquired by the National Aeronautics and Space Administration (NASA) after its use in Europe, registered as N941NA, it is based at El Paso, Texas.

The idea of vastly increasing the volume of the fuselage of a transport so that it could carry bulky items came from American John Conroy, well-known for his adaptations of various types in the 1960s. With the coming of the US moon programme, the need to move section of Saturn V rocket sections about the USA gave rise to the Aero Spacelines conversion of a Boeing 377 Stratocruiser piston-engined airliner. This was known as the 'Pregnant Guppy' and it first flew in September 1962 and several other 'Guppies' followed. It was the Super Guppy 201, designated 377SGT for Super Guppy Turbine, that was the most radical and successful. It was effectively a new aircraft, using only the wings, horizontal tail surfaces and the cockpit of Boeing C-97 Stratofreighters – the military version of the Stratocruiser. A brand new fuselage dispensed with the need to adapt fuselage sections of C-97s or 377s. The Super Guppy could carry a maximum load of 52,500lb, its freight floor was 13ft wide and 111ft 6in long; the bulbous fuselage had a maximum width of 25ft. The entire nose section hinged to port, allowing unrestricted, straight-in, loading.

Personnel and vehicles provide scale to Super Guppy 201 F-BTGV at Manchester Airport. The entire nose swung open to take bulky loads. *Alan Curry*

Built by Santa Barbara, California-based Aero Spacelines, the prototype 201, N211AS, first flew on 24th August 1970 – 26 years later it became a Leicestershire denizen. The following year it was handed over to French contractor Aeromaritime as F-BTGV. It began life shuttling large loads between Airbus sites, eventually under the Airbus Skylink banner. Another California-built example followed and the final two Super Guppies were created by UTA Industries at Le Bourget, Paris. In September 1994 the first of five Airbus A300-600 Super Transporters, or Belugas, had its maiden flight at Toulouse and the writing was on the wall for the hard-working Guppies. As noted above, NASA had its eye on one of the fleet, but the others were offered to Airbus participant counties. *Golf-Victor* arrived at Bruntingthorpe on 1st July 1996 and this amazing transport is looked after by a determined band of volunteers. Such is the pace of airliner manufacturing these days, as this book went to press, the first of five Beluga XLs, based on the A330-700, was being assembled at Toulouse to replace the Beluga fleet. Is an Airbus A300-600ST destined to park alongside *Golf-Victor?*

de Havilland Comet 4C XS235
1963 | Long range transport | Four 10,500lb st Rolls-Royce Avon Mk.525B/350 turbojets

Lot 38 was to go under the hammer at the New Bond Street, London, sales room of auctioneers Phillips during the afternoon of 8th May 1997. With an estimate in the region of £400,000 to £600,000, it wasn't a painting, although many thought it a work of art. It was the Boscombe Down-based Comet 4C navigation and radio systems test-bed, XS235 *Canopus*. It was the last of its type in airworthy condition and there was speculation that it could be given a new life as a civilian, fare-paying, 'heritage' airliner. The estimated value contrasted considerably with the previous lot: just £3,000 to £5,000 for the non-airworthy Comet 4 XV814, which had last flown on 28th January 1993 and used as a source of spares to keep XS235 flying. (The cockpit of XV814 survives, cherished by a Gloucestershire-based enthusiast.) A week before the auction, the Ministry of Defence 'pulled' XS235 "in recognition of the National Heritage [ministerial capital letters] interest" to "...allow time for further consideration of the most appropriate method of disposal".

This Comet was acquired from new by the Aeroplane and Armament Experimental Establishment as a test-bed. It was first flown at Hawarden, Chester, on 26th September 1963. Just two more Comets were to come down the production line, one for Kuwait in December and one for Egypt in February 1964. Delivered to Boscombe on 2nd December, XS235 was named *Canopus* after one of the brightest stars in the sky. The Comet undertook wide ranging tests on navigation systems such as Loran and Omega and during its time made the transition from analogue to digital processes. In 1968 *Canopus* made the first of several around-the-world flights, in this case eastbound, and undertook annual sorties over the North Pole, continuing the 'expeditions' that were initiated in May 1945 using Empire Air Navigation School Avro Lancaster I PD328 *Aries*. *Canopus* also played a major part in the development of Hawker Siddeley Nimrod MR.2 navigation systems.

The last working flight was staged from Boscombe Down on 14th March 1997 by which time *Canopus* was operated under the aegis of the Defence Test and Evaluation Organisation. Guest of honour was former de Havilland test pilot Gp Capt John Cunningham CBE DSO** DFC*, who had been at the helm of the prototype Comet on 24th July 1949. As well as conducting some trials, during the 5½ hour flight, the Comet performed flypasts at its birthplace, Hawarden, and at Warton, Wittering and Lyneham. When it touched down, XS235 had accrued 8,281 flying hours. It made another flight 13 days later and was then kept ready for a 'one-shot' ferry flight somewhere in the UK for its post-auction purchasers.

A sealed bid from the de Havilland Aircraft Museum Trust (DHAMT – Chapter 12) secured *Canopus* and huge amounts spares and documentation on 1st July 1997. The scheme was to ferry XS235 to Hatfield, where it could be dismantled and moved to London Colney. The airfield had closed in April 1994 and British Aerospace was busy winding down the site. Besides, throughout 1997 much of Hatfield was in use as the set for the Steven Spielberg film *Saving Private Ryan*. At Boscombe, ramp fees were mounting and XS235's airworthy state could not be guaranteed beyond the end of October. An offer from David Walton and the team at Bruntingthorpe was too good to let slip and on 30th October XS235 made the last-ever flight by a Comet. Flight crew were: Sqn Ldr Mark Leonczek (captain), Geoffrey Delmege (co-pilot), Cliff Ware (navigator), Nick Newton and Nick Paul (engineers). Having secured XS235's future, if not its home in Hertfordshire, DHAMT gifted *Canopus* to what was then known as the British Aviation Heritage Collection in February 1998.

By 2000 another organisation had hopes for XS235; the National Air Pageant had ambitions to operate a fleet of 'heritage' airliners. A brochure outlined the aims: "The Pageant will attempt to bring together aeroplanes which represent the heyday of Britain's airlines. For around ten weekends every summer these aircraft will take the leading roles in a pageant to be seen by thousands. Supporting roles will be played by period vehicles included fuel bowsers, ground support units, cars and coaches. Everything, down to the re-created aircraft steps, will have that authentic touch. Pilots, hostesses, groundcrew and passengers (all volunteers) will wear period uniforms and clothes and the whole spectacle will be accompanied by a fascinating commentary complete with music and sound effects from newsreels of the 1940s and 1950s. The Pageant will have a travelling photographic exhibition, brightly coloured tents and trailers... the sort of aerial circus which Alan Cobham pioneered before the war."

The intention was to operate XS235 with civilian certification ready to mark the half-century of jet air travel in 2002. *Canopus* was to be ferried to Lasham where there was a concentration of recently Comet-experienced engineers. The Comet would be flown in British Overseas Airways Corporation (BOAC) colours and to this end it was registered, to C Walton Ltd, as G-CPDA on 10th August 2000. The first Comet 4 for BOAC was G-APDA and these letters were in recognition of the original *Delta-Alpha*. (G-BPDA had been worn by a HS 748 twin turboprop.) As the Bruntingthorpe-based Vulcan to the Sky Trust (see above and Chapter 31) had discovered, design authority backing was essential for the Civil Aviation Authority to formulate certification. While the Vulcan was significantly more complex in systems than the Comet, it was 'only' seeking a permit for a reduced crew and airshow participation. The National Air Pageant was whimsically adding hostesses, passengers and the possibility of overseas travel: a level of complexity required by a full-blown, professional, airline. Design authority approval was not forthcoming and the scheme quickly fizzled out. *Canopus* settled down to being cosseted by a resolute team of ground crew and it is occasionally powered up and taxied.

Cover of the Phillips catalogue for 8th May 1997 with Lot 38, Comet XS235 on the cover. Its sale in this manner was withdrawn just prior to the auction. *KEC*

Handley Page Victor K.2 XM715
1962 | Air-to-air refuelling tanker | Four 19,750lb st Rolls-Royce Conway Mk.201 turbofans

Born in 1962, retired in 1993; the RAF got phenomenal value and considerable versatility from Victor *Teasin' Tina*. As the Hurricane was to the Spitfire, the Victor was always in the shadow of the Vulcan; yet in all roles it was more capable. The 'lone wolf' imagery of the 'Black Buck' Vulcans raiding the Falkland Islands is always remembered, yet without the Victors there could have been no such operation. Unlike Vulcans, Victors, including XM715, went to war twice, serving with great distinction in the first Gulf War. Besides Cosford and Duxford, and the 'gate guardian' at Marham, there are only two other whole Victors: XM715 and XL231 *Lusty Lindy* at the Yorkshire Air Museum – Chapter 31. Both are lovingly kept 'in steam' and either could have been chosen for a profile but as *Teasin' Tina* is emblematic of what makes Bruntingthorpe tick, it gets the vote!

Handley Page test pilot Flt Lt John W Allam eased Victor B.2 XM715 off the runway at Radlett on the last day of 1962 for its maiden flight. Ferried to Wittering on 4th March 1963 XM715 joined 100 Squadron which had reformed the previous May and was busy working up as part of Britain's strategic force. As explained above, at this time Bruntingthorpe was being run as an unmanned satellite of Wittering and the resident Victors of 100 and 139 Squadrons were known to carry out 'rollers' down the runway: it would be incredible if XM715 was one of these visitors, three decades before it took up permanent residence. On 16th April 1964 XM715 changed unit at Wittering, 'crossing the ramp' to the Victor Training Flight. A spin off of Cottesmore's 'C' Flight of 232 Operational Conversion Unit (OCU) VTF 'fed' crews into the Victor squadrons as the OCU wound down. On 8th July 1964 XM715 was ferried back to its birthplace, Radlett.

Victor XM715 in B.2(SR) in 1965, note the camera arrays in the bomb bay. *KEC*

Handley Page set to work on XM715 so that it could carry the Avro Blue Steel 'stand-off' nuclear missile under the designation B.2(BS). Changing requirements in the strategic force dictated that the bomber take on a new role even before the work was finished. The yokes for the big Blue Steel missile were removed from XM715's huge bomb bay and the Victor was rigged for strategic reconnaissance, with an impressive array of cameras, photoflash flares and the ability to carry air sampling sensors. This turned XM715 into a B.2(SR), also known as SR.2, and it was test flown in this guise on 24th May 1965. Thirty days later XM715 was taken on charge by 543 Squadron at Wyton. Routine testing in 1967 discovered evidence of fatigue cracking in the port wing root and XM715 was returned to Radlett on 19th December. With the Victor bomber force winding down, its future did not look rosy.

Handley Page was working on a requirement to turn suitable Mk.2s into three-point tankers. The Jetstream twin turboprop programme was in severe trouble and, overstretched, Handley Page Ltd went into liquidation on 8th August 1969. A financial re-launch foundered on 27th February 1970 and one of the most famous names in the British aircraft industry threw in the towel. The Victor K.2 contract was awarded to Hawker Siddeley (HS) and a migration of the stored airframes to Woodford began in April 1970. John Allam re-acquainted himself with XM715, ferrying it at low level, with the undercarriage locked down, to Woodford on 10th June 1970. Conversion to K.2 status was completed on 10th April 1975 when XM715 was test flown. The third phase of its career was about to begin. Delivered to Marham on 12th May, XM715 was taken on charge by 232 OCU. The Victor continued in this instructional role for nearly seven years, then XM715 went to war.

The first wave of Victor tankers headed out of Marham on 18th April 1982 and tucked into the increasingly crowded parking space at Wideawake airfield, Ascension Island. Operation 'Corporate', the liberation of the Falkland Islands was getting into gear. By this stage XM715 was not an OCU aircraft, it was on charge with 55 Squadron and it remained with the unit for the remainder of its RAF career. Forty-eight hours later XM715 was in action, a maritime radar recce down to South Georgia with two more long-ranging sweeps in quick succession. In late April XM715 was back at Marham, supporting HS Harrier and Sea Harrier reinforcements to Ascension. The Victor returned to Wideawake on 13th May, 'tanking' a Vulcan en route. Tasks for the Victor tanker force were intense and full of variety: XM715 supported the first HS Nimrod MR.2 operation on 15th May – the maritime patroller was away from Ascension for an astonishing 19 hours 20 minutes. Other epic out-and-back sorties involved refuelling Lockheed Hercules transports air-dropping supplies; XM715 took part in such a sortie on 2nd June. Nine days later, XM715 was one of a complex 'out' and 'retrieve' network of top-ups for 'Black Buck 7', the final Vulcan raid on the Falklands when XM607 attacked Argentine troop concentrations near Port Stanley. On the 13th June XM715 departed Wideawake, tanking Vulcan XM597 – the one that 'visited' Rio de Janeiro on 2nd June – and the following day the occupying forces surrendered at Stanley. XM715 was done with Wideawake, the Victor force was needed to sustain the Hercules 'air bridge' flights to the Falklands. (Vulcan XM607 is preserved at Waddington; XM597 at East Fortune.)

In 1984 the Vickers VC-10 tanker fleet began to enter service and by the end of the decade 55 Squadron's K.2s were getting close to retirement. Iraq's Saddam Hussein had other ideas and the invasion of Kuwait brought about the Victor's second war. The K.2s deployed to Muharraq, Bahrain, from 14th December 1990 and at one stage there were ten based there. They may have been around 30 years old, but the Victors more than proved their worth. From the first 'in anger' sortie on 16th January 1991 to the end of hostilities on 28th February the K.2s were tasked with 299 tanking 'ops' and all of them were completed, clocking a total time of 870 hours. 'Clients' included RAF Tornados and Jaguars and US Navy fighters. XM715 carried out 38 refuelling sorties and gained its *Teasin' Tina* nose-art during the conflict. The Victor force continued to soldier on until 55 Squadron disbanded at Marham on 15th October 1993. A small cadre of crews remained, under the unofficial title of Victor Disposal Flight as the final examples were ferried to their new homes. XM715 was ready for phase four of its life.

Artwork adorning Victor K.2 XM715, *Teasin' Tina* and Victor Meldrew ready to dispense 'Gulf' fuel! *Both Darren Harbar*

"Bruntingthorpe, *Meldrew One* calling". Acquired by the Walton family, XM715 was flown to Bruntingthorpe on 19th November 1993. Its crew had chosen the call-sign inspired by the lead character in the 1990 to 2000 BBC situation comedy *One Foot in the Grave*. Painted on the nose was a cartoon of *Victor* Meldrew, as played by Richard Wilson. The close-knit Victor team at Bruntingthorpe have found that *Teasin' Tina* lives up to the type's reliability and it is a firm favourite at the taxying days. The Victor delighted the audience on 3rd May 2009 when it unintentionally got airborne – albeit at extremely low level – for about 30 yards. Victor pilots always praise how the wonderful crescent wing allows the aircraft to "land itself" and it seems that its aerodynamics champ at the bit to go aloft as well. Long may *Tina* stay 'alive and kicking'!

Cold War Jets Collection aircraft

Type	Identity	Built	Origin	Acquired	Notes
Aero Spacelines Super Guppy 201	F-BTGV	1970	USA	1 Jul 1996	see profile
Boeing 747-212B	SX-OAD	1979	USA	12 Jun 2002	–
Dassault Mystère IVA	85	c1956	France	on site 1983	arrived Jul 1980
de Havilland Comet 4C	XS235	1963	Britain	30 Oct 1997	see profile
Handley Page Victor K.2	XM715	1963	Britain	19 Nov 1993	see profile
Hawker Siddeley Nimrod MR.2	XV226	1968	Britain	27 Apr 2010	–
Hawker Siddeley Buccaneer S.2B	XX900	1976	Britain	27 Oct 1994	–
Panavia Tornado GR.1	ZA326	1983	GB/Ger/Italy	1 Oct 2013	–
PZL Iskra 100	1018	1978	Poland	5 Jul 1996	–
SEPECAT Jaguar GR.1	XZ382	1977	UK/France	22 Feb 1999	–

Canberra T.17 WH740 returned its 360 Squadron markings at the East Midlands Airport Aeropark. *Roger Richards*

Across the Runway
East Midlands Airport Aeropark

Castle Donington
www.eastmidlandsaeropark.org

Just a short distance from the threshold of Runway 09, there are fantastic views of the comings and goings at busy East Midlands Airport. Two observation mounds allow unrestricted photography – no fencing in the way. What more could you want? How about a large selection of historic aircraft to browse, friendly volunteers to show you around and special events and exhibitions? The East Midlands Airport Aeropark is a superb example of what an enlightened airport management and a determined set of enthusiasts can achieve together. It is safe to say that today's Aeropark has had its ups and downs but today it is a popular visitor attraction and it serves to alleviate the airport complex on the other side of the runway from people hoping to watch the activity. The Aeropark Volunteers Association (AVA) looks after the aircraft and has established a substantial and varied collection, manages the site and looks after the visitors.

Officially opened on 21st July 1965 East Midlands Airport has grown from humble beginnings to today's thriving passenger and freight centre, with general aviation and maintenance facilities, hotels, car parks and all of the other infrastructure needed to support a throughput of four million passengers and 300,000 tonnes of freight per year. Eighty holiday and business destinations are served and the airport supports 6,000 jobs. Where the present day maintenance area is, in the southwest corner, in late 1916 was a grass aerodrome, taking the name of the village to the north, Castle Donington. The Royal Aircraft Factory BE.2s of 38 Squadron used the landing ground, but had reverted to agriculture by 1918. The area was chosen as a bomber training airfield, acting as a satellite of Wymeswold, in 1941. Vickers Wellingtons of 28 Operational Training Unit (OTU) arrived in January 1943, moving out in October 1944 to make way for the Douglas Dakotas of 108 (Transport) OTU. This unit was re-designated as 1382 (Transport) Conversion Unit in August 1945 but its role was unchanged; in May 1946 it retreated to Wymeswold. The airfield fell into disuse until it was reborn as an airport.

First steps

The Loughborough Leicestershire Aircraft Museum and Preservation Society (a bit of a mouthful and best abbreviated to LLAM) opened up to the public on 27th May 1979. It was located on hard standings on the south side, to the east of the terminal building, close to the expanding freight sheds. Founder LLAM airframe was former French Air Force North American F-100D 42239 Super Sabre that arrived in April 1978 and was restored to high standards by willing hands on the airport. The remaining exhibits, some on loan and most acquired by individual LLAM members, arrived in short order over the next three years. (Full details of LLAM can be found in the sister volume *Lost Aviation Collections of Britain*.) Two aircraft took advantage of the runway: Vickers Varsity T.1 WL626 (G-BHDD) on 8th November 1979 and Avro Vulcan B.2 XM575 on 28th January 1983. The Varsity had been acquired by Graham Vale's father, Fred, and had originally flown to Coventry Airport, Baginton, 12th April 1976, re-positioning to East Midlands three years later. The big delta was on its last flight from Waddington and manoeuvring it into position on the LLAM site took considerable man-power and planning.

Air Bridge Merchantman G-APES outside the East Midlands terminal, 1991. *Roy Bonser*

During 1983 the airport management, in a joint venture with Leicestershire Museum of Technology, announced the launch of the East Midlands Aero Park ('Aero Park' later to become just one word) to be built on the south-eastern boundary. Phase 1, a visitor centre and raised spectator viewing platform, was to open in 1984. LLAM did not opt in to this plan and its members were faced with finding a new home, followed by dismantling the airframes, transporting them, and starting all over again. A haven was found in Bruntingthorpe and the collection moved over there in November 1983 – see *Big Thunder* above for more. Graham Vale set up the East Midlands Historic Flying Group in May 1982 with the main purpose of getting the Varsity flying again. It was not long before Graham and the team decided that the venture was not feasible and they decided to join in with the Aeropark. When all options for moving the Vulcan were exhausted, it was also passed on. The new facility had its first of many airframes.

Migrating northwest

With a small display and reception building the Aeropark opened in May 1984 and was well greeted by visitors and the airport management. As well as the airport and Leicestershire Museums, help in establishing it came from Derbyshire and Nottinghamshire councils and a large donation from the NCP Car Parks organisation. As mentioned earlier, supporting the Aeropark was the AVA. Graham Vale played a major role in the running, expansion and maturity of the AVA operation to the present day. He was to spend a lot of time and energy on the Aeropark's when for a while it faced oblivion.

As a reminder of the ever-changing nature of an airport, in April 1996 it was announced that the Aeropark was to close before the end of the year as a freight handling centre was going to swallow up its site. There followed a considerable period of uncertainty where it seemed that scrapping was the only option for the larger airframes. The airport management team could have just washed its hands of the situation and concentrated on the job in hand – running a busy and expanding enterprise. Instead, the exhibits were found space away from the construction work while other options were explored. Through the dedication of a handful of AVA members and the airport team, a new site was found across the runway on the northwest perimeter close to the Donington Park motor racing circuit. The new Aeropark involved considerable investment by the airport along with support from major operators. The impressive facility opened on 9th August 2001 and the AVA has developed and refined the site ever since.

A close relationship with organisations at the airport has helped considerably in exhibits and facilities over the years. This went as far as the donation of the Argosy freighter in in 1987. Another cargo aircraft, Vickers Merchantman G-APES, was also bound for the Aeropark. An all-cargo conversion of the Vanguard airliner, *Echo-Sierra* had last been operated by the resident Hunting Cargo Airlines and it was retired in 1995. With the announcement of the closure of the Aeropark and demands on ramp space it was cut up in May 1997, but the cockpit section was handed on to the AVA. A pair of World War Two era 'exhibits' probably never get a second look from visitors yet they have greatly enhanced the Aeropark. In the summer of 2004 the AVA acquired all 98 feet of a Romney Hut; it was re-assembled refurbished and serves as a display area and workshop. A second of these wartime survivors was acquired in 2014. East Midlands Airport and the AVA can take great pride in their achievements in the Aeropark; a shining example of the power of combined operations.

Restored' to a status it never achieved, the one-off Sheriff on display at the Aeropark. *Jon Wickenden*

Aircraft Designs Sheriff G-FRJB
1982 | Light transport | Two 160hp Lycoming O-320 pistons

In Chapter 11, the first design by John Britten and Desmond Norman, the BN-1, is profiled. At the Aeropark is the final design that John Britten CBE had a hand in, the Sheriff light twin. The aircraft never flew and as such it could be argued to be of little significance, but it is an insight into the British aircraft industry and its inability to sustain a foothold in the general aviation marketplace. In February 1976 John and Desmond had decided to go their own ways and left the Britten-Norman (BN) company they had founded. By 1976 John Britten and Denis Berryman – a designer with BN – were firming up plans for a family of low-cost, rugged, easy to maintain, light twins; ranging from fixed undercarriage two-seat trainers to more sophisticated, retractable, four-seaters. John was very proud to become the High Sheriff of the Isle of Wight in 1976 and this inspired the name of the new machine. Tragically, John died at his Bembridge home on 7th July 1977; he was just 48.

John's brother, Robin, stepped in and Aircraft Designs (Bembridge) Ltd, and later Sheriff Aerospace, were formed to continue the project. In September 1981 Robin staged a press conference announcing that construction of the first example and a structural test airframe was underway at Sandown and the maiden flight was expected the following spring. Robin said that the first order had been taken, in the USA, and that there was interest in building the type under licence in Romania. The previous May the prototype had been registered as G-FRJB – honouring Forrester Robin John Britten. Wight Aviation, a BN sub-contractor, had been engaged to build fuselages and wings for a production batch. In February 1983 the first of these was registered as G-BPOP. But the following month the plug was pulled on the project and efforts to find new funds began. Early in 1984 a receiver was called in and the unfinished prototype languished at Sandown. Following approaches from East Midlands Airport the Sheriff was donated to the Aeropark Volunteers Association and moved north on 1st July 1986. Since then it has formed an unusual project at the Aeropark workshop as the work entailed 'completion' as much as restoration.

Armstrong Whitworth Argosy 101 G-BEOZ
1960 | Medium range freighter | Four 2,100shp Rolls-Royce Dart 526 turboprops

Born in Leicestershire, 25 miles to the south of its present home, and resident at East Midlands Airport since 1972, the Aeropark's *Fat Albert* could not ask for better credentials. Three Argosies survive intact in Britain: at Cosford, Coventry and G-BEOZ at East Midlands. Designed specifically as a commercial freighter, the first Argosy flew at Bitteswell on 8th January 1959 but found little favour in a market dominated by conversions of existing airliner types. Much refined, the type served as a tactical airlifter for the RAF, which ordered 56 examples, the vast majority of the production run of 71.

First to order the Argosy was Miami-based Riddle Airlines, taking five examples. Riddle had gained a contract from the United States Air Force's Logistics Command to carry freight on regular routes to bases within the USA to relieve the frontline transport fleet for more pressing duties. This system was known as LOGAIR. The East Midlands Argosy first flew from Bitteswell on 16th December 1960 wearing the 'B Condition' (or 'trade plate') identity G-1-7. As N6502R it was delivered to Riddle on 7th January 1961. Riddle lost the LOGAIR contract in June 1962 and ceased operations two years later. The Argosy fleet reverted to Armstrong Whitworth ownership but remained in the USA in the hopes that the next contractor would take them on. This indeed happened; they were transferred to New York-based Capitol Airlines in July. The LOGAIR contact was taken up by Zantop Air Transport of Willow Run, Detroit, and N6502R and the other Series 101s followed on. Zantop morphed into Universal Airlines in September 1966 and the Argosy was re-registered as N895U.

East Midlands-based Sagittair acquired four former Universal Argosies in 1971 and 1972. N895U arrived at its new base on 28th February 1972 but did not enter service, the airline ceased operations on 8th September that year. Maintenance specialist Field Aircraft Services, which looked after the Sagittair fleet, was left with them. Rather than try to dispose of the Argosies Field launched Air Bridge Carriers (ABC) in November 1972. *Niner-Five-Uniform* continued to languish on the ramp, but its day came when it was registered as G-BEOZ on 28th March 1977 and the task of putting it into service began. Named *Fat Albert*, *Oscar-Zulu* joined the ABC fleet on 30th August 1979 and in 1985 it was repainted in the colours of small package specialist Elan International. By March the following year, *Fat Albert* was engineless and parked up again on the Field ramp. Three months later it was towed across the runway, having been presented to the Aeropark.

English Electric Canberra T.17 WH740
1953 | Electronic countermeasures trainer | Two 6,500lb st Rolls-Royce Avon RA3 turbojets

There are plenty of Canberras in British museums and choosing which to profile is not easy. The Aeropark's T.17 represents a very distinctive variant that served for six years not far away at Cottesmore in Rutland. It also complements the largest aircraft in the collection, the 'spook' Nimrod R.1, both working in the dark world of electronic emissions. Built by English Electric as a B.2 bomber, WH740 was ready for collection at Warton on 16th July 1953. It was delivered a fortnight later to 18 Squadron at Scampton; the unit moving to Upwood in May 1955. It is believed that WH740 was not one of the Canberras deployed by the unit to Nicosia, Cyprus, and used in anger against Egyptian targets during Operation 'Musketeer', 31st October to 6th November 1956. Transferred to 40 Squadron, also at Upwood, WH740 served on until the unit disbanded on 1st February 1957 when it joined the Station Flight, awaiting a decision on its future.

Its next posting was exotic, WH740 was one of fifteen B.2s placed on loan to the Royal New Zealand Air Force (RNZAF) as part of that country's commitment to the British Commonwealth Strategic Reserve, South East Asia. For this, 75 Squadron RNZAF was reformed at Coningsby on 2nd June 1958 to convert air and ground crews to the Canberra. The first of the unit's B.2s touched down at Tengah, Singapore, on 14th July 1958 replacing 14 Squadron RNZAF's de Havilland Venom FB.1s and greatly increasing 'Kiwi' presence in the area. As well as its strategic role, 75 Squadron was also available to support ground operations against communist terrorists within the Malaysian peninsula. By the time of 75's arrival, the long-running conflict was nearing a successful conclusion. On 13th August 1959 the squadron's B.2s were armed and bombed insurgent camps in Pahang and four days later hit a hillside emplacement in Perak. This latter operation was the last air offensive of the entire Malayan campaign. No.75 Squadron disbanded at Tengah on 31st March 1962 and the Canberras were ferried back to the UK.

WH740 was earmarked as one of eighteen B.2s to be converted to T.17 status and it was dispatched to British Aircraft Corporation at Samlesbury by 1965. The bulbous nose of the T.17 housed electronic countermeasures (ECM) equipment designed to jam radar and radio transmissions and 'chaff' dispensers were fitted to clutter radar screens. A third crew member, an air electronics warfare officer, was crammed into the Canberra's already 'cosy' cockpit behind the pilot. The first T.17 began flight testing in September 1965 and the batch was completed by 1968.

A unique unit, 360 Squadron, operated the T.17s initially from Watton. The Latin motto 'Confundemus' summed up 360's purpose, translating as 'We shall throw into confusion'. Crewed by RAF and Royal Navy personnel, 360 played the part of the enemy against RAF and Fleet Air Arm aircraft and Royal Navy vessels, providing realistic ECM training during exercises. The squadron moved to Cottesmore on 21st April 1969 and again to Wyton on 1st September 1975; finally disbanding on 31st October 1994. By that time WH740 was long gone, having being struck off charge at Wyton on 1st December 1982. It was taken Cosford for use as an instructional airframe at 2 School of Technical Training, with the airframe number 8762M. Put up for disposal in 1991, it moved to East Midlands on 8th December 1991 and carries 360's colourful yellow lightning flashes against a red background on its flanks.

The personnel, RAF and Royal Navy, of 360 Squadron assembled on and around a Canberra T.17 for a formal group-shot at Wyton. *KEC*

Hawker Siddeley Nimrod R.1 XW664
1971 | Electronic intelligence gathering platform | Four 12,160lb st Rolls-Royce Spey 251 turbofans

In an increasingly electronic and digital age, the RAF has been in the forefront of what became known as SIGINT (signals intelligence) and is now referred to under the umbrella of ISTAR (intelligence, surveillance, target acquisition and reconnaissance). During World War Two the work of 100 Group, with its motto 'Confound and Destroy', and others pioneered such vital work. In July 1957 the first of a trio of de Havilland Comet C.2(R) SIGINT platforms joined 192 Squadron, transferring to 51 Squadron in August 1958. Along with a handful of English Electric Canberra B.6RCs, these comprised the RAF's electronic 'snoopers'. The Hawker Siddeley Nimrod maritime patroller was seen as the ideal choice to replace the Comets and the Canberras: an order for three R.1s was placed in 1969.

The Nimrod R.1s survived the maritime MR.2 force, but not for long. The last flight by an MR.2 took place on 26th May 2010 when XV229 was delivered to the fire school at Manston. The last-ever Nimrod sortie was staged by R.1 XV249 into Kemble on 29th July 2011, ready for moving to the RAF Museum Cosford. (On 16th May 1995 R.1 XW666 ditched in the Moray Forth after take-off from Kinloss; all on board were rescued. From October 1995 to April 1997 MR.2 XV249 was converted to R.1 status and joined 51 Squadron. The cockpit of R.1 XW666 is at Doncaster – Chapter 31.) Ten Nimrod MR.2s, either intact or as fuselages are with British museums. Thanks to all involved with the Aeropark, the prototype Nimrod R.1 and a veteran of four wars and a large number of 'out of area operations' post 11th September 2001 is cherished at East Midlands.

Built at Woodford, XW664 was essentially a MR.1 without the distinctive magnetic anomaly detector boom in the tail. Its cabin and bomb bay lacked any of the maritime equipment, all of the SIGINT gear was to be installed at Wyton. And that was a long and complex job, XW664 arrived at Wyton on 8th July 1971 and it was 31st October 1973 that it carried out a test flight as the first fully equipped R.1. The other two followed the same, but accelerated, process and 51 Squadron retired the last of the venerable Comets in January 1975. Probably the most secretive, and certainly the most reclusive, RAF aircraft of its era, little is known about just what systems were fitted to the R.1s during the 37 years of service. The complexity of the task is reflected in the 'behind the cockpit' crew, which could be up to 28 personnel. On 3rd May 1974 XW664 carried out 51 Squadron's first R.1 operational sortie and ten days later Air Marshal Sir Ruthven Wade presided over a ceremony at Wyton when XW664 was formally commissioned. The RAF's SIGINT capability had been massively enhanced.

By 1980 XW664 was sporting electronic support measures pods on the wingtips but circumstances were shortly to require further external modifications. With the phase out of the R.1s in 2011 the RAF produced a booklet, *History, Mystery and Gratitude*, paying tribute to its hard-working platforms. Page 10 proved instructive: "Although, at first, 51 Squadron was not planned to be involved in the [Falklands] campaign, it was later tasked to provide an aircraft and crew for operations in the South Atlantic. On 5th May 1982 a detachment led by the squadron commander, Wg Cdr B N J Speed, departed RAF Wyton in Nimrod R.1 XW664. Although the Forward Operating Base remains classified, the squadron was reported to have flown a total of ten missions in support of the campaign. They returned to RAF Wyton on 22nd May 1982..." As regards the 'forward operating base', the smart money is on Punta Arenas air base at the southern tip of Chile. Wyton-based English Electric Canberra PR.9s are believed to have kept XW664 company. Learning from the Falklands experience, during June 1982 XW664 had been fitted with an in-flight refuelling probe over the cockpit and a large ventral strake under the rear fuselage. The ability to top-up on fuel during a sortie dramatically increased the R.1s flexibility of operation. About this time XW664 and its sisters had acquired underwing pylons and occasionally sported pods that appeared to house towed decoys for self-defence.

Sqn Ldr M J Beane captained XW664 on 10th August 1990, deploying to Akrotiri on Cyprus. Iraq had invaded Kuwait and SIGINT assets were going to be of great importance. Two R.1s were resident throughout the run up and the brief air and ground war, resulting in the liberation of Kuwait on 23rd February 1991. The Nimrods of 51 Squadron played an unsung but vital role, returning to base in March. From 1990 to the present day, world history has been littered with conflict, much of it involving bitter ethnic struggles or international terrorism. The territories of the former Yugoslavia erupted in a complex series of wars from 1991 to 1995 and in June 1992 the R.1s of 51 Squadron began regular deployments to Italy to monitor the situation. Coalition forces engaged in a bombing campaign – Operation 'Deliberate Force' from 30th August to 20th September 1995 and the R.1s were engaged. In the middle of all of this, 51 Squadron left Wyton and moved into its new home at Waddington, in April 1995. After the twin towers fell in New York coalition forces were again in action, this time through 'Enduring Freedom' in Afghanistan from 7th October 2001: a war that has involved US forces to at least the time of writing. Throughout that time, the R.1s of 51 Squadron were busy, although it will be a long time before the exact nature of their operations is revealed. The so-called 'War on Terror' shifted its attention to Iraq and the second Gulf War was waged from 20th March with Baghdad being taken on 9th April 2003. The SIGINT Nimrods were again at Akrotiri and perhaps elsewhere: XW664 was covertly fighting its fourth war and were to remain regular visitors as the situation Iraq turned into a vicious insurgency with US forces not pulling out until 18th December 2011.

As the dust was settling on the second Gulf War, on 17th April 2003 XW664 was heading across the Atlantic, deploying to Naval Air Station Patuxent River, Maryland, to take part in Project 'Extract'. Throughout the life of the R.1s updates, upgrades and refits were routine and XW664 was validating an automatic electronic warfare suite developed by Raytheon Strategic Systems. Job done in six sorties, the R.1 was eastbound heading for Waddington on 4th May. 'Extract' went 'live' on the R.1s in September 2005.

The maritime Nimrod fleet was paid off in the spring of 2010 and the MRA.4 programme was axed in October. Suddenly the remaining R.1s (XW664, XW665 and XV249) became what is known as 'orphans' – sustaining such a small fleet being very expensive. Much in demand in a volatile world, the R.1s flew on to the official retirement date of 28th June 2011. At 10:29 hours on 12th July 2011 XW664 touched down at East Midlands Airport having made the short flight from Waddington. Greeted by the airport fire service, the Nimrod taxied through an arch of water spray. XW664 had notched up a total of 21,466 flying hours. Seventeen days later R.1 XV249 completed the last-ever Nimrod flight and an incredible era ended. At East Midlands, a working party from Waddington attended over a period of weeks to remove fittings and to decommission the airframe. Preparations to move XW664 across the runway took some time and it was installed in the Aeropark on 19th November 2011.

At Waddington, 51 Squadron had to wait until 12th November 2013 for the Nimrod R.1's replacement. On that day Boeing RC-135W RIVET JOINT ZZ664 (the serial honouring its forebear) arrived and it became operational on 23rd May 2014. Known in the RAF as the Airseeker R.1, the 'gizmos' inside are just as 'hush-hush' and capable as the Nimrods were in their day. ZZ664 was built by Boeing as KC-135A tanker 64-14833 and first flew at Seattle on 29th October 1964. That makes ZZ664 seven years *older* than XW664; such is progress...

East Midlands Airport Aeropark aircraft

Type	Identity	Built	Origin	Acquired	Notes
Sheriff Aerospace Sheriff	G-FRJB	1982	Britain	1 Jul 1986	see profile
Armstrong Whitworth Argosy 101*	G-BEOZ	1960	Britain	Jun 1987	see profile
Avro Vulcan B.2*	XM575	1963	Britain	21 Aug 1983	–
Beagle Terrier 2	G-ASDL	1950	Britain	Jan 2012	–
de Havilland Dove 6	G-ANUW	1955	Britain	31 Oct 2009	–
de Havilland Vampire T.11	XD534	1954	Britain	2004	–
de Havilland Vampire T.11	XD447	1954	Britain	3 Oct 2009	–
de Havilland Sea Venom FAW.22	XG737	1958	Britain	31 Oct 2009	–
DHC Chipmunk T.10	WP784	1952	Canada	11 Oct 2008	–
English Electric Canberra T.17	WH740	1953	Britain	8 Dec 1991	see profile
English Electric Lightning F.53	ZF588	1968	Britain	8 Jan 1989	–
EoN Primary	–	c1950	Britain	2012	glider
Gloster Meteor NF.13	WM367	1953	Britain	11 Oct 2008	cockpit
Gloster Meteor NF(T).14	WS760	1954	Britain	11 Nov 2006	–
Gloster Meteor TT.20	WM224	1952	Britain	12 Jan 2003	–
Hawker Hunter T.7	XL569	1958	Britain	20 Feb 1993	–
Hawker Hunter 'FR.10'	'272'	1956	Britain	23 May 2009	composite
Hawker Hunter GA.11	WV382	1955	Britain	24 Jun 2009	–
Hawker Siddeley Buccaneer S.2B	XV350	1967	Britain	11 Dec 1993	–
Hawker Siddeley Nimrod R.1	XW664	1971	Britain	12 Jul 2011	see profile
Hunting Jet Provost T.3	XN492	1960	Britain	2015	cockpit
Hunting Jet Provost T.4	XP568	1962	Britain	25 Oct 2008	–
Morane-Saulnier Rallye 100S	G-BBLM	1973	France	27 Aug 2015	–
Percival Provost T.1	WW442	1954	Britain	Sep 2013	–
Schleicher K-8	–	c1962	Germany	2012	glider
Slingsby Cadet TX.3	WT914	1952	Britain	Jun 2014	glider
Sud Gazelle AH.1	XX457	1976	France	11 Oct 2008	cabin
Vickers Varsity T.1	WL626	1953	Britain	8 Nov 1979	–
Vickers Viscount 807	G-CSZB	1957	Britain	Apr 2003	cockpit
Vickers Merchantman	G-APES	1961	Britain	1997	cockpit
Vickers VC-10 C.1K	XV108	1968	Britain	16 Nov 2013	forward fuselage
Westland Whirlwind Srs 3	XG588	1955	USA/GB	May 1986	–
Westland Wessex HC.2	XT604	1966	USA/GB	11 Jul 2002	–
Westland Lynx HMA.8	XZ721	1980	Britain	Mar 2016	–

Notes: * – illustrated in the colour section.

In-flight refuelling probe-equipped Nimrod R.1 XW664 at Wyton, circa 1984. *Peter Green Collection*

Also in Leicestershire
Charnwood Museum

This tribute to the social and industrial heritage of Loughborough and beyond includes the 1956 King's Cup-winning Auster J/1N G-AJRH to commemorate the wonders worked at nearby Rearsby. **www.charnwood.gov.uk**

Lutterworth Museum

The displays includes much about Sir Frank Whittle and Power Jets material and an incredible archive. Dramatically displayed to the south of the town on the A426 roundabout is the **Whittle Memorial**, a superb tribute to the Gloster E28/39 and Sir Frank Whittle. **www.lutterworthmuseum.com**

Stanford Hall and Percy Pilcher Museum

Within the stables block is a display devoted to Percy Pilcher. He crashed at Stanford Hall on 30th September 1899 while flying the Hawk and died of his injuries two days later. There also is a memorial to the pioneer in the grounds. (The original craft he was piloting is held in store by the National Museum of Flight Scotland, East Fortune.)

Auster J/1N G-AJRH at the Charnwood Museum. *Roger Richards*

Lancaster Base
Lincolnshire Aviation Heritage Centre

East Kirkby
www.lincsaviation.co.uk

With every year that goes by, the exhibits, buildings and grounds that are centred upon the wartime watch tower at East Kirkby get to look and feel more and more like they would have done in the years 1943 to 1945 when the Avro Lancasters of 57 and 630 Squadrons thundered in and out. With the help of a small staff and a band of loyal volunteers, the Lincolnshire Aviation Heritage Centre (LAHC) is the summation of the passion of the Panton family, particularly the grandees, Fred and Harold. Their wish to commemorate the sacrifice of the men of Bomber Command and especially their elder brother, Christopher, has resulted in a museum of unique character. This desire took physical form in the early 1970s when they acquired the former Bomber Command airfield and in September 1983 secured Avro Lancaster NX611, later to gain fame as *Just Jane*. (Fred died in 2013; his and Harold's story are so inter-woven with that of NX611 that they are detailed in the profile that appears later.)

Above and overleaf: Lancaster VII *Just Jane*, 'star' of the Lincolnshire Aviation Heritage Centre. *Ken Ellis*

East Kirkby became an operational station in August 1943 when the Lancasters of 57 Squadron arrived from Scampton. During November, 'B' Flight of 57 Squadron was used as the basis for a new unit, 630 Squadron, which was formed on the 15th. The perils of Bomber Command were experienced by the locals during the evening of 17th April 1945. A fire broke out on the bombed-up NN765 which blew up cataclysmically; killing four members of ground crew and injuring many more, both air crew and maintenance teams. Five other Lancasters were written off; 14 were damaged to some extent or another. A hangar was put out of action and farm buildings were seriously damaged. No.630 Squadron's short service life came to a halt in July

East Kirkby's watch tower has been restored to its Bomber Command days. The detailing is a delight, even down to the period bicycles in the shelter outside. *Peter Green*

1945 and the Lancasters of 460 Squadron Royal Australian Air Force moved in from Binbrook, only to disband in October. The first Avro Lincoln arrived for 57 Squadron on 23rd July 1945 but a full conversion was not achieved; it also disbanded, in November. de Havilland Mosquitos of 139 Squadron used the airfield during 1947 and early 1948 as a refuge from construction work at Coningsby. Otherwise all was quiet until building teams descended for a major reconfiguration in April 1954; East Kirkby was destined to become a United States Air Force base. Operational usage of the airfield was restricted to the 61st and 64th Air Rescue Squadrons, operating specially configured Douglas SC-47 Skytrains and these had moved on by January 1958.

Turning the clock back

As the Pantons settled to establishing their agricultural and poultry business at East Kirkby, the first act of commemoration was the dedicating of a memorial to those who had served at the airfield with Bomber Command. During the early 1980s lots of work was being carried out, particularly at the watch tower as the notion of what was to become the LAHC became a reality. Other buildings were turned into exhibition halls, including the exceptional RAF Escape Museum. The chapel is deeply emotive and visitors should keep their eyes open as they walk the grounds, there are numerous memorials to individuals and organisations. The reception hut also contains a 'NAAFI' and well-stocked shop.

In a hectic weekend, 10th and 11th December 1985, the majority of the airframes of the Lincolnshire Aviation Museum (LAM) arrived. (The full story of this collection and its successor, Thorpe Camp Visitor Centre, is chronicled in *Pathfinders* below.) With the Lancaster due to arrive from Scampton, the decision was taken that a large 'fleet' of historic aircraft was inappropriate for LAHC and over the next couple of years, much of the LAM aircraft were disposed of. The Lincolnshire Aircraft (later Aviation) Preservation Society was established in 1988 to support the LAHC and work on the Handley Page Hampden and Percival Proctor restoration projects; the latter had been part of the LAM collection. Hampden I AE436 of 144 Squadron crashed on high ground in Sweden on 4th September 1942, killing three Canadian airmen. The substantial remains were salvaged in 1976 and passed on to the RAF Museum and stored at Henlow. Seemingly forgotten, the hulk was 'discovered' by Brian Nicholls in 1987 and he persuaded the museum to part with them. (P1344, another Hampden that crashed in the Soviet Union on the same day as AE436 is undergoing a long term restoration at the Michael Beetham Conservation Centre at the RAF Museum, Cosford.) Work on AE436 began in earnest at East Kirkby in 1989 and visitors can monitor progress as the workshop has a viewing area. Tragically, Brian died, aged 34, in 1996 and AE436 is known as the Brian Nicholls Hampden Project in his honour. Another organisation working in close co-operation with LAHC is the Lincolnshire Aircraft Recovery Group (LARG) which specialises in aviation 'archaeology'. Many of the displays in the Lancaster hangar are from LARG 'digs'. The wreckage of former 416 Squadron Royal Canadian Air Force (RCAF) Supermarine Spitfire IX BL655, which crashed at Dorrington Fen on 1st July 1943, is an evocative sight.

Latest exhibit at LAHC is a superb recreation of a Lancaster forward fuselage using as many original components as possible. Like *Just Jane*, this was used in the making of the BBC television drama *Night Flight* in 2001. Created by Lancaster maestro Jeremy Hall, this impressive item was used for the close-up cockpit sequences. It is painted up in post-war RCAF colours to starboard and wartime Canadian Bomber Command markings to port, 405 Squadron's *Our Beautiful Babe*.

During the winter of 2016-2017 *Just Jane* was stripped down. This allowed for a thorough survey of the airframe and any problems discovered along the way could be rectified. After all this was completed, LAHC had an excellent base point from which to determine the extent of the work required to put the Lancaster back in the air. As well as NX611's devoted maintenance crew, the task was supported by MAAS Aviation, an Irish-Dutch organisation with extensive experience of aircraft painting. This programme was estimated to have cost around £250,000 and LAHC initiated a variety of fund-raising schemes, including the innovative 'Rivet Club'. At the time of writing, *Jane* was about to revert to its ever-popular taxi rides while the question 'To fly or not to fly?' continues to be assessed. Whatever the eventual decisions, the next phase of *Just Jane*'s life has begun. So without more ado, we'd better profile a very special Lancaster...

Avro Lancaster VII NX611
1945 | Long range heavy bomber | Four 1,620hp Rolls-Royce Merlin 24 pistons

East Kirkby is the only place outside of the 'nationals' (Mk.I R5868 at Hendon, the cockpit of Mk.I DV372 at South Lambeth, Mk.X KB889 at Duxford) and the Battle of Britain Memorial Flight (below) with a genuine Lancaster. This is down to the fortitude of two brothers, paying tribute to their elder sibling felled while serving with Bomber Command.

Just Jane started life at Austin Motors, Longbridge, as a Mk.III but was completed as the factory's first Mk.VII. It was issued to the RAF on 16th April 1945 and spent much of its time in store; mostly at 38 Maintenance Unit, Llandow. On 31st May 1951, NX611 was taken on charge by Avro at Woodford, for conversion for the French naval air arm, Aéronavale, using Western Union Alliance financing. Work complete and wearing the serial number WU-15 on 30th May 1952, it was returned to Llandow, ready for delivery to France. WU-15 was initially issued to Flottille 25F at Lann-Bihoué, Brittany, and also operated from bases in Morocco. Lockheed P2V-7 Neptunes started to arrive for 25F in 1958. WU-15 was refurbished at Le Bourget, Paris, by 1962 and given a tropical all-white colour scheme. In its new colours, WU-15 was ferried to Escadrille de Servitude 9S at La Tontouta, New Caledonia in November 1962. The last three veterans of 9S were retired in favour of Douglas C-54 Skymasters in 1964.

Formed in 1965, the Historic Aircraft Preservation Society (HAPS) had been campaigning to take on one of the surviving French Lancasters and its pleas were answered when WU-15 was delivered to Bankstown, New South Wales, in August 1964, ready to collect. When approached about the possibility of a Lancaster coming from Australia, the operators of Biggin Hill offered free ramp space providing it could 'star' at the 1965 'Air Fair'. As preparations to bring it from the other side of the world were concluded, the Lancaster was registered as G-ASXX on 22nd October 1964. Captained by Wg Cdr John Hampshire DFC RAAF, *Xray-Xray* touched down at Biggin Hill on 13th May 1965. Twenty-three days and 12,000 miles previously the crew had embarked on an epic ferry flight, starting off from Mascot, New South Wales. The word was hardly in common usage in 1965, but Britain's largest privately-owned 'warbird' had arrived. By this time, the Lancaster had about 2,411 hours 'on the clock'. After the euphoria of the arrival, hard work followed to get G-ASXX ready for British certification. This took much time and a lot of expense and it was not until 6th May 1967 that it was air-tested. It had been painted in standard Bomber Command camouflage and soon gained the codes 'HA-P' and the name *Guy Gibson*. Fortuitously, 218 Squadron used the squadron identifier 'HA' and flew Lancasters 1944 to 1945. For this and all the other flights the captain was gifted pilot Sqn Ldr Neil Williams.

Lancaster NX611's flights in Britain – the story so far!

Date	From	To	Notes
13th May 1965	Australia	Biggin Hill	arrival in UK
6th May 1967	Biggin Hill	Biggin Hill	test flight
7th May 1967	Biggin Hill	Biggin Hill	test flight
9th May 1967	Biggin Hill	Biggin Hill	test flight
17th May 1967	Biggin Hill	Biggin Hill	test flight, Permit to Fly issued
19th May 1967	Biggin Hill	Scampton	'Dam Busters' 24th anniversary celebrations
20th May 1967	Scampton	Biggin Hill	return
2nd Sep 1967	Biggin Hill	Blackbushe	static for airshow
3rd Sep 1967	Blackbushe	Biggin Hill	return
5th Jun 1968	Biggin Hill	Filton	static for airshow
5th Jun 1968	Filton	Biggin Hill	return
30th Mar 1969	Biggin Hill	Lavenham	–
7th Feb 1970	Lavenham	Hullavington	–
26th Jun 1970	Hullavington	Squires Gate	departed by road Aug 1973 to Scampton

HAPS adopted not-for-profit company limited by guarantee status in February 1967 and in January 1969 the volunteer-run organisation became Reflectaire Ltd with paid employees and ostensibly run on a commercial footing. This brought about a change of attitude with the operators of Biggin Hill, who felt that the Lancaster (and other aircraft in the collection) could no longer bask in free ramp fees. The search for a new home commenced. On 30th March 1969, the Lancaster left Biggin Hill for Lavenham, a former wartime USAAF Consolidated B-24 Liberator base offering basic accommodation. By this time, the Lancaster had new codes, 'GL-C' to honour Gp Capt Leonard Cheshire VC DSO DFC. A change of landowner at Lavenham brought about another migration. 'Feelers' were put out for the next venue in what was becoming a hand-to-mouth management exercise. The Officer Commanding RAF Hullavington offered a hangar as a temporary home and Neil Williams was again in command when G-ASXX flew there on 7th February 1970. This was to be a very short stay. In the naïve belief that a visitor centre could be opened within an operational RAF station, the public were invited – at a fee – to come and inspect the bomber and perhaps buy some souvenirs! Quickly a directive explaining that this was unacceptable was issued and Reflectaire and its airframes were on the move again.

Lancaster VII WU-15 of the Aéronavale's Flottille 25F visiting Durban, South Africa, in 1958. *Vic Pierson-KEC*

Lancaster VII G-ASXX at Biggin Hill in May 1965, shortly after arrival. *Roy Bonser*

An offer from the management at Blackpool's Squires Gate Airport was seized upon. Flight No.14, and G-ASXX's last in the twentieth century, was staged on 26th June 1970. The choice of venue had a lot to do with expediency and desperation, but Blackpool and its holiday makers seemed to offer advantages. The Reflectaire Museum opened soon afterwards, with all of the airframes kept outside. At first attendance was encouraging, but rapidly fell away to a trickle. A cash injection came in February 1971 when the Lancaster was used for scenes in an episode of the ITV series *A Family at War*; during which it was taxied. It would be 24 years before all four Merlins ran again. (For more on the Historic Aircraft Preservation Society and Reflectaire, take a look at the sister volume *Lost Aviation Collections of Britain*.)

Blackpool Airport served a notice to quit on Reflectaire on 5th November 1971 and the company was wound up by liquidators Bernard Phillips and Company of London. Reflectaire's chattels were auctioned on 29th April 1972 through Henry Spencer and Sons of Retford. Of the 60-odd lots, the one generating the most interest was No.63, Lancaster G-ASXX, with a reserve of £16,500. The highest bid received by auctioneer Rupert Spencer, was £9,500 from Gordon Briggs, an Accrington-based scrap dealer. Among the 300 or so people attending was Lord Lilford of Nateby and he settled post-sale for a reported £12,500 (£200,000 in present-day values) and set about evaluating his options. It was quickly apparent that a return to airworthiness would cost a fortune. All the while the bomber was outside in the elements and incurring ramp fees.

In November 1970 Lancaster I R5868 had been removed from the 'gate' at Scampton, leaving on low loaders bound eventually for the RAF Museum. The loss of this landmark beside the A15 was sorely missed by personnel on the base and by locals. The Officer Commanding Scampton, Gp Capt Richard Lockyer, was determined to find a replacement. But where? Approaches to Lord Lilford were fruitful and a 'heads up' agreement on a ten-year loan was agreed on 2nd August 1973. The RAF lost no time, two days later work started on dismantling the Lancaster and nine days later, it was in a hangar at Scampton. It was painted in the colours of the Scampton Station Flight as 'YF-C' as worn by no less than ED932 in 1946. This had been the machine that Wg Cdr Guy Gibson DSO* DFC* had flown during the 16th/17th May 1943 'Dams' raid. The restored NX611 was rolled out on 18th March 1974 and, minus its outer wings, was trundled along the A15 and put in place as 'gate guardian' on 10th April 1974. It was officially placed on loan in a ceremony on 17th May 1974. It was allocated the ground instructional airframe number 8375M.

On the evening of 30th March 1944 Canadian Plt Off C M Nielsen eased Handley Page Halifax III HX272 *N-for-Nan* of 433 Squadron Royal Canadian Air Force off the runway at Skipton-on-Swale. The destination was the German city of Nuremberg; *Nan* was part of an armada of 795 bombers, Lancasters, Halifaxes and Mosquitos, sent to pummel the target. On the run in HX272 was singled out by a Luftwaffe night-fighter and it was shot down in flames. Nielsen and two others survived to become prisoners of war. The rest of the crew, five souls, were killed: among them was the flight engineer, Plt Off Christopher Whitton Panton. The five dead on *N-for-Nan* were part of the 537 aircrew killed that night; 94 bombers failed to return and eleven more were written off in crashes and accidents on return. It was Bomber Command's worst loss of the war. Among those that Christopher Panton left behind were his younger brothers, Fred (13) and Harold (11). These two became ever more determined to commemorate their brother's sacrifice when the Panton family acquired the former airfield of East Kirkby in the early 1970s. They decided to preserve a bomber.

In June 1973 the RAF Museum was salvaging Halifax II W1048 from a Norwegian lake; otherwise there were no others intact. (Canada did likewise in 1995 with Mk.VII NA337 now on show at Trenton, Ontario. See Chapter 31 for the astounding *Friday 13th*, unveiled at the Yorkshire Air Museum in 1996.) Besides, East Kirkby was a Lancaster base... After the Blackpool auction, the Panton brothers approached Lord Lilford, who was moved by their story and determination. He agreed to give Fred and Harold first refusal at the end of the loan agreement with the RAF. On 1st September 1983 Fred and Harold became the owners of NX611. It was resolved to allow NX611 to adorn the entrance at Scampton for another five years, while things were prepared at East Kirkby. During May 1988 the bomber was dismantled and trucked to its new home to begin a wonderful transformation.

Jeremy Hall's Lancaster forward fuselage recreation, the Lincolnshire Aviation Heritage Centre's latest exhibit. *Richard Hall*

The Lancaster was dedicated on 8th July 1989 as the centre piece of the newly established Lincolnshire Aviation Heritage Centre. To starboard it carried the codes of 57 Squadron, 'DX-C' and to port 'LE-C' of 630 Squadron – the two 'founder' units at East Kirkby. The team that looks after NX611 had not just been using paint brushes; miracles had been worked: on 21st April 1994 the starboard inner Merlin burst into life and in July 1995 all four were running. Three years later the Lancaster gained the *Just Jane* nose-art and it, or should that be she, has been universally known as *Jane* ever since. In February 2001 NX611 was wearing fictitious codes 'CM-V' and got to charge down the runway, getting the tailwheel up in the air, for its part in the BBC television drama *Night Flight*.

Jane has regularly delighted countless visitors by taxying on the former Lancaster base and has taken a growing number of people for a never-to-be-forgotten power-on ride. For the 70th anniversary of the Nuremberg raid, the code letters on the side of Jane were altered and revealed in a moving ceremony on 29th April 2014. The port codes had become 'LE-H' – *H-for-Harold* – and the starboard ones were 'DX-F' – *F-for-Fred*. Aged 82, Fred Panton had died the previous June and it was felt to be high time that the two brothers had their name on their bomber. For some time now, the team at East Kirkby has been looking into returning *Jane* to airworthiness and, as described at the beginning of this section, major steps have been made towards that end.

Lincolnshire Aviation Heritage Centre aircraft

Type	Identity	Built	Origin	Acquired	Notes
Avro Lancaster VII	NX611	1945	Britain	May 1988	see profile
Avro Lancaster	'976'	2001	Britain	17 Jan 2017	replica forward fuselage
Druine Turbulent	–	1962	France	Dec 1985	fuselage
English Electric Canberra E.15	WH957	1955	Britain	Dec 1985	cockpit
Handley Page Hampden I	AE436	1941	Britain	Nov 1988	forward fuselage
Heinkel He 111	–	1968	Germany	Mar 1993	cockpit mock-up
Percival Proctor IV	NP294	1944	Britain	Dec 1985	–
Supermarine Spitfire Vb	BL655	1941	Britain	1993	fuselage section

Destined for a new life at East Kirkby, Tony Agar's magnificent Mosquito NF.II HJ711 *Spirit of Val. Courtesy Tony Agar*

Postscript

As this book closed for press came the news that Tony Agar was moving his near-to-taxiable de Havilland Mosquito NF.II HJ711 *Spirit of Val* was to relocate from the Yorkshire Air Museum (Chapter 31) to the Lincolnshire Aviation Heritage Centre. The move was anticipated as taking place in November 2017. This puts this truly magnificent re-creation betwixt and between both locations and it was felt best that it was not profiled at either location. **www.mossie.org/HJ711**

> **STOP PRESS:** As this book closed for press came the news that Tony Agar was moving his de Havilland Mosquito NF.II HJ711 *Spirit of Val* from the Yorkshire Air Museum (Chapter 31) to the Lincolnshire Aviation Heritage Centre. It arrived at its new home by early August 2017. This puts this truly magnificent re-creation betwixt and between both locations and it was felt best that it was not profiled... it's time will come! **www.mossie.org/HJ711**

Nurturing Wings
Cranwell Aviation Heritage Centre

North Rauceby
www.cranwellaviation.co.uk

Before we go any further, and despite the heading image, it is important to explain that the Cranwell Aviation Heritage Centre is located *near* to Cranwell – it's within the circuit, but not *on* the airfield. Doing 'circuits and bumps' from the historic airfield will be the resident Beech King Airs (and soon Embraer Phenoms), Grob Prefects and Tutors. Since the early 1990s, the centre has been vividly charting the history of the world's first military air academy. With a couple airframes, a flight simulator, loads of artefacts and presentations, the centre is a very popular waypoint when touring Lincolnshire.

What is probably the most famous RAF landmark, the imposing College Hall, had an inauspicious start. To save time and money, the job of design was given to the Ministry of Works. Unsurprisingly, the plans were utilitarian and far from inspiring. The architect, James West, was taken to see the Royal Hospital in Chelsea, commissioned from Sir Christopher Wren in 1681. This did the trick; the building is a combination of authority and grace. Completed in September 1933, College Hall was officially opened by HRH The Prince of Wales in October 1934. In front of this grand edifice is the parade ground and a large circle of grass known as the 'Orange'; graduation ceremonies are still held there today.

Cranwell's imposing College Hall. *Ken Ellis*

Cranwell's origins lie with the Royal Naval Air Service (RNAS) which wanted to establish a base to train officers and ratings to fly aeroplanes and airships. The RNAS Central Training Establishment Cranwell was commissioned on 1st April 1916. Two years later, on another 'All Fools' Day', 1st April 1918, the RNAS and the Royal Flying Corps were amalgamated and Cranwell became an RAF station. Opened on 5th February 1920, the RAF College used the wooden huts of the RNAS days while plans for permanent structures were formulated. In his message to the first intake, Marshal of the RAF Sir Hugh Trenchard set the tone: "We have to learn by experience how to organise and administer a great service, both in peace and war, and you, who are present at the college in its first year, will, in future, be at the helm. Therefore, you will have to work your hardest, both as cadets at the college and subsequently as officers, in order to be capable of guiding this great service through its early days and maintaining its traditions and efficiency in the years to come." The badge of RAF Cranwell carries the Latin motto 'Alitum Altrix' which translates as 'Nurturer of the Wings' to reflect this task and the Visitor Centre portrays over a century of this illustrious heritage superbly.

Cranwell Aviation Heritage Centre aircraft

Type	Identity	Built	Origin	Acquired	Notes
de Havilland Vampire T.11	XE946	1955	Britain	14 Feb 1996	cockpit
Hunting Jet Provost T.4	XP556	1961	Britain	mid-1997	–

Hidden Gem
Metheringham Airfield Visitor Centre

Metheringham
www.metheringhamairfield.co.uk

Construction work was still going on and accommodation was basic. Although Lincoln was only seven miles to the northwest, the personnel of 106 Squadron thought they were in the middle of nowhere – and it was freezing! Just a fortnight after arriving at Metheringham, still trying to settle in, the crews huddled into the briefing room in the early afternoon of 26th November 1943. Being battle-hardened, the announcement that the target was 'The Big City' – Berlin – was greeted stoically. The Avro Lancaster IIIs started rolling just after 17:00 hours. One aircraft had to turn back with engine trouble, limping back ED873 gave up the struggle and came down a couple of miles short of the airfield; all of the crew scrambled clear. Captained by Belgian Fg Off J van Hoboken DFC JB592 *W-for-William* was returning when it crashed north of Frankfurt. All seven on board perished – one of 47 aircraft lost by Bomber Command that night.

Above: Vertical camera shot of Metheringham, March 1945. North is to the left of the image. *KEC*

Right: The memorial, featuring the propeller of a downed 106 Squadron Lancaster, at Metheringham. *Jeff Williams*

Nobody was sad to see the under-performing Avro Manchesters leave 106 Squadron in May and June 1942, when the unit was based at Coningsby. Returning from a raid on Hamburg on 27th July Lancaster I R5748 was shot down by a Luftwaffe night-fighter and it crashed in the Netherlands. Three of the crew became prisoners of war, four were killed. The bomb aimer, Plt Off W Fuller, was never found and his name appears on the Air Forces Memorial at Runnymede. Fifty years later, wreckage from *R-for-Robert* was salvaged by a team from the Royal Netherlands Air Force and a propeller hub and twisted blade was passed on to Metheringham. Mounted on a simple brick plinth, this acts a memorial to those who served at Metheringham. It was dedicated during the opening of the Airfield Visitor Centre in 1994.

Metheringham was a one-unit airfield until 1690 Bomber Defence Training Flight arrived in September 1944, its Hawker Hurricanes, Miles Martinets and Supermarine Spitfires being used to hone the defensive skills of the crews of 106 Squadron and other units at nearby airfields. In 1945 the Lancasters of 189 Squadron and the Australian 467 Squadron arrived, only to disband before the end of the year. The Lancasters of 106 out-lived all of them; disbanding on 18th February 1946 and the land began to revert to agriculture.

During eighteen months of intensive action 106 Squadron had staged over 200 'ops' and lost 59 Lancasters, the majority of those crews where killed. Established in the 1980s, the Friends of Metheringham Airfield has worked wonders with buildings on the former communal site. The displays at Metheringham are detailed and fascinating, but the most moving is also the simplest. On a ceiling are 59 black outlines of Lancasters, a poignant reminder of the purpose of the museum.

Metheringham Airfield Visitor Centre aircraft

Type	Identity	Built	Origin	Acquired	Notes
Douglas Dakota 3	KG651	1942	USA	16 Nov 2015	–
Hunting Jet Provost T.4	XS186	1964	Britain	5 Mar 2004	–

Roll of Honour
RAF Wickenby Memorial Collection

Wickenby
www.wickenbymuseum.co.uk

Pause at the main entrance to delightful Wickenby airfield where the 'Icarus' memorial pays tribute to the personnel of 12 and 626 Squadrons who gave their lives while the two units were based there. Head for the watch tower. This offers great views of light aircraft using the runways that once reverberated to Vickers Wellingtons and Avro Lancasters. The ground floor is home to a brilliant café; the upper floor is the domain of the RAF Wickenby Memorial Collection and you'll get a very warm welcome on both levels. In the latter, you'll be astounded at the quality and comprehensive nature of the displays. The volunteers are exceptionally knowledgeable, will answer questions and happily regale you with stories. One that most struck the author follows; I thought at first it was apocryphal, but it has stood the test of time. Farm owner Mr Bowser was told one morning in 1941 by surveyors pacing out his land that it was suitable – he knew not what for. By 3pm that same day construction contractors McAlpine began to clear the site! Remember, there was a war on!

The collection has its origins in the Wickenby Register, run by the 12 and 626 Squadron Association, which was formed in 1979 and a vast amount of material was gathered. The Register was responsible for the memorial at the entrance, which was dedicated on 6th September 1981 and was refurbished in 2010. The following year the Register was disbanded and, via

The watch tower at Wickenby holds an exceptional heritage collection. *Ken Ellis*

the Friends of the Wickenby Archive, the material is lodged in the watch tower. The RAF Wickenby Airfield Museum (later the suffix was changed to 'Collection') was established fully in 1998 by the then owners who were pleased to see how much interest was expressed in Wickenby's heritage. Taking pride of place is the Roll of Honour that includes the names of all 1,491 men who were killed while serving with 12 and 626 Squadrons during World War Two, including those stationed at Wickenby, Binbrook, Eastchurch and with the Advanced Air Striking Force in France.

After McAlpine had finished its work, in late September 1942, the Wellington IIs and IIIs of 12 Squadron arrived from Binbrook. Conversion to Lancasters started almost immediately. The personnel of 12's 'C' Flight became the caucus of 626 Squadron, which formed at Wickenby on 7th November 1943, with Lancasters. No.12 Squadron returned to Binbrook In September 1945 and the following month 626 Squadron was disbanded. For two months the de Havilland Mosquito XVIs of 109 Squadron called Wickenby home but then all flying ceased. The site was used for the collection, storage and disposal of bombs and **93** Maintenance Unit was reformed for this task in January 1949. From September 1952 the work was taken on by **92** MU and its work was completed in 1956. Much of the airfield was returned to agriculture by 1966, but the northern element of the big base was retained for light aviation and Wickenby remains a vibrant flying community.

Pathfinders
Thorpe Camp Visitor Centre
Tattershall Thorpe
www.thorpecamp.org

When volunteers decided to turn a derelict and overgrown segment of the famed Woodhall Spa airfield into a heritage site there must have been times when they doubted their resolve. The place looked a mess, but as the spades were deployed in 1988 the daunting extent of the reclamation needed became clear. Located on the southern edge of the airfield, the land had formed part of No.1 Communal Site and was known locally as 'Thorpe Camp', because of is proximity to the village of Tattershall Thorpe. Built in 1940, the site included the Officers' and Sergeants' Messes, the Airmens' dining halls, the NAAFI, ration store, ablution block and latrines.

Thorpe Camp's dramatic 'guardian', Lightning F.1A XM192. Ken Ellis

When the RAF vacated the area, the camp became a target for squatters. It was then converted into temporary council housing and was used as such into the 1960s. The plot was dilapidated and nature was relentlessly reclaiming it by 1987. A section was acquired by the Woodland Trust and it was intended to demolish the buildings as they had no further use for them. Five enthusiasts, led by the irrepressible Mike Hodgson, set up the Thorpe Camp Preservation Group and in April 1993 it was registered as a charity. The aim was to restore the Communal Site and tell the story of RAF Woodhall Spa, its squadrons and civilian life in Lincolnshire during World War Two. All of the blood, sweat, tears, shovels, hammers and paint brushes triumphed on 17th July 1994 when this unique aviation heritage community opened its doors to the public. Initially, the land was leased from the Woodland Trust, but in April 1998 it was purchased outright.

Much of the small team who had toiled against the odds to clear the site, refurbish the buildings and equip them with displays had done this before. If they forgive me, they were veterans of the aircraft preservation movement, having established a pioneering museum a couple miles further south at Tattershall, nearly a quarter of a century before. This was the Lincolnshire Aviation Museum (LAM) and the choice of the title 'Pathfinders' was not just to reflect the role of Woodhall Spa's 627 Squadron it was to underline the influence of Thorpe Camp and its forebear. During the writing of sister volume *Lost Aviation Collections of Britain*, which charted the major museums that had gone by the wayside, I had considered covering LAM. But this was dismissed as its story is part-and-parcel of Thorpe Camp and, should this title ever get written, that's where it should be. So here it is...

Pioneer museum

During 1965 the Lincolnshire Aircraft Preservation Society (LAPS) was formed. Activities included aviation 'archaeology', the recovery of components from wartime crash sites and this was extended to hunting down whole airframes. In 1966 Percival Proctor IV NP294 was acquired and it was followed by Miles Gemini 1A G-AKER. LAPS stumbled along and by October 1969 had run out of steam. (The name was to be revived in 1988 at East Kirkby, see above.) Undaunted, previous members started again creating the Lincolnshire Aviation Enthusiasts Society, centred on Boston. This organisation took on the LAPS artefacts and airframes and decided that *collecting* things and secreting them away in garages was counter-productive. Their actions only made sense if there was a centralised location where they could be kept. If that could be achieved then the members had a duty to open their treasures to the public – a museum.

The search was on for an affordable, practical venue and it had to have at least one reasonably sized building. A former railway goods shed in the Old Station Yard at Tattershall was deemed suitable. Not far from Lincoln, Sleaford, Boston and Louth, Tattershall had a good 'catchment' area. It was also next door to Tattershall Castle and a short distance from the popular weekend venue of Woodhall Spa, so it had what today would be called 'footfall'. From an aviation point of view, Coningsby was just down the road and in those days the county had an array of active bases: Barkston Heath, Binbrook, Cranwell, Manby, Scampton, Stubby and Waddington; so a good throughput of 'spotters' could be expected. The goods shed was refurbished and the plot fenced: woodworking and painting skills being much more important than aircraft restoration prowess at that point! LAM was opened on 19th July 1970 by former World War Two pilot Alderman George Whitehead. Britain's first volunteer-organised aviation museum in what was to become the 'classic' sense – aircraft park, indoor exhibitions and regular weekend opening – was up and running.

Suspended from a crane intended to load and unload railway wagons, Ward Gnome G-AXEI at Tattershall, November 1978. In the foreground is the tail section of Vampire T.11 WZ549. *Roy Bonser*

Lincolnshire Aviation Museum aircraft 1969 to 1988

Type	Identity	Built	Origin	Acquired	Current status / fate
Auster AOP.9	XK417	1956	Britain	Feb 1974	private owner, Lincolnshire
Avro Vulcan B.1	–	1957	Britain	Sep 1984	cockpit, South Yorkshire Aircraft Museum – Chapter 31
Blackburn B-2	G-ADFV	1935	Britain	1982	cockpit, believed stored, Cambridgeshire
de Havilland Dove 1	G-AHRI	1946	Britain	Feb 1973	Newark Air Museum – Chapter 23
de Havilland Comet 4C	G-BEEX	1961	Britain	Sep 1982	cockpit, North East Land, Sea and Air Museum – Chapter 22
de Havilland Vampire T.11	WZ549	1953	Britain	20 Feb 1971	Ulster Aviation Collection – Chapter 34
de Havilland Vampire T.11	XD447	1954	Britain	1973	East Midlands Airport Aeropark – Chapter 15
Druine Turbulent above	–	1962	France	28 Dec 1979	fuselage, LAHC, East Kirkby,
English Electric Canberra B.2	WD954	1951	Britain	Oct 1969	cockpit, private owner, Cornwall
Fairchild Argus II	FK338	1942	USA	1981	Yorkshire Air Museum – Chapter 31
Focke Achgelis Fa 330A-1	100502	1944	Germany	1979	To Spain 2008
Handley Page Victor B.2	XH670	1959	Britain	1982	cockpit, private collector, Essex
Hawker Hunter F.51	E-424	1956	Britain	Apr 1982	South Yorkshire Aircraft Museum – Chapter 31
Mignet 'Flying Flea'	'G-AEOF'	1936	France	1970	Aviodrome, Netherlands
Mignet 'Flying Flea'	–	1936	France	Oct 1974	Newark Air Museum – Chapter 23
Mignet 'Flying Flea'	–	1936	France	1975	fuselage, Newark Air Museum – Chapter 23
Miles Gemini 1A	G-AKER	1947	Britain	Oct 1969	believed reduced to produce
North American Harvard III	EZ259	1944	USA	Oct 1969	fuselage. Registered as G-BMJW, in the Netherlands
Percival Proctor IV	NP294	1944	Britain	19 Oct 1969	LAHC, East Kirkby, above
Percival Provost T.1	WW450	1953	Britain	1980	Bournemouth Aviation Museum – Chapter 8
Piel Emeraude	G-BLHL	1959	France	7 Nov 1982	destroyed by 1998
Saunders-Roe Skeeter AOP.12	XM561	1959	Britain	28 Jan 1983	South Yorkshire Aircraft Museum – Chapter 31
Slingsby T.8 Tutor glider	BGA.794	1949	Britain	Oct 1969	airworthy, Leicestershire
Stewart Ornithopter	–	c1965	Britain	1979	South Yorkshire Aircraft Museum – Chapter 31
Supermarine Swift	–	c1955	Britain	1971	Solent Sky – Chapter 11
Ward Gnome	G-AXEI	1966	Britain	1971	private owned, Breighton, Yorkshire
Westland Dragonfly HR.3	WH991	1953	USA	May 1977	Yorkshire Air Museum – Chapter 31

It was obvious very quickly that the wooden airframes of the Gemini and Proctor were not designed for day-in-day-out exposure to the elements. The Gemini was moved on and the Proctor taken off site. The latter returned to Tattershall in 1984, occupying a genuine wartime Nissen hut that had been moved on site and re-assembled. Today, the Proctor is under long term restoration at East Kirkby. As discussed in the sections covering the Northern Aircraft Preservation Society (within Chapter 18) and the Midland Aircraft Preservation Society (Chapter 29) this was an era of rapid expansion of collections and at times when faced with the discovery of another potential airframe, the hardest word to utter was 'No'. The LAM collection reflected this and no apologies are made for including the table showing all of the aircraft secured during its tenure at Tattershall. A look through the listing reveals that a large proportion of the airframes have survived and are with other organisations: LAM served to pump-prime the next generation.

Visiting Tattershall in mid-1980, the author spoke to Mike Hodgson about LAM's most recent – and very important – acquisition. It was not an aircraft; it was the Panton Wing, a new building. Shocked that my notes survived from that time and amazed that they were in a logical place for me to find while writing this book, I'll quote from my scrawl. Mike explained: "Getting aircraft has proved to be really quite easy... Once the word gets around that you've got a few [airframes], offers for others follow, mostly from people who are looking for somewhere cheap to park them... Buildings are another matter... small ones are relatively easily handled, but there will come a time when we need a proper hangar..." The Panton Wing had been officially opened the previous April and was the gift of Fred and Harold Panton, of which much has been written earlier in this chapter. The building was named in honour of their brother Plt Off Christopher Panton who was killed on the Nuremberg raid of 1944.

Although its dimensions were modest, the most was made out of the goods shed at Tattershall. On 19th December 1970 former Central Air Traffic Control School, Shawbury, de Havilland Vampire T.11 WZ549 touched down at Coningsby. It was intended to be an instructional airframe, or destined for incineration on the fire dump. At the time the base was home to McDonnell Phantom FGR.2s and the Battle of Britain Memorial Flight. The Officer Commanding RAF Coningsby decided that he had a better use for the 1953-built jet trainer and it moved, on loan, to Tattershall on 20th February 1971. The Vampire fitted within the goods shed and there was room for another 1971 acquisition, with a Lincolnshire provenance. Former Short Stirling rear gunner Mick Ward built a single-seat monoplane of his own design at his North Scarle home. Powered by a converted 14hp Douglas motorcycle engine, it had span of 15ft 9in, considerably less than a 'Flying Flea' and appropriately was called the Gnome. Its first flight took place on the nearby disused Wigsley airfield in the hands of Ray Fixter on 4th February 1967. All of this was without the knowledge of the Air Registration Board, the predecessor of Civil Aviation Authority. The Gnome passed to Ray and he 'legitimised' it on 25th April 1969 by registering it as G-AXEI. It never gained a Permit to Fly and was presented to LAM. Inside the goods shed was a crane jib and the little monoplane was suspended from it. Today the Gnome is part of Nigel Ponsford's collection of light aircraft at Breighton.

A couple of times, it looked as though the lease on the Tattershall site could not be renewed, but ways and means were found. Options ran out in 1985 and the museum had to vacate by the year end. The Panton family offered a home at East Kirkby and in an intensive weekend, 10th and 11th December, the bulk of the collection sought sanctuary here. As related in the section of the Lincolnshire Aviation Heritage Centre, above, plans where changing there with the pending arrival of Lancaster NX611 from Scampton. It was clear there was no long term future for the LAM airframes and the process of dispersing the collection began. As this was going on, the overgrown, decaying No.1 Communal Site at Woodhall Spa was beginning to look more and more attractive. The seeds for a new and different museum had been planted.

A display of ordnance at Woodhall Spa, early 1945, with a 'Tallboy' in the background. The 'KC' marking on the bomb trolley in the foreground denotes its 'owner', 617 Squadron adopted those codes for its Lancasters from May 1943. *KEC*

'Dam Busters' and big bombs

RAF Woodhall Spa became operational in February 1942 as a heavy bomber airfield within 5 Group. On 1st March 1942 the Avro Lancasters of 97 Squadron made the short hop from Coningsby and early raids from the new base included a low level sortie against the diesel engine factory in Augsburg on 17th April. The unit moved to Bourn in 1943. Some of 97's crews remained at Woodhall to form the nucleus of a new unit, 619 Squadron, on 18th April 1943. In turn, 619 moved out in January 1944, to be replaced by Woodhall's most famous residents.

With 34 Lancasters and a pair of target-marking de Havilland Mosquitos, 617 Squadron settled in during January 1944. For the duration 617 used the Petwood Hotel in the town of Woodhall Spa to the north of the airfield as the Officers' Mess – see below. The 'Dam Busters' pioneered the use of ultra-heavy bombs, the 12,000lb 'Tallboy' and the 22,000lb 'Grand Slam' during its tenure at Woodhall. The unit re-located to Waddington in June 1945 where it converted to the Avro Lincoln the following year. Low level target marking, as developed by 617, was so successful that 627 Squadron, a Mosquito unit in 8 (Pathfinder) Group was 'loaned' to 5 Group to exploit this role. Arriving on 15th April 1944 from Oakington, the unit stayed until it was re-designated 109 Squadron in October 1945 and moved on to Wickenby. After Germany's surrender, Woodhall was used as an assembly and kitting-out point for 'Tiger Force' ground personnel destined to take RAF heavy bombers to the Far East, but the atomic bombs dropped on Japan in early August negated the need. In the early 1950s Woodhall served as a sub-site for 92 Maintenance Unit, also at Wickenby. (See *Roll of Honour*, above.)

From the late 1950s to 1965 Woodhall became a base for Bristol Bloodhound surface-to-air missiles (SAMs). With the rest of the airfield sold off for agriculture or mineral extraction, the former SAM site remained under the control of RAF Coningsby and was used for the servicing the engines of McDonnell Phantoms and later Panavia Tornados until 2003 when it was mothballed.

Arresting exhibit : magic ingredient

While the entrance to Thorpe Camp is dominated by an English Electric Lightning F.1A – profiled below – full-scale airframes, including replicas, are a small part of the centre's over-riding message. There is a workshop, dealing with everything from wings to display cases and visitors can watch activities at close quarters. Should it ever require the attention of the workshop, there is one artefact that will remain unmoved and the restoration team will have to go to it! This is a brake drum arrester gear salvaged from the end of one of Woodhall's former runways. The enormous contraption was sunk into the side of the runway and a cable was waiting to 'catch' an over-running, hook-equipped, heavy bomber. Built by Mather and Platt in Manchester in 1942, Arrester Gear serial number A9 was designed by Sir William Arrol and Company of Glasgow. Needless to say, the scheme was not widely adopted, but Woodhall was one of the first airfields to have the gear installed. Excavating this monster from its pit and moving it to Thorpe Camp was an epic operation. This forgotten piece of Bomber Command history and its supporting display has to be seen to be believed!

Farmer, author and historian, battlefield tour guide, aviation enthusiast, museum curator and manager, chairman of the British Aviation Preservation Council, leading light in establishing the pathfinding LAM and founder of Thorpe Camp are

Thorpe Camp's incredible bomber arrester gear. *Ken Ellis*

among the many roles that Mike Hodgson has taken on; frequently several of them at once! Mike is very proud of the caucus of volunteers that turn up each weekend to run the place, to look after the exhibits and generate new displays and special events. Ever aware that aircraft don't make a museum work, Mike has summed up perfectly the magic ingredient at Thorpe Camp: "We have come a long way and we still have much to do. What we have here is special and that reflects totally on the people that make this place tick."

English Electric Lightning F.1A XM192
1961 | All-weather fighter | Two 11,250lb st Rolls-Royce Avon 210 turbojets

Thorpe Camp's 'guardian' represents the first operational iteration of the exceptional Lightning; the Mk.1 entered squadron service at Coltishall with 74 Squadron in June 1960 followed six months later by the in-flight refuelling capable F.1A at Wattisham with 56 Squadron. Only two intact F.1 variants from the production batch are in British museums; the other being at Duxford. XM192 served in the county, at Binbrook, for a while but its greatest claim to fame was that Airfix chose it for the subject of a 1:72nd scale plastic kit which was released in 1962. Tens of thousands of them must have either inspired youngsters to greater things or become dust traps!

Production test pilot Keith Isherwood took XM192 for its maiden flight, from Warton, on 25th May 1961. It was issued to 111 Squadron at Wattisham, receiving the code 'K', on 28th June 1961. Soon, it took on the black spine and black and

Lightning F.1A XM192 heading a 111 Squadron line up at Wattisham in 1963. By that time the unit had adopted a less flamboyant colour scheme from the black and yellow markings of 1961. *KEC*

A ceremony in front the Lightning F.1A XM192, the 'gate guardian' at Wattisham, in September 1975. Left to right: 111 Sqn CO Wg Cdr Dick Horsfield; Flt Lt Jack Glass, the last pilot to fly XM192; Sue Wright, press officer for Airfix Products with a 1:72nd model of XM192. *KEC*

yellow fin and rudder that it again wears today. 'Treble-One' began converting to F.3s in December 1964 and on January 14, 1965 XM192 was taken on charge by 226 Operational Conversion Unit at Coltishall. Based once again at Wattisham, but with detachments to Binbrook, XM192 joined the Target Facilities Flight on 2nd October 1969. Last pilot to fly XM192 was Flt Lt Jack Glass; XM192 completing 2,186 hours in December 1973. Downgraded to instructional airframe status on 28th May 1974, it was issued the airframe number 8413M. Painted up in 111 Squadron colours, it became the Wattisham 'gate guardian' by 1975. Offered for disposal by the Ministry of Defence, it was acquired by Charles Ross, chairman of the Lightning Association, on the last day of January 1994. It was moved to Charles's home, close to Binbrook, in late May. The Lightning was on the road again on 29th June 1996, arriving at the Bomber County Aviation Museum at Hemswell, on loan from Charles. Bomber County closed its doors in 2005 and a new home was needed for XM192. A loan was negotiated with Thorpe Camp and XM192 took up its commanding position at the museum from 3rd December 2005.

Thorpe Camp Visitor Centre aircraft

Type	Identity	Built	Origin	Acquired	Notes
de Havilland Tiger Moth	–	2011	Britain	2011	replica
English Electric Lightning F.1A*	XM192	1961	Britain	3 Dec 2005	see profile
Fairchild Argus	'EV771'	1997	USA	2005	replica
Hawker Siddeley Buccaneer S.2B	XX895	1975	Britain	Jul 2016	cockpit
Panavia Tornado F.2	–	1982	GB/Ger/Italy	Oct 2016	cockpit, simulator
Percival Mew Gull	'G-AEXF'	2011	Britain	2011	replica

Notes: * – illustrated in the colour section.

Guided tours of the Battle of Britain Memorial Flight hangar at Coningsby provide close inspection and fascinating insights into the aircraft, their heritage and maintenance. *Richard Hall*

Lest We Forget
Battle of Britain Memorial Flight Visitor Centre

Coningsby
www.lincolnshire.gov.uk/bbmf

Mention Lincolnshire to any enthusiast and likely the Battle of Britain Memorial Flight (BBMF) will be the first thing they name. With respect to the superb Visitor Centre, everyone is champing at the bit to get into the Flight's hangar, a shrine full of 'national treasures'. Effectively an operational RAF squadron, these 'exhibits' not only are airworthy, they are also not always to be found at Coningsby. Accordingly this venue is beyond the remit of this book, but it *has* to get a mention.

A unique partnership between the RAF, Lincolnshire County Council and Lincolnshire's Lancaster Association provided the public with a gateway to the BBMF with the opening of the Visitor Centre in April 1986. As the aircraft of BBMF are mostly away displaying somewhere, it follows that the centre is normally closed at weekends. It is advisable to check in advance relating to the movements of the Flight, as it may be that some, or all, of the aircraft may be away visiting an event, or on over-winter maintenance. Readers are reminded that access to the BBMF hangar is by guided tour only; but these are superb, the volunteers that give them being very skilled and knowledgeable.

The origins of BBMF go back to July 1957 when the Historic Aircraft Flight was formed as an adjunct of the Biggin Hill Station Flight. It had become traditional to fly a Hawker Hurricane and a Supermarine Spitfire over London and other venues on Battle of Britain Day and the flight was conceived as a method of formalising this arrangement. On 21st February 1958 it was renamed the Battle of Britain Flight and seven days later it started a migratory existence, moving to North Weald; then in turn: Martlesham Heath (11th May 1958), Horsham St Faith (3rd November 1961) and Coltishall (1st April 1963). On 1st June 1969 the current title, BBMF, was adopted and on 6th March 1971 the permanent home at Coningsby was established.

Battle of Britain Memorial Flight aircraft

Type	Identity	Built	Origin	Acquired
Avro Lancaster I	PA474	1945	Britain	20 Nov 1973
de Havilland Canada Chipmunk T.10	WG486	1951	Canada	1995
de Havilland Canada Chipmunk T.10	WK518	1952	Canada	Apr 1983
Douglas Dakota III	ZA947	1942	USA	Jun 1993
Hawker Hurricane IIc	LF363	1944	Britain	28 Jun 1956
Hawker Hurricane II	PZ865	1944	Britain	29 Mar 1972
Supermarine Spitfire IIa	P7350	1940	Britain	5 Nov 1968
Supermarine Spitfire Vb	AB910	1941	Britain	16 Sep 1965
Supermarine Spitfire IX	MK356	1944	Britain	7 Nov 1997
Supermarine Spitfire XVI	TE311	1945	Britain	19 Oct 2012
Supermarine Spitfire PR.19	PM631	1945	Britain	14 Jun 1957
Supermarine Spitfire PR.19	PS915	1945	Britain	14 Jun 1957

Also in Lincolnshire
RAF Digby World War Two Sector Operations Room

Regular guided tours – no booking necessary – of the operations room are staged. After several years of 'scrounging', the lovingly restored room opened in May 1997. **www.raf.mod.uk/rafdigby**

RAF Ingham Heritage Group

Volunteers have been working hard to open a museum based on the former Airmen's Mess building since 2012. Keep an eye on: **www.rafingham.co.uk**

North Coates Heritage Collection

A display of artefacts, images and models relating to the history of the airfield 1914 to 1992 has been put together within the North Coates Flying Club premises. A Bloodhound Mk.1 missile is also on show. **www.northcoatesflyingclub.co.uk**

Waltham Windmill Trust and Preservation Society

An element of the extensive site surrounding the windmill is the **RAF Grimsby Exhibition**, situated in a Nissen hut. This is dedicated to the personnel and Lancasters of 100 Squadron and other units that flew from Waltham (or Grimsby) airfield, located to the east of the windmill. **www.walthamwindmill.org.uk**

When in Lincolnshire...

"Lincolnshire is a county where history was made and memories lie around every corner" so says the website of **Aviation Heritage Lincolnshire**, which aims to help visitors maximise their trip. The comprehensive website provides details of other attractions, memorials, suggests an airfield trail and even offers something called an 'app'. **www.aviationheritagelincolnshire.com**

In **Lincoln**, the first phase of this ambitious **International Bomber Command Centre** project, the memorial spire and the first sections of the 'Wall of Names' at Canwick Hill were unveiled on 2nd October 2015. Names of 26,500-plus Bomber Command aircrew will eventually be honoured in the 'Wall of Names' within the remembrance garden. Guided tours only are currently available but the centre is aiming for extended opening times in 2018: **www.internationalbombercommandcentre.com**

In the town of **Woodhall Spa** is the impressive 'Dam Buster' memorial and the newly inaugurated 617 Squadron commemoration. Another 'must' is the Petwood Hotel which was the Officers' Mess for, in turn, 97, 619 and 617 Squadrons. The 'Squadron Bar' has loads of memorabilia. **www.petwood.co.uk**

Please note that the **Heritage Centres** at **RAF Scampton** and **RAF Waddington** are available for inspection by prior arrangement only: **www.raf.mod.uk/rafscampton** and **www.raf.mod.uk/rafwaddington**

Woodhall Spa's famous Petwood Hotel; the 'Squadron Bar' is a shrine to the crews who flew from the nearby airfield. *Ken Ellis*

CHAPTER 17
GREATER LONDON

Capital Venues

London would not be the capital if it was not home to the national collections and it is, for the purposes of this book, that the **Imperial War Museum** at South Lambeth, the **Royal Air Force Museum** at Hendon and the **Science Museum** at South Kensington dominate. The 'big three' are the domain of sister volume *Great Aviation Collections of Britain*, but to start you off, respectively take a look at: **www.iwm.org.uk www.sciencemuseum.org.uk** and **www.rafmuseum.org** A number of other venues – some with restricted opening hours, or requiring prior booking – have an aviation 'flavour'...

Bentley Priory Museum

The museum tells the story of the magnificent country house's role as the headquarters of Fighter Command. The website puts it well: "Explore the important stories of 'The One' – Air Chief Marshal Sir Hugh Dowding, 'The Few' who took to the air to defend our skies and 'The Many' without whose tireless work on the ground victory would not have been possible." The grounds are 'guarded' by replicas of a Hawker Hurricane and a Supermarine Spitfire. **www.bentleypriorymuseum.org.uk**

Croydon Airport Visitor Centre

The visitor centre within the former terminal building of London Airport is run by the Croydon Airport Society. Outside, de Havilland Heron 2D G-ANUO is painted in the colours of G-AOXL of Morton Air Services which made the last passenger flight from Croydon on 3rd September 1959. **www.croydonairport.org.uk**

Above: Pre-booking is needed to visit the Uxbridge bunker, but it is well worth it. *Richard Hall*

'Flying' over a car park at Croydon is a DH Heron in the colours of Morton Air Services. *Terry Dann*

RAF Uxbridge Battle of Britain Bunker

Guided tours of 11 Group's command bunker, 60ft below ground level and in use from 1939 to 1958 are available by prior booking. There is an exceptional collection of artefacts. The grounds are 'guarded' by replicas of a Hawker Hurricane and a Supermarine Spitfire. **www.friendsof11group.co.uk**

Firepower – The Royal Artillery Museum in Woolwich closed its doors in June 2016 and its extensive exhibits have been placed in store. There are hopes that the museum will be re-born, but that will not be within Greater London. There's better news from the **Kenley Revival Project** which aims to conserve the eight extant blast pens, the fuel dump, perimeter track and taxiways and the impressive memorial at the famous airfield. Keep an eye on: **www.kafg.org.uk**

Founding Fathers
The Aeroplane Collection
at the
Museum of Science and Industry
Manchester
www.theaeroplanecollection.org
www.mosi.org.uk

It was a close run thing, although neither of the 'competitors' knew what the other was doing... An informal group of enthusiasts, who spent their weekends at Manchester Airport, Ringway, heard about a biplane at a school in nearby Lymm, Cheshire, and went to take a look on 10th February 1962. A slightly more formal band of devotees, the Solway Group of Aviation Enthusiasts (SGAE), set off on 17th March 1962 for Wigton to see if rumours about the existence of a biplane at a school were true. The timeline continues... On 3rd November 1962 the fuselage of Avro Avian G-EBZM was removed from a cellar at Lymm Grammar School and delivered to Stretford, Manchester. The two surviving wings followed the next day. Up in Cumberland seven days later the dismantled airframe of Hawker Hart K4972 was extracted from a loft at the Nelson Tomlinson School and transferred to Carlisle Airport, Crosby-on-Eden. It was some time before the two groups knew of one another.

Above: 'Star' of the Museum of Science and Industry Air and Space Gallery, The Aeroplane Collection's Avian IIIA G-EBZM. *MSI*

The lads in Cumberland carried out some restoration work on their find but on 16th October 1963 they presented K4972 to the Royal Air Force Museum and today it is displayed at Hendon. It was six years before what had become the Solway Aviation Group (later Society) took on another airframe, when de Havilland (DH) Vampire T.11 WZ507 touched down at Carlisle. The 'bug' had bitten and in 1983 a visitor centre was opened at the airport, around a growing collection of aircraft. On 18th May 1996 the full-blown Solway Aviation Museum was opened and it remains one of Britain's leading regional collections. (See Chapter 7.) By early April 1962 the gang from Ringway had chosen Northern Aircraft Preservation Society (NAPS) as a label to describe their activities. On 21st October that year the title was confirmed and a structure was being devised and in January 1963 the organisation was officially constituted. That October meeting was to clear the way to take on the Avian and the sum of £5 had been agreed as a donation to the school's aviation society. NAPS was renamed as The Aeroplane Collection (TAC) in 1974 and the organisation did not follow the path taken by its Carlisle-based 'competitors'. The Avian has remained its property ever since and, in this writer's opinion it is the star exhibit at the Museum of Science and Industry, which is why this section is far less about the Manchester museum and much more about its pioneering owners.

The fuselage of Avian G-EBZM atop the trusty 'Beagle Bus' shortly to leave Lymm Grammar School on 3rd November 1962. Left to right: John Kenyon, Chris Burke, Jeff Teagle, Paul Connatty, John Dickinson, Jim Patrick, Richard Jones. *Mike Ingham*

Avian G-EBZM was the first aircraft to have been acquired by a volunteer, enthusiast group with the overt aim of 'preservation' and NAPS was the inaugural body in a veritable explosion of such activity in the 1960s through to the early 1990s. That NAPS/TAC did not become a museum does not make the organisation's activities inferior – quite the contrary as will be seen as this narrative unfolds. The guys at Solway will be the first to declare that they have benefited from initiatives that radiated out of NAPS throughout their formative years.

As an aside, the SGAE had an obvious 'destination' for their Hart. Although it was 15th November 1972 before the RAF Museum opened at Hendon, the intention to do so was fully apparent by the early 1960s as the collecting of airframes and artefacts gathered pace at Henlow and other locations. Should NAPS have wanted to hand on the Avian to a 'higher authority', there was no such dedicated repository for light aviation; indeed there still isn't. NAPS would also have been stymied by trying to place it locally. Until the advent of the Manchester Air and Space Museum in 1983, no institution in the area had showed any great interest in things aeronautical.

Restoring City Hall

A desire to bring the former City Hall in Manchester's Liverpool Road back into use coincided with lobbying in the early 1980s to commemorate the contribution of the city and the northwest to aviation. The venue was suitable, the area was being fast-tracked for regeneration and the theme was likely to appeal to the public. From the first tentative meetings, TAC was very willing to support the venture; here was an opportunity to 'showcase' its aircraft in the city of its roots. The nature of its collection meant that the 'stick and string' era could be vividly met from TAC 'stock' but the 'heavy metal' end was lacking. Salvation was found with the RAF Museum, and items in the extensive 'reserve collection' could get an airing. It was also a well-timed place to locate the Shackleton AEW.2 which had flown into Cosford on 22nd October 1982 and looked set for a long time out of doors. This giant arrived at Liverpool Road on 27th January 1983, with the rest of the exhibits being arranged around it. (WR960's history is given in detail in sister volume *Great Aviation Collections of Britain*.) So it was that the Manchester Air and Space Museum opened up on 30th March 1983. Unlike many museums, of the twenty airframes on show that day, *all* were on loan. In the present day line-up loaned airframes are still in the majority: TAC's Avian, Bensen, Dragon Rapide, 'Flying Flea' and Roe Triplane; RAF Museum's Avro 504K, Shackleton, Belvedere, English Electric P.1A, Yokosuka Ohka. The Air and Space Museum was not the only institution to open on Liverpool Road in 1983. Yards to the west of City Hall is the former Liverpool Road Station, the oldest surviving railway terminal in the world. The Manchester to Liverpool line was opened on 15th September 1830 as the world's first double-tracked, fully timetabled, and a shedload of other 'firsts', railway. Like much of the area, it was out of use and crying out for development. The city council wisely poured money in and on 15th September 1983 the North West Museum of Science and Industry (MSI) opened its doors. It has expanded and flourished, offering 'in steam' locomotives, working stationary engines, the ever-popular toilets and sewage exhibition, inter-active elements and more. Within two years of opening up the nature of the air and space museum changed subtly but fundamentally. The logical fusion of two museums took place, with City Hall becoming the Air and Space Gallery of MSI. At

A general view of the Air and Space Museum, circa 1984. In view are: Spitfire V BL614, Shackleton AEW.2 WR960, Hunter F.1 WT619, Magister I 'T9707', Avro 707A WZ736 and in the foreground Sycamore HR.14 XL824. All but the Shackleton and 707 have moved on. *Alan Curry*

that point – by the definition adopted by this book – it ceased to be an *aviation* museum and became a 'museum *with planes in it*', albeit a goodly number. Since then there have been at least two schemes to dramatically revamp the aviation side, but none came to fruition. From early 2012, the National Museums of Science and Industry (aka the Science Museum) welcomed Manchester's MSI into its fold. It's arguable that the 2012 'acquisition' makes the Manchester MSI a 'national', but 'satellite' is a more workable definition; especially as the majority of its airframes are owned by the two organisations that pump-primed it in 1983 – the RAF Museum and TAC.

Cross-border Avian raid

But before we go any further, we should note that NAPS was not the first organisation to save Avian G-EBZM... In April 1959 a bunch of Liverpudlians staged a cross-border raid and extricated it from the fire pits at Manchester Airport. It was stored at the Huyton home of the MGAE's chairman, Bryan Heatley. This was before the gents that became NAPS had got into gear. There's always been rivalry between Liverpool and Manchester, but in those days before the Local Government Act of 1972 and the advent of unitary authorities in the early 21st century, Liverpool was firmly in Lancashire and Ringway was in Cheshire, so this was a genuine cross-border affair. Founded in 1956 the Merseyside Group of Aviation Enthusiasts (MGAE, later changing 'Group' for 'Society' and finally settling for the simpler Merseyside Aviation Society – MAS) linked it members with the monthly journal *Northern Aeronews* and its 'spotter' included features on extant historic aircraft. (*Aeronews* was later renamed *Flypast*; long before the high-street magazine of the same name – with a capital 'P' – made its appearance in 1981.)

As recounted in the profile of the Avian below, MGAE member and Ringway air traffic controller Alan Madden was concerned that G-EBZM had been presented to the airport fire crews. This seemed sacrilege and so a deal was struck with the firemen and the incomplete Avian was extracted to Huyton, Liverpool. There was no 'plan' for the biplane; it just seemed the right thing to do and a logical extension of being an enthusiast. Since the earliest days of aviation there have been plenty of occasions when someone has 'discovered' an aircraft, taken pity on it and found a garage or a barn to stash it in, with no scheme beyond that. And such impulses continue to this day... The MGAE was the first organised, enthusiast body to take such a step.

The July 1959 issue of *Northern Aeronews* shows a direction that the active members were considering. A local 'chapter' of the Popular Flying Association had been set up and MGAE members pondered what they could do: purchase a flyable aircraft; build an aircraft (a Luton Minor seemed favourite); or restore G-EBZM. Of the third option, the magazine noted: "Bearing in mind that many parts of this are missing, this would, at first sight, appear to be impossible". Despite this, the recommendation was to go with G-EBZM as members were following a lead on another example and, if that were acquired:

The Airviews hut at Manchester Airport, 1961. Left to right: John Kenyon, Tim Gresty (at rear), Jim Patrick, Norman Jenkinson, Mike Ingham, Paul Connatty. *via Mike Ingham*

"there should be little difficulty in combining the two aircraft (assuming the Air Registration Board is willing!)." On 30th June a deputation had travelled to Yorkshire and preliminary discussions seemed to have gone well. This was Ken Smith's Avian IIIA G-ACGT; later NAPS also pitched for this machine only to be given short shrift. *Golf-Tango* still exists in Yorkshire, having remained flightless since the 1930s.

So, MGAE saw the Avian as a way of getting *airborne*. Meanwhile the kind gesture to look after G-EBZM was beginning to pall with family Heatley. In mid-1960 the Avian moved to Liverpool Airport, Speke, but hangar fees needed paying, a financial clock was ticking. An offer from MGAE member Peter Schofield, a teacher at Lymm Grammar School, to take the Avian into his care was seized upon and it moved in early February 1961. The interest expressed by the nascent NAPS team clinched the future of G-EBZM; it was the founder member of a *preservation* group.

This was far from the end of MGAE's involvement in aviation heritage and arguably its most important step came in May 1961 with the publication of a supplement to *Northern Aeronews*. This was the first edition of *Wrecks & Relics*, compiled by Don Stephens, which surveyed preserved, significant, derelict and decaying airframes in Britain. At a stroke, the burgeoning preservation 'movement' had what one early preservationist called "a catalogue of what we could try for". Fifty-six years later, the title is in its 25th edition and still helping to preserve aircraft. As will be seen in Chapter 12, MSAE agitated to bring DH Mosquito TA634 to Speke in 1965. In the early 1970s, by which time the author was a member, MAS returned to acquiring aircraft. Part of the NAPS-inspired hand-out care of Hawker Siddeley at Woodford, the society took delivery of DH Vampire T.11 WZ553 at Speke on 15th March 1973 and not long afterwards Focke Achgelis Fa 330A-1 100549. The Fa 330 was easily portable and a great attraction when attending airshows with a publicity/fund-raising stall. The Vampire was another matter altogether; I remember that the main 'driver' was that it was an opportunity too good to miss out on. Certainly there was little thought of what happened beyond Thursday; in this MAS was no different from similar organisations in those days! The Vampire was disposed of on 10th March 1979 and today its fuselage 'pod' serves as a simulator in Warwickshire. The Fa 330A-1 was a founder-airframe at the Manchester Air and Space Museum, arriving at Liverpool Road on 18th September 1983, on loan. (Today it is with the Lashenden Air Warfare Museum, see Chapter 14.)

To own something – anything!

In conversation with NAPS founder-member Mike Ingham, I was keen to find out what sparked things off, not just with his particular group but what were the conditions that made aircraft preservation such a rampant enthusiast activity from the early 1960s. Such a narrative could be just as valid when discussing early organisations such as the Lincolnshire groups (Chapter 16), the North East Vintage and Veteran Aircraft Association (Chapter 22), Newark (Chapter 23) of Midland (Chapter 29). During my interviews with him, Mike was at pains to note that the establishment of NAPS and its expansion was from the very first a team effort in every way and remained so. As explained in the introduction, the intention of the narrative is not to become a 'name-fest' and Mike's reminiscences relate to the endeavours of an incredible group of individuals.

The birthplace of NAPS was a small, unpretentious hut at Manchester Airport; the motivation was 1946-built Auster J/1N Alpha G-AGXN. *Xray-November* operated by John Martin's Airviews (Manchester) Ltd on pleasure flying from May 1959. It was natural draw for enthusiasts and they provided low-cost labour, drumming up custom, helping passengers strap in, cleaning the Auster, wheeling it in and out, and the like. (G-AGXN still graces the skies, registered to the wonderfully named Gentleman's Aerial Touring Carriage Group in Hampshire. Pilot and trustee of the group is a certain Jeff Teagle, who was part of the team recovering G-EBZM in November 1962.) I hope Mike won't mind but the context is needed, in 1962 he was still at secondary school; some of the friends around him were much the same age, others older, but not by much. When things were slack, or the weather was against them, what Mike calls the 'Gang of Nine' would retreat to the hut and brainstorm.

Mike talked some of my questions through with two others from this era: John Kenyon and Jim Patrick (a former Lymm Grammar School pupil). From this, he wrote: "We have found it difficult to pinpoint just how some things happened, and I think they just did because ideas bounced off us all as we talked. The Airviews hut was the focus [and] we were all aircraft enthusiasts, very much 'Reginald S Potter' in our roots. We were a bit of a motley crew but were bound together through mutual interest and association; we certainly enjoyed each other's company. To quote John, the founder chairman, aircraft preservation did not feature at all initially, but then the Avian came about. Suddenly we all had a real 'live' aeroplane and a purpose and vision to aspire to and, as they say, the rest is history! Looking back I don't think we initially saw any further than having an aircraft – *any* aircraft – of our own. None of us can remember how the NAPS name came about. But then, once we had the Avian it was logical we were the north, we had aeroplane, and were preserving it."

Mike stressed that to *own* something was the over-riding aim. There was great excitement at the prospect of the Avian and it galvanised the small group into action. "I had no idea what an Avian was," Mike openly admitted, but he and his fellows enjoyed discovering its heritage. "The Lady Heath connection [see the profile below] was a real feather in our cap."

With the spur of the Avian, NAPS began a relentless search for other items. Having got access to lock-up garages in Stockport, space was available and soon filled! NAPS/TAC went on to build an exceptional collection of engines, a goodly number going on to grace other museums. A landmark on Lindow Common, near Wilmslow, was considered. The battered rear fuselage of Handley Page Halifax I L9504 had last been used as an instructional airframe in 1944. It was deemed too large to move and avoided the 'net'. The bulk of the NAPS/TAC story is beyond the remit of this book, but the table of the first 'decade' of acquisitions is instructive, showing the incredible level of activity.

The trusty NAPS Bedford panel van towing G-EBZM. *NAPS / TAC*

Northern Aircraft Preservation Society aircraft – the first 'decade', 1962 to 1970

Type	Identity	Built	Origin	Acquired	Current status / fate
Addyman Standard Training Glider	–	1934	Britain	29 Jan 1966	Nigel Ponsford collection, Selby
Addyman Standard Training Glider	–	c1934	Britain	29 Jan 1966	fuselage. Nigel Ponsford collection, Selby
Addyman Ultralight	–	1936	Britain	29 Jan 1966	Nigel Ponsford collection, Selby
Avro Avian IIIA	G-EBZM	1928	Britain	3 Nov 1962	see profile
Avro Avian IVM	G-ABEE	1930	Britain	1 Dec 1963	used as spares for G-EBZM, sold in Australia
Avro Anson C.19/2	VP519	1947	Britain	22 May 1970	cockpit. South Yorkshire Aircraft Museum – Chapter 31
BA Swallow	G-AEVZ	1937	Britain	28 Feb 1965	returned to airworthiness. Sold in Spain Sep 2001
Bristol F.2b Fighter	–	c1918	Britain	1 Jan 1967	fuselage frame. Used as basis for replica, displayed at Musée Royal de l'Armée, Brussels, Belgium
Chrislea Airguard	G-AFIN	1938	Britain	7 Feb 1970	Privately owned, under restoration in Devon
de Havilland Dragon Rapide	G-ADAH	1935	Britain	11 Oct 1970	see profile
de Havilland Dragon Rapide	G-AJBJ	1944	Britain	25 Oct 1969	fuselage. To Midland Aircraft Pres Soc – Chapter 29. Private owner north Wales
Focke Achgelis Fa 330A-1	100502	1944	Germany	21 Aug 1969	To Lincolnshire Aviation Museum 1979 – Chapter 16. To Spain 2008
Killick Man-Powered Helicopter	–	1963	Britain	13 May 1967	Nigel Ponsford collection, Selby
Mignet 'Flying Flea'	–	1936	France	13 Jun 1964	Museum of Science and Industry, Manchester
Mignet 'Flying Flea'	–	1935	France	12 Dec 1965	Last reported private owner, Sheffield
Miles Messenger 4A	G-ALAH	1945	Britain	Mar 1967	To RAF Museum at Henlow Jul 1970. Privately owned in Spain by 1995.
Mosscraft MA.2	'G-AFHA'		Britain	14 Feb 1965	with private owner in Midlands, thought reduced to produce
Percival Proctor IV	NP294	1944	Britain	13 Feb 1965	To LAPS 15 Oct 1966 and to LAM 19 Oct 1969. At Lincolnshire Aviation Heritage Centre – Chapter 16.
Roe Triplane I replica	–	c1953	Britain	24 Oct 1969	Museum of Science and Industry, Manchester
Saunders-Roe Skeeter AOP.12	XL811	1959	Britain	2 Dec 1968	The Helicopter Museum, Weston-super-Mare – Chapter 25
Slingsby Cadet TX.1 glider	RA848	1943	Britain	2 Jun 1968	fuselage. Nigel Ponsford collection, Selby
Slingsby Cadet TX.1 glider	RA854	1943	Britain	23 Nov 1963	Yorkshire Air Museum – Chapter 31
Woodhams Sprite	–	1960	Britain	26 May 1969	unfinished airframe. Suffolk Aviation Heritage Museum – Chapter 26

Swinging Sixties

Why had there been nothing like this enthusiast phenomenon before the 'Swinging Sixties'?. The author looked around at what 'kindred spirits' were up to, believing that there was probably a similar blossoming of activity in world of locomotives and railway carriages, but this does not seem to be the case. The famous, prolific, Woodham Brothers loco graveyard at Barry in South Wales did not give up its first steam engine until 1969 and it was the 1970s and 1980s before things really got rolling. So, aviation was not inspired by locomotion...

Back to Mike: "The 1960s were the springboard, it's regarded as a cliché but we were the generation that felt we were going to change the world." Information was getting easier to find, *Air Pictorial* (these days *Aviation News*) was a source of much enlightenment. Mike joined Air-Britain in 1962; the Ringway Spotters Club evolved into the Society of Northern Aviation Enthusiasts and the MGAE was becoming an increasing fount of 'gen', especially through *Wrecks & Relics*. Intelligence on what was out there was not a one way street. In the spring of 1963 Mike made enquiries with the officer commanding 27 Maintenance Unit at Shawbury suggesting that two recently arrived Civilian Anti-Aircraft Co-operation Unit DH Mosquitos, T.3 RR299 and TT.35 TA719 should be preserved. The reply came that two were available at £250 each. Wisely, the NAPS team realised that financially and logistically even such a charismatic aircraft was beyond their means. Mike: "Gen like that was passed on to those more capable than us... there was enough [available] for everyone" This idea of spreading the word was going to have great ramifications, as will be explained. (By July 1963 both of the Mosquitos had been snapped up. RR299 by Hawker Siddeley to fly at airshows until it crashed fatally at Barton on 21st July 1996. TA719 flew to Bovingdon to take part in the filming of *633 Squadron* and is now on show at Duxford.)

The era of post-war austerity was over, or so it seemed. Bicycles were giving way to members who had access to cars. Anyone with a van was a treasure, taking moving airframes to a new dimension: previously possession of a roof rack was a major step forward! In 1968 the decision to acquire Saunders-Roe Skeeter AOP.12 XL811 from the Ministry of Defence was made all the easier because a member had graduated as far as a trailer! But time was going to catch up with the 'founder' groups unless new blood was brought in. The fifteen-year-olds quickly became eighteen and college, university or employment would beckon. It was important to be able to hand the baton on. This meant that as well as urgent fund-raising, groups had to devote a lot of time to recruiting, or they would run out of their most precious resource – motivated, determined people.

Northern legacy

As membership grew, a regular magazine was launched for NAPS members in 1963. This was called *Control Column* and Mike Ingham became the first ever editor of a journal dedicated to aviation heritage and preservation. *Control Column* rapidly grew in scope and stature, adding further to the dissemination of information. The clamour for copies was such that in 1967 it went 'national', distributed via other groups and, eventually, through membership of the British Aircraft Preservation Council (BAPC), of which more shortly. The magazine took on a life of its own, and the financial burden on NAPS was too much and it was handed on to the Newark Air Museum – see Chapter 23.

Already mentioned for giving Avian G-EBZM sanctuary, Peter Schofield joined NAPS and became a driving force across all its activities. The notion of an information exchange and fostering good relations between preservation organisations – large and small, volunteer and state funded – appealed to him. The concept of a national body to encourage communication and stronger ties began to take form and NAPS, led by its chairman John Kenyon, was busy promoting the idea. In October 1967 the inaugural meeting of the British Aircraft Preservation Council (BAPC, later renamed the British *Aviation* Preservation Council) was held, with John, Peter and other NAPS 'names' helping to nurture the new body. (The meeting was held in Derby, courtesy of Rolls-Royce, and was organised by Newark Air Museum member Bill Harrison – Chapter 23.) Peter went on to be one of the Council's most effective, and endearing, chairmen. Following a short illness, Peter died on 13th May 2017. A large number museums, groups and individuals have him to thank in part, or in whole, for information, introductions, shrewd guidance and above all, inspiration. His part in the development of the British aircraft preservation 'movement' cannot be over-emphasized.

By the early 1970s a store of Vampire T.11s held by Hawker Siddeley at Woodford was gathering dust and the chances of finding a new market had long since vaporized. Peter spearheaded negotiations and, with BAPC acting as 'broker', the Vampires became available for the nominal sum of £35 towards transportation. NAPS took advantage of Peter's 'Vampire Air Force', receiving XD435 on 9th March 1973. (Having gone through several other owners, this machine was scrapped in Warwickshire in the mid-1990s.) The Vampire exodus was the first of similar donations; the aviation industry handing on former Royal Danish Air Force Hawker Hunters, for example. From late 1975 to 1985 large quantities of Mutual Defense Assistance Program-funded French Air Force aircraft – Dassault Mystère IVAs, Lockheed T-33As and North American F-100 Super Sabres – were flown into Sculthorpe for disposal. Through the United States Air Force Museum (now the National Museum of the USAF) examples of all three types were offered to museums and groups and BAPC took on a similar role to the Vampire hand-outs.

The dream of running a museum remained unfulfilled and in the early 1970s practicalities dictated that NAPS take on the role of fostering the preservation of light aviation and that its 'products' be lent out to other concerns for display. This was formally reflected in 1974 when NAPS was renamed as The Aeroplane Collection. This was a more realistic label as by the early 1970s, the suffix 'APS' was beginning to be associated not with enthusiasm, but amateurism as a couple of groups

Avian G-EBZM at Hooton Park, circa 1930. *MSI*

crashed and burnt in regrettable circumstances. Storage/workshop sites in and around Manchester – Stockport, Irlam, Peel Green and Hadfield, all served their purpose but from 10th May 1983 consolidation at a craft centre at Warmingham in Cheshire began, providing much-needed stability for over a decade. TAC began moving into its current home, Hooton Park, from 12th March 1994 – see Chapter 5. The TAC website sums up well its present-day role: "TAC is fully committed to supporting the Hooton Park Trust in its objective to restore the hangars and to provide access to as wide a range of people as possible to the site and its heritage. In return for its support TAC hopes that facilities will be available for it to continue its restoration work. With the experience gained at Manchester we know that a restoration project which visitors have access to is a visitor draw and a means of encouraging audience participation in preserving heritage and history. As TAC enters its next half century we increasingly see our future efforts being concentrated on single restoration projects either for Hooton Park or for other museums and groups who have the space and facilities to look after them properly but lack the necessary skills or work space for restorations."

With week-long access, MSI in Manchester remains TAC's 'showcase' highlighting the capabilities it had accrued by the early 1980s when it could furnish quality aircraft for display at a major venue. When Liverpool Road opened up in 1983, the Avro Triplane replica, the Avian and the Bensen became prominent exhibits, with the Dragon Rapide following in 1989. It is doubtful that the museum management could have turned to any other organisation to provide such scope and depth.

Avro Avian III G-EBZM
1928 | Biplane tourer/trainer | One 90hp Cirrus Aero-Engines Cirrus III piston

From 1925 de Havilland began to dominate the light aircraft market with its DH.60 Moth which evolved into an incredibly successful family that included cabin monoplanes. The year after the prototype Moth flew, Avro introduced its contender, the Avian. Different engines were offered and the Mk.IVM had a metal tube fuselage; but the Avian achieved only a fraction of the production figures of its rival. There is another Avian in Britain, Mk.III G-ACGT, privately owned and believed to be under long term restoration in Yorkshire. As discussed above, the survival of G-EBZM is recognised as a turning point in Britain's aviation heritage and it brought about the prototype volunteer aircraft preservation organisation. While it might not have been appreciated at the time, the group that became the Northern Aircraft Preservation Society (NAPS) secured an aircraft with a great provenance: built in Manchester and operated from northwest venues.

Avian G-EBZM was built at Newton Heath in July 1928 and was trundled on its own undercarriage to Woodford for flight test. Irish-born aviatrix and athlete Mary Lynn had struck up a relationship with Avro, helping to show off its capabilities. She piloted Mk.III G-EBSD to a new altitude record of 19,200ft on 8th October 1927. Three days later she married Sir James Heath. In November, as Lady Heath, she flew another Avian III, G-EBUG, from Cape Town to Croydon. In September 1928 Avro let her get her hands on G-EBZM which she took to Orly, Paris, to complete in the French Light Aeroplane Trials which were staged from 10th-21st. The event ended with a 1,345-mile reliability contest routing Paris-Nancy-Lyon-Marseilles-Toulouse-Nantes-Le Havre-Paris. Lady Heath came fourth overall to three impressive contestants: Hubert Broad in a Gipsy Moth, Edgar Percival in another Avian, and the winner, German Robert Lusser in a Klemm. (Broad was de Havilland's test pilot; Percival was four years away from creating his famous Gull; Lusser went on to design the Messerschmitt Bf 110.)

On 12th February 1929 G-EBZM was registered to Hooton Park-based Merseyside Aero and Sports Ltd, trading as the Liverpool and District Aero Club. (Hooton Park has been the base of G-EBZM's owners, The Aeroplane Collection since 1994.) From December 1932 G-EBZM joined the pleasure flying operation run by Norman Giroux, the Giro Aviation Company of Hesketh Park, Southport, operating off the beach. During its time with Giro, G-EBZM suffered two, possibly three accidents, although sources vary as to the sequence and severity. Wg Cdr Jordan dug a wing in on landing and the Avian ended up on its nose. This *may* have been the same accident reported as "an inverted landing" at Marshside Sands. The final accident took place in April 1937 when H S Robson collided with telegraph wires and it turned out to be the Avian's last flight. On two occasions G-EBZM was back at Hooton Park, being repaired by Martin Hearn Ltd. The certificate of airworthiness expired on 20th January 1938 while the Avian was being patched up. It was not renewed, with World War Two looming G-EBZM was put into store at Hesketh Park to await better times. The registration was formally cancelled on 1st December 1946.

Airline engineer Bernard Murphy bought G-EBZM from Giro in 1955, at which time de Havilland Fox Moths G-ACCB and G-ACEJ were 'working' the sands. (G-ACCB later joined the Midland Aircraft Preservation Society – Chapter 29.) Bernard took the Avian to his home in Styal, Cheshire, to work on. In 1958 his job with Eagle Aviation at Ringway ended and he found employment overseas, presenting G-EBZM to the Ringway fire crews. Thankfully Alan Madden, an air traffic controller at Ringway and a member of the Merseyside Group of Aviation Enthusiasts (MGAE), felt this was wrong. After some negotiation, in April 1959 a band of Liverpool enthusiasts arrived at Ringway and removed G-EBZM, although at this point it was minus its upper and lower starboard wings. It was stored at the home of the MGAE chairman, Bryan Heatley in Huyton, east of Liverpool. By mid-1960 the Heatley family were less than enamoured with the continued presence of the aircraft and it was moved to a hangar at Liverpool Airport, Speke, but there it incurred fees. MGAE member Peter Schofield, a teacher at Lymm Grammar School, a near halfway point between Liverpool and Manchester, opted to take the Avian into his care. He was running the school's aviation society and perhaps its restoration would be a suitable focus for its members. The Avian was delivered to Lymm in early February 1961, finding a home in a cellar.

Having heard of the existence of G-EBZM just down the road, several members of the nascent NAPS went to have a 'look see' on 10th February 1962. A meeting in Manchester on 21st October announced that the group would indeed take on the name NAPS and that £5 be donated to the Lymm Grammar School Aviation Society, in exchange for G-EBZM. Thirteen days later, the deed was done; on 3rd November 1962 the Avian was moved to Stretford, Manchester. It was housed in a building behind the greengrocers shop in Moss Road that was run by the father of NAPS member Ian Jones. The wings arrived the following day. As related at the beginning of the chapter, NAPS began a migratory life moving from one storage site/workshop to another. In the early years G-EBZM also appeared at events to publicise 'the cause'; in 1975 this included a return to Woodford for an open day, 47 years after it had first flown there.

The search for parts to complete the Avian struck gold when the damaged, steel tube-framed Mk.IVM G-ABEE, was recovered from Selhurst, Surrey, on 12th December 1963. (This machine was a composite, including much from fellow Mk.IVM G-ACKE.) Over time, this machine passed on wings, tail 'feathers', undercarriage and other elements to G-EBZM as its restoration continued. In June 1973 the Avian was loaned to Keith Fordyce's Torbay Aircraft Museum at Higher Blagdon, Devon. The following year NAPS was renamed as The Aeroplane Collection. With the advent of the Manchester Air and Space Museum, G-EBZM was an obvious 'target' for inclusion in the line-up and on 9th December 1982, it returned to the land of its birth. The museum opened on 30th March 1983 and has been one of its 'stars' ever since.

Bensen B-7MC G-APUD
1959 | Single-seat gyroplane | One 80hp converted Volkswagen 1600cc piston

Small, portable and relatively cheap to acquire, there are many gyroplanes or autogyros – particularly the designs of Russian-born American pioneer Dr Igor Bensen – within British museums. The Aeroplane Collection's (TAC) example is the best of the lot by a long, long way. It was the first Bensen to fly in Britain, built, flown, modified and learned from by the father of post-war British gyroplanes, Wg Cdr Kenneth Horatio Wallis MBE. It is perhaps sad that it is for *Little Nellie*, the inanimate star of the 1967 Bond, James Bond movie *You Only Live Twice* that Ken Wallis will be best remembered. Then again, the film did much of what Ken was determined to do, to demonstrate that the autogyro was capable of many roles and was a safe and reliable form of aviation. As well as his passion for motorcycles, fast cars, powerboats and many other aspects of engineering, Ken began to get interested in the mechanics of flight from the early 1930s. He started an RAF career in 1938 that included 'ops' in Vickers Wellingtons with Bomber Command's 103 Squadron and ended in the mid-1950s as the Station Armament Officer at Scampton. By the late 1950s his interest had focussed on autogyros and he was convinced that the type represented a multi-purpose platform for pleasure, commercial and military use. He became the president of the Norfolk and Suffolk Aviation Museum in the late 1970s – see Chapter 26.

Ken acquired a Bensen B-7 kit which he built at his home in Southwick, Sussex, and it was registered as G-APUD. He flew this for the first time from Shoreham on 23rd May 1959 and used it to help him develop a series of patents, including an off-set gimbal rotor head providing exceptionally stable flight and a spin-up drive for the rotor. All of this led to his first original design, the Wallis WA-116 Agile and he flew the prototype, G-ARRT, from Boscombe Down on 2nd August 1961. (WA-116 G-ARZB, the famed *Little Nellie*, is held by the Shuttleworth Collection at Old Warden.) *Romeo-Tango* formed the basis for a family of more than 20 autogyros, including several world record breakers, that followed up to the late 1980s.

Ken Wallis at the controls of Bensen G-APUD at Shoreham, 1959. *KEC*

Ken sold G-APUD in October 1965 to Frank Purvis, who flew it from Biggin Hill. It was there that a team from the Northern Aircraft Preservation Society (TAC from 1974) collected in in April 1972 and it was immediately put to work as a travelling exhibit. From 1981 *Uniform-Delta* was placed on loan with the South Yorkshire Aviation Society's Nostell Aviation Museum, moving with them to Firbeck in mid-1982. It was put on display at Manchester in May 1983.

de Havilland Dragon Rapide G-ADAH
1935 | Light transport | Two 200hp de Havilland Gipsy Six pistons

The name proudly carried on the nose of this venerable biplane – *Pioneer* – is so appropriate for the work of the Northern Aircraft Preservation Society (NAPS)/The Aeroplane Collection. This is another aircraft with a stunning provenance. The are four other Rapides in museum 'captivity' in Britain: G-AGSH airworthy at Old Warden; G-AKDW at London Colney; G-AHED stored for the RAF Museum; G-ALXT of the Science Museum, also in store. Being pedantic, all of these are Dominie crew trainers, built by Brush Coachworks at Loughborough, Leicestershire, for the RAF. Nowt wrong with that of course, but *Pioneer* is pre-war, pure civilian and built by the company that designed and developed it.

Built at Hatfield, G-ADAH was the 29th off the production line and destined for the launch customer, Hillman's Airways, based at Abridge, Essex; it was delivered on 23rd February 1935. Hillman's was one of three airlines merged into Allied British Airways in September 1935 but the following month it took on the simpler British Airways title. (That name was reborn, with decidedly different hardware, in 1972.) The biplane's first taste of Scotland came on 10th August 1936 when it was taken on by Northern and Scottish Airways at Glasgow's Renfrew airport. After a brief spell with Airwork at Shoreham, G-ADAH returned to Scotland, this time to Aberdeen Airport, Dyce, on 26th October 1938. Dyce had been opened by airline maverick, and later outspoken politician, Eric Leslie Gandar Dower, in July 1934 and he had started up Allied Airways to operate services across Scotland. He named G-ADAH initially *The Thurso Venturer*, but later this was changed to *Pioneer*.

Dragon Rapide G-ADAH in Allied Airways colours, out of service at Dyce, 1957. *Peter Green Collection*

With the coming of war, airline services were controlled by the National Air Communications organisation. Vital routes being maintained, and those linking remote areas of Scotland became even more important. During the summer of 1940 G-ADAH disgraced itself in an accident on Orkney and it was shipped and then trucked all the way to Pengam Moors, Cardiff, for Air Dispatch Ltd to nurse it back to health. From December 1942 to late 1944 *Pioneer* was registered to the Secretary of State for Air, but this was essentially a 'paperwork' exercise 'for the duration'. For much of the war, G-ADAH plied a 'round-robin' regular schedule: Aberdeen-Wick-Kirkwall-Shetland and return.

On 25th July 1946 G-ADAH was registered to the great man himself, Eric Leslie Gandar Dower, and it wore Island Air Services titles. By this time Gandar Dower was a member of parliament and his aeronautical ventures were on the wane. With its certificate of airworthiness lapsing in June 1947, *Pioneer* was stored at Dyce. In the early 1960s it was offered for sale at £750. When the NAPS team heard that the Rapide was available, they investigated further, but baulked at the price. (If £750 seems cheap for so much biplane, that works out at £18,750 in present-day values. In 1960 a British manual worker was taking home an average of £220 per annum.)

In August 1966 G-ADAH was acquired by the Shuttleworth Collection, the fuselage was moved to Booker, the remainder going to Old Warden. Persistence rewarded, NAPS secured the Rapide and the fuselage moved to the store at Peel Green, Salford, on 11th October 1970; the remainder following fourteen days later. *Pioneer*'s days in Scotland were not over; in November 1973 it moved to East Fortune and the Museum of Flight, on loan. It was installed at Manchester on 7th April 1989.

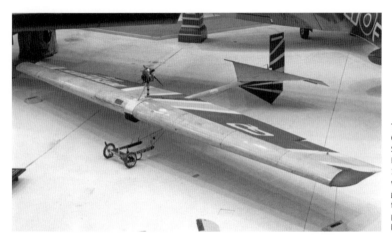

The cross-Channel Volmer Swingwing at Liverpool Road, 1983. The wheels are for ground handling, for landing the pilot used his legs! *Alan Curry*

Volmer VJ-23 Swingwing
1977 | Single place powered hang-glider | One 9hp McCulloch 101 123cc piston

In the late 1960s and beyond, hang-gliding became an established sport and vast numbers have been built worldwide. Such devices spawned the microlight, which has gone on to change the nature of light aviation. Like gyroplanes, they are light, easily portable and reasonably cheap, so there are plenty of examples in British museums. The trouble is, most have little in the way of a 'story' to go with them. The Museum of Science and Industry has several hang-gliders and microlights on its books, including locally designed and built Flexiform and Mainair types. But the stand-out example is American designed and had considerable influence on the British microlight industry.

Designed as a three-axis hang-glider by Volmer Jensen and Irving Culver in 1971, the VJ-23 Swingwing was available as factory built or from plans by Volmer Aircraft of Glendale, California. 'Three-axis' refers to it having conventional controls: ailerons, elevators, rudder. The term 'hang-glider' is because the pilot hangs from a frame and his legs act as the 'undercarriage'. David Cook of Aldringham, Suffolk, built this example from plans and fitted it with a McCulloch two-stroke engine, driving a tiny pusher propeller. With sponsorship from Duckhams Oils, David became the first person to fly the English Channel in a powered hang-glider on 9th May 1978. He flew from Deal, Kent, to Les Baraques in 90 minutes. His landing place was more or less where Louis Blériot took off from on 25th July 1909 when he became the first to fly 'La Manche', and he had the advantage of another 15hp over Cook! After this, David was much in demand to perform at airshows. He made the last flight in front of the audience at Old Warden on 8th May 1981 and presented the VJ-23 to the Shuttleworth Collection. The hang-glider moved to Manchester on 24th September 1983. David Cook was clearly 'bitten' by microlighting; he went on to found Cook Flying Machines (CFM) and to design the two-seat CFM Shadow, the first of over 300 appearing in 1983.

Museum of Science and Industry aircraft

Type	Identity	Built	Origin	Acquired	Notes
Avro Type 'F'*	–	2010	Britain	2011	replica
Avro Avian IIIA*	G-EBZM	1928	Britain	9 Dec 1982	see profile
Avro 504K	G-ABAA	c1918	Britain	Feb 1989	–
Avro Shackleton AEW.2	WR960	1954	Britain	21 Jan 1983	–
Avro 707A	WZ736	1953	Britain	8 Sep 1982	–
Bensen B-7MC	G-APUD	1959	USA	May 1983	see profile
Bristol Belvedere HC.1	XG454	1960	Britain	4 Nov 1982	see Chapter 25
Colt 56 SS	G-BLKU	1984	Britain	2004	hot air balloon
de Havilland Dragon Rapide	G-ADAH	1935	Britain	7 Apr 1989	see profile
English Electric P.1A	WG763	1955	Britain	17 Aug 1982	–
EoN 460 Srs 1	–	1964	Britain	25 Jan 2000	glider
Flexiform Sky Sails hang-glider	–	c1982	Britain	1990	–
Hawker Siddeley Trident 3B-101	GAWZP	1971	Britain	12 Jun 1986	cockpit
Hiway Spectrum	–	c1980	Britain	1986	hang-glider
Mainair Tri-Flyer	G-MJXE	1982	Britain	2001	–
Mignet 'Flying Flea'	'G-ADYO'	1936	France	2002	–
Morane-Saulnier Rallye Club	G-AYTA	1971	France	1996	–
Pegasus Quantum 15-912	G-BYMT	1999	Britain	2010	–
Roe Triplane I*	–	c1953	Britain	4 Nov 1982	replica
Skyhook Safari	–	c1979	Britain	1998	hang-glider
Volmer VJ-23 Swingwing	–	1977	USA	29 Sep 1983	see profile
Wood Ornithopter	–	c1968	Britain	20 Jan 1985	–
Yokosuka Ohka 11	–	c1944	Japan	14 Dec 1982	–

Notes: * – illustrated in the colour section.

Dynastic Hub
Avro Heritage Museum
Woodford
www.avroheritagemuseum.co.uk

From 1925 Woodford was the hub of the dynasty that had been founded by Edwin Alliott Verdon Roe in 1910. His initials and surname combined to form the world famous Avro 'brand'. The name gave way to Hawker Siddeley in 1963 which was subsumed into British Aerospace in 1977 and in 1999 the bloodline morphed into the multi-national BAE Systems. But for those of a certain age, the products of the Woodford plant will always be 'Avros'. Everything came to an abrupt halt when the government axed the Nimrod MRA.4 programme – despite five aircraft having been completed – in October 2010. During the first weeks of 2011 the airframes, sub-assemblies and jigs were all scrapped and the writing was on the wall for Woodford. Air traffic closed in August and the following year BAE Systems had vacated the site.

With the blessing of the management a small heritage centre was established in the late 1970s. In the hands of volunteers, many of whom were retirees from the factory, the task of gathering artefacts and documents began. On 12th March 1982, Vulcan XM603 touched down at its birthplace and was placed in the care of the heritage team. As Woodford turned from aerospace giant to housing development site, it seemed that the long-held prospect of a museum dedicated to Avro had been shattered. Well aware of the fantastic heritage that Woodford stands for, the management at BAE Systems announced that it would fund and oversee the creation of a museum building utilizing the structure of the airfield fire station. BAE Systems handed the completed structure over to what had become the Avro Heritage Museum (AHM) on 5th May 2015. The opening was planned for October and with a 'hard' deadline the team faced long hours of toil, achieving an incredible tribute to an aviation industry giant. Former Woodford test pilot Sir Charles Masefield presided over the official unveiling on 8th October 2015 ready for the public debut on 13th November.

Spread around three walls of the display hall is a timeline, from Roe's 1907 rubber-powered model to the last of the Nimrods. Models of all sizes, instruments, posters, photos, flight suits, brochures – all have been carefully displayed with

A general view of the Avro Heritage Museum, Woodford. *Ken Ellis*

supporting narratives. The scope is delightful and full of revelations. There's a billiard table carrying the famous Avro winged triangle trademark. During the mass cancellations post-1918 the company diversified to survive; it also built cars. With Vulcan XM603 dominating the exterior of the museum and space limited inside, the intention has never been to acquire a large number of aircraft. Eighteen days before XM603 took the skies, XM602 thundered down the Woodford runway on its debut. Last used as a crew trainer for the 'warbird' XH558, the cockpit of XM602 is integrated within the building. Since then more cockpits have arrived to expand the displays; the relevance of the Avro XIX, the replica Lancaster and the Nimrod are self-evident. The Canberra was part of a batch of 75 built by Avro while Woodford took on the design authority of the VC-10 tanker programme in the mid-1980s.

One of the building's rooms is named after a Woodford institution, Harry Holmes. He's very bashful about this: his colleagues think it's the least they could do. He'll deny it, but without his energy and drive over decades, AHM would not have seen the light of day. Harry's great uncle, Frederick J V Holmes, worked with Roe at Brownsfield Mill, Manchester, in 1912. After RAF service, Harry followed in Fred's footsteps and joined Avro in 1958, first in marketing, then public relations. He retired in 1993 and has written seminal books on Avro and the Lancaster, among others. All praise to BAE Systems for not letting the Avro legacy be reduced to a couple of road names where the airfield once was. The baton is now firmly with the AHM team and it is in the best of hands. To return to Harry: "It's a big story and a huge responsibility, but we have to keep this alive otherwise the younger generation will have no idea about a century of incredible achievements and what Avro really means."

Avro Nineteen Series 2 G-AGPG
1945 | General purpose transport / radar test-bed | Two 420hp Armstrong Siddeley Cheetah 15 pistons

Forever known as 'Aggie-Paggie' from its registration G-AGPG, the story of this purely civilian 'Anson' is one of ups and downs and determination that it has not been allowed to die. The history of the British aircraft preservation 'movement' is littered with good intentions to restore Ansons. Clearly a fundamental historic type, it's hard not to love an 'Annie'. But the heart tends to rule the head and the wallet. The operator of an airworthy example told the author in 1985 that he thought the movie *The Money Pit*, released that year and starring Tom Hanks, was about his Anson! Only when strip down starts do would-be restorers discover that this benign-looking aeroplane is complex, demanding in skills as diverse as metalworking, carpentry and fabrics – and big! There have been failed restorations that have gone by the wayside, and others 'doing the rounds' looking for their next owner. 'Aggie-Paggie' is part of that story.

There are nine Ansons in British museums; as might be expected all are former RAF examples. The introduction explains that cockpits in general don't merit a profile: here's another rule-breaker coming in under the radar, because it is such a significant type and a classic study in the vulnerability of airframes. In its time, this machine has been 'saved' for posterity at least three times.

Avro Nineteen G-AGPG at Woodford in 1946: Lincolns behind. *Avro*

As World War Two came to a close, Avro realised that the venerable Anson still had a lot of life in it. By 1945 it was a much more sophisticated creature than it was in its prototype days of a decade before. 'Metal' wings and fuselage, increased cabin volume and powered undercarriage retraction had all been introduced. As well as burgeoning military orders in crew training and communications, Avro saw a small, but worthwhile, civilian market and for this the name 'Anson' was dropped. Harking back to the 1920s and 1930s when a series of Fokker-inspired transports were produced with numbers as names, eg the Type 618 Ten, the commercial Anson was called the Nineteen, or XIX. Combining the attributes of the Mk.XI and Mk.XII with a lowered cabin access door, the first from-new example was G-AGPG. Anson production had been transferred from Woodford to Yeadon (present-day Leeds-Bradford Airport) in 1942 and it was from there that Aggie first flew on 17th August 1945. It was put to use as a demonstrator and later became a 'hack', flying crews and management about from Woodford. In May 1952 G-AGPG was upgraded to Series 2 and continued its duties. It was sold to Skyways Coach Air of Lympne on 13th July 1961; its role hardly changed, flying crews or spares around.

At Rochford, Southend, radio and radar specialist Ekco Electronics Ltd had a new commission that was beyond its current test-bed, Anson XI G-ALIH. The company took its name from its founder, Eric K Cole, and was busy developing its E320 weather radar destined for the BAC/Sud Concorde supersonic transport. *India-Hotel* had proven ideal as a radar test-bed, but its wooden-framed, low-ceiling cabin was too cramped. The Avro Nineteen was ideal, offering not just cabin space but geared engines and variable pitch props for better climb and engine-out performance. On 20th October 1967, G-AGPG was acquired and the bulbous nose from G-ALIH was fitted to Aggie by Rochford-based Aviation Traders. (Ekco donated *India-Hotel* to the Newark Air Museum, fitted presumably with G-AGPG's original nose – see Chapter 23.) In April 1969 Ekco was absorbed by Pye Telecommunications. Its job done, Aggie was moved across the airfield, joining the Historic Aircraft Museum for a reported £300. Its certificate of airworthiness lapsed on 13th December 1971, its long and interesting flying life had amounted to 1,948 hours. So, it would appear that G-AGPG had been 'saved'. Well, not really, by 1982 the museum had fizzled out and on 10th May 1983 auctioneers Phillips put most of the collection under the hammer, including G-AGPG. French operator Philippe Denis bid £2,800 for the 'Anson' and, to some sources, it was 'safe'. It lay neglected and was next reported to have been acquired by Patrick Luscombe's short-lived Lympne-based British Air Reserve; but Aggie remained at Rochford, decaying still further.

In April 1986, G-AGPG crossed the Thames and arrived at Brenzett in Kent – all courtesy of a low-loader. Saved! Brenzett Aeronautical Museum Trust (Chapter 14) was keen to increase the number of exhibits outside its building; but the team there began to realise that the battered Avro Nineteen was beyond their means. From early 1992 'feelers' were put out that it was available for trade. By 1996 Aggie had moved to Chadderton, Manchester, while the Museum of Science and Industry (above) assessed it as a possible exhibit. Surely saved? It seems not, in June 2000 it was acquired by The Aeroplane Collection (also above) and made the journey to Hooton Park. Home and dry! Well no, the good intentions of the group were thwarted and G-AGPG was transferred to the ownership of the Hooton Park Trust. The inevitable decision was made and on 1st September 2011; it was not tenable as a restoration project. Aggie was disposed of to Richard Parr's Retro Aviation in Shropshire. The wings, centre section and 'tail feathers' were to be amalgamated with the fuselage of Anson I AX246 which was being put together at Church Fenton during 2014; the whole thing moving to Greece in March 2016.

Incredible restoration work returned the gutted cockpit of G-AGPG to prize-winning condition: CockpitFest, Newark, June 2016. *Ken Ellis*

It was then that Lancashire-based collector and restorer Mike Davey stepped in and bought the sorry remains in late 2012. While it may have been reduced to a cockpit, with much missing from its interior, for the first time in three decades 'Aggie-Paggie's' long term prospects were looking decidedly up! (Mike also has aircraft on loan to the Speke Aerodrome Heritage Group – see Chapter 19.) G-AGPG was shown off at the Newark Air Museum's ground-breaking *CockpitFest* gathering in June 2013. The author had no hesitation in presenting Mike with the *Wrecks & Relics* 'Spirit of CockpitFest' award even though the project was in its early days, specifically for the brave move of saving a much-deserving airframe. Three years later and superbly restored, Mike and Aggie picked up another 'Spirit' prize. On 5th December 2016 G-AGPG was back at Woodford, going on display at the Avro Heritage Centre. Saved!

Avro Vulcan B.2 XM603
1963 | Long range heavy bomber | Four 20,000lb st Bristol Siddeley Olympus 301 turbojets

I'll probably get pilloried for this, but there is an embarrassment of Vulcans preserved in Britain. There are eleven whole airframes in museums, and three more kept 'in steam' with occasionally public access. Of the intact museum examples, only three are kept inside: Duxford, Cosford and Hendon. Of the 'runners' the Vulcan Restoration Trust's XL426 is due to roll into a hangar at Southend during 2017 (Chapter 9) and the Vulcan to the Sky Trust have intentions to house XH558 at Doncaster Sheffield Airport (Chapter 31). That leaves eight, all bar one of which are held by 'local' collections; the odd-man-out being the National Museum of Flight Scotland's famous Rio de Janeiro 'visitor' and Falklands war veteran, XM597. During

Vulcan XM603 making its final touchdown, Woodford 12th March 1982. *British Aerospace*

2017 these eight were clocking up an average of 33½ years exposed to the elements. The allure of the mighty delta is self-evident, a natural crowd-puller. Choosing which to profile was not easy, as unless they took part in the South Atlantic conflict, their careers are much the same. One was easy; XM603 is displayed at its birthplace.

On 15th November 1963 XM603 had its maiden flight, within a matter of yards of where it now stands, at Woodford. Nineteen days later it was taken on charge by the RAF at Coningsby, with 9 Squadron, moving in October to Cottesmore. In October 1965, with centralised servicing, XM603 was pooled with 9, 12, 35 Squadrons, forming the Cottesmore Wing. By the summer of 1975 the Vulcan had transferred to Waddington, its wing comprising 9, 44, 50 and 101 Squadrons. Sporting the badge of 44 Squadron by 1980, XM603 soldiered on at Waddington, completing its last operational sortie on 28th February 1982. It was delivered to its birthplace, Woodford, on 12th March 1982, captained by British Aerospace test pilot Charles Masefield. So ended 5,733 flying hours. Looked after by the Avro Heritage Society (later Centre) and the associated 603 Club, the Vulcan was painted in white 'anti-flash' colours. Ready for the opening of the centre in 2015, the Vulcan was towed to its new site and a restoration programme was commenced. In September 2016 former Woodford apprentice Leon Howard of Warmco Properties provided the necessary funding to complete the repainting of XM603; including scaffolding, tenting and materials.

Avro Heritage Museum aircraft

Type	Identity	Built	Origin	Acquired	Notes
Avro XIX Srs 2*	G-AGPG	1945	Britain	5 Dec 2016	cockpit. See profile
Avro Lancaster	–	1998	Britain	Jan 2017	replica forward fuselage
Avro Vulcan B.2	XM602	1963	Britain	20 Apr 2013	cockpit
Avro Vulcan B.2*	XM603	1963	Britain	12 Mar 1982	see profile
English Electric Canberra TT.18	WK118	1954	Britain	20 Apr 2013	cockpit
Hawker Siddeley Nimrod MR.2	XV235	1969	Britain	8 Sep 2016	cockpit
Vickers VC-10 C.1K	XV106	1967	Britain	8 Sep 2016	cockpit

Notes: * – illustrated in the colour section.

Manchester Airport's Runway Visitor Park's RJX G-IRJX with the prototype, G-ORJZ, in the foreground on a sortie out of Woodford, January 2002. *BAE Systems*

Room with a View
Runway Visitor Park

Manchester Airport
www.manchesterairport.co.uk

Just like East Midlands Airport (Chapter 15), Manchester Airport reasoned that large numbers of people would want to come and watch the airliners coming and going and it was better to be proactive and cater for them, rather than have crowds in the terminals, or parking where they shouldn't. A look around the airport from the Runway Visitor Park radiates mostly modernity, yet the site has an illustrious heritage – as a look around the displays at the centre will reveal. Ringway was used by Fairey from 1937 as an assembly and flight test centre for production from its Heaton Chapel factory, with Battles giving way to Fulmars and Fireflies, the last being tested in April 1956. By 1939 Avro was also using Ringway, both the Manchester and Lancaster prototypes having their maiden flights at the airfield. In June 1938 it became Manchester Airport, taking over from Barton. A variety of units flew from the airfield during World War Two; the most important of which was the curiously named Central Landing School (later Establishment and from 1942 to Airborne Forces Experimental Establishment). The first steps in developing parachute and glider-borne forces were made at Ringway. The airfield reverted to airport status in June 1946 and began the expansion to the mammoth it is today.

In 1992 a viewing area was created on the airport's southern perimeter, later moving to the northern site in 1997. This proved the viability of such an attraction and much more ambitious plans were launched. On 14th May 2003 the Airport Visitor Park (later the Runway Visitor Park) was officially opened with viewing mounds, picnic tables, a cafeteria, shop and visitor centre. With its proximity to the northern taxi tracks, the park not only offered intimate viewing of arrivals and departures, it was ideally placed to receive retired aircraft, flying directly into the airport. Already in hand was the second prototype Avro RJX. The story of Trident G-AWZK is profiled below and while decidedly military, the Nimrod MR.2 was welcomed as a Comet jetliner derivative and a local product. The jewel in the crown was the arrival of Concorde G-BOAC on 31st October 2003. On loan from British Airways, one of the conditions of the transfer of *Alpha-Charlie* was that it be placed within covered accommodation. Again the airport authorities showed great vision by announcing in January 2008 the investment of £1.1 million in a dramatic enhancement. Work began in July 2008 creating a glass-walled restaurant and a display hangar for the Concorde. Attendance figures have increased steadily ever since and, despite the crowds, there's still space for at least one more airliner...

Trident 3B G-AWZK at the Runway Visitor Park, Manchester Airport. *Terry Dann*

Hawker Siddeley Trident 3B-101 G-AWZK
1971 | Medium range airliner | Three 11,930lb st Rolls-Royce Spey 512-5W turbofans and one 5,250lb st Rolls-Royce RB162-86 booster

From their introduction into service with British European Airways (BEA) in March 1963 through to the mid-1980s, Tridents were common sight at Manchester Airport. Thanks to local enthusiasts, the airport management and very determined Trident die-hards at London Airport, *Zulu-Kilo* graces the visitor park and was not turned into aluminium ingots. Between 1962 and 1975 a total of 117 Tridents in three variants was produced. Just four survive intact with British museums at Sunderland, Duxford and at the Science Museum's store at Wroughton; and G-AWZK.

Built as a Series 3B for BEA, G-AWZK first flew from Hatfield on 15th October 1971 and was handed over to the customer the following day. On 1st April 1974 BEA became British Airways. Its unsung service came to an end flying BA4653 from Belfast to Heathrow on 1st November 1985, completing its 19,761st landing and 23,466 hours flying time. *Zulu-Kilo* began a new life as a vehicle positioning and towing trainer, gaining the name *The Spirit of Fleet Maintenance* on the nose. In 1991 the wings were cropped to save some space, fifteen feet from each wing tip. (This caused considerable re-engineering when the Trident was re-assembled for display at Manchester.) The Trident Preservation Society (TPS) was established in 1994 to look after the airframe. In 2001 *Zulu-Kilo* was returned its BEA colours of 1971. The horrific events of 9th September that year changed the Trident's prospects as access to it was severely restricted. It was clear that the there was a dwindling future at Heathrow. The opening of the visitor park in May 2003 gave the possibility of a new venue and discussions were productive. Moving an airliner by road is no light undertaking, the physical side pales into insignificance against the cost. With help from Manchester-based enthusiast organisation, The Aviation Society, TPS began a vigorous campaign to raise funds. Dismantling around 70,000lb of Trident 3B began in October 1994 and the majority of the tri-jet arrived at its new home on 11th September 1995. Masterminding this incredible undertaking was Neil Lomax. Neil also had a hand in the saving of Trident 1 G-ARPO which is profiled in Chapter 22. Putting G-AWZK together and up to display standard was a huge job. Captain Tony Angus, who had accepted *Zulu-Kilo* for BEA back in October 1971, presided over the official opening on 7th April 2007.

BAE Systems Avro 146-RJX 100 G-IRJX
2001 | Short-medium range airliner | Four 7,000lb st Honeywell As977-1A turbofans

Thursday 3rd September 1981 proved to be a noteworthy day for two reasons; only one of which was apparent at the time. The prototype Hawker Siddeley HS.146 prototype, G-SSSH, took to the skies for the first time, from Hatfield. It transpired that it was to be the last of its kind: a British designed airliner, built and flown in this country. Production of all versions amounted to 387 when the programme was terminated in late 2001. By British standards, that was an impressive figure, but by 2001 a four-jet regional airliner was completely outclassed by twin-jets from Brazil and Canada. Being a relatively 'young' type, 146s are still enjoying the 'secondary' market, but as well as the Manchester example, the fuselage of a 1983-built Series 100 is displayed at the de Havilland Aircraft Museum.

In 1992 a major new version of the HS.146 had its maiden flight from Hatfield on 13th May 1992. This was the RJ100 – the initials standing for 'regional jet' – and featured Honeywell turbofans and an all-digital cockpit, among other improvements. The first production example flew in November that year, but from Woodford; Hatfield was being closed down. To help with the relaunch of the 146, British Aerospace decided to revive the 'Avro' brand, as it had become a Woodford product. In order to further boost sales, the further improved RJX entered flight test on 28th April 2001, when G-ORJX took off. G-IRJX was termed 'T2', the second development RJX and it first flew at Woodford on 23rd September 2001. On 27th November 2001 BAE Systems announced that it was folding the project. The third example, G-6-391, flew on 9th January 2002, clocking just shy of nine hours before it was stored and then scrapped. G-IRJX was put into store at Woodford on 7th February 2002. Donated by BAE Systems to the visitor park, it was prepared for the short hop from Woodford to Ringway and this was achieved on 6th February 2003. That was *Juliet-Xray's* 135th landing, its total time coming out at 1,982 hours, 23 minutes. Britain's all-indigenous airliner heritage had ground to a halt. On 15th April 2003 the RJX was towed through on to the visitor park site and started its new life as a display airframe.

Runway Visitor Park aircraft

Type	Identity	Built	Origin	Acquired	Notes
BAC/Sud Concorde 102	G-BOAC	1975	GB/France	31 Oct 2003	–
Douglas DC-10-30	G-DMCA	1980	USA	19 Dec 2003	cockpit
Hawker Siddeley Trident 3B-101	G-AWZK	1971	Britain	11 Sep 2005	see profile
Hawker Siddeley Nimrod MR.2*	XV231	1971	Britain	27 Apr 2006	–
Hawker Siddeley HS.146 RJX 100 T2	G-IRJX	2001	Britain	6 Feb 2003	see profile

Notes: * – illustrated in the colour section.

Also in Manchester
Imperial War Museum North

The futuristic off-shoot of the London and Duxford based museum is housed in a building designed to represent a shattered globe. Former US Marine Corps Hawker Siddeley AV-8A Harrier 159233 'flies' within. **www.iwm.org.uk/north**

Willpower
Speke Aerodrome Heritage Group

www.spekeaero.org
and

Britannia Aircraft Preservation Trust

www.bristol-britannia.com
Speke, Liverpool

By far and away the largest and tallest control tower preserved in Britain marks the site of the former Liverpool Airport, Speke. The present day bustling and expanding Liverpool John Lennon Airport resulted from a staged 'migration' to a new and much longer runway to the south. With the entire northern zone surplus to requirements in 2000 it was going to be swallowed by commercial development. Thankfully, the incredible art deco banana-shaped terminal building with its imposing control tower, flanked by two huge hangars were all protected by 'listing'. The hangars have become business centres and gymnasia and the terminal is now the Crowne Plaza Hotel, the 're-invented' building opening (as the Liverpool Marriott Hotel South) on 29th June 2001. The southern face the terminal building looks no different than it did in 1939. An entire 'wing' was built on the northern face following the style of the original building; it is a brilliant piece of architecture that has ensured that this aviation treasure does not slide into dereliction and demolition.

But the listing process took into account another crucial element of what made Speke Airport so ground breaking. The concrete apron – one of the first and most extensive of its kind – is also protected. Certainly much of it is used for car parking, but the enlightened management of the Crowne Plaza decided that the best thing to put on an *airliner* apron was airliners! Before we go any further, the author better explain that the airliner collection at Speke is another example of how to break the 'rules' laid down in the introduction as it is available for inspection only on Saturdays. There are three reasons why the two separate organisations that work side-by-side at Speke get a full-on mention. As the title of this chapter might suggest, dealing with airliners is an expensive, time consuming, back-breaking task that involves an incredible amount of willpower and what happens at Speke is entirely volunteer run. Secondly, without the vision and support of the Crowne Plaza all of this endeavour would not have happened. Finally, the author was born-and-bred in Liverpool and cut his aviation 'teeth' on the viewing balcony that now forms part of the hotel and Speke's exclusion from this book was never going to be an option!

Above: An epic airliner rescue, HS.748 G-BEJD regaining its Dan-Air colours at Speke. *Ken Ellis*

Above us only sky

The history of Liverpool Airport is crowded and varied and cutting down to a handful of sentences is no easy task; but try we must. Liverpool Corporation acquired the land in 1928 and two years later the first flying services were staged. Construction of the incredible art deco-style control tower, hangars and terminal building began in 1937 and it was fully operational in 1939. By then the airfield was taking on a role that was very different from what had been intended. Close to the southeast perimeter, Rootes Securities opened a shadow factory in 1938 initially producing Bristol Blenheims and then Handley Page Halifaxes. The port of Liverpool played a vital role in the supply of all manner of materials from Canada and the USA. This was reflected at Speke as it became a reception centre for US aircraft shipped across the Atlantic. The most unusual of a range of RAF units based at Speke was the Merchant Ship Flying Unit, training pilots in the art of being catapulted in a Hawker Hurricane off a converted vessel in an attempt to intercept long-ranging Focke-Wulf Condor patrol bombers. At Speke, a pilot could go around and land conventionally: in the Atlantic the sortie would end with a ditching and hopefully his rescue. From the late 1940s Speke reverted to an airport. Its fortunes were mixed until the 'new' terminal was opened on the southern runway in 1986 after which it has expanded considerably. The last flying from the north site took place on 29th August 2000 and the reshaping of the entire area into a commercial estate began. The airport was named John Lennon Airport in 2001.

With a little help from my friends

The origins of the Speke Aerodrome Heritage Group (SAHG) go back to the Wirral Aviation Society and the interest of some of its members in flight simulators and full-size aircraft. A brain storming session concluded that it would be an incredible challenge to mount a simulator system inside an aircraft and to link it to the physical controls. This could be relatively easily done by acquiring a cockpit section and a growing number of sheds and gardens across Britain had become the home of a 'hooked up' cockpit. But the team wanted to share the experience, ideally with youngsters, and soon the motto 'Education through Aviation' was being bandied about. A small airliner would fit the bill: a spacious cockpit allowing for a 'wide screen' simulation to be projected across the windscreen and the cabin could be turned into part airliner, part classroom.

"If you don't ask, you don't get!" said Roy Coates, the man who led the project. He was referring to how the small group managed to achieve the donation of a Jetstream 41 prototype from British Aerospace. The company was impressed with what the group intended to do and the aircraft, which had been used for spares recovery and was engineless, and was facing the scrapheap. The same logic appealed to the hotel management when the proposal was put to them that an aircraft gracing the apron outside would be a great idea.

Soon named *Spirit of Speke*, G-JMAC arrived in January 2003 and it was powered up for its first 'flight' ten months later, an incredible achievement. School parties, special interest groups and individuals have since shared in the 'flying' classroom. With the arrival of *Alpha-Charlie*, the group adopted the name the Jetstream Club and took on charitable status. Prior to going 'live' the first of what is now an annual 'aviation fair' was staged in July 2003 to raise awareness and funds for the Jetstream project and local charities. The club and the hotel rallied round to help out Britannia G-ANCF – see below for more – and this huge project arrived in March 2007. The following year Prince G-AMLZ 'touched down' and the apron was really beginning to look like an airport once more. The decision was taken to change the organisation's name and SAHG was born in January 2010. The HS.748 in 2011 was another ambitious undertaking, but once again Speke was helping to save precious examples of airliner heritage and doing things a 'national' museum might only dream of. All of this propelled by willpower.

British Aerospace Jetstream 4100 G-JMAC
1992 | Regional airliner | Two 1,650shp Garret AiResearch TPE331-14-801H turboprops

Only five years after the maiden flight of the prototype, the Jetstream 41 programme was brought to a close in 1997; production running to 100 units. A stretched development of the Jetstream 31 feederliner, the Series 41 could seat up to 29 passengers,

G-JMAC, the fourth prototype Jetstream 41, 1992. *British Aerospace*

thanks to the fuselage being positioned above the carry-through wing presenting an unrestricted cabin floor. Jetstream 41s continue in service worldwide in dwindling numbers; G-JMAC is the only example of its type on display in Britain.

The fourth prototype, it first flew at Prestwick on 8th July 1992. It was allocated two identities before it flew; G-JXLI – J for 'Jetstream', XLI being Roman numerals for '41' – in February 1991 and this was briefly changed to G-JAMD in April 1992 before G-JMAC was chosen on 12th June 1992. *Alpha-Charlie* was withdrawn from use in 1997 and put into open storage at Woodford. After enquiries by what became the Jetstream Club, G-JMAC was delivered by road to Speke on 29th January 1993. It was given the name *Spirit of Speke* and turned into a simulator under a team led by Roy Coates. The stripped-out instrument panel was replaced by flat screens replicating all of the dials with further screens providing the view 'outside'. The control yoke, throttles and rudder pedals were linked into the 'system' to provide a totally convincing experience, made all the more so because the 'pilot' had entered a *real* airliner and not a fibreglass pod standing on hydraulic tripods. *Spirit of Speke* carried out its first 'flight' on 1st November 2003 and has been educating pilots of all generations ever since.

Hawker Siddeley HS.748-1/105 G-BEJD
1961 | Medium range airliner | Two 1,740shp Rolls-Royce Dart 514 turboprops

Juliet-Delta is a classic example of how individuals, or voluntary organisations, can achieve wonders and leave the 'nationals' in the shade. With a total of 382 produced between 1960 and 1989, including 89 under licence in India, the HS.748 is a world class airliner and general purpose transport. A military tactical version with an upswept rear fuselage with a loading ramp/parachute platform was developed for the RAF as the Andover. On 13th July 1994 Andover E.3A XS639 landed at Cosford, securing an important type for the RAF Museum. An example of a pure airliner version had been a blatant 'hole' in the story of British airliners until 2011 when enthusiastic willpower and determination secured G-BEJD – the oldest surviving intact 748.

Ordered by Aerolineas Argentinas, the Speke HS.748 first flew at Woodford on 19th May 1962 as LV-PUF and it arrived at Buenos Aires on 5th June 1962. It was re-registered as LV-HHE and named *Ciudad de Resistencia*, Spanish for City of Resistencia, the capital of Argentina's Chaco province. It was sold in April 1975 to Yacimientos Petrolíferos Fiscales, a specialist operator in the petro-chemical sector, based at Buenos Aires. In December 1976 LV-HHE was acquired by British airline Dan-Air and, registered as G-BEJD, it arrived at Manchester Airport, Ringway, on 24th December 1976. *Juliet-Delta* entered service on 8th March 1977 flying on passenger duties until early 1987 when its cabin was stripped out for use as a small item freighter. Dan-Air ceased operations in 1992 and after a brief period of storage at Manchester, G-BEJD was acquired by Janes Aviation that July. It was delivered to Blackpool Airport, Squires Gate, on the 16th, taking on the name *John Case*. Janes Aviation was renamed as Emerald Airways in September 1993 and it became the largest ever British operator of 748s. Base for services was Liverpool Airport, Speke, with maintenance carried out at Blackpool. In late 1994 G-BEJD was painted in the colours of freight operator Reed Aviation and named *Sisyphus*. Emerald ceased operations by the spring of 2005 and G-BEJD was ferried to Blackpool on 13th March. This was its 50,882nd and last landing; its total time amounting to 49,914 hours – a true workhorse.

Acquired for parting out, *Juliet-Delta* and others of the Emerald fleet languished at Blackpool until broken up or other operators were found. The oldest surviving HS.748 was facing oblivion and several people were concerned that an opportunity was slipping away. Among these were Neil Airey and Heather Graham of the Cumbria-based Lakes Lightnings collection. Negotiations were started with the airport management and G-BEJD would be passed on providing there was a plan of rescue with a credible outcome and that this was to be reached as soon as possible. At first the RAF Millom and Militaria Museum in Cumbria was sounded out but that collection closed its doors in woeful circumstances on 12th August 2010. Fate was playing a hand; the airport waited patiently and eyes turned to Liverpool. Members of the Speke Aerodrome Heritage Group (SAHG) had intervened with Percival Prince G-AMLZ in 2008 – see below. SAHG were receptive, the destination was solved, but financing moving about 15,000lb of HS.748 by road looked daunting. The idea was 'floated' on the Key Publishing aviation forum – Key being the producers of *FlyPast* magazine – and within 2½ days there were sufficient pledges, along with significant inputs of cash and muscle from SAHG members and other north westerners. *Juliet-Delta*'s fuselage arrived at Speke on 20th October 2011 with the wings and other items coming the following day. Work on this unique airframe began immediately and during 2017 it was acquiring the colours of Dan-Air once again.

Percival Prince 6E G-AMLZ
1952 | Light transport | Two 540hp Alvis Leonides 504 pistons

First flown in May 1948, the Prince enjoyed greater success with the military than in the civil market, as the Sea Prince communications and crew trainer for the Fleet Air Arm, and the Pembroke and President general duties type for the RAF and for export. When production ended in 1960 a total of 207 had been built. Two examples of the original, short fuselage purely civilian Prince survive, G-AMLZ and another in the USA. *Lima-Zulu* was one of five Prince 3s ordered for the Refining and Marketing Division of Shell Oil and it first flew at Luton on 10th September 1952. It was delivered to its operating base, London Airport, Heathrow, in November. Its service with Shell completed, for a matter of twelve days in July 1954 the registration VR-TBN was reserved for the Prince. This was for potential supply to the British protectorate of Tanganyika, East Africa, but another aircraft was supplied. *Lima-Zulu* passed through a series of owners: Winston Martin, based at Tollerton, from July 1954; Stewart Smith and Co, at Blackbushe and Heathrow, from July 1956 and Timothy Clutterbuck, at Leavesden, from October 1968. During this time, Eagle Aircraft Services at Blackbushe upgraded G-AMLZ to Prince 6E status, fitting Leonides 504s in place of the original 501s.

Prince 6E G-AMLZ at Blackbushe, 1963. *KEC*

On 23rd October 1973 *Lima-Zulu* was registered to Percival zealot John Coggins and he ferried it to his base at Coventry Airport, Baginton, the following month. This is believed to have been the aircraft's final flight. John optimistically painted the title of his pleasure flying operation, City Airways Ltd, on the side, but it never entered service. (John's Percival Prentice, G-APJB, did great service and is *still* in the pleasure flying business, with Aero Legends at Headcorn.) John sold *Lima-Zulu* to another Coventry operator of classic aircraft, Air Atlantique in 1994. It was dismantled and moved to Caernarfon Airport, Llandwrog, to become part of the Caernarfon Air World Museum (Chapter 33). The Welsh airfield was operated by Air Caernarfon, a division of Air Atlantique, in those days. After thirteen years of exposure to the elements, Jonathan Howard, a Jetstream Club member, took pity on the Prince and managed to secure it, against a non-negotiable deadline. Between the 29th September and 5th October 2007 the Prince was moved to the RAF Millom and Militaria Museum in Cumbria. There it was held in store, with occasional forays by working parties, while its long term future was worked out. As Britannia G-ANCF settled in at Speke (see below), the way was clear for *Lima-Zulu* to join the 'flight line' and it made the journey south to Liverpool on 23rd November 2008. It was reassembled and on its undercarriage by January 2011 and today is resplendent in its Shell colour scheme of 1952.

Speke Aerodrome Heritage Group aircraft

Type	Identity	Built	Origin	Acquired	Notes
American Aviation AA-1 Yankee	G-SEXY	1970	USA	2006	fuselage
British Aerospace Jetstream 4100*	G-JMAC	1992	Britain	29 Jan 2003	–
Gloster Meteor F.8#	WH291	1951	Britain	Mar 2011	–
Hawker Siddeley HS.748-1/105	G-BEJD	1961	Britain	20 Oct 2011	–
Hawker Siddeley HS.748-2A/334#	G-ORAL	1977	Britain	Mar 2011	cockpit
Percival Prince 6E	G-AMLZ	1952	Britain	23 Nov 2008	–
Short 360-100#	G-SSWM	1984	Britain	6 May 2014	cockpit

Notes: * – illustrated in the colour section. # – on loan from Mike Davey

Two-and-a-bit 'Brits'

Moving a monster like a Bristol Britannia by road is not a process to be repeated... unless all else fails. Roger Hargreaves masterminded the transport of *Charlie-Fox* no less than *four* times – no wonder his email address included the name 'Britboss'. Roger's involvement with Britannia heritage did not stop with G-ANCF. He secured the cockpit of the second prototype, G-ALRX, in 1995 and donated it to what is now Aerospace Bristol (see Chapter 10) in 2013. His standing within the airliner and engineering world was such that when Transair Cargo was retiring the last Britannia, the company presented it to the Britannia Aircraft Preservation Trust that Roger had founded in 1991. This aircraft, former RAF C.1 XM496 flew into Kemble on 14th October 1997 and is now in the care of the Bristol Britannia XM496 Preservation Society (see also Chapter 10). During an interview with him in 2009, Roger smiled about his ability to 'collect' Britannias: "For a while, I was responsible for two-and-a-bit 'Brits'!" Roger died in September 2016 aged 65: the out-pouring of sorrow and respect that followed summed up an incredible determined man. Roger is a shining example of willpower.

Roger Hargreaves in the cockpit of his beloved Britannia G-ANCF at Speke, 2008. *Ken Ellis*

Long since instilled with the aviation 'bug', Roger left school in 1968 and joined British Eagle on November 1 – *six days* later the airline ceased trading! He joined Monarch Airlines in 1969 as a traffic officer at its 'Town Terminal' in London, transferring to Luton in March 1971 to work in operations. He made his first flight in G-ANCF in October 1972 from Luton to Adelaide and return. In April 1976 he moved to African Cargo Airways along with *Charlie-Fox* – he is alleged to have been an integral part of the deal! Roger started his own aircraft charter business and called it Proteus Aero Services after the turboprop that powered the 'Whispering Giant'. Proteus ran until 1994 and after that he specialised in operations management for airline and corporate jet organisations.

Roger was involved in the preservation of about 20 aircraft, including the preserved 'Brits', the Vickers Viscount at Brooklands (Chapter 27) and the Handley Page Herald at Woodley (Chapter 3). Like anyone involved in aviation heritage's 'private sector', this involvement cost him a lot in time and money. He explained his regard for the Britannia: "It's difficult to see why I love the Britannia, it's not just having worked closely with them for so long, they kind of get into the blood."

Bristol Britannia 308F G-ANCF
1958 | Long range airliner | Four 4,440shp Bristol Proteus 765 turboprops

Despite great hopes, only 85 Britannias were built, but the type went on to a long and productive life with operators all over the world. In British museums is the cockpit of second prototype G-ALRX at Filton and whole examples at Cosford and Duxford. Former RAF C.1 XM496 is cherished by volunteers at Kemble.

Charlie-Fox was registered as such on 3rd January 1958 to Bristol Aircraft. It was built by Short Brothers and Harland at Sydenham, Belfast, and first flew wearing the 'B Condition' ('trade plate') marking G-18-4 on 19th November 1958. It had been completed as a series 305 initially destined for British Overseas Airways Corporation but the order was taken over by the Northeast Airlines with the American registration N6597C allocated. This deal also fell through and, as G-14-1, the Britannia was ferried to Filton on 24th October 1959 where Bristol fitted it out as a Series 308 for the Argentine airline Transcontinental SA as LV-PPJ. The ferry flight to Buenos Aries began on 16th December 1959 and the following year it was re-registered as LV-GJB. It was used on the Buenos Aries to New York route until the airline closed down in 1961 and it was stored.

On 16th January 1964 again registered as G-ANCF, it arrived at London Airport, Heathrow, having been acquired by Britannia advocate British Eagle International Airlines. It was converted to Series 308F convertible freighter status at the airline's maintenance base, Liverpool Airport, Speke. During its time with British Eagle, *Charlie-Fox* carried the names *New Frontier* and later *Resolution*. The airline ceased operation in October 1968 and two months later it joined Monarch Airlines at Luton. Between December 1973 and January 1974 G-ANCF was leased to International Aviation Services, trading as IAS Cargo Airlines, flying out of Gatwick. Another lease followed in February 1976 when *Charlie-Fox* took up the Kenyan identity of 5Y-AZP to serve African Cargo Airways, trading as African Safari Airways. It was sub-leased to Invicta Airlines at Manston, from June 1976. Invicta took the Britannia on full time and it resumed the registration G-ANCF on 7th January 1977. *Charlie-Fox* flew to Manston on 30th October 1980 for regular maintenance, but this was never completed; Invicta had folded. That October arrival turned out to be its last flight; it had totted up 37,074 flying hours. Stored at the Kent airfield, ownership was transferred to the New Zealand company Merchant Air, which was operating Series 312F G-AOVF – now at the RAF Museum Cosford – and needed a source of spares.

Determined not to let G-ANCF face the axe, Roger Hargreaves stepped in and acquired it, via his company Proteus Aero Services, in June 1985. The Britannia Aircraft Preservation Trust was founded in 1991 to look after *Charlie-Fox*. Roger and his friends needed to get the airliner out of Manston as soon as possible. The centre section – nearly 70 feet long ending at the outer engine nacelles – was stored courtesy of the officer commanding RAF Quedgeley, Gloucestershire. The rest travelled on 5th April 1988 to the Brooklands Museum (Chapter 27) and Roger became a strong friend of this organisation, helping to move several large aircraft to the site; starting with Vickers Varsity T.1 WF372 in November 1988. As the Bristol Aero Collection (Chapter 10) began to gain pace, Roger placed G-ANCF on loan and the bulk of the Britannia moved to Banwell, Somerset, in readiness for display, on 27th March 1993. Bristol Aero moved to Kemble and G-ANCF followed in September 1996, along with its centre section. In 2006 Bristol Aero had to forsake its large storage hangar for a smaller one at Kemble and *Charlie-Fox* faced another move. The hunt for a home resulted in a decided 'Yes' from the Jetstream Club at Speke and G-ANCF moved there on 7th March 2007. Since then a team that is best described as resolute – remember its first British Eagle name? – has worked steadily on the gargantuan task of restoring *Charlie-Fox*.

G-ANCF serving British Eagle as *New Frontier* in 1968 shortly before the airline folded. *via Roger Hargreaves*
Charlie-Fox at Speke in May 2017, in front of the hangar where it was maintained in the 1960s. *Ken Ellis*

Inside Fort Perch Rock, the Warplane Wreck Investigation Group's 'double-decker' museum: the 610 Squadron exhibition and below the aviation 'archaeology' display. *Ken Ellis*

Also in Merseyside
Fort Perch Rock

The fort, on Marine Promenade, New Brighton, has a great strapline: 'Defending Merseyside's Heritage since 1829'. This coastal defence fort is amazing enough but it is also the home of the Warplane Wreck Investigation Group with extensive displays of recovered items, including the 'Luftwaffe over Merseyside' exhibition and a section dedicated to 610 (County of Chester) Squadron. **www.fortperchrock.org**

Also, in Lancashire
Spitfire Visitor Centre

At Blackpool Airport, the Lytham St Anne's Spitfire Display Team is developing a visitor centre within Hangar 42. This is centred around a variety of full scale replica Hurricanes and Spitfires plus supporting artefacts. Occasional open days are staged while working up to longer opening times. **www.spitfiredisplayteam.co.uk**

CHAPTER 20
NORFOLK

East Anglian Threshold
City of Norwich Aviation Museum

Norwich Airport
www.cnam.org.uk

Norwich Airport has become the gateway to and from East Anglia, reaching out into Europe, and beyond. The aeronautical heritage of the region is exceptional and it is appropriate that the northern perimeter of the former wartime airfield that became the airport is home to the City of Norwich Aviation Museum (CoNAM). The collection's origins go back to 1977 when like-minded employees of the Eastern Counties Omnibus Company set up the Eastern Counties Aircraft Association. Thoughts turned to acquiring an aircraft or two and charting the history of aviation in Norwich and the surrounding area. First acquisition was Avro Anson C.19 TX228 from Duxford on 2nd March 1980. Space at the threshold of the north end of the out-of-use northwest-southeast runway was secured – just a short distance from the museum's current site. Three months later Whirlwind HAR.10 XP355 arrived and the small volunteer group began working to establish a museum. With access via the village of Horsham St Faith, land on the northern perimeter of the airport was acquired, allowing visitors to view the activity 'over the fence'. It also allowed large aircraft to be flown in to join the collection. This was achieved in fine style in January 1983 when Avro Vulcan B.2 XM612 touched down and repeated in May 2010 when HS Nimrod MR.2 XV255 was delivered. These needed to be carefully towed across the grass to get to the museum compound, a delicate exercise. CoNAM opened its doors to the public on 5th May 1985.

Above: Vulcan B.2 XM612 at Nellis Air Force Base, Nevada, during a 'Red Flag' exercise in 1979. *KEC*

Fighters and bombers

Locals differ on how to refer to the airfield; to some it is 'Horsham', to others it is 'St Faiths' with emphasis on the plural. RAF Horsham St Faith became completely operational in May 1940. It had been intended as a bomber base, but its proximity to Europe also made it ideal for long-ranging fighters. The defence of East Anglia, in particular Ipswich and Norwich, was also a vital undertaking. Bristol Blenheims and Supermarine Spitfires formed the main types operated in the first years by resident units, but Boulton Paul Defiants and DH Mosquitos also featured. The nature of the airfield – and much of East Anglia – changed in late 1942 with the coming of the Americans. Martin B-26 Marauders of the USAAF's 319th Bomb Group (BG) and Republic P-47 Thunderbolts of the 56th Fighter Group settled briefly. The long term unit most associated with the wartime Horsham was the 458th BG with its Consolidated B-24 Liberators, from January 1944 to July 1945.

Like many other airfields, the end of hostilities could have brought about a return to agriculture, but Horsham St Faith was destined for a new, and long, life with RAF fighters. DH Hornets and Mosquitos and North American Mustangs represented the twilight of the piston era. In August 1946 the first jets, Gloster Meteors, arrived and DH Vampires and Venoms, Hawker Hunters and Gloster Javelins settled on the station. Horsham St Faith closed for flying in August 1963 and the RAF finally pulled out in 1967. By that time the farsighted Norfolk County Council had decided that an airport for Norwich and its surroundings was vital. Norwich Airport opened on 30th May 1970 and that year saw the foundation of Air Anglia, the region's own airline. The two provided the launch pad for what rapidly became a regional success story.

Delivered into the airport in May 2010, Nimrod MR.2 XV255: Dassault Mystère IVA 121 on the right. *Terry Dann*

Regional heritage

Gales on 1st February 1983 badly damaged the 'founder airframe' Anson and it was placed into store. As discussed in Chapter 18, Ansons are challenging to restore and very wisely the CoNAM team decided that it was better to reduce the airframe to spares to help other projects. Alongside the acquisition of aircraft, the museum has continually expanded and developed its internal displays. The history of aviation in and around Norwich is presented to an exceptional standard; the main exhibition hall was opened in 1992. Five years later the 100 Group Memorial Museum was inaugurated in conjunction with the 100 Group Association to explain the work of the World War Two 'spoof' units. The Association regards CoNAM as its place of pilgrimage and regular reunions are staged.

The museum's geographic closeness to the airport is reflected in strong bonds with the management and operators. KLM UK and its predecessor, Air UK, have passed on considerable hardware in the form of a retired HP Herald and *two* Fokker Friendships. The expanding collection of light and general aviation types also came from the airport. As noted above a driving force in the development of Norwich Airport was Air Anglia – later part of Air UK – and displays highlight the airline's progression from light aircraft, to Douglas Dakotas and the present day Fokker 100 twinjets of KLM UK. The museum team has always embraced new concepts and while researching its history the author was amused to find a reference in the fifteenth edition of *Wrecks & Relics*, published in 1996 which read: "CoNAM breaks new ground by being the first entry with an internet address". Pixels rapidly became a major tool in the process of preserving aircraft.

Lightning F.53s 1305 (foreground) 1308 on approach, probably to Tabuk, Saudi Arabia, in the early 1970s. Both are preserved in Britain: 1305 at Norwich, 1308 at Sunderland – see Chapter 22. *BAC*

English Electric Lightning F.53 53-686
1968 | All-weather fighter / strike fighter | Two 11,100lb st Rolls-Royce Avon 302C turbojets

Visitors to Norwich need to take in *both* sides of this gleaming Lightning. To port it carries the markings it wore while serving in Saudi Arabia; to starboard it carries a British civil registration from its appearance at the Farnborough airshow in 1968. This machine was one of 35 single-seaters ordered for the Royal Saudi Air Force (RSAF) and it was first flown from Samlesbury on 11th June 1968 by Tim Ferguson. (Tim also flew the museum's Jaguar – see below.) For testing the Lightning carried the 'B Condition' ('trade plate') marking G-27-56. Slated to appear in the static at the September 1968 Farnborough display, the Lightning was allocated the civil registration G-AWON. ('B Condition' markings were not supposed to be used for cross-country flights.) *Oscar-November* was surrounded by sufficient weaponry to start a war but also caused quite a stir by the armament fit it was carrying. Under the nose was a pop-out 2in rocket pallet, the under wing pylons were fitted with *double* rocket pods while the over-wing pylons toted twin stores with rocket pods at the front and fuel tanks behind. It transpired that the over-wing 'fit' was a mock-up only and was never trialled 'in anger'.

On 17th April 1969 the Lightning was ferried out to Saudi Arabia. During its time with the RSAF, as well as the serial 53-686, this machine also wore the identities 201, 1305 and 223 at different times. The F.53 was declared operational with 2 Squadron at Khamis Mushayt in December 1969 and later flew with 13 Squadron from Tabuk. Upon retirement British Aerospace took the surviving RSAF Lightnings back and on 22nd January 1986 the Norwich Lightning arrived at Warton. For the return journey the jets were given RAF red-white-blue roundels and serials, in this case ZF592. This brought the total time on this example to 2,311 hours – low airframe utilisation. In 1989 Wensley Haydon-Baillie bought eleven F.53s and a pair of two-seat T.55s from storage at Warton. (Wensley was the brother of warbird pilot and restorer Ormond who died in a North American Mustang crash on 3rd July 1977, in West Germany.) The Lightnings were moved to the former airfield at Stretton in Cheshire and there the majority stayed, carefully dismantled and sitting in containers. Most were disposed of to Marine Salvage and moved to a yard in Portsmouth. A number of cockpits and a handful of intact airframes (including 53-686) were dispatched to Pinewood Studios, Iver Heath, Buckinghamshire, for use by film production company Carousel Pictures. Most of the cockpits were turned into 'star fighters' for the puerile 1999 release *Wing Commander*. Some of these 'extras' were taken to Luxembourg for further filming. The 'survivors' of this adventure were returned to Portsmouth by 2000. From there, 53-686 was acquired by the City of Norwich Aviation Museum and it made the journey to its new home on 6th February 2002.

Fokker Friendship 200 G-BHMY
1962 | Medium range airliner | Two 2,050shp Rolls-Royce Dart 528-7E turboprops

Until 7th April 2017 the City of Norwich Aviation Museum had the *only* intact example of a Friendship on display in Britain. Since that date, it has basked in *two* of them! On that date the museum took delivery of Series 200 G-BCDN which, like *Mike-Yankee*, served Norwich-based Air UK. The newcomer, retired by 1996 had been in use as a training airframe with KLM UK Engineering on the other side of the airfield. (The Norfolk and Suffolk Aviation Museum – Chapter 26 – has the cockpit section of yet another former Air UK Friendship, G-BDVS.) The Norwich museum also has the Handley Page competitor to the Friendship, the Herald, on view, allowing comparison – see also Chapter 3. The first Friendship had its maiden flight on 24th November 1955 and went on to spectacular success with 583 built by Fokker up to 1987 and another 206 under licence by Fairchild in the USA. A modernised and re-engined version, the Fokker 50, appeared in 1985 and 203 were built when the line closed in 1997, bringing to an end just over four decades of production. Air UK's predecessor, Air Anglia, pioneered the use of the Friendship on scheduled services in Britain and the type was based and maintained at Norwich from 1972 into the late 1990s.

Ordered by Fujita Air Lines of Tokyo, the Norwich Friendship first flew, as PH-FDL, at Amsterdam Airport, Schiphol, on 20th February 1962 and was delivered, as JA8606, on 1st March. In November the following year, JA8606 was transferred to All Nippon Airways, also Tokyo-based. By October 1971 it was serving from Jakarta, Indonesia, with Pelita Air Services as PK-PFS. By April 1997 it was operating with Seulawah Air Services, but had returned to Pelita by March 1978. A 7,000-plus mile ferry took the Friendship to its next airline at Tours, France; joining Touraine Air Transport as F-GBDK. Registered as G-BHMY on 6th May 1980 it arrived at Norwich for service with the newly founded Air UK. In that year Norwich airline Air Anglia merged with British Island Airways to form Air UK. Dutch airline KLM took greater and greater shares in Air UK and in 1998 it was renamed as KLM UK. *Mike-Yankee* was retired at Norwich in mid-1998 and in 2000 it was donated to the museum; it was towed to the site on 10th August.

SEPECAT Jaguar GR.1 XX109
1971 | Strike fighter | Two 7,305lb st Rolls-Royce/Turboméca Adour 104 turbofans

From 1974 until the base closed in March 2006, Coltishall – five miles to the northeast from the museum – thundered to the sound of the highly capable Jaguar. Chapter 11 provides more on the background to the Jaguar. Britain has a reasonable 'population' of whole Jaguars in museums. Although the Norwich Jaguar did not fly operationally from Coltishall, it served in an instructional capacity and had an important war role. It was also the fastest Jaguar ever to travel on the M55 motorway! Paul Millett took XX109, the second production GR.1, for its maiden flight from Warton on 16th November 1972. It was

Bombed-up Jaguar GR.1 XX109 blasting off from the M55 motorway near Warton, 26th April 1975.
British Aerospace

issued to 'A' Squadron of the Aeroplane and Armament Experimental Establishment at Boscombe Down on 1st May 1973 and conducted stress monitoring and weapons carriage tests, among others. It was back with the trials fleet at Warton by March 1979 by which time construction of the M55, running from Preston to Blackpool, was drawing to a close. The British Aerospace Jaguar marketing department couldn't miss the opportunity to prove that such an 'improvised' airstrip could be used by the new strike fighter. On 26th April 1975 deputy chief test pilot Tim Ferguson landed XX109 on the westbound carriageway. Apart from his ground crew, he was greeted by a phalanx of the press and plenty of public, many of whom had trudged a long way across fields to witness the event. In a 'bombing-up' demonstration, XX109 was fitted with a quartet of dummy bombs and then Tim took off, running under a bridge carrying the Weeton to Wrea Green road and took off, returning to Warton. (See Lightning 53-686, above, for more of Tim.) The hard-working XX109 was retired at Warton in 1986.

On 21st October 1986 Flt Lt Mike Rondot flew the Jaguar to Coltishall where it started a new life as a weapons loading trainer, with the instructional serial 8918M. With the approach to the Gulf War, during the summer of 1990 the Aircraft Evaluation, Development and Investigation Team was established at Coltishall to perfect 'Special Fit' modifications for the Jaguar force that was being deployed to the Middle East; XX109 was used for much of this work. It also helped perfect the Gulf 'pink' colours adopted by the Jaguars. In 2003 XX109 gave up its pink scheme and was painted in early Jaguar camouflage and the markings of 54 Squadron. The museum secured XX109 and it arrived on 1st September 2004. It has retained its 54 Squadron markings, with the addition of the code 'GH' to honour volunteer Graham Hall, who helped in its restoration. The museum has two Jaguar cockpits, GR.1 XZ375 *The Avid Guardian Reader* and T.2 XX830. Mike Rondot, who delivered XX109 to Coltishall, flew XZ375 on 'ops' during the Gulf War. After a 25-year RAF career Mike lives in Norfolk and is an aviation artist of considerable repute.

City of Norwich Aviation Museum aircraft

Type	Identity	Built	Origin	Acquired	Notes
Avro Vulcan B.2	XM612	1964	Britain	30 Jan 1983	–
Blackburn Buccaneer S.1	XN967	1963	Britain	2006	cockpit
Cessna 401A	G-OVNE	1969	USA	2006	–
Dassault Mystère IVA	121	c1956	France	31 Jan 1982	–
English Electric Canberra B.15	WH984	1955	Britain	30 Nov 2005	cockpit
English Electric Canberra T.17	WJ633	1954	Britain	2007	cockpit
English Electric Lightning F.53	53-686	1968	Britain	6 Feb 2002	see profile
Evans VP-2	G-BTAZ	1990	USA	2006	–
Fokker Friendship 200	G-BCDN	1963	Netherlands	7 Apr 2017	–
Fokker Friendship 200*	G-BHMY	1962	Netherlands	10 Aug 2000	see profile
Gloster Meteor F.8	WK654	1952	Britain	25 Nov 1995	–
Gloster Meteor NF.11	WM267	1953	Britain	11 Sep 2006	cockpit
Handley Page Herald 211	G-ASKK	1963	Britain	May 1985	–
Hawker Hunter F.6A	XG172	1956	Britain	2 Feb 2001	–
Hawker Hunter T.7	XL564	1958	Britain	Jul 2015	cockpit
Hawker Hunter F.51	E-409	1956	Britain	7 Oct 1995	–
Hawker Siddeley Harrier T.4N	XW268	1970	Britain	8 May 2008	–
Hawker Siddeley Nimrod MR.2	XV255	1970	Britain	24 May 2010	–
Lockheed T-33A	16718	1951	USA	31 May 1986	–
McDonnell Phantom FGR.2	XV426	1969	USA	2007	cockpit
Morane-Saulnier Rallye Club	G-ASAT	1962	France	12 Jun 2012	–
Piper Aztec 250	G-AYMO	1965	USA	May 2016	–
SEPECAT Jaguar GR.1	XX109	1972	GB/France	1 Sep 2004	see profile
SEPECAT Jaguar GR.1	XZ375	1976	GB/France	2006	cockpit
SEPECAT Jaguar T.2	XX830	1974	GB/France	2006	cockpit
Supermarine Scimitar	–	c1958	Britain	c1998	cockpit
TTL Banshee 300	3088	c1986	Britain	2012	target drone
Westland Whirlwind I	–	2006	Britain	2006	replica forward fuselage
Westland Whirlwind HAR.10*	XP355	1962	USA/GB	15 Jun 1980	–

Notes: * – illustrated in the colour section

Part of the extensive displays at the City of Norwich Aviation Museum. *Ken Ellis*

Garden Wings
Fenland and West Norfolk Aviation Museum

West Walton Highway

Providing many opportunities for aviation 'archaeology' the Fens of Cambridgeshire and Norfolk gave rise to the Fenland Aircraft Preservation Society. The group amassed a lot of material and in the early 1980s set about finding a means of exhibiting it. Lee Bamber of Bamber's Garden Centre at West Walton Highway, northeast of Wisbech and just inside the Norfolk border, offered accommodation and both parties went on to expand. The group opened the collection to the public on 20th June 1987. At this stage it was devoted to the incredible number of artefacts, both from 'digs' and vigorous 'scrounging' across the region.

In March 1989 a DH Vampire T.11 was taken on and space was arranged for what became a static park. RAF personnel from the Victor Major Maintenance Unit at nearby Marham restored and refinished the Vampire and it was handed back on 30th April 1991 completed to a very high standard – those were the days! In the period 1995 to 1997 the floor space was doubled and more buildings were brought on site. To emphasize the group's geographic remit, in 1995 the name Fenland and West Norfolk Aviation Museum (F&WNAM) was adopted.

The depth and level of presentation of material at West Walton Highway is exceptional. Easily the most unusual exhibit is the mangled cockpit section of one of the two Russian Federation MiG *Fulcrums* that famously and publically collided on 21st July 1993 – thankfully without serious injury. A more traditional display is the reconstructed instrument panel from Supermarine Spitfire II P7913 *City of Birmingham IV*. This was recovered from Marshland Fen, where it crashed on 8th June 1943. It had been operated by the Central Gunnery School which was based just six miles to the north of the museum at Sutton Bridge. If this sounds pedestrian, I turn to F&WNAM's secretary, Bill Welbourne, to provide the context: "it was being flown by Flt Lt George Frederick 'Screwball' Beurling DSO DFC DFM*, the most highly decorated and the highest scoring fighter 'ace of World War Two. Talking about the 'nationals' drooling over the exhibits of 'regionals', how the Canadians would love to get their hands on the only known remains of Beurling's *eight* crashes." I rest my case!

Lightning T.5 XS459 at the Fenland and West Norfolk Aviation Museum. *Ken Ellis*
Display of undercarriage legs at West Walton Highway. *Ken Ellis*

Fenland and West Norfolk Aviation Museum aircraft

Type	Identity	Built	Origin	Acquired	Notes
Avro Shackleton MR.3/3	WR971	1956	Britain	2002	fuselage
de Havilland Vampire T.11	XD434	1954	Britain	Mar 1989	–
English Electric Lightning T.5	XS459	1965	Britain	Apr 1994	–
Hawker Siddeley Buccaneer S.2B	XN983	1965	Britain	2002	cockpit
Hunting Jet Provost T.3	XM402	1959	Britain	10 Sep 1995	–
Hunting Jet Provost	–	c1960	Britain	2000	procedure trainer
Mikoyan MiG-29 *Fulcrum*	526	c1990	USSR	2000	cockpit

Always On Duty
RAF Air Defence Radar Museum

Neatishead
www.radarmuseum.co.uk

On the edge of the Norfolk Broads, close to the town of Hoveton, is a cutting edge installation that forms part of the defence of Britain's airspace and is home to an unsung museum. RAF Neatishead is the world's longest continuously operating radar site, established in 1941 as a Ground Control Intercept station. At first it used mobile radars but soon more sophisticated equipment came on line. A hardened control room, called the 'Happidrome' was built and is now part of the museum. Post-war Neatishead became a Sector Operations Centre and this role continued to 2004. The base still functions as part of the UK Air Surveillance and Control System as a Remote Radar Head, with control of other sites in North Norfolk.

Originally called the Air Defence Battle Command and Control Museum, the collection was officially opened in 1994 with five rooms in the main building available on a pre-booked basis. On 1st January 1999 it took on its present name and the opening hours and facilities have expanded. Twenty rooms are dedicated to every aspect of radar, air defence and battle management: themes include a Battle of Britain 'Ops' Filter Room, a Cold War era 'Ops' Room, a Royal Observer Corps field post and the RAF Coltishall Heritage Memorial Room.

RAF Air Defence Radar Museum aircraft

Type	Identity	Built	Origin	Acquired	Notes
Handley Page Victor	–	c1957	Britain	5 Apr 2017	cockpit
SEPECAT Jaguar GR.1A	XX979	1975	GB/France	2008	cockpit

Bloody Hundredth
100th Bomb Group Memorial Museum

Thorpe Abbotts
www.100bgmus.org.uk

The skies of East Anglia reverberate frequently to the whine of Boeing KC-135R Stratotankers operating out of the United States Air Force base at Mildenhall. Many of these are on rotation from Stateside bases but one of the tanker units calls the region home – the 100th Air Refuelling Wing. Proudly worn on the tails of the big jets is the letter 'D' in a square: this adorned Boeings of a very different era when the 100th was based at Thorpe Abbotts, 30 miles to the east. After a couple of days recovering from the transatlantic ferry flights, the crews of the 100th Bomb Group (BG) gathered at Podington in Northamptonshire in the first days of June 1943 while the ground echelon arrived after a perilous sea journey. From 9th June the B-17 Flying Fortresses began to drop into Thorpe Abbotts, the 100th's base for the next 30 months. Frequently American combat units took on nicknames that reflected the nation's innate bravado: 'Helton's Hellcats' or 'Fame's Favoured Few'. Not so the 'Bloody Hundredth'; the unit suffered swingeing losses throughout much of its stay: 753 aircrew lost their lives in the quest for Europe's freedom.

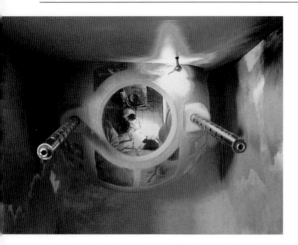

Graphic reproduction of a claustrophobic and vulnerable Sperry ball turret as fitted in the belly of a B-17 at the 100th Bomb Group Memorial Museum. *Richard Hall*

From late 1942, construction crews carved an airfield out of land to the east of Diss. The 100th BG was Thorpe Abbott's only resident unit, the B-17s living in the open all around the perimeter of the base. At its height, USAAF Station 139 Thorpe Abbotts had 7,000 people living within its bounds or billeted around and about. This influx eclipsed the nominal population of the neighbouring town; a guide at the museum described this 'invasion' as "transforming, life was never to be the same again".

The 100th Bomb Group Memorial Museum was founded by a group of locals in 1977 and among many themes depicted two are paramount: the sacrifice of the men of the 100th and their social legacy. By the time the museum was in the making, the former Flying Fortress base had been decaying for over three decades. The control tower had survived and its restoration was completed in May 1981, becoming a centre for reunions by veterans of the 100th and their families. The displays within are full of poignancy, fascination and humour; visitors can stand alongside the watch office on the top floor and imagine anxious hours waiting for the sound of returning bombers. Two new Nissen huts were introduced to the site increasing the exhibition space and the Varian Centre provides a place to gather over a 'cuppa' and ponder over how the locals view of the 'Yanks' evolved from 'over-paid, over-sexed and over here' strangers into strong bonds that have traversed an ocean and stood the test of time.

The 'Bloody Hundredth's' control tower, Thorpe Abbotts. *Richard Hall*

Ol' Buck's Liberators
453rd Bomb Group Museum

Old Buckenham
www.453museum.com

Despite being underweight and much in demand in Hollywood, the star of *Destry Rides Again* was determined to enlist and do his bit for the war effort. His 27th movie, *Ziegfeld Girl*, was released in 1941 and he did not return to the world of movies until 1946. Unlike some other actors, James 'Jimmy' Stewart, was not going to pop in and out of action; he was there for the duration. He'd held a commercial pilot's licence since 1938, but that didn't count for much, his weight-versus-height was a problem but more so was his age, in 1941 he was 33, and combat was a young man's domain. James Stewart was undaunted and by the end of 1943 he was in Britain, clocking 12 'ops' in Consolidated B-24 Liberators of the Tibenham-based 455th Bomb Group (BG). Major James Maitland Stewart DFC arrived at 'Ol Buck' on 30th March 1943, becoming the resident 453rd BG's operations officer. A staff job was not sufficient, he flew whenever possible, completing another eight combat missions and he ended the war as a colonel, commanding the 2nd Combat Bomb Wing. A glittering film career awaited James, kicking off with the five-star *It's A Wonderful Life* of 1946 all the way through to the not-so-great *The Green Horizon* of 1981. He retired from the Air Force Reserve as a Brigadier General in 1968, having flown at least one Boeing B-52 Stratofortress mission over Vietnam two years before. During his time at Old Buckenham, James may well have encountered a 24-year-old radio operator/gunner, Staff Sgt Walter Matuschanskavasky – he made his screen debut as Walter Matthau in 1955. Heralded as "the best airfield café/bar in the UK" – and who am I to argue? – Old Buckenham honours its famous operations officer with the atmospheric 'Jimmy's' diner.

Having staged through the Azores, the B-24s of the 453rd settled down at 'Ol Buck' 48 hours before Christmas Day 1943. By the time the unit pulled out in May 1945, it had carried out 259 missions. James Stewart would have been the first to downplay his role and praise the men, both air and ground, of the 453rd and honour the 366 who died in all circumstances while serving at Old Buckenham. A memorial to these men was rededicated within a garden of remembrance in 2013. Using a newly built Nissen hut, the museum itself was inaugurated on 11th November 2015, in readiness for its first season the following year. The building is named in honour of the late Pat Ramm, who was a local schoolboy when the 453rd arrived. He was 'adopted' by the ground crew of the B-24s *Hattie Belle* and *Sleepy-Time Gal*. Pat became the local contact for the 453rd BG Memorial Association in the late 1970s and he was able to reacquaint himself with many of the personnel that he had known. To quote the museum's website: "With these friendships came artefacts, uniforms and a myriad of other items to add to those which had been generously given to Pat by his USAAF friends at the end of the war. Thus began the seeds of the 453rd Bombardment Group Museum."

Major James Stewart perched on the railing at the top of Old Buckenham's tower, 1944. *KEC*

Also in Norfolk
Langham Dome

The website declares this as: "small building, big story". The museum is based around a rare survivor of an anti-aircraft gunnery training dome. The story of Langham airfield is also told. **www.langhamdome.org**

RAF Bircham Newton Memorial Project

Volunteers have erected memorials and established a treasure trove of a visitor centre dedicated to the famous RAF station (1918-1962) and its satellite field at Docking. **www.rafbnmp.org.uk**

Station 146 Control Tower Museum

The control tower at Seething has been restored and contains a museum dedicated as a living memorial to the Liberator-equipped 448th BG. The brochure sums it all up well: "One building: a whole airfield of memories". **www.seethingtower.org**

93rd Bomb Group Museum

Based on USAAF Station 104 Hardwick's Communal Site A, an incredible museum has been established dedicated to the personnel and Liberators of 'The Travelling Circus'. **www.93rd-bg-museum.org.uk**

Above: The memorial to the 453rd Bomb Group at 'Ol Buck'. *Ken Ellis*
Seething's control tower, home of an impressive museum. *Ken Ellis*

389th Bomb Group Memorial Exhibition and Home for the 466th BG Attlebridge

Volunteers have restored Hethel, Station 114's wartime chapel and the buildings around it; a unique element of Eighth Air Force history. **www.hethel389th.wordpress.com**

Muckleburgh Collection

Bannered as Britain's largest working military collection, there is much to fascinate at Weybourne, including 'live' tank demonstrations and a small collection of aircraft. **www.muckleburgh.co.uk**

Muckleburgh Collection aircraft

Type	Identity	Built	Origin	Acquired	Notes
Fieseler Fi 103 V-1	–	2001	Germany	2001	replica flying-bomb
GEC-Marconi Phoenix	ZJ385	c1995	Britain	2011	drone
Hawker Siddeley Harrier GR.3	XZ968	1980	Britain	1 Feb 1995	–
Northrop Shelduck D.1	'XT581'	2013	USA	2013	replica target drone

Norfolk Tank Museum

At Forncett St Peter, an impressive arsenal of Cold War era hardware has been assembled. Visitors can see armoured fighting vehicles in action and under restoration. Saro Skeeter AOP.12 XL739 is also part of the collection. **www.norfolktankmuseum.co.uk**

And in Norwich

Well worth a visit is the **2nd Air Division Memorial Library** inside The Forum on Millennium Plain in the middle of Norwich. As well as a vast archive, there is plenty of memorabilia on show, along with the amazing 'Friendly Invasion' mural. **www.2ndair.org.uk** In Martineau Lane, south of the city centre, **County Hall** is 'guarded' by plinth-mounted SEPECAT Jaguar S.07 XW563 which has been named *Spirit of Coltishall*.

The 2nd Air Division Memorial Library in Norwich. *Ken Ellis*

CHAPTER 21
NORTHAMPTONSHIRE

Shady Business
Carpetbagger Secret Warfare Museum

Harrington
www.harringtonmuseum.org.uk

"Most of the men actually engaged in the Carpetbagger mission never did know the whole story. For security reasons we attempted to give to any one individual only that information which he needed to conduct his portion of the total mission. I can understand why many of the people who participated give the impression of being confused. Our security program was successful." The words of Lt Col Robert W Fish, commanding officer of the 801st Bomb Group (BG) describing the 'tight ship' that was run by Harrington's Special Operations Group, as quoted in Ben Parnell's *Carpetbaggers – America's Secret War in Europe* (Eakin Press, Austin, Texas, 1987). From late November 1943 Harrington airfield was used as a relief landing ground by the Vickers Wellingtons of 84 Operational Training Unit at nearby Desborough. In March 1944 the 801st BG moved in, supplemented by the 492nd BG in August. They adopted the nickname 'Carpetbaggers': nefarious characters of no fixed abode, carrying out shady business.

Main equipment was Consolidated B-24 Liberators, but Boeing B-17 Flying Fortresses, Douglas C-47 Skytrains, Douglas A-26 Invaders and de Havilland Mosquitos were also utilised. The area around the base was thinly populated but passers-by cannot have failed to notice that most of the aircraft were painted black overall, a sign of the clandestine nature of the missions the 'hush-hush' unit flew. The 801st kept close links with its RAF equivalent, 161 Squadron, at Tempsford just 25 miles to the southeast. Most of the 801st BG's task was in support of the activities of the Office of Strategic Services (forerunner of the Central Intelligence Agency) and Britain's Special Operations Executive: dropping supplies to partisans, conveying 'Joes' (agents) to drop zones, communications relay with agents in place and occasional pin-point bombing. By the summer of 1945, all had gone quiet and the airfield settled back into agriculture.

Above: Carpetbagger B-24H Liberator 42-51211 *Miss Fitts* taking off on the southwest-northeast runway at Harrington, with the Foxhall Cottages, west of Orton, in the background. *Carpetbagger Aviation Museum*

From missiles to museum

The RAF returned in 1959 with construction teams creating substantial concrete pans and blast walls. By early 1960 the skyline at Harrington changed as 218 Squadron's new equipment pointed skywards. Three Douglas Thor intermediate range ballistic missiles were at readiness, should the Cold War demand that the unthinkable become reality. These ominous weapons were stood down in August 1963, probably as part of the quid pro quo that followed the Cuban Missile Crisis of the previous October. The Thor launch pads have been granted Grade 2 listing and although on private land, these chilling relics can be seen from local roads.

As the airfield was being transformed into a missile base, Bernard Tebbutt and his family were busy acquiring land and former USAAF buildings on the northwest edge and this became Sunnyvale Farm. A visit by the 801st/492nd Bomb Group Association in 1986 convinced Bernard that the Carpetbaggers deserved greater

Just a section of the extensive displays within the hardened group operations building at Harrington. *Ken Ellis*

recognition. With the help of the Northamptonshire Aviation Society, a memorial was unveiled in 1987. From this things began to snowball, the Association requested that Sunnyvale Farm be the venue of the fiftieth anniversary reunion, scheduled for late March 1994. The Harrington Aviation Museum Society was formed and the hardened group operations building and others were transformed into an exhibition devoted to USAAF Station 179, the Carpetbaggers and their colleagues at Tempsford. The opening of the museum, on 26th March 1994, was the highlight of an exceptional gathering at Harrington. Included in the collection is the forward fuselage of 1959-built Westland Widgeon G-APWK, which arrived on sire in 1998. Originally named the Carpetbaggers Aviation Museum, the collection has recently taken on the more descriptive title Carpetbagger Secret Warfare Museum and it really does deserve the over-used label 'unique'.

Fly Well with Style
Sywell Aviation Museum

Northampton Airport
www.sywellaerodrome.co.uk/museum.php

'You can fly well at Sywell' was the sales pitch when the lovely airfield opened for business in 1928. The adage holds equally well today. The superb art deco clubroom and terminal was completed in 1934. Developments since, across the Sywell complex, delightfully have reflected this style: even the refuelling office is a deco treasure! In June 1935 de Havilland Tiger Moths and other types filled the circuit with the formation of 6 Elementary and Reserve Flying Training School. RAF Tigers flew from the grass aerodrome throughout the war up to the spring of 1953 when 6 Reserve Flying School disbanded. The 1935 school was run by Brooklands Aviation and during the war it was a major contractor building sub-assemblies, and repairing, refurbishing and modifying a large range of types. The main wartime Brooklands speciality was the Vickers Wellington, 1,840 examples being worked on at Sywell. Armstrong Whitworth built a shadow factory at Sywell, building 100 Avro Lancaster IIs, powered by Bristol Hercules radials. Brooklands continued to work on RAF types post-war, ending with Vickers Varsities in the 1950s. In the 21st century Sywell is a bustling aeronautical and commercial community and rightly regarded as a gem in the world of general aviation.

Buildings as artefacts

In 1998 a group of individuals began to germinate the idea of a museum at Sywell, highlighting the history of the aerodrome and the varied heritage of Northamptonshire. The airport management was happy to embrace the idea and a site in the viewing area was set aside. Three Nissen huts, previously located at Bentwaters were trucked in and assembled, end to end. Visitors stepping inside will probably be oblivious that what they are standing in is an exhibit in its own right; these huts

Hunter F.2 WN904 guarding the Sywell Aviation Museum. *Ken Ellis*

were used by the armaments section at Bentwaters, for fusing bombs and storing firing pins. Famed aviator Alex Henshaw MBE presided over the opening of the Sywell Aviation Museum (SAM) on 21st July 2001. During the war, Alex was a frequent visitor, testing repaired Wellingtons. On 6th September 1943 he was at the helm of Mk.III BK272 when its port engine failed on a test flight out of Sywell; he was able to bring it back without incident.

Two more Nissen huts arrived in dismantled form in 2010 as SAM prepared for expansion. This pair had come from Snape Farm in Derbyshire, where there had been a prisoner of war camp during World War Two. The first of these was formally opened in Easter 2011 as the Paul Morgan Hall. Paul was a gifted motor engineer and a partner in a high-tech Northamptonshire company serving Formula 1 and other ultra-high performance cars. He had built up an impressive 'warbird' stable which he based at Sywell. Tragically he was killed in an accident in Hawker Sea Fury FB.11 WH588 on 12th May 2001, aged 53. Outside the 1934 art deco terminal building there is a poignant sculpture-cum-fountain with a 'missing man' formation to commemorate Paul. The Morgan Hall houses SAM's cockpit collection and working Link trainer. The following Easter the second Snape Farm Nissen hut was inaugurated and it accommodates the museum's extensive USAAF exhibitions. Housed on a delightful aerodrome with a superb heritage; SAM pays fine tribute to its base and its county. People might regard it as 'small' until they have completed a visit and realised what a significant, singular and satisfying experience they've had.

Hawker Hunter F.2 WN904
1954 | Day fighter | One 8,000lb st Armstrong Siddeley Sapphire 101 turbojet

The Hunter fighter programme was of such importance that the decision was taken to develop in parallel two versions with different powerplants. The favoured engine was the Rolls-Royce Avon, but if that were to encounter problems, delays could prove catastrophic. The third prototype Hunter first flew on 30th November 1952, fitted with an Armstrong Siddeley Sapphire as the prototype F.2. Production of the 45 Mk.2s was given to Armstrong Whitworth at Coventry with assembly and flight test at Bitteswell. Avon-powered F.1s and the Sapphire F.2s were intermediate versions with the longer endurance and ground attack capable F.4s (Avon) and F.5s (Sapphire) following in 1954. By that time the Avon was established and after 105 F.5s, the Sapphire was dropped. The Sywell Hunter is the only intact F.2; the Tangmere Military Aviation Museum (Chapter 28) has the only whole F.5 in existence.

Three Hunter F.2s had their maiden flights at Bitteswell on 19th July 1954, including Sywell's WN904. It was dispatched for service preparation to 5 Maintenance Unit (MU) at Kemble on 13th September and was issued to 257 Squadron at Wattisham on 20th October, taking up the code 'Q'. By 12th January 1956 it was with Gloster, probably at Hucclecote, licking

The Sywell Aviation Museum's USAAF exhibition. *Ken Ellis*

its wounds following a Category 4 (repairable only at an MU or in a factory) flying accident. It may have been that WN904 that had run short of fuel and made a precautionary landing at Kenley; ripping its way through the perimeter fence and across a public road in the process! Repaired, WN904 was sent to 5 MU again, on 7th December 1956. By then the other F.2 unit, 263 Squadron, had converted to F.5s and its original unit, 257, was to disband in March 1957. The brief age of the F.2 over, WN907 was transferred to 1 School of Technical Training (SoTT) at Halton, with the instructional airframe serial 7544M, on 22nd November 1957. In May 1961 it moved again, this time to 12 SoTT at Melksham and once more, to 9 SoTT at Newton in 1964. The Hunter was declared surplus in early 1974 and on 11th May it was trucked to Duxford to join the Imperial War Museum's collection. In November 1986 Duxford took delivery of Hunter F.6A XE627 and, once again, WN904 had been ousted and was in need of a new home. In mid-1989 it moved to the other side of Cambridge to the former Hunter airfield of Waterbeach to become 'gate guardian' for 39 Engineer Regiment. Waterbeach began to wind down as an Army base in 2011 and WN904 was once more facing uncertainty. The Sywell Aviation Museum put in a bid and on 2nd August 2012 its first whole airframe settled in.

Sywell Aviation Museum aircraft

Type	Identity	Built	Origin	Acquired	Notes
de Havilland Tiger Moth	G-AOES	1941	Britain	Mar 2013	fuselage
de Havilland Vampire T.11	XD599	1954	Britain	10 Oct 2004	cockpit
de Havilland Canada Chipmunk T.10	WG419	1951	Canada	2008	cockpit
English Electric Canberra TT.18	WH887	1954	Britain	25 Oct 2014	cockpit
Hawker Hunter F.2*	WN904	1954	Britain	2 Aug 2012	–
North American Harvard T.2B	KF650	1945	USA	2014	forward cockpit
Slingsby Grasshopper TX.1	WZ820	1952	Britain	2001	glider

Notes: * – illustrated in the colour section

CHAPTER 22
THE NORTH EAST
(Cleveland, Durham, Northumberland and Tyneside)

Combined Ops
North East Land, Sea and Air Museum

Usworth, Sunderland
www.nelsam.org.uk

It is rare to find an aviation enthusiast who isn't also drawn to military vehicles, classic cars, steam railways or trams. Motive power seems to provide a universal attraction. That was the logic when the Military Vehicle Museum (MVM), previously housed in Newcastle, began to move in alongside the North East Aircraft Museum in January 2012 and with this the North East Land, Sea and Air Museum (NELSAM) came about. Members of the North East Military Vehicle Club established the MVM in 1983 in the former Newcastle Science and Engineering Museum. By 2005 the display building was in need of repair and MVM closed its doors, aiming to re-open at a different site. This new venue was flooded in 2008 and the plan was shelved. Sunderland City Council came to the rescue with the offer of land alongside the North East Aircraft Museum and a building donated by the Port of Sunderland was moved to Usworth. In December 2013 construction of a shed began to house the trams of the North East Electrical Traction Trust.

The Royal Aircraft Factory FE.2s and Bristol Scouts of 36 Squadron moved into an aerodrome variously called Hylton or Town End during the summer of 1918. The unit disbanded there in June 1919 and the flying field began to be forgotten. With the establishment of the Auxiliary Air Force, the former airfield – now referred to as Usworth – came back to life and 607 (County of Durham) Squadron's Westland Wapitis were fully operational by 1932. By the outbreak of World War Two, 607 was flying Gladiators and it left Usworth in October 1939. The bulk of the airfield's war lay with 55 and then 62 Operational Training Units with Avro Ansons, Bristol Blenheims and Vickers Wellingtons. By the middle of 1944, Usworth

Above: An epic recovery and appropriate markings: Trident 1C G-ARPO at NELSAM. *David S Johnstone*

was acting as a re-settlement camp under the somewhat uncaring title Aircrew Disposal Unit! Post war, the airfield was home to 23 Reserve Flying School (de Havilland Tiger Moths, DH Canada Chipmunks and Percival Prentices) and Durham University Air Squadron (Tiger Moths, North American Harvards and Chipmunks), with RAF flying ceasing in late 1957. Sunderland council adopted the site as a municipal airport in July 1963.

Never say NEVVAA

With the establishment of a civil flying centre, one of the first operators was the Sunderland Flying Club. On 17th January 1969 Vickers Valetta C.2 VX577 flew in from Kemble, having been acquired to act as a clubroom-cum-attraction. This may well have been the last-ever flight of the type. First flown at Brooklands on 9th January 1950, this had last served with the Metropolitan Communications Squadron at Hendon. The flying club was a place where enthusiasts congregated and in March 1974 the North East Vintage and Veteran Aircraft Association (NEVVAA) was formed by some of the stalwarts. Lambton Pleasure Park, within the grounds of Lambton Castle at Chester-le-Street, offered display space which at first was occupied by items from aviation 'archaeology' recoveries from the region. A year later Westland Dragonfly HR.5 WG724 arrived and in May it was joined by Gloster Meteor F.8 WL181 – both are still with the collection. During 1976 both were damaged by vandals and negotiations were in hand for land at Usworth.

In May 1977 NEVVAA changed its name to the Northumbrian Aeronautical Collection. There is a lot of folklore about why the pendulous name North East Vintage and Veteran Aircraft Association was chosen in the first place. Malcolm Scott, member No.2 said it was because they thought they'd **neva** get an aircraft while another founder members said that it was because they wanted to "stand out from all the APSs" – aircraft preservation societies – that were prevalent. Former Danish Air Force Hunter F.51 E-419 was the first aircraft to be delivered direct to Usworth. The Valetta, previously carrying Northern Parachute Centre titles, was taken on by the volunteers in 1979. Twelve months later, another name was adopted, the North East Aircraft Museum, and this was to remain in use for 32 years. With the organisation having used several titles, for the rest of this narrative and the profiles, it will be referred to as 'North East' for simplicity.

Torch man, spare those aircraft...

We take a diversion now to discuss two airframes that were once part of the North East collection – albeit on loan – but departed by 2008. This book doesn't dwell much on *former* exhibits, but this is a famous occasion when an amateur group saw a need and without hesitation acted. Both airframes in question are now with the 'big boys': 1946-built Bristol Brigand TF.1 RH746 with the RAF Museum and 1953 world air speed record holder Supermarine Swift F.4 WK198 with the Brooklands Museum. In May 1981 a trip to the Manchester area by members of the North East museum to purchase an aero engine had drawn a blank. The team turned to the seventh edition of *Wrecks & Relics* to see if there was anything else they could fill the time with. They read of the Unimetals Industries Ltd scrapyard at Failsworth, Clayton Vale, and that a threat of closure hung over it.

Signage salvaged from the last days of Sunderland Airport. *Ken Ellis*

The fuselages of Brigand TF.1 RH746 (left) and Swift F.4 WK198 at Usworth shortly after the rescue from Failsworth. *Alan Curry*

Off they went and – so the story goes – arrived to find a man astride WK198 about to light his oxy-acetylene torch. Much had already gone or was in the process of being cut up but the Brigand (a unique survivor) and record-breaking Swift fuselages were too good to pass up. A hasty amount of bargaining went on. Oddly purchase was not possible, but the loan of several items was agreed and the lads shot back to Sunderland to arrange the trucks. It could be argued that without a 'crew' like the boys from North East, the rescue could not have happened. On-the-spot decision making was needed; the 'what-ifs' could wait. The Clayton Vale valley was to be redeveloped and the scrapyard had lingered far too long as it was. Bulldozers were to plough through the property within the week. Sunderland had proved it had the flexibility and the manpower to undertake such a recovery. On 17th May 1981, a fleet of lorries left the soon to be obliterated Unimetals yard. As well as the Swift and the Brigand, the forward fuselage of Boulton Paul Balliol T.2 WN516 and the forward fuselage of Fairey Firefly AS.5 WD889 completed the haul.

As the airframes were on loan, there was always an element of becoming a hostage to fortune. The owner of the yard negotiated a new arrangement for the Brigand and on 19th April 2001 it moved to the Bristol Aero Collection at Kemble (Chapter 10) before it was purchased by the RAF Museum in April 2010 and is now in store at Cosford. The Swift remained at Usworth until 2nd April 2008 when it was transferred to the RAF Millom and Militaria Museum in Cumbria. For the second time the Swift's prospects looked slim when the Millom museum collapsed, but thankfully the Brooklands Museum stepped up to the plate and WK198 was moved by road to its new home on 3rd February 2011. (The Balliol cockpit is displayed at Tettenhall – Chapter 24 – while the Firefly sections are with a private owner in Devon.)

One door shuts, another opens

The arrival of the Vulcan, detailed below, in January 1983 was a fantastic morale booster for the museum. Fifteen months later things looked very bleak. Sunderland council had been negotiating with Nissan to establish a car factory in the area and the publically owned land that the airport occupied was perfect for both parties. The venture was going to provide a deprived area with thousands of jobs, directly and indirectly, but at North East, the possibility of relocation looked daunting if not impossible. Both the council and Nissan were determined to minimise any 'collateral damage' and a long term lease on a four-acre site just outside the boundary of the airfield was offered. Planning permission for small hangars was granted and the evolution of the North East museum commenced. The massive Nissan plant was opened in September 1986 and has since been expanded.

With its new site, the museum extended to full time opening in 1987. An application was made in 1991 for planning permission for a hangar offering 20,000 square feet of display space. In 1993 this superb, self-financed edifice was erected and opened. During the night of 2nd September 1996 the old control tower and other buildings were torched by vandals; although not on museum land it was a sign of the times. On 24th January 1997 the Valetta was reduced to a smoking ruin. Readers will recall that 21 years previously, at Lambton Castle hoodlums had struck at North East airframes but not with such devastation. Horrific this might have been, VX577 had been inert and exposed to the elements (meteorological and anti-social) for 28 years and would have stretched the museum's restoration prowess and budget to the limits. The RAF Museum has Valetta C.2 VX573 on charge but has never restored, or displayed it; leaving the Norfolk and Suffolk Aviation Museum (Chapter 26) with the only example (VX580) on public display. Determined to get more exhibits indoors, a hangar extension and shop were opened in 1998. With military vehicles and trams providing a combined 'ops' flavour to the site, the newly named NELSAM enters a new era.

Valetta C.2 VX577 and Meteor F.8 WL181 in 1986 with first phase of the new site. To the left is 'The Three Horse Shoes' public house – required visiting! *Alan Curry*

Vulcan B.2 XL319 framing the bare structure of the huge display hall, 1992. *Alan Curry*

Aero and Engineering Lone Ranger G-MBDL
1981 | Single-seat microlight | One 22hp Zenoah G-25 piston

Lancaster, California-based Striplin Aircraft flew its prototype Lone Ranger single-seat microlight for the first time on 23rd October 1980. This was followed by the side-by-side two-seater Sky Ranger. Both were conventional in layout featuring tricycle undercarriage and three-axis controls. Striplin lost no time in granting licences and David Wilson established Aero and Engineering Services (AES) at Washington, Tyne and Wear, to produce a British version of the Lone Ranger. Early examples were fitted with a converted Chrysler engine, but the Japanese-built Zenoah was the main choice. Around a dozen Lone Rangers were built before AES closed its doors. Having been manufactured just three miles from the museum, North East was keen to acquire an example. *Delta-Lima* did not gain a permit to fly; it joined the museum in 1989.

Northeast product, AES Lone Ranger G-MBDL.
Craig Dunlop

Vulcan B.2 XL319, wearing 230 OCU markings, tucks up the gear during a display at Woodford, 1977. *Alan Curry*

Avro Vulcan B.2 XL319
1961 | Long range heavy bomber | Four 20,000lb st Bristol Siddeley Olympus 301 turbojets

When Vulcan XL319 touched down at Usworth on 21st January 1983 the North East Museum had the advantage of being based on an aerodrome so that 'drop ins' were a possibility. Within a year Usworth was on countdown for closure as the entire site was transformed into the world-class Nissan car factory. Two Vulcans are profiled in this book: turn to Chapter 18 for a study of Woodford's XM603 and more general comments. For the sum of £5,000 (£20,000 in present-day values) a museum could take delivery – to a suitable runway – of a Vulcan B.2. Falklands veterans Sqn Ldr John Reeve and Sqn Ldr Neil McDougall DFC piloted XL319 on its last-ever flight, into Usworth from Waddington. It was still wearing 44 Squadron markings, although the unit had disbanded on 21st December 1982. Members of the North East team were euphoric, especially as they were the first independent museum to receive a Vulcan.

Built at Woodford and first flown on 1st October 1961, Vulcan B.2 XL319 was awaiting collection eighteen days later and was delivered to 617 Squadron, the famed 'Dam Busters', at Scampton on 23rd October 1961. The Vulcan was finished in the overall white colour scheme referred to as 'anti-flash' but in 1964 it adopted the camouflage scheme it wears today. In April that year the centralised servicing scheme meant that Vulcans were not 'owned' by individual units and were 'pooled'; the Scampton Wing at that stage comprising 27, 83 and 617 Squadrons. Scampton became the home of 230 Operational Conversion Unit (OCU) in December 1969, the outfit having previously been based at Finningley. XL319 was transferred to the OCU on 14th May 1970. The following year it was back in the charge of 617 Squadron, but reverted in 1972 to 230 OCU in 1972. XL319 was issued to 35 Squadron at Scampton on 16th October 1978 and it was still with the unit when it disbanded on 28th February 1982. It made the short hop across Lincoln on 1st March 1982 to Waddington; the base's wing was composed of 9, 44, 50 and 101 Squadrons. The delta was confirmed as going to Sunderland on 20th January 1983, taking off for the last time the following day.

Frederick Brown's Helicopter at Usworth. *Alan Curry*

The Frederick Brown Luton Minor at Ken Fern's Stoke-on-Trent workshop during its restoration, 1997. *Ken Ellis*

Bensen B-7
1965 | Single-seat gyroglider
Brown Helicopter
1962 | Single-seat helicopter | One McCulloch piston
Luton Minor 'G-AFUG'
1944 | Single-seat ultra-light | One 40hp Aeronca-JAP J-99 piston

In 1975 members of the North East Veteran and Vintage Aircraft Association were shown into a barn at Stanley, just to the west of Chester-le-Street, where they were establishing a collection of aircraft at Lambton. Three rotorcraft and a parasol monoplane were nestled there. Arnold Pickering was offering them on behalf of this late father-in-law, Frederick Brown. Needless to say the gesture was graciously taken up and the North East lads had acquired a fascinating collection with the strongest of local provenance. The cache remained in Stanley until 1977, when it was passed on to the museum. This is a case of the whole being more significant than the parts. Any one of these airframes in another collection would most likely not raise an eyebrow. As a grouping they represent an important regional asset; an insight into the endeavours and skills of a local and a 'snapshot' on the world of homebuilding.

Frederick Brown was fascinated by flight and proved to a capable carpenter and, later, an engineer. There were two phases to Frederick's aeronautical adventures, the war years and the early 1960s. His first project was a Luton LA.4 Minor single-seat parasol monoplane which he built, from plans published in *Practical Mechanics* magazine, from 1939 to 1944. He lived in a small miner's cottage in Front Street, Stanley, and the 20-foot long fuselage and 25-foot span single-piece wing were worked on in a passage alongside the dwelling, in the hallway and in a bedroom. As with most plans-built aircraft of the 1930s, the construction of the all-wood airframe was relatively easy; finding a practical and affordable engine was the difficult part. At first Frederick used a small V-twin that had powered a three-wheeler car but he was not happy with this, substituting a 40hp ABC Scorpion twin-cylinder. All the while Frederick was designing and building a five-cylinder radial; but this does not seem to have ever been finished. The final choice lay with an Aeronca-JAP J-99. At some stage, possibly from the very beginning given the restricted space he was working in, Frederick designed the wing to fold, allowing the Minor to be towed behind a car. It seems likely that this machine never flew. In late 1980 the Minor was brought out of storage and loaned to the Nene Valley Aviation Society at Sywell; moving to Sibson in 1984. It returned to Sunderland in 1986 and that year travelled to Ken Fern's workshop at Stoke-on-Trent where he worked his magic refurbishing and refinishing the little monoplane. The completed machine was delivered to Sunderland in October 1998 wearing the 'period' registration G-AFUG'. (In the summer of 2001 the museum acquired an example of the two-seat Luton LA-5 Major, G-ARAD which had been built between 1960 and 1973 and was fitted with a 90hp Continental C90. It is doubted that this machine achieved flight.)

The timeline for Frederick Brown's 'rotary period' probably runs as follows. By 1961 Frederick was constructing a small single-seat helicopter of his own design. This was intended to be powered by a twin-cylinder engine that had also been designed and built by Frederick. It is not known if this engine came to fruition. It was fitted with a McCulloch which Frederick claimed came from a World War Two era target drone. This would most likely make it a 72hp McCulloch 4318 four-cylinder as fitted to the Radioplane (Northrop from 1952) Shelduck drone; tens of thousands were built from 1947 onwards. Less engine, the unique Brown Helicopter was presented to the museum in 1975. Next it seems that Frederick acquired the plans to what he called a 'Gizmer Autogyro', an American design which this author has never been able to trace. It is believed that the McCulloch from the Brown Helicopter was fitted to this single-seater. Autogyro zealot Fred Fewsdale of Darlington tested this machine at Middleton St George (now Durham Tees Valley Airport) around about 1963 but it was damaged in a running up accident. Although presented to the North East team in 1975 when it came to handing on Frederick's creations in 1977, the 'Gizmer' was not present. Frederick Brown's last rotorcraft was a kit-built Bensen B-7 gyroglider. (See Chapter 18 *Founding Fathers* for more details of Bensens.) Frederick re-used the rotors from the 'Gizmer' on this craft. As before, it is not known if this example achieved flight.

Fábrica Militair de Aviones Pucará A-522
c1980 | Ground-attack / Counter-insurgency aircraft | Two 978shp Turboméca Astazou XVIG turboprops

To properly portray Britain's aerial adversaries of the Falklands conflict, April to June 1982, UK museums would need to get hold of a Dassault Super Etendard or a Douglas A-4 Skyhawk that were flown valiantly and to great effect against the British task force. However, that does not seem to be a credible option. Easily the most interesting type fielded to the Falklands by Argentina was the Pucará. Intended for use against guerrilla forces and not for use in heavily contested airspace, the twin turboprop was severely hampered during the conflict. One managed to shoot down Army Air Corps Westland Scout AH.1 XT629 on 28th May 1982, killing the helicopter's pilot. Otherwise, the Pucarás deployed were very much in the firing line. Four complete Pucarás are in museum hands in Britain: Duxford, Cosford, Flixton and A-522. The prototype Pucará first flew from Cordoba on 20th August 1969 and up to 1993 a total of 110 are believed to have been built. The major customer was the Fuerza Aérea Argentina, taking its first in 1976, but small numbers were also received by Colombia, Sri Lanka and Uruguay.

A-522 served with Grupo 3 de Ataque at Reconquista and in March 1982 had a total flying time of 761 hours. It was one of a dozen Pucarás deployed to the Falklands in mid-May to make up for attrition losses. As well as being vulnerable to RAF Harriers and Fleet Air Arm Sea Harriers and to shoulder-launched missiles from ground forces, the Pucarás suffered from chronic operational availability. After the surrender, A-522 was assessed at Port Stanley as being only slightly damaged and 18 Squadron Boeing Chinook HC.1 ZA720 airlifted it to the SS *Contender Bezant* on 6th September 1982 for shipping to Britain. Off-loaded at Southampton Docks on 23rd September it was moved to Abingdon and allocated the instructional airframe serial 8768M. Ear-marked for the Royal Air Force Museum it was roaded to St Athan on 25th October 1982. It was transferred to the Fleet Air Arm Museum at Yeovilton and arrived there on 7th December 1982. Several airframes became spares donors for A-515 which was being returned to airworthiness for evaluation by the Aeroplane and Armament Experimental Establishment at Boscombe Down, as ZD485. (This first flew on 28th April 1983. Its last sortie was to the RAF Museum Cosford on 9th September 1983.) A-522 was among those used to support ZD485 and probably helped Yeovilton to eventually decide to that it was surplus to requirements in 1994. This Pucará was not the first to come to Sunderland... The Museum of Army Flying had delivered A-528 in 1993 on short term loan. On 24th July 1994 a cost effective shuffle was achieved: A-522 arrived at Sunderland from Yeovilton and the same low-loader took A-528 away to the Norfolk and Suffolk Aviation Museum at Flixton.

Hawker Siddeley Trident 1C G-ARPO
1965 | Medium range airliner | Three 9,850lb st Rolls-Royce Spey 505-5F turbofans

In Chapters 18 and 19 we've already seen some airliner recoveries and restorations which would be astounding if they were carried out by nationally-funded bodies. But these were conceived, managed, funded, 'staffed' and completed entirely by volunteers determined to make a difference. The story of *Papa-Oscar* is another 'against the odds' epic. First flown at Hatfield on 13th January 1965, Trident 1C G-ARPO was delivered to British European Airways (BEA) at London Airport, Heathrow, on the last day of that month. It plied the airways with the regularity that Tridents became famed for; changing its colour scheme after BEA was absorbed into British Airways on 1st April 1974. Captain Andy Butcher was at the controls for what turned out to be *Papa-Oscar*'s last commercial flight, from Glasgow to London on 16th March 1983. It was stored at Heathrow while its future was sorted. It was ferried to Teesside Airport (once Middleton St George, now Durham Tees Valley Airport) on 12th December 1983; its last-ever flight, clocking up 26,471 hours. It was used by the Civil Aviation Authority's fire and rescue school but thankfully was reserved for evacuation exercises and 'smoke environment' training. Airframes around it were reduced to ashes in real 'burns'.

The incredible rescue of Trident 3B G-AWZK from Heathrow and its removal to the Runway Visitor Park at Manchester Airport, Ringway, by Neil Lomax and team in 2005 had shown what was possible. Tony Jarrett found himself project leader of 'Save the Trident' and a bid for G-ARPO was launched. By this time contractor Serco was running the fire school at Durham Tees Valley and negotiations for the airframe that was surplus to requirement resulted in an agreement in principle in September 2009. Serco would donate the Trident if a credible plan for its future – with no cost to the company – could be drawn up. Sunderland was always envisaged as the destination and the North East team offered not just the venue but all the help they could. Before *Papa-Oscar* could go anywhere, the smoke-soaked cabin needed careful checking out for toxins or worse: health and safety procedures (for once!) having a purpose. On 31st July 2011 the fuselage of G-ARPO arrived at its new home, with the tail, wings and engines following on the 18th and 19th August. A brief moment of celebration was followed by nearly four years of intensive labour to turn a fire-rescue airframe into a jetliner. The wise decision was taken to paint *Papa-Oscar* in the colours of Newcastle-based Northeast Airlines. Although the Trident had never served with the airline, the name helped reflect the jetliner's custodians and commemorate a well-regarded regional operator. Known as BKS Air Transport until 1st November 1970, Northeast purchased a quartet of Trident 1Es from 1969. It was absorbed by British Airways in late 1973. The Trident was unveiled on 11th June 2015 with the 'Save the Trident' team proving as good as their word. *Papa-Oscar* is opened up on special occasions at Sunderland.

North American F-86D Sabre 51-6171
1953 | All-weather fighter | One 7,630lb st General Electric J47-17 turbojet

A swept wing and after-burner for fast response, reliable intercept radar, a revolutionary fire control system, the ability to deliver a withering salvo of rockets into a Soviet bomber stream, service with a NATO member. These are impressive attributes, but were not why the only 'Sabre Dog' in Britain is given a profile. First reason: for two years F-86 6171 defended UK airspace as part of the United States Air Forces in Europe (USAFE). Second: this is a great example of how a small regional museum can engage with a foreign government, acquire an exotic aircraft and overcome endless bureaucracy while trucking a weapon of war across Europe. With the advent of the F-86 Sabre in 1947, North American Aviation changed the nature of day fighters but two years later took an even greater step. The all-weather version was so significantly different from its forebear that it was initially designated YF-95A. The prototype YF-86D first flew on 22nd December 1949 – an incredible leap in capability in such a short time. The APG-36 four-quadrant search radar had a range of 30 miles and was linked to a Hughes E-4 fire-control system. Once the target was acquired, a 'tray' holding two dozen folding-fin 'Mighty Mouse' high-velocity unguided rockets dropped down under the forward fuselage, ready to unleash a deadly barrage. Also known as the 'Dogship' (from its 'D-for-Dog' designation) the 2,504 F-86Ds manufactured changed the face of all-weather engagements – for a while.

The North East F-86D was built at Inglewood, California, for the USAF as 51-6171 and was issued for service with Air Defense Command on 8th September 1953. It served with three Stateside units: the 37th Fighter Interceptor Squadron (FIS) at Ethan Allen Air Force Base (AFB), Burlington, Vermont, from new; the 325th FIS at Hamilton AFB, Novato, California, from October 1954 and the 83rd FIS at Paine Field, Washington State, from August 1955. While with the 325th, 51-6171 was part of its aerobatic demonstration team, the 'Sabre Knights' until the unit deactivated in August 1955. Today, the starboard side of the F-86D is painted in the scheme it wore with the team. In February 1956 the Sabre was at Brookley AFB, Alabama, undergoing a rework at the Mobile Air Materiel Area. Assigned to USAFE, after the transatlantic ferry flight in March 1956 it was accepted by Shorts, probably at Aldergrove, Northern Ireland. Based at Bentwaters, 51-6171 served with the 512th FIS, part of the 406th Fighter Interceptor Wing. The port side of the F-86D wears the colours from its time at Bentwaters. The 406th Wing was deactivated in March 1958 and the 512th moved to Sembach, West Germany, under the control of the 86th Air Division. In July 1958 the US Navy's Sixth Fleet deployed to the eastern Mediterranean, landing a force of US Marines at Beirut, Lebanon, on the 15th in response to incursions by Syrian forces. In support of the action, the 512th's Sabres were detached to Adana in Turkey. The situation was stabilized and US forces withdrew in October.

By June 1959 the Sabre was at Châteauroux in France within the 3130th Field Maintenance Group before moving to Turin where Fiat prepared it for service with the Helliniki Aeroporía (Hellenic – Greek – Air Force). It was removed from USAF inventory in May 1960 and served with the Greeks as 6171 for less than a decade. By early 1980 6171 was parked up at Hellinikón, near Athens, and that was when the North East team sent out the first 'feelers' about acquiring surplus aircraft from the Hellenic Air Force. Five years of calls, paperwork and visits paid off when Republic F-84F Thunderstreak 26541, also at Hellinikón, was released and a crew dismantled it and trucked it across Europe – through six countries. This paved the way for the Sabre Dog and the same process was repeated during the early summer of 1987 and 6171 arrived at its new home that July.

Short 330-100 G-OGIL
1981 | Regional airliner | Two 1,198shp Pratt & Whitney Canada PT6A-45R turboprops

When the North East Aircraft Museum took delivery of Short 330 G-OGIL in April 1993, a proud volunteer declared: "This is the first wide-bodied airliner to go on display in the UK!" Things being the way they are that month also saw the second prototype 330, G-BDBS, arrive at the Ulster Aviation Society's growing collection at Langford Lodge. Whichever was first, Sunderland was open to the public on a regular basis whereas their Northern Ireland colleagues were working on a prior-arrangement basis. A North East first!

Shorts followed up the success of its Skyvan utility transport by using its box section fuselage and wings to create a family of commuter airliners. The first 30-seater SD3-30 (later Short 330), G-BSBH, had its maiden flight on 22nd August 1974. A stretched version of the 330, with 36 seats and the former's twin tails replaced by a raked single fin, appeared as the Short 360 in 1981. Including the C-23 Sherpa military freighter for the US Air Force, production of 330s and 360s amounted to 321 units with the last example being delivered in 1998. There is a cockpit of a 330 at Speke (Chapter 19), otherwise G-BDBS and G-OGIL are the only British museum examples.

The Sunderland 330 first flew at Sydenham, Belfast, on 8th April 1981 wearing the 'B Condition' ('trade plate') identity G-14-3068; it was allocated the civil registration G-BITV two days later. Ordered by Inter-City Airlines, based at East Midlands and Aberdeen Airports it was in service by the end of April 1981 but in June it was registered to the parent company, Alidair. *Tango-Victor* went on to be flown by a series of British operators: British Air Ferries, Southend (from August 1983); Air Ecosse, Aberdeen (February 1984); Fairflight, Biggin Hill (April 1985) and Connectair, operating Caledonian Link services from Gatwick (December 1986). Re-registered appropriately as G-OGIL, the 330 entered service with Gill Aviation, based at Newcastle Airport, Woolsington, in July 1990. At 06:10 hours on 1st July 1992 at Newcastle a defective nosewheel led *India-Lima* to hit a vehicle, hangar doors and fellow Short 330 G-BIFH; thankfully without injury to anyone. This put paid to G-OGIL's flying life, which amounted to 16,776 hours. After spares and engine recovery, Gill Aviation donated the 330 to the museum.

North East Land, Sea and Air Museum aircraft

Type	Identity	Built	Origin	Acquired	Notes
AES Lone Ranger	G-MBDL	1981	USA/GB	1989	see profile
Auster 5 Alpha	G-ANFU	1945	Britain	1985	–
Avro Anson C.19	G-AWRS	1946	Britain	6 Aug 1981	–
Avro Vulcan B.2	XL319	1961	Britain	21 Jan 1983	see profile
Bell Sioux AH.1	XT148	1965	USA	20 Nov 1993	cockpit
Bensen B-7	–	c1965	USA	1977	see profile
Bristol Sycamore 3	WA577	1949	Britain	1981	–
Brown Helicopter	–	1962	Britain	1977	see profile
Carmam M.100S	DUC	c1978	France	2009	glider
Dassault Mystère IVA	146	1956	France	30 Apr 1982	–
de Havilland Dove 8	G-ARHX	1961	Britain	1992	–
de Havilland Vampire T.11	WZ518	1953	Britain	11 Oct 1975	–
de Havilland Comet 4C	G-BEEX	1961	Britain	1989	cockpit
de Havilland Sea Venom FAW.22	XG680	1956	Britain	Jul 1981	–
de Havilland sea Vixen FAW.2	XN696	1961	Britain	2 Mar 2011	cockpit
de Havilland Canada Chipmunk T.10	WB685	1950	Canada	1986	–
Electra Flyer Olympus	–	c1985	USA	1989	hang-glider
English Electric Canberra TT.18	WJ639	1954	Britain	Aug 1988	–
English Electric Lightning F.53	ZF594	1968	Britain	Apr 1989	–
Fieseler Fi 103 V-1	–	2010	Germany	2011	replica flying-bomb
FMA Pucará*	A-522	c1980	Argentina	24 Jul 1994	see profile
Gloster Meteor F.8	WL181	1954	Britain	18 Mar 1975	–
Gloster Meteor NF.11	WD790	1952	Britain	30 Oct 1985	cockpit
Handley Page C-10A Jetstream	–	c1968	Britain	1993	cockpit, mock-up
Hawker Hunter F.51	E-419	1956	Britain	12 Jul 1977	–
Hawker Siddeley Trident 1C	G-ARPO	1965	Britain	31 Jul 2011	see profile
Hunting Jet Provost T.4	XP627	1962	Britain	25 Nov 1980	fuselage
Lockheed T-33A	54439	1955	USA	5 Jun 1979	–
Luton Minor	'G-AFUG'	1944	Britain	1977	see profile
Luton Major	G-ARAD	1960	Britain	4 Jun 2001	–
Mignet 'Flying Flea'	'G-ADVU'	1993	France	1994	–
North American F-86D Sabre*	16171	1953	USA	Jul 1987	see profile
North American F-100D Super Sabre	42157	1954	USA	Apr 1978	–
Republic F-84F Thunderstreak	26541	1953	USA	9 Oct 1985	–
Saunders-Roe Skeeter AOP.12	XM555	1959	Britain	12 May 2015	–
Short 330-100	G-OGIL	1981	Britain	Apr 1993	see profile
Slingsby Grasshopper TX.1	WZ767	1952	Britain	Apr 1985	glider
Sud Gazelle 1	G-SFTA	1973	France	Nov 1986	–
Westland Dragonfly HR.5	WG724	1952	USA/GB	Mar 1975	–
Westland Widgeon*	G-APTW	1959	USA/GB	1993	–
Westland Whirlwind HAR.9	XN258	1959	USA/GB	1993	–
Westland Wessex HAS.3	XM833	1960	USA/GB	Apr 2010	–

Notes: * – illustrated in the colour section

Also in the North East
Bamburgh Castle Aviation Artefacts Museum

In the West Ward of the exceptional castle within the former laundry is a superb aviation exhibition in two rooms cover the region's aviation history, including wreckage from local 'digs'. **www.bamburghcastle.com**

The former Gill Aviation Short 330 is an impressive exhibit at NELSAM. *Ken Ellis*

At Fishburn Aerodrome, north of Sedgefield, enthusiasts are busy gathering a selection of airframes and assembling hangars that will become the **Fishburn Historic Aircraft Centre**. As this book went to press, no plans for opening had been released.

Fishburn Historic Aircraft Centre aircraft

Type	Identity	Built	Origin	Acquired	Notes
de Havilland Sea Vampire T.22	XG743	1954	Britain	2016	–
de Havilland Dove 6	D-IFSB	1952	Britain	2 Feb 2016	–
de Havilland Venom FB.54	J-1790	1957	Britain	2 Feb 2016	–
Mignet 'Flying Flea'	'G-ADRZ'	c1990	France	Oct 2015	–
Soko Kraguj	G-RADA	1976	Yugoslavia	22 Apr 2017	–
Supermarine Spitfire replica	'BR954'	c2012	Britain	2016	–
Thurston Tawney Owl	G-APWU	1959	Britain	Oct 2015	–

Today Newark, Tomorrow a 'National' Newark Air Museum

Newark
www.newarkairmuseum.org

J ust short of one hundred airframes 'on the books' – the vast majority on public view – and countless other exhibits from missiles to medals; two huge display halls, an engine and an exhibition gallery, a workshop, education room, a superb café, an incredibly well stocked shop and a large number of special events constitute the Newark Air Museum. At Duxford, the Imperial War Museum has just over 80 aircraft *of its own*, not with the associated Duxford Aviation Society or the based 'warbird' operators, on show or stored. Yes, one of those is a Royal Aircraft Factory BE.2 of 1916 and another is B-52 Stratofortress with eight engines and a span of 185ft, and there are more hangars and display halls – but you get my drift.

Above: Air-to-ground of the Newark Air Museum with the south site in the background. *Newark Air Museum*

While it uses lottery and grant money whenever possible, the Newark Air Museum (NAM) has grown from the humblest of enthusiast beginnings without a whiff of state funding. It is among a handful of other 'regionals' that have a stature above and beyond their apparent status.

To milk the Duxford analogy one last time, both museums are based on former operational airfields. Standing alongside Avro Vulcan B.2 XM594 visitors should look down, below their feet is a concrete dispersal used by an Avro bomber of another generation, a Lancaster of 1661 Heavy Conversion Unit (HCU). NAM occupies land immediately to the south of the eastern end of the east-west runway of the former RAF Winthorpe. Opened in September 1940 it was a basic grass airfield acting as a satellite to nearby Swinderby, which at the time was home to a pair of Polish Fairey Battle units, 300 and 301 Squadrons. In 1942 it was rebuilt with three concrete runways. On New Year's Day 1943 the Avro Manchesters and Lancasters of 1661 HCU moved in from Waddington. The unit also operated Handley Page Halifaxes and Short Stirlings, but by February 1945 it was all-Lancaster. The HCU disbanded on 24th August 1945. By that October Winthorpe had become a satellite of Syerston and was used as a drop zone for that station's 1333 Conversion Unit, with Douglas Dakotas, Halifaxes and Airspeed Horsa assault gliders. In 1947 the airfield was transferred to Maintenance Command and, from 1953 to 1958 was home to the Central Servicing Development Unit. Winthorpe closed as an RAF station on 30th June 1959.

In 1964 much of the former airfield was purchased by the Newark and Nottinghamshire Agricultural Society and it was inaugurated as the Newark Showground the following year. As detailed below, by the summer of 1967 NAM began to establish its presence at Winthorpe. On the sixtieth anniversary of the opening of RAF Winthorpe a memorial garden to those who had served there was unveiled on the museum's south site. Mounted on top of the monument is the propeller hub from Stirling III EF186 of 1661 HCU which crashed near Grantham on 4th December 1944, killing all nine on board.

A very special shed, still going strong

Keeping to the bomber theme; there is an exhibit in Display Hangar 1 that often gets overlooked and deserves 'bigging up': it is one of the most significant pieces of Bomber Command history in Britain. In March 1974, the Newark Air Museum (NAM) was presented with a fuselage section of a Lancaster that had served for decades as a garden shed in Gainsborough. With the 9 Squadron codes 'WS-J' still evident on its sides, it was soon confirmed as Mk.I W4964.

Built by Metropolitan-Vickers in Manchester, W4964 was issued to 9 Squadron at Bardney in the spring of 1943. It took on the codes 'WS-J' and the name *Johnnie Walker – Still Going Strong* was applied to the nose along with the image of a striding gent from a well-known bottle of whisky. On the night of 11th September 1944 a force of 38 Lancasters from 9 and 617 Squadrons headed for Yagodnik, near Archangel in the Soviet Union. Twenty-one of the bombers were carrying 12,000lb 'Tallboy' bombs; the remainder were equipped with mines. The RAF bombers held no malice for the USSR; they were using Yagodnik as a forward operating base. Their target was the German warship *Tirpitz* lying in Kåfjord in northern Norway. For a variety of reasons, only 27 Lancasters were available for the raid. On 15th September the force took off at 09:30 hours. As they approached Alta Fjord, low cloud and a smoke screen billowing around the ship greatly hampered the attack. W4964 was captained by Flt Lt Dougie Melrose and bomb aimer Fg Off Sammy Morris spotted the warship's stern and at 10:55 released the 'Tallboy' from 15,000ft. Post-raid analysis confirmed that Melrose's 'Tallboy' had hit the battleship about 50ft

Lancaster I W4964 'Johnny Walker' and crew after its 100th sortie, September 1944. Left to right: Flt Lt J D Melville, skipper; Fg Off S A Morris, bomb aimer; Sgt E C Selfe, flight engineer; Fg Off J Moore, navigator; Sgt E Stalley, gunner; Sgt E Hayle, gunner; Fg Off R Woolf, wireless operator.
Peter Green Collection

Last serving as a garden shed in Gainsborough, the fuselage section of Lancaster W4964.
Howard Heeley-Newark Air Museum

astern of the bow, penetrating straight through to the keel, exploding beneath the ship allowing 1,000 tons of water to flood in. Long feared for its potential to wreak havoc on Atlantic convoys, the *Tirpitz* was to remain a priority for Bomber Command, but the attack of 15th September 1944 had rendered it impotent. That 'op' had been W4964's hundredth: only 36 Lancasters became 'century' bombers. *J-for-Johnnie* went on to complete another six 'ops'; the veteran was retired in October and on 9th December 1944 it became instructional airframe serial 4922M. It was struck off charge in November 1949 and chopped up. An enterprising householder recognised the potential of an upper section of fuselage and, with wooden walls 'fore and aft' it served in a Lincolnshire garden until its long-term future was assured by NAM.

Founders: people and airframes

The museum's origins lie with a pair of individuals and their association with the local Air Training Corps. Neville Franklin worked at a local engineering business as a draughtsman and Charles Waterfall ran a newsagents shop in Newark. Both set their sights high, they wanted a Spitfire for what became the museum. Only Neville was to achieve this, but in a private capacity with a pair of Seafire airframes. Spitfire or not, between them they set in motion the machinery that produced today's world-class collection. With the Air Training Corps headquarters providing the focal point for Charles, Neville and a growing band of enthusiasts, in 1965 they investigated rumours of a biplane lying forlornly at Cranwell. The skeletal fuselage of Westland Wallace II K6035 plus sections of other examples were found mouldering in the undergrowth on the north airfield. This was a miraculous survival; the big biplane had been downgraded to an instructional airframe in late 1940 and used as a decoy and, eventually, forgotten. As is so often the case, the 'finding' was easy, it was the 'housing' that was difficult. Neville persuaded his employers, Abbott and Company in Northern Road, Newark, to let him have some space in the large yard alongside the premises. This turned out to be a big 'ask', 'Abbott's Yard' became a part of NAM's folklore and the store of airframes, engines and other bits and pieces was not completely vacated until 1979! Neville sourced wings for the Wallace in 1970 but it would have been a very challenging restoration. Representing a generation of RAF general purpose biplanes of the 1920s and 1930s that otherwise have become extinct it was handed over to the RAF Museum in April 1977. The original deal was it would be exchanged for a 'Red Arrows' Folland Gnat: a cash sum of £5,000 was eventually accepted. Entrusted to Skysport Engineering of Hatch, Bedfordshire, the fuselage of the Wallace was restored and unveiled at Hendon in March 1993.

Newark co-founder Neville Franklin (right) receiving a presentation model of a Meteor from Wg Cdr King, officer commanding 85 Squadron, West Raynham, 1973.
Peter Green

The skeletal fuselage of Westland Wallace II K6035 in the undergrowth at Cranwell North, 1965.
Peter Green Collection

Charles went on to become the museum's first chairman and a major benefactor of exhibits. Neville took over the editorship and publication of the aircraft preservation magazine *Control Column* in 1968. The journal had been started by the Northern Aircraft Preservation Society – Chapter 18 – and it was expanded and refined by Neville. The last edition appeared in 1988. The second airframe acquired by the nascent museum was Miles Magister G-AKAT, last operated by the Magister Flying Group at Leicester. Charles, Neville and Doug Revell acquired it in 1967, going initially to Abbott's Yard. It was disposed of in 1986 going to Tony 'Taff' Smith at Breighton and restored to flying condition and it remains airworthy today. During the early history of the museum, individuals, or combinations of the membership would club together to acquire exhibits; donating them to NAM or presenting them on permanent loan. Two other airframes that arrived before the museum was officially constituted moved on. Auster Aiglet Trainer G-AMUJ, which had been involved in an accident near Sleaford on 6th June 1960, was recovered from a farm near Ancaster in 1967. Restoration would have been a complex undertaking and it was transferred to a nearby workshop specialising in Austers in the late 1980s and reduced to spares. The nose section of an Airspeed Horsa assault glider was acquired from the Historic Aircraft Preservation Society and this was passed on to the Museum of Army Flying at Middle Wallop; NAM's Bell Sioux AH.1 helicopter was eventually acquired in exchange.

Newark's second airframe, Magister T9738 (G-AKAT) was disposed on in 1986 and today is airworthy at Breighton. *Andy Wood*

A permanent home

By the end of 1967 the bare bones of a museum were in place, including eight airframes: the Auster, Horsa, Magister and Wallace mentioned above and the Lee Richards replica, Monospar, Prentice and Tiger Moth/Jackaroo listed in the table below. A 'temporary' storage site had been found and 30 or so members were lending their time. A meeting in Newark on 27th May 1968 brought about NAM as a legal entity. While Neville Franklin had arranged 'temporary' storage space another member, Neville Armitage, provided the breakthrough to a display site. He was secretary of the Newark and Nottinghamshire Agricultural Society and permission was granted to 'park' NAM's first 'heavyweight' – Supermarine Swift FR.5 – at Winthorpe. The relationship was cemented in 1971 and a small compound and workshop was established. During that May's agricultural show over 1,000 people got a preview of the collection.

On 3rd September 1969 Avro Anson XI G-ALIH was delivered, having been presented by Ekco Electronics at Southend. (For more on Ekco and another of their Avro twins, G-AGPG, see Chapter 18.) Disaster struck on 11th May 1971 when a fire all but destroyed *India-Hotel*. The fuselage was gutted; the outer wings and its Armstrong Siddeley Cheetah radials survived. A replacement was sourced, also from Southend, during the summer of 1972 – see the profile. ACM Sir Ralph Cochrane presided over the official opening of the Newark Air Museum on 14th April 1973. As it transpired, this site was a temporary home. In 1978 NAM was on the move again, transferring to the much greater possibilities offered by the northern portion of the overall area the museum occupies today.

The burnt out remains of Anson XI G-ALIH, Winthorpe, May 1971. *Peter Green Collection*

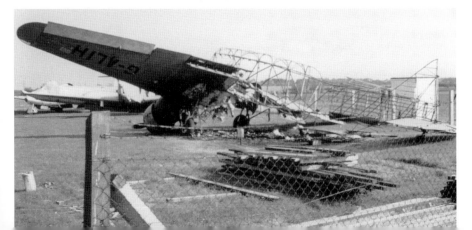

Above: Grins amid the sleet as Vulcan B.2 XM594 is handed over, 7th February 1983. Falklands veteran Sqn Ldr Neil McDougall DFC (second from right) captained the aircraft. Civilians on the left are: Stuart Stephenson, Roger Bryan and Howard Heeley, all Newark Stalwarts. *Via Newark Air Museum*

Left: The east-west runway at Winthorpe, now a car park, is named in honour of XM594. *Ken Ellis*

Turning finals for Winthorpe

The east-west runway at Winthorpe and a grass strip south of it provided NAM with a means of aerial 'deliveries' until 2004. The strip was operated by the Newark Gliding Club and for a brief period the club flew SZD Pirat glider CDX in a co-operative venture designed to give museum members air experience. In 2004 the club vacated Winthorpe moving to Darlton, near Tuxford. The glider is presently in deep store at the museum. The first aircraft to fly in for the museum – and the first direct arrival – was Percival Prentice G-APIY (previously RAF VR249) acquired by Neville Franklin from Southend. It was the first of an impressive line: Vickers Varsity T.1 WF369 in April 1976; Handley Page Hastings T.5 TG517 in June 1977; Saab Safir 56321 (more of which anon) in July 1982 and Avro Vulcan B.2 XM594 in February 1983. Preparations for the Vulcan landing were extensive, involving several inspections of the runway surface and three 50m portable roadways provided by local company Trakway of Sutton-in-Ashfield, allowing the big delta to taxi up to the museum site. In honour of this high powered arrival, the east-west runway, now used as a car park for major events at the showground has been named 'Vulcan Way'.

After 26 years of faithful service to Leicestershire County Council, Auster J/1 Autocrat G-AGOH was retired and touched down at Winthorpe on 12th July 1995 having been presented on loan to NAM. *Oscar-Hotel* would appear to be an odd local government servant, but it saved its rate payers considerable fees during its time resident at Leicester's Stoughton aerodrome. It was used for an extensive archaeological survey of the county, for photo-mapping road schemes and buildings and other aerial work that would normally have to be hired in. The choice of the Auster was not just to do with the work: built in 1945 at Rearsby it was a Leicestershire product. It was always intended that it would become a museum exhibit upon retirement. When the time came, there being no space for it on public view at the Snibston Discovery Park, Coalville, approaches were made to NAM and the offer was readily accepted. The Auster was removed by road on 24th April 2007 and installed at Coalville only for that museum to close in July 2015. The last aircraft to fly into NAM used the glider strip on 15th February 2003. This was Antonov An-2 SP-FBO, a large general transport biplane built in Poland by WSK-Mielec. On short-term loan to the museum, the Antonov was dismantled and removed in December 2003, bound ultimately for the USA.

Exotic Nordic hardware

If there is a technical term it would probably be 'speculative enquiry', but it boils down to an 'any chance of a so-and-so' letter. Such trawling exercises have been used by museums to good effect, but mostly only targeting Britain. A handful of collections have cast the net wider and NAM 'scored' in this fashion with a trio of Scandinavian exhibits. Letters to the Royal Norwegian Air Force paid off with the offer of a SAAB Safir trainer in the type's twilight years. Entering service in 1956, the Norwegians got exceptional service out of their fleet of 25 and the example put aside for NAM was the very first of these. Lts Stig Halvorsen and Peter Reymert piloted 56321 from Værnes, Trondheim, to touch down where Lancasters had once roared.

    With the retirement of the Royal Danish Air Force Drakens pending, a letter was dispatched in mid-1993. There was no response and it was put down to nothing ventured nothing gained. A telephone call in January 1994 got everyone's attention: could the museum accept a Draken the following month? Regarding the question as rhetorical, the museum moved quickly; the paperwork for importing a weapon of war requiring careful attention, one slip and the project could be scuppered. As with all SAAB jets, the ability to fly from roads or even semi-prepared strips was built into the Draken and the Danes gave consideration to flying it in to Winthorpe. In the end, the need to render safe items like the ejection seat, canopy explosive chords and to remove sensitive equipment meant that the fighter had to stage its last flight into an RAF base with the capabilities to support such specialist work. AR-107 landed at Scampton on 25th February 1994; it made the road journey to its new home in late June. It was a similar story with the Viggen, which was directed to Cranwell, arriving there on 7th February 2006 and moving by road convoy to Winthorpe in June.

Newark's Safir as originally delivered to the Royal Norwegian Air Force, 1956. *SAAB*

Hard core, buildings and vision

By the mid-1980s NAM faced a situation that other museums are familiar with: lots of exhibits with no roof over them. In 1986 plans were released for an ambitious display hall with an estimate cost of £200,000. Fund raising got into gear and planning permission was granted in 1989. Wherever savings could be made, without compromising the building's integrity or safety, they were implemented. As with any organisation relying on volunteers, this often meant the application of 'elbow grease'. Top soil was extracted from the site, followed by the back-breaking task of laying down hard core ready for the concrete floor to be poured on. The savings in labour costs were substantial. The first aircraft were rolled into Display Hangar No.1 on 11th April 1990 – six months after the first ground had been broken. Two aircraft were placed inside the new hall in May 1991 and in doing so, NAM's increasing stature was simultaneously validated. The RAF Museum has long operated a loans policy, but it does not hand out exhibits willy-nilly. Strict conditions need to be met. Endorsing NAM's achievements, Airspeed Oxford I MP425 and North American Harvard IIB FE905 arrived from Cardington on short term loan to complement the museum's trainer theme. Both machines departed in May 1994.

NAM's long term strategy looked to the south. In 1996 negotiations with the neighbouring farm brought about the purchase of 12.4 acres. With the existing plot leased from the showground, this acquisition gave the museum a degree of independence, a dramatic increase in area and the ability to have access directly off the road from the A17 and A46. Straight away additional covered exhibition space could be contemplated. The offer of the frame of a wartime T2 hangar from the nearby bomber base of Bottesford from John Rose of the Roseland Group was graciously accepted. This was covered display space *and* historic artefact all in one. The metalwork arrived on site in October 1997 but hundreds of sections were stolen shortly afterwards and the scheme came to nought. This was a blow, but a much more ambitious scheme was gaining pace.

Newark has a good track record for devising novel fund raising. Back in 1981, the acquisition of Gloster Javelin FAW.8 XH992 needed £1,250 – £5,000 in present-day values. Prior to this a museum member, or a small group of them, would club together for the purchase. The idea for a 'bond issue' was floated – 1,250 one-pound bonds were printed, allowing a contribution to be made for a very moderate sum, or much more, depending on the size of the benefactor's pocket. Thanks to the generosity of Newark-based Brick-Works UK, a buy-a-brick scheme was launched in 1997. For ten pounds the donor received a pristine building brick and the loan of a marker pen to allow them to sign or put a message on their offering towards the planned Display Hangar No.2 to be built on the south field site.

To divert away from structures for a moment... One of the author's better initiatives while he was at the helm of *FlyPast* was to put the magazine's support behind an innovation that had its first airing at the museum in June 2000. This was *CockpitFest* which remains one of the most popular of the special events staged by the museum. The brainchild of NAM's Bill O'Sullivan *CockpitFest* is a real 'grass roots' event allowing enthusiasts to bring their projects, unrestored and hopeful through to gleaming and museum class to an informal annual gathering of like-minded people. The real joy of the event is the ability for the public to inspect the cockpits at close quarters and talk to the owners. It's nice to have helped establish a national institution!

Having demonstrated the skills of Newark volunteers in moving tons of material about; the wheel barrows and spades were called to action again in 2002. A drainage ditch divides the north and south sites and a wide 'taxi-track' was built across it to enable the moving of aircraft with ease from one zone to the other. A substantial hard standing was created by laying 500 tons of crushed concrete with a rigid plastic grid on top to provide cohesion. To quote Colin Savill in his book *Preservation Pioneers* on NAM's history: "The concrete had come from one of the former RAF Worksop's runways thus providing a somewhat unusual form of aviation preservation." Plans for the second display hall were announced in 2002 and in March the following year the sum of £453,000 was approved by the Heritage Lottery Fund towards the project. Much larger than the first exhibition hall, No.2 was officially opened on 13th November 2004, permitting aircraft up to the size of the Vickers Varsity to be accommodated.

Sometimes in the museum world, the ability to say 'No' can be the best response to circumstances. In 2010 the offer of a Hawker Siddeley Nimrod R.1 from the winding down 51 Squadron at Waddington was carefully assessed by museum trustees. As the crow flies, Winthorpe is about ten miles from Waddington. With a length of 123ft and an empty weight of around 86,000lb, dismantling a Nimrod so that it could be taken through southern Lincoln to join the A46 and then down a minor road to the museum would represent a huge cost; one that very likely would spiral upwards in the light of the practicalities. Re-assembly and restoration on the south site could be carried out at more relaxed pace, but would absorb a vast amount of volunteer time. Tempting as the Nimrod was, 'No thanks' was the sensible conclusion. The focus remains on improving the infrastructure at NAM. The latest project will greatly enhance the catering and toilet facilities with a new education centre as a medium term goal. The present-day café – home of the best cheese toasties on the planet – is part and parcel of the Newark success story; the catering and the welcome within is a crowd-puller in its own right. From humble beginnings in an engineering yard, the Newark Air Museum has transcended being a regional treasure to become a national asset.

Throughout the writing of this chapter, Preservation Pioneers : Newark Air Museum 1963-2015 *by Colin Savill was a constant companion. Published by the museum in 2016 it is a detailed yet very human history. If all museums chronicled their exploits in this manner,* this *book would never have been needed! Order via:* **www.newarkairmuseum.org**

Avro Anson C.19 Srs 2 VL348
1946 | General purpose transport | Two 420hp Armstrong Siddeley Cheetah 15 pistons

Turn to Chapter 18 and the profile of Avro XIX G-AGPG for general notes on Ansons. Built by Avro at Yeadon, now Leeds-Bradford Airport, VL348 was ready for collection by the RAF on 21st December 1946. It was August the following year before it entered service, joining the Reserve Command Communications Flight at White Waltham. This was the start of sixteen busy years of service and like many Ansons on 'comms' work, it flew for a procession of different units with gaps for repairs, upgrades or storage. In VL348's case, these were as follows: 62 Group Communications Flight (GCF), Colerne from February 1951; the Colerne Station Flight and 81 GCF, also at Colerne, from August 1952; 24 GCF, Halton, from March 1958, Colerne Station Flight again from October 1958; 24 GCF from January 1960 and finally 22 GCF at Ternhill from July 1963. Four months later VL348 was retired to nearby 27 Maintenance Unit at Shawbury and declared a non-effective airframe on 23rd November 1965. It was sold to Tippers Air Transport and civil registered as G-AVVO on 6th October 1967 and ferried to its base at Halfpenny Green on 10th November. It was acquired by the British Historic Aircraft Museum at Rochford, Southend, on 3rd September 1968. The venture failed to get anywhere and *Victor-Oscar* languished in the open. The succeeding Historic Aircraft Museum opened in May 1972 but, as it also had Avro XIX G-AGPG (Chapter 18), VL348 was surplus. As explained in the opening narrative, Newark had suffered the lost of Anson XI G-ALIH in a fire on 11th May 1971, so was on the look out for a replacement. A deal was struck on VL348 and it arrived at Winthorpe in November 1972. The wings of VL348 were in poor shape and those from G-ALIH were salvaged and fitted to the new exhibit.

Avro Shackleton MR.3/3 WR977
1957 | Maritime patrol and anti-submarine platform | Four 2,455hp Rolls-Royce Griffon 57A pistons and two 2,500lb st Armstrong Siddeley Viper 203 turbojet boosters

The ultimate development of the Shackleton, with tricycle undercarriage, wing tip tanks, enhanced avionics and weapons the Mk.3 was a quantum leap on from the prototype of 1949. The first Mk.3, WR970, had its maiden flight on 2nd September 1955. The RAF took 34 up to 1959 and the South African Air Force ordered eight. Mk.3s served until the advent of the Hawker Siddeley Nimrod in the early 1970s. As noted below, WR977 was flown to the RAF Museum 'satellite' at Finningley in November 1971 for preservation, but this was not to be. In September 1988 the final Mk.3 instructional airframes were offered for disposal at Cosford and to the amazement of many, one was not wheeled over to the Aerospace Museum (precursor of the RAF Museum Cosford). This left AEW.2 WR960 in 'exile' at the Museum of Science and Industry in Manchester (Chapter 18) as the RAF Museum's only example. As well as Newark's WR977 there are two whole MR.3s in museums: at Gatwick and at Duxford. The Imperial War Museum's XF708 is stored within the restoration area of the huge 'AirSpace' display hall and as such Newark's WR977 is the nation's 'lead' MR.3.

The maiden flight of WR977 took place at Woodford in August 1957, possibly on the 16th. After appearing in the static at the Farnborough airshow 2nd-9th September, it was ferried to 23 Maintenance Unit at Aldergrove by Avro test pilot Tony Blackman on the 14th. The complex search and attack systems and changes in weaponry meant that the Shackleton fleet was put through a 'rolling' update programme. Three elements of this were so extensive that they were termed as 'Phases'

Shackleton MR.3/3 WR977 with 42 Squadron, 1968. *Peter Green Collection*

and this was reflected in the designation: WR977 ended up as a Phase 3, or MR.3/3. Its host squadrons were as follows: 220 Squadron at St Eval from October 1957 coded 'L'; 220 was re-numbered as 201 Squadron at St Mawgan on 1st October 1958; 206 Squadron, also at St Mawgan, as 'B' from November 1959; 201 Squadron at St Mawgan as 'O' from April 1963; 42 Squadron at St Mawgan as 'B' from May 1966; a loan to 206 Squadron at Kinloss from July 1969; 42 Squadron again from August 1969 and finally 203 Squadron at Luqa, Malta, as 'B' from August 1970.

WR977 returned to Woodford in May 1959 for Phase 1 modifications to the systems, lasting six months. The more comprehensive Phase 2 took place at the Avro out-station at Langar from January 1962, this work being completed in April 1963. The upgrade to Phase 3 was carried out at Langar from July 1965 to April 1966. The systems were again improved and the weapons fit could include the Mk.10 'Lulu' nuclear depth charge and acoustic homing torpedoes. The most complex modification improved the Shackleton's performance in over-load and 'hot and high' conditions; a Viper turbojet was installed in the rear of each outboard engine naclle to provide boost on take off. In its new guise WR977 was taken on charge in April 1966 by 42 Squadron and the following year, its Vipers were put to the test. After Rhodesia's unilateral declaration of independence from the British Commonwealth in November 1965, the RAF maintained a patrol of the waters off the port of Beira, Mozambique to prevent sanction-busters. From January to April 1967 WR977 was deployed to Majunga, Madagascar, for these duties, known as Operation 'Mizar'.

As noted above, WR977's last operator was 203 Squadron at Luqa and from mid-1971 the unit took on its first Nimrod MR.1s. Redundant; WR977 was ferried to St Mawgan on 7th November 1971 where it was slated to go to Thorney Island for fire-rescue training. This was rescinded and instead, WR977 took off two days later bound for Finningley which had a growing collection of aircraft as an out-station for the RAF Museum. Captaining the aircraft was Flt Lt Ted Buddin and on landing WR977 clocked up 6,696 flying hours. Finningley was picked as the venue for HM Queen Elizabeth's Silver Jubilee Review of the RAF in 1977 and there was a hasty reshuffling of the RAF Museum airframes. WR977 was put up for tender with a deadline for removal of 1st May 1977. Long-term museum benefactor Stuart Stephenson offered the £1,000 (£11,000 in present-day values) the Ministry of Defence was asking. A team took a look, bit the bullet and decided the job could be done. Dismantling began on 12th April and the main sections left the Yorkshire airfield on deadline. The job of putting it all back together again began a week later! Blackburn Beverley C.1 XL149 was offered at the same time; after much debate, the Newark team wisely assessed they could not cope with two giants at once. XL149 was scrapped at Finningley and Newark managed to secure the cockpit, later passing it on to the South Yorkshire Aircraft Museum (Chapter 31). During the spring of 2016 a comprehensive external restoration of WR977 was commenced, this was completed in the spring of 2017.

de Havilland Tiger Moth 'G-MAZY'
1941 | Basic trainer | One 130hp de Havilland Gipsy Major piston

To many people the generic name for a biplane is 'Tiger Moth'. First flown in 1931 and with over 8,000 built, there are plenty of Tigers extant. Interest levels and residual values mean that any airframe has the potential to be turned into a 'flyer' so few have percolated to the 'regional' collections. Unsurprisingly, the 'nationals' have one each: Duxford, East Fortune, Hendon, Middle Wallop, Old Warden and Yeovilton. The de Havilland Aircraft Museum has one in crop-spraying guise and Brooklands has another in deep store and there are several that are best described as partial replicas. Although the Newark example has an 'open' provenance, its exceptional restoration and partially 'skeletal' status make it an outstanding exhibit.

Tiger Moth 'G-MAZY' on display inside Hangar No.1; its port side is uncovered to reveal the structure. *Ken Ellis*

In 1967 Neville Franklin attended an auction at Thruxton that included stock from the former Jackaroo Aircraft company that converted Tiger Moths into a four-seat cabin version known as the Thruxton Jackaroo in the late 1950s. In those days a reasonable outlay could purchase a large amount of Tiger Moth airframes and accessories. Neville brought the cache back to Abbott's Yard in Newark; later it was moved to the Winthorpe site. And so it all remained forgotten. In 1987 a kit-of-parts was dispatched to the workshop of the Cotswold Aircraft Restoration Group (CARG) at Innsworth, Gloucestershire. The museum had commissioned CARG to create a Tiger Moth to static standards and soon it was agreed that a 'see-through' finish to the port side would be a great idea. When it came to choosing a colour scheme the bold – and brilliant – decision to choose an all-blue civilian 'persona' was made. The choice of 'registration' was left to the man who spent untold hours working on this superb creation: Harry Hodgson decided on 'G-MAZY' to honour his late wife, Maisie. The completed Tiger Moth returned to Newark on 25th June 1995 and it instantly became one of the most popular exhibits. Harry died the following year and this exhibit is a fine epitaph.

de Havilland Heron 1B G-ANXB
1953 | General purpose transport | Four 250hp de Havilland Gipsy Queen 30 pistons

Although there were only 149 built, by British standards for commercial aircraft the Heron was a decided success story. A 'growth' version of the twin-engined Dove, the prototype first flew on 10th May 1950 and production ran to 1964. The first examples had fixed undercarriage, retractable gear became the norm from the mid-1950s. As would be expected, the de Havilland Aircraft Museum has one, another 'guards' the former Croydon Airport. But Newark's *Xray-Bravo* has a provenance that outshines all of these, including the prototype which survives in Australia.

Built at Hawarden and tested with the 'B Condition' ('trade plate') markings G-5-11, G-ANXB was one of two ordered by British European Airways (BEA) for ambulance flights across Scotland and services from Glasgow Airport, Renfrew and later Abbotsinch, to the Hebrides, including the beach airstrip at Barra. With their medical role, the Herons were appropriately named: G-ANXA *Sir John Hunter* after the 18th century Scottish surgeon; G-ANXB *Sir James Young Simpson* after the 19th century anaesthetics pioneer. As an aside, the nature of this flying was not without risk. A third Heron, G-AOFY, was introduced in 1957 but on 29th September that year a flight to Islay to pick up a patient encountered difficulties and it crashed. The two of crew and a nurse were killed: *Xray-Alpha* was renamed *Sister Jean Kennedy* to commemorate the nurse.

Xray-Bravo was the first of the original two to be delivered, on 12th February 1955, entering service with an ambulance flight on 4th March. In 1972 BEA ordered a pair of Short Skyliners – all-passenger versions of the Skyvan – and it fell to G-ANXB to fly the last service on 31st March 1973. In October that year G-ANXB was acquired by Norwich-based Peters Aviation and it was joined by G-ANXA in 1974. With its certification lapsing in early 1979 G-ANXB was dismantled and stored at Biggin Hill. It was there that present-day Newark Air Museum president 'Mich' Stevenson and then chairman Roger Bryan clubbed together to acquire the Heron on behalf of the collection. This was a far-seeking acquisition, *Xray-Bravo* travelled north by road on 27th October 1981 and it was returned to its colour scheme of the early 1970s. The Heron is one of many jewels at Newark.

Newark's Heron 1 G-ANXB as delivered to British European Airways, March 1955. *BEA*

With the spray boom retracted and flush with the underside of the rear fuselage, Canberra B.2/8 WV787 showing off the multiple nozzles of the icing rig, at Boscombe Down, 1969. *KEC*

English Electric Canberra B.2/8 WV787
1952 | Icing trials test-bed | Two 6,500lb st Rolls-Royce Avon 101 turbojets

With a British service life stretching from 1951 to 2006 the Canberra is rightly well represented within museums. Newark boasts three whole airframes and two cockpits, nicely encompassing the main versions; a basic B.2 bomber-based T.19 aircrew trainer and a PR.7 tactical photo-recce platform. The cockpits are a B.2-derived T.17 and a PR.9 strategic recce variant. The imposing all-black WV787 is a superb example of another of the Canberra's many roles, test and trials, and how the museum refused to let it succumb to an ignominious fate when it was retired for service.

Built by English Electric at Preston, WV787 was awaiting collection at Samlesbury on 26th August 1952 and six days later was transferred to Armstrong Siddeley at its Bitteswell test centre. There it was fitted with a pair of the company's Sapphire Sa.7 reheated turbojets; first flying in its new guise in March 1954. The Canberra's next destination was Seighford on 5th June 1958 where Boulton Paul was contracted to carry out dramatic surgery. The Sapphires were removed and Avon 101s were re-instated. Its new role was as a radar test bed and the 'goldfish bowl' cockpit and bulkheads were not best suited for this. The entire forward fuselage was detached and the nose from a bomber-interdictor B(I).8 was fitted. The Mk.8 featured a fighter-like canopy offset to port with a navigator/bomb aimer housing 'in the dark' of the fuselage alongside the pilot. Grafted on to the more pointed nose of the Mk.8 was a Ferranti Blue Parrot (ARI.5930) radar. This was destined for the Blackburn NA.39, later to be named Buccaneer, which had first flown on 9th July 1958. WV787 was to take over from Ferranti's previous Blue Parrot test-bed, Douglas Dakota TS423, to handle the high-speed, low level nature of the naval strike bomber's role. (TS423 is still airworthy, as N147DC with Aces High, based at Dunsfold.) Entering service with Ferranti on 28th October 1959, WV787 was based with the company at Edinburgh Airport, Turnhouse.

There was still more to be had from WV787. It was ferried to Flight Refuelling's airfield at Tarrant Rushton where it was prepared for use as an icing tanker for the Aeroplane and Armament Experimental Establishment, Boscombe Down. The bomb bay was fitted with a tank and a swivelling 'boom' was installed under the rear fuselage. A complex array of nozzles at the end of the boom provided different spray patterns on to the 'victim' aircraft flying behind and below. In its new form as a tanker, WV787 was taken on charge at Boscombe on 10th November 1966. Among the Canberra's many 'clients', the most famous was the BAC/Sud Concorde supersonic transport, but in April 1982 it was testing anew de-icing system on BAC One-Eleven G-ASYD – see Chapter 27. In 1972 WV787 was used briefly as the aerodynamic test-bed for the Canberra T.22, a conversion of PR.7s airframes to be used as Blue Parrot crew trainers. On 23rd December 1983 WV787 was retired to Abingdon where it was allocated the instructional airframe serial 8799M. At the Oxfordshire base, the Canberra was slated for battle damage repair training – the art of how to patch up an aircraft and get it back into service, quickly. At this point Newark intervened, querying why an airframe with such a varied research and development history should have holes blown in it. The Ministry of Defence was not moved and the aircraft was on the receiving end of simulated hits by projectiles using small explosive charges. Meanwhile pressure mounted, with the aviation press backing calls for a reprieve. The ministry relented and Newark succeeded in acquiring WV787; it arrived at Winthorpe on 24th November 1985. The chance of such a change of mind from present-day disposal 'agencies' is remote!

General Aircraft Monospar ST-12 VH-UTH
1935 | General purpose light transport | Two 130hp de Havilland Gipsy Major pistons

Hanworth-based General Aircraft Ltd (GAL) is best remembered for the Hotspur training glider and the huge Hamilcar tank-carrying assault glider, both of World War Two. Formed in 1934 the company was established to exploit the 'Monospar' cantilever spar construction method invented by Swiss-born Helmuth John Stieger. GAL developed a series of twin-engined types, including the ST-10, ST-12 and ST-25, production reaching 105 units up to 1939. The company also built a ten-passenger twin-engined airliner, the ST-18 Croydon, in 1939, but it remained a one-off. Newark's ST-12 is the only example of the type to survive in Britain, but it deserves a place in a museum for much more than its rarity: general aviation types from the 1930s that are not prefixed 'de Havilland' provide a broader view of what was available at the time; as a cabin monoplane with an innovative structure it was an advanced machine for its day; its return to Britain and its survival is a fascinating story.

The Newark ST-12 was one of half a dozen ordered by New England Airways of Lismore, New South Wales, Australia, and was delivered in 1935, as VH-UTH *Captain Cook*. New England was renamed Airlines of Australia in 1936. The Monospar was later flown by the Tasmanian Aero Club from Launceston and finally the Illawarra Flying School at Bankstown, Sydney. VH-UTH was stored through the war and beyond. In March 1957 it was acquired by Dr John Morris for Australian $11,000 and it was rebuilt to flying condition. Morris was scheduled to attend a post-graduate medical course in Dublin commencing in the autumn of 1961 and he intended that the ST-12 be his method of getting there. Bruce Harrison joined the venture as navigator/mechanic. The pair embarked on a six-week, 12,000 mile journey, departing Bankstown on 18th August 1961. They cleared customs at Lympne on 30th September, flying on to Biggin Hill later that day. In January 1969 Robert Hale Ltd published *Two Men in a Flying Machine*, Morris's account of the flight.

After its arrival, the machine does not appear to have flown much; it certainly never got near Dublin. By 1962 it was in store at Panshanger and in 1966 it had gravitated to Booker. With the help of Norman Jones of the Tiger Club, the engineless Monospar was acquired on behalf of the museum and in March 1968 it was moved to the storage site at Abbott's Yard in Newark. By 1995 the museum decided on restoring VH-UTH and the wings were dispatched to the Cotswold Aircraft Restoration Group (CARG) workshop at Innsworth, Gloucestershire, in June 1995 and its fuselage following in April 1998. With the closure of the Innsworth site looming, CARG disbanded and VH-UTH was returned to Newark on 3rd October 2007. Since then Newark's team has continued the Cotswold group's exceptional workmanship and this rare survivor was nearing completion in 2017.

Monospar VH-UTH in No.1 Hangar at Newark. *Ken Ellis*

Test-bed Meteor FR.9 VZ608 with the intake for the RB.108 lift jet in the closed position. *Rolls-Royce*

Gloster Meteor FR.9 VZ608
1951 | Turbojet test-bed | Two 3,500lb st Rolls-Royce Derwent 8 and one 2,130lb st Rolls-Royce RB.108 turbojets

As might be expected, there are a large number of Meteors in the British museums; the type having been prolific in RAF service. Newark is well blessed with Meteors, its T.7 VZ634 and NF(T).14 adding to the museum's training theme while NF.12 WS692 represents the type's all-weather interceptor role. Newark's FR.9 fighter-reconnaissance variant is the only survivor of the variant, but it is for its part in the development of vertical take-off (VTOL) technology at Hucknall, sixteen miles west of the museum, that this example is by far the most significant.

Built and flown at Hucclecote as a standard FR.9 in 1951, VZ608 was issued to Rolls-Royce at Hucknall in March that year. From 29th June 1953 it was involved in reverse thrust trials for the Derwent engine. On 1st June 1955 it was re-allocated to act as a test-bed for the RB.108 lift jet which Rolls-Royce was developing for the Short SC.1 VTOL programme. The SC.1 was to be powered by a battery of four RB.108s vertically mounted within the fuselage providing lift, with another mounted in in the tail for propulsion. The lift RB.108s swivelled plus or minus 30-degrees to provide a degree of thrust, forward or backwards and VZ608's role was to provide in-flight data on the engine and to help perfect the geometry of the intakes. Design consultants for the modification was F G Miles Ltd of Shoreham, run by the famous brothers Frederick and George Miles. The RB.108 was fitted in what had been a fuel tank behind the pilot. VZ608 made its first flight with the third engine fitted, but inert, on 18th May 1956. Sorties with the RB.108 running on take-off were made from 2nd August and the first start up in flight occurred on 23rd October. Just over 135 hours of flying time was devoted to the project. (The first hovers were carried out by an SC.1 at Sydenham on 23rd May 1958. Both SC.1s survive: XG900 at the Science Museum, London, and XG905 at the Ulster Folk and Transport Museum, Belfast – they are dealt with in *Great Aviation Collections of Britain*.) To continue to support SC.1 testing at the Royal Aircraft Establishment, VZ608 was used for ground-running trials from May 1960 to June 1964 after which the project was wound down. The RAF struck VZ608 off charge on 29th September 1965 but it remained at Hucknall and was used for rescue exercises. Approached by Newark, Rolls-Royce agreed to handing the FR.9 over, but wanted a replacement Meteor. F.8 WH443 was located at a civil defence establishment at Falfield in Gloucestershire and museum volunteers moved it to Hucknall in 1970 with VZ608 arriving at Winthorpe on 15th February 1970.

Handley Page Hastings T.5 TG517
1948 | Crew trainer | Four 1,675hp Bristol Hercules 106 pistons

The Hermes airliner and the Hastings long range military transport represented Handley Page's response to the post-war marketplace. The Hermes was disappointing, with just 29 being built. The Hastings saved the day, 151 were manufactured up to 1953 and the type enjoyed considerable longevity, finally retiring in 1977. The fuselage of Hermes G-ALDG is part of the Duxford Aviation Society's airliner collection and Imperial War Museum Duxford has Hastings C.1A TG528 and the RAF Museum Cosford T.5 TG511: Newark's Hastings is the only example of this impressive airlifter preserved by a British 'regional'. When Hastings C.1 TG517 was declared as ready for collection at Radlett on 12th July 1948 the Berlin Airlift had been in operation eighteen days. The big transport was issued to 47 Squadron at Fairford on 4th October, but the unit moved to Dishforth in November. From the moment it joined 47, Dishforth was only home for heavy line maintenance, the rest of the time the transport was based at Schleswigland in northern Germany, close to the Danish border. From there the squadron took part in the airborne supply of everything needed to keep the British, French and US sectors of the German capital functioning as a response to the USSR's land blockade. The autobahns were opened again on 12th May 1949 and 47 Squadron returned its hard-working airlifters to Dishforth. In August the unit changed base to Topcliffe and on 20th June 1950 TG517 was transferred to 53 Squadron, sharing the ramp at the Yorkshire base.

Newark Air Museum, Newark, Nottinghamshire: Handley Page Hastings T.5 TG517. *Ken Ellis*

Newark Air Museum, Newark, Nottinghamshire: Vickers Varsity T.1 WF369. *Ken Ellis*

Newark Air Museum, Newark, Nottinghamshire: Handley Page Jetstream T.1 XX492. *Ken Ellis*

The Helicopter Museum, Weston-super-Mare, Somerset: Westland Wessex HCC.4 XV733.
Roger Richards

The Helicopter Museum, Weston-super-Mare, Somerset: Piasecki HUP-3 Retriever 622.
Roger Richards

Norfolk and Suffolk Aviation
Museum, Flixton, Suffolk: Vickers
Valetta C.2 VX580. *Ken Ellis*

Norfolk and Suffolk Aviation
Museum, Flixton, Suffolk: English
Electric Lightning F.1 XG329.
Ken Ellis

Norfolk and Suffolk Aviation Museum, Flixton, Suffolk: Dassault Mystère IVA 79, Lockheed T-33A 55-4433,
de Havilland Sea Vixen FAW.1 XJ482. *Ken Ellis*

Martlesham Heath Control Tower Museum, Martlesham Heath, Suffolk: North American P-51Ds of the 360th Fighter Squadron, 356th Fighter Group, 1945, from the tower. *via Roger Freeman*

Martlesham Heath Control Tower Museum, Martlesham Heath, Suffolk: the view from the tower today. *Ken Ellis*

Brooklands Museum, Brooklands, Surrey: Vickers Wellington Ia N2980. *Ken Ellis*

Brooklands Museum, Brooklands, Surrey: Vickers Merchantman G-APEP. *Terry Dann*

Brooklands Museum, Brooklands, Surrey: Vickers VC-10 1103 A40-AB. *Terry Dann*
Brooklands Museum, Brooklands, Surrey: BAC One-Eleven Srs 475AM G-ASYD. *Terry Dann*

Gatwick Aviation Museum, Charlwood, Surrey: Hawker Siddeley Harrier GR.3 XV751 and English Electric Lightning F.53 ZF579. *Richard Hall*

Gatwick Aviation Museum, Charlwood, Surrey: Hawker Siddeley Harrier GR.3 XV751, English Electric Lightning F.53 ZF579 and Hawker Hunter T.7 XL591. *Richard Hall*

Gatwick Aviation Museum, Charlwood, Surrey: Gloster Meteor T.7 VZ638. *Richard Hall*

Wings World War Two
Remembrance Museum,
Balcombe, Sussex: Nakajima Ki-43
Hayabusa. *Daniel Hunt*

Tangmere Military Aviation
Museum, Tangmere, Sussex:
Hawker Hunter F.5 WP190.
Les Woodward

Tangmere Military Aviation
Museum, Tangmere, Sussex:
Supermarine Swift WK281.
Les Woodward

Midland Air Museum, Coventry Airport, Warwickshire: Mikoyan Gurevich MiG-21SPS *Fishbed* 959. *Richard Hall*

Midland Air Museum, Coventry Airport, Warwickshire: Dassault Mystère IVA 70. *Ian Humphreys*

Midland Air Museum, Coventry Airport, Warwickshire: Mil Mi-24 *Hind-D. Richard Hall*

Midland Air Museum, Coventry Airport, Warwickshire: Hawker Siddeley HS.125 Srs 1 G-ARYB. *Ken Ellis*

Midland Air Museum, Coventry Airport, Warwickshire: Panavia Tornado GR.4 ZA452. *Ian Humphreys*

Midland Air Museum, Coventry Airport, Warwickshire: de Havilland Canada U-6A Beaver. *Ken Ellis*

Boscombe Down Aviation Collection, Old Sarum, Wiltshire: Royal Aircraft Factory BE.2c replica '2783'. *Ken Ellis*

Boscombe Down Aviation Collection, Old Sarum, Wiltshire: Gloster Meteor D.16 WK800. *Jon Wickenden*

Boscombe Down Aviation Collection, Old Sarum, Wiltshire: Hawker Hunter F.6A XF375. *Steve Hobden*

Yorkshire Air Museum, Elvington, Yorkshire: Handley Page Halifax II 'LV907'. *Ken Ellis*

Yorkshire Air Museum, Elvington, Yorkshire: de Havilland Mosquito NF.II HJ711. *Ken Ellis*

Yorkshire Air Museum, Elvington, Yorkshire: Hawker Siddeley Nimrod MR.2 XV250. *Ken Ellis*

South Yorkshire Aircraft Museum,
Doncaster, Yorkshire: Cessna
F.150G G-AVAA. *Jon Wickenden*

South Yorkshire Aircraft Museum,
Doncaster, Yorkshire: Piper Apache
160 G-APMY. *Jon Wickenden*

South Yorkshire Aircraft Museum, Doncaster, Yorkshire: Westland Whirlwind HAR.1 XA870. *Ken Ellis*

Dumfries and Galloway Aviation Museum, Dumfries, Scotland: North American F-100D Super Sabre 54-2163 in the foreground. *Ken Ellis*

Dumfries and Galloway Aviation Museum, Dumfries, Scotland: Fairey Gannet AEW.3 XL497. *Ken Ellis*

Dumfries and Galloway Aviation Museum, Dumfries, Scotland: Lockheed T-33A FT-36. *Ken Ellis*

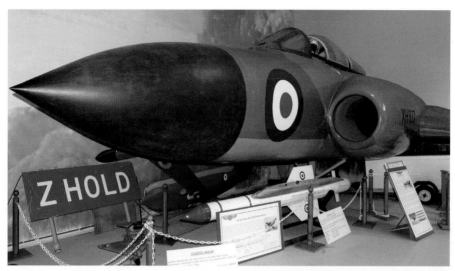

Caernarfon Airport Airworld Museum, Caernarfon Airport, Wales: Gloster Javelin FAW.7 XH837. *Terry Dann*

Caernarfon Airport Airworld
Museum, Caernarfon Airport,
Wales: Westland Whirlwind
HAR.10 XJ726. *Terry Dann*

Caernarfon Airport Airworld
Museum, Caernarfon Airport,
Wales: Hawker Siddeley Harrier
T.4A XW269. *Terry Dann*

Stow Maries Great War Aerodrome, Stow Maries, Essex: Royal Aircraft Factory BE.2e replica 'A2767'. *Terry Dann*

In October 1950 TG517 returned to Radlett for a transformation. It was one of sixteen converted for meteorological reconnaissance duties with the designation Met.1 and given a dark sea grey paint scheme enlivened with a white 'cheat' line. It also moved from Transport to Coastal Command, going on charge with 202 Squadron at Aldergrove. The flying was exacting and perilous, involving flights in all weathers over the Atlantic acquiring regular 'met' data during a long steady climb to height. In April 1959 another role had been determined for TG517 with its third designation, this time T.5. The Hastings was delivered to Blackbushe on 15th April 1959 where contractor Airwork turned the 'cloud-chaser' into a trainer for bomb aimers, with two positions within the fuselage and a radar scanner mounted ventrally behind the trailing edge of the wing. The colour scheme reverted to standard transport white top decking, blue 'cheat' line and aluminium lower fuselage, and red panels for ease of identification.

There were eight T.5s and they served with the Bomber Command Bombing School at Lindholme. The unit changed its name to the Strike Command Bombing School in December 1967 and in September 1972 moved to Scampton. In July 1974 the surviving Hastings were absorbed into the Radar Training Flight (RTF) of 230 Operational Conversion Unit at Scampton. Veteran TG517 already had 'ops' on its 'CV' with its time in the frontline during the Berlin Airlift, and in the winter of 1975/1976 it was again to find itself involved in a crisis – this time a bizarre one. A dispute had arisen between Iceland and Britain over fishing rights and the small Nordic nation was determined to enforce what it deemed as its territorial rights. Some sort of maritime reconnaissance was needed to 'keep and eye' and to 'wave the flag' over British fishing fleets, but it was considered that appearance of a nuclear capable Hawker Siddeley Nimrod might be regarded as 'escalation'. Scampton's Hastings had the endurance and clearly represented no military threat. TG517 carried out four such Icelandic sorties before things calmed down. Each of these is commemorated with a fish painted under the cockpit, in similar style to the bomb 'tallies' of World War Two. During this time, the RTF was termed '1066 Squadron' to emphasise the age of its aircraft! The RAF announced that the Hastings was to retire on the last day of June 1977 and Newark put in a bid for an example. TG517 flew into Winthorpe on 22nd June, completing 29 years of loyal service. Captaining the final flight was Sqn Ldr Ken 'Jacko' Jackson AFC, who became officer commanding the Battle of Britain Memorial Flight that year.

Hawker Siddeley Sea Harrier FA.2 ZA176
1981 | V/STOL shipborne air defence fighter | One 21,500lb st Rolls-Royce Pegasus 106 vectored-thrust turbofan

Hawker Siddeley claimed that its exceptional Harrier 'jump jet' could operate from civilian ships with moderate space if needs must. In the mid-1980s Dunsfold test pilot Heinz Frick put forward the revolutionary 'Skyhook' concept which could have led to Harriers with no undercarriage being 'caught' by a crane-like device and loaded onto wheeled dollies aboard a converted merchant vessel; transforming shipborne aviation. He was bound to have been bolstered by an adventure that befell Sqn Ldr Ian 'Soapy' Watson and ZA176 off West Africa in 1983. (Turn to Chapter 27 for more on 'Skyhook'.) Having blasted off from the aircraft carrier HMS *Illustrious* on 7th June 1983, RAF exchange officer Watson was flying ZA176 of 801 Squadron Fleet Air Arm. A navigation/comms system failure eventually led to a fuel shortage and the likelihood of a 'bang out' and a search of a huge sea area. 'Soapy' spotted the SS *Alraigo*, a Spanish container ship. Here was salvation; having made his intentions as clear as possible, 'Soapy' carefully put ZA176 down on top of the containers, as it shut down it sat back on its tail, but with minimum damage. The *Alraigo* headed for Santa Cruz on Tenerife where the Sea Harrier was off-loaded and doubtless shedloads of compensation was promised. It was an exceptional piece of flying involving a world-beating aircraft. Apart from 'Soapy' helping to validate Heinz's 'Skyhook' theories, the test pilot had a personal involvement: he had carried out its maiden flight, at Dunsfold on 25th November 1971.

Built as a Sea Harrier FRS.1, after sign-off at Dunsfold and pre-service preparation at St Athan, ZA176 joined 809 Squadron at Yeovilton on 8th April 1982. Fleet Air Arm usage of Sea Harriers was both complex and simple: complex because they changed squadron allegiances at the drop of a hat; simple because they were all shore-based at Yeovilton. In its time, 1982 to 2003, ZA176 served with 800 Squadron four times, 801 five times, 809 twice and 899 three times. Six days before ZA176 entered service with 809 Squadron, Argentine forces had landed on the Falkland Islands and the pace with British armed forces was turning frenetic. On 1st May 1982 ZA176 was flown via Banjul in Gambia to Wideawake airfield, Ascension Island; Operation 'Corporate' was taking shape. It was loaded on to the SS *Atlantic Conveyor* bound for a rendezvous with the aircraft carrier HMS *Hermes* in the South Atlantic. ZA176 departed the *Conveyor* on 18th May, landing on *Hermes* and became part of 800 Squadron. (Seven days later the *Atlantic Conveyor* was hit by an Exocet missile launched by a Dassault Super Etendard; it sunk while under tow on the 28th.) During its time in *Hermes* 800 Squadron flew a staggering 1,126 sorties and ZA176 was heavily involved, occasionally flown by Lt Clive Morrell. Unscathed, ZA176 was on board *Hermes* for the return to Britain, 3rd July 1982.

There was no respite, turnaround was quick and in early August, back with 809 Squadron and having gained the name and nose-art *Hot Lips*, ZA176 was embarked in HMS *Illustrious*, going back to the South Atlantic to maintain British patrols off the Falklands. After the 'adventure' with the *Alraigo* in June 1983, ZA176 was back in service, with 899 Squadron, the following month. On 17th February 1992 it was flown to its birthplace, Dunsfold, for conversion to FA.2 (originally F/A.2) status with Blue Vixen radar, more powerful Pegasus vectored-thrust turbofan and enhanced weapons fit. It first flew in this guise on 1st October 1993, re-joining 899 Squadron the following month. With the impended wind-down of the Sea Harriers, ZA176 was retired at Yeovilton in September 2003, moving to the museum in July the following year. Considering the type's combat history – including over the former Yugoslavia – comparatively few Sea Harriers are in British museums, the bulk with the 'regionals'.

Probably over the River Trent, Tiger Cub G-MBUE in 1982. *MBA*

Micro Biplane Aviation Tiger Cub G-MBUE
1982 | Single-seat microlight | One 50hp Fuji Robin EC44 piston

Newark is among a small number of museums that recognises the importance of light aviation exhibits. Within the collection are two prototype single-seaters: the Tiger Cub and the Taylor Monoplane – see below. With 23 years separating them, they have widely differing construction techniques and configurations but were designed to achieve the same thing: affordable flying. (There is potentially a third prototype at Newark, the Luscombe Rattler Strike of 1983; claimed by its builder to be a 'pre-production' example, although it would appear to be a one-off. Offered from the start with a side-mounted 7.62mm Hughes Chain Gun or fourteen 2in unguided air-to-ground rockets, this can be dismissed from the 'flying for fun' category!)

Micro Biplane Aviation (MBA) was formed in 1981, establishing a factory at Worksop, Nottinghamshire, in the following year. They initially designed the Micro-Bipe, powered by a 250cc engine and with conventional, three-axis, controls. The aim was to produce a robust single-seater and by opting for a biplane layout, the wing span could be kept small, allowing it to be towed on an off-the-shelf vehicle trailer. This evolved into the Tiger Cub, with a semi-enclosed fuselage, option for tailwheel or tricycle undercarriage and a 50hp engine. The prototype was G-MBUE, although it was initially registered in April 1982 as a Micro-Bipe. Kits were offered at £3,112 or completed at £4,500 – the latter £18,000 in present-day values. As many as 150 Tiger Cubs had been built when MBA shut down in 1984. *Uniform-Echo* was acquired in 1986 by Retford-based Neal Cuthbertson and he set about converting it from 'tail-dragger' to 'trike'. A heavy landing in September 1988 put the Tiger Cub out of action until early 1989. This local product was donated to Newark by Mr Cuthbertson in July 1994. With the demise of MBA and a series of accidents, a lot of Tiger Cub owners put their machines into store. With its small dimensions – 13ft 4in length, span 21ft – and low residual values; as well as the Newark example, there are four Tiger Cubs in British collections.

Above: Swift FR.5 WK277 in service with 2 Squadron,
1960. *Peter Green Collection*

Right: A sketch showing Dizzy Addicott's intention to turn
WK277 into a record-breaking jet and rocket-propelled car.
Via Newark Air Museum

Supermarine Swift FR.5 WK277
1955 | Day fighter / reconnaissance | One 7,145lb st Rolls-Royce Avon 114 turbojet

Much was expected of the RAF twin-pronged fighter programme of the early 1950s, the Hawker Hunter and the Supermarine Swift. Although the Swift became the first British swept-wing fighter to enter RAF service, it proved to be problematic and it reached production figures that were only a fraction of the Hunter's. Reconfigured from the interceptor role, the Swift found a niche in the low-level fighter-reconnaissance role. Either built from new or converted from F.4s, 94 Swift FR.5s were created. The type served with two squadrons, 2 and 79, in RAF Germany from 1956. To underline the ascendancy of the Hawker product, the FR.5s were replaced by Hunter FR.10s. Four intact Swifts are in British collections: the RAF Museum's Swift FR.5 'guests' at Tangmere; FR.5 WK275 at Doncaster-Sheffield, missile development F.7 XF114 at Southampton and Newark's WK277. The fuselage of record-breaking F.4 WK198 is at Brooklands – Chapter 27. Newark's machine saw frontline service and nearly had another career in very different form, making it the obvious one to profile.

Built at South Marston as an F.4, WK277 was ferried to Chilbolton for testing on 30th April 1955 and by November was involved in autostabiliser trials. It was back at South Marston in April 1956 for conversion to FR.5 guise. Work completed, it was issued to 23 Maintenance Unit (MU) at Aldergrove on 7th March 1957 and stored. Flt Lt Derek Burton of Benson-based 147 Squadron, the ferry specialists, flew WK277 to Jever in West Germany on 3rd March 1959. It was taken on charge by 2 Squadron, adopting the code 'N' and the black bars and white triangles either side of the fuselage roundel that it wears today. Moving to Gütersloh on 9th September 1961, WK277 completed 25 months of operational service on 7th April 1961 when it was dispatched to 60 MU at Church Fenton. During those 25 months, WK277 spent two periods under repair following Category 3 flying accidents – repairable on site but not at unit level – on 22nd July 1959 and 3rd October 1960: great value for money! WK277 was delivered to 2 School of Technical Training at Cosford on 9th November 1961, becoming instructional airframe 7719M.

It was from Cosford that Wisley-based Vickers test pilot Desmond 'Dizzy' Addicott, a long-term motorsport fanatic on two or four wheels, bought WK277 for £225 (£4,500 in present-day values). Dizzy had been involved in a series of wet runway braking trials for the Ministry of Supply from 1958 to 1962, using specially modified Swift F.7 XF114 (preserved at Solent Sky, Chapter 11), and was impressed by its 'ground-hugging' abilities. He formulated a scheme to turn a Swift fuselage into a world land speed record 'car', using a 'tweaked' Rolls-Royce Avon RA7R turbojet giving around 15,000lb st with reheat and a pair of 4,000lb st Bristol Siddeley BS605 rocket motors. The rockets were to be mounted on stub 'wings' attached to the rear fuselage to carry the main wheels of the tricycle layout. WK277 was taken to Wisley for the transformation to be carried out, but eventually management at British Aircraft Corporation wanted it moved. Dizzy sold the Swift to Holder's Garage at Congresbury, Somerset, and the project was forgotten. Newark benefactor Norman Pratlett acquired WK277 from Congresbury in August 1969 and presented it on permanent loan.

Taylor Monoplane prototype G-APRT nestled under Anson C.19 VL348. *Ken Ellis*

Taylor Monoplane G-APRT
1959 | Single-seat light aircraft | One 40hp Ardem 4CO2 Mk.X piston

As noted under the Tiger Cub above, Newark has two prototype British light aircraft of very different eras. The JT.1 Monoplane proved to be a popular homebuild of the 1960s and 1970s, with upwards of 160 completed or started worldwide. While the Tiger Cub has the advantage of being a Nottinghamshire product *Romeo-Tango* is important as it was the first British post-war homebuild design and therefore a major milestone. School teacher John Taylor of Ilford, Essex, designed the all-wooden JT.1 in 1958 with the intention of providing a practical airframe that could be built for £100 (£2,500 in present-day values). The engine was extra and the Monoplane was capable of taking a wide choice. Construction took about 14 months and Wg Cdr O V Holmes took G-APRT for its first flight, at White Waltham, on 4th July 1959. It was then powered by a 38hp JAP J-99 but in 1966 was fitted with a Rollason Ardem converted Volkswagen motor car engine. John Taylor sold *Romeo-Tango* in October 1961 and it went through a long line of owners, from all over Britain. With over 640 hours 'on the clock', the Monoplane was donated to Newark, arriving by road, in April 2012.

Romeo-Tango is the only example of a JT.1 in a British museum, but it is not the only John Taylor design in 'captivity' and here is an appropriate place to mention it. Responding to a competition for a 'midget racer' organised by Rollason Aircraft in 1964, John designed the JT.2 Titch and came second; the winner was the Luton Group's Beta. John built the prototype JT.2, G-ATYO, powered by an 85hp Continental C85-12F and he was at the helm for its first flight on 22nd January 1967. While flying *Yankee-Oscar* on 16th May 1967, John was killed in a crash. Plans were offered and around 60 have been built worldwide – far out-running the rival Beta. An early plans-built example was constructed by John Bygraves of Gamlingay, Bedfordshire. Fitted with a 100hp Continental O-200-A, it first flew in 1975. It was delivered on 28th July 2003 to the Norfolk and Suffolk Aviation Museum – Chapter 26.

Vickers Varsity T.1 WF369
1951 | Aircrew trainer | Two 1,950hp Bristol Hercules 264 pistons

At the time of writing, two Varsities were kept indoors by British museums: Newark's WF369, the oldest example and RAF Museum Cosford's WL679. As the latter spent its entire career in test and trials, WF369 is the nation's 'lead' example, all the more so as it opened its career just across the Nottinghamshire border at Swinderby. Intended to replace the Vickers Wellington T.10, the Varsity was a tricycle undercarriage development of the Valetta transport. A gondola under the centre section housed a small weapons bay and at the forward end a bomb aimer could lie prone to learn his craft. This was a truly all-purpose crew trainer: multi-engine pilot, navigator, bomb aimer, radar and air electronics disciplines could all be tackled. The prototype first flew on 17th July 1949 and the last of 163 appeared in 1954. The last trainer examples, like Newark's, were withdrawn in 1976, the type completing a quarter of a century of instruction.

WF369 had its maiden flight at Brooklands on 21st November 1951 and entered service the following month with 201 Advanced Flying School at Swinderby. It transferred to 2 Air Navigation School at Hullavington in October 1954. Still at Hullavington, WF369 join the Air Electronics School and moved with the unit to Topcliffe in January 1962. Mergers resulted in a new name, the Air Electronics and Air Engineers Operators School, in January 1967. From the autumn of 1973 the Varsity was issued to its final base, Finningley, with the multi-tasking 6 Flying Training School, with the individual code 'F'. With the wind down of the fleet, Newark's retiring chairman, Harold Bradshaw, was successful in a bid for one to be presented to the museum. Piloted by

Sqn Ldr Kimmins, WF369 touched down at Winthorpe on 1st April 1976 making its 7,612th landing and completing 8,646 hours of flying time. It is displayed in the main aircraft hall alongside the Handley Page Jetstream T.1 that took over the multi-engine training role in 1976 and the Hawker Siddeley Dominie T.1 that became the RAF's navigator trainer from 1965.

Newark Air Museum aircraft

Type	Identity	Built	Origin	Acquired	Notes
Armstrong Whitworth Argosy C.1	XN819	1961	Britain	Feb 1984	cockpit
Auster AOP.9	XS238	1962	Britain	1999	fuselage
Aviasud Sirocco 377GB	G-MNRT	1986	France	28 Jun 2005	–
Avro Anson C.19	VL348	1946	Britain	Nov 1972	see profile
Avro Shackleton MR.3/3	WR977	1957	Britain	1 May 1977	see profile
Avro Ashton 2	WB491	1951	Britain	26 Feb 2003	forward fuselage
Avro Vulcan B.2	XM594	1963	Britain	7 Feb 1983	–
Bell Sioux AH.1	XT200	1965	USA	1978	–
Bensen B-8	G-ASNY	1964	USA	20 Apr 2009	–
Blackburn Beverley C.1	XB261	1955	Britain	25 May 2004	cockpit
Blackburn Buccaneer S.1	XN964	1963	Britain	26 Feb 1988	–
Bristol Sycamore 3	WT933	1951	Britain	17 Jun 1980	–
Cessna 310	G-APNJ	1956	USA	4 Mar 2004	–
Clutton FRED Srs 2	G-BJAD	1981	Britain	9 Jan 2002	unflown
Dassault Mystère IVA	83	1956	France	Sep 1978	–
de Havilland Tiger Moth	'G-MAZY'	1941	Britain	25 Jun 1995	see profile
de Havilland Dove 1	G-AHRI	1946	Britain	13 May 1989	–
de Havilland Heron 1B	G-ANXB	1953	Britain	27 Oct 1981	see profile
de Havilland Vampire T.11	XD593	1954	Britain	30 Mar 1973	–
de Havilland Venom NF.3	WX905	1953	Britain	16 May 1989	–
de Havilland Sea Venom FAW.21	WW217	1955	Britain	18 Dec 1983	–
de Havilland Sea Vixen FAW.2	XJ560	1959	Britain	10 Aug 1986	–
de Havilland Canada Chipmunk T.10	WB624	1950	Canada	14 Sep 1995	–
Eipper Quicksilver MX	G-MJDW	1982	USA	15 Dec 2007	–
English Electric Canberra B.2/8	WV787	1952	Britain	24 Nov 1985	see profile
English Electric Canberra PR.7	WH791	1954	Britain	29 Nov 1998	–
English Electric Canberra PR.9	–	1952	Britain	14 Nov 2000	cockpit
English Electric Canberra T.17	WH863	1953	Britain	10 Jul 1990	cockpit
English Electric Canberra T.19	WH904	1953	Britain	1 Oct 1985	–
English Electric Lightning T.5	XS417	1964	Britain	5 Sep 1988	–
English Electric Lightning F.6	XR757	1965	Britain	Jun 2015	cockpit
Fairey Gannet AEW.3	XP226	1962	Britain	7 Nov 1982	–
Folland Gnat T.1	XR534	1963	Britain	2 Dec 2000	–
Folland Gnat T.1	–	1962	Britain	1994	procedure trainer
General Aircraft Monospar ST-12	VH-UTH	1935	Britain	18 Mar 1968	see profile
Gloster Meteor T.7	VZ634	1951	Britain	16 Dec 1985	–
Gloster Meteor FR.9	VZ608	1951	Britain	16 Dec 1985	see profile
Gloster Meteor NF.12	WS692	1953	Britain	31 Oct 1981	–
Gloster Meteor NF(T).14	WS739	1954	Britain	21 Jan 1984	–
Gloster Javelin FAW.8	XH992	1959	Britain	22 Aug 1981	–
Handley Page Hastings T.5*	TG517	1948	Britain	22 Jun 1977	see profile
Handley Page Jetstream T.1*	XX492	1975	Britain	9 Dec 2004	–
Hawker Sea Hawk FB.3	WM913	1954	Britain	1 Jul 1984	–
Hawker Hunter F.1	WT651	1954	Britain	17 Jan 1992	–
Hawker Hunter T.7	XX467	1958	Britain	3 May 2017	–

Newark Air Museum aircraft continued...

Type	Identity	Built	Origin	Acquired	Notes
Hawker Siddeley Dominie T.1	XS726	1965	Britain	24 Sep 2014	–
Hawker Siddeley Sea Harrier FA.2*	ZA176	1981	Britain	21 Jul 2004	see profile
Hunting Jet Provost T.3	XN573	1961	Britain	15 Apr 1989	cockpit
Hunting Jet Provost T.3A	XM383	1960	Britain	12 Nov 1994	–
Hunting Jet Provost	–	1960	Britain	Feb 1998	procedure trainer
Hiway Skytrike	G-MBVE	1982	Britain	21 Jun 1995	–
Lee Richards Annular Biplane	–	1964	Britain	1975	replica
Lockheed T-33A	51-9036	1951	USA	1979	–
Lockheed TriStar	–	1975	USA	Feb 2016	simulator
Luscombe Rattler Strike	G-BKPG	1983	Britain	16 Dec 200	–
Maxair Hummer	G-MJCF	1982	USA	17 Jan 2006	–
MBA Tiger Cub 440	G-MBUE	1982	Britain	16 Jul 1994	see profile
McDonnell Phantom FGR.2	XV490	1969	USA	Jun 2016	cockpit
McDonnell Phantom	–	1969	USA	1992	simulator
Mignet 'Flying Flea'	–	1936	France	9 Mar 1994	–
Mignet 'Flying Flea'	–	1936	France	9 Mar 1994	fuselage
Mikoyan-Guervich MiG-23ML	458	1975	USSR	22 Feb 2002	–
Mikoyan-Guervich MiG-27K	71	1979	USSR	22 Feb 2002	–
Mooney M.20A	G-APVV	1959	USA	13 Dec 1995	–
Morane-Saulnier Rallye Club	G-BFTZ	1968	France	27 Jan 1996	–
North American Harvard IIB	42-12417	1942	USA	24 Aug 2010	–
North American F-100D Super Sabre	54-2223	1954	USA	May 1978	–
Percival Prentice T.1	VR249	1948	Britain	8 Jul 1967	–
Percival Provost T.1	WV606	1954	Britain	Feb 1972	–
Powerchute Kestrel	G-CCLT	1993	Britain	27 Oct 2003	powered parachute
SAAB 91B-2 Safir	56321	1956	Sweden	14 Jul 1982	–
SAAB S.35XD Draken	AR-107	1971	Sweden	29 Jun 1994	–
SAAB AJSH.37 Viggen	37918	1976	Sweden	25 Jun 2006	–
Saunders-Roe Skeeter AOP.12	XL764	1958	Britain	16 Jul 1980	–
Scottish Aviation Bulldog T.1	XX634	1974	Britain	9 Jan 2006	–
Scottish Aviation Bulldog T.1	–	c1973	Britain	Jun 2005	procedure trainer
SEPECAT Jaguar GR.1	XX753	1975	GB/France	1 May 2010	cockpit
SEPECAT Jaguar T.2A	XX829	1974	GB/France	21 Mar 2012	–
Slingsby Grasshopper TX.1	XA239	1953	Britain	2004	glider
Slingsby Cadet TX.1	RA897	1944	Britain	2004	glider
Slingsby Motor Cadet	G-AXMB	1971	Britain	18 Aug 2002	motor-glider
Slingsby T.67 Firefly	–	1995	France/GB	2011	procedure trainer
Sud Gazelle 03	XW276	1970	France	Apr 1999	–
Supermarine Swift FR.5*	WK277	1955	Britain	18 Aug 1969	see profile
SZD Pirat	CDX	1968	Poland	2007	glider, airworthy
TASUMA CSV 30	–	1998	Britain	2013	UAV, plus two others
Taylor Monoplane	G-APRT	1959	Britain	10 Apr 2012	see profile
Vickers Varsity T.1*	WF369	1951	Britain	1 Apr 1976	see profile
Volmer VJ-24W	G-MBBZ	1981	USA	16 Oct 1998	–
Ward Gnome	–	2000	Britain	Nov 2007	unflown
Westland Whirlwind HAS.7	XM685	1959	USA/GB	17 Jun 1980	–
Westland Wessex HC.2	XV728	1968	USA/GB	18 Aug 1998	–
Zurowski ZP.1	–	1977	Britain	26 Apr 1985	unflown helicopter

Notes: * – illustrated in the colour section

The cockpit of Argosy C.1 XN819 is in running order as a procedure trainer. *Ken Ellis*

Below: Newark's latest exhibit, Hunter T.7 XX467 en route to the museum, 3rd May 2017. *Howard Heeley-Newark Air Museum*

DERBYSHIRE

Silk Mill – Museum of Making

The only museum in the county with aviation content available on a regular basis was in Derby and closed its doors several years ago for a major redevelopment. It did display an incredible array of Rolls-Royce aero engines and it is hoped that the same will be the case when it re-opens. Scheduled re-opening is 2019 or 2020, keep an eye on **www.derbymuseums.org**

CHAPTER 24

SHROPSHIRE

Royal Air Force Museum Cosford

Some call this 'RAF Museum North' but Cosford is regarded as a sister museum to Hendon and not a subsidiary. Home to the imposing National Cold War Exhibition and three other huge exhibition hangars, Cosford is, of course, a national institution and is covered in depth in the sister volume *Great Aviation Collections of Britain*. **www.rafmuseum.org**

Wartime Aircraft Recovery Group Aviation Museum

Located alongside the control tower at Sleap aerodrome, the group's impressive collection is centred on artefacts from many aviation 'archaeology' excavations and a Hawker Fury and a Supermarine Spitfire replica. Open Sundays in the summer months. **wargsleap@gmail.com**

STAFFORDSHIRE

The Potteries Museum and Art Gallery

Reginald Joseph Mitchell, the designer of the Supermarine Spitfire, was born in 1885 at Talke, near Stoke-on-Trent, and the museum, in Hanley, pays tribute to him. Included in the displays is 1945-built Spitfire XVI RW388 which is being restored under the gaze of visitors. **www.stokemuseums.org.uk**

Above: Hurricane IV 'P3395' (KX829) with Spitfire IX ML427 just visible behind it at Thinktank. To the right is John Cobb's 1938 record-breaking Railton Special car. *Thinktank*

Formal portrait of Stoke's local hero, R J Mitchell. *KEC*

WEST MIDLANDS

Thinktank – Millennium Discovery Centre

At Millennium Point, near New Street Station in Birmingham, is the much re-vamped Birmingham Science Museum. The newly opened Spitfire Gallery highlights Birmingham's role in manufacturing the fighter, centred on the massive Castle Bromwich factory. **www.thinktank.ac**

Thinktank aircraft

Type	Identity	Built	Origin	Acquired	Notes
Hawker Hurricane IV	KX829	1943	Britain	1961	–
Supermarine Spitfire IX	ML427	1944	Britain	1958	–

Tettenhall Transport Heritage Centre

Based in a former railway goods yard, the centre was officially opened in March 2017. It concentrates on the transport heritage of Wolverhampton and the general area and includes some of the Staffordshire Aircraft Restoration Team's airframes. **www.tettenhallthc.tumblr.com**

Tettenhall Transport Heritage Centre aircraft

Type	Identity	Built	Origin	On site from	Notes
Boulton Paul Balliol T.2	WN516	1953	Britain	Apr 2015	cockpit
Boulton Paul Balliol T.2	WN534	1954	Britain	2014	cockpit
de Havilland Vampire T.11	XD445	1954	Britain	Apr 2015	–
de Havilland Canada Chipmunk T.10	WK576	1952	Canada	2014	cockpit
English Electric Canberra T.17	WJ576	1953	Britain	Apr 2015	cockpit
Flexiform Sky Sails Striker	G-MJIA	1982	Britain	2012	–
MBA Tiger Cub	G-MMFS	1983	Britain	2014	–
Microflight Spectrum	G-MVJM	1988	Britain	2015	–
Slingsby Cadet TX.1	'PD685'	c1945	Britain	2014	glider, fuselage
Slingsby Grasshopper TX.1	WZ755	1952	Britain	2012	glider

Rotors Across the World
The Helicopter Museum

Weston-super-Mare
www.helicoptermuseum.co.uk

Helicopters hold a fascination for most people and this is reflected in the stock of most aviation collections, in Britain and globally. To devote an entire museum to the subject of rotorcraft would appear to be a risky business but since it opened in November 1989 The Helicopter Museum has confounded all the critics. It's not just chugging along; it has consistently expanded and is a major Somerset and regional tourist attraction. Rightly calling itself the 'World's Largest Dedicated Helicopter Museum', it has superb relations with Britain's rotorcraft manufacturer, Leonardo (formerly AgustaWestland and Westland) as well as European and American producers and enjoys Royal recognition. Including the reserve collection, there are close on 100 rotorcraft of all shapes and sizes at Weston-super-Mare: all of this started out as one man's personal gathering of documents and artefacts in 1958.

Enthusiast, historian, writer, publisher, helicopter owner and pilot, Elfan Ap Rees is the man with the vision that led to today's national rotorcraft museum. Elfan has been publisher and editor of *Helicopter International* magazine since 1977. He took the plunge in May 1969 and acquired Bristol Sycamore Mk.3 G-ALSX and it is still part of the collection. Other airframes followed and by the early 1970s he was at the head of a small group of like-minded enthusiasts most working for, or having been employed by, Westland. Acquiring helicopters was the easy bit, finding somewhere to put them was difficult. Loaning out was the answer, for example the Sycamore went to the Skyfame Museum two months after Elfan had bought it. Space at Weston-super-Mare (WSM) airfield was begged and borrowed and some of the helicopters were parked up there.

Above: Queen's Flight Wessex HCC.4 XV733 at its base, Benson, September 1969. *Roy Bonser*

The airfield opened as a municipal airport in 1936 and three years later 39 Elementary and Reserve Flying Training School started up, the first of several units that were resident through to 1945. A short distance to the east, the RAF opened up a large non-airfield complex at Locking, including 5 School of Technical Training and 1 Radio School in 1938; this closed down in 1965. Construction started in 1940 of two Bristol-run shadow factories, on the Oldmixon (western) edge of the airfield and at nearby Elborough; these built Beaufighters and Hawker Tempest IIs up to 1946. Contractor Western Airways assembled a batch of Bristol 170s and modified aircraft as large as Britannias at WSM. (See the Campbell Cougar below for another task.) The airfield became the home of Bristol's helicopter division post-war, with Sycamores and Belvederes being produced and tested. In 1960 Westland acquired Bristol's helicopter interests. Westland Industrial Products Ltd took over some of the factory area, supporting a wide range of activities at the Yeovil headquarters, including Merlin and Puma refurbishment into the early 2000s. Fixed wing flying at WSM came to an end in 1978.

Putting a roof on it

By 1974 the informal gathering of 'rotor heads' had a title, the British Rotorcraft Museum (BRM). To test the water, open days were staged during the summers of 1978 and 1979 and the number of visitors was encouraging. There was no doubt that WSM was *the* place for the collection, with its helicopter associations and the holidaymakers of Weston-super-Mare itself just a short distance away to the west. As BRM's fleet grew, steps were taken to protect the volunteers with the formation of a limited company and at the same time charity registration was finalised in 1981. The latter status helped Westland in its decision to support the new venture and a lease of 4.5 acres of its land was arranged. By 1988 BRM had grown to fifty airframes and a vast amount of artefacts. Former Fleet Air Arm helicopter pilot, HRH Prince Andrew, the Duke of York, presided at the opening of newly renamed International Helicopter Museum (IHM) in November 1989. At the ceremony, Elfan explained the change of name to the author; he wanted to see notable helicopter types from all over the world join the collection and he had discovered that a proportion of visitors thought that a 'rotorcraft' was an agricultural implement!

Gales in late January 1990 damaged several helicopters; it was a stark reminder that covered space was a priority. In April 1993 the Raoul Hafner Building was opened, providing workshop and storage space. (See the profile of the Revoplane below for more on Hafner.) Much of the expansion at this time was self-financed; the Cierva Memorial Building, a display

The restored Pilots' Block and Control Tower houses an exhibition on the history of Weston-super-Mare airfield. *Courtesy THM*

hall costing £25,000 was ready in 1996. At this point the museum took on its third name: The Helicopter Museum. This was not to downgrade its international ambitions; it was to meet strict Museum and Galleries Commission accreditation guidelines but also to emphasize its unique place in British collections. In 1999 the land that had been leased from Westland was purchased from the GKN Group, by then the owners of the helicopter manufacturer. This cleared the way to explore the world of the Heritage Lottery Fund (HLF) which had come into being in 1994. A huge, 23,500 square foot display hall – the equivalent of four standard-size hangars – was projected. The plans were rewarded by a grant of £334,500 from HLF. While this project got going, a HLF fast-track grant was applied for to purchase former Queen's Flight Wessex HCC.4 XV733 which was to be sold by auctioneers Phillips on 25th October 2001 – see the profile below.

Prince Andrew was back to officially open the Duke of York Hangar in 2002. The Hafner Building was bulging at the seams and THM announced a new Conservation and Engineering Hangar – the Duke of Edinburgh Hangar – to replace it, with funds generated entirely by the museum. On 20th July 2007, the Duke, accompanied by HM Queen Elizabeth II, opened the new facility and the Hafner Building became a display hall. The team was only just getting into their stride: HLF funding enabled the Learning and Archive Centre in 2011 and a Coastal Community Fund grant of £134,000 restored the derelict wartime Pilots' Block and Control Tower to house an exhibition devoted to the entire history of WSM airfield in 2016. Although fixed wing flying had ceased in the late 1970s, the museum has operated a fully approved heliport since 1989. Civil and military helicopters frequently 'drop in' and during the 'high season' helicopter experience flights are available to visitors.

Soviet Bloc warriors

A look through the THM 'fleet' listing reveals an incredible array of overseas types. As the collecting policy of the museum is rotorcraft whatever their origins, *all* could well qualify for a profile. Staunchly nationalistic, the opportunity to zoom in on important waypoints in the British industry precludes greater depth for all but one of the cosmopolitan inmates at WSM. With the fall of the Berlin Wall in November 1989, the long-held prospects for acquiring Soviet hardware began to be realised. Poland was the first country targetted, ultimately providing four helicopters. First to arrive, in June 1991, was a PZL-Swidnik SM-2 air ambulance, an enlarged and refined version of the Mil Mi-1 *Hare*. An example of the latter was received in September 1993 and a civilian turboshaft-powered Mi-2 *Hoplite* four years later; both had been licence-built in Poland. Five years of negotiations were rewarded in February 2010 when a Mi-8 *Hip* transport helicopter joined the collection. Over 10,000 twin-turbine *Hips* were built, taking over from the Mi-4 *Hound* as the principal Warsaw Pact troop carrier.

Powered a potent 1,700hp Shvetsov ASh-82V piston engine, the first Mi-4 appeared in 1952; the THM example served in Czechoslovakia and arrived in September 1994. Two helicopters were sourced in the former East Germany, both from design bureaux established by Siberians. Nikolai Ilyich Kamov's signature co-axial rotor system is still employed in present day products from the factory. Arriving at WSM in June 1995 the Ka-26 *Hoodlum* had been used by civilian operator Interflug for crop dusting. The Kamov was exchanged for Westland Whirlwind Series 3 G-AYNP from the reserve collection. The jewel of the Soviet types is the Mi-24 *Hind,* which is profiled below.

The fuel tanker provides scale to the huge XCH-62 prototype at Philadelphia, Pennsylvania, circa 1972. *Boeing Vertol*

The Rotodyne early in its flight test programme; it is unpainted and the main undercarriage is braced. *Fairey*

Size matters at the world's largest

Two exhibits at WSM perhaps do not draw the eye as much as they should. Three undercarriage legs, two 17ft tall, are all that remains of the largest American helicopter, the Boeing Vertol XCH-62. This was a response to a 1968 US Army requirement for a heavy lift helicopter (HLH), capable of lifting 23 tonnes slung under the fuselage – loads including tanks or containers. The twin-rotor design was to have 93-foot diameter rotors and it would stand 38ft 7in off the ground. Power was to be supplied by a trio of 8,000shp Allison XT701 turboshafts. One prototype, 73-22012, was ordered and construction was well in hand at Philadelphia, Pennsylvania, when the plug was pulled on the project on 1st October 1974. The National Aeronautics and Space Administration supplied a stay of execution, funding static testing of the transmission system. The huge XCH-62 was stored in the open at the plant in the hope that the HLH programme would be revived. This was not to be and in 1987 the forlorn, incomplete prototype was moved to the US Army Aviation Museum at Fort Ricker, Alabama. Kept outside and continuing to decay, in 2005 the museum staff bit the bullet and the XCH-62 was scrapped on 11th October 2005. Approaches to Fort Rucker by THM revealed that the undercarriage legs had been kept and, yes, they were available. Three years of paperwork followed – the USA has stringent rules relating to the export of redundant military hardware – before the legs arrived in Somerset.

Much more survives of Britain's largest ever rotorcraft, the Fairey Rotodyne twin-turbine transport compound helicopter. Sections of the fuselage and the rotor head are impressive, but do not convey what a monster this was. The Rotodyne was make-or-break for Fairey's long-standing faith in compound technology. A pair of 2,800shp Napier Eland turboprops acted as conventional propeller turbines. These were mounted on stub wings with a tip-to-tip span of 46ft 6in that generated half of the lift in forward flight. The Elands also created compressed air to drive the enormous 90ft diameter four-bladed rotor through tip jets. The 58ft 8in long fuselage could seat 30 passengers, or accept freight via twin clam-shell doors in the rear, which also permitted use as a tactical military transport. After many months of ground runs and tethered 'hops', chief test pilot Sqn Ldr Ron Gellatly AFC and his deputy John Morton took the sole prototype, XE521, on its first untethered sortie at White Waltham on 6th November 1957. It was not until April 1958 that the first transition from helicopter (rotor-borne) to compound (rotor-plus-wing lift, rotor plus jet efflux propulsion) flight was achieved. Early airline interest waned and the world's military remained unconvinced. Westland acquired Fairey's helicopter assets in February 1960 and two years later the Rotodyne programme was axed. Sections were presented to the College of Aeronautics at Cranfield and from there they were acquired by Elfan Ap Rees. The remnants of the XCH-62 and the Rotodyne are important exhibits at THM, providing visitors with 'What if?' moments.

Bristol Sycamore Mk.3 G-ALSX
1951 | General purpose helicopter | One 550hp Alvis Leonides 73 piston

First flown at Filton on 30th April 1951, G-ALSX was the seventh production Sycamore and destined for a long life, mostly devoted to demonstration, trials and communications. Of the first of those *Sierra-Xray* attended the Paris Salon at Le Bourget, France, in June 1951 and June 1953; the Society of British Aircraft Constructors display at Farnborough in September 1951 and 1952; and it set off for a sales tour of Europe in May 1952. Trials work included deck landings on the carrier HMS *Triumph* in December 1951 and HMCS *Magnificent* in early 1957, just before the Royal Canadian Navy returned the vessel to the Royal Navy. Two unusual duties were attendance at the Festival of Britain celebrations in London during the summer of 1951 and helping in search and rescue operations during the horrific floods in the Netherlands, February 1953.

Early in 1958 Bristol sold G-ALSX to Williamson Diamond Mines for the use of its founder, Canadian geologist and adventurer, Dr John Williamson. Bristol Freighter Mk.31 F-BFUO of French operator Société Commercial Aérienne du Littoral flew to WSM to pick up the helicopter. Registered in Tanganyika (the present-day Tanzania) as VR-TBS, the Sycamore was carefully shoe-horned into the Freighter. Dr Williamson died, aged 51, in 1958 and the helicopter was returned to the UK on 1st December 1959. Re-registered as G-ALSX in March 1960, the Sycamore was used to support the testing of the Type 192 – the Belvedere twin-rotor prototype. As before, it was variously based at Filton and WSM. In that year Bristol became part of the British Aircraft Corporation and the company's rotorcraft assets were acquired by Westland of Yeovil. G-ALSX took up 'B Condition' ('trade plate') markings as G-48/1 as it carried out revalidation trials for the type's wooden rotor blades to help Westland continue to support existing operators.

The Sycamore was retired in 1966 with a total flying time of 1,233 hours, 50 minutes. In May 1969 it was acquired by Elfan Ap Rees and placed on loan to the Skyfame Museum at Staverton two months later. Skyfame was forced to close its doors in January 1978 and the Sycamore, along with most of the collection, migrated to the care of the Imperial War Museum at Duxford. During 1987 the Sycamore returned to WSM to join what was then the British Rotorcraft Museum. There are three Sycamores on display with 'nationals', all production examples, and several at 'local' regional collections. Weston's G-ALSX 'ticks all the boxes' – early production example, test and trials life, museum collecting policy and local 'roots' – and is easily Britain's 'best of breed'.

Bristol Belvedere HC.1 XG452
1960 | Transport helicopter | Two 1,650shp Napier Gazelle 2 turboshafts

The Belvedere was the first twin-rotor *and* turboshaft-powered helicopter in RAF service, 26 HC.1s were accepted after a long and protracted development programme. This stemmed from the Type 173 which first flew on 24th August 1952 – see Chapter 10. XG452 was the fifth and last prototype/development machine and it was built at the Oldmixon factory, WSM; making its first flight on 26th February 1960. The following month it was brought up to full production standard, including 'drooping', or 'gull-wing', tail surfaces. In March 1960 the plant at Weston changed hands, Westland having acquired the Bristol helicopter division. XG452 was at the Aeroplane and Armament Experimental Establishment (A&AEE) at Boscombe Down by May 1960. It was to take part in tropical trials at Idris, Libya, to be followed by high altitude evaluation in the French Alps. On the outbound legs, it was decided to set several point-to-point records. The helicopter positioned to Gatwick on 12th June and two days later departed to Rome, Italy. The next 'hop' was to Luqa on Malta and thence to Idris, reached with a total flying time of 13 hours, 57 minutes. The return trip included high altitude trials in the French Alps before transiting through the USAF air base at Chambley in northeast France. XG452 attended the Farnborough airshow in September 1960.

After checks and modifications XG452 was re-issued to A&AEE on 7th November 1962. Flying included paratroop dropping and radio trials. By 21st January 1963 XG452 was with at the Rolls-Royce test airfield at Hucknall. Engine manufacturer Napier had been acquired by Rolls-Royce the previous year and support of the Gazelle engine had become the Derby company's responsibility. On 21st April 1965 XG452 was at WSM where it was used for flight control system trials before being upgraded to the latest modification state and painted in a high gloss camouflage scheme. In early August 1967 XG452 encountered vibration problems and the decision was taken to withdraw it from service; it had 'clocked' 487 flying hours. By that time the type was in its twilight years with the RAF; Belvederes completed just 7½ years of operational service in March 1969. Allocated the instructional airframe number 7997M in December 1967, by February of the following year XG452 was at 2 School of Technical Training at Cosford. By 1972 it had moved to nearby Ternhill where it languished with the fire section.

Offered for disposal in 1977, XG452 was acquired by Elfan Ap Rees, but he quickly realised that the 89ft 9in long, 11,700lb empty weight Belvedere was a quantum leap in logistics and therefore expenditure. A quote to move it by road came in at £4,000 – that would be a daunting £44,000 in present-day values. The Royal Navy came to the rescue, deciding that the journey by low-loader to WSM could be put down to a training exercise by the Mobile Repair and Transport Salvage Unit; XG452 arrived at its birthplace on 5th November 1977. A group of former Oldmixon employees, calling themselves the Belvedere Preservation Group, set to initial restoration and it was returned to its aluminium and white colours. On 15th June 1978 XG452 was given the British civil registration G-BRMB – British Rotorcraft Museum Belvedere – but this identity was cancelled in July 1996. Also at THM is the cockpit of Belvedere HC.1 XG462 and the museum owns sister ship XG454 currently on loan to the Museum of Science and Industry in Manchester – Chapter 18. The only other example is XG474 at the RAF Museum Hendon. While RAF helicopter operations have been dominated by the incredible Boeing Chinook twin-rotor since 1981, the Belvedere – born at Weston-super-Mare – is a very significant milestone in the story of *British* rotorcraft.

The one-off Campbell Cougar, G-BAPS. *Roger Richards*

Campbell Cougar G-BAPS
1973 | Single-seat autogyro | One 130hp Rolls-Royce/Continental O-240-A piston

Autogyro pioneer Don Campbell acquired the rights for the US-designed Bensen series of single-seaters by the early 1960 and started a small production run at Membury. Campbell was killed in an airliner crash in 1967 but the company he had founded, Campbell Aircraft, continued to develop the Bensen theme. This led to the Campbell Cricket single-seater, designed by Peter Lovegrove. The prototype first flew in November 1969 and a production run was begun with Western Airways at WSM acting as a sub-contractor. THM has two Crickets in the collection – see the table.

Determined to widen the market appeal of the autogyro, Campbell devised the Curlew two-seater, but did not go ahead with completion of the prototype. In 1972 Campbell came to an agreement with Western Airways to build a prototype of the Cougar, a two-seat autogyro aimed at the 'sports', training and aerial work markets – the latter with an eye on the use of rotorcraft for sheep 'droving' in Australia. The prototype, G-BAPS, with a single-seat cockpit, was completed at WSM and made its first 'hops' down the runway on 20th April 1973. The plan was to reconfigure *Papa-Sierra* with a side-by-side enclosed cockpit as interest in the type grew. Within a month of the start of test flying, the prototype was flown across the English Channel and it was displayed in the static at Le Bourget for the Paris Salon in May 1973. Development flying continued at Weston but Campbell Aircraft ceased trading in 1975. The British Rotorcraft Museum acquired this unique, locally-built, prototype in May 1976.

Cierva Rotorcraft Grasshopper 1 G-ARVN
1961 | Single-seat helicopter | Two 105hp Walter Minor pistons
Cierva Rotorcraft Grasshopper 3 G-AWRP
1969 | General purpose helicopter | Two 135hp Rolls-Royce/Continental O-300-A pistons

Dismantled within THM's reserve collection, the unorthodox-looking Grasshopper 1 can claim to be Britain's first co-axial helicopter. Two sets of counter-rotating rotor blades, one above the other, are driven by two shafts, one inside the other, from a common gearbox. What this adds in complexity is offset by a smaller rotor diameter and the ability to dispense with a tail rotor which cancels out the torque generated by a conventional single rotor array. Several nations have dabbled in co-axial designs, but *the* exponent of the concept was Nikolai Ilyich Kamov; he and his successors mastering the concept with military and commercial designs still in production. (The Kamov Ka-26 and the Gyrodyne QH-50 drone on show at WSM are superb examples of co-axial technology.)

Cierva Rotorcraft Grasshopper G-ARVN during early trials in 1961. *Servotec*

Designer Jacob Shapiro conceived the two-seat Grasshopper 1 and it was built at Feltham, London, by his company Servotec Ltd and marketed by Rotorcraft Ltd. Intended as a proof-of-concept prototype, G-ARVN featured a car-like cockpit behind the rotor shaft and a V-format tail and it began flight trials in the hands of Basil Arkell in the spring of 1961. It was powered by a pair of 65hp Walter Mikrons but was underpowered and it was rebuilt with a pair of Walter Minors. Registered as *Victor-November* in February 1962, it resumed testing but was grounded the following year and put into store at Redhill, where Servotec and Rotorcraft had relocated.

The original Cierva Autogiro Company was formed in Britain in 1926; on the board was Air Cdre J G Weir, who also developed rotorcraft under the Weir name in Scotland. Cierva and Weir merged in 1943, trading under the former name. The company ceased production and development in 1951 but re-emerged in 1965 when it acquired Rotorcraft, becoming Cierva Rotorcraft. Development began at Redhill of the Grasshopper Series 3, a five-seater using Shapiro's co-axial dynamic system and three examples were laid down. The prototype, G-AWRP, began testing in the summer of 1969; it was displayed at the Farnborough airshow in September 1970. The second prototype, G-AXFM, was used as a ground-running rig and the third, G-AZAU, was not completed when work ceased in the mid-1970s. All three Series 3s were acquired from storage at Shoreham by helicopter operator and enthusiast, Jim Wilkie, who had established Wilkie Helicopters and the Helicopter Museum of Great Britain, initially at Heysham, but centred on Blackpool Airport by 1990. This venture came to an end with an auction on 13th January 1993 and beyond this the Grasshoppers were moved to Weston-super-Mare later in the year. Eventually, the museum acquired the remains of G-ARVN from Redhill, bringing together all of the elements of a fascinating, if abortive, episode of British rotorcraft technology.

EH Industries EH 101 PP3 G-EHIL
1988 | Transport helicopter | Three 1,920shp General Electric CT7-6A turboshafts

When the third prototype EH 101 arrived by road from Yeovil on 26th November 1999 it looked as though it had taken the crown of the largest exhibit at THM. Six years previously another helicopter with very similar attributes dominated the other inmates at WSM. Like the EH 101, the Sud Super Frelon was powered by three turboshafts and designed as an anti-submarine or transport helicopter; both could be configured for civilian operation. Looks can be deceptive: the Frelon has an empty weight of 15,130lb, a length of 63ft 7in and an overall height of 16ft 2in while the EH 101 clocks in at 15,360lb, 55ft 5in and 19ft, respectively. So the Anglo-Italian 'newbie' is heavier and towers over its French neighbour, but the latter has the length!

A joint development by Westland and Agusta under the EH Industries banner, the very first EH 101, ZF641, first flew at Yeovil in October 1987 and survives as an instructional airframe with the Fleet Air Arm at Culdrose. Named Merlin in RAF and Royal Navy service, the big helicopter is still in production, under the designation AW101. Agusta and Westland adopted the corporate name Leonardo in 2016. The RAF Museum at Hendon displays PP8 ZJ116 which, like G-EHIL, is in commercial transport guise. *India-Lima* was first flown on 30th September 1988 and it was used for handling, performance and rotor blade trials, icing trials in Denmark and much of the civil certification assessment. During 1990 PP3 was engaged in evaluating a Westland group innovation, Active Control Structural Response – ACSR – a vibration reduction system pioneered on the WG.30 (see below) which could be also employed on large fixed-wing types. For some trials G-EHIL adopted the military serial ZH647. PP3 was flown for the last time, at Yeovil, in February 1999 by which time it had accumulated a total flying time of 653 hours, in 581 flights. After that it was readied for its move to WSM.

Hafner R-II Revoplane
1932 | Single-seat helicopter | One 45hp Salmson 9Adr piston

Here's a treasure the Science Museum missed out on, the oldest surviving helicopter in Britain and an example of the early work of rotorcraft pioneer, Raoul Hafner. He went on to design Britain's first production helicopter, the Sycamore and the twin-rotor Type 173 that led to the Belvedere. From 1929 Austrian-born Hafner and Bruno Nagler collaborated to develop helicopters. The R-I was followed by the R-II which was tested at Aspern, near Vienna, in 1930-1931. Hafner moved to Britain in 1932, probably at the behest of his backer, Scottish cotton magnate Major Jack Coates, perhaps because of the increasingly repressive regime of the Austrian chancellor, Engelbert Dolfuss. The R-II followed Hafner and was assembled at Heston in 1933. Tests continued, but it was underpowered and it was relegated to a test rig for Hafner's rotor hubs and control systems.

It is in this capacity that the R-II really 'scores' as an exhibit; Hafner went on to devise the AR.III gyroplane which trail-blazed collective and cyclic controls and the so-called 'Spider' rotor hub that transformed the development of British helicopters.

With Hafner's move to Bristol to lead its helicopter efforts, the R-II was put into store, re-appearing in the static at the Fifty Years of Flying event at Hendon in July 1951, before being moved to the new helicopter cente at WSM. In 1961 was 'rediscovered' in its crate and it was refurbished by Westland apprentices. It was moved to the Shuttleworth Collection at Old Warden in 1966 before being passed on to the Torbay Aircraft Museum at Higher Blagdon on 11th August 1972. It joined what was then the British Rotorcraft Museum at WSM in 1979. It was given a major restoration by Westland volunteers and personnel from the Glider Support Unit at nearby RAF Locking that year. Raoul Hafner died, aged 75, in a boating accident in 1980; his widow, Eileen, donated this very significant rotorcraft to the museum in 1996.

The Hafner Revoplane at the Fifty Years of Flying event at Hendon in July 1951. *KEC*

Mil Mi-24D *Hind* 96+26
1981 | Attack / transport helicopter | Two 2,200shp Klimov TV3-117 turboshafts

To portray the Communist bloc arsenals during the Cold War, jets from the Mikoyan-Gurevich stable, ideally a MiG-15 *Fagot* or a MiG-21 *Fishbed* are essential and a Tupolev Tu-95 *Bear* would be the ultimate. But there is another Cold War icon that symbolised Soviet thinking and looked the part – the brutish Mil Mi-24 *Hind* gun-slinger. The most famous product of the design bureau named for Siberian Mikhail Leontyevich Mil, the *Hind* was derived from the dynamic system of the Mi-8 *Hip* transport helicopter – THM also has one of those in its collection. Designed in the late 1960s it was intended to lay down formidable fire power from a 12.7mm chin-mounted multi-barrel machine gun and unguided rocket pods and wire-guided AT-2 *Swatter* anti-tank missiles on substantial stub wings. That big fuselage was not wasted; the Hind could airlift eight fully equipped troops into battle and then go on to wreak havoc. The idea of massed ranks of *Hinds* coming over the horizon gave many a NATO planner sleepless nights. By 1973 Hinds were in widespread use in East Germany, with the Luftstreitkräfte and Soviet 'guest' forces. Perhaps as many as 2,400 *Hinds* were built up to the late 1990s and were widely supplied to Soviet bloc nations and 'client' states. The number of wars, conflicts and skirmishes that *Hinds* have been involved in is enormous. As well as the WSM example, the Midland Air Museum has a *Hind*. Imperial War Museum Duxford had former East German Mi-24 96+21 on loan from 1996 to 2012 when it moved on to the Pima Air Museum in Arizona, USA. This is another type the 'nationals' have missed out on.

The WSM *Hind* was first flown on 2nd April 1981 and delivered to the East German Luftstreitkräfte at Basepohl, near Stavenhagen, six days later, with the serial number 421. It was flown by Kampfhubschraubergeschwader 57 (KHG 57), the first East German air regiment equipped with Mi-24s; the unit also had a large force of Mi-8 *Hips* on strength. Later, 421 was issued to KHG 5, still at Basepohl. With the reunification of Germany in September 1990, KHG 5 was stood down and the

The Mi-24 *Hind* alongside Sud Super Frelon F-OCMF at Weston-super-Mare, 1997. *Roger Richards*

Hinds were given the four-number serials long adopted by their cousins to the west; in 421's case it became 96+26. KHG 5 morphed into Heeresfliegergruppe 80 (HFLG 80) but utilization was thought to be low; 96+26 was last flown on 24th February 1992. Its total time was quite a revelation: 1,793 hours, 43 minutes. The commonly held opinion was that the Soviet bloc, especially the Warsaw Pact members, achieved minimal sortie time. Assuming HFLG 80 did little flying, in the nine years 421 was operational with the East Germans it averaged very nearly 200 hours per year: some NATO nations during that timeframe would be envious of that. Enquiries by THM to Germany solicited a call in 1994 that the museum could have a Hind; it must move it as soon as possible in 1995 and the Luftwaffenmuseum at Gatow, Berlin, wanted something appropriate in exchange. A deal was struck over Saunders-Roe Skeeter AOP.12 XM556 held in the reserve collection – the Luftwaffe operated six Skeeter Mk.50s and the Marineflieger four Mk.51s, all as trainers, from 1958. A dismantling team departed WSM 8th February 1995, followed by the Skeeter a week or so later, and returned with 96+26 on the 20th.

Westland Dragonfly HR.5 WG719
1952 | General purpose helicopter | One 500hp Alvis Leonides 521/1 piston

The Dragonfly was the first helicopter produced by Westland; a much-developed and re-engined version of the American Sikorsky S-51. Built as an HR.3, WG719 was first flown at Yeovil on 19th September 1952 by Derrick Colvin and taken on charge by the Fleet Air Arm eighteen days later. It was shipped to Malta and joined the Station Flight at Hal Far by December. Courtesy of the light cruiser HMS *Bermuda*, it travelled to Greece to help in relief work following the earthquake that hit the Ionian Islands in early August 1953. While attempting to land in difficult conditions and terrain, WG719 rolled down a slope on 20th August and was damaged, thankfully without harm to the two on board. Repaired, it joined 705 Squadron in October 1954, initially at Gosport, later at Lee-on-Solent. From 1956 it was upgraded to HR.5 status with a more powerful Leonides radial, improved instrumentation and radio equipment. WG719 next flew with the Yeovilton Station Flight from April 1958, moving on to the Fleet Requirements Unit at Hurn in August 1959 and the Britannia Flight at Dartmouth in September 1963. It was retired to Fleetlands following an in-flight engine failure on 14th May 1965 at which stage WG719 had accrued 1,421 hours. Sold to Twyford Moors Helicopters on 5th May 1970; it languished at the company's heliport in Southampton before being sold to Widgeon operator Helicopter Hire, purely for its winch.

The airframe was then purchased by Elfan Ap Rees and moved, on loan, to the Fleet Air Arm Museum, WG719 moved to Yeovilton on 15th June 1974. In March 1976 it joined the British Rotorcraft Museum at WSM. On 15th June 1978 it was given the British civil registration G-BRMA – for British Rotorcraft Museum – but this identity was cancelled in March 1989. Following a partial restoration by volunteers in the summer of 1985 WG719 was at RAF Shawbury for repaint and temporary display, after which it returned to Weston for display, for a while marked with the incorrect serial 'WG718'.

Westland Widgeon Series 2 G-AOZE
1957 | General purpose helicopter | One 520hp Alvis Leonides 521/2 piston

With a new forward fuselage allowing for a pilot and four passengers, more power and much improved rotor and gearbox, Westland created a 'second generation' Dragonfly. The Widgeon could be regarded as the first British production helicopter aimed specifically at commercial operators. As a 'sub-set' of the Dragonfly, the Widgeon does not score highly in terms of technological advance, but as an early example of a civilian helicopter, it has good provenance. Between 1955 and 1959 three Dragonflies were converted to Widgeon status and a dozen new-build examples were created. With three whole examples plus the forward fuselage of another in British 'local' museums, the proportion of surviving Widgeons is remarkably high.

The Helicopter Museum's Widgeon G-AOZE in the static at Fairford, July 2003. *Roger Richards*

G-AOZE was built at Yeovil in 1957 and was sold to Bristow Helicopters being shipped out to the Persian Gulf in July that year. Bristow undertook contracts on a worldwide basis, specialising in support of oil exploration and extraction. In June 1962 the Widgeon was relocated to Bristow's operation in Nigeria and was registered in that country as 5N-ABW. It survived the Biafran civil war, 1967-1970, and was shipped to Bristow's Redhill headquarters in 1970. It was not flown again and was acquired by Warden Park School of Cuckfield, Sussex, in 1968 and, after a while on the playground, moved into a purpose-built 'hangar' where it was used as an instructional airframe for Certificate of Secondary Education courses. (The cockpit of Avro XIX D-IDEK – scrapped in 1979 – and former Bristow Whirlwind Series 3 VR-BEP, now at the East Midlands Airport Aeropark – Chapter 15 – were also employed at Warden Park.) Curriculum changes forced the engineering facility at the school to close in 1986 and the Widgeon moved to WSM.

Westland Whirlwind Series 1 G-ANFH
1954 | General purpose helicopter | One 600hp Pratt & Whitney Wasp R-1340-40 piston

Presently held in the reserve collection, with intentions for restoration, is a film 'star' with an impressive number of credits to its name. From 1954 to 1969 Whirlwind G-ANFH served British European Airways (BEA), initially on experimental schedules and later on charter work. It took part in the unremarkable Hammer horror *The Damned*, released in 1961, and two 1966 spy 'spoofs', the low budget *Where the Bullets Fly* with Tom Adams and one of Dean Martin's successful Matt Helm franchise, *Murderer's Row* with action scenes staged on the French Cote d'Azur. These pale against *Fox-Hotel's* role in the closing sequences of Richard Lester's *Hard Day's Night* released in 1964 and starring four lads from Liverpool called George, John, Paul and Ringo. Those sequences took place at BEA's Gatwick heliport and from playing fields in northwest London. In case the identities of the Whirlwind's passengers were lost on anybody, prior to filming the logo on the port side had been modified to read 'BEA-TLES'.

Based on the Sikorsky S-55, the Whirlwind was considerably redeveloped by Westland and aimed mostly at military roles. With the piston engined Series 1 and 2 and the turboshaft-powered Series 3, the company also had success in the commercial market. G-ANFH first flew at Yeovil on 15th October 1954 and was delivered to BEA's Helicopter Experimental Unit (HEU) at Gatwick on 2nd November as part of what the airline called the King Arthur Class, carrying the name *Sir Ector*. With a cabin that could take up to eight seats BEA Whirlwinds flew eight round trips daily from London Airport, Heathrow, to a heliport on London's South Bank from July 1955 to May 1956. A further experimental 'feeder' service ran from heliports in Leicester and Nottingham to Birmingham Airport, Elmdon, from July to November 1956. *Fox-Hotel* took part in both of these trials.

During 1959 BEA began to change its livery and dropped the 'speed key' logo, replacing it with a red square containing the letters 'BEA'. For the HEU fleet, the 'choppers' – including G-ANFH – were painted overall red with black and white trim and a white logo square. On 9th September 1961 *Fox-Hotel* flew from Hendon to Windsor Great Park, to celebrate the 50th anniversary of Britain's first 'aerial mail', staged over the same route by Gustav Hamel in a Blériot in 1911. At least on one occasion, in 1959, *Fox-Hotel* was fitted with a spray boom on the forward fuselage; the HEU took on a lot of contract work applying pesticides to fields. In April 1964 the airline's helicopter operations, predominantly the scheduled service to the Isles of Scilly plus charter work, were rationalised into BEA Helicopters; the term HEU having long since been dropped. *Fox-Hotel* soldiered on until February 1969 when it was sold to Autair at Luton, with around 4,000 flying hours to its credit. The

Whirlwind Series 1 G-ANFH in the red British European Airways colour scheme, 1962. *KEC*

transfer to Autair was brief, G-ANFH changing hands within the month to Bristow Helicopters at Redhill. Among other contracts, Bristow based the Whirlwind at Squires Gate, Blackpool, acting in support of nascent oil and gas exploration being carried out in the Irish Sea. Retired in 1971, *Fox Hotel* was stored at North Denes before returning to Redhill. The museum took charge of G-ANFH in 1978. While there are other examples of civilian Whirlwinds, both at WSM and elsewhere, *Fox-Hotel* has an exceptional aeronautical and social provenance.

Westland Whirlwind HAR.10 XR486
1964 | VIP transport helicopter | One 1,050shp Bristol Siddeley Gnome 10101 turboshaft
Westland Wessex HCC.4 XV733
1969 | VIP transport helicopter | Two 1,350shp Bristol Siddeley Gnome 11401/11501 coupled turboshafts

There are two helicopters at Weston-super-Mare resplendent in highly polished Signal Red and Royal Blue colours; a Whirlwind and a Wessex. From 1959 to 1998 such helicopters were well-known sights, either in reality or on TV screens, as they flew members of the Royal family all over the UK in the service of the Queen's Flight and, from 1st April 1995, 32 (The Royal) Squadron. Since 1998 the Royal Household has been responsible for its own helicopter operations, chartering a civil-registered Sikorsky S-76C when needed.

Trials with a Westland Dragonfly HC.4 in 1959 with the Benson-based Queen's Flight led to the introduction of a pair of Whirlwind HCC.8s in early 1960. These piston-engined machines were superseded by two HCC.12s, XR486 and XR487. The Mk.12 was essentially an HAR.10 military general purpose type with a VIP cabin and enhanced navigation aids. XR487 started crew training at Benson on 26th March 1964 and it was joined by XR486 on 6th June. Tragedy struck on 7th December 1967 when XR487 suffered rotor failure at about 500 feet and it crashed at Brightwalton in Berkshire; killing all four Queen's Flight personnel on board, including the officer commanding, Air Cdre J H L Blount DFC. Whirlwinds in general were grounded until a 'fix' was devised and inspections carried out. As a single-engined type, HM The Queen did not fly in the early helicopters, but HRH Prince Philip and other members of the Royal Family regularly did so.

Resulting from the crash, an order for a pair of twin-engined Wessex HCC.4s – based on the tactical transport HC.2 – was placed in 1967. With the delivery of the HCC.4s in 1969, XR486 was transferred to 15 Maintenance Unit at Wroughton on 27th July. Its career was not over; it joined 32 Squadron at Northolt on 2nd January 1970. Having had much of the 'Royal' fittings removed, the designation of XR486 was changed to HAR.10 on 15th February 1971. Retirement came on 9th December 1981 when the Whirlwind was issued to St Athan as instructional airframe 8727M. Offered up for disposal in October 1989 it was acquired by helicopter operator Roger Windley and flown to his premises at Tattershall Thorpe in Lincolnshire. Civil registered as G-RWWW – for Roger Windley's Whirlwind – it was granted permission to fly in Queen's Flight colours. Ownership was transferred to Whirlwind Helicopters Ltd in December 1993 at Redhill. *Double-Whisky* was retired by the summer of 1996 with just over 3,000 hours 'on the clock'. Acquired by the museum, the Royal Whirlwind arrived at WSM by road on 8th June 2000.

The second of the pair of Wessex HCC.4s, XV733 first flew at Yeovil on 13th May 1969 and was delivered to Benson on 11th July. HM Queen Elizabeth II had her first-ever helicopter flight, in XV733, in August 1977. Following the amalgamation of the Queen's Flight with 32 Squadron, usage of the Wessex was scaled down. XV733's last Royal sortie took place on 11th March 1998 and two days later it was ferried from Benson to storage at Shawbury. The helicopter was the 'star' of an auction staged by Phillips at its New Bond Street, London, salesroom on 25th October 2001. Thanks to a 'quickie' grant from the Heritage Lottery Fund, XV733 was 'hammered' to THM for £57,000. It moved by road to WSM on 15th November 2001. The other Wessex HCC.4, XV732, is with the RAF Museum Hendon. Whirlwind XR486 is a unique survivor and with XV733 also at the museum, almost the entire history of Queen's Flight helicopters is on display.

A glimpse of the VIP interior of Whirlwind HCC.12 XR486 at Benson in September 1964. *Roy Bonser*

Westland Wessex 60 Srs 1 G-AVNE
1967 | Transport helicopter | Two 1,350shp Bristol Siddeley Gnome H1200 Mk.660 coupled turboshafts

Following on from the Dragonfly/Widgeon and the Whirlwind, the Wessex was a heavily re-engineered version of a Sikorsky design, the S-58. It was aimed essentially at the military market, both in transport and anti-submarine versions. Towards the end of its production life, in 1965 Bristow Helicopters ordered 20 examples of a civil version, to replace its fleet of Whirlwinds and Widgeons engaged in worldwide contracts, specialising in support of oil exploration and extraction. Based upon the RAF's HC.2 tactical transport, the Wessex 60 could carry up to 16 passengers and featured a substantially enhanced navigation and communications fit. Throughout the remainder of the 1960s to the early 1980s, the Wessex 60 became the backbone of Bristow's operations.

The seventh Wessex 60 built; the museum's example was delivered to Bristow at Redhill in March 1968 as G-AVNE. In the summer of 1970 it was shipped to Indonesia, becoming PK-HBQ and from there moved to Bristow contracts in Australia (as VH-BHC) and Malaysia (as 9M-ASS). From March to November 1974 it was registered as G-AVNE again, but was shipped to Warri in Nigeria, becoming 5N-AJL, serving in the offshore oil support role until 1981. A series of accidents to Wessex 60s, culminating in 13 fatalities when G-ASWI crashed in the North Sea on 13th August 1981 resulted in the type's grounding. Along with the remainder of the fleet, *November-Echo* was returned to Redhill and, for purposes of flying in the UK, was given the Westland 'B Condition' ('trade-plate') identity G-17-3. The Wessex 60s were mostly stored at Westland's Oldmixon plant at WSM, although two were moved to Hurn in 1984 for potential operation by Sykes Aviation. These plans did not come to fruition and *November-Echo* was one of five that joined the museum in November 1987.

Westland Lynx Series 1 G-LYNX
1979 | General purpose helicopter | Two 1,350shp LHTEC CTS800 turboshafts

Alongside its larger and more powerful successor, the Wildcat, the Lynx is still in production at Yeovil 46 years after the first flight of the prototype. THM boasts the fifth prototype, an early shipboard version and the one-off stretched Mk.3, but G-LYNX as a world record holder holds all the 'cards'. With the Lynx paid off by the Fleet Air Arm on 17th March 2017 and the Army Air Corps not far behind, more of the type will hopefully join collections. Three 'nationals' hold examples: an AH.7 at Duxford, and AH.1 and an AH.7 at Middle Wallop AH.1 and Yeovilton with a pair of HAS.3s. As well as those at Weston presently there are four with 'regionals'.

Trevor Egginton flying specially-marked record-breaking Lynx G-LYNX in 1986. *Westland Helicopters*

The tenth production Lynx was built to AH.1 standard for use by Westland as a demonstrator and for development work and was appropriately civilian registered as G-LYNX and termed a Lynx Series 1. First flown at Yeovil on 18th May 1979 it was used for trials with the Franco-German Euromissile HOT and Rockwell AGM-114 Hellfire missiles and later a 20mm cannon installation. For some of this work a military identity was needed and the serial number ZB500 was allocated. It took part in the September 1980 airshow at Farnborough and was used for a while by Rolls-Royce at Hucknall.

Collaboration between Westland the Royal Aircraft Establishment in the early 1980s known as the British Experimental Rotor Programme (BERP) had created very efficient, composite, blades. The tips of the rotors were swept back (in a paddle shape) which delayed the onset of blade stall. Tested for the first time in August 1985 on a standard AH.1, the BERP blades made it a staggering 70mph faster than its colleagues. This encouraged the management and at a board meeting at Yeovil on 15th May 1986 it was decided to take on the USA and the USSR: an attempt would be made on the helicopter world speed record. A Sikorsky S-76A held the Class E1E (3,000 to 4,500kg category) record at 211mph and the absolute record rested with a Mil A-10 (a modified Mi-24 *Hind* gunship) at 229mph. The 'magic' number they were looking for was not Imperial, it was metric: Westland was going to be the first with a helicopter that could fly at 400km/h.

G-LYNX was chosen and subjected to an intensive ten-week transformation. The two 900shp Rolls-Royce Gem 2 turboshafts were replaced by 1,200shp Gem 60s with a water-methanol injection system. A low-set tailplane with end-plates was borrowed from a WG.30 to reduce the load on the tail rotor. State-of-the-art BERP III rotor blades completed the refit. On 11th August 1986 Westland chief test pilot Trevor Egginton and flight test observer Derek J Clews flew G-LYNX on an out-and-back 15km (9.32-mile) straight course over the Somerset Levels, near Glastonbury, to achieve 249.1mph. Four out-and-backs were flown and the speed was averaged over two runs; the last being the fastest as the weight reduced with fuel consumption. The speed of 249.1mph converted to 400.87km/h which was a fabulous feather in the cap for Westland. This combination beat the Soviets by a comfortable 20mph and the USA by a demonstrative 38mph. In June 2013 some of the world's press heralded the Eurocopter X3 as the world's fastest helicopter when it achieved 293mph, but that was a *compound* – rotor and propeller powered – helicopter, G-LYNX boasted no such augmentation and still holds the glory!

G-LYNX attended the Paris Salon at Le Bourget, France, in June 1987. From January 1991 it gave up its Gem turboshafts for LHTEC CTS800s and it was involved in intensive trials up to its retirement at Yeovil the following year. The Lynx was handed over to THM on 18th January 1995, but has been back to its birthplace twice. It was restored by AgustaWestland apprentices between October 2007 and July 2011. It was back again in 2016 – the thirtieth anniversary of the record flight – for Leonardo (as the company had become) to celebrate the centenary of the Westland brand.

Westland WG.30-100 G-BGHF
1979 | Transport helicopter | Two 1,135shp Rolls-Royce Gem Mk.530 turboshafts

Production of the WG.30 was terminated after forty units in 1988 and THM has four on the books at present: the prototype; the Series 200 prototype G-ELEC (first flown 3rd September 1983) and the prototype tactical transport TT300 G-HAUL (first flown 5th February 1986) and an example flown briefly on scheduled services in the USA, Series 100 N5840T, which is providing selfless service in the museum playground! Perhaps unsurprisingly, there are no examples in any other British museum. The WG.30 represents a rare Westland failure. It was an extrapolation of the Lynx connecting the military helicopter's dynamic system to a bigger, boxy fuselage. Intended to re-establish Westland in the commercial market, the WG.30 was aimed at the oil support operators but by the end of the programme Westland was desperately trying to find military customers. Launch customer British Airways Helicopters disposed of its trio after only four years; scheduled operations in the USA with Airspur and PanAm were all out of service by 1988. Largest operator was India, but after a couple of accidents the survivors of a fleet of 21 were grounded in early 1990. Chief test pilot Roy Moxam was at the controls on 10th April 1979 for the maiden flight of G-BGHF at Yeovil. During 1980 it took part is a series of exercises with the British army and in September 1983 was in India for an extensive sales tour. It was retired in 1986 and stored at Yeovil. With the demise of the project, it was transferred to WSM in December 1988. While the WG.30 is an episode Westland would sooner forget; the generosity of the company helped the museum considerably. As well as the three prototypes, a batch of seven Series 100s that had been operated in the USA was handed over to THM on 10th January 1997. The museum was able to exchange these, enabling other exhibits and projects to become reality.

The Helicopter Museum aircraft

Type	Identity	Built	Origin	Acquired	Notes
Aerospatiale Super Puma	G-TIGE	1982	France	30 Nov 2015	–
Agusta 109A-II	MM81205	1986	Italy	6 Oct 2010	–
Air & Space 18A	G-BVWL	1966	USA	22 Nov 2007	–
Barnett J4B	G-BWCW	1995	USA	29 Oct 2015	–
Bell Sioux AH.1	XT190	1965	USA	8 Jun 1995	–
Bell 47H-1	OO-SHW	1956	USA	1986	–
Bell UH-1H Iroquois	66-16579	1967	USA	29 Aug 1992	–
Bell 206C JetRanger	MM80927	1974	USA	2012	–
Bensen B-6	–	1984	USA	c2000	gyro-glider
Bensen B-8M #	G-ASCT	c1962	USA	1993	–
Bensen B-8M	G-BIGP	1981	USA	2010	plus another
Bensen B-8M Gyro-Boat	–	c1965	USA	11 Oct 2003	gyro-glider
Bölkow Bö 102 Helitrainer	D-HMQV	1960	Germany	c1977	tethered pilot trainer
Bölkow Bö 105M	81+00	1984	Germany	3 May 2007	–
Brantly B.2B	G-ATFG	1965	USA	21 Jan 2004	–
Brantly B.2B	G-OAPR	1965	USA	Apr 1989	airworthy
Bristol Sycamore Mk.3	G-ALSX	1951	Britain	May 1969	see profile
Bristol Sycamore HR.14	XL829	1957	Britain	17 Oct 2007	–
Bristol Belvedere HC.1	XG452	1960	Britain	5 Nov 1974	see profile
Bristol Belvedere HC.1	XG462	1961	Britain	1989	cockpit
Campbell Cricket #	G-AXRA	1969	Britain	Oct 2013	–
Campbell Cricket	G-BYMP	1999	Britain	16 Jan 2014	–
Campbell Cougar	G-BAPS	1973	Britain	May 1976	see profile
Cierva C.30A	AP506	1934	Britain	1986	–
Cierva Grasshopper 1 #	G-ARVN	1963	Britain	1993	see profile
Cierva Grasshopper III	G-AWRP	1969	Britain	1993	see profile
Cranfield Vertigo #	–	c1982	Britain	1991	man-powered helicopter
EHI EH-101 PP3	G-EHIL	1988	UK/Italy	26 Nov 1999	see profile
Fairey Ultra-Light Helicopter	G-AOUJ	1956	Britain	1979	–
Gadfly HDW-1 #	G-AVKE	1967	Britain	1978	–
Gyrodyne QH-50D	–	1966	USA	2 Oct 2014	shipborne drone

The Helicopter Museum aircraft continued...

Type	Identity	Built	Origin	Acquired	Notes
Hafner R-II Revoplane	–	1930	Austria	1979	see profile
Hiller UH-12C	G-ASTP	1961	USA	12 Oct 1989	–
Hughes OH-6A Cayuse	67-16506	1968	USA	Aug 1999	–
Husband Modac Hornet	–	2002	Britain	13 Nov 2004	–
Julian CD Wombat	G-WBAT	1990	Britain	9 Jul 2013	–
Kamov Ka-26 *Hoodlum*	DDR-SPY	1973	USSR	12 Jun 1995	–
McCulloch J-2	G-ORVB	1971	USA	21 Dec 2008	–
Mil Mi-1 *Hare*	2007	1959	USSR	2 Sep 1993	–
Mil Mi-2 *Hoplite*	SP-SAY	1985	USSR	24 Nov 1997	–
Mil Mi-4 *Hound*	09147	c1957	USSR	Jan 1994	–
Mil Mi-8PS *Hip*	618	c1979	USSR	5 Feb 2010	–
Mil Mi-24 *Hind-D*	96+26	1981	USSR	20 Feb 1995	see profile
Murray M-1 Helicopter	–	1954	Britain	Oct 1995	–
Piasecki HUP-3 Retriever*	622	1954	USA	Oct 1991	–
Piasecki H-21C Shawnee	FR-41	1957	USA	27 Jan 2016	–
PZL-Swidnik SM-2	1005	1961	Poland	10 Jun 1991	–
Robinson R22	G-OTED	1981	USA	Feb 2002	–
Saunders-Roe Skeeter AOP.12	XL811	1959	Britain	1993	–
Saunders-Roe AOP.12 #	XL736	1958	Britain	21 Jan 2011	–
Saunders-Roe AOP.12 #	XM557	1959	Britain	21 Jan 2011	–
Saunders-Roe AOP.12 #	XN345	1960	Britain	21 Jan 2011	–
Saunders-Roe P.531-2	XP165	1960	Britain	10 May 1983	–
Sikorsky S-55C #	S-881	1954	USA	1991	plus S-887
Sud Alouette II	A-41	1967	France	19 Feb 2008	–
Sud Super Frelon	F-OCMF	1967	France	28 Apr 1993	–
Sud Gazelle AH.1	ZB686	1983	France	2011	–
Sud Dauphin 2	F-WQAP	1979	France	19 Mar 2003	–
Sud-Ouest Djinn	FR-108	1959	France	1991	–

Robinson R22 G-OTED dwarfed by the Super Frelon F-OCMF. *Roger Richards*

Sud Dauphin 2 F-WQAP at THM. It set three world speed records in February 1980 between the London and Paris city heliports, including Paris-London in 63 minutes at 200.07mph. *Roger Richards*

The Helicopter Museum aircraft continued...

Type	Identity	Built	Origin	Acquired	Notes
Watkinson CG-4	–	1977	Britain	1978	man-powered autogyro
Westland Dragonfly HR.5	WG719	1952	USA/GB	Nov 1973	see profile
Westland Widgeon Srs.2	G-AOZE	1957	USA/GB	1986	see profile
Westland Whirlwind Srs.1 #	G-ANFH	1953	USA/GB	1980	see profile
Westland Whirlwind HAS.7 #	XG596	1957	USA/GB	11 Jul 1977	–
Westland Whirlwind HAS.7	XK940	1957	USA/GB	6 Jun 200	–
Westland Whirlwind HAR.10	XD163	1954	USA/GB	1982	–
Westland Whirlwind HAR.10 #	XP404	1962	USA/GB	1991	–
Westland Whirlwind HAR.10	XR486	1964	USA/GB	8 Jun 2000	see profile
Westland Whirlwind Srs.3 #	G-ANJV	1954	USA/GB	1982	–
Westland Whirlwind Srs.3	G-AODA	1955	USA/GB	7 Aug 1993	–
Westland Wessex HAS.1	XM330	1959	USA/GB	16 May 1994	–
Westland Wessex HC.2 #	XR526	1964	USA/GB	26 Aug 1999	–
Westland Wessex HAS.3	XM328	1960	USA/GB	Mar 2004	–
Westland Wessex HAS.3 #	XS149	1963	USA/GB	1987	–
Westland Wessex HCC.4*	XV733	1969	USA/GB	15 Nov 2001	see profile
Westland Wessex HU.5 #	XS486	1964	USA/GB	13 May 2004	–
Westland Wessex HU.5 #	XT472	1966	USA/GB	1987	–
Westland Wessex 60 Srs.1 #	G-ATBZ	1965	USA/GB	Jul 1988	–
Westland Wessex 60 Srs.1	G-AVNE	1967	USA/GB	24 Nov 1987	see profile
Westland Scout AH.1 #	XP886	1963	Britain	2011	–
Westland Wasp HAS.1	XT443	1966	Britain	18 Jan 1995	–
Westland Lynx 00-05	XW839	1974	Britain	11 Jan 1996	–
Westland Lynx HAS.2	XX910	1974	Britain	5 Dec 2000	–
Westland Lynx Srs.1	G-LYNX	1979	Britain	18 Jan 1995	see profile
Westland Lynx 3	ZE477	1984	Britain	1989	–
Westland WG.30-100	G-BGHF	1979	Britain	22 Dec 1988	see profile
Westland WG.30-100	N5840T	1982	Britain	10 Jan 1997	–
Westland WG.30-200	G-ELEC	1983	Britain	7 Dec 2001	–
Westland WG.30 TT300	G-HAUL	1986	Britain	1991	–
Westland WG.25 Mote	–	1975	Britain	2012	drone helicopter
Wetland Wisp	–	1976	Britain	2012	drone helicopter
Westland WG.33	–	1978	Britain	1980	engineering mock-up
Westland Wideye	–	1979	Britain	2012	drone helicopter, plus mock-up
Westland Sharpeye	'ZS782'	1982	Britain	2012	drone helicopter engineering mock-up
Yamaha Motors R-50	–	1986	Japan/USA	2012	agricultural drone

Notes: * – illustrated in the colour section. # – reserve collection

Also in Somerset
Fleet Air Arm Museum

Located at Royal Naval Air Station Yeovilton, the headquarters of naval aviation, the Fleet Air Arm Museum tells the story from primitive biplanes to the onset of the Lockheed Martin F-35s. The 'Leading Edge' hall concentrates on aviation technology and is the home of the British prototype BAC/Sud Concorde, G-BSST. The award-winning 'Carrier' exhibition involves a 'flight' to an aircraft carrier deck and a tour of its operational quarters. This is a national collection and it is covered in depth in the sister volume *Great Aviation Collections of Britain*. **www.fleetairarm.com**

CHAPTER 26
SUFFOLK

'Warthog' Twin Base
Bentwaters Cold War Museum

Bentwaters
www.bcwm.org.uk

From the centre of the airfield at Bentwaters to its neighbour, Woodbridge, deep in the Rendlesham Forest is just three miles. From 1958 this proximity was exploited as the McDonnell F-101 Voodoos of the 81st Tactical Fighter Wing (TFW) occupied both airfields – the unique twin base was born. For many enthusiasts, these two airfields had an appeal all of their own and the rapid pull out of the USAF in the early 1990s left a void that seemed impossible to fill. As Bentwaters settled into light industry, storage, leisure and housing developments in 2001 the Bentwaters Aviation Society (BAS) began to see if some form of museum could be established. At first, thoughts centred on leasing a room in the control tower but when the team was shown to the Wing Command Post on the northern perimeter, ambitions were expanded. Inside were a war operations room and the so-called 'battle cabin': there was nothing like this available to the public anywhere in Britain. Work started on refurbishing the appreciably sized, air strike-hardened building in May 2003 – a determined band of eight volunteers achieved miracles. The Bentwaters Cold War Museum (BCWM) was opened on 20th May 2007 and visitors can attest to the hard graft and attention to detail that has created a memorable experience. With consoles and barrages of communications equipment, maps and status boards the tensions and disciplines generated while controlling jets as they were vectored to their objectives is brought vividly to life. The building was used as the command post for Operation 'El Dorado Canyon' on 15th April 1986 during a punitive raid on Colonel Muammar Gaddafi's Libya by British-based General Dynamics F-111s. During the run up and execution of the First Gulf War 1990-1991, Bentwaters was the point of support for the deployed Fairchild A-10A Thunderbolt II forces.

From Day One the wish was to acquire suitable aircraft, but finding machines with a direct Bentwaters link proved to be nigh on impossible, so it was decided to acquire jets from that era. The first to arrive, in 2005 was Gloster Meteor D.16 WH453 which had last served as a target drone; it is being restored to its original fighter guise as an F.8 in the BCWM's workshop. Since then, largely thanks to the generosity of BAS members, an impressive array of hardware has been gathered. In May 2016 the arrival of an A-10A that served from Bentwaters in the 1980s was a major coup.

Above: A-10A Thunderbolt IIs were stationed at the twin bases of Bentwaters and Woodbridge, 1978 to 1993. *KEC*

The Bentwaters Wing Command Post, an incredible glimpse of the Cold War. *Graham Haynes – BCWM*

Twins with different backgrounds

Until the advent of the 81st TFW in July 1958, the twin bases had very different histories. Woodbridge was carved out of the Rendlesham Forest to create a huge emergency airfield – a safe haven for Allied aircraft limping their way back from operations over Europe. A 12,000ft runway – including over-runs – was laid down, with three 'lanes' to accommodate a surge in arrivals and FIDO fog dispersal equipment was installed. The base was ready for operations in November 1943 and it handled over 4,000 emergency landings. The secluded location meant that Woodbridge was also a great place for units that would benefit from not being overlooked and from May 1944 the Bomb Ballistics Unit was resident for two years. Its Avro Lancasters, de Havilland Mosquitos and Handley Page Halifaxes worked in association with the highly secret ranges up the coast at Orfordness. The Blind Landing Experimental Unit was formed at Woodbridge in July 1945, moving to Martlesham Heath the following April. The airfield was handed over to the USAF in June 1952 with Republic F-84 Thunderjets of the 79th Fighter Bomber Squadron its first inmates. With the setting up of the twin base concept in 1958, Woodbridge mirrored the activity of Bentwaters up to the deactivation of the 81st TFW on 1st July 1993. The airfield was taken over by the British Army on 1st September 2006, becoming the home of 23 Engineer (Air Assault) Regiment.

A conventional three-runway airfield, Bentwaters was the domain of RAF tactical fighter units from December 1944 with North American Mustangs and Supermarine Spitfires. The Gloster Meteor IIIs of 124 Squadron heralded the jet age in October 1945. The last RAF presence was 230 Operational Conversion Unit with Meteors and de Havilland Vampires from October 1946 to August 1949. After that Bentwaters was prepared for the USAF. North American F-86A Sabres of the 91st Fighter Interceptor Squadron arrived in April 1954 and Sabre units were in the majority until July 1958 when the 81st TFW settled in at both Bentwaters and Woodbridge. The 81st flew F-101s, giving way to McDonnell F-4 Phantom IIs and on 24th August 1978 the first three 'Warthogs' – as the A-10As were nicknamed – arrived. Between the twin bases in the late 1970s the 81st had an establishment of 108 aircraft. The Thunderbolts worked hard, regularly deploying to forward operating bases at Aalhorn, Leipheim, Norvenich and Sembach in West Germany and engaged in exercises across Europe. In the spring of 1988 the 81st lost two squadrons to Alconbury as part of the 10th TFW. With the Berlin Wall in pieces and Germany unified, the political and strategic landscape of Europe had changed beyond belief. Wind down of the 81st was rapid, and the last two A-10s departed for Spangdahlem in Germany on 23rd March 1993. The Americans pulled out completely on 1st July 1993 – the 'Peace Dividend' in Suffolk had been swift.

Unloading A-10A 80-0219 at Bentwaters, 23th May 2015. *Graham Haynes – BCWM*

Fairchild GA-10A Thunderbolt II 80-0219
1981 | Close support strike | Two 9,065lb st General Electric TF34-GE-100 turbofans

Anyone spending time close to the gunnery ranges at Donna Nook on the Lincolnshire coast in the late 1970s through to the early 1990s would have been listening for the turbine whine of A-10A 'Warthogs'. This would be followed by a sensation that is difficult to describe. Aiming for the flag-like targets, the pilot would press the 'go-button' and a deep 'thrrrrrummmm' would be heard *and* felt as a puff of smoke erupted from the nose of the jet. Within milliseconds there would be a series of dull thuds as shells impacted the shoreline. That's what the Thunderbolt II was all about: a seven-barrel General Electric GAU-8/A Avenger Gatling-like gun dispensing 30mm armour-piercing shells at 4,500 rounds per minute. Pilots had to be disciplined; the normal peacetime loading was 750 rounds – just ten seconds of 'squirt' time. On pylons underneath the wing and the centre section a staggering 16,000lb of sundry ordnance could also be carried. Fairchild won the USAF's A-X competition for an aircraft intended to stop Soviet tanks lurching out from behind the 'Iron Curtain'. The prototype flew in May 1972 and 716 units followed. Fairchild acquired Republic in September 1965 and with that legacy there was only one name for the new machine – Thunderbolt, after the hard-hitting, robust P-47s of World War Two. Around 280 A-10As were on the USAF's operational inventory in 2017 with no sign of retirement: the threats may have changed, but the need for this unique machine remains.

Until 2015 only one A-10A 'Warthog' was preserved in Britain, in the American Air Museum at Duxford. The volunteer team at the Bentwaters Cold War Museum (BCWM) had long coveted the example that was Alconbury's 'gate guardian'. Persistence was rewarded on 24th May 2016 when 80-0219 arrived on a low-loader. With respect to the other aircraft in the BCWM collection, the A-10A is not 'of the era', or likely to have visited, for seven years this very machine was operational at Bentwaters – it's come home. Congratulations to all who made this possible. Built at Hagerstown, Maryland, 80-0219 touched down at Bentwaters on 14th December 1981 and joined the resident 81st Tactical Fighter Wing's (TFW) 509th Tactical Fighter Squadron. It transferred with the 509th to the 10th TFW at Alconbury in May 1988. A technical problem on 4th April 1989 resulted in an over-run of Alconbury's runway and its flying days were over. It was decided to turn it into a display airframe and technically the designation was changed to GA-10A – the 'G' denoting permanently grounded. With the continued contraction of the USAF enclave at Alconbury, BCWM engaged in negotiations to take on 80-0219. In February 2016 a formal agreement was reached, the Warthog was presented on loan from the National Museum of the USAF, Dayton, Ohio.

Bentwaters Cold War Museum aircraft

Type	Identity	Built	Origin	Acquired	Notes
English Electric Lightning F.53	ZF581	1967	Britain	22 May 2011	–
Fairchild GA-10A Thunderbolt II	80-0219	1981	USA	24 May 2015	see profile
Gloster Meteor D.16	WH453	1951	Britain	18 Jan 2005	–
Hawker Hunter GA.11	XE707	1955	Britain	1 Jul 2010	–
Hawker Siddeley Harrier GR.3	ZD667	1986	Britain	Feb 2013	–
McDonnell Phantom FGR.2	XV401	1968	USA	Aug 2013	–
McDonnell Phantom FGR.2	XV497	1969	USA	24 Nov 2012	–
SEPECAT Jaguar GR.1A	XX741	1974	GB/France	16 Aug 2009	–

A Walk in the Woods
Norfolk and Suffolk Aviation Museum

Flixton
www.aviationmuseum.net

Pubs have played an important role in the development of the exceptional Norfolk and Suffolk Aviation Museum. A meeting at 'The Fleece' in Bungay in 1973 found sufficient like-minded enthusiasts keen to lend a hand establishing a museum. The following year the Norfolk and Suffolk Aviation Society was formed and Jim Patterson, a veteran flyer from World War One who ran the Post Office in Flixton village, offered the used of a Nissen hut at the back of his premises. Before Jim really took what his offer meant, an Avro Anson C.19 VL349 and a replica Supermarine Spitfire along with lots of artefacts from aviation 'archaeology' excavations had arrived! Salvage of Gloster Meteor F.8 WF643 from Coltishall was completed in May 1975 and that also moved in. Autogyro pioneer, Wg Cdr Kenneth Horatio Wallis MBE presided over the official opening on 8th May 1976 and even provided a display in his Wallis WA-116 G-ATHM. This was the start of a long relationship between and Ken and the museum; he was soon to become is president. (For more on Ken see *Founding Fathers* in Chapter 18.)

Hunter FGA.9 XG254 outside Flixton's main display hangar. *Ken Ellis*

USAAF Station 125 Bungay, looking southeast in late 1944. A Liberator of 446th BG is outside the hangar; the control tower can be seen above the hangar, beyond the taxi track. *KEC*

Flixton was the obvious location for a museum, the village lying on the western edge of Bungay airfield, USAAF Station 125, with the Communal Site immediately to the south of the church. From December 1942 it was home to the Consolidated B-24 Liberators of the 329th Bomb Squadron; the rest of the 93rd Bomb Group (BG) settling on Hardwick. In June 1943 the 329th joined its comrades at Hardwick and Bungay was prepared for an entire bomb group. The B-24s of the 'Bungay Buckaroos', the 446th BG, arrived on 4th November 1943, to begin a long association with the little village, with Bungay and Norwich. After 273 combat missions, the B-24s departed for the USA on 5th July 1945. The 446th BG Association has maintained strong bonds with the village, and later the museum, ever since. From 1946 to 1955 Bungay was used for munitions storage and beyond that the runways hosted crop sprayers and for a while a parachute club was also resident. One runway remains, reduced to half-width, and some of the perimeter track can be discerned but otherwise, there is little to see. At the museum, the men of the 446th are commemorated in fine style.

Fund raising and museum raising

Visitors to the shed behind the Post Office were increasing and it was unfair to put upon Jim Patterson for much longer. This is when another hostelry entered the story; Andrew Gilham was then the landlord of the 'Buck', on the northern edge of the village and well-patronised by the 446th during the war. Behind the pub were two meadows and Andrew offered to lease them to the society. The airframes and artefacts at the Post Office yard were vacated and the new site was up and running for visitors on 24th April 1977, by which time the society had taken the name Norfolk and Suffolk Aviation Museum (N&S). These two fields are still in use by the museum, but later the opportunity to purchase land between them and the banks of the River Waveney to the north was taken up. Much of this parcel of land would not lend itself to be an aviation museum, but with amazing vision N&S developed it into the 350-yard long Adair Walk, offering a peaceful stroll along a wheelchair-friendly raised boardwalk down to the river. The first section is edged with trees planted on behalf of visitors and members in memory of their loved ones and there is a willow plantation. When in season, varieties of wild plants, butterflies, dragonflies and damselflies add to the splendour of this area. This is a wonderful diversion and an incredible example of an aviation museum remembering that there is much more to life than just aircraft!

Exhibits and displays have been funded by the generosity of N&S members and from constant fund raising. In particular, present-day museum chairman Ian Hancock became a significant benefactor; at the time of writing he had ten aircraft on loan to the museum. Ian also penned the biography of Ken Wallis. An appeal to raise £50,000 to finance a display hangar in September 1983 was launched by Ken. This was brought about significant reshaping of the site. For flood protection purposes the northern portion needed to be raised. This was achieved with the help of Waveney District Council which arranged for the delivery, without cost, of thousands of tons of rubble. The council was always in need of sites to 'park' such material – a win-win situation. The concrete base went down in 1988 but it was 1996 before the self-funded hangar was up and running.

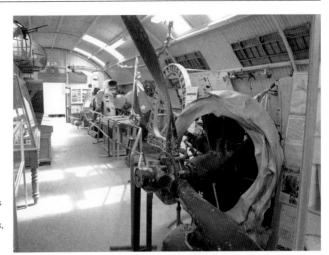

The substantial remains of Vickers Wellington I L4288 of 9 Squadron which crashed at Sapiston, Suffolk, on 30th October 1939 within the Bomber Command hall. *Ken Ellis*

Museums within a museum

In October 1991 N&S welcomed the Royal Observer Corps Museum to the site and individual buildings dedicated to different themes have become a hallmark ever since. A Nissen hut dedicated to the 446th BG was unveiled by 'Buckaroo' veterans in 1993. Other displays include Bomber Command, air-sea rescue, bomber decoys – a particular fascination of museum stalwart and curator Huby Fairhead – and simulated flying training through the impressive collection of Link Trainers – of which more anon. On 28th July 1998 Ken Wallis presented his Wallbro Monoplane replica G-BFIP on loan to N&S. In 1910 Horace Samuel and Percival Valentine Wallis – respectively Ken's father and uncle – built and flew a steel tubed-framed monoplane powered by a 25hp JAP engine. Built by the brothers Wallis, it was named the Wallbro. The monoplane did not last long; it was destroyed in its shed during a violent storm. In 1974 Ken and his cousin, Geoffrey, and Percival's son, embarked on the construction of a replica, powered by a converted McCulloch engine. Ken was at the controls for its first flight, from Swanton Morley, in 1978.

Ipswich Borough Council made a substantial donation to the museum in 2000. The former Ipswich Airport was being redeveloped and a Boulton and Paul hangar, erected in 1936, was dismantled and handed over. A successful application was made to the Heritage Lottery Fund for £77,000 to conserve and re-erect what would be a display hall and an exhibit in its own right. The ever-willing Ken Wallis was on hand to officially open this on 25th April 2004. Ken's steadfast support of N&S was honoured in 4th July 2010 when the 5,000 square foot Ken Wallis Hall was inaugurated. The following year, on 15th May, Ken supplied on loan another Wallis type to go in the new building: Wallis WA-116 G-AVDH, which stood in for studio shots of famous *Little Nellie*, G-ARZB, in the 1967 Bond, James Bond movie *You Only Live Twice*. Ken Wallis died, aged 97, on 1st September 2013 and, sadly, both the Wallbro and the WA-116 were removed the following April, returning to the Wallis family. During January 2015 N&S came to the aid of the Boulton Paul Heritage Project, taking on two replicas (the P.6 biplane and the forward fuselage of an Overstrand biplane bomber) and other artefacts that had previously been held in store at the RAF Museum Cosford. The Norfolk and Suffolk Aviation Museum – East Anglia's Aviation Heritage Centre – is one of Britain's most distinctive collections and continues to evolve and adapt.

de Havilland Sea Vixen FAW.1 XJ482
1958 | Shipborne all-weather fighter | Two 11,250lb st Rolls-Royce Avon 208 turbojets

The N&S Sea Vixen was the ninth production Mk.1, the first issued to a Fleet Air Arm (FAA) unit and a part of a famous aerobatic team. First flown at Christchurch on 30th September 1958, it was delivered to Yeovilton on 3rd November, ready the formation of 700Y Squadron the following day. The squadron was the Sea Vixen Intensive Flying Trials Unit and XJ482 carried out deck landings on HMS *Victorious* in early May 1959. It was briefly seconded to the Royal Aircraft Establishment Thurleigh on 21st May. By July it had been ferried to the Vickers test airfield at Wisley for cold weather 'soaks' in a climatic chamber, presumably at nearby Brooklands. XJ482 re-joined FAA service on 5th November 1959 at Yeovilton, with 766B Squadron. The unit was tasked with all-weather training and the suffix 'B' was applied to the element operating Sea Vixens; the remainder was flying de Havilland Sea Venom FAW.21s. The Venoms had gone by late 1960 and the unit dropped the 'B'. XJ482 was carrying the code '713' – which it wears today – by this time. Stardom beckoned from March 1962 when it became a part of 'Fred's Five', an aerobatic team led by Lt Cdr Peter 'Fred' Reynolds. The debut was staged at Upavon on 16th June 1962 and the season's commitments included appearances at Farnborough that September; the team disbanded at the end of the year. XJ482 was

Sea Vixen FAW.1s of 766 Squadron 'Fred's Five' performing at Upavon in June 1962: XJ478, Flixton's XJ482, XJ493, XJ565 and XJ575. Two others from this formation are extant: XJ575 is at the de Havilland Aircraft Museum (Chapter 12) and the cockpit of XJ575 is at Wellesbourne Mountford (Chapter 29). *Roy Bonser*

retired to the Air Engineering School at Lee-on-Solent as an instructional airframe, serial A2598 in August 1969, and it spent some time as the station's 'gate guardian'. Flight Refuelling at Tarrant Rushton was developing a target drone version of the Sea Vixen, the D.3, and it purloined XJ482 as a static rig for what the firm called the 'Universal Drone Pack', later moving it to the factory site at Wimborne Minster. It was from here that N&S acquired the airframe and it was delivered, courtesy of the Navy's Mobile Aircraft Repair, Transport and Salvage Unit, on 25th November 1979.

Felixstowe F.5 nose section
1918 | Maritime patrol and anti-submarine flying-boat | Two 350hp Rolls-Royce Eagle VIII pistons

For the second time in this book, we come to an exhibit that last served in someone's garden. (See Chapter 23 for Newark's 'centenarian' Lancaster.) Within the eclectic mix at Flixton, this exhibit is by far the star – the largest surviving element of a Great War flying-boat extant in Britain. This is another example of a 'local' exhibit that's really a 'national'. (The hull of a US-built F-5L is held in deep store by the American National Air and Space Museum.) Although Curtiss H.12 'Large America' flying-boats were operated successfully by the Royal Naval Air Service (RNAS), the type proved to have hydrodynamic shortcomings. The station commander of RNAS Felixstowe, Wg Cdr John Cyril Porte, who had worked with Glenn Curtiss in 1914, led a redesign that combined the wings and tail surfaces from the Curtiss with an entirely new hull. This was evolved through the F.2, F.2A, F.3 to the definitive F.5,

The nose section of the Felixstowe F.5 flying-boat; an amazing survival and a very significant exhibit. *Ken Ellis*

the prototype flying in May 1918. F.5s continued to serve with the RAF through to 1925; some were still on charge with the Felixstowe-based Flying Boat Development Unit in 1924. Over thirty were built, by Boulton and Paul at Norwich assembling and flying them from Felixstowe; Phoenix Dynamo (precursors of English Electric) at Bradford with assembly and flight test at Brough, Shorts at Rochester and S E Saunders at Cowes.

An article in the *East Anglian Daily Times* for 15th September 1989 got the N&S team's attention. It reported that developer working near Felixstowe had found ten feet of the bow of a wooden flying-boat standing with its nose in the air, having been used as a potting shed for six decades. With the help of Felixstowe Museum and the History and Museum Society of Felixstowe, the precious and fragile artefact was salvaged and taken to Flixton. Investigations revealed that it was an F.5

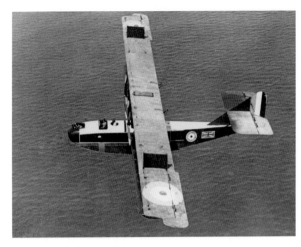

A Felixstowe F.5, the RAF's first practical maritime patroller. *KEC*

and that very likely it had been built by Boulton and Paul. The Norfolk and Suffolk Aviation Museum had got its hands on an exhibit that was probably built in Norfolk and served in Suffolk! A painstaking restoration was carried out by Ken Collinson and Derek Small, including a replica Lewis gun in the nose position. Ironically, in 1999 the RAF Museum handed on another section of an F.5, about eight feet long. Size doesn't necessarily matter: the Flixton F.5 is an exceptionally important exhibit.

Flexiform Solo Striker / Moult Trike G-MTFK
1987 | Single-seat microlight | One 250cc Fuji piston

Love them or loathe them, there are many microlights in British collections. And rightly so, vast numbers have been operated, designed and built in Britain, providing many pilots with the ability to fly and own an aircraft, to turn almost any field into an aerodrome and to be rid of hangar fees. Development has broadly taken two routes: the flex-wing and the more traditional three-axis (ailerons, elevators, rudder) format. It is the former category – flex-wings – that concerns us here. While working on how to bring back to earth spacecraft, National Aeronautics and Space Administration (NASA) engineer Francis Rogallo, and his wife Gertrude, designed a collapsible delta wing that could give a capsule a degree of control, a considerable improvement on a group of parachutes relying on wind conditions. The Rogallo wing, as it became known, was not adopted by NASA but it spawned the global sport of foot-launched hang-gliding in the 1960s. This soon evolved into powered hang-gliders and to the more sophisticated microlights: all using the Rogallo wing. Hang-gliders are controlled by the pilot shifting his weight using a triangular shaped frame. On a microlight, a 'pod' is hung from the jib-like main-post, in this minimalistic 'fuselage' sits the pilot (and a passenger on many types), with an engine at the back driving a pusher propeller. There is no rudder. All this sits on tricycle undercarriage and from this the 'pod' gets its name: 'trike'. Conventional fixed-wing pilots often find converting to flex-wings difficult; push forward on the triangle frame and the microlight climbs, pull back and it descends: the opposite response from a stick or a yoke on a three-axis system. Moving the frame from side to side produces roll, twisting it creates yaw. The controls change the position of the trike in relation to the wing and once that is grasped, piloting becomes intuitive.

Fox-Kilo has a span of 37ft 4in and empty weight of around 250lb. With low residual values flex-wing microlights are cheap to acquire, take up little space and can easily be suspended above other exhibits. With colourful wings and the 'I could do that!' appeal, they are both curator- and visitor-friendly; no wonder there are so many preserved. The wing is the complex element of a microlight and most of the major manufacturers concentrated on building and marketing wings, allowing purchasers to choose a trike from another source or, in the case of G-MTFK, for the owner to create their own. Based in Macclesfield, Cheshire, Flexiform Sky Sails Solo Striker, Dual Striker and Striker Light wings were built in the hundreds, but the company manufactured only about 30 two-seat trikes in the early 1980s. Beccles-based David Ivan Moult built his own trike, powered by a 250cc Fuji, for his Flexiform Solo Striker wing. The combination was registered as G-MTFK on 23rd March 1987 and its constructor's number reflected the owner/builder's initials – DIM-01. It was flown from Bungay airfield and had the honour of being the last aircraft to fly from the former Eighth Air Force base. *Fox-Kilo* was retired in 1990, with one last taxi taking place on 3rd July 1994 after which David Moult presented it to the museum.

Above: Flixton's unique simulated flying training display: in the foreground is the 1950s D4 Provost version. *Ken Ellis*

Left: The cockpit of the Aviation Trainers Ltd-built D4, simulating the Percival Provost. *Ken Ellis*

Link Trainers: ANT 18, D4, D4/2

All of the exhibits profiled in this book flew or were *intended* to fly, except for these. Many museums have an example of a Link Trainer, but N&S has turned these under-rated devices into a specialisation. A section of the museum is devoted to them and, by connecting one of its ANT 18s to a modern-day computer simulator programme is introducing youngsters to these quaint, stubby winged pioneers. Link Trainers were lovingly referred to as 'Blue Boxes' by instructors and pupils alike from the 1930s to the 1950s. Several concerns had tried to build ground-based trainers to give the 'feel' of flying from as early as 1910, but it was American Edwin Albert Link who developed the first practical instrument – 'blind flying' – simulator. Link's name became a generic brand for this form of training. His father ran the Link Piano and Organ Company at Binghampton, New York. He was convinced that he could extend the company's product base and in 1930 he patented 'An effective Aeronautical Training Aid – a novel, profitable amusement device', which had three-axis movement – pitch, roll and yaw. It was not a success, but Link persevered concentrating on blind flying training and soon got the attention of the Army Air Corps. Instrument training was a protracted, expensive and risky business.

The breakthrough came with the Model C of 1936 which could rotate through 360 degrees horizontally thereby adding a compass. Instruments were operated either mechanically or by vacuum and a simple form of analogue computer took the pupil, completely 'in the dark' under the hood, for a 'flight'. The N&S website has a superb section on this fascinating subject and provides a great briefing: "The simulated course is automatically recorded and traced by the three-wheeled course plotter – the self-propelled and steerable 'crab' – across paper, or a map on the instructor's desk. A duplicated instrument panel is also present, electronically harmonised with those in the Trainer's cockpit. This miniature aeroplane is pivoted on a universal joint mounted on an octagonal turntable, which in turn is free to rotate in azimuth on a square base. Between the fuselage and the turntable are four supporting bellows, which are inflated or deflated by a vacuum turbine. Its valves are operated as the pupil moves the control column, and realistically recreates most of the sensations and 'feel' of flying." Stall and spin recovery could be simulated as could rough weather. By the late 1930s Link trainers were in great demand and exports blossomed, with the Luftwaffe as an early customer and the RAF acquiring its first in 1937. Post-war the D4 was introduced which extended its capabilities to radio navigation techniques. Today's multi-million pound simulator industry owes a huge debt to the pioneer work of Edwin Link.

N&S has four Link Trainers, almost certainly the largest concentration in Britain. Led by Ray Kidd, a small team of volunteers has worked miracles, with two examples fully functioning. Just like their airborne counterparts, looking after the Links requires extensive knowledge and sourcing spares is a constant task. Appearing in 1940, the Army-Navy Trainer Model 18 – ANT 18 – was based upon the North American AT-6 Texan and SNJ trainers. The museum has two of these, one was acquired from an Air Training Corps unit in North London. Based on the Percival Provost, the N&S D4 was built in the early 1950s by Aviation Trainers Ltd, utilising Link sub-assemblies. The D4/2 is Jet Provost-based and manufactured in 1955. This provides a hands-on cockpit experience for school visits and special events.

Percival Provost T.1 WV605
1954 | Basic trainer | One 550hp Alvis Leonides 126 piston

The Percival Prentice did not cover itself in glory as the RAF's basic trainer, so much so that a replacement was being sought by the late 1940s. With the Provost, Percival surpassed itself, production running to 464 units, including extensive exports. The last Provosts were retired from RAF service in 1969, but since 1955 the Provost-derived Jet Provost had entered service and it led to a dynasty including the pressurised T.5 and the Strikemaster, the last example flying in 1982. Eight intact Provost T.1s are with British museums. Built at Luton, WV605 was issued to 22 Flying Training School (FTS) at Syerston on the last day of March 1954. It transferred to Feltwell and 3 FTS on 25th August 1954. Final service came with 6 FTS at Ternhill from 15th June 1957; the school moved to Acklington on 24th July 1961. Retired to 27 Maintenance Unit at Shawbury on 13th March 1964, WV605 was acquired by Macclesfield College of Further Education, Cheshire, as an instructional airframe on 31st October 1966. The college presented the Provost to the Shuttleworth Trust in 1970, who in turn loaned it to the Torbay Aircraft Museum at Higher Blagdon, Devon, in 1971. Having acquired an example of its own (WV679 which is now at Wellesbourne), Torbay returned WV605 to Shuttleworth, and it was put into store at Henlow. Acquired by N&S it moved to its new home on 14th September 1978. Two years later it was painted in the colours and codes – 'T-B' – that it wore while flying in Norfolk skies form Feltwell,.

Vickers Valetta C.2 VX580
1950 | VIP transport | Two 1,976hp Bristol Hercules 230 pistons

For reasons best known unto itself, while honouring Malta by naming its new tactical transport after the island's capital, the RAF spelt it Valetta with one 'I', not two. Be that as it may... The Valetta was a tactical transport version of the Vickers Viking airliner; the prototype of the military version having its maiden flight in June 1947. Production amounted to 252 Valettas from 1948 to 1952. The majority were the C.1 parachute and freight version, 20 were finished as C.2 VIP transports and 40 as T.3 trainers. The RAF Museum keeps C.2 VX573 in deep store at Cosford and there is a cockpit section at Doncaster That makes the N&S machine the only intact example on public display. The museum is well aware that in 2018 VX580 will have chalked up half a century exposed to East Anglian weather and has instigated a limited restoration programme. The Valetta is a complex aircraft and this task is no simple undertaking.

First flying from Brooklands on 1st February 1950, VX580 was destined for a busy and cosmopolitan career with the RAF. From 28th August 1950 VX580 was with the Handling Squadron at Manby for an eight-day stint; the unit compiled the Pilot's Notes reference series and there can't have been many alterations from the text for the C.1 version. After that VX580 settled into a life of serving a variety of transport outfits, interspersed with update programmes and periods of storage. It plied the airways with: appropriately the Malta Communications Squadron at Luqa (from February 1953); 114 Squadron at Kabrit, Egypt (from December 1954); the Aden Station Flight at Khormaksar (January 1955); the Middle East Air Force Communications Squadron at Nicosia, Cyprus (October 1955); and finally the Metropolitan Communications Squadron at Northolt from 28th June 1962. Flt Lt William Gospill captained VX580 on a sortie from Northolt to Coltishall on 12th December 1968 where a group of Air Scouts and their leaders were picked up for the short flight to Horsham St Faith, Norwich Airport. Christmas had come early for the Air Scouts, after landing they were gifted the Valetta with the intention that it be turned into a classroom. VX580 was presented to N&S in March 1982 and working parties began to dismantle the big machine. Roading the 62ft 11in long fuselage would be a challenge, but the centre section plus engine nacelles left

A Chinook HC.1 of 7 Squadron delivering Valetta C.2 VX580, 27th May 1983. *Norfolk and Suffolk Aviation Museum*

a width of about 28ft. Taking the airframe apart to reduce this would be very difficult. Enter 7 Squadron at Odiham, the unit offered to lift the fuselage slung underneath one of its Boeing Chinooks as a training exercise. On 27th May 1983 HC.1 ZA675 flew into Norwich Airport and picked up the Valetta, depositing it gently at Flixton after a half-hour flight.

A replica of the 'Colditz Cock' glider; the original was built over the winter of 1944-1945 in an attic of Colditz Castle, Germany, by inmates of the Offizierslager IV-C prisoner of war camp. *Ken Ellis*

Norfolk and Suffolk Aviation Museum aircraft

Type	Identity	Built	Origin	Acquired	Notes
Antonov C.14	–	1992	Russia	2003	hang-glider
Avro Anson C.19	VL349	1947	Britain	Jan 1974	–
Avro Vulcan K.2	XL445	1962	Britain	29 Jul 2005	cockpit
Beagle Terrier	G-ARLP	1948	Britain	5 Jul 2016	–
Bensen B-7	'LHS-1'	1966	USA	1978	–
Boeing PT-27 Kaydet	'FJ801'	1942	USA	26 Jun 2012	composite
Boulton Paul P.6	'X-25'	2001	Britain	19 Jan 2015	replica
Boulton Paul Overstrand	'K4556'	2011	Britain	19 Jan 2015	replica forward fuselage
Bristol Sycamore HR.14	XG518	1955	Britain	24 Feb 1997	–
Bristol Sycamore HR.14	XG523	1955	Britain	25 Jan 1997	cockpit
Colditz Cock	JTA	2000	Germany	2004	replica glider
Dassault Mystère IVA*	79	1954	France	18 Nov 1978	–
de Havilland Vampire T.11	XK624	1956	Britain	11 Apr 1980	–
de Havilland Sea Vixen FAW.1	XJ482	1958	Britain	27 Nov 1979	see profile
EoN Primary	CDN	1948	Britain	27 Apr 1997	plus another
English Electric Canberra B.2/6	WG789	1952	Britain	6 Mar 2002	cockpit
English Electric Canberra PR.3	'WE168'	2000	Britain	2002	cockpit re-creation – see note
English Electric Canberra T.4	WH840	1954	Britain	Mar 1994	–
English Electric Canberra B(I).8	XM279	1959	Britain	Mar 1994	cockpit
English Electric Lightning F.1*	XG329	1959	Britain	1993	–

Norfolk and Suffolk Aviation Museum aircraft continued…

Type	Identity	Built	Origin	Acquired	Notes
Eurowing Goldwing	G-MMWL	1983	Britain	15 Jul 2007	–
Fairchild 24C8F	N16676	1936	USA	18 Mar 2003	–
Felixstowe F.5	–	1918	Britain	1990	nose section – see profile
Flexiform Striker/Moult Trike	G-MTFK	1987	Britain	Jul 1994	see profile
FMA Pucará	A-528	1979	Argentina	24 Jul 1994	–
Fokker D.VIII	'694'	1984	Germany	1991	scale replica
Fokker Friendship 200	G-BDVS	1963	Netherlands	17 Dec 1996	cockpit
Folland Gnat T.1	–	1965	Britain	19 Jan 2015	cockpit, procedures trainer
Gloster Meteor F(TT).8	WF643	1951	Britain	10 May 1975	–
Gloster Javelin FAW.9R	XH892	1957	Britain	6 May 1982	–
Goldfinch Amphibian 161	–	1996	Britain	23 Sep 2008	–
Gowland Jenny Wren	G-ASRF	1966	Britain	11 Sep 2004	–
Grunau Baby III	DUD	1954	Germany	2002	glider
Hawker Hurricane I	P3708	1940	Britain	23 May 2010	fuselage
Hawker Sea Hawk FGA.6	WV838	1954	Britain	23 Aug 2011	cockpit
Hawker Hunter T.53	ET-272	1958	Britain	19 Jan 2015	cockpit
Hawker Hunter FGA.9	XG254	1956	Britain	19 Feb 2002	–
Hawker Siddeley Sea Harrier FA.2	ZA175	1981	Britain	27 Jul 2004	–
Hunting Jet Provost T.3A	XN500	1960	Britain	7 Oct 2007	–
Lightwing Rooster 1	G-MJVI	1983	Britain	24 Feb 2004	–
Lockheed T-33A	55-4433	1955	USA	21 Jul 1978	–
Lovegrove Discord	–	1996	Britain	Apr 2010	–
Lovegrove Sheffy	G-CDFW	2004	Britain	3 Apr 2010	–
Luton Major	G-APUG	1964	Britain	17 Oct 2006	–
Maupin Woodstock One	HCG	1992	Britain	25 Sep 2010	glider
MBA Tiger Cub	G-MJSU	1983	Britain	8 Aug 2002	–
Mignet 'Flying Flea'	–	c1936	France	Jan 1998	–
Mikoyan-Gurevich MiG-15*bis*	3794	1956	USSR	14 Aug 2007	see profile
North American T-28C Trojan	146289	1957	USA	28 May 1981	fuselage
North American F-100D Super Sabre	42196	1954	USA	18 Mar 1978	–
Penrose Pegasus 2	HKJ	1993	Britain	24 Feb 2002	glider
Percival Sea Prince T.1	WF128	1952	Britain	25 Sep 1981	–
Percival Provost T.1	WV605	1954	Britain	14 Sep 1978	see profile
Skycraft Super Scout 250	G-MBUD	1982	Australia	11 Nov 2007	–
Slingsby Grasshopper TX.1	XA226	1953	Britain	21 Apr 2004	glider
Supermarine Spitfire II	'P8140'	1968	Britain	1974	replica
Supermarine Spitfire XVI	'TD248'	1945	Britain	2000	re-creation
Taylor Titch	G-BABY	1975	Britain	28 Jul 2003	–
Thunder Ax7-65Z	G-BJZC	1982	Britain	2006	hot air balloon
UFM Icarus II	–	1974	USA	6 Nov 2005	hang-glider
Vickers Valetta C.2*	VX580	1950	Britain	27 May 1983	see profile
Wasp Falcon 4	–	1976	France	2003	hang-glider
Westland Whirlwind HAS.7	XN304	1959	USA/GB	19 Jul 1982	–
Westland Whirlwind HAR.10	XR485	1963	USA/GB	19 Feb 1981	–

Notes: * – illustrated in the colour section. Canberra WE168 was a 'gate guardian' at Manston – see Chapter 14.

It may be surreal to drive through a housing estate to find a control tower, but the Martlesham Heath Control Tower Museum is an incredible time capsule. *Ken Ellis*

Suffolk Centenarian
Martlesham Heath Control Tower Museum

Martlesham Heath
www.mhas.org.uk

Suffolk is a county that specialises in control tower museums. All have a story of endeavour and heroism to tell, but one has a lineage that surpasses all the others. Even if it is in the middle of a housing estate... A century ago the entire area lived up to its name: Martlesham *Heath*. Synonymous with tests and trials, this was 'The Heath's' theme from the very beginning. The Testing Squadron moved in from Upavon in late 1916, although the station was not commissioned until 16th January 1917. The Martlesham Heath Aviation Society opened the control tower museum in September 2000 and its volunteers have been working towards the airfield's hundredth birthday ever since. The last flying took place in March 1979 and since then the landscape has changed considerably. Much of the airfield is covered in houses, amenities and, at the junction of the runways, is the 'Douglas Bader' public house. The dual carriageway A12 slices its way through the eastern side, severing the impressive RAF headquarters buildings from the former airfield.

The Testing Squadron was renamed the Aeroplane Experimental Station on 16th October 1917. It expanded to take in Orfordness on the coast, well away from prying eyes. By March 1920 it had changed its name to Aeroplane Experimental Establishment and took on its most well-known identity, the Aeroplane & Armament Experimental Establishment (A&AEE), on 24th March 1924. With the prospect of German bombs raining down and the airfield ideally placed for fighter and intruder operations A&AEE de-camped west to Boscombe Down in September 1939. Over 22 years over 400 different types, civil and military – were test at the station making it one of the most important trials airfields in the country. Between 1939 and 1944 a dazzling array of RAF fighter units called Martlesham home, sometimes only for a matter of days. The majority flew Hawker Hurricanes or Supermarine Spitfires, but others had Boulton Paul Defiants, Bristol Blenheims, Hawker Typhoons, North American Mustangs and Westland Lysanders. The Supermarine Walrus amphibians of 277 Squadron contrasted with the sleek fighters from December 1941 to April 1944 when it was replaced by the similarly equipped 278 Squadron until September 1944. As illustrated in the colour section, Martlesham's tower looked out on fighters bedecked with stars and stripes from October 1943 when the 356th Fighter Group arrived. Initially flying Republic P-47 Thunderbolts, P-51 Mustangs took over from November 1944.

Test and trials again became the dominant role from July 1946 when the Blind Landing Experimental Unit and the Bomb Ballistics Unit arrived, both from Woodbridge. These merged in November 1949, becoming the Armament and Instrument Experimental Unit the following year. Once again Martlesham witnessed a rich variety of types including, jets – Avro Ashton, English Electric Canberra and Short Sperrin. The Battle of Britain Flight – Chapter 16 – was one of the last resident units, from 1958 to 1961. This brief overview cannot do justice to the mammoth lineage that is Martlesham Heath; that is left to the painstaking team at the control tower, where visitors will find details of *every* type tested, all of the units, the personalities, the tragedies and the successes from a century of aviation.

Also in Suffolk
Halesworth Airfield Station 365 Memorial Museum

Established on the former 8th Air Force airfield of Halesworth (also known as Holton); this museum includes an exceptional range of exhibits centred on the 56th Fighter Group and the 489th Bomb Group. **www.halesworthairfieldmuseum.co.uk**

Parham Airfield Museum

Framlingham aerodrome incorporates the **390th Bomb Group Memorial Air Museum** and the **Museum of British Resistance**. The tower houses a superb museum dedicated to the 390th and USAAF Station No.153. The Resistance Museum is dedicated to the work of the Auxiliary Units – the so-called 'Stay Behind' cells in the event of an invasion. **www.parhamairfieldmuseum.co.uk**

The Red Feather Club

The official museum of 95th Bomb Group, operated and managed by the **95th Bomb Group Heritage Association** at Horham. It has brought back to life the former NCOs' club at USAAF Station 119, once home to the B-17s of the 95th. Included in the exhibits are the famous murals painted by S/Sgt Nathan Bindler. **www.95thbg-horham.com**

Rougham Tower Association

A surprising amount of the former B-17 Flying Fortress base survives, including the superbly-preserved tower. Displays are dedicated to the men and the memories of the 322nd and 94th BGs and there are poignant memorials and expanding museum facilities – a great place of pilgrimage. **www.rctam94th.co.uk**

Suffolk Aviation Heritage Museum

On the southern edge of the former Martlesham Heath airfield at Foxhall, the museum is within a cavernous communications centre known to the USAF as 'The Roc'; it was last used by the 2164th Communications Squadron USAFE in the early 1990s. Within the collection is the cockpit of English Electric Canberra PR.7 WH798. **www.suffolkaviationheritage.org.uk**

493rd Bomb Group 'Helton's Hellcats' Museum

Centred on the control tower at Debach, USAAF Station 152, the museum has been painstakingly put together. As has the website, which includes a vast amount of material: for example, the locals pronounce it 'Deb-idge', while Americans call it 'Dee-bark'. **www.493bgdebach.co.uk**

Wattisham Station Heritage

Run by the Wattisham Museum Society, the museum is situated in what was the Station Chapel during the airfield's USAAF days, the displays are dedicated to every aspect of Wattisham's incredible history from 1937 to date. The team has the use of a 'Cold War' hardened aircraft shelter which serves both as a workshop and storage site for the airframes. Located on a busy Army Air Corps base, visits are on a pre-booked basis only. **www.wattishamstationheritage.org**

Wattisham Station Heritage Aircraft aircraft

Type	Identity	Built	Origin	Acquired	Notes
English Electric Lightning F.3	XP743	1964	Britain	Jun 2009	cockpit
Hawker Hunter FGA.9	XG194	1956	Britain	28 Nov 2009	–
McDonnell Phantom FGR.2	XT914	1968	USA	8 Mar 2012	–
Sud Gazelle AH.1	XX444	1976	France	2015	–
Westland Scout AH.1	XT617	1965	Britain	2015	–
Westland Lynx AH.7	XZ605	1979	Britain	28 Apr 2014	–

CHAPTER 27
SURREY

Birthplace of Aviation
Brooklands Museum

Weybridge
www.brooklandsmuseum.com

Brooklands can claim to be the cradle of motor sport and this combination of vehicles and aeroplanes is unique. This makes Brooklands a dual-theme museum, another singularity. Although only a fraction of the race track and the aerodrome remain, the atmosphere of high performance cars, pioneering aircraft and word-class aviation industry is heady... and set to increase. As these words hit the keyboards, the Brooklands Museum is in the throes of an incredible regeneration that will transform how it portrays the tremendous legacy of the site. Before we examine this: an apology. This book is already busting the limits the publisher set; mention of the motoring side of Brooklands will have to be fleeting, fascinating though it is.

Above: The magnificent 1907 clubhouse at Brooklands, complete with classic cars. *Brooklands Museum*

A replica of Alliott Verdon Roe's Type I biplane that nearly flew at Brooklands in June 1908. It is kept in a reconstruction of the shed that Roe built for it. *Ken Ellis*

Hugh Locke King owned an estate to the south of Weybridge and work began in 1906 to create the world's first purpose-built motor racing circuit there. As is so often the case when designers and builders get involved, the scheme became much more ambitious than Hugh envisaged: the track was to be 100ft wide, have two sections with 30ft high banking, and an additional finishing straight running through the middle of circuit – 3¼ miles of racing history. All of this came together in just nine months with the bill amounting to around £145,500. That might not sound much in terms of present-day Surrey prices, but in Edwardian Britain that would come to millions in 2017 values. The first official race was staged on 6th July 1907.

Pioneers and flying schools

The allure of speed and power has always created a bond between motorists and aviators and Brooklands became the place where the two pursuits could combine. Manchester-born Alliott Verdon Roe was attracted to the Brooklands track; it was an ideal place for flying. He assembled his first biplane there and, powered by 6hp JAP twin-cylinder he tested from September 1907 but it was not successful. With a 24hp French Antoinette installed it managed a few 'hops' in June 1908 before the 30-year old Roe was asked to leave Brooklands. These trials are commemorated by a faithful replica of the Roe I and the shed that it lived in at today's museum. After being 'evicted' from Brooklands, Roe moved to the Lea Marshes in Essex and there, on 13th July 1909 he coaxed his triplane, powered by a 9hp JAP to make the first sustained flights by a Briton in a British designed and built flying machine with an indigenous engine. (The Roe Triplane is preserved at the Science Museum in London.)

At Brooklands, the British Automobile Racing Club realised that aviation was to be encouraged and that the middle of the circuit was an ideal place for what could well become another major crowd-puller. In 1909 they gave approval for its use for flying and a row of garage-like hangars began to appear. In October that year Frenchman Louis Paulhan gave Britain's first public flying demonstration. Aviators, the serious, the deluded, the rich, the just-getting-by flocked to Brooklands. For a vivid image of what this golden age was like there can be no better source than Ken Annakin's wonderful 1965-released film *Those Magnificent*

A section of the famous race track banking and bridge. *Ken Ellis*

Men in Their Flying Machines which was inspired by the *Daily Mail* 'Circuit of Britain' air race hosted by Brooklands in 1911. If the crashes into the sewage farm seem too fanciful, there was one just within the perimeter of the circuit and racing cars and aeroplanes *did* 'visit' it. Two examples: Hubert Oxley in a Roe Type IV triplane on 17th October and Gordon England in a Weiss Monoplane on 22nd December, both in 1910. Mr Oxley was learning to fly at the Roe school – he'd been allowed back – and a whole string of outfits offering tuition grew up. Flying training was to remain a major undertaking at the aerodrome up to 1939.

Industrial giants

Some of the pioneer aviators at Brooklands turned their hands to creating what became the British aircraft industry and it was natural that the Surrey airfield should become a centre for aircraft manufacture. Alliott Verdon Roe has already been mentioned, but his destiny lay in Manchester and at Hamble. *The* name that was to resonate in one form or another all the way to the Harrier was Thomas Octave Murdoch Sopwith. He established a school at Brooklands by January 1911 and went on to create the huge empire that carried his name. After World War One the Sopwith company was forced to close its doors, but it was reborn as Hawker Aircraft in honour of designer-test pilot Harry Hawker in November 1920. Sopwith turned the new concern into a giant, establishing the Hawker Siddeley Group in 1935 that encompassed Armstrong Whitworth, Avro, Gloster as well as Hawker. Vickers set up its aviation division at Brooklands, becoming part of the British Aircraft Corporation (BAC) in 1960. Hawker Siddeley and BAC became British Aerospace in 1977. Turning to the Brooklands Museum website, there is a barrage of figures that are more than instructive: "Some 18,600 new aircraft of nearly 250 types were first flown, manufactured or assembled at Brooklands... Of 11,461 Wellingtons built by Vickers by 1943, 2,515 were built at Brooklands – one fifth of the total number... Altogether, 3,012 Hurricanes were produced at Brooklands..."

Early production Wellington fuselages at Brooklands, 1939. *Vickers*

The famous racing track had been damaged by the Luftwaffe in 1940 and a runway extension in 1951 broke through the Byfleet banking: the days of motor racing were over. Vickers had acquired the whole site for £330,000 in 1946 and built types from the Viking to the VC-10 at Brooklands; most having their maiden flights end just a short distance to the southwest at Wisley where Vickers established its flight test centre in 1944. With the establishment of BAC, the Brooklands factory built elements of the prototype TSR.2 low-level bomber programme which was axed in 1965, the very successful One-Eleven twin-jet airliner and major sections of the Concorde supersonic transport. The closure of the Brooklands factory was announced in the summer of 1986 and by 1990 it had been demolished making way for redevelopment.

Transformation

Founded in 1969, the Brooklands Society alerted people to the need to preserve the heritage of the site: both aeronautical and automotive. Weybridge Museum was very keen on this initiative and in 1977 it and the Brooklands Society, the Brooklands-based Vintage Aircraft Flying Association and with the help of British Aerospace staged an exhibition, 'Wings over Brooklands'. This vividly demonstrated the importance of the site. Curating the display was Morag Barton, who became pivotal in the generation of today's museum. In preparation for closing the factory, British Aerospace sold off the northwest corner of the site and the pace had to quicken and negotiations with Elmbridge Borough Council and the Gallaher Ltd resulted in 1984 with a 99-year lease of 30 acres at the north end of the site, including banking, part of the finishing straight, the hill-climb track, the 1907 clubhouse and its surroundings. With Morag Barton at the helm, the Brooklands Museum Trust was inaugurated in 1987 and the site was opened to the public in 1991. The freehold of the museum site was gifted to Brooklands Museum Trust by Japan Tobacco International in January 2010.

Stratospherics and Re-Engineering

On of the most fascinating elements of Brooklands is the Stratosphere Chamber. This was the brainchild of Barnes Wallis, head of the Vickers research and development department. From 1945 the great man had an office within the clubhouse. Wallis was investigating airliners with extremely long range and needed a high altitude and climatic test chamber. This awesome structure was built with the help of the Vickers-Armstrong shipyard at Barrow-in-Furness. The techniques needed were not the finesse of aviation, the 200-ton mammoth required the skills of shipwrights and the giant project was completed in September 1947. The chamber is 50ft long and has a diameter of 25ft – this allowed whole aircraft, or sections, to be subjected to simulated altitudes of up to 70,000ft and a temperature range of minus 65°C to plus 55°C. Restoration of the chamber was a long and complex job. In March 2014 it was opened by Mary Stopes-Roe, Barnes Wallis's daughter. Today the cockpit section of Vickers Merchantman G-APEJ is displayed inside.

The cockpit of Merchantman G-APEJ inside the Stratosphere Chamber. *Terry Dann*

Under the banner 'Re-Engineering Brooklands' a complex and challenging project, devised by museum director Allan Winn, was launched in 2014, a Heritage Lottery Fund-aided £8 million project. Since World War Two, a Bellman hangar had been sited on the finishing straight, effectively cutting off motor racing from the remaining banking and the clubhouse. During 2016 this listed building was relocated and turned into the 'Brooklands Aircraft Factory' devoted to the history of aircraft construction. The 'Loch Ness' Wellington – profiled below – is the centrepiece. A brand-new two-storey building – 'Flight Shed' – exhibits aircraft and supporting artefacts while below is an archive store, a reading room and a workshop. Outside, the clubhouse will once again overlook an uninterrupted finishing straight. By the time these words are read this amazing development will have been unveiled.

British Aircraft Corporation One-Eleven 475AM G-ASYD
1965 | Medium range airliner | Two 12,550lb st Rolls-Royce Spey 512DW turbofans

Air Enthusiast magazine (Ed: K Ellis) for May/June 2003 carried a history of G-ASYD, by Stephen Skinner. It was entitled *The Long and the Short of It* and sums up well the twin-jet's exceptional career. Vickers morphed into the British Aircraft Corporation in January 1960 and while VC-10 production continued at Brooklands, it was decided that the next airliner product, the One-Eleven 'bus-stop jet' would be assembled and test flown at Hurn, Bournemouth. The prototype had its first flight on 20th August 1963 and 249 were built between 1965 and 1991 (nine of which were completed in Romania). G-ASYD – Syd, as this One-Eleven was always known – was the prototype Series 400 with heavier operating weights and greater range. Peter Baker and Brian Trubshaw were at the controls for the first of what would be four maiden flights, on 13th July 1965. Two months later, Syd was at Torrejon, near Madrid, for tropical trials. It made the first of four appearances at the Farnborough airshow in September 1966. On 4th February 1967 Syd was retired from tests and customer demonstrations and began a major metamorphosis at Hurn. The fuselage was cut in two places and the fuselage was stretched by 13ft 6in to create the prototype high-capacity Series 500. Brian Trubshaw and Roy Radford took Syd into the air in this new guise on 17th June 1967.

During April 1969 it was flown into the tight confines of Brooklands for a special engineering assessment; this was to be its only visit until it joined the museum. Returned to the factory floor at Hurn in 1970 G-ASYD was shortened back to its original 93ft 6in for its next 'life' as the prototype Series 475 'hot and high' airliner with the ability to fly from semi-prepared airstrips. Roy Radford and Dave Glaser did the honours on 27th August 1970 and in May-June 1971 it was pounding a specially prepared gravel runway at Waterbeach as part of the certification process. In June 1974 Syd was testing Rolls-Royce developed hush-kits for its Spey 512 turbofans. Aiming at the potentially lucrative Japanese inter-city market, G-ASYD was turned into its fourth incarnation at Hurn in 1977. No stretch this time, the Series 670 offered increased fuel reserves and greater performance for high density and frequently utilised routes. For the fourth first flight Roy Radford and John Cochrane took Syd into the air on 13th September 1977. The Japanese market never materialised and by 1980 G-ASYD was back to Series 475 status. Development work became the norm; in 1980 relaxed stability trials – achieved by transferring water ballast between tanks in the fuselage – and gust alleviation tests were carried out. On 30th April 1982 Syd had an airborne appointment with another museum-piece-to-be. Tucking in behind spray tanker English Electric Canberra B.2/8 WV787 on a sortie out of Boscombe Down, G-ASYD was testing a new de-icing system. (WV787 is at Newark – Chapter 23.) In the early 1990s more technology was trialled, this time a Lucas Industries developed light-activated control system. Wearing 'Fly-By-Light' titles on the fuselage, Syd flew with its spoilers and ailerons triggered by inputs sent by fibre-optic cabling. British Aerospace Filton division chief test pilot John Fawcett captained G-ASYD on its final flight to Brooklands, carrying out its 5,004th landing, on 14th July 1994, bringing to an end nearly thirty years of test and trials work.

One-Eleven 475 G-ASYD during rough strip trials at Waterbeach, May-June 1971. *BAC*

The forward fuselage of Concorde 202 about to leave the Brooklands production line for Filton, 1971. *Brooklands Museum*

British Aircraft Corporation/Sud Concorde 100 G-BBDG
1974 | Supersonic airliner | Four 38,050lb st Rolls-Royce/SNECMA Olympus 593
Mk.610-14-28 turbojets

When the last Concorde to fly, G-BOAF, touched down at its birthplace at Filton on 25th November 2003, there was another example there that was biding its time waiting to depart. Piloted by Peter Baker and Roy Radford, *Delta-Golf*, Concorde 202, the second production example and the first British production machine, had made the last of 633 flights, completing 1,282 hours, 9 minutes of flying time when it rolled to a stop on Christmas eve 1981. Its development flying was over, but it would be held on a care and maintenance basis, just in case. By late 1982 it was declared redundant and it began to be 'robbed' for spares. On 1st April 1984 British Airways (BA) bought 202, not to operate, but as a source of spares for the rest of the fleet. It was moved into a purpose-built 'temporary' hangar on Filton's northern perimeter in May 1988 and, out of sight, it was forgotten by airfield workers and passers by. With the last-ever services to take place on 24th October 2003, BA was assessing where it was going to deliver – on loan – its Concordes. Brooklands had an excellent case, but it would be impossible to fly one of the supersonic transports in to what was left of the runway. That being the case, the long-grounded G-BBDG was the obvious choice and on the 30th the museum was informed that its application for a Concorde had been successful. For a brief while, G-BOAF had a sister on the airfield, but from 5th May 2004 thanks to the specialists at Air Salvage International, *Delta-Golf* began to leave Filton. The final low-loader arrived at Brooklands on 5th June and G-BBDG was structurally re-assembled from March to December 2005. Preparing the airliner took considerable work, but on 26th July 2006 the 'Concorde Experience' was officially opened and on 1st August the public were welcomed on board. *Delta-Golf* continues to get close attention from its team of 'carers'; the 'droop snoot' works again, but that took four years of graft to achieve.

Construction of the forward and rear fuselage of Concorde 202 began at Brooklands in April 1970 and the sections were roaded to the assembly line at Filton. By November 1971 the aircraft was beginning to be recognisable. Peter Baker and Brian Trubshaw took *Delta-Golf*, wearing British Airways colours, for its maiden flight on 13th February 1974. This sortie lasted 105 minutes, a dozen of which were at supersonic speed. Brooklands has documentation accounting for every trip that 202 made; we'll take a trawl some of the highlights. *Delta-Golf* became a common sight at Casablanca, Morocco, for tropical 'soak' trials, but it also visited the Middle East, including Teheran, Iran, in August 1974; Singapore in September 1974 and Cape Town, South Africa in March 1976. Throughout this time it was based at the Concorde test centre at Fairford. In February 1975 it was used to familiarise PanAm flight crew with the type and from June 1975 began the serious work of converting BA personnel. Fairford closed in November 1976 and G-BBDG moved to its birthplace, Filton, although the need for support flights was waning. In 1978 *Delta-Golf's* BA colours were removed and it awaited retirement.

The sixth prototype P.1127, XP984, precursor of the Harrier. *Ken Ellis*

Hawker P.1127 XP984
1964 | V/STOL fighter prototype | One 15,500lb st Bristol Siddeley Pegasus 5 vectored thrust turbofan

The prototype Hawker P.1127 XP831 – the development airframe that evolved into the world-beating Harrier – is on display in the Science Museum, London. Brooklands and Yeovilton have the only other survivors of six prototypes. Bill Bedford was at the controls for XP984's maiden flight, from Dunsfold, on 13th February 1964. The sixth and last P.1127, XP984 was the first with the so-called 'seventh wing' and had leading edge extensions. The P.1127 programme was a steep learning curve and modifications through experience were always being applied. During a test flight south of Dunsfold in XP984 on 19th March 1965 Hugh Merewether was diving through 28,000ft when the Pegasus packed up. This was not a new experience for Hugh; on 5th April 1962 XP972 had gone all quiet on him following a high g-force turn. He managed to force land it at Tangmere, but the precious prototype was destroyed by fire; Hugh was unhurt. Bill Bedford had 'banged out' of the second prototype, XP836, from just 200ft on 14th December 1961. So with the prospect of losing another P.1127, Hugh hoped for other prospects as XP984 plummeted down. He was rewarded by a helpful gap in the overcast at 4,000ft that revealed Thorney Island. Hugh made a successful dead stick landing there. A compressor blade had fractured: with a new engine XP984 was back in the air in late October and Hugh was awarded an OBE.

In December 1965 Sqn Ldr F A Trowern flew XP984 to West Germany for demonstrations. Trowern was with the West Raynham-based Tri-Partite Evaluation Squadron, part of the Central Fighter Establishment, which was operationally testing the interim Kestrel FGA.1s with a mixture of British, American and German pilots. Beyond this XP984 had further wing modifications and was involved in trials from the aircraft carrier HMS *Bulwark* and off-base operations from a specially prepared clearing in woodland at the Royal Aircraft Establishment (RAE) Thurleigh. On 11th September 1968 the P.1127 was issued to RAE Farnborough for work on head-up displays for operational Harriers. XP984 was back at Thurleigh by 1973 and it was written off when it swerved off the runway on 31st October 1975. Its total flying time came to 204 hours 5 minutes. It became an instructional airframe (serial number A2658) at the Royal Naval Engineering College at Manadon, Devon, on 12th February 1976. With the college due to close in mid-1995, XP984 was moved to Lee-on-Solent for disposal in October 1994. It was entered as Lot 190 in the Ministry of Defence auction, staged by Sotheby's at Billingshurst on 26th November 1994 with an estimate of between £2,000 and £4,000. Thankfully someone convinced the 'suits' at the Ministry that this machine should be withdrawn. In June 1995 XP984 returned to Dunsfold where it was restored and on 28th September 2000 it was presented to Brooklands.

Hawker Siddeley Harrier T.52 G-VTOL
1971 | V/STOL conversion trainer / demonstrator | One 21,500lb st Bristol Siddeley Pegasus 103 (11PV) vectored-thrust turbofan

Brazil, France, Germany, India, the Middle East, Spain and many more. These and others were destinations for Hawker Siddeley's famous private venture demonstrator two-seat Harrier. It performed airshow routines, demonstrated its capabilities from airfields, airstrips, aircraft carriers or heli-decks, flew operational evaluations, or gave 'top brass' a ride. With prospects for sales increasing, the company took the plunge and built a special version of the T.2 conversion trainer, under the designation T.52 and the appropriate civil registration G-VTOL. It first flew at Dunsfold on 16th September 1971 and it worked hard for the next fifteen years. Occasionally it would need to carry armament and the military serial ZA250 was allocated to cover such eventualities. Initially fitted with a Pegasus 102, it was later given a Mk.103. Because of its globe-trotting nature, G-VTOL was far more comprehensively equipped than a tactical Harrier; it had an automatic direction finder and an instrument landing system. G-VTOL was part of a long line of company-owned demonstrators, going back to Hawker Hart G-ABMR of 1931 and concluding with Hawk Mk.50 G-HAWK of 1975. (The Hart is with the RAF Museum Hendon; the Hawk is an instructional airframe with BAE Systems.)

Harrier Mk.52 G-VTOL during mock-up Skyhook trials at Dunsfold, April 1985. *British Aerospace*

The man most associated with G-VTOL is John Farley, whose airshow displays never ceased to stop audiences in their tracks as he put the aircraft through its paces. John thinks G-VTOL was a very important investment and that it was essential for it to be a two-seater. It allowed operational pilots to safely experience V/STOL flying at first hand and – if it was necessary – non-pilots could be given a ride. As John remarked: "the subcontractors threw in their bits for free – it was very cost effective..." Trials work was also part of G-VTOL's job. Visitors to Brooklands will notice the name 'Skyhook' on G-VTOL's nose at Brooklands, this relates to a system invented by Hawker Siddeley test pilot Heinz Frick to allow far more vessels to operate Harriers, increase the number of aircraft a ship could accommodate and improve the fighter's range. The concept was to 'capture' a hovering Harrier using a specially-modified crane with a 'grab' that would secure the fighter from above at the centre section. The aircraft could then be 'parked' on a trolley and manoeuvred into a hangar deck. It was entirely possible, using Skyhook, to have Harriers without undercarriage, saving on complexity and weight and hence increase range. Using G-VTOL, BAe carried out feasibility trials in the early 1980s but nothing further came of the project. G-VTOL was retired at Dunsfold by 1986 and on 6th April 1989 it joined the Brooklands collection.

Vickers Wellington Ia N2980
1939 | Medium bomber | Two 1,050hp Bristol Pegasus XVIII pistons

New Year's Eve 1940 was just another workday – the war did not pause for festivities. Wellington Ia N2980 *R-for-Robert* of 20 Operational Training Unit (OTU) climbed out of its base at Lossiemouth in mid-afternoon. After the navigation exercise was completed the eight crew would have plenty of time to get ready for whatever revelry they intended. At the helm was Sqn Ldr David Marwood-Elton, alongside him was co-pilot Plt Off J F Slatter, both 20 OTU 'regulars'. The other six on board, all but one sergeants, were anxiously coming to grips with their respective 'trades': wireless operator/air gunner W Wright, navigators C Chandler, E Ford, R E Little and Plt Off Lucton and rear gunner J S Fensome. The Bomber Command novices had every reason to be nervous; it was a pig of day and getting worse.

Marwood-Elton was heading southwest towards Fort Augustus, at the southern end of Loch Ness. He'd climbed to 8,000ft, a safe enough height for the mountains that lay all around them. They were flying through dense 'clag' and the snow squalls were getting more and more threatening. It was then that the starboard Pegasus XVIII engine packed in. This was no time for prevaricating: Marwood-Elton immediately adopted the drills he'd learned. They were losing height, out of sight of

Minus its rear fuselage, the bulk of Wellington *R-for-Robert* is brought to the Loch Ness shoreline in September 1985. *Brooklands Museum*

the surface and surrounded by mountainous terrain – bale out, and do it now. Getting six men out took a while and the pilots had no choice but had to stay at the controls while this took place. Suddenly, Marwood-Elton spotted a gap in the cloud and saw a stretch of intense blackness – water. Dropping *Robert*'s nose, he aimed for it, figuring a forced-landing in Loch Ness was much more preferable to a parachute descent into the gloom. He made a textbook touchdown. He and Slatter got out on to the wing, extracted the dinghy and paddled ashore. Chandler, Ford, Little, Lucton and Wright all baled out successfully. Rear gunner Fensome seems to have pulled his ripcord too soon and damaged his parachute on the tailplane; he fell to his death. *Robert* sank into the depths. It had chalked up 330 hours, 20 minutes flying time. That might not seem a lot, but for an operational Wellington in the early years of the war, this made it a veteran.

Vickers test pilot Joseph 'Mutt' Summers put the throttles forward on Wellington Ia N2980 at Brooklands on 16th November 1939 to start pre-delivery tests. Four days later the 'Wimpey' was issued to 149 Squadron at Mildenhall, taking on the code letters 'OJ-R' – *R-for-Robert*. On 18th December it was one of 24 Wellingtons from 9, 37 and 149 Squadrons destined to take part in the fateful 'Battle of Heligoland Bight'. Only ten returned, *Robert* among them. Moving to Feltwell in Norfolk on 30th May 1940 the Wellington joined 37 Squadron and flew 14 'ops' with the unit. Upgrading to Mk.Ics in October, 37 Squadron gave up N2980 on the 6th and it was ferried to 20 OTU, where it kept its individual code letter 'R'.

American Marty Klein used very high-tech sonar equipment in 1976 in an attempt to find the famed 'Loch Ness Monster'. He picked up lots of traces, but not one swimming dinosaur. Instead, he found what he thought was a Catalina flying-boat in the depths of the loch. Heriot Watt University in Edinburgh had been developing remotely-operated vehicle (ROV) technology for the offshore oil industry and in 1978 decided that finding the 'Catalina' would be an excellent practical trial for the submersible. The images that the ROV brought back showed that this was no Catalina, it was a Wellington. A Royal Navy team diving team in 1979 proved that it was N2980. The condition of *R-for-Robert* was deteriorating – a fishing boat net had snagged the nose and the wings were suffering. With all the publicity it was becoming a well-known 'target' for divers and souvenir hunting was bound to start. Heriot Watt's Robin Holmes decided that the Wellington should be salvaged and he set up a charity in 1984 to achieve this, the Loch Ness Wellington Association. He set about seeking sponsors and, among others, *FlyPast* magazine lent its support. On the second attempt, the Wellington came to the surface on 21st September 1985. On the shore was Sqn Ldr David Marwood-Elton, aged 74; he had come to re-acquaint himself with 'his' Wellington. A team from British Aerospace delivered N2980 to its birthplace, Brooklands six days after its salvage. The museum embarked upon an exacting restoration of the 'Loch Ness' Wellington, putting it back on its undercarriage and returning it to the condition it was in when it took off from Lossiemouth on New Year's Eve 1940. Well almost, the wise decision was taken to only partially cover the airframe and to leave the rest as vivid testament to the geodetic structure devised by its designer, Barnes Wallis.

Vickers Viking 1A G-AGRU
1946 | Medium range airliner | Two 1,675hp Bristol Hercules 634 pistons

Designed and built at Brooklands, assembled and test flown just down the road at Wisley, Viking 1A G-AGRU is the only example of its type in Britain and a very significant survivor. Along with the Valetta tactical transport (Chapter 26) the Viking was derived from the Wellington and replaced the bomber in the factory. The prototype first flew at Wisley on 22nd June 1945 and up to 1949 Vickers had built 163 Vikings. Ordered by British European Airways (BEA), G-AGRU was the twelfth off the production line and it first flew at Wisley at 19th July 1946. With the name *Vagrant*, it was delivered on 9th August 1946. It was leased to the Irish airline Aer Lingus from December 1946, returning to BEA in February 1947. Sold to British

South American Airways on 2nd February 1948 it was briefly operated from London Airport, Heathrow. Registered as VP-TAX it joined British West Indian Airways on 15th June 1948, named *Barbados*, operating schedules out of Trinidad. Re-registered as G-AGRU by British International Airlines, it was leased to the Kuwait Oil Company. It was badly damaged in a landing accident at Basra on 16th October 1955, but was returned to duty. East Anglian Flying Services of Southend took on *Romeo-Uniform* on 19th January 1959 and in November 1962 the company took on the name Channel Airways. The Viking was withdrawn from use and in open storage at Southend by September 1963.

A new, and bizarre, career awaited G-AGRU. Dutch entrepreneur John Bouvy approached Channel Airways about acquiring the Viking for use as a café at Soesterberg in his homeland. Agreeing to keep it in Channel Airways colours, the airline gifted G-AGRU to Bouvy. On 9th January 1964 was ferried by Captain Brian Deakin to Soesterberg. It was moved off the airfield to a nearby site on the Utrecht to Amersfoort road and became the founder of the very popular Avio-Resto Café. Trade was so good that Bouvy was back in Britain four years later, this time to Luton where he acquired Vikings G-AGRW and G-AHPB from Autair. They were flown across on 15th February 1968. The three Vikings were given names of Dutch aviation pioneers, respectively: *Henri Wijnmalen*, *Flores Albert van Heijst* and *Marinus van Meel*. Avio Resto closed in 1979 and G-AGRU was snapped up by the British Airways collection and taken to Cosford where it was repainted in BEA colours as *Vagrant*. G-AGRW moved to Austria and is displayed next door to a McDonald's eatery. G-AHPB went to a museum in Germany, before moving on to Switzerland where it was scrapped in the 1990s. The projected British Airways museum at Cosford did not fully materialise and G-AGRU was trucked to Brooklands on 27th June 1991. Initially on loan, it was donated to the museum by British Airways in 2005.

Vickers Merchantman G-APEP
1961 | Medium range freighter | Four 4,985shp Rolls-Royce Tyne 506 turboprops

Trying to capitalise on the experience of the phenomenally successful Viscount, Vickers devised a larger sister: the prototype Vanguard first flew at Brooklands on 20th January 1959. Between 1961 and 1964 a disappointing 44 units were built for British European Airways (BEA) and Trans Canada Air Lines. They gave good service and found further use in the secondary market, particularly as freighters; BEA's aircraft receiving a major modification under the name Merchantman. The world's only intact Vanguard/Merchantman is preserved at its birthplace. *Echo-Papa* had its maiden flight at Brooklands on 29th November 1961 and was delivered to BEA at London Airport, Heathrow, fourteen days later taking up the fleet name *Superb*. Over the winter of 1969-1970 G-APEP was converted to Merchantman status by Aviation Traders at Southend and it flew in its new guise as a freighter on 23rd February 1970. It was back in service with BEA's cargo division in April. Based at East Midlands Airport, Castle Donington, Air Bridge Carriers (ABC) acquired G-APEP on 8th November 1979 and revived the name *Superb*. In August 1992 ABC was renamed Hunting Cargo Airlines. *Echo-Papa* carried out its last revenue-earning flight on 30th September 1996 and on 17th October conducted the last-ever Vanguard/Merchantman flight when it flew to Brooklands.

Merchantman G-APEP showing its side-loading freight door. *Ken Ellis*

Vickers VC-10 Series 1103 A40-AB
1964 | Long range VIP transport | Four 21,000lb st Rolls-Royce Conway 540 turbofans

The last Vickers aircraft to be flown from Brooklands, the VC-10 occupies a position in British airliner folklore only surpassed by Concorde. Aircrew and passenger appeal was exemplary, but that did not boost the production figures beyond 54 from 1962 to 1970. The prototype first flew on 29th June 1962. Six intact VC-10s are preserved in Britain and two of those are with Brooklands. Plush VIP-equipped A40-AB, the last civil VC-10 in service, is on site, while kept 'live' at Dunsfold is the last

Above: VC-10 G-ASIX departing Brooklands on its maiden flight, 17th October 1964, bound for Wisley. It returned 23 years later, in VIP guise. *BAC*

Left: Oman Royal Flight VC-10 framing Viscount 806 G-APIM and Varsity T.1 WF372. *Ken Ellis*

VC-10 built, former RAF K.3 ZA150 which flew from Brooklands on 16th February 1970 destined for East African Airways as 5H-MOG. Additionally, the museum has the fuselage of former British Overseas Airways Corporation Series 1101 G-ARVM and an engineering test shell. Series 1103 G-ASIX had its maiden flight at Brooklands on 17th October 1964. It was one of three ordered by Gatwick-based British United Airways and was delivered on the last day of October. British United amalgamated with Caledonian Airways in November 1970, becoming British Caledonian and *India-Xray* took on the fleet name *Loch Maree*. Upon retirement, G-ASIX was acquired by the government of Oman in October 1974 and it was flown to Hurn where it was overhauled and outfitted as a VIP transport for the Sultan of Oman's Royal Flight. Registered A40-AB and based at Muscat, it became the personal transport for His Majesty The Sultan of Oman, Qaboos bin Said Al Said. In July 1984 the VC-10's replacement, Boeing 747SP A40-SO was delivered but fitting it out was going to take a long time and the VC-10 had several more years ahead of it. Upon retirement, *Alpha-Bravo* was generously donated to the museum and it made its last flight, from Heathrow to Brooklands, on 6th July 1987. The VC-10 was kept on the airfield, but it was moved across the famous bridge over the River Wey to the 'factory' site in June 2004.

Brooklands Museum aircraft

Type	Identity	Built	Origin	Acquired	Notes
Avro 504K	'G-AACA'	c1975	Britain	29 Jan 1987	replica
BAC TSR.2	–	1963	Britain	Aug 1992	cockpit
BAC One-Eleven 475AM*	G-ASYD	1965	Britain	14 Jul 1994	see profile
BAC/Sud Concorde 100	G-BBDG	1974	GB/France	5 Jun 2004	see profile
BAC/Sud Concorde	–	1972	GB/France	1995	simulator
Beagle 206 Srs 1X	G-ARRM	1961	Britain	10 Dec 2011	see note
de Havilland Canada Chipmunk T.10	WP921	1952	Canada	1995	cockpit
Handley Page Jetstream T.1	XX499	1976	Britain	21 May 2008	–
Hawker Fury I	'K5673'	1994	Britain	1996	replica
Hawker Hurricane II	Z2389	1940	Britain	14 Oct 1997	–
Hawker Hunter F.51	E-412	1956	Britain	10 Sep 2005	–
Hawker Hunter F.51	E-421	1956	Britain	18 Mar 1989	–
Hawker P.1127	XP984	1964	Britain	28 Sep 2000	see profile
Hawker Siddeley Harrier T.52	G-VTOL	1971	Britain	6 Apr 1989	see profile
Hunting Jet Provost T.3A	XN586	1961	Britain	22 May 2014	–
Roe I Biplane	–	1988	Britain	1988	replica
Royal Aircraft Factory SE.5a	'F5475'	1994	Britain	1996	replica
Santos-Dumont Demoiselle XX	–	1999	France	Jan 1999	replica
Sopwith Tabloid	'3'	2013	Britain	27 Nov 2013	replica
Sopwith Camel F1	'B7270'	1977	Britain	1988	replica
Supermarine Swift F.4	WK198	1953	Britain	3 Feb 2011	fuselage, see Chapter 22
Vickers Vimy	–	1997	Britain	2008	cockpit, replica
Vickers Vimy	NX71MY	1994	Britain	15 Nov 2009	replica
Vickers Viking	'G-EBED'	1974	Britain	1988	replica
Vickers Wellington Ia*	N2980	1939	Britain	27 Sep 1985	see profile
Vickers Wellington	–	2011	Britain	2000	forward fuselage
Vickers Viking 1A	G-AGRU	1946	Britain	27 Jun 1991	see profile
Vickers Varsity T.1	WF372	1951	Britain	13 Nov 1988	–
Vickers Valiant BK.1	XD816	1956	Britain	Sep 1988	cockpit
Vickers Viscount 806	G-APIM	1958	Britain	11 Feb 1990	–
Vickers Viscount 813	G-AZLP	1958	Britain	14 Nov 2013	cockpit
Vickers Viscount 837	XT575	1960	Britain	14 Jan 1996	cockpit
Vickers Merchantman	G-APEJ	1961	Britain	26 Aug 1995	cockpit
Vickers Merchantman*	G-APEP	1961	Britain	17 Oct 1996	see profile
Vickers VC-10 Srs 1101	G-ARVM	1964	Britain	19 Oct 2006	fuselage
Vickers VC-10 Srs 1103*	A40-AB	1964	Britain	6 Jul 1987	see profile
Vickers VC-10 K.3	ZA150	1970	Britain	24 Sep 2013	at Dunsfold
White Monoplane	G-CHOI	2013	Britain	2013	replica

Notes: * – illustrated in the colour section. Does not include airframes in deep store off site. Beagle 206 G-ARRM arrived back at Brooklands on 3rd August 2017 from Farnborough – it is profiled in Chapter 11.

In early March 2017 the team at Gatwick Aviation Museum managed to get Lightning F.53 ZF579's Avons running. Buccaneer S.1 XN921 to the left. *Richard Hall*

New Era
Gatwick Aviation Museum

Charlwood
www.gatwick-aviation-museum.co.uk

People of vision and drive are needed to set up museums and run them. There are times when the zeal required dominates when compromise might be a better option. Such was businessman Peter Vallance: a man who relished playing Don Quixote.

Peter Vallance amid his aircraft collection at Charlwood. *Ken Ellis*

In Peter's case, the windmills he was forever tilting at took the form of Mole Valley District Council and planning permission. The author met and interviewed Peter several times. We had robust disagreements about his flaunting regulations and he was very much of the 'if you're not with me, you're against me' school. Peter Valance died on 14th January 2013; his battle unresolved. His methods outraged many people, but like them or not he put today's superb museum on the map.

In 1981 Peter bought 40 acres of land at Orchard Farm, just to the north of London Gatwick Airport's twin runway 08 threshold, near the village of Charlwood. It was a rundown poultry farm with lots of sheds and Peter set about turning it into business units and he soon had a dozen small firms on site. Shortly after the purchase, this land was designated as green belt. Peter later added to his parcel of land by acquiring another 13 acres. With the property determined as in breach of planning consent, Mole Valley served a notice to cease in 1983. Two years later an appeal gained temporary, four-year, planning permission for the trading estate largely to lessen the impact on the enterprises that had established themselves at Charlwood.

Falling in love with a Sea Hawk

On 10th October 1987 Sea Hawk FB.3 WM983 arrived for use as a 'gate guardian' at Orchard Farm – this was the beginning of the aircraft collection. The all-red naval fighter attracted a lot of attention and Peter got 'bitten' by the aircraft collecting 'bug'. To quote Peter, he: "fell in love with that little red Sea Hawk, its history enthralled me. I wanted more!" Within decade he had close on twenty airframes on site and was encouraging people to come a take a look: he was running a museum in all but name. As the table shows, Peter did not do things by halves: he acquired three Percival twins, two Westland Whirlwinds and a pair of Avro Shackletons. The advent of the maritime patrollers gave rise to my favourite Peter Vallance expression: "You can't have enough Shackletons!"

The founder member of the Gatwick Aviation Museum, Sea Hawk FB.3 WM983. *Ken Ellis*

With expiry of the temporary permission in 1989 an application was put in to Mole Valley for the continued use of Orchard Farm as a trading estate – this was refused. In January 1992 Peter announced that he would be opening up to the public and would erect a hangar including a balcony so that the public could watch the airliners at the airport. A council inquiry that year deemed that the trading estate could continue, but only if the aircraft were removed within a twelve-month deadline. Peter repeatedly contested every element of the ruling. Enforcement action commenced in 1994, but a very patient council allowed a 'period of grace'. In mid-1997 a plan was floated to move the collection to Shoreham aerodrome, but this came to nought. The Gatwick Aviation Museum was launched in 1999 and in April 2004 regular Sunday openings started – none of this had approval. Peter presented a new claim for planning permission in February 2001, involving the removal of the existing buildings and the erection of structures suitable to put the aircraft under cover and a classroom facility. And so the cycle of appeal and rebuttal went on: on 6th July 2011 and a year later the same thing. After that hearing Peter told a local newspaper: "The only way they're going to take me out of here is feet first in a hearse." These were prophetic words. Never the diplomat, often cantankerous and constantly out-spoken nevertheless it was hard not to have admiration for his enthusiasm and drive for Peter Vallance.

Former Peter Valance / Gatwick Aviation Museum aircraft

Type	Identity	Built	Origin	Acquired	Current status / fate
Avro Shackleton MR.3/3	WR974	1957	Britain	Jul 1989	privately owned, Bruntingthorpe
English Electric Canberra B.2	WH903	1954	Britain	Dec 1988	cockpit, Yorkshire Air Museum
English Electric Canberra PR.7	WH773	1953	Britain	May 1990	Laarbruch Museum, Germany
Fairey Gannet AEW.3	XL472	1959	Britain	Dec 1990	spares source, St Athan
Handley Page Victor K.2	XL164	1961	Britain	12 Dec 1995	cockpit, Bournemouth Aviation Museum
Hunting Jet Provost T.3A	XN494	1960	Britain	19 Aug 2008	instructional airframe, Pool, Cornwall
Percival Sea Prince T.1	WF118	1951	Britain	12 Nov 1989	stored, St Athan
Percival Pembroke C.1	XK885	1956	Britain	Nov 1989	stored, St Athan
Percival Provost T.1	WW442	1954	Britain	1992	East Midlands Airport Aeropark
SEPECAT Jaguar GR.1	XX734	1974	UK/France	May 1999	Boscombe Down Aviation Collection
Sud Gazelle 1	G-TURP	1981	France	1997	paintball site, Essex
Westland Whirlwind HAR.10	XP351	1962	USA/GB	15 Oct 2003	stored locally
Westland Whirlwind HAR.10	XP398	1962	USA/GB	Jul 1988	stored locally
Westland Wasp HAS.1	XS463	1965	Britain	19 Aug 2008	Bournemouth Aviation Museum

Sea Vixen FAW.2(TT) XS587 inside Gatwick's impressive display hangar. *Richard Hall*

New beginning

Peter may have been a maverick, but thankfully, provisions had been made and most of the collection passed into a trust. The trustees and volunteers were determined to carry Peter's dream through to completion. The watchword for the future was to drop the confrontational stance and to work *with* the authorities. To this end, a slimming-down of the collection was initiated from the spring of 2013 and during the summer of 2017 the last departure – hybrid Hawker Hunter F.51 E-430 – will be complete the operation. The museum's website is refreshingly open about aims and capabilities: others could learn from this approach: "For those that know something of our history, they will probably be aware that the collection was much larger just a couple of years ago. It was reduced for a number of reasons. Firstly, as a show of faith to the planning authorities that we were very mindful of the issues regarding the aircraft being outside in a green belt area.

"We reduced the impact by disposing of ten aircraft. We sold off less relevant airframes, duplicates and artefacts that added no particular value. Also just as important, was the assessment that with only a small but dedicated group of volunteers and quite [a] few aircraft, we simply could not prevent the steady deterioration that all of the airframes were experiencing by living outside. Better then to try to ensure their survival by passing them on to other organisations that would have the resources to preserve or ideally restore them." Wise words... The Gatwick team went on to work miracles and the ever-patient Mole Valley District Council responded positively. An impressive display hall, including an education room, an exhibition on Gatwick and more was offered up and accepted. The building was officially opened on 25th March 2016 and instantly the Gatwick Aviation Museum became credible with a collection to be proud of. The route may have been tortuous, but the 'new' museum has a determined and experienced team with a long term view. Peter's legacy is assured.

Blackburn Buccaneer S.1 XN923
1962 | Shipborne low-level strike aircraft | Two 7,100lb st de Havilland Gyron Junior 101 turbojets

The Buccaneer was designed specifically for low-level penetration against capital ships or land targets with either conventional or nuclear weapons. The first of six NA.39 prototypes first flew on 30th April 1958. These were followed by 54 production S.1s which began entering service in July 1962 for a relatively brief operational career as the even more capable and re-engineered S.2s started to arrive in 1965. The Fleet Air Arm Museum has NA.39 XK488 and S.1 XN957 and, as well as XN923, four other intact S.1s are in British museums.

The Gatwick S.1 has had an extensive trials and development background and retains its test colour scheme. Built at Brough, XN923 was taken by road to the Blackburn flight test centre at Holme-on-Spalding Moor where it had its maiden flight on 11th March 1962. It was issued to the Fleet Air Arm's Intensive Flying Trials Unit, 700Z Squadron, at Lossiemouth on 8th May 1962. This service was brief and on 20th July XN923 moved to Boscombe Down to join the Aeroplane and Armament Experimental Establishment (A&AEE) and begin a dozen years of trials work. During this time the bulk of XN923's flying was with A&AEE, but it also spent time with the manufacturer at Holme and with the Royal Aircraft Establishment (RAE) at Thurleigh and in one case, Farnborough. Tasks with A&AEE included tropical trials at Idris, Libya in September 1962; the first in-flight refuelling hook-ups, from a tanker-equipped de Havilland Sea Vixen in December 1962; deck clearance tests

Hard-working Buccaneer S.1 XN923 at Charlwood. *Ken Ellis*

on HMS *Ark Royal* and *Victorious* in 1963; testing the Sperry master reference gyroscope from *Hermes* and *Ark Royal* in 1964. A lot of sorties drop-testing the aerodynamically faired under wing 'slipper' tanks and pylon mounted 250-gallon tanks were conducted by XN923 at Holme, Boscombe and Thurleigh. Ejection seat trials were performed by RAE Thurleigh in the summer of 1965. The S.1 was issued to RAE Farnborough on 23rd June 1967 for a period of ground-based weapons assessments which were tested in flight from the remote RAE airfield at West Freugh, near Stranraer, from September 1970. Ferried south to Boscombe on 17th May 1974, XN923 was retired and used for a while on electromagnetic compatibility tests before being stored externally. It was acquired by Gatwick and moved to the Charlwood site on 23rd March 1990. The volunteers have succeeded in restoring XN923 to the extent that its Gyron Junior engines can be run.

Hawker Siddeley Harrier GR.3 XV751
1969 | V/STOL tactical support fighter | One 21,500lb st Bristol Siddeley Pegasus 103 vectored thrust turbofan

RAF tactical support changed radically in April 1970 when the Harrier GR.1 entered service with 1 Squadron at Wittering. In 1988 the first of the dramatically enhanced Anglo-US Harrier GR.5s started to come on stream and in turn GR.7s and GR.9s continued to fly the vertical/short take-off and landing (V/STOL) flag until the entire RAF/Fleet Air Arm combined force was axed on 28th January 2011. Thanks to comparatively enlightened disposal policies in the 1980s GR.1 and GR.3 Harriers are well represented in British museums; much better than the 'big winged' GR.5s, GR.7s and GR.9s. Gatwick's XV751 was the 14th production GR.1 and was first flown on 28th May 1969 by John Farley at Dunsfold. It was delivered to Wittering on 2nd June 1969, entering service with the Harrier Conversion Team. This was before the two-seat operational trainer T.2 had entered service and pilot conversion to the Harrier was a carefully staged, step-by-step affair. While entering a transition from level to vertical flight at West Raynham on 6th August 1969 the pilot of XV751 had an extremely lucky escape when it plummeted downwards, ending up inverted in a cabbage field on the edge of the airfield. The pilot was only slightly injured: XV751 was trucked to Dunsfold for repair. While at Dunsfold it was fitted with the latest Pegasus 103 engine and it re-designated a GR.1A accordingly. XV751 was test flown on 22nd October 1970 and was returned to Wittering on 24th February 1971 and the following month it was issued to 233 Operational Conversion Unit. The Harrier was back at Dunsfold in March 1973, this time for upgrade to GR.3 status. As well as a Pegasus 103, it gained radar warning receivers on the fin and extreme tail and the nose profile was considerable altered by a laser ranging and marked-target seeker in a 'thimble'-shaped fairing. After this work, XV751 was taken on charge by 20 Squadron at Wildenrath, West Germany. With 20 Squadron due to disband, XV751 moved across the ramp in February 1977 and joined 3 Squadron and moved with the unit to its new base at Gütersloh

When received at Charlwood, Harrier GR.3 XV751 was painted in Sea Harrier-like colours. *Ken Ellis*

in April. By February 1979 XV751 was back at Wittering, serving with 1 Squadron. A return to 3 Squadron and Gütersloh was made in early 1986. From 1988 the unit was converting to GR.5s and XV751 was retired to St Athan; its flying days over. It was stripped of its engine and much of the operational equipment. On 16th May 1991 XV751 'enlisted' in the Navy and even received a Sea Harrier-like grey colour scheme, becoming an instructional airframe with the Air Engineering School at Lee-on-Solent. Surplus to requirements at Lee, XV751 arrived at Charlwood on 14th October 1995 and has been restored to the colours it wore with 3 Squadron.

Gatwick Aviation Museum aircraft

Type	Identity	Built	Origin	Acquired	Notes
Avro Shackleton MR.3/3	WR982	1958	Britain	Jul 1989	–
Blackburn Buccaneer S.1	XN923	1962	Britain	23 Mar 1990	see profile
de Havilland Venom FB.50	J-1605	1952	Britain	27 Oct 1989	–
de Havilland Sea Vixen FAW.2(TT)	XS587	1965	Britain	Sep 1990	–
English Electric Canberra B.2	WK146	1954	Britain	2001	cockpit
English Electric Lightning F.53*	ZF579	1967	Britain	18 Apr 2000	–
Gloster Meteor T.7*	VZ638	1949	Britain	Jul 1988	–
Hawker Sea Hawk FB.3	WM983	1954	Britain	Oct 1987	–
Hawker Hunter F.51	E-430	1956	Britain	1988	see narrative
Hawker Hunter T.7*	XL591	1958	Britain	2002	–
Hawker Siddeley Harrier GR.3*	XV751	1969	Britain	14 Oct 1995	see profile
Percival Sea Prince T.1	WP308	1952	Britain	12 Nov 1989	–

Notes: * – illustrated in the colour section

CHAPTER 28
SUSSEX

Preserve and Protect
Tangmere Military Aviation Museum

Tangmere
www.tangmere-museum.org.uk

Some airfields have what can only be described as a stellar heritage and Tangmere is one of those. Today the control tower lies bare and the airfield is used for storage, light industry, agriculture and a plant nursery under acres of glass. In the village, St Andrew's church is a place of pilgrimage its many headstones tended by the Commonwealth War Graves Commission. Since June 1982 the Tangmere Military Aviation Museum, located on the western perimeter, has paid tribute to the airfield's past, commemorates its personnel and charted the development of aerial warfare in general. A meeting of enthusiasts in 1981 led to the founding of the all-volunteer run museum and West Sussex County Council donated a large display hall to get things going. Since then the museum has expanded considerably: the latest of several exhibition halls being dedicated to the memory of Meryl Hansed. This houses Hunter F.5 WP190 – painted in the colours of 1 Squadron, as based at Tangmere – and English Electric Lightning F.53 ZF578, both of which were donated by Raymond Hansed. As well as the Cold War hardware on show, the museum has a vast amount of material from World War Two and the Battle of Britain in particular. The remains of Hurricane I P3179 are extremely poignant. On 30th August 1940 Sgt Dennis Noble of 43 Squadron took off from Tangmere in P3179 and engaged a Luftwaffe Junkers Ju 88 off Brighton. The German aircraft got the better of the Hurricane and it crashed in a street at Hove, killing its 20-year-old pilot. The hulk was recovered in 1996 and presented to the museum three years later.

Above: Neville Duke's world record-breaking Hunter Mk.3 WB188 at Tangmere. *Ken Ellis*

A record breaker with a record breaker: Gp Capt Hugh Wilson CBE AFC with Meteor IV EE549 at Cranwell in June 1952. Wilson flew Meteor IV EE454 'Britannia' to take the world air speed record to 606.25mph on 7th November 1945. This was beaten on 7th September 1946 by Gp Capt 'Teddy' Donaldson while flying EE549 from Tangmere. *Peter Green Collection*

Crowded heritage

Royal Aircraft Factory SE.5s of 92 Squadron were among the first residents at the newly established aerodrome from the spring of 1918. The United States Army Air Service brought Airco DH.4s to Tangmere in November 1918, but stayed only fleetingly as the Armistice obviated their presence. The airfield was closed by 1920 but was reborn in 1926 with the arrival of the Gloster Gamecocks of 43 Squadron. (The museum's postal address is Gamecock Terrace, Tangmere.) Briefly used for coastal patrol Avro Ansons in 1937-1938, the airfield played host to intense deployments of Hawker Hurricanes, Supermarine Spitfires and other fighters throughout the war. Tangmere also gained fame as the forward operating base for the Westland Lysanders of 161 Squadron as they plied to and from France dropping off and picking up agents. An early post-war inmate was 1 Squadron, from April 1946. Initially equipped with Spitfire Mk.21s, the unit converted to Gloster Meteor IIIs the following year. No.1 returned to Tangmere twice in the 1950s, disbanding at the airfield in June 1958, having flown Hunter F.5s. Flying from the site came to an end in October 1963 when the English Electric Canberras of 98 Squadron and the Vickers Varsities of 115 Squadron departed, both going to Watton. Disposal of the airfield began in the mid-1970s.

Flat out for world records

In June 1946 the RAF revived a unit that had made history in September 1931 by securing the Schneider Trophy in perpetuity for Great Britain. (See Chapter 11.) This was the High Speed Flight, then flying Supermarine S.6 floatplanes, but this time the pilots were issued with specially modified Meteor IVs, known as Star Meteors. Commanding the special unit was Gp Capt E M 'Teddy' Donaldson DSO AFC and among the pilots he had gathered together were Sqn Ldr Neville Duke DSO DFC and Sqn Ldr Bill Waterton AFC – destined to become test pilots for Hawker and Gloster, respectively. On 7th September 1946 Teddy piloted Star Meteor EE549 around a calibrated 3-kilometre course off Littlehampton to establish a new world air speed record of 615.8mph – Mach 0.81.

This was not to be the only world record clinched at Tangmere. Neville Duke returned in September 1953 in the prototype Hunter, WB188, specially modified and designated Mk.3. Operating from Tangmere and flying the same 'race track' off the Sussex coast that had been used by the High Speed Flight, on 7th September 1953 Neville took WB188 to 727.6mph to take the record and on the 19th took the 100km closed-circuit record to 709.2mph for good measure. The rival Supermarine team was determined to steal Neville's laurels and in Libya on 25th September 1953, Mike Lithgow piloted Swift F.4 WK198 to 735.7mph to keep the headlines going. In 1992 the RAF Museum paid the Tangmere museum a huge compliment by presenting on loan the two aircraft that had flashed through the skies off Littlehampton: Meteor IV EE549 and Hunter Mk.3 WB188. This faith was extended in 1995 when Swift FR.5 WK281 was also delivered by road. This was to extend the record

Sea Vixen FAW.2 XJ580, in the colours of 899 Squadron, in the aircraft park at Tangmere. *Les Woodward*

break theme and to commemorate Mike Lithgow's record in Libya. (The fuselage of Mike's record-breaking WK198 is held at the Brooklands Museum – Chapter 27 – and was rescued by the North East Aircraft Museum – Chapter 22.) Gp Capt Donaldson died on 2nd June 1992 and he is buried at St Andrew's church, Tangmere. In the 1990s Neville Duke graciously agreed to be the museum's honorary president: today the Neville Duke Hall remembers the great test pilot's links with Tangmere.

Tangmere Military Aviation Museum aircraft

Type	Identity	Built	Origin	Acquired	Notes
de Havilland Vampire T.11	XH313	1956	Britain	22 Oct 2008	–
de Havilland Sea Vixen FAW.2	XJ580	1960	Britain	27 Jun 2000	–
de Havilland Canada Chipmunk T.10	WZ876	1953	Canada	Oct 2014	cockpit
English Electric Canberra B.2	WE113	1952	Britain	Jun 2011	cockpit
English Electric Lightning	–	1962	Britain	Dec 2008	simulator
English Electric Lightning F.53	ZF578	1967	Britain	Jun 2002	–
Gloster Meteor IV Special	EE549	1946	Britain	19 Sep 1992	–
Gloster Meteor F.8	WA984	1951	Britain	Dec 1990	–
Hawker Hurricane I	'L1679'	1992	Britain	Aug 1994	replica
Hawker Hurricane I	P3179	1940	Britain	1999	cockpit
Hawker Hunter F.3	WB188	1951	Britain	19 Sep 1992	–
Hawker Hunter F.4	WV332	1955	Britain	2003	cockpit
Hawker Hunter F.5*	WP190	1955	Britain	2 Jun 2002	–
Hawker Siddeley Harrier GR.3	XV744	1969	Britain	14 Mar 2013	–
Hawker Siddeley Sea Harrier FA.2	ZA195	1983	Britain	21 Feb 2008	–
Lockheed T-33A	51-9252	1951	USA	1985	–
McDonnell Phantom FGR.2	XV408	1968	USA	30 Nov 2005	–
Percival Provost T.1	XF840	1955	Britain	2014	fuselage
Supermarine Spitfire prototype	'K5054'	1992	Britain	1997	replica
Supermarine Swift FR.5*	WK281	1956	Britain	1995	–
Westland Wessex HU.5	XS511	1964	USA/GB	2004	–

Notes: * – illustrated in the colour section.

Part of the Wings museum 'Ghosts of the Tundra' display, a P-63C Kingcobra. *Daniel Hunt*

Recalling Ghosts
Wings World War Two Remembrance Museum

Balcombe
www.wingsmuseum.co.uk

Lying on the edge of a field in East Anglia was a fascinating, battered piece of metal. It was the late 1970s and brothers Daniel and Kevin Hunt were on a family holiday. The discovery was taken home and later found to be a gunsight from a 0.5in Browning machine gun. This small artefact, probably from a waist gun of a USAAF 2nd Air Division Consolidated B-24 Liberator, was the catalyst for today's Wings World War Two Remembrance Museum. Collecting, researching and restoring ever since, Daniel and Kevin soon came to the conclusion that they had gathered so much material that the easiest way to handle it all was to found a museum!

The Gas Decontamination Block at Redhill aerodrome in Surrey was turned into a museum and was opened to the public in 2003. This was just the start and the World War Two building was soon too small. On 15th March 2008 the next phase of the Wings Museum was unveiled in Hangar 9. Closing in November 2009 for the winter season, the volunteer team discovered that they had to vacate the hangar. A new venue was found at Balcombe and after back-breaking work and long days the museum opened up again on 20th March 2010 in a 12,000 square foot hangar-like building. Redhill has not been forgotten at Balcombe; there is a display charting the history of the airfield and curator Daniel Hunt has researched every operational sortie staged from there. A Book of Remembrance lists nearly eighty pilots who lost their lives flying from Redhill.

Among the themes adopted by the museum, 'Ghosts of the Tundra' is the only exhibition of its kind in Europe. This includes extensive remains salvaged from the former Soviet Union on both the European front – against the Germans – and the Siberia front where the Russians briefly fought the Japanese up to, and beyond, the official surrender of 2nd September 1945. A Soviet-operated Bell P-63 Kingcobra and an Imperial Japanese Navy Nakajima B5N2 *Kate* uncovered on the Kuril Islands to the north east of Japan in the Sea of Okhotsk have been placed within a diorama. The remains of a Soviet Air Force Douglas A-20G Havoc are depicted in a forest setting, just like the area in which it crashed over seventy years ago. The propeller blades have been nicked by bullet strikes and there are holes in the rear fuselage from 20mm cannon shells. Underneath the faded red star is the ghostly traces of an American 'star and bar'.

Wings World War Two Remembrance Museum aircraft

Type	Identity	Built	Origin	Acquired	Notes
Auster J/1U Workmaster	G-OJAS	1952	Britain	2003	fuselage
Bell P-63C Kingcobra	43-11137	1943	USA	2003	cockpit, plus another
Bristol Beaufighter If	–	1941	Britain	Sep 2015	cockpit
Curtiss SB2C-5 Helldiver	–	1942	USA	2016	forward fuselage
de Havilland Canada Chipmunk T.10	WD377	1951	Canada	2015	cockpit
Douglas A-20G Havoc	43-21664	1943	USA	Mar 2006	fuselage
Douglas C-47A Skytrain	42-100611	1942	USA	Sep 2007	fuselage
Douglas B-26K Invader	64-17657	1964	USA	Feb 2010	cockpit
Hawker Hurricane II	BD731	1941	Britain	2003	substantial remains
Hunting Jet Provost T.3	XM468	1960	Britain	2016	cockpit
Miles Hawk Trainer III	G-AUIA	1940	Britain	2003	fuselage
Nakajima B5N2 *Kate*	339	c1944	Japan	2003	forward fuselage
Nakajima Ki-43 Hayabusa*	–	c1944	Japan	2012	cockpit, plus another
North America B-25J Mitchell	43-36140	1943	USA	2003	forward fuselage

Notes: * – illustrated in the colour section.

Also in Sussex
Newhaven Fort

Within the late 19th century fortification are displays on the air war over Sussex and a feature on the Royal Observer Corps as well as more general material on World War Two. **www.newhavenfort.org.uk**

Robertsbridge Aviation Centre

Run by the Robertsbridge Aviation Society, this museum is open only on the last Sunday of the month from March to November, but is well worth seeking out. As well as a collection of cockpits, there is a vast number of artefacts, mostly from World War Two. **https://sites.google.com/site/robertsbridgeaviation/**

Robertsbridge Aviation Centre aircraft

Type	Identity	Built	Origin	Acquired	Notes
de Havilland Sea Vixen FAW.1	XJ488	1958	Britain	1997	cockpit
English Electric Canberra PR.3	WE173	1953	Britain	1996	cockpit
English Electric Lightning F.3	XP701	1963	Britain	1991	cockpit
Gloster Meteor T.7	WA630	1949	Britain	1991	cockpit
Hawker Hunter F.2	WN907	1954	Britain	17 Mar 2002	cockpit
Hunting Jet Provost T.4	XR681	1963	Britain	2002	cockpit

CHAPTER 29
WARWICKSHIRE AND WORCESTERSHIRE

Honouring Whittle
Midland Air Museum

Coventry Airport
www.midlandairmuseum.co.uk

Fifty years ago, a classified advertisement in the *Coventry Evening Telegraph* sparked the formation of the Midland Aircraft Preservation Society (MAPS), which in turned spawned the Midland Air Museum. Chapter 18 examined the origins of the prototype 'APS' – the Northern Aircraft Preservation Society – and I was keen to investigate the formative years of MAPS by way of a comparison. John Berkeley was chairman of MAPS and the Midland Air Museum from 1972 to 1987 when Ray Ball took over briefly, with John returning from 1988 to 1993, and he patiently answered my questions. While the NAPS founders were united by a regular weekend meeting at Manchester Airport, the MAPS equivalent, John said: "could be divided into two groups – aeromodellers (*flying*, not plastic kits) or train spotters, who changed to plane spotting with the advent of diesels." The main source of information on what was going on was the magazine *Air Pictorial* (these days *Aviation News*) as well as establishing a good 'grapevine' at Coventry and at air events, particularly the Shuttleworth Collection at Old Warden. There was an interest in aircraft built in the area and the engines made by Armstrong Siddeley but: "There was an increasing awareness that locally made aircraft were getting thin on the ground." This was the spur that led to setting up a preservation organisation.

Above: Tornado GR.4 ZA452 at the Midland Air Museum. *David Horton*

Founder members of MAPS with the first aircraft acquisition, Pixie III G-EBJG. Left to right: Rick Clarke, Mick Abbey, Gordon Riley, Dave Phillips and Roger Smith. *Coventry Evening Telegraph*

John continued: "We had the time and the determination, but no money, so that really set the limits to what we could achieve. More and more, we were getting to know owners of aircraft and they knew of others, the net was widening. Our knowledge went up and up accordingly... We had no ultimate scheme... I for one could not have envisaged what we achieved in that first decade. The collecting policy was very basic; we were looking for airframes that were light, portable and either cheap or free." One idea stuck quite early on: "We took pride in the knowledge that Sir Frank Whittle was a Coventrian [born in the city's Earlsdon district, 1907] and so jets began to play an increasingly important part in our interest." As MAPS began to spread the word about what it was up to and its ambitions, at local events and airshows, something began to sink in: "...we had a vision to honour Whittle, a man many Coventrians had no idea was born in their city".

Made in Coventry

Coventry Airport, Baginton, owes its origins to Armstrong Whitworth (AW) which was out-growing its factory and small airfield at nearby Whitley Abbey. The land at Baginton, not far away to the south, was deemed ideal for a large factory to build the company's latest product, the appropriately named Whitley medium bomber. The prototype first flew at Whitley Abbey on 17th March 1936 but by then the Baginton plant was nearing completion, with its own grass airfield alongside. With the outbreak of war, a procession of fighter units was based for local defence of the heavily industrialised area. The longest resident was 308 (Polish) Squadron which arrived in September 1940 with Hawker Hurricane Is, departing with Supermarine Spitfire IIs in June 1941. The RAF withdrew in late 1943, leaving Baginton largely to AW. By 1944 Bitteswell, to the east at Lutterworth was being used increasingly for flight testing and by the late 1940s began to take over the assembly role. Replacing the Whitley on the production line were Avro Lancasters and, from 1945 to 1949 Avro Lincolns. Experimentation with flying wings and the abortive Apollo four-turboprop airliner were followed by production for other design houses. As a member of the Hawker Siddeley Group, AW took part in the manufacture of Gloster Meteors from 1949 and AW was given design responsibility for the long-nosed night-fighter versions. Hawker Sea Hawks, Hawker Hunters and Gloster Javelins succeeded one another in the Baginton factory. The final product was homespun, the Argosy commercial freighter and tactical airlifter, the last example flying in 1966.

With a long and proud lineage in motor cars, both Armstrong Siddeley and Alvis moved into aero engine manufacture. At Parkside, Armstrong Siddeley began with the six-cylinder in-line Puma of 1917, before making its name with a family of radials. From April 1943 the ASX turbojet was developed leading to the Sapphire and the company also created the Mamba turboprop. Alvis made radial engines from mid-1935: its Leonides being its most famous product, made up to 1966. As mentioned earlier, Frank Whittle was not only born in the area, but tapped into experience within Coventry and the area; founding Power Jets Ltd in March 1936. The first Whittle Unit was run at Lutterworth on 12th April 1937. British Thomson-Houston of Rugby and Coventry-based Rover – another motor car manufacturer – became involved with developing Whittle's engines and getting them to a stage where they could be mass manufactured. In November 1942 Rolls-Royce was put at the helm of the project.

Dismantling Vampire F.1 VF301 at Debden, March 1973. *Gordon Riley*

First steps

To help celebrate the half-century of MAPS, John Berkeley wrote *Museum in the Making* in the May 2017 edition of *FlyPast*. There being no point in re-inventing the wheel, the following is heavily based on John's feature and I am very grateful to him for allowing this. As related above, an advertisement in the *Coventry Evening Telegraph* was the clarion call for like-minded people in the area to join forces and seventeen people attended a meeting on 24th May 1967. Roger Smith, a 19 year-old apprentice draughtsman at Dunlop Aviation placed that advert and founded MAPS. Significantly, many of those early members were already active with restoration projects of their own: Carl Butler with his two Mosscrafts, MA.1 G-AFHA and MA.2 G-AFJV; John Coggins and his collection of Prentices; Roy Nerou had Klemm L.25 G-AAHW; Ken Wooley with Foster Wickner Wicko G-AFJB and several others. They were followed shortly after by the likes of Don Burgoyne and Joe Wood both of whom had built and 'flown' Mignet 'Flying Fleas' G-AECN and G-AEBT respectively in the mid-1930s.

Between 1910 and 1966 Coventry produced over 14,000 aircraft and no fewer than 3,530 Royal Aircraft Factory RE.8s were built in the city during World War One, nearly 90 per cent of the total. It is fitting that the new society's very first acquisition was an RE.8 propeller. The first airframe was donated by James Rowe: the remains of Parnall Pixie III G-EBJG, which participated in the Lympne Light Aeroplane Trials in both 1924 and 1926. James's family farm at Stratford-upon-Avon had served as a landing ground for the town during the 1920s and 1930s. The Pixie had flown from a field off the A5 road near Nuneaton while owned by local businessman Stanley Dodwell from 1935. James Rowe continued to support MAPS, with a converted pigsty on his farm remaining in use as a store until 1988.

At first MAPS relied almost entirely on the generosity of donors, content to pass on redundant airframes. As a result several gliders, either damaged or with glue failure, found their way into the growing collection. Some were relatively familiar types, such as the Slingsby Cadet, DFS Grunau Baby and DFS Kranich, while the experimental Nyborg TGN.3 sailplane was a true one-off. [See the table for early MAPS acquisitions that did not become part of the museum.] The main priority was to raise funds and attract new members by visiting airshows with a publicity and sales stand, and, wherever possible, displaying an airframe. In February 1954, the wings of 'Flying Flea' G-AEGV were discovered in a garage in Northampton and these were later acquired by society chairman Bob Ogden and donated to MAPS. Members built a new fuselage and it became the ideal travelling exhibit, capable of being transported in a van. In 1972, a record 22 venues were attended and, before the end of 1973, membership had passed the 100 mark, drawn from across the region.

Heavy metal – increased costs and decreased mobility

After five years, it was decided to take a more proactive approach towards acquisitions and the first to be targeted was de Havilland Vampire F.1 VF301, serving as a 'gate guardian' at RAF Debden in Essex. The procedure back then was to contact R T Kenworthy at the Ministry of Defence (MoD) in Harrogate and express an interest. He would respond by post with a fixed price, probably based on the aircraft's empty weight. No competitive tendering, just a simple take-it-or-leave-it transaction and, in the case of VF301, an asking price of £100! [Average annual salary in Britain in 1972 was £2,262.] The Vampire was quickly followed by a second early jet, Gloster Meteor F.4 EE531, still in its wartime camouflage and gathering dust in a Royal Aircraft Establishment hangar at Lasham. At £175, and with dismantling and transport costs, the search began for a sponsor. Fortunately, the Birmingham telephone directory turned up a car dealership in Moseley named Meteor Ford and, freshly repainted, EE531 became the centrepiece of a forecourt display in the summer of 1973. Neither of these aircraft had been declared as surplus by the MoD and acquiring them was an important step towards the future direction of the museum.

Aerial view of the extended original site, 1983. *via John Berkeley*

Having accumulated nine engines and fifteen airframes during the first five years, the need for a permanent base was becoming urgent, with lock-up garages and converted pigsties simply no longer fit for purpose. Many possibilities had already been explored, from as far afield as Halfpenny Green, now Wolverhampton Airport, to the old Stratford aerodrome. Although Lord Brooke at Warwick Castle offered the use of a small site in the town centre, this would have provided no scope for expansion. Thanks to Roger Smith being employed at the National Agricultural Centre at Stoneleigh, near Kenilworth, that venue came to the rescue. In August 1972, MAPS displayed several aircraft and engines at the first Town and Country Festival and, following the event, was offered storage and workshop facilities on the site. This arrangement lasted for the next five years and without it MAPS could not have continued to expand and develop.

In an effort to bring the Society's problem to a much wider audience, four aircraft were moved to the BBC television studios in Birmingham for a live *Pebble Mill at One* transmission on 26th November 1973. Although the switchboard was jammed with offers of help, none came from within the Midlands! Eventually, after strenuous canvassing, Coventry City councillors commissioned a report on the society's proposal to establish a museum at Coventry Airport. Following the project's approval, the council formally transferred its responsibility for recording and preserving the city's aviation heritage to MAPS. This was the start of a unique relationship, supported by individual councillors, a succession of Lord Mayors and the local press, that played a vital role in the future. The initial site on the edge of the airport was small but gave an uninterrupted view of the main runway and was opened to the public as the Midland Air Museum for the first time on 2nd April 1978.

Percival Q.6 G-AFFD nearing the end of a restoration to fly at Seething. *Ken Ellis*

Midland Aircraft Preservation Society aircraft 1967 to 1978

Type	Identity	Built	Origin	Acquired	Current status / fate
Auster AOP.9	–	c1953	Britain	1967	static test airframe; believed scrapped at Fairwood Common c1975
Beagle Airedale	G-ASAH	1963	Britain	1973	exchanged for G-AFFD, last known at Chelsea College, Shoreham, 1977
Clay Cherub	'G-BDGP'	c1965	Britain	Sep 1978	ground trainer; disposed of 1978, thought scrapped c1982
de Havilland Fox Moth	G-ACCB	1933	Britain	Nov 1968	fuselage, private owner Nuneaton, under restoration, with wings from Tiger Moth G-AOUY
de Havilland Dragon Rapide	G-AJBJ	1944	Britain	1972	with private owner, stored in North Wales
DFS Grunau Baby IIB	VT921	c1943	Germany	Mar 1969	glider, to Thetford for restoration to fly; unknown
DFS Kranich 2 B-1	SE-STF	1944	Germany	31 Jan 1970	glider, at Allebergs Segelflyg Museet, Falköping, Sweden
Hawker Hurricane	'H3422'	1968	Britain	1972	replica, private owner, Cornwall
Hawker Hurricane	'V7467'	1968	Britain	1974	replica, Jet Age Museum – Chapter 10
Messerschmitt 'Bf 109'	–	1973	Germany	1973	replica, Kent Battle of Britain Museum – Chapter 14
Miles Messenger 4A	G-ALAR	1948	Britain	c1970	private owner, stored in Stratford-on-Avon area
Nyborg TGN.3	–	1932	Britain	Nov 1967	glider, to MAPS member for restoration, destroyed while in store
Percival Q.6	G-AFFD	1938	Britain	6 Apr 1974	under restoration to fly, Seething, Norfolk
Supermarine Spitfire	'N3313'	1968	Britain	7 Feb 1973	replica, Kent Battle of Britain Museum – Chapter 14

Special relationships

Although the long term objective was to establish a museum centred around the life and work of Sir Frank Whittle, throughout the 1970s and 1980s the aim was also to create a broad, well-balanced collection of aircraft, helicopters and gliders and three very special relationships were to play a crucial part in that process. The first was with the College of Aeronautics at Cranfield, now Cranfield University. Early on, it had amassed a remarkable collection of airframes, known as the 'Library of Flight' some of which had already found their way into major museums. [More details in sister volume *Lost Aviation Collections of Britain*.] Thanks almost entirely to the generosity of the then Head of Aircraft Design, Professor Denis Howe, a stream of aircraft and major components were transferred to Coventry. Amongst these were all that remained of several early British jets, such as the outer wing of Gloster E1/44 TX150 and the cockpit canopy of the sole Supermarine 545 XA181. The cost, 44 years ago was £15! Other parts followed, together with four rather more substantial acquisitions: in order of arrival: the Fairey Ultra-Light Helicopter, Flettner Fl 282B Kolibri, Boulton Paul P.111A and Westland Whirlwind Series 3 – the first three are profiled, see below. Because of its significance and rarity, it was decided that every effort should be made to return the Flettner to Germany to be professionally restored and exhibited. With Cranfield's full agreement, enquiries began in 1976 with the aim of arranging an exchange for one of the top priorities on the acquisitions list. Four German collections were anxious to negotiate a deal but, unfortunately, none were able to offer something suitable. Nevertheless, those efforts continued into the 1990s, with the offer of a Mikoyan-Gurevich MiG-15 *Fagot* from the Deutsches Museum in Munich.

Former Danish F-104G Starfighter R-756 was delivered inside a C-130 Hercules in 1987. *David Horton*

On 24th November 1975 a trio of former French Air Force North American F-100D Super Sabres flew into Sculthorpe from Châteaudun. These machines had been funded under the USA Mutual Defence Aid Program and were to be ferried to Britain for scrapping. Many more F-100s were to follow, along with Lockheed T-33As and Dassault Mystère IVAs. In common with several other collections, interest was expressed in obtaining one of each, to be held on indefinite loan from what was then the USAF Museum (now the National Museum of the USAF). This was the museum's second special relationship. Despite the museum team's previous experience, dismantling the ten-ton F-100D was challenging. Having scarcely even seen one at close quarters and with none of the special equipment required for dismantling, it proved quite a challenge. If, after the three-hour journey to Sculthorpe, one of the specially-made tools was to break, it was back to Coventry to make a new one in a local school workshop. Eventually, the nearly 50-foot long fuselage arrived safely in March 1978, followed by the wings a month later.

During the spring of 1981, new-found friends at the US Defense Property Disposal Service asked if the museum would be interested in a US Army de Havilland Canada U-6A Beaver which had been operated on intelligence-gathering missions along the Berlin Wall. Ramstein Air Force Base very kindly offered to ship it inside a Boeing CH-47 Chinook as a 'training exercise'. In March 1982 this bond was further strengthened with a meeting at the US Embassy where it was agreed that the then Defense Security Assistance Agency would assist in acquiring other surplus aircraft on the same terms. Ten years later, that support, aided by the excellent relationship with Tom Brewer at the USAF Museum, had enabled the acquisition of no fewer than eleven aircraft and one cockpit section; more than any other British museum. In January 1986, interest was expressed in a Royal Danish Air Force (RDAF) Lockheed F-104G Starfighter. This arrived in April 1987, courtesy of a RDAF Lockheed C-130 Hercules. Once again, being located on an operational airport proved invaluable.

The SAAB J29 29640 inside the Sir Frank Whittle Jet Heritage Centre at Coventry. *Richard Hall*

Research also revealed that batches of RAF Hunter F.6s had been funded by the US and one of these, Coventry-built XF382, was located at Brawdy and quickly dismantled during November 1986. Attention turned in 1991 to the number of former USAF aircraft in use for battle damage repair training and interest was expressed in three of these, a McDonnell F-101 Voodoo at Alconbury and McDonnell F-4C Phantoms at Upper Heyford and Woodbridge. It was believed that this might be the only opportunity to preserve examples of these types in Britain and the fact that Phantom 63-7699 was also a genuine Vietnam 'MiG-killer' was a great bonus.

The third special relationship was of a very different kind, but no less important. As a voluntary organisation, the museum's most important and valuable resource was its members. By the early 1980s, the sheer pace of development demanded additional manpower. Thankfully, the Thatcher government had introduced the Community Programme, providing temporary work for the long-term unemployed. In 1983 the first of three such schemes began, employing twenty people on a mixture of site work and restoration. It was the start of a seven-year partnership, a unique collaboration that finally led to the opening of a dedicated aircraft restoration workshop at Edgwick in the city centre in 1985. This was largely staffed by a team made redundant with the closure of the Hawker Siddeley facility at Bitteswell. The first project tackled at Edgwick was the former Southend museum Saab J29F 29640, which included some re-skinning.

The Whittle Project

Following a city centre event in 1981 to mark the 40th anniversary of the maiden flight of the Power Jets Whittle W.1 propelled Gloster E28/39 at which the first appeal for funds to erect a hangar/workshop was launched, the then Lord Mayor confessed that he had no idea that Sir Frank Whittle was born in Coventry. This demonstrated how much effort would be required to create a permanent and fitting tribute to the pioneering work of the 'Father of the Jet Engine' in the region where he lived and worked. It was left to Roger Smith to have a commemorative plaque cast and mounted on Whittle's birthplace. The museum's Blériot XI was installed in October 1984 as the centrepiece of the main terminal building at Birmingham Airport. Based on original parts, the Blériot had been reconfigured as a 1911 Humber Monoplane fitted with a Humber 30hp three-cylinder engine, on loan from Coventry Museum. Use of the Blériot led to an excellent relationship with senior management of the airport's owners, the West Midlands County Council. In December 1985 a formal application was made for financial support to create the Sir Frank Whittle Jet Heritage Centre and on 2nd April 1986, just a few hours before the West Midlands council ceased to exist, a cheque for £110,000 was handed over – worth half a million at today's rates.

The first museum plot had been a mere 540 by 450 feet but, by 1986, the move had been made to the adjacent 4.5 acre site. The construction contract for the Whittle building was signed on 30th October 1986 with a planned completion date of February the following year. Sir Frank Whittle had given his blessing to the project back in 1981 and an excellent rapport had been created with The Reactionaries, an association of former employees and associates of Whittle's company, Power Jets. A Robin hangar recovered from the wartime Daimler factory in Coventry would provide all-important workshop facilities as well as being an exhibit in its own right. Within a year, planning for a mezzanine exhibition area had begun, to accommodate a 'Wings over Coventry' gallery, presenting the story of eighty years involvement with aviation. The official opening took place on 21st May 1991, performed by Lord Kings Norton, once chairman and managing director of Power Jets. At the end of its first quarter century, the Midland Air Museum had a collection of close to fifty aeroplanes, had rebalanced a city's appreciation of its industrial heritage and led the way in securing local recognition for the most significant Coventrian of the twentieth century. Fifty years on, the pioneers who responded to a classified advert in the local paper and who joined the ranks beyond that can be justifiable proud of their achievements.

The P.111A VP935 during an early flight, 1950. *Boulton Paul*

Boulton Paul P.111A VT935

1950 | Delta wing research aircraft | One 5,100lb st Rolls-Royce Nene 3 turbojet

Boulton Paul was contracted to build a pair of single-seat pure delta (ie no horizontal tailplanes) P.111 trans-sonic research aircraft under Specification E27/46. Only VT935 was completed in this form, the other aircraft became the P.120 with a 'T' tail. VT935 was built at Pendeford, Wolverhampton, between 1947 and 1950 and had its first taxi trials in the hands of the Boulton Paul chief test pilot, Flt Lt Alexander Ewen 'Ben' Gunn. Unusually, Ben was not given the responsibility of the maiden flight. As the aircraft was destined for the research fleet of the Royal Aircraft Establishment (RAE), this task fell to the officer commanding the Farnborough Aero Flight, Sqn Ldr Robert Smythe. The delta was taken by road to Boscombe Down and Smythe carried out the honours of 10th October 1950. No slight was meant on Ben Gunn's capabilities, indeed he got to pilot VT935 the same day, flying it a total of four times over three days. VT935 was demonstrated at the September 1951 Farnborough airshow, and again at the 1953 event. A belly landing at Boscombe on 5th January 1952 had VT935 travelling back up the roads to Pendeford. Boulton Paul repaired it and took the opportunity to upgrade it to P.111A status, including 'petal' airbrakes. Back at Boscombe, Ben carried out its first flight in this new guise on 2nd July 1953. It was officially accepted by the RAE Aero Flight at Farnborough on 24th February 1954 and transferred to RAE Thurleigh on 16th February 1956. Retired from flying in March 1957, it was acquired by the College of Aeronautics at Cranfield and was delivered by road on 21st April 1959 becoming part of the famous 'Library of Flight' collection. Approaches from Midland were successful and the museum became VT935's custodian when it arrived at Coventry on 13th July 1975 – its fifth road journey. As a midlands product and a jet, the P.111A was ideal for the museum, but with research aircraft being normally regarded as a 'national' asset it was also quite a coup for a 'regional' collection.

de Havilland Vampire F.1 VF301
1946 | Day fighter | One 3,100lb st de Havilland Goblin 3 turbojet

An incredible number of Vampires are held in collections across Britain. A trio of early Vampires exist; development Mk.1 LZ551 at Yeovilton, F.3 VT812 at Hendon and Midland's VF301 – the oldest surviving operational example – another one for the 'nationals' to envy. Built by English Electric at Samlesbury, VF301 was issued to the newly formed 226 Operational Conversion Unit at Molesworth on 27th September 1946; relocating to Bentwaters on 10th October. Then came service with two operational squadrons and the opportunity to be in harm's way: 595 Squadron at Pembrey from 19th February 1947 and 631 Squadron at Llanbedr from 24th September 1948. Both units were tasked with anti-aircraft co-operation, flying what were called gun-laying exercises – giving the Army and RAF Regiment 'ack-ack' gunners the chances to aim – and perhaps fire blanks – at a fast flying jet. After a spell with de Havilland in early 1951 for refurbishing, VF301 joined 103 Flying Refresher School at Full Sutton on 29th August 1951. This unit allowed long desk-bound pilots to get up to scratch prior to operational postings, or to keep their flying experience topped up. Final use came with 208 Advanced Flying School at Merryfield, from 21st July 1952. As explained in the introduction, space precludes every visit to a maintenance unit (MU) and the like, but the final 'active' days of VF301 are quite instructive. On 28th October 1952 the Vampire suffered an accident at Merryfield which was defined as Category 3 – repairable on site, but not by the resident facilities. The following day a working party from the Colerne-based 49 MU arrived to begin work. By 12th January 1953 VF301 had been moved to 5 MU at Kemble for re-assessment. Fourteen days later VF301 was issued to de Havilland for what was termed 'repair in works' and this treatment was notified as complete on 30th April. All done and dusted, thirteen days after that the Vampire was declared a non-effective airframe – ready for disposal! It was issued to Debden as a 'gate guardian' (with the instructional airframe serial 7060M) on 25th August 1953. As described in the narrative, it was taken on by Midland in April 1972 – £100 well spent!

Fairey Ultra Light Helicopter G-APJJ
1957 | Light helicopter | One 252shp Turboméca Palouste BnPe 2 turboshaft

Two of the five Fairey Ultra-Lights that flew are preserved – an exceptional survivor percentage. G-AOUJ at The Helicopter Museum (Chapter 25) is undergoing a long term restoration process, and Midland's Juliet-Juliet. Along with the huge transport Rotodyne – also in Chapter 25 – Fairey applied its tip-driven rotor blade technology to the other end of the scale, light helicopters. Specification H.114T gave rise to a development contract for a small helicopter capable of carrying out surveillance, training and casualty evacuation yet be small enough to be transported on the back of a three-tonner truck. A Palouste turbojet, built under licence by Blackburn, was modified to act as a compressor driving 'jets' in the rotor tips and provide a degree of thrust. Referred to only as the Ultra-Light Helicopter, the first prototype flew for the first time at White Waltham on 14th August 1955. Official backing for the project was withdrawn in 1956 but Fairey followed up four Ministry-funded examples with the private venture G-APJJ. Built at Hayes, it was first flown at White Waltham in 1958 and appeared at that year's Farnborough airshow. After some further development flying, Fairey also abandoned the venture in 1959. G-APJJ was taken on by the Royal Aircraft Establishment Thurleigh where it was used for non-flying rotor behaviour testing; some of this involving the helicopter being mounted on the top of a single-deck bus that was driven at speed while cameras recorded the blade's antics. After Thurleigh, G-APJJ stayed in Bedfordshire, being presented to the College of Aeronautics at Cranfield; it was acquired by Midland in 1975.

The P.111A VP935 during an early flight, 1950. *Boulton Paul*/Fairey test pilot John Morton flying Ultra-Light Helicopter G-APJJ. *Blackburn*

Above: HH-43B Huskie 62-4535 at Alconbury in 1970.
KEC

Left: The Midlands Flettner undergoing trials at Kiel-Holtenau, 1944. *Kurt Lastig, via Steven Coates*

Flettner Fl 282B V20 Kolibri 280020
1943 | Light observation helicopter | One 160hp BMW-Bramo Sh 14A piston

Although only the bare forward fuselage frame, undercarriage and complex rotor head survives, this is an airframe of world significance. German rotorcraft pioneer Anton Flettner succeeded in getting his Kolibri (humming bird) observation helicopter to be operationally evaluated by the Kriegsmarine, certainly in the Baltic, possibly in the Mediterranean. Using complex shafting and gearing the Fl 282's radial engine drove two synchronised inter-meshing rotors that did away with the need for a torque-cancelling tail rotor. Flight trials began in 1941 with a batch of 20 – perhaps 24 – prototypes which were built at the Flettner factories at Johannistal, near Düsseldorf, and Bad Tölz, south of Munich. In 1942 trials were conducted with a Kolibri flying on and off decking built on top of a gun turret of the cruiser *Köln* in the Baltic. By the following year, the type had proved itself and arrangements were being made to construct a thousand examples. Events overcame this promising helicopter and four were discovered by occupying forces, with two going to the USA and one to the USSR. The Midland example, the V20 (versuchs – experimental) twentieth prototype, 'CJ+SN', was captured at Travemünde on the Baltic coast and dispatched to 6 Maintenance Unit at Brize Norton in July 1945. It was issued to the newly established College of Aeronautics at Cranfield on 1st August 1946 for study. At this point it was complete, including its rotors, but shortage of space at Cranfield had led to the removal of its rear fuselage and cropping of its intermeshing rotor blades and by the early 1970s it was only the bare forward fuselage frame.

Midland collected the Kolibri from Cranfield in May 1975 and six years later – on 6th March 1981 to be exact – another inter-meshing design arrived at the museum; a more modern development of the inter-meshing concept. This was Kaman HH-43B 62-4535. Aeronautical engineer Charles Huron Kaman turned his hand to rotorcraft experimentation from 1945. (He also designed high-tech guitars, but I digress...) His prototype K-125 first flew in 15th January 1947 with inter-meshing blades. Kaman termed the rotor system 'synchropter'. By the early 1960s the USAF was operating the much-developed HH-43 Huskie for short-range crash rescue and fire suppression at bases across the world. The Midland example served with the 40th Aerospace Rescue and Recovery Wing at Upper Heyford and later Alconbury, until the type was withdrawn in 1972. It was moved to Woodbridge by 1976 for battle damage repair training until salvaged by the museum. The Kaman organisation is still a firm adherent of the inter-meshing concept, with the K-MAX flying crane in limited production since 1991.

Gloster Meteor F.4 EE531
1946 | Day fighter | Two 3,500lb st Rolls-Royce Derwent 5 turbojets

In the 'Milestones of Flight' gallery at the RAF Museum Hendon is the earliest surviving Meteor, F9/40 prototype DG202 – the third example to fly – and the Jet Age Museum (Chapter 10) has the cockpit of F.III EE425. Although the Midland Meteor did not serve with an operational unit, it was decidedly a production example and could well have gone to the front line. Nevertheless, it had a fascinating career. Mk.IV EE531 was declared as awaiting collection at Hucclecote on 31st March 1946

Meteor F.4 EE531 at Lasham, 1973. *Gordon Riley*

– that is ready for the 'customer' to take possession. By October it was noted with Gloster for modifications: it was slated for tests of the Hispano Mk.V 20mm cannon and a retractable gyro gunsight. At this point it goes 'off the radar', the mods were completed on 20th May 1947 and responsibility for EE531 was vested with the Controller of Supplies (Air) until the last day of 1949. In the abbreviated world of the military CS(A) was a 'book keeping' exercise, normally while aircraft were with the manufacturers, contractors or service test institutions. EE531 was *likely* on charge with the Aeroplane and Armament Experimental Establishment at Boscombe Down, but there is no trace of this in the aircraft movement card until 10th March 1950. A comment in Tim Mason's exceptional *The Cold War Years : Flight Testing at Boscombe Down 1945-1975* (Hikoki, Ottringham, 2001) sheds a little light: "Records for the work of this aircraft at A&AEE are scant, probably because it had a nasty accident at Port Said in May 1947 on its way to Khartoum." Tropical trials spring to mind. At this point we pause to note that EE531 was born as an F.IV but in 1948 it became an F.4 as the military changed its designations from Roman numerals to Arabic. Life at Boscombe from March 1950 was involved with "VT fuse experiments", referring to 'variable time' or proximity fuse shells. By 25th August 1953 EE531 was retired and on that date was issued to Digby with the instructional serial 7090M. This did not transpire and the Meteor next surfaced in the late 1960s at the Royal Aircraft Establishment out-station at Lasham, as a non-flying airframe with the Aerial Development Unit. Here it was sourced by the Midland Aircraft Preservation Society and it was acquired on 26th June 1973.

Panavia Tornado GR.4 ZA452
1983 | All weather strike / reconnaissance | Two 16,000lb st Turbo Union RB.199 Mk.103 turbofans

From the summer of 1980 the RAF took delivery of 390 Tornado 'swing-wing' strike or air defence fighters and the type has been 'blooded' in a depressing number of wars and conflicts up to the present day. Now in their twilight years, the surviving GR.4s are looking like an endangered species in terms of disposals to museums. Given the type's longevity and ceaseless contribution to national security, a more considered transfer to museums is required. As might be expected, the 'nationals' – Duxford, Cosford and Hendon, the Science Museum (at Wroughton) and Scotland's East Fortune – have examples of the GR.1 and F.3. At the time of writing there were five whole Tornados with 'regional' collections, the Midland example being the first operational – and Gulf War veteran – GR.4 to join a museum. Tornado GR.1 ZA452 was first flown at Warton on 5th May 1983 and was issued to the Aeroplane and Armament Experimental Establishment at Boscombe Down. It was issued to the RAF on 15th May 1984, initially joining 20 Squadron at Laarbruch, West Germany. From August 1990 the RAF Tornado force began to be deployed to bases in Saudi Arabia as the coalition gathered following the Iraqi invasion of Kuwait. Tornado GR.1s of 2, 9, 14, 16 and 20 Squadrons settled in at Tabuk from early October – ZA452 among them. The 'lead' unit at Tabuk was 16 Squadron and ZA452's unit code 'GK' inspired one of the names painted on its nose: *Gulf Killer*: it also carried the legend *I Luv Gaynor XX*. From the night of 16th January 1991 to withdrawal in early March, Tornados carried out approaching 2,000 missions – ZA452 clocking 32 sorties. On return from the Gulf ZA452 was one of 26 airframes allocated for conversion to GR.1B status, capable of carrying the British Aerospace Sea Eagle anti-ship missile. Other than the prototype GR.1B, ZA407, which was reconfigured at Warton, all of the remainder were worked on at St Athan. The Sea Eagle units, 12 and 617 Squadrons, gathered at Lossiemouth from 1993; ZA452 serving with 12, coded 'FC'. On 1st August 2002, ZA452 returned to its birthplace at Warton for upgrade to GR.4 status and it re-entered service on 9th June 2003. After nearly a decade of further service ZA452 was ferried to Leeming, the Tornado 'graveyard'. The Yorkshire base is home of the RTP – reduce to produce – programme, stripping the jets of all usable material before passing the carcase on to scrap merchants. By one means or another, ZA452 escaped the final stage, settling on Coventry in September 2013.

Viscount 708 F-BGNR with Air France, at Heathrow, 1959. *KEC*

Vickers Viscount 708 F-BGNR
1954 | Medium range airliner | Four 1,540shp Rolls-Royce Dart 506 turboprops

From 1953 to 1964 Vickers built 445 Viscounts, by far and away the most successful British airliner ever. The prototype first flew on 16th July 1948 initially with Series 700s and, from 1956, the stretched Series 800. There are two other Series 700s in British museums; the oldest surviving Viscount, G-ALWF, at Duxford and the fuselage of G-AMOG in store at East Fortune. Series 806 G-APIM is displayed at Brooklands (Chapter 27) and there are several cockpits in museums. *November-Romeo* was one of a dozen Series 708s ordered by Air France. It first flew, at Hurn, on 6th May 1954 and was delivered to the state airline at Orly, Paris, on 29th June. It was transferred to the French domestic services operator, Air Inter, at Le Bourget, Paris, on 20th February 1962. Retired in 1973, it made its last flight to Perth Airport, or Scone, in Scotland on 8th October 1973. It had been acquired by Airwork for its Air Service Training college as an instructional airframe. By the early 1990s the Viscount was out of use and in December 1996 it was purchased by restoration specialist Skysport. It was not until 12th January 1998 that the task of dismantling for road transport was complete and the airliner travelled south of the border to Hatch in Bedfordshire; it was not re-assembled. Martin Garrett and Robert MacSkinning purchased F-BGNR in January 2007, forming the Viscount 35 Association at the same time. (F-BGNR was the 35th Viscount built.) Negotiations with Midland resulted in the airliner's arrival at Coventry on 6th September 2007 and the following July ownership was transferred to the museum. *November-Romeo* was put back on its undercarriage by September 2012; the first time in fourteen years.

Midland Air Museum aircraft

Type	Identity	Built	Origin	Acquired	Notes
Armstrong Whitworth Argosy 101	G-APRL	1959	Britain	20 Feb 1987	−
Avro Vulcan B.2	XL360	1962	Britain	4 Feb 1983	−
BAe/McDD Harrier GR.5	−	c1990	GB/USA	2008	procedure trainer
Beagle 206-1	G-ASWJ	1965	Britain	Jan 1993	−
Blériot XI	−	1959	France	Dec 1991	based on original parts,
Boulton Paul P.111A	VT935	1950	Britain	13 Jul 1975	see profile
Bristol Beaufighter	−	1942	Britain	Oct 1989	cockpit
Chargus Vortex 120	G-MJWH	1983	Britain	1989	hang-glider
CMC Leopard	G-BRNM	1989	Britain	26 Mar 2008	−
Crossley Tom Thumb	−	1937	Britain	29 Jul 1969	unflown

Midland Air Museum aircraft continued...

Type	Identity	Built	Origin	Acquired	Notes
Dassault Mystère IVA*	70	1956	France	1 Jun 1979	–
de Havilland Vampire F.1	VF301	1946	Britain	Nov 1972	see profile
de Havilland Vampire T.11	XD626	1954	Britain	10 Aug 1982	–
de Havilland Vampire T.11	XE855	1954	Britain	28 Aug 1982	pod
de Havilland Dove 2	G-ALCU	1947	Britain	28 Mar 1980	–
de Havilland Sea Vixen FAW.2	XJ579	1960	Britain	18 Aug 1992	cockpit
de Havilland Sea Vixen FAW.2	XN685	1961	Britain	14 Sep 1992	–
de Havilland Canada U-6A Beaver*	0-82062	1958	Canada	10 Jul 1981	–
Druine Turbulent	–	1958	France	13 Sep 1978	non-flying demonstrator
English Electric Canberra PR.3	WF922	1952	Britain	24 Jun 1984	–
English Electric Canberra T.17A	WH646	1952	Britain	1995	cockpit
English Electric Lightning F.6	XR771	1966	Britain	15 Jul 1988	–
English Electric Lightning T.55	55-713	1967	Britain	14 Jan 1989	–
EoN Olympia 2	ANW	1947	Britain	2005	glider
Fairey Gannet T.2	XA508	1955	Britain	26 Sep 1982	–
Fairey Ultra-Light Helicopter	G-APJJ	1957	Britain	1975	see profile
Flettner Fl 282B V20 Kolibri	280020	1944	Germany	May 1975	see profile
Folland Gnat F.1	XK741	1957	Britain	7 Jun 1975	fuselage, composite
Gloster Meteor F.4	EE531	1946	Britain	1973	see profile
Gloster Meteor F.8	VZ477	1950	Britain	4 Jun 1992	cockpit
Gloster Meteor NF.14	WS838	1954	Britain	15 Mar 1986	–
Gloster Javelin FAW.5	XA699	1957	Britain	19 Sep 1981	–
Handley Page Victor B.1A	XH592	1958	Britain	2015	cockpit
Hawker Sea Hawk FGA.6	WV797	1954	Britain	6 Feb 1986	–
Hawker Hunter F.6A	XF382	1956	Britain	1 Dec 1986	–
Hawker Siddeley HS.125 Srs 1*	G-ARYB	1962	Britain	2 Dec 1993	–
Hawker Siddeley Buccaneer S.2B	XX899	1976	Britain	Apr 1996	cockpit
Hawker Siddeley Sea Harrier FA.2	ZE694	1988	Britain	16 Feb 2005	–
Hunting Jet Provost	–	c1960	Britain	2002	procedure trainer
Kaman HH-43B Huskie	62-4535	1952	USA	7 Mar 1981	–
Lockheed T-33A	51-7473	1951	USA	26 Oct 1993	–
Lockheed T-33A	51-4419	1951	USA	1979	–
Lockheed 188AF Electra	G-CHNX	1959	USA	2013	cockpit
Lockheed F-104G Starfighter	R-756	1964	USA	30 Apr 1987	–
McDonnell F-101B Voodoo	56-0312	1956	USA	7 Mar 1992	–
McDonnell F-101B Voodoo	57-0270	1957	USA	Apr 1992	cockpit
McDonnell F-4C Phantom II	63-7414	1963	USA	May 1992	–
McDonnell F-4C Phantom II	63-7699	1963	USA	7 Oct 1993	–
Mignet 'Flying Flea'	G-AEGV	c1969	France	1972	original wings, contemporary fuselage
Mikoyan-Gurevich MiG-21SPS*	959	c1966	USSR	25 Jun 2001	–
Mil Mi-24D *Hind**	06	c1977	USSR	15 Sep 2005	–
North American F-86A Sabre	48-0242	1948	USA	22 Apr 2005	–
North American F-100D Super Sabre	54-2174	1954	USA	29 Mar 1978	–
Parnall Pixie III	G-EBJG	1924	Britain	Aug 1967	substantial remains
Panavia Tornado GR.4*	ZA452	1983	GB/Ger/Italy	Sep 2013	see profile
Percival Prentice T.1	VS623	1949	Britain	26 Jul 1982	–
PZL Iskra 100	408	c1977	Poland	2005	–

Midland Air Museum aircraft continued...

Type	Identity	Built	Origin	Acquired	Notes
SAAB J29F 'Tunnen'	29640	c1954	Sweden	27 Apr 1985	–
Slingsby Cadet TX.1	–	c1954	Britain	12 Jun 1968	glider
Slingsby Grasshopper TX.1	XK789	1955	Britain	1999	glider
Vickers Viscount 708	F-BGNR	1954	Britain	6 Sep 2007	see profile
Westland Whirlwind HAS.7	XK907	1957	Britain	8 Mar 1981	cockpit
Westland Whirlwind Srs 3	G-APWN	1959	USA/GB	1984	–
Westland Scout AH.1	XR635	1965	Britain	10 Sep 2012	–
Wheeler Slymph	G-ABOI	1931	Britain	Apr 1968	–

Notes: * – illustrated in the colour section.

Croome Park's Secret
RAF Defford Museum

Defford, Worcestershire
http://deffordairfieldheritagegroup.wordpress.com

Between the village of Defford and the stately home of Croome Court are the ghostly remains of an airfield that for the bulk of its life was shrouded in secrecy and myth. With much of its landscape shaped by Lancelot 'Capability' Brown, Croome Park was the ancestral home of the Earls of Coventry. In 1940 land was requisitioned from the resident Earl and tracts of Defford Common were also taken over and construction of an airfield was initiated. Defford became the home of the Vickers Wellington-equipped 'B' Flight of 23 Operational Training Unit – headquartered at Pershore five miles to the northeast – from September 1941. This unit vacated on 18th May 1942 and seven days later the Telecommunications Flying Unit (TFU) settled in. Previously located at Hurn, near Bournemouth, the TFU was the airborne arm of the Telecommunications Research Establishment (TRE) which had been housed at Worth Matravers in Dorset and itself relocated to Great Malvern. The word 'Telecommunications' was a deliberately obtuse description for the work being carried out which mostly centred on the war-winning radar and similar devices. Dorset was too close to enemy activity and move to quieter airspace was sensible and Defford was also far away from prying eyes. TFU was renamed the Radar Research Flying Unit, and TRE became the Royal Radar Establishment (RRE), in November 1955. Flying came to an end at Defford in September 1957 when the trials unit moved to Pershore. The scientific theme had been perpetuated, some of the airfield is used for radio astronomy.

Radically modified aircraft of all types flew from Defford, carrying out vital experimentation. Thankfully, the National Trust and the Defford Airfield Heritage Group (DAHG) thought this should be properly commemorated with a museum. The National Trust has been at Croome Park since 1996, restoring the parkland and opening it up to the public. Several former RAF buildings on what was the airfield's domestic site are within the trust's territory and, recognising the heritage they represent, these structures have been preserved and put to use. Formed in 2010 DAHG sets out to record and research the history of the airfield and has entered a partnership with the National Trust. A variety of grants permitted the refurbishing of

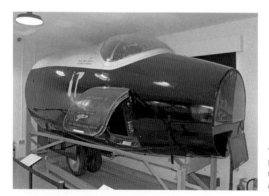

two of the wartime buildings to their 1942 external appearance. The former Decontamination Annexe was opened on 28th September 2014 as the first phase of the RAF Defford Museum. This was followed in February 2016 by what had been the Ambulance Garage and Mortuary. The garage houses the cockpit section of former RRE workhorse, English Electric Canberra B.2 WD956. Visitors to Croome Park pay the National Trust's admission charge; there is no additional payment to visit the fascinating RAF Defford Museum.

The cockpit of Canberra B.2 WD956 with the RAF Defford Museum – it flew from the airfield, 1958 to the mid-1960s.
Les Woodward

Wellington Ic R1629 served with TRU during 1942 and featured an unusual rotatable radar array on the upper fuselage.
Peter Green Collection

Also in Warwickshire
Wellesbourne Wartime Museum

Run by the Wellesbourne Aviation Group since 1986 at Wellesbourne Mountford aerodrome, the museum is centred on the underground Battle Headquarters. As well as a small number of airframes – see table – the history of the aerodrome, including 22 Operational Training Unit, is extensively presented, along with a comprehensive exhibition of aviation 'archaeology' artefacts. Also based at Wellesbourne, and closely associated with the museum, is the XM655 Maintenance and Preservation Society which keeps Vulcan B.2 XM55 'in steam'. **www.xm655.com**

Wellesbourne Wartime Museum aircraft

Type	Identity	Built	Origin	Acquired	Notes
de Havilland Vampire T.11	XK590	1956	Britain	Jan 1984	–
de Havilland Sea Vixen FAW.2	XJ575	1960	Britain	Mar 1990	cockpit
Percival Provost T.1	WV679	1954	Britain	Jan 1992	–
Yakovlev Yak-52	RA-01378	1983	USSR	1999	–
Avro Vulcan B.2	XM655	1964	Britain	11 Feb 1984	ground runs

Vampire T.11 XK590
under its canopy at
Wellesbourne Mountford.
Ken Ellis

CHAPTER 30
WILTSHIRE

Tried and Tested
BDAC – Old Sarum Airfield Museum

Old Sarum
www.boscombedownaviationcollection.co.uk

When the Aeroplane and Armament Experimental Establishment (A&AEE) moved into Boscombe Down in September 1939 it became one of the most secret of Britain's airfields. These days it is the domain of the trendy sounding commercial enterprise QinetiQ (a play on kinetic force – note *both* capitals) but the role is much the same, the evaluation of capabilities – or limitations – of aircraft, weapon and security systems for the British armed forces and other clients. Charting the history of this incredible airfield in tangible form would be a challenge and a group of former A&AEE personnel and enthusiasts set up the Boscombe Down Museum Project in 1999 to address the need. They were offered a hardened aircraft shelter (HAS) and apron on the western perimeter and the loan of redundant aircraft from the test and trials fleet. With great speed, airframes, weaponry, equipment and artefacts were generated and the first open day was staged on 1st July 2000. The sensitive nature of the base meant that visitors could only be received in a very restricted manner; nevertheless the project made great strides and the organisation was reconstituted as the Boscombe Down Aviation Collection (BDAC) by 2003.

Above: BDAC's 'guardians', the forward fuselage of Comet C.2 XK699 and Hunter F.6A XF375. *Steve Hobden*

Middle Wallop-based Whirlwind HAR.2 XK986 of the Joint Experimental Helicopter Unit lifting Auster AOP.6 VF582 (7595M) in front of the World War Two hangars – one of which is now occupied by BDAC – at Old Sarum. In the background is the fuselage of Hastings C.1 TG617. *Westland*

Previously part of a 'Private-Public Partnership' alongside the Ministry of Defence-owned Defence Science and Technology Laboratory, QinetiQ was sold off in 2006, becoming a wholly commercial venture. In October 2010 the inevitable happened; previously housed on a near 'grace and favour' basis, BDAC faced rent at the full commercial rates applicable to the property it occupied. A stay of execution was secured through to 2012 when the final open days were staged. By then BDAC had entered into negotiations with John Jervais, the owner of a hangar on the equally historic Old Sarum aerodrome, a mere five miles to the south. A ten-year agreement on this 'Belfast Truss'-style hangar, built by German prisoners of war in 1918, was signed and the enormous logistics of the move contemplated. Long since established as a 'can do' team, the BDAC crew was confidently handing out cards to visitors announcing the inaugural day at the new venue – 1st July 2012.

Eyes for the guns

Just north of Salisbury Ford Farm airfield, as Old Sarum was initially known, was ready to receive the Royal Aircraft Factory BE.2s and Airco DH.6s of 98 and 99 Squadrons, Royal Flying Corps, in August 1918. Old Sarum's proximity to Salisbury Plain determined the airfield's main role in January 1921 when the School of Army Co-operation moved in from Stonehenge. Up to the outbreak of war in 1939, the unit went through a progression of types, commencing with the ubiquitous Bristol F.2b to the versatile Westland Lysander. During 1939 trials were held for a new type of aircraft – the air observation post, eyes for the guns. The workmanlike Taylorcraft D was chosen from a variety of hopefuls and from this the Auster dynasty was founded. Up to 1944 Auster squadrons dominated at Old Sarum. Post-war, the airfield became home of the School of Land/Air Warfare, developing tactics for battlefield support and introducing helicopters, 1947 to 1963. The last major unit was the Joint Helicopter Development Unit (JHDU) with Bristol Sycamores and Westland Whirlwinds up to 1968. Military presence at Old Sarum finished in 1979 and ever since the aerodrome has been a thriving general aviation centre.

The cockpit of former ETPS Hawk T.1 XX343 awaiting visitors at Old Sarum. *Ken Ellis*

Dusty hangar to living museum

"The most hectic three weeks I've ever known – everyone has worked miracles." These are the words of BDAC's Sqn Ldr John Sharpe as he summed up the incredible migration from Boscombe Down to Old Sarum carried out in the early summer of 2012. Lorry after lorry arrived with airframes and exhibits all to be unloaded, re-assembled and readied for public display. Meanwhile the hangar – a massive increase in covered exhibition space from the HAS at Boscombe – needed to be prepared, a reception area and conference facilities created and the myriad other things that most museums undertake over a period of months, if not years – certainly not in weeks. As if anyone doubted it, BDAC was open for business at its new home, on time on 1st July 2012. With the public streaming in, another BDAC stalwart, Ron Fulton commented: "Our prospects are challenging but very exciting. We could not do this without our hard-working volunteers; they have transformed a dusty hangar into a living museum. You could say that we have been tried and tested and come out with full marks."

With its emphasis on flight testing and evaluation, much of the BDAC collection could be deemed as 'heavy metal' with a fascination for all visitors, but not relevant to the heritage of Old Sarum. One of the exhibits travelling south was BE.2b replica '2783', construction of which was begun to mark the 90th anniversary of Boscombe Down in 2007. A team of volunteers took five years to complete this exacting project and it is just at home at Old Sarum which also started with the reliable, Geoffrey de Havilland designed biplane. The collection's Sycamore helicopter is representative of the airfield's JDHU days. In April 2015 the acquisition of an Auster 5 was a major milestone as it served with 653 and 661 Squadrons, both of which were based at Old Sarum during World War Two. Restoration of the Auster continues.

To maximise exhibits inside the necessarily cramped HAS at Boscombe Down an emphasis was placed on cockpits and these have allowed for one of BDAC's hallmarks: accessibility. Visitors will find a selection open to close inspection, some of which can be sat in allowing all ages to saver the feel and atmosphere of a frontline jet. Restoration of BDAC's airframes is to the highest standards as proven by a series of major 'wins', including Grand Champions, over the period 2005 to 2009 at the annual *CockpitFest* staged at the Newark air Museum. To back this up, within the hangar a marvellous detail is an 'ops' room-like blackboard which gives exhibit status, including what's new, what's being restored and which cockpits are open to the public.

The change of venue has allowed the collection to spread its wings, both in terms of exhibition space and regular, longer, opening times – six days a week in the high season. This unique and diverse collection deserves a far wider audience than could be achieved within the restricted cloisters of Boscombe Down. While maintaining its test and trials/A&AEE remit, the BDAC team is busy extending the scope to Old Sarum and the Wessex region. Across the BDAC website are phrases like "We are *not* at MoD Boscombe Down" to try and head less prepared visitors in the right direction. To emphasize its location, the name 'Boscombe Down Aviation Collection' has been reduced to the acronym 'BDAC' for continuity while the organisation morphs into its new persona – the Old Sarum Airfield Museum.

Gloster Meteor D.16 WK800
1959 | Manned / unmanned target drone | Two 3,600lb st Rolls-Royce Derwent 8 turbojets

With each museum comes a dilemma. A pleasant one... What aircraft to profile? The difficulty is that this book is trying to highlight the sheer breadth of top-class aircraft that are available for inspection at 'humble' regional collections, but not repeating a particular type. Here's *another* Meteor... The Mk.16 is a rare bird, but ultimately it is 'just' a Mk.8 designed to dispense with the pilot. There is another example, WH453 at the Bentwaters Cold War Museum – Chapter 26. Why not that one? It's under long term restoration and the museum intends to bring it back to F.8 status and the colours of 72 Squadron, with which it served from 1954 to 1956. BDAC's main collecting policy is trials and testing and WK800 spent its final years on high-tech evaluation of missile calibration gear – big tick. WK800 was a frontline aircraft – not at Leuchars, Wattisham or Laarbruch, but at Kimpo in South Korea with the Royal Australian Air Force (RAAF) – another tick. Then it changes career and becomes a drone, at first flying from Woomera in Australia, then in North Wales – you get the picture.

Built at Hucclecote, Meteor F.8 WK800's maiden flight ended a short distance to the southwest at Moreton Valence, the Gloster flight test airfield. After one hour, fifteen minutes of flying time, it was signed off by a test pilot in September 1952. That may seem little time, but the F.8 was a mature programme and, with the Korean War in its second year, Gloster was churning them out rapidly. By January 1953 the jet was at 47 Maintenance Unit at Sealand in North Wales, in preparation for shipping to the Far East. Other than the Short Sunderland flying-boats operating out of Hong Kong and Iwakuni, Japan; the main British aircraft contribution to the Korean conflict was the Fleet Air Arm with Fairey Fireflies and Hawker Sea Furies from carriers. WK800 was destined for the RAAF and 77 Squadron. The Australian unit had originally been equipped with North American P-51D Mustangs but picked up Meteor F.8s at Iwakuni in April 1951. From late June the unit was at Kimpo and on 1st December a dozen Meteors faced what some estimate to have been *fifty* Mikoyan-Gurevich MiG-15 *Fagots* that were lying in wait. The Meteors were outclassed against the swept-wing Soviet types, but gave a good account of themselves, downing two 'bogies' but six Meteors failed to return. After that 77 Squadron was tasked with point defence of their air base and ground support. WK800 arrived in Korea on 3rd May 1953. The ceasefire came into effect on 27th July 1953 but 77 Squadron stayed on standby, departing for home in December 1954.

Meteor WK800 was shipped to its new home, Australia, at which point it is recorded that it had a total flying time of 5 hours, 50 minutes. It would seem that comprised, test at Gloster, ferry to Lyneham, ferry to Sealand and test in Korea: no combat flying. On 12th October 1955 it was flight tested again, this time in Australia and no longer as WK800, it was now RAAF A77-876. That month it was issued to 78 Wing, headquartered as Williamtown, New South Wales; the wing comprising

Meteor D.16 WK800 at Teversham after conversion to the RVMDI test-bed with ten 'radomes' distributed around the airframe, 1987. *MCE*

75 and 77 Squadrons. A77-876 was stored from late 1956 to May 1958 when it joined 23 (City of Brisbane) Squadron of the RAAF's Citizen Air Force at Amberley, Queensland. Retired in February 1960, it was declared surplus on 17th October 1960. Flight time at this point was 767 hours – the Australians finally getting value for money out of it. The Meteor was granted a stay of execution and transferred to the Weapons Research Establishment (WRE). It was issued to Fairey Aviation Australasia Pty at Bankstown, New South Wales, in November 1960. There it was converted to a U.21A drone, using a kit-of-parts supplied by Flight Refuelling in Britain. (The U.21A was the equivalent of the British operated U.16.) From November 1962 it flew from the WRE's base at Woomera in South Australia, with the RAAF's 1 and 2 Air Test Units. Retired in July 1969, A77-876 had amassed 1,013 hours.

It was shipped back to the UK and taken to Flight Refuelling's test centre at Tarrant Rushton for conversion to U.16 status, reclaiming its identity as WK800. It was cleared for service in early July 1971 and delivered to its new home, Royal Aircraft Establishment (RAE) Llanbedr on 26th July 1971. By the early 1980s the designation 'U' for unmanned had been changed to 'D' for drone thus becoming a D.16. On 7th April 1983 WK800 was ferried to Teversham to be converted by Marshall of Cambridge Engineering (MCE) into a test-bed for the Radar Vector Miss Distance Indicator (RVMDI) a sophisticated system for calibrating the performance of missiles. Fitted with no less than ten mini-'radomes' containing transceivers on the fuselage and the outer wings, WK800 was first flown in this guise in January 1987 by Flt Lt Tim Mason. (Tim, an author as well as a pilot, is mentioned in the profile of another Meteor, F.4 EE531, in Chapter 29.) Included in the trials was a spell at RAE Farnborough where the D.16 was flown 'against' inert BAE Rapier surface-to-air missiles. The extensive programme was completed with the delivery of WK800 to Llanbedr on 27th June 1988 to commence unmanned RVMDI flights. All of this was put in jeopardy on 19th April 1989 when a pilot-less take-off down Llanbedr's southerly runway went wrong and was aborted. The D.16 hurtled through the net barrier at the end of the runway, slewing to the right and ending up on its belly with its starboard undercarriage leg collapsed. The wounded Meteor was dragged into the hangar and its fellow D.16; WH453 mentioned above, was grounded to supply vital parts. WK800 was back in the air on 13th February 1991. With the programme complete, WK800 made its last flight on 11th October 2004 to Boscombe Down while its future was determined. It was sold to Trevor Stone in 2008 and placed on loan with BDAC the following year.

Hawker Hunter F.6A XF375
1955 | Day fighter | One 10,000lb st Rolls-Royce Avon 203 turbojet

A similar rationale to that for Meteor D.16 WK800 – above – applies to the BDAC Hunter. Here's *another* Hunter, but spot on with the collecting policy. It served for fifteen years from Boscombe Down, and in its early days flew in the test and trials role. Built by Armstrong Whitworth as an F.6, XF375 had its maiden flight on 14th July 1955 and, after sign off, was delivered to Rolls-Royce on 31st August 1955. It was used for Avon turbojet trials, mostly from the company's test airfield at Hucknall, but also from Wymeswold. In January 1959 it was issued to English Electric at Warton where it was used for Lightning development trials, playing the role of a 'target'. It began its long sojourn with the Empire Test Pilots' School, initially at Farnborough and two dates compete for this honour: 21st December 1962 or 23rd April 1963. The school decamped and relocated to Boscombe Down on 12th December 1967. It received the F.6A modifications, including the fitment of a rear-mounted braking parachute during the 1970s. The Hunter's last flight took place on 5th February 1982 when it was ferried to Cranwell for use as an instructional airframe, serial 8736M. With this it completed 4,221 flying hours. In October 1991 XF375 was put up for disposal and purchased by the Old Flying Machine Company, moving by road to Duxford. It was allocated the British civil registration G-BUEZ in April 1992; but no work was carried out to return it to airworthy status. Acquired by a private owner it was trucked to Spanhoe aerodrome on 18th November 2002 and re-assembled. Acquired by BDAC in April 2007 it was moved to Boscombe Down and repainted in its striking ETPS colours – see the colour section. It made the short journey to Old Sarum on 29th June 2012.

Boscombe Down Aviation Collection aircraft

Type	Identity	Built	Origin	Acquired	Notes
Auster 5D	G-ALYG	1944	Britain	10 Apr 2015	–
BAC One-Eleven Srs 402	XX919	1966	Britain	2001	cockpit
BAC Jet Provost T.5	XS231	1965	Britain	Sep 2009	cockpit
Bristol Sycamore HR.14	XJ380	1956	Britain	2007	–
British Aerospace Jetstream 31	G-PLAH	1984	Britain	Mar 2017	cockpit
de Havilland Comet C.2	XK699	1957	Britain	12 Nov 2013	forward fuselage
de Havilland Sea Vixen FAW.1	XJ476	1957	Britain	2007	cockpit
de Havilland Canada Chipmunk T.10	WD321	1951	Canada	Jan 2008	–
English Electric Canberra B.2(mod)	WH876	1953	Britain	22 May 2001	cockpit
English Electric Canberra T.4	WJ865	1954	Britain	Apr 2007	cockpit
English Electric Lightning F.2A	XN726	1961	Britain	1 Apr 2000	cockpit
GAF Jindivik 103B	A92-466	c1975	Australia	2006	target drone
Gloster Meteor NF.11	WD686	1952	Britain	27 Apr 2017	–
Gloster Meteor D.16*	WK800	1952	Britain	Jan 2009	see profile
Hawker Sea Hawk FGA.4	WV910	1955	Britain	2000	cockpit
Hawker Hunter F.1	WT648	1954	Britain	2002	cockpit
Hawker Hunter F.2	WN890	1954	Britain	Jun 2005	cockpit
Hawker Hunter F.6A*	XF375	1955	Britain	Oct 2007	see profile
Hawker Hunter F.6	XG290	1956	Britain	2000	cockpit
Hawker Siddeley Andover CC.2	XS790	1964	Britain	2000	cockpit
Hawker Siddeley Harrier GR.3	XV784	1970	Britain	2002	cockpit
Hawker Siddeley Sea Harrier FA.2	XZ457	1979	Britain	Jul 2003	–
Hawker Siddeley Hawk T.1	XX343	1981	Britain	2000	cockpit
Hunting Jet Provost T.3A	XN503	1960	Britain	Oct 2004	cockpit
Hunting Jet Provost T.4	XR650	1963	Britain	2000	–
Panavia Tornado F.2	ZD936	1985	GB/Ger/Italy	2002	cockpit
Royal Aircraft Factory BE.2c*	'2783'	2007	Britain	2007	replica
SEPECAT Jaguar S.06	XW560	1969	GB/France	2004	cockpit
SEPECAT Jaguar GR.1	XX734	1974	GB/France	5 May 2013	–
SEPECAT Jaguar GR.1A	XX761	1975	GB/France	2002	cockpit
Short MATS-B	ZA220	c1982	Britain	20 Jul 2016	target drone
Slingsby T.21B	'XN149'	1962	Britain	30 Nov 2014	powered glider
Supermarine Swift F.7	XF113	1956	Britain	2000	cockpit
Supermarine 544	WT859	1956	Britain	2002	cockpit
TTL Banshee 400	3150	c1999	Britain	30 Nov 2013	target drone
Westland Scout AH.1	XP899	1963	Britain	14 Sep 2015	–
Westland Wasp HAS.1	XT437	1965	Britain	2001	–

Notes: * – illustrated in the colour section

Wasp HAS.1 XT437 underneath the 1918 wooden trusses of the BDAC hangar at Old Sarum. *Ken Ellis*

Also in Wiltshire
REME Museum

Having relocated from Aborfield, Berkshire, in late 2015, the museum opened its doors again on 6th June 2017. The new venue is the former RAF Lyneham, now Prince Philip Barracks. REME stands for Royal Electrical and Mechanical Engineers and the large and diverse collection reflects both the heritage and the present role. Aviation content is small, but interest levels are high! **www.rememuseum.org.uk**

REME Museum aircraft

Type	Identity	Built	Origin	Acquired	Notes
Westland Scout AH.1	XV141	1968	Britain	1999	–
GEC-Marconi Phoenix	ZJ449	c1995	Britain	7 Oct 2008	drone

CHAPTER 31
YORKSHIRE

Innovators
South Yorkshire Aircraft Museum

Doncaster
www.southyorkshireaircraftmuseum.org.uk

In the spring of 1999, the author was invited up to the former Doncaster Airport to meet with a delegation of members of the South Yorkshire Aircraft Museum. We toured an empty Bellman hangar and other buildings that were available for lease. There were some desperately concerned looks on faces; they wanted to know what I thought. To many it seemed a massive leap; perhaps one too far. The team had been running a delightful museum at the farm of the genial Carl Speddings – a fellow enthusiast – but they had outgrown it. Previously used by Yorkshire Water as a centre for its vans and other vehicles, 4.5 acres plus all the buildings thereon were on offer. Adopting philosopher mode I explained that they *had* to go for it, it was too good an opportunity to later look back on and utter: 'If only...' I also explained that if *anyone* could make a go of the venture, it was the South Yorkshire team! If I played even the tiniest part in tipping the scales to 'Yes' then I'm very pleased: the set up at Doncaster has never ceased to make me feel very proud.

Above: Harrier GR.3 XV752 guards the entrance to the South Yorkshire Aircraft Museum. *Ken Ellis*

On 11th July 1976 the Nostell Aviation Museum was opened within the grounds of Nostell Priory, near Wakefield. Run by the South Yorkshire Aircraft Preservation Society, the collection went from strength to strength. One of the founding airframes was Mignet 'Flying Flea' G-AEKR which today graces Doncaster's Museum and Art Gallery, see below. Changes on the site at Nostell meant that the enterprise had to close its doors in 1982. Undaunted, an offer from Carl Speddings to come to Home Farm at Firbeck was taken up and the lorries started rolling. The first visitors could inspect what was named the South Yorkshire Aircraft Museum (SYAM) in May 1982 but for the next nine years, they were admitted on a prior arrangement only basis – this was a working farm after all. Home Farm lies on the northeast perimeter of the all-grass Firbeck airfield which was inaugurated, as the home of the Westland Lysanders of 613 Squadron, in September 1940. The last powered aircraft – the Auster IIIs of 659 Squadron – left in August 1943 and from then until the site returned to agriculture in early 1948, it was the domain of gliders. From 1991 SYAM opened regularly on Sundays and Bank Holidays. After the move to Doncaster was achieved, Firbeck was used as a storage site; the last airframes departing in 2000.

Transformation

Despite its limited opening times, visitor figures grew and grew at Firbeck, as did the exhibit list. So the search was on for new premises in the late 1990s. The team signed the lease for the site at Doncaster and once again fleets of low-loaders were needed to re-locate the museum in 1999. Herculean efforts turned a disused and vandalised site into a display hall, exhibition rooms, reception, shop, workshop and store. All was ready for a 'quiet' opening on 24th August 2000, followed by a formal unveiling on 29th May 2001. For the new start the name Aeroventure as chosen for a 'brand', but this was dropped in 2010 in favour of the more 'does what it says on the can' South Yorkshire Aircraft Museum.

Doncaster's first aeronautical claim to fame was in October 1909 when Britain's first aviation meeting was staged on the race course – more of this anon. The Royal Flying Corps occupied the turf from January 1916 when the Avro 504s and Royal Aircraft Factory RE.8s of 15 (Reserve) Squadron settled in. After the Armistice flying ceased, but in the 1930s fields to the southwest of the race course were adopted as a municipal airport with trial services to Croydon being staged. Equipped with Hawker Hinds, 616 (South Yorkshire) Squadron Auxiliary Air Force was formed at Doncaster on 1st November 1938. By the following year the squadron was flying Fairey Battles and it departed for Leconfield that October. A variety of units were based there throughout World War Two, including the North American Mustang I equipped 169 Squadron in 1942. With the closure of Firbeck in February 1948, 24 Gliding School arrived and this was Doncaster's last RAF unit; disbanding in late 1949. Beyond that, the airfield was used by aero clubs and maintenance organisations, but by the 1980s usage had declined and redevelopment of the site began. Today the most tangible remains are the buildings occupied by SYAM.

The SYAM exhibit table – see later – is extensive and eclectic, reflecting the team's determination to show as wide a spread of aviation as possible. The engine hall is very comprehensive and among themes covered are aviation in Doncaster and South Yorkshire, a World War Two 'ops' room and an impressive Great War exhibition. The Falklands conflict display – 'Eleven Weeks in 1982' – is the only permanent exhibition of its kind in the UK. This is so well regarded that the museum is used as a venue for several Falklands reunion organisations.

Protectors of Endangered Helicopters

A magazine article outlining the work of the Yorkshire Helicopter Preservation Group was entitled 'Protectors of Endangered Helicopters' and it well sums up YHPG's purpose. The story of the group begins in the summer of 1994 when Ray 'Mac' McElwain acquired long-derelict Westland Dragonfly HR.5 WH991 and moved it to the Yorkshire Air Museum at Elvington – see later. Ray gathered a team of volunteers around him and, after a four-year restoration; the completed helicopter was rolled out on 27th September 1998. The team looked around for replacement projects and in short order the prototype Whirlwind HAR.10 XJ398 and former United Nations HAR.10 XP345 were taken on. At the same time the ad hoc organisation was formalised and the YHPG was formed. A change of policy at Elvington meant that independent groups could no longer function on site and from 2001 YHPG was looking for a new home. This need dovetailed beautifully with the establishment of Aeroventure just down the road at Doncaster. Alan Beattie and Mike Fitch of YHPG held discussions with the SYAM team and the low-loaders started to shuttle along the A19 on 14th July 2002. By the spring of the following year, YHPG had established a workshop and the team was back in business undertaking quality restorations of significant helicopters.

Acquisitions and 'supply drops'

In 1982 when SYAM was established at Firbeck, and ever since, the throughput of airframes, engines, artefacts and related items has been astounding. The present-day airframe inventory is impressive, making SYAM one of the largest of the 'locals'. But this is the tip of the iceberg, the SYAM crew adopted a selfless policy of taking on airframes with the certain knowledge that they were not on the 'wants list', but might well be so for another organisation. This has meant that Firbeck and now Doncaster have acted as a hub for the coming and going of an incredible procession of aircraft, engines, all the way down to humble components. There must be trailers parked at Doncaster that have more miles on them than the International Space Station! The author began the task of collating a table to reflect these 'supply drops' but he soon realised it would be too vast. It is likely that most of the 'locals' covered in this book have SYAM to thank for some prized item within their collection.

Of the personalities at SYAM, one stands out and I know that heads will be nodding in agreement whenever these words are read: Bill Fern. He is a tireless finder of things aeronautical with the rare skill to trade them and place them just

A replica of Léon Delagrange's Blériot XI is the centrepiece of the Early Aviation Hall. *Ken Ellis*

where they are needed at precisely the right time. The author can pay him no higher tribute than the majority of out-of-date information in the biennial *Wrecks & Relics* is entirely down to Bill shuffling as many aircraft around as he possibly can in the months leading up to the book's press date! Bill, curator Naylan Moore, another dynamic finder-in-chief and restorer, and the rest of the team makes sure that SYAM continues to be a never-ending stream of exhibits, ideas and improvements.

As noted above, Doncaster race course was the venue for the first-ever aviation meeting, 15th to 18th October 1909; among those attending was Samuel Franklin Cody. To commemorate this epoch, the museum commissioned Ken Fern, gifted craftsman and creator of many a fine wooden airframe, to build a full-scale replica of a Blériot XI to celebrate the centenary. Flown by Frenchman Léon Delagrange, the monoplane established a world speed record of 49.9mph during his time at Doncaster. To capitalise on Doncaster's aviation roots, the Blériot was installed as the centrepiece of SYAM's Early Aviation Hall and this was officially opened on 26th May 2017.

There are many significant exhibits at Doncaster and cutting it down to five profiles was a difficult task but I want to highlight one more airframe and some of the non-aviation displays. Many visitors probably sweep past the forward cabin of Westland Scout AH.1 XP902, heading for some of the 'sexier' exhibits. A growing number of guests find this machine the single most important aircraft they have ever encountered. Phil Jarvis carried out a simple modification; behind XP902's cabin is a gentle access ramp, and the port-side pilot's seat has been removed. This is a wheel chair accessible cockpit giving it a significance way beyond its provenance. This fantastic innovation was given a special award at the Newark Air Museum's *CockpitFest* gathering in 2002. This is a concept that every museum should adopt – take a look at *Land of the Giant* below for an exhibit that has taken up the idea.

Award-winning, wheel chair-friendly Scout AH.1 XP902 at Newark's 2002 CockpitFest. *Ken Ellis*

Within the museum is an education centre complete with lots of pads of paper, crayons and plenty of stimulating material. Not far away is a room that has become very popular with younger visitors – a dressing-up room, full of different sorts of uniform from a variety of eras. Bill Fern was very candid about his initial views of this. "Most of us thought the idea was going nowhere, but for very little investment we could give it a go. Blow me; it's now one of the most popular places in the museum!" Families are by far and away the majority of visitors at Doncaster, the team has made sure it's a welcoming place for all. As a devotee of Ronnies Barker and Corbett, I recommend you find the 'Doncaster at War' exhibit and the replica shop which sums up the wonderful mind-set at SYAM. It is, of course, called 'Arkwrights' and close examination reveals four candles and fork handles on the shelves!

Cessna F.150G G-AVAA
1967 | Two-seat trainer/tourer | One 100hp Continental O-200-A piston

From 1961 the face of British aero clubs changed radically. Gone was the hotchpotch of increasingly British-built types: mostly Austers and a dwindling number of Tiger Moths. The indigenous industry had failed to come up with any replacements; its final fling in that direction was the Beagle Pup, but by then the tide of American imports was overwhelming. In September 1957 Cessna flew the prototype 150 and in 1977 the 'refreshed' Cessna 152 was introduced. When production ended in 1986 just under 32,000 examples had been built, including licence manufacture by Reims Aviation in France. This made the Cessna 150 and 152 family the most popular light aircraft ever and today the type is still to be found flogging the circuits of British aerodromes in healthy numbers. Not far behind the Cessna two-seaters in production figures were dedicated trainer versions of the Piper Cherokee, but that machine was essentially a four-seater tourer. SYAM has two other US designs in this category, the Erco Ercoupe and the American Aviation AA-1B – the latter of local significance as it flew from Doncaster in the mid-1970s – but they were minority players. At first sight the SYAM's 150 might appear commonplace and foreign at that. This is a very significant exhibit; generations of 'Brits' have had their first experience of flight, of going solo, or cross-county in a 150 or a 152 and continue to do so today. *Double-Alpha* is the only example in a UK museum, a shining example of an innovative collecting policy and a true 'People's Plane'.

SYAM's Cessna was built in 1967 by Reims Aviation to the order of Airwork Services at Scone aerodrome, Perth, and it was used by the associated Scottish Aero Club. From August 1978 it began a long association with Sussex, going through a series of private owners based at Goodwood and Shoreham. Its final owner, from July 1993, was a lady owner with a Southampton address at which point it had achieved 11,207 flying hours. By 1995 it had moved to Shobdon where a rebuild was abandoned and in 1997 it started a new career as a museum exhibit.

Cessna F.150G G-AVAA, a true 'People's Plane'. *Ken Ellis*

DC-3 N4565L of the Hibernian Dakota Flight at Fairford in 1985. Note the air stair door and the panoramic window. *KEC*

Douglas DC-3-201A N4565L
1939 | Medium range airliner | Two 1,100hp Wright GR-1820-G102 pistons

Doncaster's 'Dakota' is no such thing, SYAM's largest and bravest exhibit, is a rare item: a pre-war genuine airliner DC-3. There is one other example of a 'pure' DC-3 in Britain, EI-AYO kept under wraps at the Science Museum's store at Wroughton. All others are former RAF or USAAF workhorses; respectively Dakotas or C-47 Skytrains and the RAF Museum at Cosford and the Imperial War Museum respectively has an example of each. As well as the Doncaster machine, there are two other whole examples with 'local' collections: at Metheringham (Chapter 16) and at the Yorkshire Air Museum (see later). While former RAF or USAAF Ninth Air Force examples will have flown from British airfields, the Douglas DC-3 is one of the most iconic of aircraft and as such rates as a 'crown jewel'. Besides, N4565L provides a refreshing change.

Built at Long Beach, California, to the order of New York-headquartered Eastern Air Lines as NC21744, fleet number '346', this venerable transport entered service in February 1939. It stayed with Eastern for fourteen productive years before being disposed of in December 1953, first becoming N80CA, then N51D and then N512 with a variety of owners. By December 1958 it was with Trans International – thought to be a broker or lessor – as N129H. The DC-3 was in Argentina as LV-PCV by April 1961, taking up the more permanent identity LV-GYP in July 1961 with Servicios Aereos Santa Isabel of Buenos Aires. Then it was subjected to major surgery, a radar nose, panoramic windows and a twelve/thirteen seat interior for use as an executive shuttle for the Ford Motor Company of Argentina. In this guise *Yankee-Papa* served on until disposed of in late 1981 and by the summer of the following year it was to be found in open storage at Ezeiza, Buenos Aires.

Here the story might have ended had it not been spotted by Airspeed International of Miami, Florida, which registered the DC-3 as N4565L in December 1983. *Six-Five-Lima* was 'adopted' by the well-known film, ferry and display pilot John 'Jeff' Hawke and it was flown to Dublin in 1984. (The ferry registration N3TV was applied for, but not used, for this venture.) Countless hours of enthusiast labour were put into a thorough restoration of the aircraft under the aegis of the Hibernian Dakota Flight. All of this was in readiness for what was hoped would be a large number of 'bookings' on the airshow scene. The completed aircraft was given the name *Aisling* ('dream' or 'fantasy') and 'flew' the Irish tricolour prominently on the fin. Its first appearance was at the July 1985 International Air Tattoo at Fairford where the DC-3's half-century was one of the themes but beyond that *Aisling* saw little usage. Painted in all-over gloss black with a massive cartoon 'smile' under the nose, *Six-Five-Lima* arrived at Ipswich on 2nd October 1986 and was parked up. During January 1987 it was damaged in gales and suffered further as the months became years. A downward career path was being mapped out for the veteran. The airport authorities tried to auction the DC-3 in February 1990, in lieu of parking fees, but this fizzled out amid a complex trail of paperwork. Hawke was killed in 1991 when the Piper Aztec he was piloting solo crashed into the Adriatic Sea.

Only beyond this could the DC-3, and other airframes in similar circumstances, be disposed of. Mike Woodley, of film and airshow specialists Aces High, acquired *Aisling* for spares in 1994 and passed the airframe on to the 390th Bomb Group Memorial Air Museum at Framlingham – Chapter 26. The fuselage arrived by road on 2nd March 1995 with the wings following later. To be fair to the team at Framlingham, it 'seemed like a good idea at the time'. They had fallen victim to the seductive notion that an airframe would bring greater numbers of visitors. Once Britain's population of 'spotters' had driven up, gawped, clicked and left – probably without giving a passing thought to the quality of the exhibits within the wartime control tower – the DC-3 proved to be no great 'pull'. Plans for a hangar were ambitious and distracting from the main purpose: honouring the men and B-17Fs of 'Wittan's Wallopers' – the 390th. Feelers were put out concerning its disposal and on 6th August 2003, the DC-3 arrived at Doncaster.

Piper Apache 160 G-APMY
1958 | Light transport | Two 160hp Lycoming O-320-B2B pistons

The logic regarding *Mike-Yankee* is very similar to the Cessna 150 above. The prototype Piper Twin-Stinson of March 1952 led to the phenomenally successful Apache and Aztec family; flanked by the Cessna 310 series and the Beech Baron from 1953 and 1960, respectively. These machines, and other types, were a quantum leap ahead of the mixed bag of types being used for business aviation in Britain, and they dominated the market place. Needless to say, G-APMY is the only example of its type in a British museum: the Newark Air Museum displays 1956-built Cessna 310 G-APNY.

Built at Lock Haven, Pennsylvania, this Apache was delivered to Irish Air Charter at Dublin as EI-AJT in April 1958. Its time in Ireland was fleeting, being registered to The United Steel Companies Ltd – the titling it wears today – as G-APMY on 15th May 1958 and it spent the next decade based at Gaston, near Redford and just eighteen miles away from the museum. It was traded in via Piper agents CSE Aviation at Kidlington, in November 1968 before serving: Cab air at Elstree from March 1969, Skidoos at Lympne from March 1971 and finally Mooney Aviation at Halfpenny Green from August 1976. The Apache was withdrawn at Halfpenny Green by late 1981 and it was acquired by the Kelsterton College of Technology at Connah's Quay, north Wales, as an instructional airframe. Recognising its significance, SYAM acquired it and brought it to Firbeck in April 1996.

Sea King HAS.6 XV677 was more or less a carcass when it first appeared at Doncaster. *Ken Ellis*

Westland Sea King HAS.6 XV677
1970 | Anti-submarine helicopter | Two 1,535shp Rolls-Royce Gnome 1400-IT Mk.12/127 turboshafts

"It was late 2004 and news had come to light of a Sea King that was due to be turned into pop cans. Phil Jarvis and I decided to set the wheels in motion to try and save her. [XV677] was being used at HMS *Sultan* at Gosport as a ground instruction airframe, which included skin repairs. She had been totally stripped of all serviceable parts with just the main fuselage section remaining but [it was] a solid base to start the restoration of the first Sea King in a UK museum." So wrote co-owner Nigel Porembski in the YHPG house journal as he launched 'Project 677'. Eleven years later the transformation of XV677 is exceptional, it bears little resemblance to the hulk that arrived at Doncaster in July 2006. Nigel was quite right, yet again SYAM was innovating; two years later the Fleet Air Arm Museum took on HAS.6 XZ574 on 9th June 2008, but it remained at Gosport until it was unveiled at Yeovilton on 4th August 2016. Since then Yeovilton has received another HAS.6 and the Imperial War Museum at Duxford HAS.6 XV712 on 27th May 2010. The first former RAF air-sea rescue HAR.3, XZ592, was delivered to Morayvia (Chapter 32) in July 2015. At the time of writing, it seemed as though more Sea Kings are destined for 'glamping' (that's posh camping) than museums...

First flown at Yeovil on 18th December 1970, Sea King HAS.1 XV677 was issued to storage at Culdrose the following month. It was December 1972 before it was in operational service, with 820 Squadron at Culdrose; transiting to 814 Squadron at Prestwick from February 1974 and to 706 Squadron at Culdrose in August 1978. It had been upgraded to HAS.2 status at Fleetlands in 1977 and on 3rd May 1982 was issued to 825 Squadron. Nine days later, it was loaded on board the SS *Queen Elizabeth II* for the voyage to the South Atlantic as part of Operation 'Corporate'; the liberation of the Falklands Islands.

Transferred to the SS *Canberra* on the 27th, XV677 was operating from the terra firma of the Falklands from 2nd June. It returned to Britain on board the MV *Atlantic Causeway* the following month. By October 1982 it was again at Culdrose, this time serving with 819 Squadron. It was further upgraded to HAS.5 guise in 1984 and again to HAS.6 in 1989, both times at Fleetlands.

Having taken off from a launch site in Maine, USA, 37 hours previously Richard Branson and Per Lindstrand looked nervously at one another on 3rd July 1987. Their attempt to be the first to fly the Atlantic in a hot-air balloon was not going to end as planned. *Virgin Atlantic Voyager*, designed and built by Lindstrand, was in trouble and the pair decided to ditch in the Mull of Kintyre, Scotland. Sea King XV677 was one of the helicopters dispatched to bring the balloon adventurers ashore. Inside the main display hangar at Doncaster is another of Per Lindstand's balloons, the much more modest LBL.77A built at the Swede's workshop in Oswestry, Shropshire, in 1993 – a fascinating, if tenuous link with XV677. By April 1990 XV677 was on charge with 810 Squadron at Culdrose. It joined its last operational unit in July 1993: this was 814 Squadron, shore-based at Culdrose, but also working from the deck of HMS *Invincible*. On 7th June 1999 XV677 was retired, with a total of 8,009 flying hours, to the Defence College of Aeronautical Engineering at Gosport: which is where Nigel Porembski came in at the beginning of this profile. It arrived by road at Doncaster in July 2006 and its circumstances have improved ever since.

Carrying the name 'HMS Endurance' on its nose, Lynx HAS.3S(ICE) XZ246 at Doncaster. *Ken Ellis*

Westland Lynx HAS.3S(ICE) XZ246
1978 | General purpose helicopter | Two 1,120shp Rolls-Royce Gem Mk.204 turboshafts

With the decommissioning of Fleet Air Arm Lynxes on 23rd March 2017 it can expected that more of the type will percolate through to museums, although at the time of writing, Yeovilton had a HAS.3; Farnborough (Chapter 11) a HAS.2 and The Helicopter Museum (Chapter 25) an early HAS.2. (Chapter 25 also gives background to Lynxes.) Doncaster's example, typically, is distinctive, having flown in the most challenging conditions from two ice patrol ships, both named HMS *Endurance*. For the bulk of the Fleet Air Arm Lynx, the helicopters were shore-based with a 'holding' squadron and then detached to Ships' Flights, operating from the heli-deck on the stern and living inside a cramped hangar. HAS.2 XZ246 had its maiden flight at Yeovil on 12th July 1978 and in October it was at Yeovilton with 702 Squadron, spending time on the frigates HMS *Amazon* and HMS *Broadsword*. From 26th May 1982 XZ246 was operated by 815 Squadron at Yeovilton and later Portland; embarking in the destroyer HMS *Newcastle* and the frigate HMS *Alacrity*. In July 1986 XZ246 was at Yeovilton being converted to HAS.3(ICE) status (and further to HAS.3S(ICE) in 1995) ready for service with HMS *Endurance*. It was first embarked in March 1987 and was detached to *Endurance* up to its final voyage in 2008. The original *Endurance* was retired in 1991; its replacement, initially HMS *Polar Circle*, took over that year, acquiring the historic name in 1992. Last unit to fly XZ246 was 815 Squadron at Yeovilton from 24th February 2010 for just over a month when it was delivered to Fleetlands for storage pending disposal. By 2014 it was with contractor Everett Aero and stored at Bentwaters; XZ246 moved to Doncaster in August 2016.

South Yorkshire Aircraft Museum aircraft

Type	Identity	Built	Origin	Acquired	Notes
AD Skyship 500	G-BECE	1976	Britain	Jan 2008	airship gondola
Aermacchi MB.339AA	0767	1981	Italy	Nov 2013	–
American AA-1B Trainer	G-BCLW	1974	USA	27 Apr 2013	–
Auster 5	RT520	1944	Britain	1983	fuselage
Auster J/1N Alpha	G-APKM	1958	Britain	12 Apr 2015	spares recovery
Auster 6A	G-ARGI	1946	Britain	Jan 2000	–
Auster AOP.9	WZ711	1954	Britain	Jun 2016	–
Austin Whippet	'K-158'	1990	Britain	Jan 2000	replica
Avro Anson C.19/2	VP519	1947	Britain	2011	cockpit
Avro Vulcan B.1	–	1958	Britain	2011	cockpit
Avro Vulcan B.2	XL388	1962	Britain	7 Apr 2003	cockpit
Beagle Airedale	G-ARYZ	1962	Britain	12 Apr 2015	–
Beagle Pup 150	HB-NAV	1971	Britain	2009	cockpit
Bell Sioux AH.1#	XT150	1965	USA	7 Aug 2008	–
Bell Sioux AH.1#	XT242	1966	USA	13 Feb 2003	–
Bell JetRanger	G-BAML	1967	USA	2004	–
Bell 206B JetRanger II	G-TPTR	1979	USA	28 Apr 2017	–
Bensen B-8	–	1965	USA	2009	–
Blackburn B-2	G-ACBH	1932	Britain	21 Feb 2012	fuselage
Blackburn Beverley C.1	XL149	1957	Britain	2005	cockpit
Blériot XI	–	2009	France	2010	replica
Bristol Sycamore HR.14	XE317	1954	Britain	1997	–
Cessna 140	G-BTYX	1976	USA	12 Apr 2015	–
Cessna 140	N76402	1969	USA	12 Apr 2015	–
Cessna F.150G*	G-AVAA	1967	USA	26 Nov 1997	see profile
de Havilland Tiger Moth II	N9399	1939	Britain	2004	fuselage
de Havilland Vampire NF.10	WP255	1951	Britain	1991	cockpit
de Havilland Vampire T.11	XD377	1953	Britain	1999	cockpit
de Havilland Vampire T.11	XE935	1955	Britain	1986	–

A corner of the SYAM main display hangar: Bulldog T.1 XX669 with the Bensen B-8 gyrocopter 'flying' above. *Ken Ellis*

South Yorkshire Aircraft Museum aircraft continued...

Type	Identity	Built	Origin	Acquired	Notes
de Havilland Vampire T.55	333	1958	Britain	Feb 2003	cockpit
de Havilland Venom NF.3	WX788	1954	Britain	Feb 2002	–
de Havilland Canada Chipmunk T.10	WB733	1950	Canada	1995	–
de Havilland Canada Chipmunk T.10	WK626	1952	Canada	1997	fuselage
Douglas DC-3-201A	N4565L	1939	USA	6 Aug 2003	see profile
English Electric Canberra B.2	WD935	1951	Britain	2003	cockpit
English Electric Canberra T.4	XH584	1955	Britain	1993	cockpit
English Electric Canberra PR.7	WH779	1954	Britain	11 Jan 2015	cockpit
English Electric Canberra T.17	WJ565	1953	Britain	22 Mar 2003	cockpit
English Electric Canberra T.19	WJ975	1953	Britain	2005	cockpit
English Electric Lightning F.3	XP706	1963	Britain	19 Nov 2002	–
Enstrom 280C	HB-XMO	1980	USA	20 Oct 2015	cockpit
Erco Ercoupe 415D	G-AVTT	1947	USA	21 Feb 2014	–
Eurowing Goldwing	G-MJPO	1982	Britain	2003	–
Gloster Meteor T.7	WA662	1950	Britain	1994	–
Gloster Meteor F.8	WL131	1953	Britain	Sep 1995	cockpit
Handley Page Jetstream 200	G-ATXH	1967	Britain	2005	cockpit
Handley Page Jetstream T.1	XX477	1973	Britain	1 Nov 2008	fuselage
Hawker Typhoon I	–	1942	Britain	2007	cockpit, plus another
Hawker Tempest V	SN280	1945	Britain	2010	cockpit
Hawker Hunter FGA.9	XG297	1956	Britain	1995	cockpit
Hawker Hunter GA.11	WT741	1955	Britain	2005	cockpit
Hawker Hunter F.51	'WV314'	1956	Britain	1988	–
Hawker Hunter T.53	N-302	1958	Britain	1996	cockpit
Hawker Siddeley Buccaneer S.2	XN979	1964	Britain	2003	cockpit
Hawker Siddeley Buccaneer S.2B	XZ431	1977	Britain	2016	cockpit
Hawker Siddeley Harrier GR.1	XV280	1967	Britain	2016	cockpit
Hawker Siddeley Harrier GR.3	XV752	1969	Britain	5 Dec 2011	–
Hawker Siddeley HS.125-1B/522	G-BOCB	1966	Britain	2001	cockpit

Two of YHPG's exhibits: United Nations-schemed Whirlwind HAR.10 XP345 with Whirlwind HAR.1 XA870 behind. *Ken Ellis*

South Yorkshire Aircraft Museum aircraft continued...

Type	Identity	Built	Origin	Acquired	Notes
Hawker Siddeley HS.748-2A/266	G-OPFW	1972	Britain	4 Sep 2010	cockpit
Hawker Siddeley Nimrod R.1	XW666	1973	Britain	2001	cockpit
Hiway Stytrike	G-MJKP	1982	Britain	2001	–
Hunting Jet Provost T.3A	XM350	1958	Britain	1995	–
Hunting Jet Provost T.3	XM411	1960	Britain	1999	cockpit
Hunting Jet Provost T.3	XN511	1960	Britain	1997	cockpit
Hunting Jet Provost T.4	XS216	1964	Britain	2003	cockpit
Linstrand LBL.77A	G-BUUV	1993	Britain	2011	hot air balloon
Mainair Tri-Flyer	G-MMDK	1983	Britain	2009	–
McDD/BAe Harrier T.10	ZH655	1994	USA/GB	Oct 2016	cockpit
Mignet 'Flying Flea'	G-AEJZ	1936	France	2004	–
North American Harvard II	FX322	1944	USA	2006	cockpit
Panavia Tornado F.2	ZD938	1985	GB/Ger/Italy	28 Jun 2011	cockpit
Percival Prentice T.1	G-AOKO	1949	Britain	9 May 2000	–
Percival Sea Prince T.1	WF122	1951	Britain	29 Aug 2003	–
Piper Apache 160*	G-APMY	1958	USA	Apr 1996	see profile
Robinson R22	G-DELB	1988	USA	Nov 1997	–
Robinson R22	EI-JWM	1990	USA	2004	–
Saunders-Roe Skeeter AOP.12	XM561	1959	Britain	1993	–
Saunders-Roe P.531-2	XP190	1961	Britain	27 Aug 1992	–
Scottish Aviation Bulldog T.1	XX669	1975	Britain	2006	–
SEPECAT Jaguar GR.1	XX736	1974	GB/France	2007	cockpit
Slingsby Sedbergh TX.1	WB969	1950	Britain	Oct 2001	glider
Slingsby Grasshopper TX.1	WZ822	1952	Britain	May 1997	glider
Slingsby Prefect TX.1	WE987	1950	Britain	Dec 2001	glider
Slingsby Cadet TX.1	WT913	1952	Britain	2003	glider
Slingsby Cadet TX.3	XE797	1953	Britain	30 Oct 2016	glider, cockpit
Slingsby Cadet TX.3	XN238	1959	Britain	May 1997	glider, cockpit
Stewart Ornithopter	–	c1965	Britain	9 May 2016	–
Sud Gazelle AH.1	XX411	1975	France	May 2002	–
Vickers Valetta	–	1952	Britain	2001	cockpit
Vickers Varsity T.1	WJ903	1952	Britain	14 Mar 1997	cockpit
Waco CG-4 Hadrian	–	1997	USA	2003	cockpit, replica
Westland Dragonfly HR.5	WN499	1953	USA/GB	3 Jun 2006	–
Westland Whirlwind HAR.1#	XA862	1953	USA/GB	13 Jul 2005	cockpit
Westland Whirlwind HAR.1*#	XA870	1954	USA/GB	1 Dec 2002	–
Westland Whirlwind HAR.9	XN386	1960	USA/GB	1999	–
Westland Whirlwind HAR.10#	XJ398	1957	USA/GB	27 Jun 2003	–
Westland Whirlwind HAR.10#	XP345	1962	USA/GB	6 Jul 2002	–
Westland Wessex HAS.1#	XS887	1966	USA/GB	9 Dec 2007	–
Westland Wessex HU.5	XS481	1963	USA/GB	Jun 1998	–
Westland Scout AH.1	XP902	1963	Britain	1999	cockpit
Westland Scout AH.1	XV139	1967	Britain	Jun 2009	–
Westland Sea King HAS.6	XV677	1970	USA/GB	25 Jul 2006	see profile
Westland Lynx HAS.3S(ICE)#	XZ246	1978	Britain	Aug 2016	see profile
Whittaker MW-5-K	G-MVNT	1990	Britain	2009	–
Whittaker MW-8	G-MYJX	1993	Britain	2007	–

Notes: * – illustrated in the colour section. # Yorkshire Helicopter Preservation Group airframes, dates given are for arrival at Doncaster. Includes airframes in deep store.

Halifax *Friday the 13th* ready for the unveiling ceremony at Elvington, September 1996. *Josh Lyman*

White Rose Base
Yorkshire Air Museum

Elvington
www.yorkshireairmuseum.org

Had history unfolded differently, Elvington would have had three bomber eras: instead it has had two, both featuring the incredible Handley Page Halifax. With a 'traditional' three-runway layout, the airfield received the Halifax IIs and Vs of 77 Squadron from October 1942. This unit moved on to nearby Full Sutton on 15th May 1944. The following day the first of two French units was formed at Elvington: 346 Squadron, otherwise known as Groupe de Bombardement (GB) 2/23 'Guyenne'. On 20th June 347 Squadron, GB 1/25 'Tunisie' was established. Both flew a mixture of Halifax IIIs, Vs and VIs. The French developed a considerable rapport with Elvington and York in particular and this is reflected in the imposing memorial close to the village. Both units departed for their homeland on 20th October 1945. The Franco-Yorkshire links have been maintained through to the present; with the supply of engines to the Halifax project and the handing on of former French Air Force jets in the form of the Dassault Mirage IIIE in 1995 and the recently delivered Mirage IVA – both the first and only examples of their kind preserved in Britain. Other than a brief spell as a relief landing ground for the Airspeed Oxfords of 14 Flying Training School from Holme-on-Spalding Moor between 1952 and 1953, all was quiet at Elvington.

Halifax VI NP763 of 346 'Guyenne' Squadron, based at Elvington, 1945. This colour scheme has been applied to the starboard side of YAM's Halifax. *Peter Green Collection*

Elvington's watch tower. *Ken Ellis*

In September 1953 the airfield was handed over to the United States Air Force and in 1954 most of the airfield was regenerated, only the eastern perimeter and its buildings, including the watch tower, went unscathed. A giant 9,800ft runway – 08/26 – was laid down. On the southern border of the runway's eastern threshold was a vast aircraft parking ramp of just over 49 acres; more than twice the area occupied by the present-day museum. Elvington was to receive squadrons of Douglas B-66 Destroyers, nuclear-capable twin-jet bombers deployed at the drop of hat from the USA should the Cold War take a turn for the worse. This would have been the airfield's second bomber phase, but it seems that not one B-66 ever touched down on that exceptional runway. All American personnel had gone by December 1958. The RAF took over the facilities in 1962, using the airfield for 'touch and goes' by Hunting Jet Provosts and later Short Tucanos from Church Fenton and Linton-on-Ouse, until February 1992. Then the runway again went quiet; apart from the occasional aerial delivery of an exhibit to the Yorkshire Air Museum (YAM).

Return of the Halifax

The eastern portion of Elvington airfield had survived as a form of 'time capsule' but by the late 1970s it was in poor state and neglected. By 1983 a group of enthusiasts, under the guidance of Ian Robinson, had secured a lease on 12 acres of the site and what became YAM was born. Such was the maturity of the museum that in 1993 it was in a position to acquire this land outright. Work on clearing undergrowth, repairing and restoring buildings commenced, with the watch tower as a priority. From the earliest days of the museum project there was a determination to have a Halifax as the centrepiece of the aircraft collection. The author was

Ian Robinson (left) with the Earl of Halifax in front of the newly restored rear fuselage from HR792. *YAM*

honoured to be asked to write the foreword for Ian Robinson's book *Home is the Halifax* which was published by Grub Street in August 2010, just two months before he died at the age of 84. Ian glossed over the blasphemy that I was a Lancastrian and was very pleased with my summing up of the rationale for the Halifax project: "The thinking was straightforward. There should be a Halifax on show at Elvington, where once Handley Page's under-praised stalwart flew on 'ops'. There was no chance of an original, so the job was to *recreate* one, using as many genuine, or kindred, components as possible. A hen coop that once bashed the circuit at Stornoway, a Berlin Airlift-era Hastings, engines from a French transport, contributions from friends and colleagues worldwide, all to help with the formation of a masterpiece – *Friday the 13th*. Cries from pedants of "It's not a *proper* one!" didn't faze Ian and his team. But the detractors couldn't see how moved former air and ground crew were at being reunited with *their* warhorse... Since its inception, *Friday* has always been a 'People's Plane' – Ian and the Yorkshire Air Museum would have it no other way."

Reviving an airfield

Work on the site advanced so quickly that YAM staged its first open day on 11th August 1985 and it was officially opened on a full-time basis on 31st May 1986. Close to the watch tower is the extensive 'NAAFI', the museum's now legendary restaurant and other buildings have been transformed into a chapel (with memorial garden), the exceptional Air Gunners' Memorial Room and the 'Pioneers of Aviation' exhibition, opened in 2010, among others. Opened on 24th July 2013 was the purpose-built ACA Building which houses YAM's extensive archive. Although a new-build, this structure was carefully designed to blend in with the 1940s architecture. The archive is named for the Air Crew Association, which was 'stood down' in December 2011, handing over its extensive records to the Air Crew Association Archive Trust which contributed over £200,000 towards the construction and fitting-out of building.

In 1988 the museum inaugurated the Handley Page building, as the first covered aircraft display hall. In 2002 this structure was given a major refurbishment and it was renamed the Handley Page Restoration Hangar to indicate its new role. This is a popular destination for visitors as the refit included a viewing area, allowing close inspection of work in hand on aircraft, vehicles and engines. As the aircraft collection grew and the Halifax project progressed, the need for a main display hangar was addressed. A T2 hangar, last in use at Keevil in Wiltshire, was acquired and in July 1995 the Heritage Lottery Fund granted £135,000 towards its erection and fitting out. Known as the 'Canadian Memorial Hangar' in honour of the Royal Canadian Air Force bomber units that served from Yorkshire and the museum's very active Canadian branch, which contributed £30,000 towards the hangar appeal, it was inaugurated at the same time as Halifax *Friday the 13th* was unveiled – 13th September 1996. Touching down on the runway on 25th November 1993 was André Tempest's Handley Page Victor K.2 *Lusty Lindy*. A dedicated team has kept this V-bomber 'in steam' ever since and it is regularly taxied. In recent times it has been joined by an increasing number of aircraft that have been restored to ground-runnable status, including the Dakota which moved under its own power for the first time in seventeen years in 2014. Where once Halifaxes thundered into the air bound for targets in occupied Europe, now on special, regular, 'Thunder Days' Elvington once again reverberates to the sound of aviation in action.

Douglas Dakota IV KN353
1944 | General purpose transport / Medium range airliner | Two 1,200hp Pratt & Whitney R-1830-92 Twin Wasp pistons

See under the South Yorkshire Aircraft Museum for general notes on DC-3s and Dakotas. The YAM machine was built by Douglas at its Oklahoma City plant for the United States Army Air Force as C-47B Skytrain 44-76384 but was transferred three days later under Lend-Lease to the RAF at Montreal, Canada, becoming Dakota IV KN353. It faced a long journey, it was destined for 300 Wing, controlling transport flights from headquarters at Camden, New South Wales. The 'Dak' was accepted by 300 Wing in Australia on 3rd March 1945. It was taken on charge by the Camden-based 243 Squadron who used it for wide-ranging re-supply and trooping flights extending as far as Kai Tak, Hong Kong, from August 1945. Disbanding in mid-April 1946, 243 Squadron handed KN353 to 96 Squadron which was operating from Hong Kong, mostly to and from Singapore. On 15th June 1946 the unit was re-numbered as 110 Squadron which decamped to Changi, Singapore, in September 1947. Surplus to requirements, KN353 flew in stages to Britain, being taken on charge at 12 Maintenance Unit, Kirkbride on 29th October 1947 where it entered deep storage.

Dakota G-AMYJ with Harvestair at Southend in November 1983. It has a wind-driven pump under the centre section and spray bars for oil dispersant under the tail planes. *KEC*

Life as a civilian started with the Croydon-based Transair registering the Dakota as G-AMYJ on 25th February 1953. Its military life was not quite over as the airline regularly operated under contract to the Ministry of Defence and in 1954 *Yankee-Juliet* was allocated the serial XF747 to cover such flights, particularly when ferrying troops carrying live weapons. Jersey Airlines was G-AMYJ's next operator, from 8th May 1959, the airline changing its name to British United Island Airways (BUIA) on 1st August 1963. A sequence of British airlines followed: Morton Air Services of Gatwick from 30th November 1965; a return to BUIA on 1st November 1968; South West Aviation at Exeter on 6th May 1969 and Intra Airways of Jersey from 14th September 1972. An exotic interlude was next for the Dakota, registered in Egypt as SU-AZF it moved to Cairo for a spell with Nile Delta Airways from 6th July 1976. It was back with Intra, as G-AMYJ, from 3rd February 1978. Humberside Airport, Kirmington, was the Dakota's next base, flying with Eastern Airways from 29th November 1978. *Yankee-Juliet* was briefly on the books of well-known Dakota operator Air Atlantique in October 1981 but it was passed to another famous DC-3 flyer, Aces High of Fairoaks in January 1982. Harvestair of Southend took on G-AMYJ on 3rd March 1982, joining its fleet of pollution dispersant sprayers under contract to the Department of the Environment. The Dakota was returned to Air Atlantique, at Coventry, on 26th February 1990 and by the last day of 1995 had 'clocked' a grand total of 29,951 flying hours. It was withdrawn from use at Coventry by the spring of 1997 and stored. YAM had long been looking for a 'Dak' and Air Atlantique donated *Yankee-Juliet* to the museum in December 2001. Returned to military colours, long and hard work by a team of volunteers was rewarded by the venerable Dakota's first taxi on 12th October 2014.

Handley Page Halifax 'LV907'
1944 | Long range heavy bomber | Four 1,800hp Bristol Hercules 100 pistons

No false claims are made for YAM's Halifax; it is what it is. Some would call it a replica, but that is too sterile a definition: *Friday the 13th* is a re-creation, an evocation of all that the Handley Page bomber stood for. As described in the narrative above, the Halifax venture went hand-in-hand with the setting up of YAM itself. The wartime buildings, especially the watch tower, provided the body of the museum, but it needed a heart. When the first steps were being taken on the project there was the cockpit of Halifax VII PN323 with the Imperial War Museum and all of Mk.II W1048 *S-for-Sugar*, which had been salvaged from Lake Hocklingen in Norway during June 1973 by the RAF Museum. (This epic recovery is detailed in the sister volume *Great Aviation Collections of Britain*.) In 1995 – the year before *Friday* was unveiled – a Canadian team succeeded in recovering more or less intact Mk.VII NA337 out of the waters of Lake Mjosa in Norway and it is today displayed at Trenton, Ontario. Other than its nose turret, Hendon's *Sugar* has not been restored and it is presented in 'as found' condition, on its belly. At Elvington, *Friday* towers over the visitors providing a magisterial image of the great bomber. The composite some-new, some-old nature of *Friday* means that its 'rating' as a museum artefact is not dazzling but the sheer scope of the project and what it stands for makes it a truly remarkable exhibit.

The rear fuselage of former 58 Squadron Halifax II HR792 on Norman McKenzie's farm on the Isle of Lewis, May 1979. *KEC*

The cornerstone of the project was the survival of the rear section of Rolls-Royce Merlin-engined Mk.II Series 1A HR792 at Norman MacKenzie's farm on the Isle of Lewis in the Hebrides. Coastal Command had positioned 58 Squadron at Stornoway on Lewis for anti-submarine patrols from August 1944. While taking off on 13th January 1945 the undercarriage of HR792 was retracted too early and it slithered to a halt on its belly, with no injuries to the crew. (Before you ask: 13th January 1945 was a Saturday, not a Friday!) It was beyond the capabilities of the based personnel to repair and it made no sense to dismantle the war-weary Mk.II to take it to the mainland for repair. It was struck off charge and scrapped and grateful local inhabitants found a new purpose for some of it. Norman McKenzie was asked two questions in 1983: Did he still have his Handley Page hen coop? Could YAM have it? The answer was 'yes' both times. The first piece of a complex 'jigsaw puzzle' arrived in Yorkshire in 1984.

Leads were being followed up on a global basis for parts and crash sites were scoured; a surprising number of these were fruitful. But there would have to be an element of new-build in the final product. The offer of facilities and a workforce – in the form of apprentices – at British Aerospace Brough was pivotal to the prospects of the project. All of this was valueless without drawings – to 'reverse engineer' a Halifax would be prohibitive in time and expenditure. Harry Fraser-Mitchell of the Handley Page Association came to the rescue; the plans survived, they were copied and microfilmed. Work was split between Brough and Elvington – see the table for details of *Friday's* major sections and their origins.

Yorkshire Air Museum Halifax project

Major sections	Source
Forward fuselage and cockpit	Built from scratch at Elvington by YAM volunteers
Centre fuselage	Refurbished from a section believed to have originated at Linton-on-Ouse
Mid-fuselage	Former 58 Squadron Mk.II HR792 previously in use as a hen coop on the Isle of Lewis – see narrative
Rear fuselage	Built from scratch by apprentices at British Aerospace, Brough
Tailplane, elevators	Refurbished from wreckage salvaged from high ground near Coniston, Lake District. Believed to be from Mk.V LL505 of 1659 Conversion Unit, Topcliffe, crashed 22nd Oct 1944
Tail fins	Built from scratch by apprentices at British Aerospace, Brough
Rudders	Built from scratch at Elvington by YAM volunteers
Centre section and wings to outer engines	From Handley Page Hastings C.1 TG536, struck off charge 2nd Jan 1974 at the fire school, Catterick
Outer wings	Unflown Hastings C.1 spares found in a scrapyard in the south of England – still in their transportation crates!
Engines	From French Air Force stocks, four 2,040hp SNECMA-built Bristol Hercules 739s, as used on Nord Noratlas tactical transports

The two unused Hastings outer wing sections arriving at Elvington, 1989. *YAM*

Fabricating the forward fuselage of *Friday* inside the Handley Page hangar at Elvington. *Steve Hague*

The Halifax was the basis of a two-pronged programme to set Handley Page up for the post-war aviation market place. The Hermes airliner was not a great success, but the Hastings military airlifter kept the factory busy. Both types shared the World War Two bomber's wing structure. This was another boon; while the fuselage structure was relatively simple, the complexities of the wings might well have been a stumbling block. The search was on for a Hastings that could donate its wings and the answer lay in Yorkshire – 40 miles to the north at the RAF fire and rescue school at Catterick. Thankfully 1948-built Hastings C.1 TG536 had not been 'torched' and the commanding officer was more than happy to put the centre section and wings to better use. A working party from Elvington was dispatched to carry out the surgery. Even more miraculous was the discovery in 1989 of outer wing panels, unused and still in wooden packing cases, in a scrap yard in southern England.

There are many other stories that can be related regarding the 'ingredients' that make up *Friday*, but that is best left to Ian Robinson's book *Home is the Halifax*. One more will have to suffice; it embodies the international nature of the project and the depth of work required to make it happen. The search for engines for the Halifax was proving fruitless: the carcass of TG536 at Catterick had had its Hercules 106 engines removed upon arrival in 1974. Elvington's 'French connection' delivered the goods. Groupe Lourds (translating as 'heavy group', an association of French heavy bomber aircrew) tracked down a quartet of Bristol Hercules 739s that had been made under licence by SNECMA for use on French Air Force Nord Noratlas tactical transports. This donation was incredible, but the logistics of bringing such cumbersome items across the Channel would not be easy. That had been thought of as well; a French Air Force Transall C-160 airlifter delivered them to Elvington's generous runway on 20th August 1987. Derek Reed, YAM's present-day manager, liaised with myriad agencies to achieve the hand-over. He explained at the time: "It would be wrong to think that all we had to do was nod to this brilliant offer, step back and wait for it all to happen. There were import clearances, insurance, flight plans, runway inspections, translations of documents and constant phone calls, fork lifts... and so the list went on." Multiply this sort of activity across all of the elements, large and small, that went into *Friday* and the enormity of the venture becomes apparent.

The starboard side of the YAM Halifax is painted in the colours worn by Mk.VI NP763 'H7-N' of 346 'Guyenne' Squadron that served from Elvington. The choice of the port side was the subject of considerable debate: some felt that 347 'Tunisie' Squadron was the most deserving, others that 77 Squadron was more appropriate. In the end, one of the most well known Halifaxes was chosen: 158 Squadron's veteran of 128 'ops', Mk.III LV907 *Friday the 13th*. There could only be one date for the unveiling ceremony of the finished Halifax: Friday 13th September 1996 was a momentous occasion and one on which to reflect what can be achieved with much good will, generosity, dogged determination and a hen coop!

Shaw Europa G-YURO
1992 | Two-seat light aircraft | One 80hp Rotax 912-UL piston

'Flying' inside Elvington's 'Canadian' hangar is a sleek light aircraft and not far away is a glider in RAF colours. Their purpose and construction techniques are radically different, 49 years separate them but both are linked by geography: Kirkbymoorside on the southern edge of the North York Moors. (See below for the glider's pedigree.) Having been inspired by the futuristic all-composite designs of American Burt Rutan, Ivan Shaw produced a twin-engined version of Rutan's Vari-Eze two-seater in 1981, the Shaw Twin-Eze, appropriately registered G-IVAN. Further experimentation led to Ivan formulating a simple, practical, all-composite two-seater, capable of being de-rigged in moments so that it could be towed home on a trailer. This

The prototype Shaw Europa, G-YURO, shortly after arrival at Elvington, July 1997. *Steve Hague*

was the Europa and Ivan flew the prototype G-YURO, from Rufforth, west of York, on 12th September 1992. Two years later the Europa Aircraft Company was producing kits from a factory at Kirkbymoorside, later still from nearby Wombleton. The product line was extended beyond the original 'monowheel' layout to offer a tricycle undercarriage and a bigger winged motor glider version. By 2004 over 1,000 kits had been sold to over 30 countries and it is reported that 700 are flying. This makes the Europa the most-produced British post-war light aircraft by a long way. Its work complete, G-YURO had been retired by 1997 and was presented to YAM as the starting point of a Yorkshire and British success story.

Slingsby Cadet TX.1 RA854
1943 | Single-seat training glider

Yorkshireman and former Royal Flying Corps pilot Frederick 'Sling' Slingsby took up gliding in the early 1930s and transformed his furniture making business at Scarborough into a glider manufacturing dynasty at Kirkbymoorside. Initially his products were marketed under the Kirby name, but from 1939 the business was known as Slingsby Sailplanes. On 11th January 1936 Fred flew the prototype Kirby Cadet single-seat glider from Sutton Bank and it entered limited production. In 1943 orders were placed for Cadet TX.1s for the Air Training Corps. Total production for military and civil use came to 431. The YAM example was part of a batch of 30 built by Otley Motors, at Otley, north of Bradford. It entered service with 41 Gliding School (GS) at Knowle, Warwickshire in 1943 and by 1949 was at 186 GS at Woodvale. By the late 1950s RA854 was with the Woodford Gliding School, at the famous Avro airfield. It

Slingsby Cadet TX.1 RA854 in Elvington's 'Canadian' hangar. *Ken Ellis*

was donated to the Northern Aircraft Preservation Society (Chapter 18) on 23rd November 1963. Stored, mostly at Wigan, the glider was released to Ken Fern in 1996 and later passed to Yorkshire-based light aircraft collector Nigel Ponsford. With its considerable Yorkshire provenance, it was acquired by YAM in April 2000. In a similar manner to microlights, as discussed in Chapter 26, all manner of gliders have proved to be a popular exhibits in British museums. Some early gliders suffered from glue failure making them readily, and cheaply, available. Their light structure permits display suspended from roof structures, as is the case with YAM's example. Seven Cadet TX.1s are preserved in British museums.

Yorkshire Air Museum aircraft

Type	Identity	Built	Origin	Acquired	Notes
Air Command 532	G-TFRB	1990	USA	Nov 2001	–
Avro 504K	'9828'	1968	Britain	Oct 1994	replica
Avro Anson T.21	VV901	1949	Britain	8 Jun 1993	–
Beagle Terrier 2	VW993	1948	Britain	1988	–
Blackburn 1911 Monoplane	–	1978	Britain	10 Jan 1995	replica
Cayley glider	–	1972	Britain	12 Aug 1999	replica
Dassault Mirage IIIE	538	1968	France	1995	–
Dassault Mirage IVA	45	1966	France	30 Mar 2017	–
de Havilland Vampire T.11	XH278	1955	Britain	10 Feb 2002	–
de Havilland Devon C.2/2	VP967	1948	Britain	6 Oct 2010	–
Douglas Dakota 3	KN353	1944	USA	10 Dec 2001	see profile
English Electric Canberra B.2	WH903	1954	Britain	1992	cockpit
English Electric Canberra T.4	WH846	1954	Britain	19 May 1988	–
English Electric Lightning F.6	XS903	1966	Britain	18 May 1988	–
Fairchild Argus II	FK338	1942	USA	2000	–
Fairey Gannet AEW.3	XL502	1961	Britain	11 Mar 2005	–
Gloster Meteor F.8	WL168	1954	Britain	12 Apr 1996	–
Gloster Meteor NF(T).14	WS788	1954	Britain	16 Mar 1992	–
Gloster Javelin FAW.9	XH767	1957	Britain	4 Feb 2001	–
Handley Page Halifax*	–	1944	Britain	1984	see profile
Handley Page Victor K.2	XL231	1962	Britain	25 Nov 1993	–
Handley Page Herald 213	G-AVPN	1964	Britain	20 Oct 1997	cockpit
Hawker Hurricane I	'P3873'	1999	Britain	Oct 2000	replica
Hawker Hunter T.7	XL572	1958	Britain	12 Jan 1995	–
Hawker Hunter FGA.78	'N-2'	1968	Britain	25 Apr 1992	–
Hawker Siddeley Buccaneer S.2A	XN974	1964	Britain	19 Aug 1991	–
Hawker Siddeley Buccaneer S.2B	XV168	1966	Britain	18 Aug 2013	–
Hawker Siddeley Buccaneer S.2B	XX901	1977	Britain	26 May 1996	–
Hawker Siddeley Harrier GR.3	XV748	1969	Britain	21 Oct 2000	–
Hawker Siddeley Nimrod MR.2*	XV250	1971	Britain	13 Apr 2010	–
Hunting Jet Provost T.3	–	1962	Britain	Oct 1992	cockpit, plus another
Hunting Jet Provost T.4	XP640	1962	Britain	Oct 1993	–
Lockheed CT-133 Silver Star	21417	1954	USA	25 Jun 1993	–
Mainair Tri-Flyer	G-MJRA	1982	Britain	2001	–
Messerschmitt Bf 109G	'15919'	1994	Germany	May 1994	replica
Mignet 'Flying Flea'	'G-AFFI'	1975	France	1989	–
Panavia Tornado GR.4	XZ631	1978	GB/Ger/Italy	22 Mar 2005	–
Panavia Tornado GR.1	ZA354	1982	GB/Ger/Italy	29 Apr 2005	–
Port Victoria Kitten	'N540'	1975	Britain	1996	replica
Royal Aircraft Factory BE.2c	'6232'	1962	Britain	Oct 1994	replica
Royal Aircraft Factory SE.5a	'F943'	1982	Britain	1987	replica
Saunders-Roe Skeeter AOP.12	XM553	1959	Britain	2009	–
Shaw Europa 001	G-YURO	1992	Britain	1997	see profile
Slingsby Cadet TX.1	RA854	1943	Britain	6 Apr 2000	see profile
Supermarine Spitfire I	'R6690'	1996	Britain	Sep 1996	replica
Waco CG-4A Hadrian	'319764'	1968	USA	25 Apr 1992	–
Westland Dragonfly HR.5	WH991	1953	USA/GB	Oct 1994	–
Wright Flyer	–	1966	USA	Nov 1999	replica

Notes: * – illustrated in the colour section. See Chapter 16 for details of previous long-term resident Mosquito NF.II HJ711*.

Beverley C.1 XB259 dominates the skyline at Fort Paull. *Ian Humphreys*

Land of the Giant
Fort Paull Armouries

Paull
www.fortpaull.com

There has been a fort at Paull, on the north shore of the Humber, since 1542 and the current fortifications were completed in the 1860s. It was owned by the Ministry of Defence until the 1960s and from 2000 it was opened to the public under the title Fort Paull Armouries. Readers may well have guessed that this venue does not fall within the book's definition of dedicated aeronautical museum. Inside the fort's walls is a remarkable survivor; the last intact Blackburn Beverley. With a wingspan of 162ft, height of 38ft 9in and an empty weight in the region of 80,000lb it is one of the largest aircraft preserved in Britain. The team at Fort Paul showed their determination in acquiring this giant, dismantling it and moving it by road, re-assembling it, restoring its interior. A display devoted to the Blackburn company and the Beverley in particular was established in its cavernous interior. XB259 is a classic example of how a significant aircraft can 'slip through the net' and rely on the intervention of determined individuals for its salvation.

Blackburn Beverley C.1 XB259
1955 | Medium range, high capacity transport | Four 2,850hp Bristol Centaurus 273 pistons

Originally a General Aircraft design, what was originally known as the Universal Freighter was taken on by Blackburn at Brough when the companies merged in 1949. The prototype first flew on 20th June 1950 and was followed by a considerably redesigned second example on 14th June 1953. The RAF ordered 47 and the first of these was XB259 which had its maiden flight from Brough – just down the River Humber from its current location – on 29th January 1955. For an undisclosed reason, the civil registration G-AOAI was allocated to XB259 from 15th to 30th March 1955. The aircraft was used for trials by the manufacturer and these included a spectacular demonstration in December 1956. With Blackburn chief test pilot Harold 'Timber' Wood at the controls and XB259 loaded to its maximum all-up weight of 135,000lb and fitted with no less than ten Napier Scarab solid-fuel rockets strapped to fuselage blasted the Beverley into the air in just 1,200ft.

Transferred to the Royal Aircraft Establishment at Farnborough on 16th September 1959, XB259 served with the Structures and Mechanical Engineering Flight on a wide variety of trials into the early 1970s. Offered for disposal, it was ferried to Luton on 14th March 1973. It had been acquired by Court Line; the airline intended to use the Beverley to transport Rolls-Royce RB.211 turbofans for its Lockheed TriStars. This scheme came to nothing and as the airline's financial situation worsened – it was to be put into liquidation in August 1974 – XB259 was offered for sale. It was acquired by North Country Breweries for use as a control tower and clubhouse by Hull Aero Club at its aerodrome at Paull – within sight of where the Beverley is now. On 30th March 1974 XB259 made the last ever-flight by a Beverley, touching down on the grass at Paull with no difficulties at all. Crew for the flight were: captain Sqn Ldr Peter Sedgwick, co-pilot Flt Lt Brian Peaty and engineer John Oakes.

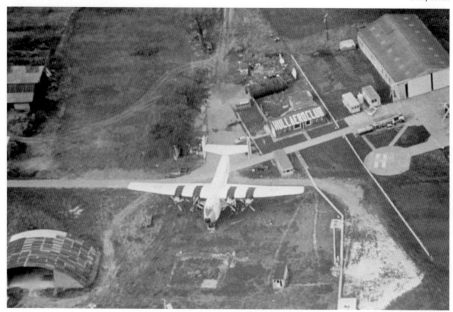

An aerial view of Paull aerodrome in September 1977 with Beverley C.1 XB259 in front of the Hull Aero Club building. To the right is the Bristow Helicopters hangar. *KEC*

All was well until 1981 when the aero club's lease on the aerodrome expired. Before long, the Beverley was all alone amid fields with a land owner who was losing patience with its presence. XB259 was purchased by an individual from Gateshead for its scrap value, but before this could happen entrepreneur Francis Daly offered him a reported £6,000 for it. Daly presented it to the Museum of Army Transport (MoAT) which was being established, very appropriately, at the town of Beverley, just north of Kingston upon Hull. The museum opened its doors on 7th June 1983 and sections of XB259 began to arrive on site from early August. A team composed mostly of former Blackburn employees began the difficult job of restoring and then re-assembling the giant. They did a superb job, the tail boom was again fitted out with parachute seats and the freight bay was turned into a display. In March 1990 the RAF Museum reluctantly scrapped Beverley C.1 XH124 at Hendon and XB259 became the last intact example of its breed. With falling visitor figures, MoAT called in the receivers in January 1997. Alan Bushell, co-founder of the Baltic Pine time company and a military vehicle collector stepped in and took over the museum on 12th November 1997. During 2001 XB259 was repainted, forsaking its overall white colours of its days at Farnborough for RAF tactical sand and brown camouflage.

In August 2003 MoAT again went into receivership; this time not to bounce back. A deadline for bids for the contents, including the Beverley was set for 26th January 2004. During this time, the Yorkshire Air Museum (YAM) – see above – looked into the possibility of staging a rescue but declined as the real long term solution was to put the monster under cover, at prohibitive cost. It was then that Brian Rushworth, the owner of Fort Paull, stepped in and acquired XB259 for what is thought to have been £36,000. The big airlifter faced its second dismantling, road journey and re-assembly operation; the move was completed on 23rd May 2004. The Beverley has become a popular attraction at Fort Paull and the opportunity has been taken to install a gentle access ramp allowing wheel chairs to enter its huge fuselage.

Fort Paul Armouries aircraft

Type	Identity	Built	Origin	Acquired	Notes
Blackburn 1916 Triplane	–	2007	Britain	2008	replica
Blackburn Beverley C.1	XB259	1955	Britain	23 May 2004	see profile
Hawker Hunter F.6	XF509	1956	Britain	10 May 2008	–
Scottish Aviation Bulldog T.1	XX557	1973	Britain	2001	cockpit

Doncaster Museum and Art Gallery
displays a 'Flying Flea' and a
Bensen B-7. *Ken Ellis*

Also in Yorkshire
Doncaster Museum and Art Gallery

As well as a display on the 1909 aviation meeting at Doncaster race course, a locally built Bensen gyrocopter and a 'Flying Flea' are on show. The original G-AEKR had it first flight from Doncaster Airport in May 1936 but was sadly, burnt out in a hangar fire at RAF Finningley in 1970. A replica was made and this particular 'Flea' was a founder member of the Nostell Aviation Museum – see *Innovators* above. **www.doncaster.gov.uk/museums**

Doncaster Museum and Art Gallery aircraft

Type	Identity	Built	Origin	Acquired	Notes
Bensen B-7	–	1961	USA	22 Mar 1997	–
Mignet 'Flying Flea'	'G-AEKR'	1972	France	2001	–

Eden Camp Modern History Theme Museum

Each hut in this former prisoner of war camp at Malton has a different theme and the level of presentation is breath-taking. There is much to fascinate the aviation follower, including a Link trainer display, plotting room, items on 617 Squadron, the Comete escape line, two Hawker Hurricanes, a Supermarine Spitfire and a Fieseler V-1 flying-bomb replicas. **www.edencamp.co.uk**

Sewerby Hall and Gardens

Amy Johnson officially opened the house in 1936 and to celebrate this connection with the famous flyer, there are two rooms of memorabilia and displays as a permanent exhibition. **www.sewerbyhall.co.uk**

Streetlife Museum of Transport

There are five extensive galleries ranging between bicycles, cars, horse carriages and railways at this Hull museum. Also on show is a replica of Blackburn Lincock G-EBVO biplane of 1928. **www.hullcc.gov.uk**

Vulcan to the Sky Trust

Doncaster Sheffield Airport, the former RAF Finningley, is home of XH558, the last Vulcan to fly in Britain. Visits are possible on a prior arrangement basis, but there are high hopes that a visitor and education centre will be established. **www.vulcantothesky.org**

Vulcan to the Sky Trust aircraft

Type	Identity	Built	Origin	Arrived	Notes
Avro Vulcan B.2(MRR)	XH588	1960	Britain	29 Mar 2011	–
English Electric Canberra B.2/6	WK163	1955	Britain	19 May 2016	–
Supermarine Swift F.4	WK275	1955	Britain	23 Nov 2016	–

CHAPTER 32
SCOTLAND

Scottish Independence
Dumfries and Galloway Aviation Museum

Dumfries
www.dumfriesaviationmuseum.com

On the night of 3rd/4th June 1944 Vickers Wellington X HE476 came down on approach to Dumfries airfield. Thirty years later local enthusiasts salvaged both Bristol Hercules engines, one of which still boasted its wooden propeller. This fourteen-cylinder radial became the founder of the museum's exceptional engine collection, now standing at 70 items. The Wellington recovery led to the setting up of the Dumfries and Galloway Aviation Group in 1976. All eyes turned to the former airfield as a base and the old flight hut, last used by the local gliding club, was occupied. That year the first whole airframe, Vampire T.11 XD425, arrived with Meteor T.7 WL375 following soon afterwards. (The Vampire is now with Morayvia – see below, WL375 is still at Dumfries.)

More artefacts appeared and, after feverish preparation, the Dumfries and Galloway Aviation Museum (D&G) was officially opened on 17th July 1977 by Michal Cwynar. Polish-born Michal had served briefly at Dumfries in 1940-1941 flying Fairey Battles with the resident 10 Bombing and Gunnery School (10 B&GS). Having downed a Junkers Ju 87 'Stuka' during the invasion of his homeland, Poland, while piloting a PZL P.11 in September 1939, Michal was keen to go back on the

Above: View from the tower at Tinwald Downs; in the background is one of the huge storage hangars used by 18 Maintenance Unit. *Ken Ellis*

The top flor of the Dumfries watch tower portrays flying control from the 1940s. *Ken Ellis*

The Dumfries and Galloway three-storey tower is believed to be a unique survivor. To the left is Jet Provost T.4 XP557; centre F-100D 54-2163. *Ken Ellis*

offensive and by the summer of 1941 he was with 315 Squadron on Spitfires and later Mustangs. With five 'kills', one shared, a 'probable' and three V-1 'doodlebugs' accounted for and a Distinguished Flying Cross, the Virtuti Militari and the Cross of Valour worn proudly on his chest, Michal chose to settle in Scotland. He became the museum's patron, carrying out this duty until his death, aged 92, in 2008.

Nobody was surprised when the flight hut proved inadequate for the growing organisation and in 1979 a tenancy in the unique three-storey watch tower – D&G's centrepiece ever since – was finalised. This tower is the only survivor of what is thought to have been just seven to this design, one of which was at Heathrow. The top floor was completely re-glazed in 2016 with frames that exactly mimic the originals, but are double-glazed. The long term plan is to return the tower to its 1940s status; there is plenty of photographic evidence to help outfit each room. Presently, the top floor is set out as flying control would have been; the middle level contains exhibits on RAF Dumfries and local airfields while the ground floor is the engine hall.

Masters of their own destiny

David 'Davie' Reid, curator, chairman and 'founding father', took great delight in explaining to the author the quiet revolution that was going on at D&G in its fortieth anniversary year. "We have no illusions, we know we're never going to get everything under cover, but we've got a plan that can go a long way down that road. We don't want anything grand – that's not our style – and we are going to achieve it with the minimum of help and at a pace that suits us." The pragmatism exhibited at D&G should inspire other organisations; in four decades it has become the oldest established independent aviation museum and the second largest in Scotland. Not bad for a bunch of enthusiasts who started out trying to recover the wreck of a Wellington off the end of the runway.

Surrounding the museum is the bustling Heathhall industrial estate, most of which utilizes the many 'half round' Type J and K storage hangars built in 1939. Immediately opposite the museum entrance is a stretch of concrete, the last remnants of the northwest-southeast runway. Planned in 1938 as an Aircraft Storage Unit, Dumfries (also known as Tinwald Downs) was ready for business when 18 Maintenance Unit (MU) started up on June 17, 1940. That year 10 B&GS, the unit that Michal Cwynar flew with, moved in and construction of runways began. During the war, 10 B&GS morphed into 10 Air Observer School, later 10 (Observer) Advanced Flying Unit and finally, in June 1945, 10 Air Navigation School, only to disband 29 days later. The founder unit, 18 MU, has a much longer tenure, closing its doors in 1957.

A decade ago, the rent for its site rose considerably. Members debated the implications; income was such that the increase *could* have been met, instead it was seen as a wake-up call. It was time to go independent, allowing long term development. With help from the then Labour MP, Russell Brown, the freehold on the control tower and surrounding land was made available. A fund-raising campaign was launched and in 2014 additional ground was acquired, permitting future expansion and improvements. The volunteers had become masters of their own destiny and set about launching a building plan to turn D&G into an all-weather attraction to prove it.

A new perimeter fence was needed and this was made possible through a grant facilitated by a local wind farm. The Dumfries lads have always been champions of re-cycling and the old fence was sent to their good friends just south of the border at Carlisle Airport, the Solway Aviation Museum – Chapter 7. The reception building and lecture theatre is another example of salvage and reclaim. This had been in use as temporary accommodation by nearby Moffat Academy and was declared surplus. Taken away by a D&G team on three articulated lorries in the morning, it was bolted together at Dumfries that afternoon. Local hauliers and other specialists have proven to be very helpful to the museum throughout its existence.

The escape capsule from F-111E 68-060 at Dumfries and Galloway. *Ken Ellis*

Nissens and Romneys

With a clear span of 150ft, a length of 300ft and a working height of 30ft, a nearby Type J hangar would have provided all of the covered area that D&G could ever have dreamed of. Keeping such a complex building, approaching its 80th birthday, in tip-top condition would be a never-ending task and all such thoughts were quickly dumped. Likewise, the notion of a single, modern, box-like, display hall was abandoned as out of keeping with the site and requiring far too much investment 'up-front'. Ever realistic, D&G's plans settled upon technology well within the capabilities of its volunteers and friends – a 'farm' of Nissen and Romney huts. Such structures would have been found all over the airfield in the 1940s and each one could provide easy and appropriate accommodation for different elements of the collection.

The local authority was very helpful and planning permission for the first tranche of buildings was granted with construction starting in 2016. After acquiring a genuine World War Two era Nissen hut which was facing scrapping locally, the museum has been gathering such buildings ever since. Storage of the frames and fittings took up little space and this policy has paid off. The nature of the semi-circular structures is such that almost any length can be achieved, "cut like a cake to size" as Davie said. D&G holds enough structure to create another 270ft of building.

Two more original Nissens, a bespoke Nissen-like structure and two of the larger Romneys, running behind the watch tower along the museum's northeast perimeter were ready for the fortieth birthday celebrations. They house the archive, a hall dedicated to RAF Dumfries and the completed Spitfire restoration – see below, the workshop and the Airborne Forces exhibition. The archive is forever expanding, including a wealth of audio interviews, Davie remarked: "not a week goes by when we don't get offered something for exhibition". Within the Airborne Forces hall is D&G's fully restored 18ft section of Airspeed Horsa assault glider. In the pipeline are two more Nissens that will start off a new row on the site's northwest edge. These will accommodate some of the extensive 'aerowreckology' items and a World War One hall. There is plenty of scope for more of these modular structures.

In the D&G aircraft park several jet fighters are displayed, including a Lightning and a Draken, transferred from the Imperial War Museum. One of the exhibits that always raises comment is the battered flight deck from a 'swing-wing' F-111E – which could also be considered as a piece of aviation 'archaeology'. Crewed by Captains James Stieber and weapons systems operator Robert Gregory, the 20th Tactical Fighter Wing F-111 from Upper Heyford was on a low level mission to the ranges at Wainfleet on the Lincolnshire coast on 5th November 1975 when a bird strike shattered the canopy, severely injuring Stieber. Emergency egress from the F-111 was achieved by a self-contained module, including the entire flight deck, explosively detaching. Parachutes brought the pod, which could float, down. As F-111 68-060 barrelled into the North Sea, helicopters from the 67th Aerospace Rescue and Recovery Squadron at Woodbridge located Stieber and Gregory. They also salvaged the life-saving capsule, destined to become a museum artefact at Dumfries.

The F-111 capsule provides Davie with an example of why aviation museums appeal so much to the general public: "I read a magazine article that called specialist collections 'a different kind of weird' – that's certainly us!" The author asked Davie, with four decades under his belt, if in the early days he thought that all this time later the museum would not just be still functioning, but flourishing. He beamed: "No, it was beyond any of our expectations, but we are so proud that we proved ourselves wrong!"

Fairey Gannet AEW.3 XL497
1961 | Shipborne early warning aircraft | One 3,875shp Armstrong Siddeley Double Mamba 102 coupled turboprop

Sharing only its powerplant, wings and tailplanes, the airborne early warning version of the anti-submarine Gannet – which first appeared in 1949 – was a radical redesign. The prototype of the portly radar picket had its maiden flight on 20th August 1958; the first of 44 for the Fleet Air Arm. The type entered service with 849 Squadron in February 1960 and soldiered on until December 1978. Three other intact AEW.3s are in British Museums: at the Fleet Air Museum, Newark and Elvington.

Gannet AEW.3 XL497 during its 'gate guardian' days at Prestwick, 1982. *Carl Friend*

Built at Hayes, XL497 was trucked to White Waltham and had its maiden flight on 3rd November 1960. It joined the headquarters (HQ) flight of 849 Squadron, at Culdrose, on 10th February 1961. As well as the HQ flight, the squadron operated several flights, detaching to aircraft carriers. With very few exceptions, 849 'owned' all of the AEW.3s throughout their lives. In November 1965 XL497 was with the Aeroplane and Armament Experimental Establishment at Boscombe Down for trials relating to new equipment 'fits' and it visited again for similar reasons in December 1973. XL497 was shipped to the Far East in January 1966 and was flight tested at Changi, Singapore, before joining HMS *Ark Royal*, as part of 849's 'C' Flight. The next dozen years with 849 were as follows: July 1966 on HMS *Eagle* with 'D' Flight; July 1969 with HQ Flight then at Brawdy, in November 1970 re-locating to Lossiemouth; August 1974 on *Ark Royal* with 'B' Flight. On 7th December 1978 the Gannet was placed on the 'gate' of HMS *Gannet* at Prestwick, fifty miles northwest of D&G. All Gannet operations ceased when 849 Squadron disbanded eight days later. D&G acquired XL497 and it moved to Dumfries on 13th April 2005.

Supermarine Spitfire IIa P7540
1940 | Day fighter | One 1,140hp Rolls-Royce Merlin XII piston

There's a reason why so few Spitfires are in 'local' museums; the sleek fighter is the domain of well endowed civilian operator/owners, or with the 'nationals'. Possession of the 'right' builder's plate can facilitate the creation of effectively a new-build and there is money to be had tracking down such project cornerstones. That makes the P7540 all the more remarkable: while it has 'plastic' wings, as much of the original as possible has been incorporated: it's truly a Scottish Spitfire. The Battle of Britain started on 10th July 1940 and its end was declared as 31st October 1940: D&G are the proud owners of a genuine Battle of Britain veteran.

Built at the vast 'shadow factory' at Castle Bromwich, P7540 was issued to 6 Maintenance Unit at Brize Norton for operational preparation. It was issued to 66 Squadron at Gravesend on 29th October 1940, only for the unit to move the following day to West Malling and later to Biggin Hill. Decamping to Exeter on 24th February 1941, P7540 was left behind by 66 Squadron and handed on to 609 Squadron which arrived at 'The Hill' that day. The Spitfire briefly joined 266 Squadron at Wittering on 14th June 1941 before transferring on 6th July to Kenley, where it was issued to the Czechoslovak 312 Squadron, taking on the codes 'DU-W'. Fighter squadrons were in a constant state of flux in 1940 and 1941 and 312 moved to Martlesham Heath fourteen days after P7540 had arrived, before settling for a 'rest' at Ayr on 19th August. The last flight of W-for-William took place on 25th October 1941; the fighter was last seen flying at ultra-low level down the six-mile length of Loch Doon, about 45 miles west of Dumfries. A wing tip hit the water and the Spitfire disappeared in a plume of spray. A search was initiated, but proved fruitless. The Spitfire was struck off charge on 2nd November 1941 with apparently just 21 hours, 25 minutes flying to its credit.

A view inside the fuselage of Spitfire IIa P7540 during restoration. *Ken Ellis*

No trace of Fg Off Frantisek Hekl was ever found. That was not the case for P7540, although that took another 41 years. D&G member Bruce Robertson persuaded local sub-aqua divers to search for the wreck. Dividing the southern tip of Loch Doon into search squares divers began what became a five-year odyssey to locate the Spitfire, with sub-aqua clubs from as far away as Blackpool lending a hand. Then in July 1982 the rear fuselage was discovered and brought to the surface. Descents continued and around 90 percent of P7540 was recovered. The salvage involved 567 individual dives, 109 divers and 337 hours of underwater time. Over the years, the D&G Spitfire has been through several restoration phases and venues; including a 'poly tunnel' at Tinwald Downs. Tempering all efforts was the need to display the finished P7540 under cover, and not just in the corner of a building. With the Nissen and Romney huts beginning in 2016, the Spitfire was allocated its own display hall and all of the plans could dovetail together, ready for the unveiling on 16th July 2017.

Dumfries and Galloway Aviation Museum aircraft

Type	Identity	Built	Origin	Acquired	Notes
Airspeed Horsa	–	1944	Britain	1990	forward fuselage
BAC Jet Provost T.5A	XW363	1971	Britain	2010	–
Bristow Sycamore 3	WA576	1951	Britain	7 Jun 1987	–
Dassault Mystère IVA	318	c1957	France	1981	–
English Electric Canberra T.4	WJ880	1955	Britain	1995	cockpit
English Electric Lightning F.53	ZF584	1968	Britain	22 May 2006	–
Fairey Gannet AEW.3*	XL497	1961	Britain	13 Apr 2005	see profile
General Dynamics F-111E	68-0060	1968	USA	1985	escape pod
Gloster Meteor T.7	WL375	1952	Britain	1977	–
Handley Page Jetstream T.1	XX483	1974	Britain	2002	cockpit
Hawker Hunter F.4	WT746	1955	Britain	1999	–
Hawker Siddeley Buccaneer S.2B	XT280	1965	Britain	Feb 2003	cockpit
Hawker Siddeley Trident 3B-101	G-AWZJ	1971	Britain	1999	forward fuselage
Hunting Jet Provost T.4	XP557	1962	Britain	25 Mar 2005	–
Lockheed T-33A*	FT-36	1955	USA	8 Sep 1981	–
North American F-100D Super Sabre*	54-2163	1954	USA	11 Jan 1979	–
SAAB J35A Draken	35075	c1961	Sweden	19 Aug 2005	–
Scottish Aviation Twin Pioneer 3	G-AYFA	1958	Britain	Sep 2013	cockpit
Supermarine Spitfire IIa	P7540	1940	Britain	Jul 1982	see profile
Westland Wessex HU.5	XT486	1966	USA/GB	13 Jun 2007	–

Notes: * – illustrated in the colour section

Along the Firth
Highland Aviation Museum

Inverness Airport

Work to establish the Highland Aviation Museum began in 1998 as the Highland Aircraft Preservation Society brought its collection of artefacts to the Dalcross Industrial Estate. Located on the former technical site of RAF Dalcross – the present-day Inverness Airport – the museum opened its doors in May 2005. The aircraft collection is intended to reflect the post-1945 skies of northern Scotland, with the Tornado and Nimrod illustrating recent equipment. The Nimrod forward fuselage is a particularly impressive item, all 54 feet of it.

As well as the airframes there is an extensive exhibition devoted to the history of Dalcross. The airfield was built on low lying land on the banks of the Moray Firth, to the north of the town and was operational from July 1941 when 2 Air Gunnery School formed. This unit continued to fly at the airfield, with a wide variety of types, until it disbanded in November 1945. Fighter and light bomber units were briefly detached, but it was training that was the lasting theme. Another long-standing outfit was 19 (Pilot) Advanced Flying Unit, from October 1942 to the spring of 1944. With the return of peace, Dalcross was inaugurated as Inverness Airport in 1947, with British European Airways operating regional services and ambulance flights. The RAF returned in May 1951 with the Airspeed Oxford T.1s of 8 Flying Training School based until the unit disbanded in December 1953.

Above: Tornado GR.1 ZA362 at Inverness. *Roger Richards*

The forward fuselage of Nimrod MR.2 XV254 is an imposing exhibit at Inverness. *Roger Richards*

Highland Aviation Museum aircraft

Type	Identity	Built	Origin	Acquired	Notes
BAC Jet Provost T.5A	XW419	1971	Britain	19 May 2015	–
Blackburn Buccaneer S.1	XK532	1961	Britain	23 Dec 2002	–
English Electric Lightning F.1A	XM169	1960	Britain	23 Jun 2004	cockpit
Hawker Hunter F.1	WT660	1954	Britain	4 Oct 1999	–
Hawker Siddeley Buccaneer S.2B	XV867	1968	Britain	2005	cockpit
Hawker Siddeley Nimrod MR.2	XV254	1971	Britain	20 Jul 2010	forward fuselage
Hunting Jet Provost T.3	XN607	1961	Britain	23 Jun 2004	cockpit
Panavia Tornado GR.1	ZA362	1981	GB/Ger/Italy	9 Jun 2005	–
Vickers Valiant B.1	XD875	1957	Britain	2003	cockpit

First to the Front
Montrose Air Station Heritage Centre

Montrose
www.rafmontrose.org.uk

Just north of the town of Montrose, between the main road and the sea is a patch of unremarkable looking land with some buildings scattered about. A replica Spitfire 'gate guardian' is a tell-tale sign, but this is just a temptation to beckon visitors. After an absorbing time at the Montrose Air Station Heritage Centre visitors appreciate that they have trodden in the footsteps of history. As denoted by the Spitfire, during World War Two Montrose was the domain of operational fighter units until mid-1942 when training became the task. The principal unit in that role was 2 Flying Instructors School (FIS), from January 1942 and it was its aircraft that were the last to beat the circuit, disbanding in July 1945.

With great respect to World War Two, it is the airfield's earliest days, just prior to the outbreak of the Great War, that sets it apart. In April 1912 twelve Royal Flying Corps (RFC) 'Air Stations' were to be established under the instructions of the First Lord of the Admiralty, Winston Churchill, to protect the Royal Navy bases at Rosyth, Cromarty and Scapa Flow. The first of these was at Montrose and on 13th February 1913, five aircraft of 2 Squadron took off from Farnborough and flew north. The 450-mile journey was completed in stages over the following 13 days. They settled at Upper Dysart Farm, a short distance south of

Superb BE.2a replica '471', from the day when Montrose went to war.
Courtesy Montrose Air Station Heritage Centre – Neil Werninck

Montrose's typical 1940s room.
Courtesy Montrose Air Station Heritage Centre – Neil Werninck

Montrose, on the 26th. Thus it became the first operational military airfield to be established in Britain. Major Burke, Commanding Officer of 2 Squadron, considered their location at Upper Dysart as far from ideal and started surveying the Montrose area for somewhere more suitable. He identified a site at Broomfield Farm a mile north of Montrose and was given authority to relocate. By the end of 1913 Army engineers had erected three hangars of Indian Army design, known as the 'Major Burke's sheds', on the site. The Royal Aircraft Factory BE.2s and a selection of other types of 2 Squadron moved in during the New Year of 1914.

On 3rd August 1914 the aircraft of 2 Squadron slipped out of Montrose and flew to Farnborough; war with Imperial Germany was declared the following day. The ground echelon departed for Glasgow docks on the 8th for a ship to take them to Boulogne. Four days later 2 Squadron was at Dover. At 06:25 hours the unit set off across the English Channel and at 08:20 Lt Hubert Dunsterville Harvey-Kelly was the first British airman to touch down, landing BE.2a 471 at Amiens; bound for the frontline in France. This biplane was the obvious choice when Montrose volunteers built a full scale faithful static replica BE.2a – Britain's first use of aerial force projection. Throughout the rest of the war, Montrose was busy as squadrons formed ready for active duty. By April 1918 this included units of the United States Army Air Service.

Protecting a century plus of heritage

This rich heritage was too good to let slip by. In April 1983, the Montrose Aerodrome Museum Society was formed with the specific task of protecting the surviving World War One era flying sheds. Acquiring aircraft of appropriate eras was at first difficult as the enthusiasts found their feet in the project and the loan of Hawker Sea Hawk FGA.6 XE340 from the Fleet Air Arm was a start; it arrived in November 1994. Ian McIntosh established the Montrose Air Station Museum Trust, which later became the Ian McIntosh Memorial Trust. In 1992, the trust took the momentous step of purchasing the former watch office and ground which became the basis of the Montrose Air Station Museum.

As the operation became more established, the grounds were extended and more buildings added. In 2005-2006, a Nissen workshop and a Romney building were erected. The Romney was officially opened on 7th April 2007, becoming the main display hall. Over the next decade more buildings and exhibits were added. An unusual acquisition was a former Mechanised Transport Hut from the local council that was in a derelict state and would not have survived much longer. Located adjacent to the main headquarters building, it dated back to 1917. It was formally inaugurated on 5th May 2012 and houses the reception, shop and 1940s room. During 2017 a new building was to be erected to provide a controlled environment restoration facility. To make space for this it was necessary to move an existing structure a short distance in February.

As mentioned above, acquiring suitable airframes to portray the incredible spread of history at Montrose proved to be a challenge. The BE.2 replica reflects the pioneering essence of Montrose, while an early breakthrough was the Sopwith Camel replica. The type was used at the air station by 80 Squadron when it formed in August 1917 and was part of the equipment of 32 Training Depot Station 1918 to 1919. Bedecked in the colours of 602 (City of Glasgow) Squadron, the Spitfire replica stands for the many units that were based at Montrose for short periods, during World War Two: 602's Spitfires served from the airfield in the summer of both 1940 and 1941. During a revision of the RAF Museum's airframe 'stock', the Miles Hawk became available, Montrose expressed interest and it arrived in February 2017. It represents the later and broadly similar Magister, which served from the airfield with 2 FIS. With respect to the airframes, particularly the evocative BE.2, the greatest appeal at Montrose is the 'feel' of the buildings and their surroundings; from this spot the Royal Flying Corps set off to the frontline to do battle.

Miles Hawk Major DG590 on display at Montrose. *Courtesy Montrose Air Station Heritage Centre – Neil Werninck*

Miles Hawk Major DG590
1935 | Two-seat trainer / tourer | One 130hp de Havilland Gipsy Major piston

Following on from the ground-breaking Miles Hawk two-seat monoplanes, the more refined Hawk Major entered production in 1934 and two years later a total of 73 had been completed. The 'Major' led to the Hawk Trainer series from 1935 which was ordered in large numbers by the RAF as the Magister – 1,200-plus being built. The Montrose Hawk Major was built to the order of Willoughby Rollo Norman and was tested by Charles Powis at Woodley on the last day of July 1935, as G-ADMW. Charles was managing director of Phillips and Powis Aircraft (Reading) Ltd, the company that built the aircraft designed by F G Miles: the company was renamed Miles Aircraft in 1943. Willoughby and his brother, Anthony Norman, entered the Hawk Major, which they kept at Heston, in the September 1935 King's Cup air race, which started and finished at Hatfield: they came 20th. By April 1938 G-ADMW was with Portsmouth Aero Club at the municipal aerodrome and with the onset of war, it was put into store by September 1939. Following inspection, it was impressed for military service on 21st January 1941 and it was issued to 5 Maintenance Unit at Kemble, taking on the serial DG590. It was not until January 1943 that it was put into service with the Station Flight at Wyton, serving the needs of 2 Group's Headquarters. By May the Hawk Major had moved on to the Station Flight at Swanton Morley, but it was in store at Kemble by December.

Offered for disposal in December 1945 DG590 was sold to Miles Aircraft for £100 – in present-day values, around £3,000. It was returned to the British civil register as G-ADMW and by June 1947 was bashing the circuit at Woodley with the Reading Aero Club. It was based at Tollerton in 1948 and from 1951 to 1952 at Leicester. The registration was cancelled as sold in the USA in May 1952, but this does not seem to have been carried through as it was registered to John Paul Gunner of Winchester in September 1952. Gunner went on to fly *Mike-Whisky* through to 1965, latterly from Ternhill. He presented it to the Air Historical Branch of the Ministry of Defence on 2nd August 1965, with the intention of it joining the nascent RAF Museum – which opened at Hendon on 15th November 1972. In the fervour of the time, assembling likely exhibits and using RAF resources to the full, G-ADMW was painted in the colours it wore as the impressed DG590 at Ternhill. It was delivered by air to Henlow in November 1965 where RAF Museum machines were gathered and stored. It was allocated the ground instructional airframe number 8379M in 1973. The Hawk was to spend many years in store, relieved only by loan to the Museum of Army Flying at Middle Wallop from 1988 to 1991. After 'Wallop, DG590 was issued to Wyton, the museum's temporary store, and in 2003 it was moved to the long-term facility which had been established at Stafford. Always peripheral to its central collecting policy, during a wide-ranging review of its artefacts, the RAF Museum wisely decided to dispose of DG590. Montrose made an application for this, the oldest surviving Miles aircraft in Britain (although the Miles-designed Southern Martlet G-AAYX at the Shuttleworth Collection was built in 1930) and was successful in securing it. The Hawk Major made the journey north on 15th February 2017.

Montrose Air Station Heritage Centre aircraft

Type	Identity	Built	Origin	Arrived	Notes
de Havilland Vampire T.22	XA109	1953	Britain	3 Aug 2011	–
Gloster Meteor T.7	WF825	1951	Britain	3 Dec 2009	–
MBA Tiger Cub 440	G-MMLM	1984	Britain	2011	–
Miles Hawk Major	DG590	1935	Britain	15 Feb 2017	see profile
Royal Aircraft Factory BE.2a	'471'	2015	Britain	2015	replica
Sopwith Camel	'B5577'	c1972	Britain	2006	replica
Supermarine Spitfire V	'EP121'	2012	Britain	17 Jul 2013	replica

First Sea King HAR.3 to be preserved in Britain; Morayvia's XZ592. *Jim Simpson*

Back to School
Morayvia

Kinloss
www.morayvia.org.uk

When it was announced in March 2010 that the Hawker Siddeley Nimrod maritime patrollers based at Kinloss would be retiring prematurely, it was a severe blow to the people of the area. Along the coast to the east the base at Lossiemouth was assured, taking on Eurofighter Typhoons, and it was hinted that the Army would adopt Kinloss. The Nimrod units disbanded on 26th May 2011 and RAF Kinloss closed its gates on 31st March 2012. After that the base morphed in Kinloss Barracks, home of 39 Engineer Regiment. As the disbandment ceremony approached, the Nimrod Heritage Group (NHG) was formed ideally to secure as much memorabilia as possible concerning the maritime patrol aircraft, which had been based at Kinloss since 1970. Nimrod MR.2 XV240 was put on public display at Kinloss on 9th September 2009 and had the dubious distinction of being one of Britain's most short-lived 'gate guardians' when it was scrapped in December 2011 during the hasty wind-down of the RAF's presence. NHG managed to secure the forward fuselage of XV240 and it was moved to a storage site at nearby Elgin.

The Cyrillic legend '*Mopaйbua*' translates as Morayvia on Antonov An-2 HA-MKE.
Jim Simpson

In July 2011 HNG changed its name to Morayvia – a play on words combining the Moray Firth and aviation – while it expanded its remit to an aviation and technology charitable organisation. In February 2012 Morayvia acquired the last Nimrod at Kinloss, XV244, and negotiations to keep the sub-hunter at Kinloss were successful and later it was given the name *Duke of Edinburgh*. A lease on the former primary school at Abbeylands, Kinloss, was granted and preparations were made to turn the buildings into a visitor and education centre – the playground proving to be an ideal aircraft park. The emphasis was to acquire airframes that could allow access to the cockpits or interior, with ease, especially for children. Arriving on 16th July 2015 was Westland Sea King HAR.3 XZ592, the first of the RAF search and rescue version to join a museum. (Royal Navy Sea Kings were based at Kinloss throughout the 1980s.) As part of Morayvia's involvement with the Science and Technology Experience Project, grant aid allowed the purchase of a mobile planetarium and wraparound projection screen for use at Abbeylands and also as out-reach to local communities. Morayvia opened to the public on 10th October 2015.

Morayvia aircraft

Type	Identity	Built	Origin	Arrived	Notes
Antonov An-2P *Colt*	HA-MKE	1974	USSR	2 Jun 2016	–
de Havilland Vampire T.11	XD425	1954	Britain	2016	cockpit
English Electric Canberra TT.18	WJ721	1953	Britain	3 Jun 2015	cockpit
Handley Page Herald 214	G-ASVO	1964	Britain	Apr 2017	forward fuselage
Hawker Hunter F.5	WN957	1954	Britain	2016	cockpit
Hawker Siddeley Nimrod MR.2	XV240	1970	Britain	Dec 2011	forward fuselage
Hawker Siddeley Nimrod MR.2	XV244	1971	Britain	Feb 2012	at Kinloss Barracks
Hunting Jet Provost T.4	XS176	1963	Britain	11 Nov 2012	cockpit
MBA Tiger Cub 440	G-MJSV	1983	Britain	2016	–
SEPECAT Jaguar GR.3A	XZ113	1976	GB/France	11 May 2017	–
Westland Sea King HAR.3	XZ592	1978	USA/GB	16 Jul 2015	–

Also in Scotland

National Museum of Flight Scotland at the former East Fortune airfield to the east of Edinburgh, is the home of Scotland's 'national' aeronautical collection. It, and the **National Museum of Scotland** in central Edinburgh, are covered in depth in the sister volume *Great Aviation Collections of Britain*. **www.nms.ac.uk/flight**

Kelvingrove Art Gallery and Museum

This superb building, in Glasgow, has incredible collections, including Supermarine Spitfire F.21 LA198 which 'flies' in the main hall. **www.glasgowmuseums.com**

Riverside Museum

Another Glaswegian venue, this collection is sub-titled 'Scotland's Museum of Transport and Travel' and includes a replica Pilcher Bat glider. **www.glasgowmuseums.com**

Scalloway Museum

At Lerwick on Shetland, the museum includes among its exhibits Luton Minor G-AMUW. This was a homebuild project started in the early 1950s on Orkney, but it was never flown. **www.scallowaymuseum.org**

CHAPTER 33
WALES

Snowdon's Skies
Caernarfon Airport Airworld Museum

Caernarfon Aerodrome
www.airworldmuseum.co.uk

By its very nature, North Wales has little in the way of flat land. The all-dominating Snowdonia mountain range – crowned by the 3,559ft of Snowdon itself – meant that options to build airfields during World War Two were few and far between and confined to the coast. The Morfa Dinlle peninsula southwest of Caernarfon was deemed as suitable for an airfield at Llandwrog. A working party from the construction firm McAlpine began work in September 1940. The first aircraft to use Llandwrog were the Airspeed Oxfords and Avro Ansons of the Shawbury-based 11 Service Flying Training School from 11th June 1941. This unit used the airfield as a relief landing ground (RLG) until the airspace became crowded from 7th July with the formation of 9 Air Gunnery School (AGS). Using Ansons, Armstrong Whitworth Whitleys, Bristol Blenheims, Boulton Paul Defiants and Westland Lysanders, the AGS had only brief life, being disbanded at Llandwrog on 13th June 1942. After that, Llandwrog was used as an RLG for the aircraft based at Penrhos, on the southern side of the Lleyn Peninsula. Llandwrog closed for flying in June 1945.

Above: A view inside Caernarfron Airworld Museum: Cadet TX.3 XA282 and Hunter F.1 WT694 in the foreground. *Ken Ellis*

Formed at Llandwrog on 29th July 1946 was an outfit that has entered the folklore of the area: 277 Maintenance Unit (277). This was a specialist explosives disposal unit and stacks of shells were 'parked' all over the airfield's perimeter tracks and hard standings. Remote, coastal, quiet, Llandwrog was ideal for the storage and later disposal of thousands of tons of German chemical warfare weapons. Some locals would have it that the airfield was a centre for chemical warfare development – but that was far from the case. In September 1953 the delicate work of 277 MU was over and it disbanded. The airfield then became a sub-site of the ultra-secretive 31 MU which worked from the depths of Glynrhonwy Quarry near Llanberis. Whatever went on there and at Llanbedr came to a halt in October 1956. Llandwrog reverted to agricultural use.

A view of the purpose-built display hall for what was then called the Caernarfon Air Museum, from the control tower, April 2001. In the foreground is Hunter T.7 XL618 which left the collection in June 2014 and is now in Germany. *Ken Ellis*

Regeneration

Liverpool-based flying school and warbird operator Jim Keen, acquired Llandwrog in 1976 and set about turning it into Caernarfon Airport. By 1986 Keen Air Services had passed it to Snowdon Mountain Aviation, trading as Air Caernarfon, which determined to further regenerate the airfield by adding tourism to its uses. de Havilland Dragon Rapide G-AIDL was based for pleasure flying duties, either up to Snowdon or along the Menai Strait. Hand-in-hand with this, the company started to acquire airframes and exhibits for a museum in a purpose-built display hall. The Caernarfon Air Museum opened to the public on 11th May 1989. Air Atlantique took over operation of the airfield and the museum in 1992 and two years later the museum took on its present name. The Dragon Rapide slipped from fully resident, to occasional deployments for the season, from Air Atlantique's main base at Coventry, until the 'service' was withdrawn in the late 1990s. The museum has been managed independently, as a charitable trust, since that time.

Clouds with rocks inside

Using wreckage salvaged from Snowdonia crash sites, one of the most dramatic exhibitions at Caernarfon depicts an Anson that has landed on its belly in mountainous surroundings. The crew of that imaginary incident was lucky; many others were killed outright when their aircraft collided with rock outcrops hit when the weather clamped down, or a navigation plot went tragically awry, or a combination of both. Others, injured and shocked, huddled near their wrecked aircraft, hoping for rescue. Some aircrew would trudge away looking for help. The lucky ones were carried off the high ground, others succumbed to their injuries or to exposure.

Clever use of artwork and crash site components forms Caernarfon Airworld's mountain rescue diorama. *Ken Ellis*v

Not far away from the Anson diorama is an RAF Land Rover, conspicuous with its yellow-painted roof. This is part of a display dedicated to a Llandwrog 'product' – the RAF Mountain Rescue Service (MRS). Flt Lt George Graham was posted to the airfield as a medical officer on the 13th May 1942. As an experienced climber, he took the lead when the staff of Llandwrog's Station Sick Quarters were 'scrambled' to help locate and care for downed RAF aircrew. Graham devised a system to filter reports, so that teams were sent less and less on fruitless wild goose chases. He also set about training RAF personnel and local volunteers in the skills required for scouring mountains and how to recover the injured. In early 1943 vehicles were allocated to the nascent MRS. In that year, 571 aircrew lost their lives in 220 crashes in other mountainous and upland districts of Britain and other mountain rescue units were set up, in Scotland, the Lake District and Yorkshire. In the 1950s there were teams in Aden, Cyprus and Hong Kong. RAF Valley on Anglesey became the MRS centre for Wales, liaising with the helicopter search and rescue (SAR) squadrons. From April 2015 the RAF and Fleet Air Arm gave up SAR and the service was transferred to Bristow Helicopters under HM Coast Guard. The badge of the present-day MRS depicts a coil of rope with a pair of climbing axes and has the appropriate motto 'Whensoever'. The volunteer MRS team at Valley co-ordinates with these civilian bodies and is regularly involved in exercises. Snowdon can be seen from the Caernarfon Airport Airworld Museum and the mountains still occasionally claim an aircraft. Museum visitors may well be able to see one of the two Bristow-operated Sikorsky S-92 SAR helicopters that are based at the airfield that gave rise to their rescue predecessors of 1943.

Caernarfon Airport Airworld Museum aircraft

Type	Identity	Built	Origin	Arrived	Notes
Blériot XI	–	2011	France	2011	replica
Bristol Sycamore HR.12	WV781	1952	Britain	1986	forward fuselage
de Havilland Tiger Moth	'N5137'	1939	Britain	26 Nov 1997	–
de Havilland Vampire T.11	XK623	1956	Britain	1986	–
Gloster Javelin FAW.7*	XH837	1957	Britain	1987	forward fuselage
Hawker Sea Hawk FB.5	WM961	1954	Britain	1988	–
Hawker Hunter F.1	WT694	1954	Britain	Sep 1995	–
Hawker Siddeley Harrier T.4A*	XW269	1971	Britain	2 Oct 2012	–
Mignet 'Flying Flea'	'G-EGCK'	c1936	France	Dec 2002	–
Slingsby Cadet TX.3	XA282	1952	Britain	1986	–
Vickers Varsity T.1	–	c1952	Britain	1988	procedure trainer
Westland Whirlwind HAR.10*	XJ726	19955	Britain	1986	–

Notes: * – illustrated in the colour section

When 'Boats Reigned Supreme
Pembroke Dock Flying-Boat Visitor Centre

Pembroke Dock
www.sunderlandtrust.org.uk

While chugging across the waters of Milford Haven in the late 1990s a fisherman looked skyward in exasperation; yet another lobster pot had snagged. A diver went down for a look-see and found a three-bladed propeller. After more descents, he and colleagues discovered a radial engine and then the remains of a Sunderland flying-boat. In August 2003, the Channel 4 television programme *Wreck Detectives* brought its team to the Haven and the 1,010hp Bristol Pegasus nine-cylinder radial and propeller came to the surface. Probably nobody gave it any thought as the corks popped, but this salvage became a catalyst for the creation of a unique British museum. Launched on to the River Medway at Rochester in mid-1940, Sunderland

Wartime RAF Pembroke Dock looking east – thirteen Sunderlands are visible. *Courtesy Pembroke Dock Flying-Boat Visitor Centre*

I T9044 was issued to 210 Squadron, becoming *F-for-Freddie*. It alighted on Milford Haven on 9th November and was moored offshore from the vast RAF flying-boat base of Pembroke Dock – known to personnel as 'PD'. On the night of the 12th a fearsome gale ripped through the area and T9044 sank, settling into the estuary bed. There it lay forgotten until it caught one lobster pot too many.

The purpose-built naval dockyard at Pembroke Dock closed in 1926, but the RAF appreciated the sheltered waters of Milford Haven and what became Britain's biggest flying-boat base opened in June 1931 when the Supermarine Southamptons of 210 Squadron arrived. Sunderlands came to dominate the skyline at PD, 210 bringing the first examples during 1938. Units chopped and changed throughout the war, and Supermarine Walrus amphibians and Consolidated Catalinas also plied from the Haven. The Sunderland had a long and special career with the RAF, the last British-based examples serving from PD until 201 and 230 Squadrons stood down in February 1957. Britain's last flying-boat station finally closed in 1959.

Remembering 'PD'

Publicity about the salvaged 'Peggie' engine brought offers of artefacts, documents, photographs and volunteers. Something had to be done to remember PD's flying-boat era *and* there was the tantalising prospect of raising T9044. The Pembroke Dock Sunderland Trust was formed and a search for exhibition space was initiated. Within the docks a former locomotive shed became available. After a lot of hard work, the Flying-Boat Centre was officially opened on 25th September 2009 by Trust Patron Wg Cdr Derek Martin, who had once piloted T9044. (Derek, a founder-member of the Guinea Pig Club, died in April 2014, aged 93.) A workshop was established where items brought up from T9044 could be worked on, ready for display. In five years 31,000 visitors proved the potential of the PD story.

What was needed was a heritage centre dedicated to the docks *and* the flying-boats. The impressive Georgian era Garrison Chapel owned by Pembrokeshire County Council, faced an uncertain future and the Trust, the council, local and Lottery funding bodies, thought it would be ideal. Transforming the building into the Pembroke Dock Heritage Centre, moving over from the loco shed, creating new displays, a café, gift shop, administrative and staff areas was a formidable undertaking. On 29th April 2014, HM Queen Elizabeth II and Prince Philip, the Duke of Edinburgh, opened the converted chapel.

The chapel was well versed with the Sunderland, for nearly a decade, its grounds hosted what became the RAF Museum's example. In 1960, preservation pioneer Peter Thomas approached the French Aéronavale about acquiring one of the last two

Sunderland MR.5 ML824 outside the chapel in the mid-1960s. This building is now the visitor centre.
Courtesy Pembroke Dock Flying-Boat Visitor Centre

flying Sunderlands and was given a resounding: "Oui!" He secured a place for it at PD and on 24th March 1961 ML824 alighted in Milford Haven and was brought out of the water. Six years later 20,000 people had toured it but it was realised that its long-term was with the RAF Museum and it moved to Hendon in 1971. Greater details of this can be found in the sister volume *Lost Aviation Collections of Britain*. Within the chapel today is the restored Pegasus from T9044 and the public is able to view a workshop area where items that continue to be recovered by the dive team are restored. A recent artefact brought up from the depths of Milford Haven is a very rare Vickers Gas-Operated machine-gun (a VGO as the gunners would call it) from the front turret. Pembroke Dock is a shrine to a long-lost era when flying-boats reigned supreme.

Also in Wales
Carew Control Tower

Based in the unique watch tower at the former airfield, visitors are in for a treat at this superbly put-together and very friendly museum. Long-term restoration project Avro Anson C.19 VM325 is also held. **www.carewcheritoncontroltower.co.uk**

National Waterfront Museum:

Part of the National Museum of Wales, this museum in Swansea holds what could be called the Welsh 'national' aircraft: the Watkins CHW of 1909. As the principality lacks a 'national' aviation museum, this aircraft was covered in depth in the sister volume *Great Aviation Collections of Britain*.
www.museumwales.ac.uk/swansea

Welsh Spitfire Museum

Run by the Pembrokeshire Spitfire Aeroplane Company and recently relocated to a workshop in the town of Haverfordwest, visitors can see progress on the restoration of Mk.VIII JG668 plus supporting displays. **http://welshspitfire.org**

The unique watch tower at Carew Cheriton is the centrepiece of an exceptional museum. *Ken Ellis*

CHAPTER 34

NORTHERN IRELAND

There are two museums with aviation content in Northern Ireland. The **Ulster Folk and Transport Museum** at Holywood has an exhibition, among a wide range of other exhibits, including re-located and reconstructed historic buildings from all over the county. With regular opening hours, this was determined as a 'national' collection and covered in depth in the sister volume *Great Aviation Collections of Britain*.

However, the Ulster Aviation Society runs the **Ulster Aviation Collection** at Long Kesh. At present it has limited opening hours that fall beyond the remit of this book, but as this is the only dedicated aviation museum in Northern Ireland and with forty-plus aircraft it was rightly 'upgraded' in *Great Aviation Collections of Britain* to 'national' status. The full story of this incredible collection can be found in that volume – go get it!

Above: Just a small section of the Ulster Aviation Collection at Long Kesh. Clockwise: Canberra PR.9 XH131, Short 330 G-BDBS, Grumman Wildcat V JV482, Hawker Sea Hawk FB.3 WN108, Team Hi-Max G-MZHM and Robinson R22 G-RENT. *Ken Ellis*

BIBLIOGRAPHY

Books, DVDs, websites – Most websites are given in their respective chapters

Action Stations Revisited, Vol 1 Eastern England and *Volume 2 Central England and London Area*, Michael J F Bowyer, Crécy
   Publishing, Manchester, 2000 and 2004
Aircraft of the Royal Air Force since 1918, Owen Thetford, Putnam Aeronautical Books, London, ninth edition, 1995
Air Wars and Aircraft – Air Combat 1945 to the Present, Victor Flintham, Arms & Armour, London, 1989
An Illustrated History of British European Airways, Phil Lo Bao, Browcom, Feltham, 1989
Armstrong Whitworth Aircraft since 1913, Oliver Tapper, Putnam, London, second edition, 1978
Aviation in Leicestershire and Rutland, Roy Bonser, Midland Publishing, Hinckley, 2001
Avro Aircraft since 1908, A J Jackson, Putnam, London, second edition, 1990
Avro Lancaster – The Definitive Record, Harry Holmes, Airlife, Shrewsbury, 2001
Avro's Maritime Heavyweight – The Shackleton, Chris Ashworth, Aston, Bourne End, 1990
Avro 748 – The Full Story of the 748m Andover and ATP, Richard J Church, Air-Britain, Staplefield, 2017
Bases: The Encyclopaedia of Airfields and Military Flying Units in Britain since 1912, DVD, Air-Britain, Tonbridge, 2012
Blackburn Aircraft since 1909, A J Jackson, Putnam, London, second edition, 1989
Bristol Aircraft since 1910, C H Barnes, Putnam, London, third edition, 1988
British Civil Aircraft Registers 1919 to 1999, Michael Austen, Air-Britain, Tunbridge Wells, 1999
British Experimental Jet Aircraft, Barrie Hygate, Argus Books, Hemel Hempstead, 1990
British Homebuilt Aircraft, Ken Ellis, Merseyside Aviation Society, Liverpool, second edition, 1979
British Museum Aircraft, Ken Ellis and Phil Butler, Merseyside Aviation Society, Liverpool, 1977
British Naval Aircraft since 1912, Owen Thetford, Putnam, London, revised ed 1971
British Research and Development Aircraft – 70 Years at the Leading Edge, Ray Sturtivant, Haynes Publishing, Sparkford, 1990
caa.co.uk : the excellent GINFO database run by the Civil Aviation Authority
Category Five – A Catalogue of RAF Aircraft Losses 1954-2009, Colin Cummings, Nimbus, Yelvertoft, 2009
Cold War Years – Flight Testing at Boscombe Down 1945-1975, Tim Mason, Hikoki, Ottringham, 2001
de Havilland Biplane Transports, Paul Hayes and Bernard King, Gatwick Aviation Society/Aviation Classics, Coulsdon, 2003
demobbed.org.uk : great database on former military from the stalwarts of the Wolverhampton Aviation Group
English Electric Aircraft and Their Predecessors, Stephen Ransom and Robert Fairclough, Putnam, London, 1987
English Electric Canberra, Ken Delve, Peter Green, John Clemons, Midland Counties Publications, Earl Shilton, 1992
English Electric Lightning – Birth of a Legend, and *English Electric Lightning – The Lightning Force*, Stewart A Scott, GMS
   Enterprises, Peterborough, 2000 and 2004
Fairey Aircraft since 1915, H A Taylor, Putnam & Co, London, 1974
Falklands: The Air War, Rodney Burden, Michael Draper, Douglas Rough, Colin Smith, David Wilton, Arms & Armour, London 1986
Fleet Air Arm Aircraft 1939 to 1945, Ray Sturtivant with Mick Burrow, Air-Britain, Tunbridge Wells, 1995
Fleet Air Arm Fixed-Wing Aircraft since 1946, Ray Sturtivant, Air-Britain, Tunbridge Wells, 2004
Fleet Air Arm Helicopters since 1943, Lee Howard, Mick Burrow and Eric Myall, Air-Britain, Tunbridge Wells, 2011
Force for Freedom – The USAF in the UK since 1948, Michael J F Bowyer, Patrick Stephens, Sparkford, 1994
Gloster Aircraft since 1917, Derek N James, Putnam, London, second edition, 1987
Grate Expectations, Edmund Wells, Cleese-Chapman, ITV London, 1967
Great Aviation Collections of Britain, Ken Ellis, Crécy Publishing, Manchester, 2013
Hawker Hunter – Biography of a Thoroughbred, Francis K Mason, Patrick Stephens, Bar Hill, 1981
Helicopters and Autogyros of the World, Paul Lambermont with Anthony Pirie, Cassell, London, 2nd Edition, 1970
History of Aircraft Piston Engines, Herschel Smith, Sunflower University Press, Manhattan, Kansas, USA, 1981
Home is the Halifax, Ian Robinson MBE, Grub Street, London, 2010
Lost Aviation Collections of Britain, Ken Ellis, Crécy Publishing, Manchester, 2011
Meteor, Bryan Philpott, Patrick Stephens, Wellingborough, 1986
Miles Aircraft – The Early Years, Peter Amos, Air-Britain, Tonbridge, 2009
Museum Guide & Year Book, 2008-9 and 2010-2011, The Helicopter Museum, Weston-super-Mare, 2009 and 2011
Nimrod R.1 – History, Mystery and Gratitude, Royal Air Force Air Media Centre, High Wycombe, 2011
On the Wings of a Gull – Percival and Hunting Aircraft, David W Gearing, Air-Britain, Tonbridge, 2012
One-Eleven Story, Richard J Church, Air-Britain, Tonbridge, 1994
RAF Flying Training and Support Units since 1912, Ray Sturtivant with John Hamlin, Air-Britain, Staplefield, 2007
RAF Squadrons, Wg Cdr C G Jefford MBE, Airlife, Shrewsbury, 1988
Register of 'Anonymous' Aircraft – British Aviation Preservation Council Register, Ken Ellis, Flying Flea Archive, Rutland, 2004

Secret Years – Flight Testing at Boscombe Down 1939-1945, 2nd edition, Tim Mason, Crécy Publishing, Manchester, 2010

Shorts Aircraft since 1900, C H Barnes, Putnam, London, 1967

Sitting Ducks and Peeping Toms – Targets, Drones and UAVs in British Military Service since 1917, Michael I Draper, Air-Britain, Staplefield, 2011

Squadrons and Units of the Fleet Air Arm, Theo Ballance, Lee Howard and Ray Sturtivant, Air-Britain, Staplefield, 2016

superguppy.co.uk : devoted to Bruntingthorpe's Super Guppy F-BTGV

Supermarine Aircraft since 1914, C F Andrews and E B Morgan, Putnam, London, 1981

Survivors, 3rd edition, Roy Blewett, Gatwick Aviation Society with Complete Classics, Croydon, 2017

Testing to the Limits: British Test Pilots since 1910, Vols One and Two Ken Ellis, Crécy Publishing, Manchester, 2015 and 2016

US Military Aircraft Designations and Serials since 1909, John M Andrade, Midland Counties, Earl Shilton, 1979

Veteran and Vintage Aircraft, Leslie Hunt, self-published, Leigh-on-Sea, 1965; also the 1968, 1970 and 1974 editions

Vickers Valiant – First of the V-Bombers, Eric B Morgan, Aerofax, Hinckley, 2002

Vulcan: Last of the V-Bombers, Duncan Cubitt with Ken Ellis, Osprey, London, 1993

War Prizes – An Illustrated Survey of German, Italian and Japanese Aircraft Brought to Allied Countries during and after the Second World War, Phil Butler, Midland Counties Publishing, Earl Shilton, 1994

Westland Aircraft since 1915, Derek N James, Putnam, London, 1991

Weston-super-Mare and the Aeroplane 1910-2010, Roger Dudley and Ted Johnson, Amberley, Stroud, 2010

victorxm715.co.uk : devoted to Bruntingthorpe's Victor K.2 *Teasin' Tina*

www.yhpg.co.uk : the Yorkshire Helicopter Preservation Group's site

and, of course...

Wrecks & Relics, all 25 editions: 1st and 2nd editions by D J Stephens, published in 1961 by the Merseyside Group of Aviation Enthusiasts, Liverpool and in 1962 by the Merseyside Society of Aviation Enthusiasts, Liverpool. 3rd edition by S G Jones, published by MSAE in 1968. 4th edition onwards by Ken Ellis; published 1974 and each 'even' year thereon. Publishers were as follows: 4th by MSAE, 5th to 10th by Merseyside Aviation Society, Liverpool. 11th to 13th Midland Counties Publications, Earl Shilton. 14th to 20th Midland Publishing, Earl Shilton. 21st onwards by Crécy Publishing Ltd, Manchester.

Magazines

British Roundel, published by Roundel Research 1997 to 2006

Control Column, published initially by the Northern Aircraft Preservation Society, then by Neville Franklin, 1963 to 1988

Northern Aeronews, published by the Merseyside Group of Aviation Enthusiasts; in the early 1960s renamed *Flypast*, the MGAE becoming the Merseyside Society of Aviation Enthusiasts and then the Merseyside Aviation Society, 1956 to 1985

Roundel, journal of the British Aviation Research Group, 1976 to 1996

and, of course...

FlyPast, published by Key Publishing from 1981, Britain's top-selling aviation monthly – **www.flypast.com**

It's not all about provenance, technical importance, operational use and local connections, sometimes it should be about fun! Never ceasing the raise a smile with visitors of all ages, the Newark Air Museum's 'Red Barrows'! *Ken Ellis*

Index

Photographs and the contents of tables throughout the book are *not* indexed. As the chapters deal with individual museums and organisations, these are noted as such, eg Ch.4, as well as any other page references. References to the Royal Air Force, Fleet Air Arm and other air arms and units are legion, and are *not* listed. Numbered squadrons, conversion units and the like, are *not* listed. UK place names are given with their pre-1974 counties. Pages in **bold** denote an exhibit profile.